A Complete Orchestra of War

A History of the 6th Division on the Western Front
1914–1919

Peter Hodgkinson

Helion & Company Limited

This book is firstly dedicated to my parents; Norma Hodgkinson (1923-2016), and engineer and author, Allan Hodgkinson (1922-1987). The support that they gave me throughout their lives was steadfast.
It is further dedicated to three soldiers of the Great War. My grandfather, 168093 Private Peter Rimmer ASC (27 Motorised Ambulance Convoy); my great-uncle, Private 206165 William Robert Moxey ASC; and another great-uncle, 14004 & 113481 Corporal Henry John Boyd, 12th Battalion 'Bristol's Own' Gloucestershire Regiment and RE (Special Brigade). Without these men's stories in my childhood, my passion for the Great War would have been the less.

Helion & Company Limited
Unit 8 Amherst Business Centre
Budbrooke Road
Warwick
CV34 5WE
England
Tel. 01926 499 619
Email: info@helion.co.uk
Website: www.helion.co.uk
Twitter: @helionbooks
Visit our blog http://blog.helion.co.uk/

Published by Helion & Company 2019
Designed and typeset by Mary Woolley (mary@battlefield-design.co.uk)
Cover designed by Paul Hewitt, Battlefield Design (www.battlefield-design.co.uk)

ISBN 978-1-912866-19-9

British Library Cataloguing-in-Publication Data.
A catalogue record for this book is available from the British Library.

Contents

List of Illustrations

List of Tables

List of Maps

In Colour Plate

Acknowledgements

First, my thanks go to Professors John Bourne and Peter Simkins, for their comments on generalship, and encouragement and support over many years.

Further thanks are due to the Imperial War Museum for access and the Documents Collection and individual copyright holders for permission to quote from the papers of H.C. Boxer, E. Buffey, J.W. Gamble, K.M. Gaunt, E.A. Luther, F.G. Chandler, E.E. Simeons, C.P. Quayle, C.L. Nicholson, M.V.B. Hill, E. Morley, T.C. Rainbird, J. du P. Langrishe. The author and the Imperial War Museum would be grateful for any information which might help to trace those whose identities or addresses are not currently known in respect of the papers of A. St J. Blunt, F.G. Minter, P.H. Jones, J.A. Liddell, G.W. Grossmith, B.J. Brookes, A.H. Muggeridge, R.B. Wilkinson, G. Clifthill, and E.K. Smith.

Abbreviations

AAG	Assistant Adjutant General
AAQMG	Assistant Adjutant & Quartermaster General
ADC	Aide de Camp
ADS	Advanced Dressing Station
AMS	Assistant Military Secretary
ANZAC	Australia & New Zealand Army Corps
AQMG	Assistant Quartermaster General
ASC	Army Service Corps
BEF	British Expeditionary Force
BGC	Brigadier General Commanding
BGGS	Brigadier General General Staff
BGRA	Brigadier General Royal Artillery
CB	Companion of the Order of the Bath
CO	Commanding Officer
CRA	Commander Royal Artillery
CRE	Commander Royal Engineers
CSM	Company Sergeant Major
CWGC	Commonwealth War Graves Commission
DAAG	Deputy Assistant Adjutant General
DAAQMG	Deputy Assistant Adjutant & Quarter Master General
DAC	Divisional Ammunition Column
DAQMQ	Deputy Assistant Quarter Master General
DCM	Distinguished Conduct Medal
DDMS	Deputy Director Medical Services
DLI	Durham Light Infantry
DMS	Director of Medical Services
DSO	Distinguished Service Order
EY	East Yorkshire
FGCM	Field General Court Martial
FOO	Forward Observation Officer
GHQ	General Headquarters
GOC	General Officer Commanding

GSO	General Staff Officer (1,2 or 3)
HE	High explosive
HQ	Headquarters
HRH	His Royal Highness
HWL	*Hauptwiderstandlinie* (line of resistance)
IWM	Imperial War Museum
KCB	Knight Commander of the Most Honourable Order of the Bath
KRRC	King's Royal Rifle Corps
KSLI	King's Shropshire Light Infantry
LTM	Light trench mortar
MC	Military Cross
MG	Machine-gun
MGC	Machine Gun Corps
MM	Military Medal
MO	Medical Officer
MT	Motor transport
MVO	Member of the Royal Victorian Order
NCO	Non-Commissioned Officer
OHL	*Oberste Heeresleitung* (German Supreme Army Command)
OR	Other ranks
psc	Passed staff college
RAMR	Royal Artillery Mounted Rifles
RE	Royal Engineers
RFA	Royal Field Artillery
RGA	Royal Garrison Artillery
RHA	Royal Horse Artillery
RIR	Reserve Infantry Regiment
RMA	Royal Military Academy
RMC	Royal Military College
RNVR	Royal Naval Volunteer Reserve
RSM	Regimental Sergeant Major
RTO	Regimental Transport Officer
SAA	Small arms ammunition
TNA	The National Archives (UK)
TMB	Trench Mortar Battery
VC	Victoria Cross
VDH	Ventricular disease of the heart
WY	West Yorkshire

Introduction

Thomas Owen Marden, the fourth and final commander of 6th Division wrote his *Short History* in 1920 as 'there was no one else to do it.' His object was to provide 'all who served with the division' a record 'to show that they belonged to a division which played no inconspicuous part in the Great War.' Offered at a price now unknown, 'every copy sold helps towards the erection of battlefield memorials to be placed in France and Flanders.'[1] This was certainly not a self-serving offer – 6th Division has no memorial to its endeavours.

Clocking in at 80 pages, Marden presented a pure operational history, as was the style of the writers of the divisional histories of the 1920s and 30s. It presents, as might be expected, 6th Division in its very best, heroic light. Modern historiography demands something different. Not that this eschews heroism or triumph. Rather, it seeks in the tradition of the new breed of 'revisionist' historians – Peter Simkins, John Bourne, Gary Sheffield et al – to get behind the narrative of operations to understand *how* the British Army evolved into the fighting force that won the Hundred Days campaign in 1918. This involves analysing both success and failure. Analysis of the latter, however, is not in the service of supporting the image that became so powerful in the 1960s, that of futility, failure, and of 'lions led by donkeys.' Rather it is in the service of understanding how the army made progress by learning from its mistakes.

Progress was in the service of one thing, to overcome the supremacy of the defence – to master, as Albert Palazzo states, 'the defender's use of firepower to dominate the battlefield and thereby prevent the attacker from achieving a favourable decision.'[2] The concept of the British Army's 'learning curve', stemming from the work of Peter Simkins and other revisionists, became popular yet fell under the shadow of criticism for being simplistic. It was, of course, at best a shorthand description of the operational and tactical progress of the BEF. There was (as the originators of the concept fully understood) never a smooth ascending curve of increasing competence – there was, rather, a rollercoaster of ups and downs. This uneven progress, as William Philpott has pointed out, was the result of a 'dynamic process of adjustment to new technologies, more sophisticated and flexible tactics, novel operational doctrines,

1 T. O. Marden, *A Short History of the 6th Division*, pp. v-vi.
2 A. Palazzo, *Seeking Victory on the Western Front*, p. 6.

complex logistics and fundamental change in the systems of command, control, communications and intelligence.'[3] Further, one need look no further than the writings of Carl von Clausewitz (1780-1831),[4] to understand why such a progress could not be smooth. Clausewitzian concepts such as uncertainty ('the fog of war'), friction, and the independent will of the enemy always indicated why this could never be so. As Clausewitz stated: 'Friction is the force that makes the apparently easy so difficult.'[5] The concept 'encompasses uncertainties, errors, accidents, technical difficulties, and the unforeseen, and their effects on one's decisions, actions, and morale.'[6] Further, war is self-evidently a human activity, and one in which one side's will is pitted against the independent will of the other. Thus, the Germans underwent their own learning process. Each step in either side's development brought forth from their opponent a reaction and counter-development. When the Germans attacked with gas at Ypres on 22 April 1915, in May the British developed a flannel gas helmet.[7] When the British attacked with tanks on 15 September 1916, the enemy soon identified that accurate field gun fire could disable them. Stuart Mitchell, in his study of 32nd Division summarises that:

> Learning at the divisional level was a complex process of interlocking factors, which at any one time could shape different aspects of the organisation. In 1916 poor leadership hamstrung command. In 1917 structure greatly improved while battle wisdom continued to be shared around the lower levels. The final year of the war saw a decline in certain respects, but overall improvement had been sufficient for this to outstrip the equivalent German learning process.[8]

This new history seeks to chart the progress of 6th Division from its heroic, desperate efforts on the Aisne and at Armentières in 1914; to its first bold step in the new war at Hooge in August 1915; to catastrophe at the Quadrilateral, Ginchy, on the Somme in September 1916 amidst the general tactical and organisational failings of the BEF; to its participation in the new 'deep battle' of Cambrai in November 1917; to valiant near-annihilation on 21 and 22 March 1918, the first two days of the German Spring Offensive; and, finally, to its (still flawed) participation in the Hundred Days offensive that concluded the war.

What was a division? Overall, it consisted of approximately 18,000 men (12,000 of whom were infantry) and 5,500 horses, just under 900 wagons and carts, not to

3 *Royal United Services Institute* <https://rusi.org/commentary/beyond-learning-curve-british-armys-military-transformation-first-world-war> (Accessed 5 September 2016).
4 Carl von Clausewitz, *On War*.
5 Clausewitz, op. cit. p.139-140.
6 M. Vego, 'Science vs the Art of War', p.66.
7 The invention of Major Cluny McPherson of the Newfoundland Medical Corps.
8 S.B.T. Mitchell, 'An Inter-Disciplinary Study of Learning in the 32nd Division on the Western Front, 1916-1918', p. 26.

mention the 76 artillery pieces (field, howitzer and medium-heavy) that formed the divisional artillery. It possessed three Field Companies of Royal Engineers; a Divisional Train, Army Service Corps; elements of the Army Ordnance Corps and a Divisional Ammunition Column; three Field Ambulances Royal Army Medical Corps; a Veterinary Section; mounted troops, Military Police, and chaplains. Its organisation would evolve during the war to encompass a Machine Gun Battalion, a divisional Trench Mortar organisation, and a Pioneer battalion.[9] It was an army in miniature. The BEF that disembarked in France on 16 August 1914 was made up of five infantry divisions and a single cavalry division. By the winter of 1916-17 it comprised approximately 58 infantry divisions, a size which remained relatively consistent for the remainder of the war. Achieving and managing such spectacular growth is a feat that is scarce given credit.

The division was the largest formation with which the individual Tommy could identify in terms of belonging. Field-Marshal Viscount Slim, the celebrated commander of Fourteenth Army in the Burma campaign in World War Two, wrote: 'It is good fun commanding a division anywhere. It is one of the four best commands in the service – a platoon, a battalion, a division and an army.' He singled out the level of the division 'because it is the smallest formation that is a complete orchestra of war and the largest in which every man can know you.'[10]

This volume naturally takes the reader through the various operations that the 'complete orchestra of war' that was 6th Division was involved in. It examines the commanders of the division, brigades and battalions, attempting to understand how commanders and command evolved during the war. It considers the division's training, the development of its firepower, logistics and engineering, and how these came together in the final, triumphant, 96 days of the war. It is the story, in miniature, of how the British Army developed 'the means by which they could create the necessary favourable superiority relationship that would restore decisiveness to battle and bring victory.'[11]

9 See Appendix I.
10 W.J. Slim, *Defeat into Victory*, p.14.
11 Palazzo, op. cit. p.40.

Chronology[1]

1914

September

(III Corps, Second Army)

8 Division embarked Southampton.

9 Commenced disembarkation St. Nazaire.

10 Commenced entraining.

12 Into billets Coulommiers - Mortcerf - Marles-Chaume.

13-19 March to the Aisne – into General Reserve.

19 18 Brigade to I Corps.

20 Attack on 18 Brigade near Troyon.

21 16 Brigade to II Corps, 17 Brigade to I Corps.

October

2 Division (less 16 and 17 Brigades) concentrated at Serches-Jury, under III Corps.

6 17 Brigade rejoined division.

9 Division (less 16 Brigade) entrained at St. Sauveur near Compiegne.

10-11 Division arrived at St. Omer. 19 Infantry Brigade joined.

12 March to Hazebrouck to cover detrainment of 4th Division.

13 16 Brigade entrained for Cassel. Division marched east, fighting from 13.00 on line La Couronne-Merris-Fontaine Houck.

14 Division reached line of Rivière du Leet-Blanche Maison, east of Bailleul.

15-16 18 Brigade crossed River Lys at Sailly, and 17 Brigade at Bac St. Maur during the night. Steenwerck occupied.

16 Line advanced to Rouge du Bout-Rue Dormoire. 16 Brigade rejoined division.

17 Line Rouge du Bout-Bois Grenier-Chapelle d'Armentières reached without opposition.

1 After T.O. Marden, *A Short History of 6th Division*, Appendix III, pp.85-101.

18 Advance onto Pérenchies ridge. Line at night after considerable fighting: Radinghem– Ennetières - Prémesques-Halte to west of Pérenchies-l'Epinette.
20 German attack all along line. Division driven back to Touquet-Bois Blancs-Le Quesne-La Houssoie-Rue du Bois-1'Epinette.
21 19 Brigade (sent to fill gap between II and III Corps) driven back from Le Maisnil-Fromelles to La Boutillerie-Touquet.
22 Heavy attack on 19 Brigade in evening repulsed.
23 17 Brigade relieved by 4th Division. Attacks on 1st KSLI and 2nd York & Lancaster (16 Brigade) repulsed.
24-25 Continuous attacks on divisional front throughout day.
25-26 Retirement of about half a mile during night to prepared line to straighten front: Touquet-Flamengerie Farm-Rue du Bois.
27-28 Attack by night on 18 Brigade trenches, which were captured but retaken by counter-attack.
28-29 Attack by night on 19 Brigade repulsed.
29-30 Strong attack by night on 19 Brigade captured trenches – enemy driven out by counter-attack.

November/December 1914
Holding trenches: Armentières front.

1915

January 1915
Holding trenches: Armentières front.

February
11 Brigadier-General W. Doran relieved of command of 17 Brigade and replaced by Brigadier-General G.M. Harper.

March
12 L'Epinette attacked and captured by 1st North Staffordshire. 16 Brigade moved to Vlamertinghe, but returned next day.

April
Holding trenches: Armentières front.

May
Mining and counter-mining in the Frelinghien and Le Touquet sectors.
27 Major-General Sir J. Keir promoted to command VI Corps, Brigadier-General W. Congreve takes over command of the division. Brigadier-General H. Ainslie takes over command of 18 Brigade.
31 Front handed over to 27th Division. 19 Brigade left Division.

31 Took over new front in Ypres Salient under VI Corps.

June
(VI Corps, Second Army)
2 Relief completed on front from Ypres-Roulers railway to Wieltje.
5 17 Brigade extended front to just short of Turco Farm.
16 Divisional artillery co-operated with 3rd Division attack on Bellewarde Farm.
17 Brigadier-General C.L. Nicholson takes over command of 16 Brigade from Brigadier-General E.C. Ingouville-Williams, promoted to command 34th Division.
20 Gas attack on 16 Brigade.
22 Divisional artillery co-operated with 14th Division attack.

July
6 Divisional artillery co-operated with 4th Division attack near Pilckem.
30 Attack on 14th Division at Hooge.
31. 16 Brigade move up for counter-attack at Hooge – operation cancelled.

August
2-3 Division relieved for operation to retake Hooge.
6 Division takes over front at Hooge. Bombardment commenced.
9 Brigadier-General Ainslie surrenders command of 18 Brigade. Successful attack on Hooge by 16 and 18 Brigades.
15 Brigadier-General R.J. Bridgford takes over command of 18 Brigade.

September
Holding line: Ypres Salient.
24 Brigadier-General J.W.V. Carroll takes over command of 17 Brigade from Brigadier-General G.M. Harper promoted to command 51st Division.

October
14 17 Brigade left for 24th Division and 71 Brigade arrived.

November
14 Major-General Sir C. Ross takes command of Division. Major-General Congreve promoted to command of XIII Corps.
19-20 Division relieved – to rest/training at Houtkerque and Poperinghe.

December
14 Into line: Roulers railway to Wieltjc.
19 Phosgene gas attack.

1916

January
24 11th Essex raid on mound on Verlorenhoek Road.

February
(XIV Corps, Second Army)
14-15 Two enemy raids near Wieltje and Trenches B9/10. Both repulsed.

March
9-10 Bombing raid by 1st Buffs on crater at I 12.
15-16 Successful raid by 2nd DLI.
15-18 Division relieved – to Houtkerque, Wormhoudt, and Calais for rest/training.

April
15-18 Division back into line, holding 5,500 yard front with left on canal.
19-20 Enemy occupied Willow Walk trenches from the 8th Bedfords in Morteldje Salient. Counter-attack unsuccessful.
21 Willow Walk trenches retaken by 1st KSLI.

May
14-15 Enemy attacked four bombing posts of 1st Buffs – beaten off three times, but captured them at fourth attempt.
27 Brigadier-General M.T. Shewen replaced in command of 71 Brigade by Brigadier-General FitzJ. M. Edwards.

June
3 1st West Yorkshire drove enemy out of posts on a frontage of 450 yards of 'Old British Front Line' and re-occupied them.
13 Brigadier-General W.K. McKlintock replaced in command of 18 Brigade by Brigadier-General H.S. Tew.
17-18 Division relieved – to Bollezeele, Houtkerque, and Wormhoudt.

July
15-17 Division into line north-west of Hooge to north of Wieltje.
26 Brigadier-General W.L. Osborn takes over command of 16 Brigade from Brigadier-General C.L. Nicholson, promoted to command 34th Division.

August
2 -3 Entrained at Hopoutre, Proven and Esquelbec, and detrained at Candas and Doullens.
3-4 Marched to Acheux-Raincheval area.
5-7 Division went into line on the Ancre, preparing for attack.

19 Brigadier-General H.S. Tew replaced in command of 18 Brigade by Brigadier-General R.J. Bridgford.
21 Unsuccessful raid by 9th Suffolk and 2nd Sherwood Foresters.
24 Unsuccessful raid by 14th DLI.
26-27 Division relieved.

September
(XIV Corps, Fourth Army)
6-8 Division moved into XIV Corps area.
11 Into line on front between Leuze Wood and Ginchy.
13 Unsuccessful attack by 71 Brigade on Quadrilateral.
15 Battle of Morval – 16 and 71 Brigades failed to take the Quadrilateral.
18 Fresh attack on Quadrilateral after bombardment by 16 and 18 Brigades – successful.
25 Battle of Flers-Courcelette – 16 & 18 Brigades successfully attacked Lesboeufs and south to Morval.
30 Relieved by 20th Division.

October
6 Brigadier-General FitzJ. M. Edwards replaced in command of 71 Brigade by Brigadier-General E. Feetham.
8-9 Division into line, relieving 20th Division.
12 Battle of the Transloy Ridges. 18 and 71 Brigades attack towards Le Transloy – unsuccessful.
15 Attack renewed – partially successful.
18 Fresh attack by 71 Brigade, only partially successful on left.
20 Division relieved – to Corbie.
28 Division assembled in reserve to I Corps.

November
(I Corps, First Army)
25 Division into line on Canal Sector, La Bassée.

December
Division side-slipped slightly to south.

1917

January
26 Raid by 1st West Yorkshire in Cambrin Sector.
29 Raid by 8th Bedfordshire in Hohenzollern Sector.

February

4. Enemy raided 1st West Yorkshire.
9 Raid by 2nd Sherwood Foresters in Quarries Sector under smoke barrage by Special Company RE.
10 Raid by 2nd DLI on Mad Point.
12 71 Brigade scouting party raid partly successful.
15 Enemy attempted raid in Hohenzollern Sector repulsed.
16-17 Relieved by 21st Division – to Bethune-Busnes-Robecq.

March

2-4 Into line in Loos Sector from Double Crassier to Railway Alley.
18 Enemy carried out several simultaneous raids. That on 2nd York & Lancasters was dispersed by Lewis gun fire. That on 1st Buffs was repulsed after hand-to-hand fighting. That on 1st West Yorkshire penetrated the line and six men were captured.
19 Unsuccessful enemy raid on 2nd York & Lancaster.
24 Raid by 11th Essex on area round Posen Crater penetrated to enemy support line and remained for one and a half hours.
25 Enemy raided 9th Norfolk and 2nd Sherwood Foresters and captured nine prisoners, penetrating some distance between the battalions.
30 Raid by 1st Buffs, Loos.

April

5 Enemy raid on 2nd Sherwood Foresters at Border Redoubt driven off.
8 Patrol raid by 2nd DLI in Loos Sector – held up by wire.
10 Successful raid by 9th Suffolks in Quarries Sector.
12 Raid by 2nd York & Lancaster.
13 Enemy withdrew from The Triangle, closely followed by 2nd York & Lancaster.
14 Small enemy raid on 1st West Yorkshire driven off by counter-attack.
15 Ground gained towards Hill 70 by 1st Buffs and 2nd York & Lancaster in the face of increasing opposition.
16 Systematic bombardment of Hill 70 trenches commenced. Enemy counter-attacked and drove 1st Buffs back slightly, but failed against 8th Bedfordshire. 1st West Yorkshire attempted raid but were driven back by artillery fire.
17 Gas released on enemy in ideal conditions. Enemy attacked right flank of 8th Bedfordshire but were driven back.
18 Raid conducted by 1st Leicestershire. 1st KSLI and 8th Bedfordshire made more ground.
19 1st KSLI took north end of Novel Alley, but three attempts to push forward by 8th Bedfordshire unsuccessful. 14th DLI relieved 8th Bedfords and 11th Essex placed under orders of 16 Brigade.
20-21 Line partially withdrawn to allow bombardment.
21 Successful attack by 14th DLI in conjunction with 46th Division.

21-22 14th DLI repulsed two enemy counter-attacks.
22 Attack by 14th DLI and 11th Essex in conjunction with 46th Division. 11th Essex were unable to progress. Whilst 14th DLI took their objective, they were gradually driven back to their original line.
22 Position became stationary with enemy in Nash Alley.
23 Small enemy raid dispersed.
27 Enemy raid in Quarries Sector.
28 Raid by both 9th Norfolk (stopped by wire), and 1st West Yorkshire (also unsuccessful).
29 7,000 gas shells fired by enemy on Vermelles, Philosophe, and Maroc.

May
2 46th Division took over portion of southern line.
5 Enemy patrol entered lines.
9 Enemy attempted raid on 2nd DLI, but were driven off.
13 Heavy enemy bombardment in 14 Bis Sector. Enemy raid broken up as it came out of trenches by artillery fire.
15-16 Enemy raided Boyau 46 and captured four men.
20-21 Raid by 1st West Yorkshire.
22 Raid by 1st Leicestershire in Quarries Sector.
28 Raid by 2nd Sherwood Foresters under cover of a smoke barrage.

June
1 Raid by 1st KSLI near Hendon Alley.
4 Further raid by 1st KSLI on same trenches.
6 Small raid by 2nd DLI – unsuccessful.
8 Enemy mounted a small raid on 9th Suffolks at Newport Sap – repulsed.
10 9th Suffolks raided as far as the enemy support trenches.
12-13 9th Norfolks attempted a raid on Merthyr Sap, but could not gain entrance.
15 14th DLI carried out a successful daylight raid near Nash Alley.
23-24 The enemy entered a post of 11th Essex.
24 Raid carried out by 1st Buffs near Halifax Alley. The raiders remained in the enemy trenches for three and a half hours.
27-28 Raid by 2nd DLI and 11th Essex in connection with operations of 46th Division. The raiders remained in the enemy's trenches for one hour, repelling all counterattacks.

July
1-2 Small enemy raid on Novel Alley – unsuccessful.
3 Small enemy raid on 1st West Yorkshires in Novel Alley – unsuccessful.
7-8 Strong enemy raid near Boyau 70 repulsed by 1st Buffs and 1st KSLI.
9-10 Raid by 14th DLI. Small German raid on Novel Alley was driven off.
12 Patrol raid by 8th Bedfordshire in Hulluch Sector.

16 Raid by 9th Norfolks.
20 Three patrols from 2nd York & Lancaster raided enemy's posts.
23 Raid by 1st Leicestershire in Quarries Sector. Raiders remained one and a half hours in enemy's trenches.
Division relieved by 46th Division. Troops to Ourton-Monchy Breton area.
31 9th Norfolk and 1st Leicestershire went by bus to Bac St. Maur to assist 57th Division.

August
5 9th Norfolks and 1st Leicestershire returned.
19 Brigadier-General P.W. Brown took of command of 71 Brigade. Brigadier-General E. Feetham promoted to command 39th Division.
21 Major-General Ross sent home – Major-General T.O. Marden took command of division.
24-27 Division went into line on Hill 70 front.

September
9 2nd Sherwood Foresters raided enemy in Hill 70 Sector unsuccessfully
13 8th Bedfordshire raided enemy – unsuccessful.
15 Brigadier-General R.J. Bridgford replaced by Brigadier-General G.S.G. Craufurd in command of 18 Brigade.
20-21 Enemy raid on llth Essex failed.
24 Side-stepped with a view to attack on Cité St.Auguste.
29 Enemy raided 2nd York & Lancasters but were repulsed.

October
4 Large enemy raid on 18 Brigade repulsed.
19 Raid with heavy bombardment on 14th DLI unsuccessful.
20-23 Relieved by llth Division – to St. Hilaire area.
26 Brigadier-General W.L. Osborn replaced in command of 16 Brigade by General H.A. Walker.
29 Marched south to join III Corps.

November
(III Corps, Third Army)
4-12 Training with tanks.
20 Battle of Cambrai. Division broke both systems of Hindenburg Line, capturing Ribecourt and Premy Chapel Ridge, entering Marcoing. Over 1,100 prisoners and 23 guns captured. All objectives gained with few casualties by 12.00.
21 14th DLI supported cavalry in advance to Cantaing.
26-27 18 Brigade extended front to Cantaing. 1st Buffs cleared and occupied Noyelles.

30 Enemy counter-attack in force. 16 Brigade moved from divisional reserve to near Beaucamps and counter-attacked Gouzeaucourt. Attack by night on La Vacquerie-Gonnelieu unsuccessful.

December

2-3 16 Brigade relieved part of 29th Division north of St Quentin Canal.

3 Enemy attacked 1st KSLI and 14th DLI north of canal. Three counter-attacks by DLI, but finally driven back. 8th Bedfordshire and 2nd York & Lancaster put in to restore situation – partially successful.

3-4 Front withdrawn to line of canal.

4 General withdrawal of British line to Hindenburg Support System.

10 Relieved by 19th Division.

(VI Corps, Third Army)

11 16th Brigade to VI Corps.

12 18 Brigade to VI Corps, both brigades placed at disposal of 3rd Division, and went into line to relieve two of their brigades on Bullecourt front for a few days.

At rest – Basseux area.

1918

January

(IV Corps, Third Army)

17 Division commenced move up to Fremicourt.

February

4 Enemy made silent raid on three posts in Boursies area.

13 Division side-stepped into Lagnicourt Sector.

March

3 1st KSLI raided the Magpie's Nest.

16 1st Leicesters repeated raid.

21 German Spring offensive commenced. Heavy casualties – brigades held out in the Reserve (Corps) Line till dark.

22 Fighting all day on Corps Line. Remnants of division relieved at night.

25 Move by train to Second Army.

April

(XXII Corps, Second Army)

3-4 Into line in Ypres Salient on high ground between Menin and Zonnebeke.

13 71 Brigade left to join 49th Division on Neuve Eglise front.

16 Line withdrawn to battle zone - enemy followed up in the afternoon.
18 Enemy raided post unsuccessfully.
25 Capture of Kemmel by enemy from the French.
26 71 Brigade returned to Division.
26-27 Further withdrawal to west end of Zillebeke Lake-White Chateau.

May
8 Unsuccessful enemy attack on Ridge Wood.
(II Corps, Second Army)
11-14 Side-slipped to south and came under II Corps.
19 11th Essex raided Manor Farm successfully.
22 2nd DLI raided pillboxes on Bedford front.
28-29 Attack by 11th Essex in conjunction with French *46th Division*.

June
5. 2nd York & Lancaster raided Lankhoff Farm unsuccessfully.
7-8 Division relieved – to Dirty Bucket Camp and Jan-ter-Biezen area. 71st TMB co-operated in French *46th Division* operation.
19 18th TMB lent to French *7th Division* for a raid.
27-28 Relieved French *46th Division* on Dickebusch front.

July
6 Enemy raid on Scottish Wood repulsed.
9 Patrol of 2nd Sherwood Foresters rushed a post near Ridge Wood by day.
14 Attack by 18 Brigade on Ridge Wood. Seven officers, 341 ORs, 23 machine-guns, one heavy and two light trench mortars captured.

August
2 1st Buffs carried out daylight raid on the Brasserie.
8 Minor operation by 18 Brigade in connection with 41st Division's operation (one company 1st West Yorkshire), unsuccessful. One company 2nd DLI on right successful.
21-24 Relieved by 27th American Division – to Wizernes area.
31 Division marched to Arques.

September
(IX Corps, Fourth Army)
1 Division entrained for Fourth Army.
2-4 Detrained and billeted in area Heilly-Ribemont-Franvillers.
13-14 Relieved 32nd Division at head of IX Corps. 18 Brigade took over front in Holnon Wood with 11th Essex.
15 11th Essex attacked and captured trenches just clear of Holnon Wood.

17 1st West Yorkshire attacked Holnon Village and 11th Essex attacked Badger Copse to establish starting line for general attack on 18 September. 11th Essex eventually successful, 1st West Yorkshire unsuccessful.
18 General attack to capture high ground overlooking St Quentin. 71 Brigade on right with 2nd DLI attached to capture Holnon, 16 Brigade on left. The latter advanced 3,000 yards, the former were held up by the Quadrilateral. 71 Brigade made little progress as the French failed to capture Round and Manchester Hills on right flank.
19 Attack renewed on Quadrilateral but unsuccessful.
20-23 Digging new assembly trenches – Quadrilateral bombarded with heavy artillery.
24 Attack on whole IX Corps front, 18 Brigade on right, 16 Brigade on left. Half of the Quadrilateral captured by nightfall. 1st Leicestershire, attached to 18 Brigade, captured Douai Trench east of Holnon at 22.30 by moonlight.
25 Gradual completion of capture of the Quadrilateral. Selency village captured.
30 Relief of division by the French.

October
1-3 Resting in Tertry area.
4 Relieved 46th Division. 16 Brigade took over line with 139 Brigade (46th Division) at Sequehart under 6th Division.
8 General attack towards Bohain – 71 Brigade on left, 16 Brigade on right, 1st West Yorkshire (attached to 16 Brigade) attacking up valley to Méricourt. All objectives gained by night.
8-9 Took over part of line by night from 30th American Division.
9 Pursuit to the Selle began. Bohain captured during night by 9th Norfolks.
10 Advance by 71 Brigade to high ground 2,000 yards east of Bohain.
11 Reconnaissance in force by 71 Brigade brought to a standstill.
12 18 Brigade make failed attack on Bellevue Spur.
16 16 and 18 Brigades moved to north for general attack on 17th. Brigadier-General H.A. Walker (16 Brigade) wounded.
17 Battle of the Selle. Attack through Vaux Andigny, 16 Brigade on left, 18 Brigade on right – successful.
19-20 Brigadier-General W.G. Braithwaite takes command of 16 Brigade.
23 General attack to gain high ground overlooking Sambre Canal at 01.30. 18 Brigade successful on right, 71 Brigade delayed on left but gained objectives by the afternoon.
23-24 16 Brigade relieved 71st by night and pushed on, completing capture of final objective.
30 Successful attack on farm on the Happegarbes Spur by 1st Buffs.
30-31 Division relieved – into rest at Fresnoy le Grand.

November
11 Armistice signed.
20 March to the Rhine commenced.
December
5 HQ Group and 71 Brigade crossed River Meuse.
13 71 Brigade crossed German frontier to Malmedy.
15 18 Brigade crossed frontier.
16 16 Brigade crossed frontier.
23 To final area Rondorf-Kendenich (Cologne).

1919

March
15 6th Division ceases to exist.

1

From the Aisne to Armentières: Operations 1914

Mobilization

The first entry in the War Diary of the headquarters of 6th Infantry Division was made at 23.00 on 3 August, and reads simply: 'War declared with Germany.'[1] At that point the division, the last numbered of the six Regular British infantry divisions which were to form a three corps British Expeditionary Force (BEF) in the event of continental war, was split between Ireland and England.[2] Under the command of Major-General John Lindesay Keir,[3] HQ was stationed with 17 Brigade (Brigadier-General Walter Robert Butler Doran) at Cork, whilst 16 Brigade was based at Fermoy.[4] 16 Brigade (Brigadier-General Edward Charles Ingouville-Williams) had begun to move on 30 July, and it is an interesting reflection on the tensions in that country that the Blackwater detachment of the 1st King's Shropshire Light Infantry, in County Wexford, was stopped at Enniscorthy 'by inhabitants who refused to allow them to proceed to their post.'[5] 18 Brigade (Brigadier-General Walter Norris Congreve), over the water, was split between Lichfield, York and Sheffield. The Irish contingents only began to embark at Cork and Queenstown on the 15th, but time had not been wasted.

1 War Diary, HQ 6th Infantry Division, TNA WO95/1581. 6th Division had been formed in 1812 by Sir Arthur Wellesley for service in the Peninsular War.
2 The Expeditionary Force would comprise Aldershot Command (1st & 2nd Divisions); Southern Command (3rd Division); Eastern Command (4th Division); and Irish Command (5th and 6th Division); plus a cavalry division.
3 See Chapter 2 in respect of both Keir and his brigadiers.
4 The Field Artillery was at Mallow, Waterford, Fermoy, Ballincoig, Kilkenny and Cahir, the Engineers at Fermoy, Cork and Limerick. The 24th Heavy Battery was in Eastern Command, at Woolwich.
5 War Diary, 16 Infantry Brigade, 30 July 1914, TNA WO95/1605. The situation was resolved by the police.

16 Brigade carried out battalion training between July 31 and 4 August, and 'route marches and tactical operations' from 10 to 13 August.[6]

General Keir had taken over command of the division during the month before war was declared from Sir William Pulteney Pulteney, who would be the division's corps commander (III Corps) during their first nine months on the Western Front. *The Times* reported of the September 1913 Irish manoeuvres: 'Commanders and staffs gave proof of competence and the troops of vigour and high training.'[7] The report of the Inspector-General of Home Forces submitted in 1914 stated that 'whilst the march discipline of the division was somewhat disappointing ... speaking generally, the work of the division was excellent.'[8] The 6th Division thus appeared to be in good shape at the outbreak of war. Held back against invasion, it assembled in camps around Cambridge and Newmarket. Thomas Marden, the division's ultimate commander, noted the 'many kindnesses shown ... by the people of Cambridge; the canteens and recreation rooms instituted for the men, and the hospitality shown by colleges and individuals to the officers.'[9] Training continued. 16 Brigade, camped at Coldham's Common, near Cambridge, carried out route marches and company and battalion training 20-22 August, and on 25 August it pursued an Advanced Guard tactical scheme. Cambridge University Officer Training Corps took the part of the enemy, and the two forces met on high ground four miles west of Newmarket. On the 28th, the brigade carried out 'an attack practice on the supposition that both flanks of the attack were covered by the advance of other brigades.'[10] From the following day until 7 September, company, battalion and brigade exercises were carried out daily. 18 Brigade similarly carried out training at a battalion, brigade and divisional level, and 'particular attention was paid to musketry training and march discipline.'[11]

Mobilization generally went smoothly.[12] One key aspect of this process, which provided impetus for training, was the fact that the Regular Army was significantly

6 War Diary, HQ 16 Infantry Brigade, August 1914, TNA WO95/1605.
7 *The Times*, 18 September 1913.
8 Quoted in A. Leask, *Putty*, p.183. The issue of Irish home rule was brought to a head in terms of the question as to whether the army would enforce this on Ulster in early 1914. Pulteney apparently stated that 25 percent of 6th Division's officers would appose this, and in terms of the plan that 6th Division would move to Dublin if there was disturbance in the north, echoing the cavalry officers of the 'Curragh Incident', confirmed on 19 April that his officers 'would not enforce home rule on an actively reluctant Ulster.' (Leask, op. cit. pp.182-4).
9 T.O. Marden, *A Short History of the 6th Division*, p.1.
10 War Diary, HQ 16 Infantry Brigade, August 1914, TNA WO95/1605.
11 War Diary, HQ 18 Infantry Brigade, August-September 1914, TNA WO95/1614. 'Ordinary training' proceeded between 1-5 September. The details of training within 17 Brigade were not recorded.
12 Except for 18 Brigade, who were detailed to assist for a week with the Forth coastal defences, suffering a lengthy train journey with the disruption of the railways, especially in relation to their stores.

understrength and had to recall reservists.[13] The previous year, the six Regular divisions had been found to be 60 percent below war establishment.[14] Charles Messenger observes, however, that 'the reporting of reservists to their depots took place more quickly than expected and a large number of infantry battalions were ... at full strength by the end of the third day of mobilization.'[15] In 18 Brigade, 2nd Sherwood Foresters received 350 reservists on the second day of mobilization, which brought it up to 30 officers and 929 men.[16] 2nd Durham Light Infantry were particularly understrength, 301 reservists arriving on the 6th, and 384 the following day.[17] In 17 Brigade, 2nd Leinster were equally depleted and received three tranches of reservists – 288 on the 6th, 317 on the 7th, and 88 on the 8th.[18] In 16 Brigade, 259 reservists arrived on the 6th, 252 on the 7th and 43 on the 8th for 1st Buffs.[19] 1st Leicestershire received 296 on the 7th, 230 on the 8th, and noted on the 9th: 'Mobilization complete except 1 Captain, 1 Subaltern, 3 Sergeants, 30 men required.' On the following day, as if to order, a further two NCOs and 33 men arrived.[20] If the units that reported the numbers of reservists received are representative, 6th Division was 56 percent under strength – the situation reported in 1913 had not been rectified. As it only began to entrain on 7 September, the last of the six divisions of the BEF to reach the continent was both at full strength and had taken the opportunity of extended training not afforded to the first five.

On 8 September the departure from Southampton began. The destination was St Nazaire at the southern base of the Brittany peninsula and the ships lay off the port for a day or two before disembarkation could take place. 16 Brigade recorded that 'all vehicles and horses had to be slung from (the) ship by ships cranes which worked badly and caused much delay and a certain amount of damage to vehicles.'[21] The movement of an infantry division was a substantial operation in ships not designed to carry them and arriving in ports with little experience of receiving a fighting force. By 12 September, however, the division had concentrated by train 35 or so kilometres south-east of Paris in the area Coulommiers-Mortcerf-Marles-Chaumes. Located in the *département* of Seine-et-Marne, the locale was famous for its brie cheeses. Tasting of this delicacy was barely possible, as the following day the division began a wet

13 The Army Reserve, consisting of previous Regulars, was approximately 145,000 strong. There was also the Special Reserve, created in 1908 out of the old Militia.
14 TNA WO/106/50, cited in C. Messenger, *Call to Arms*, p.21.
15 Messenger, op. cit., p.44.
16 War Diary, 2nd Battalion Sherwood Foresters, 6-7 August 1914, TNA WO95/1616.
17 War Diary, 2nd Battalion Durham Light Infantry, 6-7 August 1914, TNA WO95/1617.
18 War Diary, 2nd Battalion Leinster Regiment, 6-8 August 1914, TNA WO95/1612.
19 War Diary, 1st Battalion East Kent Regiment, 6-8 August 1914, TNA WO95/1608.
20 War Diary, 1st Battalion Leicestershire Regiment, 7-10 August 1914, TNA WO95/1611.
21 War Diary, HQ 16 Infantry Brigade, 10 September 1914, TNA WO95/1605.

march of 100 kilometres as the crow flies (and longer by road) north-east,[22] towards the Aisne river, south of Soissons. They were marching towards the sound of the guns.

The Aisne

The sound of the guns had been a good deal closer three days earlier. Between 6 and 10 September the exhausted BEF, following the battles of Mons and Le Cateau and subsequent retreat, together with the French *Fifth* and *Sixth Armies*, had fought the First Battle of the Marne. On 27 August the German Chief of the General Staff, Helmuth von Moltke,[23] had realigned the right wing of his invading armies and followed the retreating left wing of the French armies. In performing this manoeuvre a gap had opened up between Alexander von Kluck's *1st Army* and Karl von Bülow's *2nd Army*.[24] Into this gap Joseph Joffre,[25] the French Commander-in-Chief, projected his forces. After five days of fighting, it was the enemy's turn to retreat, in the direction of the River Aisne. As Hew Strachan has observed, whilst the Marne fighting was 'tactically indecisive … strategically and operationally the Marne was a truly decisive battle in the Napoleonic sense.'[26] Germany, now condemned to fighting on two fronts, could likely no longer win the war outright.

For the enemy, this withdrawal was a two-stage affair. Firstly, they had to regroup. The gap between the German *1st* and *2nd Armies* had to be closed. Secondly, they had to decide how to regain the initiative. The first problem was solved by the arrival of the *VII Reserve Corps* (General von Zwehl),[27] part of the newly formed *7th Army*, at the Aisne. On 13 September, as this formation was taking up position (and as 6th Division began its march), I Corps, under Sir Douglas Haig, crossed the river on the British right.[28] II Corps, commanded by Sir Horace Smith-Dorrien, crossed in the

22 The weather had broken on 10 September.

23 Helmuth von Moltke the Younger (1848-1916), a veteran of the Franco-Prussian War (1870-71), was Chief of the General Staff of the German Armies, 1906-14. He had been responsible for amendments to the so-called 'Schlieffen Plan.'

24 Alexander von Kluck (1846-1934) was a veteran of the Austro-Prussian (1866) and Franco-Prussian Wars (1870-1) and had been Inspector General of the *7th Army* at the outbreak of war. Karl von Bülow (1846-1921) had also served in both wars and was Inspector General of the *3rd Army* at the outbreak of war.

25 An artilleryman, Joseph Jacques Césaire Joffre (1852-1931) had been Commander-in-Chief of the French Army since 1911. He had served in the Sino-French War (1884-85) and Timbuktu (1894).

26 H. Strachan, *The First World War – Volume 1: To Arms*, p.261.

27 Johann von Zwehl (1851-1926,) a veteran of the Franco-Prussian War (1870-1), was on the reserve list in 1914. Under his command *7th Reserve Corps* had just reduced Maubeuge. His corps arrived on the Aisne with hours to spare having completed a 40-mile march in 24 hours, a fifth to a quarter of its infantry having fallen out. [J.E. Edmonds, *Military Operations: France & Belgium 1914, Vol. 1*, p. 393].

28 At Bourg-et-Comin (1st Division) and Chavonne and Pont Arcy (2nd Division). Sir Douglas Haig (1861-1928) would become Commander-in-Chief of the BEF on 10 December 1915, replacing Sir John French.

centre,[29] whilst III Corps, formed in France on 31 August 1914 under Sir William Pulteney (and the parent formation whom 6th Division were to join), crossed on the far left of the British front.[30] The BEF was sandwiched between the French *Sixth Army* on their left, and the *Fifth Army* on their right. (See Map 1 colour section).

The second part of the German conundrum, how to regain the initiative, was not satisfactorily solved. The Marne had finished the career of von Moltke, who had been replaced by Erich von Falkenhayn.[31] The new commander-in-chief realised that that hope for a decisive victory lay in his right wing and envelopment of the Allies. The friction of war meant that he would never quite marshal the force to do this. On the Aisne, however, his armies made every effort to push the Allies back across the river, and a savage battle ensued over the next two days. The three British corps attempted to push up the ridge on the 14th, cross the Chemin des Dames road, and reach the plateau beyond. *II Corps, III Corps,* part of *IV Corps,* and *IX Corps,* from the German *1st Army,* with elements of *II Cavalry Corps,* and *VII Reserve Corps* effectively blocked the advance, which was made at great cost. I Corps, which achieved most progress, sustained 3,500 casualties on 14 September. After a day of German counter-attacks on the 15th, both sides, fought to a virtual standstill, began to entrench.

6th Division had been destined to join III Corps on its arrival on 18 September, but instead was directed by Sir John French, the commander of the BEF, into reserve.[32] From thence, 18 Brigade was swiftly attached to I Corps. At 07.00 on the 19th, after a night in the open under heavy rain, the brigade was directed to relieve 1 and 2 Brigades of 1st Division on the extreme right of the British line abutting the French. Their position was also the furthest point of the advance. This was the location of the Sugar Factory, near Cerny, which had been the site of violent fighting by 2 Brigade on the 14th in an attempt to push on to the Cerny-en-Laonnois plateau, the brigade sustaining over 1,000 casualties.

The first action that a brigade of the 6th Division would see, therefore, would not be under its own divisional commander. The relief having been completed only at 23.00

29 At Vailly (3rd Division) and Condé and Missy (5th Division). Sir Horace Lockwood Smith-Dorrien (1858-1930) would be sacked by Sir John French from the command of Second Army following a request to withdraw during the Second Battle of Ypres. His treatment is widely regarded as unfair, and he was disliked by both French and Haig.

30 4th Division crossed at Venizel late at night on the 12th. Sir William 'Putty' Pulteney Pulteney (1861-1941) was a respected officer of the Scots Guards who continued in command of III Corps until February 1918.

31 Promoted major-general in 1912, Erich von Falkenhyn was the Prussian Minster of War in August 1914. He had seen active service in the Boxer Rebellion (1900).

32 John Denton Pinkstone French (1852-1925), had served as a midshipman in the Navy before joining the cavalry. He became a national hero during the Second Boer War, rising to command the Cavalry Division. He had commanded I Corps at Aldershot before becoming Chief of the Imperial General Staff in 1912, a post he resigned at the time of the 'Curragh incident.' A womaniser with an excitable temperament, he was out of his depth in his command of the BEF.

on the 19th, Walter Congreve was in his brigade's front line at 06.00 the following morning. He did not like what he saw. The position, particularly its right, lay at the head of a steep ravine, in which nestled the hamlet of Troyon. The right lay on the Chemin des Dames itself, the left tailed increasingly down the slope away from the road. The trenches were 'not deep enough against shell fire', and the field of fire was 'very short, as (the) trenches (were) all behind (the) crest.'[33] Private J. Warwick of 2nd Durham Light Infantry (DLI) was no more impressed than his GOC: 'Rain was coming down in torrents and our trenches were practically up to the thighs in water.'[34] Warwick's battalion was in the centre, whilst on the left were 1st East Yorkshire, with 1st West Yorkshire on the right flank. 2nd Sherwood Foresters formed a reserve downhill in Troyon, brigade HQ being positioned just above the hamlet. Congreve was undoubtedly expecting to be attacked, and indeed, General von Heeringen,[35] commanding the German *7th Army*, ordered an attack along the whole *VII Reserve Corps* front on the 20th. The corps, containing the *13th* and *14th Reserve* Divisions,[36] had been exhausted after its efforts on 14 and 15 September after a long march, but had had time to recover. This attack resulted from Falkenhayn's order for operations across all the German Armies down to Verdun, his tactic being to pin the French and British forces and prevent them moving forces further north (where both foes were planning envelopment).

At 10.15 Congreve received news of a heavy attack on the West Yorkshires. The battalion had anticipated Congreve's concerns, and had spent the night improving their trenches and constructing overhead cover, reflecting well on the professionalism of the CO, Lieutenant-Colonel Francis Towsey.[37] At 04.30, after an hour or so of shellfire, an infantry attack descended on the 'French Turkos' to their right, who were soon seen disappearing over the Paissy Hills to the rear.[38] The 'anxious' Towsey ordered D Company forward into the gap, whereupon they came under fire from the returning Moroccans. Private Thomas Rainbird described how 'it was awful, every one of us exposed to a raking fire and no cover … my mates were falling all over the place.' This friendly fire resulted in 26 wounded and two fatalities. Retaliation was inevitable: 'Naturally our boys opened fire on them … in spite of the CO's shout of "Don't Fire."'[39] The Yorkshiremen then retired. Showing the required leadership

33 War Diary, HQ 18 Infantry Brigade, 20 September 1914, TNA WO95/1614.
34 J. Warwick, quoted in P. Kendall, *Aisne 1914*, p.297.
35 Josisas von Heeringen (1850-1926) had recently served as Prussian Minister of War and General Inspector *2nd Army*.
36 Reserve divisions were not as effective as their regular counterparts, and by 1917 both were regarded as 'mediocre.'
37 Fifty-year-old Francis William Towsey had been commissioned in 1885 and had assumed command of his battalion in March 1914. He had seen active service in Lushai (1892), and the Ashanti Expedition (1895-96).
38 *Tirailleurs d'Afrique.*
39 T.C. Rainbird, Private Papers, IWM Docs 11755.

General situation of 18 Brigade, Troyon, 20 September 1914.

Attack on 1st West Yorkshire 20 September 1914, above Troyon Village (now destroyed).

Disastrous attacks of 1st East Yorkshire and 2nd Durham Light Infantry against the Chemin des Dames, 20 September 1914.

from the front, Towsey made two personal reconnaissances, his companion on the second, Lieutenant Thomas Meautys, becoming the division's first officer fatality.[40] Firing continued all morning, but at 13.30 Towsey received the ill news that his front companies had been taken prisoner.

An investigation into what happened was later ordered by 1st Division. The battalion's view that the enemy had advanced from the exposed right flank under a white flag, and 'when our men went out to meet them they were surrounded and heavily fired on',[41] was accepted as correct. The retirement of the French had allowed the enemy to infiltrate, and although the company of West Yorkshires to the right of the line had attempted to form a defensive flank, they had been 'annihilated', the Germans sweeping down the trench with white flags tied to their bayonets, killing and taking prisoners.[42] Their demand for surrender was met by Major Alexander

40 War Diary, 1st Battalion West Yorkshire Regiment, 20 September 1914, TNA WO95/1618. Lieutenant Thomas Gilliat Meautys was commissioned in September 1909 and was one of three brothers all of whom were killed during the war.

41 War Diary, 1st Battalion West Yorkshire Regiment, 20 September 1914, TNA WO95/1618.

42 2nd Kings Royal Rifle Corps had suffered a similar incident on 17 September (Kendall, op. cit. pp.278-284). The Germans would claim the same tactic was employed by the British at Ypres in October 1914.

Ingles with the cry of 'All who will not surrender follow me!',[43] and he retired a short distance with some 150 followers. Attempting to retake their trench, Ingles and most of his men were killed.[44] The retirement had exposed 2nd DLI, next in line, to a flank attack, and the report noted that 'possibly the machine guns of the D.L.I. & E.Y. which had been turned round to clear the Germans off the hill accounted for some of the damage' when Ingles made his return.[45] Thomas Rainbird had been wounded by shrapnel which had gone through his shoulder and exited his back, and could only lie 'watching my comrades fighting till the finish.' Taken prisoner, Rainbird was hauled to his feet and marched through the German lines where 'their dead numbered at least 6 to 1 of ours – they were being piled up outside their trenches as we passed.'[46]

Brigade HQ could see what was happening uphill. About half an hour before Towsey was alerted, they could see a 'mass of Germans … on line of trench supposed to be held by W.Y.'[47] In response, Congreve immediately ordered the Sherwood Foresters forward – indeed, the War Diary of 1st Division implies Congreve went with them.[48] The two companies leading could see Rainbird and his fellow prisoners being led off by a German column, and they soon came under machine-gun fire from both the front and left flank, sustaining heavy casualties. The impetus of the two companies following carried them forward 'with great dash' and they secured the front line.[49] Towsey himself had not been inactive. He had led his HQ and C Company towards the firing line – 'they fixed bayonets and advanced at the double.'[50] Meeting heavy enfilade fire, however, they did the sensible thing and retired whence they came, only able to stabilise their flank and advance again when a company of 2nd Royal Sussex (2 Brigade) and 15th Hussars came up.

The afternoon then saw failures of command and control that left Congreve frustrated. Some of the DLI 'left their trenches owing to some mistaken order to retire' and the brigadier personally went forward to stop the retirement. To his further frustration, the battalion then made an 'unauthorised counterattack', about which he could do nothing. 'Heavy losses were sustained without any corresponding result as soon as (the) trenches were left.'[51] 1st East Yorkshire similarly, and equally unwisely, joined in the DLI's counterattack. 'On crossing a small ridge machine guns and

43 Kendall, op. cit. p.303.
44 Major Alexander Wighton Ingles, born 1869, had been commissioned in March 1902. He had served in South Africa 1899-1901, and had only achieved his majority in March 1914.
45 War Diary, HQ 18 Infantry Brigade, 20 September 1914, TNA WO95/1614.
46 Rainbird, op. cit. Thomas Charles Rainbird would be released from the Torgau POW camp on 1 December 1918.
47 War Diary, HQ 18 Infantry Brigade, 20 September 1914, TNA WO95/1614.
48 War Diary, HQ 1st Infantry Division, 20 September 1914, TNA WO95/1227.
49 War Diary, 2nd Battalion Sherwood Foresters, 20 September 1914, TNA WO95/1616.
50 War Diary, 1st Battalion West Yorkshire Regiment, 20 September 1914, TNA WO95/1618.
51 War Diary, HQ 18 Infantry Brigade, 20 September 1914, TNA WO95/1614.

shrapnel opened up', and significant casualties resulted before they could return to their trenches.[52] Thereafter, the situation settled.

The West Yorkshires' losses had been exceptionally heavy. Only five officers and about 250 ORs could be accounted for at the end of the day. Major Ingles, two captains, three lieutenants and one subaltern were known to be dead; [53] whilst three captains, two lieutenants and two subalterns were missing. Towsey himself was wounded, as was another lieutenant.[54] Seventy-one other ranks were known to have been killed, 110 were wounded, and 436 missing. It was a stunning disaster – the heart had been ripped out of the battalion, which reformed into one company under the command of Major George Lang, the second-in-command.[55] The Sherwood Foresters had lost four officers killed and eight wounded in their crucial counterattack,[56] with approximately 40 ORs killed and 140 wounded. The 2nd DLI had lost two senior officers, Major D'Arcy Mander killed and Major Alexander Robb dying of wounds;[57] whilst a captain and two subalterns were dead. A further three lieutenants and a similar number of subalterns were wounded. [58] Amongst the other ranks, 36 were dead and 92 wounded. The futile charge of the East Yorkshires had cost not only the life of their commanding officer, Lieutenant-Colonel Richard Benson,[59] who would die of wounds nine days later, but two captains were also wounded and one was missing, two lieutenants were wounded with one missing, and a second-lieutenant was missing,[60] along with 73 ORs dead, missing and wounded. A reflection of the savagery of the fighting of 1914, the

52 War Diary, 1st Battalion East Yorkshire Regiment, 20 September 1914, TNA WO95/1618.

53 Captains M. Fisher and J. F I'Anson, Lieutenants T.G. Meautys, O.C.W. Thompson and W.L. Elliot, and Second-Lieutenant E.W. Wilson.

54 Lieutenant H.E. Pickering.

55 Forty-seven-year-old George Godfrey Lang was commissioned in 1887 and had achieved his majority in September 1907. He would command the battalion for a year from September 1915.

56 Lieutenants L.A. Bernard, B.C. Ash and P.M. Murray and Second-Lieutenant R.P.D Milner were killed, with four captains (C.C. Parkinson, R.S. Popham, G.F. Luther and J.H. Mathias) and four subalterns (R.E.C. Weigall, I.G. Macbean, W.A.W. Crellin and B.G. Allen) wounded.

57 Major D'Arcy Wentworth Mander, aged 44, was commissioned in December 1892, and had achieved his majority in November 1912. Major Alexander Kirkland Robb aged 42 had been commissioned in May 1893 and had achieved his majority in August 1913. Robb had served on the North-West Frontier 1897-98, with the Tirah Expedition, whilst Mander had no war experience.

58 Captain H.V. Hare and Second-Lieutenants C.M. Stanuell and R. Marshall were killed. Lieutenants W.B. Twist, W.A. Grey-Wilson and W.H. Godsal (Adjutant), and Second-Lieutenants J.R. Galos, C.H. Baker and C. Moarns were wounded.

59 Lieutenant-Colonel Richard Erle Benson, aged 52, had been commissioned in May 1884, and had served in South Africa in 1902. He was appointed CO in August 1911.

60 Captains P.B. Maxwell and D.F. Anderson (Adjutant); Lieutenants V.E. Inglefield and F.H. Sasse were wounded, whilst Captain E.L.P Edwards, Lieutenant B.S.C. Hutchinson and Second-Lieutenant A.E. Meller were missing.

brigade had lost precisely a quarter of its infantry strength, its officers taking heavy losses, and two battalions lacked their COs. The 1,044 casualties comprised nearly half of approximately 2,200 suffered by the whole BEF that day. The day also took its toll on the attackers – as night fell, *VII Reserve Corps* reported that 'its troops were so exhausted that, at best, it could only hold the line.'[61] Ordered to attack the next day, von Zwehl protested that 'the daily repetition of attack orders could not obtain any success.' One of his brigades 'could only put 200 rifles with nine or ten officers into the fight out of it six battalions.' The enemy general continued: 'The enemy was too stubborn and used his artillery too skilfully.'[62] At cost, 18 Brigade had done its job.

The Sherwood Foresters noted that 'This was a most important action as the safety of the British right and the bridge over the R(iver) Aisne at Bourg depended on the maintenance of the trenches.'[63] Indeed, worryingly, at the end of the day, 'there were no signs of the French & a big gap was apparently left open that night.'[64] 1st Division, commanded by Major-General Samuel Lomax,[65] was keeping a close eye on the position of 18 Brigade, however, and Congreve was clearly keeping his temporary divisional commander well informed. At 09.00 on the 20th Lomax sent Congreve the following message: 'Our brigade (2nd or 4th alternates) watches your right flank by day, and artillery stops the enemy's advance by day – 2nd Brigade at Paissy protects your right by night. Cavalry Brigade communicates directly with you.'[66] The division moved 1st Queen's from 3 Brigade as a reserve battalion later in the afternoon, but it is clear that the arrival of the Hussars was something of a surprise to Congreve – communication was not quite as fluid as Lomax hoped.

The battle had been fought in atrocious conditions. 'Men state that owing to rain & mud their rifle bolts would hardly work and that ammunition was short.'[67] There had evidently been confusion abounding in the front line, brought about by the enemy's flank assault. The two episodes of friendly fire were tragic. Yet 1st Division and 18 Brigade HQs had worked well together in manging resources to ensure there was no enemy breakthrough. Congreve evidently had his finger on the pulse of everything that happened and had positioned his brigade HQ so that he had direct sight of his three units in line. A failure of command lay in the hasty actions of the 2nd DLI and 1st East Yorkshire, whose COs clearly, and unwisely, took the

61 Edmonds, op. cit. *Vol. 1*, p. 449.
62 Edmonds, op. cit. *Vol. 1*, p. 450.
63 War Diary, 2nd Battalion Sherwood Foresters, 20 September 1914, TNA WO95/1616.
64 War Diary, HQ 18 Infantry Brigade, 20 September 1914, TNA WO95/1614.
65 Samuel Holt Lomax (1855-1915) would become a casualty on 31 October 1914, at Ypres, when a shell hit Hooge Chateau, and died in early 1915. Commissioned into the Scottish Rifles in 1874, Lomax had served in the 9th Cape Frontier War (1877) and the Zulu War (1878). Serving in various staff posts he had commanded 10 Infantry Brigade (from 1904) and 1st Division from 1910.
66 War Diary, HQ 1st Infantry Division, 20 September 1914, TNA WO95/1227.
67 War Diary, HQ 18 Infantry Brigade, 20 September 1918, TNA WO95/1614.

responsibility of the 'man on the spot', and decided to counterattack. They did so without any proper reconnaissance of their position, having only come into line the previous night. Breasting the rise in front of them, they were open to slaughter. Their attack represented offensive spirit in the absence of military good sense. Benson was in no position to answer to his actions. Lieutenant-Colonel Bernard McMahon of the 2nd DLI, who was in his second year of battalion command, remained in post.[68] He was, however, side-lined to the School of Musketry at Hythe in January 1915. No criticism attached to Towsey whose battalion was the victim of the French flight. Indeed, despite a significant lapse when in temporary command of the brigade at Hooge in August 1915 (see Chapter 3), he would proceed to command 122 Infantry Brigade from September 1915 to mid-1918. The brigade remained in line until after dark on 25 September and observed: 'Constant shelling and losses on Chemin des Dames trenches were very wearing to the troops. Night alarms were persistent but got better as the men got more accustomed to snipers & less jumpy at night work.'[69] The troops, many of whom would never have seen combat before, were learning their craft. They were also compelled into other activities which would become only too familiar, namely the daily strengthening of their trenches, which the Royal Engineers began to wire (trip wire in this case), and labouring work when out of the line.

Meanwhile, the remaining two brigades were put under the command of other divisions. 17 Brigade went into line to relieve 6 Brigade (2nd Division) and 4 Guards Brigade on the night of 21/22 September, to hold the line Cour de Soupir farm to Fort de Metz and remained there until 1 October. As Lance-Corporal Edward Luther of 3rd Rifle Brigade discovered, the trenches 'seemed unfinished & were not deep or wide enough' and under shelling, 'we were obliged to lay down on the bottom all day long' at first. Their position was 'just below the crest-line, the enemy's trenches were only 250 yards from us.'[70] Corporal Charles Arnold, of the same battalion, lost seven members of his platoon on their first exposure to shrapnel shelling on the morning of the 22nd: 'We who had never experienced warfare before were paled and shocked by the suddenness of this catastrophe.' He had joined up in 1907, but nothing had prepared him for being under shellfire.[71] During this period the brigade suffered 177 casualties, nearly a third of these (55) sustained in an ill-conceived and understrength attack by the Rifle Brigade on 24 September on a knoll and trench, conducted presumably because the spot in question afforded observation. Luther described how: 'One night our C.O. decided to rush the German trenches. This was kept quite secret until a few minutes before the time to form up came.' An officer of the battalion noted

68 Bernard William Lynedoch McMahon, born 1865, had previously served as brigade-major at Aldershot and a was a veteran of South Africa 1899-1901. Musketry was his specialism.
69 War Diary, HQ 18 Infantry Brigade, 25 September 1914, TNA WO95/1614.
70 E.A. Luther, Private Papers, IWM Docs 12283. Luther would be discharged on health grounds in February 1915.
71 C.W. Arnold (A. Wilson ed.), *The War Diary of an English Soldier*, p.24.

that the attack, however, 'was not the surprise it was intended to be.'[72] The leader of the assault, Major Anthony Boden,[73] paying the price for leading from the front, was killed. The attacking C Company retired almost immediately in the face of rifle fire and three machine guns, and 'back right on to the supporting Company's bayonets.'[74] The episode reflects somewhat poorly on the highly popular CO, Lieutenant-Colonel Reginald Alexander. The division would learn that even small enterprises in trench warfare needed very careful planning.

Meanwhile, towards the left of the BEF's position, 16 Brigade relieved 7 and 9 Brigades (3rd Division) near Vailly on the night of 21/22 September. Brevet Colonel Julian Hasler, 1st Buffs, took command of the whole front, showing 'quick appreciation of the situation', and repelled an enemy attack at 20.00.[75] They remained holding the line until 12 October. Their casualties were comparatively light, numbering 23 killed, 97 wounded and five missing. Although brigade HQ was shelled out of the house it occupied on 25 September, things were sufficiently leisurely for the war diarist to give a detailed description of 'an excellent example of the advantages to be derived from the occupation of a retired position.' The enemy held a re-entrant and their trenches were positioned away from the edge of the plateau. Any attack by 17 Brigade would have had to cross the rise of the plateau edge, and then be subject to 'enfilade and even reverse fire.'[76] If the writer was Captain Roland Mangles *psc*,[77] the brigade-major, then he had had the luxury of time and opportunity to thoughtfully review the relative positions, and the error made in haste by 1st East Yorkshire and 2nd Durham Light Infantry ten days earlier would not have been repeated.

Marden gives the total of divisional casualties on the Aisne as 1,482.[78] Brigade war diaries reveal a total of 1,395 infantry casualties. Twenty-two officers had been killed, 32 wounded and 12 were missing. In the other ranks, 207 fatalities had been recorded, 659 men were wounded and 463 missing.

72 R. Berkeley, *The History of the Rifle Brigade in the War of 1914-1918, Vol. I*, p.28.
73 Major Anthony Drummond Boden, aged 43, was commissioned in July 1892 and achieved his majority on 6 March 1909. He had served in South Africa 1900-1902.
74 Luther, op. cit.
75 M. Connelly, *Forward the Buffs!* Kindle edition location 880. Connelly notes that Major Edward Finch Hatton was wounded, 'revealing an immediate and abiding lesson of operations on the Western Front, the vulnerability of officers who were expected to lead from the front and set an example.'
76 War Diary, HQ 16 Infantry Brigade, 30 September 1914, TNA WO95/1605.
77 Roland Henry Mangles DSO *psc*, had been commissioned in December 1894. He had served as brigade signalling officer in South Africa 1900-2, had special employment with the War Office in 1910 and been GSO3 there 1910-12, and had been appointed brigade-major with 16 Brigade in March 1912. He had also been involved in operations on the Niger in 1897-8 when serving with the West Africa Frontier Force.
78 Marden, op. cit. p.81.

Battle of Armentières: Advance from Hazebrouck

Beyond the narrow frontage of the entrenched camps on the Aisne heights, operations were developing apace. On 17 September General Joffre, who held exactly the same view on the virtues of a flanking movement as Falkenhayn, had already ordered his *6th Army* into action on the River Oise towards Noyon on the right wing of the German *1st Army*, an attack which came to a halt the following day. On the 22nd, the reconstructed French *2nd Army* went into action a little further north between Péronne and Noyon and was similarly unable to progress beyond the second day. In this fashion battles took place in a progressively northerly direction as the French and Germans attempted to turn their respective flanks.[79] These manoeuvres had reached Arras in the first days of October, when on the 5th, Falkenhayn ordered cavalry further north to perform yet another. Proving insufficient, *6th Army*, under Crown Prince Rupprecht of Bavaria,[80] followed in the cavalry's wake. Previously engaged at Metz, and typical of combatant formations on both sides, 'it had carried out a succession of right hooks, which had depleted its resources.'[81] The German *4th Army* was therefore reconstituted with a hastily assembled reserve corps and sent to operate on *6th Army's* right to complete the flanking manoeuvre between the coast and Ypres.

Towards the end of September, Sir John French began to press Joffre for the transfer of the British forces back to the left of the allied line, ostensibly for logistical reasons, although the protection of British interests in terms of the Channel ports and ease of withdrawal were no doubt in his mind. An unenthusiastic Joffre countered with a proposal to move the BEF in stages. II Corps left the line on the Aisne on 2 October and arrived at Abbeville on the 8th and 9th. The corps concentrated near Béthune from 11 October on the left of the main French forces and would advance towards Aubers to become involved in the Battle of La Bassée. III Corps were the next to move, beginning on 6 October, and 17 and 18 Brigades of 6th Division arrived at Hazebrouck on the 12th. The corps would move towards Bailleul and Armentières to the north of II Corps. Last of all, on the 19th, I Corps concentrated at Hazebrouck and would advance further north towards Ypres and immortality. 16 Brigade entrained with them on 13 October and arrived in Cassell the following day, re-joining 6th Division on the 17th.

French's orders of 12 October set out as the objective of the easterly advance the line Armentières-Wytschaete. On the right, II Corps would be in touch with the French left at Vermelles, the overall aim being of 'passing the Army to the north of Lille and

79 This series of clashes has become inappropriately immortalised as the 'Race to the Sea.'

80 Crown Prince Rupprecht of Bavaria (1869-1955), who had entered the army from school although he combined it with a legal career, was commanding *I Bavarian Army Corps* at the outbreak of war, when he was promoted to command *6th Army*.

81 J. Sheldon, *The German Army at Ypres 1914 and the Battle for Flanders* (Barnsley: Pen & Sword, 2010) Kindle edition location 127.

driving the enemy before it',[82] turning the German northerly flank. By 14 October, however, more infantry of *6th Army* were concentrating in the area, and no driving was to be had – no sooner had II Corps begun to consider their advance, than the French lost Vermelles to their south. With enemy reinforcements arriving daily, and after relentless counterattacks and forced withdrawal, the II Corps advance ground to a halt in front of places that would become painfully familiar names over the next two years, Givenchy, Neuve Chapelle and Aubers.

III Corps, to the north of II and 45,000 strong, advanced simultaneously. 6th Division proceeded on the right of the corps, 4th Division to the left. (See Map 2, colour section). The objective for 6th Division was refined on the 13th as an attack on Outtersteene and then eastwards to Bailleul.[83] The advance to contact was made with a cavalry screen of the 19th Hussars across flat country towards the Bailleul ridge, on which lay Meteren at the northern edge of the corps advance, and Merris and Outtersteene at the south. Lance-Corporal Luther of 3rd Rifle Brigade described meeting the enemy advance guard who were 'swept … off the field', with the unit killing or capturing 'numerous Uhlan patrols.'[84] At the foot of the ridge was a stream, the Meterenbecque, and the enemy were entrenched on its eastern side. At 09.00 the Royal Flying Corps spotted two artillery batteries and about 500 infantry moving towards Meteren, and with the Cavalry Corps moving on the left of III Corps but unable to turn Meteren from the north,[85] a frontal assault was called for by the full weight of both divisions. Attacking that afternoon, 4th Division took Meteren, the enemy retreating under the force of the attack, but 6th Division struggled. In 17 Brigade's area on the left of the division the attack was made by 3rd Rifle Brigade to the north of Merris, and 1st North Staffordshire just to the south. The four companies of the Rifle Brigade, starting at 13.30, were only able to gain the ridge on their right, the left and centre being held up by machine guns which could not be advanced upon because the divisional artillery kept firing 200 yards short just in front of the infantry until dusk. The battalion advanced in 'artillery formation', and came upon the 'final position in extended order & laid down', where 'we were within 200 yards of them & they started leaving their cover & running away.'[86] The battalion suffered 69 casualties, including the CO, Lieutenant-Colonel Alexander, wounded by shrapnel in the thigh.[87] 1st North Staffordshire took Outtersteene at a cost of 54 casualties

82 Army Operation Order No. 35, 12 October 1914. [J.E. Edmonds, *Military Operations France and Belgium 1914, Vol. 2*, p.503].

83 On the 12th, 19 Brigade (Brigadier-General Hon. Frederick Gordon – see Chapter 2) was attached to 6th Division, although it remained in corps reserve. The brigade had been formed on 21 August 1914 and had immediately been engaged in the Battle of Le Cateau (26 August 1914).

84 Luther, op. cit.

85 Edmonds, op. cit. *Vol. 2*, p.96.

86 Luther, op. cit.

87 War Diary, 3rd Battalion Rifle Brigade, 13 October 1914, TNA WO95/1613.

without meeting the same degree of resistance as the Rifle Brigade. They too found the artillery support limited – their attack went in with no artillery cover, the guns unhelpfully beginning to shell Outtersteene at 16.45 once the North Staffords had occupied it. In fairness to the artillery, the only points for artillery observation were on the German side.

18 Brigade found itself attacking on the right of the division on a frontage which Brigadier-General Congreve found 'far too great for its strength', and in the wet and mist runners met great difficulties in reaching both brigade and division. Congreve observed that 'touch was not well kept, and it was impossible to direct the attack after it had been launched.'[88] The brigade suffered 120 casualties and made little progress, despite the resistance not being particularly strong, Congreve's view being that the attack was begun too late in the day. He placed some of the blame on 1st East Yorkshire who had been reluctant to advance too far with only wandering groups of French cavalry on their flank. It was a day on which command and control had struggled. This was in large part due to the weather which had rendered brigades' control over their battalions very difficult, and meant that contact between infantry and artillery broke down.[89] III Corps summarised the problem thus: 'The weather was very wet and misty and the country much enclosed.' The weather 'prevented full advantage being taken of our greatly superior artillery, and the infantry fought the action largely without artillery support';[90] the enclosed nature of the country aiding the defender.[91]

Marden probably does not quite do justice to the division's activity the following day when he states: 'The character of the advance may be illustrated by an incident on the 14th October, when a platoon of the 1st R.F. (of the Reserve Brigade) was detailed to rescue General Keir's car, which had run into snipers near Merris. Fortunately the G.O.C. was not in it.'[92] In the late afternoon, the 4th Division pushed its brigades forward into Ballieul, 6th Division advancing to the south of the town, dogged by 'rearguards of cavalry and machine guns, the difficulty of reconnaissance, and the impossibility of artillery support in such close country.'[93] II Corps, to the south of 6th Division, stood still whilst this advance was made. Despite what seemed slow progress, the arrival of the BEF in the area had required change in Falkenhayn's plan. From 14 October, *6th Army* was ordered to act defensively, whilst the British would be allowed to advance to its north and *4th Army* would, as Crown Prince Rupprecht put

88 War Diary, HQ 18 Infantry Brigade, 13 October 1914, TNA WO95/1614.
89 The War Diary for the HQ of 6th Division is missing for October, so it is difficult to establish a picture of command and control one step further removed.
90 War Diary, HQ III Corps, October 1914, TNA WO95/668.
91 III Corps suffered 708 casualties that day, German casualties being estimated at 1,000.
92 Marden, op. cit. p.7.
93 Edmonds, op. cit. *Vol. 2*, p.99.

it, 'form the base of a sack into which, it is hoped, the enemy will thrust in an attempt to surround *Sixth Army*.'[94]

On the 15th, resistance slackened (the enemy withdrawing north of Armentières), Steenwerck was occupied and at midday III Corps was ordered forward to the River Lys, which wound its way round Armentières, to repair the bridges and occupy the town. Following this, the advance would continue north-eastwards astride the river, to attack the flank of the enemy occupying Lille. To the south, II Corps would again begin its advance towards La Bassée. The crossings of the Lys made by 6th Division were at Bac St Maur and Sailly about 3,500 yards south-west of the town, 4th Division crossing closer to Armentières itself. At Bac, the enemy had failed to destroy the bridge – being a swing type, they had merely opened the bridge and left it parallel to the far bank. 12 Field Company Royal Engineers only had to cross the Lys on a raft and use the mechanism on the far bank to swing the bridge back into position.[95] At Sailly the centre span of the bridge was in place but the two end spans had been destroyed. 38 Field Company RE effected repairs by the light of a burning church.[96]

The following day, Sir John French's orders were for II, III and the Cavalry Corps to again move eastwards,[97] as Crown Prince Rupprecht hoped. By the 17th, as 4th Division entered Armentières, 17 Brigade had reached la Chapelle d'Armentières, south-east of the town, with 18 Brigade some 1,500-2,000 yards to the south. On this day, the old formation of the division was completed again, as 16 Brigade finally came up into reserve. Both 17 and 18 Brigades now faced the Pérenchies ridge (of which the Aubers ridge, of later ill-repute, was a southerly extension), and which ran roughly from Lille to Armentières. 'Masked as it was, in October 1914 by trees, this low clay ridge … appeared to rise abruptly from the ground.'[98] It was only 45 feet in height, but on top of it the Germans were believed to be entrenching with excellent observation.

That evening, in order for III Corps to pursue its north-eastwards movement up the Lys valley without threat to its right flank, orders were issued for 6th Division to carry out a reconnaissance of the ridge starting at 06.30 on the 18th, with 'infantry supported by artillery in sufficient strength to test character of defence.'[99] Depending on the resistance, an attack would either be delivered or not, in the light of the position of 4th Division. Seizing the ridge would not only reduce the enemy observation but would allow domination of the Armentières-Lille road which bisected it, and inhibit any German advance. General Keir ordered his two front line brigades forward, each with an artillery brigade, but specified that the brigadiers were 'not to engage more

94 Diary entry, Crown Prince Rupprecht of Bavaria, 14 October 1914, quoted in Sheldon, op. cit. location 1124.
95 War Diary, 12 Field Company Royal Engineers, 15 October 1914, TNA WO95/1599.
96 War Diary, 38 Field Company Royal Engineers, 15 October 1914, TNA WO95/1599.
97 O.A. 500, 15 October 1914, Edmonds, op. cit. *Vol. 2*, p.507.
98 Edmonds, op. cit. *Vol. 2*, p.107.
99 III Corps Operation Order No.28. Appendix 22 Edmonds, op. cit. *Vol. 2*, p.510.

than half their infantry' without informing him first.[100] 18 Brigade advanced to the south, towards la Vallée and le Paradis, 17 Brigade to the north, towards Prémesques and Pérenchies, a front of some 3,000 yards.

The initial advance of 17 Brigade went reasonably smoothly on the right for 2nd Leinster, but not on the left, and fire from the north-east of Pérenchies, where there was no sign of 4th Division, halted the progress of 3rd Rifle Brigade. The left of the battalion had to drop back and Brigadier-General Doran was forced to revert to divisional HQ and ask to use his reserve. In pressing on, the Rifle Brigade suffered 70 casualties, and the reinforcing 1st Royal Fusiliers, meeting 'hot fire',[101] a further 39. Pérenchies remained out of reach, and in occupying Prémesques, to the south-east, the Leinsters now suffered 105 casualties,[102] although 'they 'had got nearer to Lille than British troops were to be for many a long day.'[103]

Walter Congreve's 18 Brigade, supported by 38 Brigade Royal Field Artillery, arrived on its line at 13.00 with little opposition and was instructed to further its advance. 2nd DLI advanced on the right, 1st East Yorkshire on the left. The Durhams' attack on Ennetières-en-Weppe was successful, albeit with 109 casualties.[104] The East Yorkshires advanced on Capinghem noting that 'little (was) known of enemy except that he was in position.' The Germans were discovered in 'considerable strength', and machine guns took a toll on the left where the Yorkshire advance was in the air due to 17 Brigade's slower progress. Seventy-two casualties were sustained in reaching a position half a mile short of Capinghem.[105] 16 Brigade had been ordered forward later that morning to the right of the 18th – the three original brigades of the division now being in line together for the first time – but finished further back. This left Congreve's brigade at the tip of a salient surrounding Ennetières. He 'pointed out weakness of line', but the orders from III Corps were that he should hold the position. The brigade set about digging and erecting barricades.[106] 38 Brigade RFA remained active, the guns having a better day, noting that 'at nightfall some of the enemy's guns were located by their flashes', and their guns remained in action all night.[107]

In 16 Brigade, 1st Buffs had advanced with the French *10th Cavalry Division* to their right,[108] with orders to wheel north-east after taking Radinghem to turn the enemy's flank from the south. Supported by 2nd York & Lancaster, they took Radinghem with no opposition. General Ingouville-Williams was critical of what

100 Edmonds, op. cit. *Vol. 2*, p.111.
101 War Diary, 1st Battalion Royal Fusiliers, 18 October 1914, WO95/1613.
102 War Diary, 2nd Battalion Leinster Regiment, 18 October 1914, WO95/1612.
103 Leask, op. cit. p.218.
104 War Diary, 2nd Battalion Durham Light Infantry, 18 October 1914, WO95/1617.
105 War Diary, 1st Battalion East Yorkshire Regiment, 18 October 1914, WO95/1618.
106 War Diary, HQ 18 Infantry Brigade, 18 October 1914, WO95/1614.
107 War Diary, 38 Brigade Royal Field Artillery, 18 October 1914, WO95/1598.
108 The projected sweep of III Corps up the Lys valley would have had the French cavalry on the right flank, the British on the left.

happened next, however. The two units 'failed to consolidate themselves before debouching' from Radinghem in a southerly direction and found themselves 'rushing across' a plateau about 300 metres in width towards a wood surrounding the Chateau de Flandre.[109] Here they were met with a storm of Maxim gun fire and shrapnel. Whilst the war diary of the York & Lancasters does not mention it, merely describing being driven back, one company under Major Gerald Bayley was working round from the left,[110] and in threatening the enemy with being outflanked, the Germans pulled back. Ingouville-Williams noted, with a likely sigh of relief: 'This no doubt saved the situation or at least reduced our casualties.'[111] Accounts of the fighting are confused, which no doubt represents what happened on the ground. Mark Connelly, using the regimental history, gives an account of the capture of the chateau and its stirring defence.[112] An article of the time describes how 'room after room in the great house was cleared of the Germans.'[113] The Buffs' own war diary simply describes the defence of Radinghem itself later that day, holding a line in front of the wood, and the map in 16 Brigade's war diary confirms this.[114] The York & Lancasters had suffered 133 casualties,[115] the Buffs 81. The contemporary account makes little of the events at the chateau (from which the Buffs withdrew prior to nightfall), whilst post-hoc accounts make it a glorious event. In truth, the glory was less in the occupation of this building and more in the grim resistance that followed. The Buffs held on to Radinghem, having been ordered to hand over to the French cavalry who proved far too few in numbers for the task.

Thomas Marden described the 'reconnaissance in force' to the ridge as 'brilliantly carried out.' This overstates the case. Whilst the advance to contact had gone well, contact itself had not – the German resistance had been stiff, and considerable casualties were suffered. In ordering 6th Division to press on mid-morning, General Pulteney had come to the conclusion that the enemy was weak in numbers. The Official Historian concluded that this was to a certain extent the case – 'It was indeed the weakest period of the German defence.' It was strong enough, however. Over the 25 mile front from La Bassée to Menin there were three German Corps (*VII, XIX and XIII*) of *6th Army* and eight cavalry divisions facing two and half British corps, one and a half French Territorial divisions, and seven cavalry divisions.[116] The odds were tilted in the enemy's favour, and the advance of 6th Division had been stopped

109 War Diary, HQ 16 Infantry Brigade, 18 October 1914, WO95/1605.
110 Gerald Edward Bayley, commissioned in 1894, would command 1st York & Lancaster between May 1915 and November 1916, before being promoted to command 65 Brigade.
111 War Diary, HQ 16 Infantry Brigade, 18 October 1914, WO95/1605.
112 Connelly, op. cit. location 900.
113 *The Sphere*, 13 March 1915.
114 War Diary, 1st Battalion Buffs, 18 October 1918, TNA WO95/1608.
115 Marden specifically notes Major Edward Craig Robertson as killed in this engagement. Whilst he was indeed wounded, he would die at Loos on 29 September 1915.
116 Edmonds, op. cit. *Vol. 2,* p.112.

in its tracks. On the convex line, only part of the ridge was in British hands, and that in a precarious position. This was not the division's fault in 17 Brigade's area to the north, where the advance had been undermined somewhat by 4th Division's lack of progress. In the south, however, the two units of 16 Brigade had showed the same impulsive haste as had the two units of 18 Brigade in the first action on the Aisne, and had been pushed back. In context, however, the progress of the whole BEF had been slow. To the north of the Cavalry Corps, the progress of the newly formed IV Corps under Sir Henry Rawlinson, had approached glacial in the view of GHQ. It has been suggested that 'Smith-Dorrien, Rawlinson and above all Pulteney had not displayed great enthusiasm for Sir John's grand offensive.' They had indeed showed caution, reflected in late starts in III Corps, and 'for this, Pulteney, in particular, has been condemned.'[117] Anthony Leask poses the question as to whether III Corps, acting 'with greater boldness might have captured or destroyed a large German force' with its back to the River Lys.[118] The answer is, of course, that even if Pulteney had possessed the information to realise that he might achieve this, his duty was to protect his corps from unjustified risk, particularly on his right flank, protected only by French cavalry. Similarly, in advancing with caution on the Pérenchies ridge, 'if the ridge was strongly held, he could be taken in the flank with the river behind him … it was a matter of maintaining balance.'[119] Any such criticism underestimates the resistance encountered on the 18th. Both sides would begin to experience the enduring trope of the Great War over these days, that successfully attacking an enemy who was dug in was no easy matter. Jack Sheldon succinctly emphasises 'the enormous advantage enjoyed by the defence when it is conducted from even the most rudimentary trenches against troops advancing in the open.'[120] He further reminds us of the changes in the Flanders landscape over time. Where there are now large open fields, there were many hedges and 'scrubby wooded areas' coppiced for firewood, which channelled movement and proved ideal for concealment.[121] A simple wired hedge could prove a significant problem for an attacker. However, the caution displayed prevented the BEF from being driven into the sack of envelopment and destruction that had been in preparation. The following day, as III Corps recorded: 'Information … indicated that strong German forces were advancing with their right extending to the sea', and Sir John French's offensive was 'temporarily abandoned.'[122] 6th Division would have a day to dig in before the German hammer blow would fall. And as it did so, as Sir John French would later put it, if slightly histrionically: 'It was simply "up to us" to hold on

117 D. Lomas, *First Ypres 1914*, p.39.
118 Leask, op. cit. p.250.
119 Leask, op. cit. p.251.
120 Sheldon, op. cit. location 147.
121 Sheldon, op. cit. location 176.
122 War Diary, HQ III Corps, October 1914, TNA WO95/668.

like grim death to our positions by hard, resolute fighting, until relief in some shape could come.'[123]

Battle of Armentières: The German 6th Army Attack

On 20 October, the German *4th* and *6th Armies* attacked 'in very superior numbers' on a front from the sea to Ypres and to the south of Armentières.[124] *XIX Corps,* under General von Laffert,[125] was in the line opposing III Corps at Armentières, and having been 'reduced to such straits by the attack of II and III Corps … the *XIII Corps*' under General von Fabeck,[126] 'had to be sent south on the night 18th/19th against the right of the III Corps and left of the II Corps.'[127] The Battle of Armentières is overshadowed in the historiography by the titanic struggle further north at Ypres, but at moments was no less desperate.

The position of 2nd Sherwood Foresters in Ennetières, lying in a spur on the Pérenchies ridge, 20 October 1914.

123 J.D.P. French, *1914*, (New York: Houghton Miflin, 1919), p.232.
124 Edmonds, op. cit. *Vol. 2,* p.138.
125 *XIX (Saxon) Corps* comprised *24th* and *40th Divisions*. Maximilian von Laffert was a Saxon cavalry officer. He suffered a heart attack whilst in command and died in July 1917.
126 *XIII Corps* comprised *26th* and *25th (Reserve) Divisions*. Herrmann Gustav Karl Max von Fabeck was a Prussian infantry officer who had commanded *XIII Corps* since 1913. After commanding *8th Army* for a few weeks he fell ill in October 1916 and died that December.
127 Edmonds, op. cit. *Vol. 2,* p.122.

The attack of the reinforced enemy fell particularly heavily on 6th Division, the whole of which held a salient, and in turn on 18 Brigade in the centre of its pronounced and uncomfortable tip, 'a position over-extended and tactically unsound for defence.'[128] 2nd Sherwood Foresters, 1st West Yorkshire and 1st East Yorkshire were in line, the whole front held extending about three miles, that of the Sherwood Foresters being some 2,600 yards in length, their position sticking out like a finger on a narrow spur containing the village of Ennetières. A heavy bombardment commenced at 07.00, and the enemy began to mount attacks, advancing 'by bounds, in lines of men at several paces' interval, covered by machine-gun fire, the firing opening at eight hundred to one thousand yards.'[129] Units of the German *26th Division* (always rated first-class) were pressing the salient's south side, the *25th (Reserve) Division* (rated second-class) to the north. Whilst the enemy were resisted, Major Philip Leveson-Gower,[130] commanding the battalion, became increasingly preoccupied concerning the fact that a gap existed on his right between his unit and 1st Buffs of 16 Brigade. Reports of the enemy pushing towards this began to arrive from 08.20. An hour and a half later, the situation worsened, the battalion's position being shelled from 'the north, east & south, so practically every trench was under enfilade fire.'[131] Leveson-Gower used his reserves to reinforce his right, and even despite Congreve sending two platoons of the 2nd DLI to assist, at 13.00 a renewed attack was made and by 15.15 his vulnerable right was threatened by yet a further assault, covered by an artillery barrage that 'enfiladed and took in reverse my trenches on the right flank.'[132] Personally placing his platoons, Leveson-Gower found that his left was now also threatened, and he collected transport troops and stragglers to reinforce this flank and defend Ennetières village. His men fell back, however, and as darkness began to fall, his right flank was turned, by '3 bodies of about a battalion and a machine gun each.' Leveson-Gower had earlier asked for permission for his company at the tip of the salient to withdraw, but Congreve, mindful of corps orders, had refused. Ten officers and 484 other ranks were made prisoner as the salient was progressively overrun, and Leveson-Gower had no alternative but to retreat, noting later: 'The loss of position was entirely due to this flank attack that was overpowering in numbers, there being

128 Leask, op. cit. p.219.
129 Edmonds, op. cit. *Vol. 2,* p.138.
130 Commissioned into the Derbyshire Regiment, Philip Leveson-Gower, born 1871, had served on the North-West Frontier 1897-8 and 1899-1901, and had achieved his majority in May 1908. He would command 49th Brigade from February 1916 until May 1918. He ordered a disastrous counter-attack on 21 March 1918, the opening of the German Spring offensive, which resulted in the destruction of 6th Connaught Rangers, and was not offered command of the refitted brigade.
131 War Diary, 2nd Battalion Sherwood Foresters, 'Report on Position and Events at Ennetterres (sic) 20th Oct 1914', TNA WO95/1616.
132 War Diary, 2nd Battalion Sherwood Foresters, 'Report on Position and Events at Ennetterres (sic) 20th Oct 1914', TNA WO95/1616.

no adequate reserve to meet it.'[133] The withdrawal on la Vallée, at the base of the spur, had not been entirely orderly, and Colonel Robert Fox of 38th Brigade RFA played an important part in rallying those retiring from the enemy onslaught. Brigadier-General Wellesley Paget,[134] CRA 6th Division noted: 'Colonel Fox omits all mention of his own part in the proceedings but … it was his quick grasp of the situation and personal efforts in leading the infantry back to the ridge that restored the line of battle and enabled the guns to be got away.'[135] The 2nd Sherwood Foresters had, however, been reduced to three officers and 230 ORs. Leveson-Gower was correct about the weight of attack. He had borne the brunt of four companies of the *122nd Regiment* and the *2nd Battalion, 125th Regiment* on his right flank, and also units of the *25th Reserve Division*, some two and a half battalions in total.[136] Congreve's brigade suffered 1,124 casualties that day. His two other battalions had also had a very tough time. On the left of the brigade's line the 1st East Yorkshires had been faced with the problem of their 17 Brigade neighbours, 2nd Leinster, being driven back and losing Prémesques at the start of the assault and becoming thus exposed were ordered to retire at mid-day. This left 1st West Yorkshire in the brigade's centre in an invidious position, and as the Sherwood Foresters retired, so did they. Congreve responded to the competing demands for reinforcement by inserting elements of the 2nd DLI where he perceived danger, but it was not enough. The line could be saved intact, but the weight of the enemy onslaught could nowhere be resisted.

For the second time in the campaign, a successful German flanking attack against 6th Division had netted a substantial number of prisoners. The *122nd Regiment* claimed 576 that day.[137] On both occasions the enemy's success had been due to the British determination to hold an unsatisfactory, exposed position for the sake of retaining high ground. The reason for holding such a position – observation – was logical, but the good reasons were undermined on both occasions by the friction of war having left opportunity for penetration on an exposed flank. Congreve accepted Leveson-Gower's view of the Sherwoods' disaster. 'The loss of the position was undoubtedly due to the want of a reserve with which to strengthen the right flank and to the darkness which prevented accuracy in shooting.' Congreve further emphasised the power of the enemy attack: 'The men were overwhelmed by weight of numbers, and officers and N.C.O.s being gone, I fear, surrendered.' Whereas the history of

133 War Diary, 2nd Battalion Sherwood Foresters, 'Report on Position and Events at Ennetterres (sic) 20th Oct 1914', TNA WO95/1616.
134 Wellesley Lynedoch Henry Paget had commanded the artillery of 6th Division since September 1910.
135 War Diary, HQ III Corps, '38th Brigade RFA', October 1914, TNA WO95/668. Robert Fanshawe Fox would serve as BGRA 4th Division from September 1915 to June 1916, when he was made Inspector-General of Royal Horse and Royal Field Artillery.
136 Edmonds, op. cit. *Vol. 2,* pp.140-1.
137 Edmonds, op. cit. *Vol. 2*, p.140.

the 1st and 2nd Battalions Sherwood Foresters would have it otherwise,[138] Congreve concluded that 'they certainly were never surrounded.'[139]

On the division's left, whilst the Leinsters of 17 Brigade had been forced back early in the morning, 3rd Rifle Brigade held their position, causing the enemy considerable casualties. An artillery observation officer at battalion HQ effectively directed fire, both counterbattery and on the enemy's trenches, albeit too late to catch an armoured train of reinforcements that drew up within 800 yards of their position.[140] Lance-Corporal Edward Luther remarked how: 'It only stayed a few minutes & backed away again to Lille which we could see away in the distance about 4 miles down the line.'[141] Despite their success, the cost to the enemy was great. Luther recorded that in the aftermath of the attack 'the field was littered with dead Germans.' He and his comrades went out about 300 yards and directed wounded Germans to the British trenches. One soldier of the *139th Infantry Regiment* described how 'out of his Regiment of about 1,200 strong, he considered only about 90 could have got away safely.'[142] Left exposed, however, the Rifle Brigade withdrew at 01.00 the following morning.

In 16 Brigade, on the division's right, the war diary of 1st Buffs betrays no awareness of a gap between them and the Sherwood Foresters to their left. The Buffs were holding the brigade frontage whilst the other units were preparing a second line halfway between the front and Bois Grenier. They held the line successfully during the morning, but *51st Infantry Brigade* renewed their assault at 14.00, and by 15.50 Major Robert McDouall's plaintive report from the front line was: 'Situation very serious – am holding on – no officers left but Rice – Maxims knocked out.'[143] Twenty minutes later the battalion was being forced back, especially on its left, where the full weight of the enemy's attack on the Sherwood Foresters was telling, and they were slowly driven back and ordered to retire about 2,500 yards in a north-easterly direction at 22.00. (See Map 3, colour section).

At the end of the day, 6th Division had suffered a significant reverse. They had been forced to fall back 'two miles on the right and centre and a quarter of a mile on the left',[144] where 4th Division had had a less trying day. Sir John French, however, did not seemingly grasp the gravity of the situation, issuing orders on the evening of

138 H.C. Wylly, *1st and 2nd Battalions the Sherwood Foresters (Nottinghamshire and Derbyshire Regiment) in the Great War*, Kindle Edition location 4133.
139 War Diary, HQ 18 Infantry Brigade, October 1914, TNA WO95/1614.
140 War Diary, 3rd Battalion Rifle Brigade, 20 October 1914, TNA WO95/1613.
141 Luther, op. cit.
142 Luther, op. cit.
143 War Diary, 1st Battalion Buffs, 20 October 1914, TNA WO95/1608. Robert McDouall would command 1st Buffs from November 1914 to June 1915, would serve as a GSO2 and GSO1, then command 141 Infantry Brigade from August 1916 to October 1917, and 142 Infantry Brigade from April 1918 to the Armistice.
144 Edmonds, op. cit. *Vol. 2*, p.142.

the 20th that II, III, IV and the Cavalry Corps were to 'hold the enemy opposed to them to its ground and at the same time take every opportunity of seizing tactical advantages.'[145] The enemy were simply not allowing this to happen. The causes of the division's reverse were several. Firstly, it held a salient. Secondly, it held a considerable length of line and its resources were thus stretched, with little slack for reinforcement. Thirdly, the enemy had attacked with great weight at a crucial point in that line. This was not accidental – the Germans pitched their effort at the point where they clearly realised the British were most vulnerable and did so with the benefit of having been reinforced. Fourthly, the three brigades were tired – 2nd Sherwood Foresters of 18 Brigade, for instance, had been under fire for two days, constantly digging to improve their position. Keir, conscious that it was Pulteney who had ordered that the line be held despite Congreve's anxieties, set down a defence of 18 Brigade. He emphasised 'the unsatisfactory position which the Notts & Derby Regiment was (in) thro(ugh) no fault of its own' and the 'the orders received from the Third Army (Corps) were definite.'[146] The orders of III Corps had their logic, as previously observed. 18 Brigade thus became the victim of its own success two days earlier. The division was, however, now withdrawing towards a line it would hold for the following months, and which the BEF would hold until the German 'Georgette' offensive of 9 April 1918.

The situation of 6th Division in terms of protective artillery fire, if there was another major assault on their lines, was potentially serious – the artillery was running low on ammunition.[147] The situation on the ground was also worrying. The front held by III Corps was very extended and it was noted: 'During these days anxiety was always present as to the tasks allotted to General Conneau for filling the gap between 2nd and 3rd Corps.'[148] This gap existed roughly between Aubers and Radinghem. Louis Conneau commanded the interposed French *1st Cavalry Corps*, and he was not seen as co-operative. This was a particular concern for 6th Division, and 19 Brigade were pushed into line on the division's right on the 21st. This move did not go smoothly, however. The brigade reached Le Maisnil-en-Weppes, but came under attack from a superior German force from *XIII Corps*. Captain James Jack, staff captain to the formation, described how towards the end of the afternoon: 'The situation is growing acute … Le Maisnil is burning … I am horrified to meet two companies of the Argylls retiring down the slope, their positions having become untenable.' The French had given way, 1st Middlesex were also pulling back, and their CO, 'Colonel Ward, always so kind to me, has been killed.'[149] The brigade retired 2,000 yards to Bas

145 Quoted in Leask, op. cit. p.220.
146 War Diary, HQ 18 Infantry Brigade, copy of note from Major-General J.L. Keir, October 1914, TNA WO95/1614.
147 See Chapter 11.
148 War Diary, HQ III Corps, October 1914, TNA WO95/668.
149 J. Terraine (ed.), *General Jacks' Diary*, p.69. Fifty-one-year-old Lieutenant-Colonel Bertram Edward Ward had been commissioned in 1882, and having been an adjutant of Volunteers and Superintendent of Gymnasia in Cork, had escaped previous war service.

Maisnil having suffered 208 casualties, and organised its defence. In doing so, the gap between them and II Corps widened again to three miles, and it was only the arrival of the Jullundur Brigade of the Indian Corps on the 24th that allowed Conneau to be relieved.

One man in particular was very negative about the British position. On 22 October, Sir Horace Smith-Dorrien, commanding II Corps, wrote to General Pulteney, asking for his support in approaching Sir John French with the position that troops were exhausted, showing 'loss of nerve', were short of reserves to the rear and officers on the ground, and that he had 'no confidence in being able to maintain the line.'[150] Pulteney's reply, if there was one, does not exist. He would have borne in mind that Sir John disliked Smith-Dorrien. Pulteney would, no doubt, have agreed about the issue of reserves, which had certainly been part of the reason that 6th Division was forced back on the 20th. But his two divisions were less depleted – during the period 9-18 October III Corps had suffered 1,553 casualties whilst the tally for II Corps was 2,596. And there was no real evidence of damage to the morale of 6th Division, despite Marden noting a total of 4,696 casualties in the Battle of Armentières to the end of October 1914.[151] This figure may well be a slight underestimate. The four infantry brigades recorded a total 4,756 casualties alone. Thirty-four officers had been killed, 91 wounded, and 24 were missing. In the other ranks, fatalities totalled 563, whilst 2,418 were wounded, and 1,626 missing.

In the greater scheme of things, if the two corps commanders were aware of it or not, a seminal moment on this part of the front, and virtually everywhere, had been reached. As Hew Strachan notes: 'It was the moment when the generals of 1914 confronted the end of manoeuvre, when corps-level movements and aspirations to higher strategic control were confounded by the tactical considerations of positional warfare.'[152]

Holding on: 21 October – 31 December 1914

Opposed by the German *XIII Corps*, with the *48th Reserve Division* of the *XXIV Reserve Corps*, the *XIX Corps* and the *I Cavalry Corps*, the two divisions of III Corps were stretched out over a 12 mile front and facing a force which the Official Historian estimates as now double the British. In the aftermath of the general attack of 20 October, *XIII Corps* continued to search for 'a weak spot' in the British line.[153] Corporal Charles Arnold of 3rd Rifle Brigade wrote of the enemy: 'They are a brainy lot these fellows, and noticing a big gap there between us and our next line of trenches they rushed it at night' (the night of 20/21 October). 'A lot got through so we had

150 War Diary, HQ III Corps, G.312, October 1914, TNA WO95/668.
151 The Royal Artillery suffered seven officers wounded with one OR killed, nine wounded and two missing.
152 H. Strachan, 'Foreword', in Sheldon, op. cit. location 76.
153 Edmonds, op. cit. *Vol. 2*, p.226.

them behind us as well as in front.'[154] The most serious weak spots, of course, existed where 16 Brigade held the right (southern) face of the salient, even if it was now less pronounced, and (at least for the next three days) at the juncture of III Corps and the French cavalry, where 19 Brigade stretched out towards the French. The progress of II Corps having been brought to a halt early in the advance, with little progress followed by retreat since, the line to the south of III Corps stretched back towards them in a south-westerly direction. To the north the front curved to the north-east around Armentières, and then in a north-north-easterly direction, joining the Cavalry Corps near Ploegsteert. Despite having been forced back, the apex of this salient was still held by 6th Division.

The enemy was preparing for a further attack on II and III Corps on 23 October, and on the 22nd pressed at the weak spot on the front of 16 Brigade. Noting that 4th Division had been reasonably successful in holding the enemy attacks, the Official Historian made specific note of the position of the 6th:

> The 6th Division ... whose experience of the war was shorter, did not fare so well, and owing to the heavy attacks on it, and the various retirements, its defences were not in such good condition as those of its sister division; nor were its facilities for artillery observation so good.[155]

Whilst the matter of 'experience' was probably irrelevant, as noted earlier, 6th Division's problems of topographic situation were manifold. To make matters worse, on the 23rd 'a terrific attack' opened following the renewed assaults on the Belgian and French forces together with I and IV Corps to the north the previous day. The enemy attacked 'in the darkness, with great courage', but by 06.00 the attack broke down. As the light came up 200 dead lay in front of 1st King's Shropshire Light Infantry of 16 Brigade, and 'the wounded must have far exceeded this number as the Germans were nonplussed by our wire entanglement.' Hand-to-hand fighting took place in the unit's trenches, and well-placed British machine guns did considerable execution. The enemy were then seen sapping forward to within 50 yards of the KSLI trenches, and between 17.00 and 18.00 attacked again only to suffer a further repulse. The battalion had suffered only three killed and 38 wounded, but amongst the latter was the CO Lieutenant-Colonel Cecil Higginson.[156] The same attacks fell on 2nd York & Lancaster, on the brigade's right, the enemy advancing up 'dongas', a term for a dry

154 Arnold, op. cit. p.31.
155 J.E. Edmonds, op. cit. Vol. 2, p.227.
156 War Diary, 1st Battalion King's Shropshire Light Infantry, 23 October 1914, TNA WO95/1609. Forty-eight-year-old Cecil Pickford Higginson had been commissioned into the Shropshire Light Infantry in 1886. Having passed Staff College he served as a brigade-major and DAAG in South Africa in 1901. Subsequently he had served as a brigade-major and DAAQMG in peacetime, taking up battalion command on 19 August 1913.

watercourse acquired in South Africa, and pushing elements of their front line back. The brigade defences were in isolated sections of trench and the enemy succeeded in capturing those between 16 and 19 Brigades. Brigadier-General Ingouville-Williams kept his frontline units judiciously reinforced, and whilst the trenches of the York & Lancasters were retaken with a series of bayonet charges, the enemy were able to effect enfilade fire from the gap between the brigades, and there was a necessary falling back to safer positions. Ingouville-Williams and Walter Congreve met that evening to plan an adjustment to their lines which they regarded as 'very weak.' It consisted (they noted) of a salient, the line positioned in relation to geographical features that made it very vulnerable to the enemy ranging artillery upon their units. In particular, the part of the salient that faced south was vulnerable in enfilade, the whole position enjoying only limited fields of fire. Whilst a new line was established during the night, the two brigadiers informed General Keir that it would be necessary to withdraw another 500 yards to the rear.[157]

On the 24th the German *6th Army* renewed its attack once more, as heavy fighting continued at Ypres. Again, it was 16 Brigade who suffered the most. As Congreve and Ingouville-Williams reconnoitred the line being prepared for this further planned withdrawal at 05.00, cheering was heard from the north, the nature of it indicating to the two men that 1st Leicestershire (who with 1st Buffs had beaten off the previous day's assault), were in difficulties. Within half an hour reports were received that the Leicesters had been forced to fall back, accurate shelling having driven them out of their trenches, and 'that some posts were surrounded and that there were no officers left.' In fact, the Leicesters had closed the gap in their line. That night, the brigades fell back to their new positions in heavy rain. It is evident that these were days of high anxiety. Divisional HQ would become alarmed on the basis of limited information, and brigades would proffer reassurance. Congreve thus noted on the morning of the 24th (and no doubt tried to impress on Keir): 'Situation not as bad as believed.'[158] General Keir was clearly (and justly) worried about the weight of the attack falling on his line, and a deal was brokered by General Pulteney overnight that 4th Division would take over 17 Brigade's position on the left of the 6th Division line and would now be holding eight of the 12 miles of front. Given that 6th Division was, in theory, the BEF's strongest division (with the attachment of 19 Brigade), it is an indication that the weight of the German attack was falling disproportionately hard on them.

An enemy attempt to rush the Leicesters' trenches at dawn on the 25th was beaten off, but over these two days the battalion suffered 224 casualties. On the 25th, James Jack recorded on the 19 Brigade front, which was stretched to two miles, that: 'The Germans pound our trenches daily for about three hours in the mornings and three in the evenings. Our artillery reply is relatively feeble.' The artillery support was generally regarded as inadequate by the infantry for, as was acknowledged: 'Owing

157 War Diary, HQ 16 Infantry Brigade, 23 October 1914, TNA WO95/1605.
158 War Diary, HQ 18 Infantry Brigade, 24 October 1914, TNA WO95/1614.

to shortage of ammunition, fire of batteries was greatly restricted. Searching and sweeping forbidden.'[159] On the next day no infantry attack was made, but on the 27th a heavy bombardment indicated a further assault. On the 16 Brigade front there was a crescendo of rifle fire and shelling at 19.00, although no attack developed. On the front of 18 Brigade, however, the trenches of 1st East Yorkshire were assaulted near Rue du Bois and the enemy repulsed with heavy loss, 100 dead being counted. The Germans attacked the following day yet again near the same spot, the salient between Rue du Bois and the la Bassée-Armentières railway. Here, 2nd Durham Light Infantry were manning a road barricade, and the enemy, creeping up through ruined houses, got into (and beyond) the British trenches to the south of it. The Durhams' response was hampered by rifles jamming due to dirt. Supports belonging to the 1st East Yorkshires and reserves of the Lancashire Fusiliers from 4th Division pushed them back, and a machine-gun at the road barricade did due execution. 18 Brigade buried nearly 200 of the enemy.[160]

Following a reasonably quiet day on the 28th, the pattern of the 27th was re-enacted on the 29th. This time the blow fell against the whole front of 19 Brigade further south, a night attack starting at 00.30 and ending at dawn. Within two minutes 'the couple of 18-pounder batteries supporting the brigade are hard in action; a few seconds later these are joined by the 4.5 howitzer batter and the two 6-inch howitzers further away.' Despite this, Captain Jack went on to describe that the enemy advanced 'with consummate courage, cheering and bugles blowing.'[161] The German persistence was extraordinary. They penetrated a gap between two companies of 1st Middlesex, but of the 50 who forced their way through, 'these men were all bayoneted by "B" Coy.'[162] Unfortunately, going forward in personal reconnaissance, Lieutenant-Colonel Frank Rowley was wounded, the second CO the unit had lost in eight days.[163] Three hundred of the enemy of *223rd* and *224th Infantry Regiments* (*XXIV Reserve Corps*) were killed and 40 were captured. In contrast, 19 Brigade suffered 74 casualties, 23 fatal. With this last, brutal flurry of violence, the 6th Division front fell quiet, at least in terms of infantry attack. As the blow of the reorganised *Army Group Fabeck* fell against Ypres on 30 October, however, the 4th Division front to the north was severely tested.

159 War Diary, CRA 6th Infantry Division, 25 October 1914, TNA WO95/1588. It was added: 'Shooting at night very sparingly resorted to and limited to occasional bursts.'

160 Edmonds, op. cit. *Vol. 2*, p.229. It was noted that elements of *24th Division*, from the weakened *XIX Corps*, were used in this attack.

161 Terraine, op. cit. p.75.

162 War Diary, 1st Battalion Middlesex Regiment, 29 October 1914, TNA WO95/1365.

163 Frank George Mathias Rowley had had taken command of the battalion eight days earlier when Lieutenant-Colonel B.E. Ward, had been killed. Rowley, aged 48, had served as a brigade-major and DAAG in India and had achieved his majority in December 1903. He would go on to command 56 Infantry Brigade from June to November 1916, 107 Brigade from March to June 1917, and 138 Brigade from June 1917 to the Armistice.

The enemy had intended to rupture the Arras-La Bassée-Armentières front in these series of actions of late October, but 'a break-through had not been possible.'[164] At one level, their tactics correctly identified the weakest parts of 6th Division's line. In practice, the division's response had been stout and the attacks were conducted at considerable cost to the already weakened German forces for little result. The persistence reflected a growing desperation on the German part. Falkenhayn's plan for envelopment of the Allies' left flank was never quite played with a full hand of cards – the weight of force required was simply not there. The *4th Army* conducting the thrust was full of reservists with more than its fair share of undertrained *freiwilliger*, and the French, British, and Belgians managed to make a competent defence in just enough numbers. The grand turning manoeuvre turned into a series of costly and unsophisticated assaults, setting the scene for what was to come. Even in a more limited tactical sense, pinning III Corps to its front whilst the more crucial struggle went on at Ypres to the north was (perhaps unknowingly) missing the point, as III Corps had precious little reserve to transfer to I and IV Corps.

In Ingouville-Williams and Congreve, the attacks were made against competent brigade commanders, who clearly had the confidence of Sir John Keir, once the notion of the offensive had been abandoned, in knowing when to cede a bad position. Despite being increasingly outnumbered four or five divisions to two, III Corps had had just sufficient strength and sticking power to resist the assaults. In terms of manpower, however, Sir John French ordered the slim reserves of 4th Division north towards Ypres behind the Cavalry Corps on 30 October, leaving the equally slim reserves of 6th Division covering the whole III Corps front. Having already advised GHQ on the 28th that he could not take offensive action, this led General Pulteney to press the point with French on 1 November 'that the line was so extended and the men so exhausted that he doubted whether a serious attack could be stopped.'[165] Sir John, in response, ordered two battalions from II Corps north, to compensate 4th Division. It was a reflection of how thin the line was. Between 15 and 31 October, III Corps had lost 207 officers and 5,572 ORs. Of these, 125 officers and 3,585 ORs were from 6th Division, whose front had sustained more of the violence. The division's strength on 15 November was, however, such that two of its formations were not too badly depleted, there having been a stream of reinforcement by reservists from home depots during the period. 16 Brigade had 72 officers and 3,505 ORs, whilst 17 Brigade boasted 74 officers and 3,625 ORs. 18 Brigade, who had borne the brunt of the fighting on the Aisne and in the Battle of Armentières, and had lost substantial numbers as prisoners, had only 58 officers and 2,870 ORs, but had been bolstered by the arrival of the

164 *OHL* sources quoted in Edmonds, op. cit. *Vol. 2*, p.223.

165 Edmonds, op. cit. *Vol. 2*, p.231. It was claimed in the *Official History* that the average loss of the seven original British Divisions was 6,500 in 1914, with the average German loss put at 6,800, with the acknowledgement that it was virtually impossible to compute enemy losses accurately (p.468).

division's first Territorials, 1/16th London Regiment (Queen's Westminster Rifles), numbering 800. 19 Brigade, meanwhile, was similarly depleted, with 58 officers and 2,830 ORs.[166]

As the line in front of 6th Division quietened in November, the main concern for III Corps was further north, where the enemy were pressing Ploegsteert on the left of 4th Division. Pulteney continued to be anxious for his front to be contracted to rest his troops. He reported to GHQ on 15 November that his front consisted 'of a front line and a supporting line at an average distance of 1,000 to 2,000 yards apart. There is little means of communication between these lines', and assembling troops for attack-counterattack could only take place in the dark.[167] (Pulteney also wrote to GHQ on the subject of the inadequacies of the artillery. He was severely rapped on the knuckles by Sir John French for having circulated the document in type, and not having discussed its contents discreetly). To 6th Division's south, where the Indian Corps had come into line, fighting petered out on 2 November. As the month proceeded, a routine of being shelled and sniped developed. 19 Brigade, who had beaten off a night attack on 4 November, still reported itself outgunned. In early November it noted: 'Their artillery opposite our line includes a battery of heavy howitzers, a battery of 4.5 howitzers, and at least one horse artillery battery, the guns of which are pushed up at short range.' Supporting the brigade were 'two field batteries 24th B(riga)de RFA, one howitzer battery and 2 six-inch howitzers.'[168] These, of course, had been swiftly brought into action and caused carnage on 30 October. The enemy shelling, naturally, led to casualties. With its battalions relatively up to strength, trench wastage in 18 Brigade in November totalled 159. In 17 Brigade the total was 223, the most senior casualty being Lieutenant-Colonel William Reeve (2nd Leinster), wounded in the arm by a sniper. He lost his left forearm.[169] The brigade lost another CO on 29 December, when Lieutenant-Colonel Alexander of 3rd Rifle Brigade died of wounds sustained on Boxing Day. One of his officers wrote: 'Poor Colonel Alexander, he was always so jolly and merry, but I often trembled for his safety when he came to our trenches. He was fairly tall, and his head and

166 War Diary, HQ III Corps, October 1914, TNA WO95/668.
167 War Diary, HQ III Corps, G.394, 15 November 1914, TNA WO95/668.
168 War Diary, HQ 19 Infantry Brigade, 2-7 November 1914, TNA WO95/1364.
169 William Tankerville Monypenny Reeve was commissioned in 1877, and had fought against the Ashantis in 1900, later commanding the Gold Coast Regiment. He took command of his battalion on 13 August 1912. Following his injury, '"They asked me if I had tied my tie myself", he told a relative on coming away from a Medical Board. "I said 'yes.' It was true", he added with an almost apologetic smile, "though my wife did have to straighten it out a little".' tonbridgeatwar.daisy.websds.net/Authenticated/ViewDets.aspx?RecID=308&TableName=ta_factfile (accessed 1 November 2017). After a few weeks back at the front in June 1915, his arm proved too painful. He took command of the 1st Garrison Battalion, Essex Regiment, but contracted a fatal illness on arrival in Lemnos, en route to the Gallipoli campaign.

shoulders showed easily over the parapet. We all miss him.'[170] 19 Brigade suffered 377 casualties during this period, although over 120 of these were accounted for in a night attack near Ploegsteert carried out by 2nd Argyll and Sutherland Highlanders of 19 Brigade, who had been temporarily moved north.

Defence now largely dominated the opposing armies' mindsets, with the exception of British attacks on 14 December, which did not involve 6th Division who simply made a demonstration, and a retaliatory strike by the enemy against the Indian Corps on the 20th. On 6th Division's front, the enemy kept sapping forwards and opening parallel trenches, this being unsurprising as their front line was between 200 and 400 yards away. The whole front had by now been wired by both sides, 18 Brigade noting the enemy putting out 'a good deal of very stout barbed wire entanglement' on 4 December.[171] Work proceeded in III Corps on a second line, and 6th Division settled down to developing systems attuned to trench warfare. Thus on 22 November, Walter Congreve called a conference of his COs to discuss a 'proposed system of relief of battalions in (the) trenches.'[172] By the end of November, two battalions of the brigade were in line, two in reserve, one in brigade and one in divisional reserve. The rotation operated so that a battalion 'was in the trenches 14 days, then Division reserve 14 days & then to pass to Brigade reserve for 7 days.'[173] Work continued on establishing communication trenches, but it was only on 25 November that it was now possible to carry out reliefs during the day. A night sniping system was established whereby points were noted where noises of enemy movement were heard during the dark and rifles laid on compass bearings taken from the map.[174] The division was learning the craft of trench warfare, and training companies of the Artists Rifles began to go into their trenches from 3 December.

On 2 December, King George V and the Prince of Wales visited 6th Division – fortunately the day was fine – and men from each of the brigades lined the road. Five Distinguished Conduct Medals were presented. Otherwise, there was little to cheer the division. As Marden notes: 'The weather during November and December was

170 Reginald Alexander, known as 'Jullunder' in the regiment, has been described as 'probably the greatest regimental character of his era. He was a high-spirited practical joker, story teller, bon viveur and fearless soldier.' A fellow officer described him as: 'A fine judge of racing though he never bet a penny, large, loud-voiced, and possessed of a fund of unrepeatable stories and a strong dislike for going to bed as long as there was someone to talk to and a mess waiter to bring him whiskies and sodas.' A veteran of South Africa 1900-2, he had commanded the battalion since 15 October 1913. Curiously, his death is not mentioned in the regimental history.
Auction Archive <https://www.dnw.co.uk/auction-archive/special-collections/lot.php?specialcollection_id=467&lot_id=73562> (Accessed 1 November 2017).

171 War Diary, HQ 18 Infantry Brigade, 4 December 1914, TNA WO95/1614.

172 War Diary, HQ 18 Infantry Brigade, 22 November 1914, TNA WO95/1614.

173 War Diary, HQ 16 Infantry Brigade, 25 November 1914, TNA WO95/1605.

174 War Diary, HQ 16 Infantry Brigade, 30 November 1914, TNA WO95/1605.

truly appalling.'[175] The winter of 1914-15 is legendary in the historiography of the BEF, but beyond human misery, it operationally limited what the armies could do. Of the three routes used to supply 6th Division, only one was fit for motor transport. October had been wet and misty, but intermittent snow began to fall on 15 November, alternating with days of heavy rain. At the end of November, despite this, 16 Brigade were able to report: 'The health of the troops continues very good. Ample warm underclothing has been issued.' Goatskin coats were, however, described as 'not very practical' as they collected dirt and mud and hampered movement.[176] The positive position reported by 16 Brigade did not last, 1st Leicestershire beginning to note men being admitted to hospital suffering from frostbite in December. Private Bernard Brookes of 1/16th London Regiment, which had joined on 11 November, described how 'a large number of men by this time were suffering from such complaints as rheumatism, frost bite, trench feet and suchlike, which caused them to be removed ... the cold had been very intense and we had been standing in water, at times up to our hips.'[177] The potential impact on morale is indicated by the fact that drunkenness was becoming a problem and III Corps issued an order on 27 November forbidding the sale of alcohol to the troops except beer. In dealing with the inevitable dirt, divisional baths had been established on the Lys at Bac St Maur. The weather took its toll not only on the men, but on the trenches that were supposedly protecting them. By 5 December 16 Brigade's dug-outs were falling in,[178] and on 7 December 18 Brigade reported 'ramparts falling in badly' after a day of continuous rain, with the 'communication trenches in very bad state' two days later. Private Percy Jones, 1/16th London, near Burnt Farm in early December, 'heard that New Street was impassable .... the trench was about knee deep in water for half its length and in places waist deep. Blind Alley was a canal, pure and simple, most of the dug-outs being under water ... the trench through the Orchard held quite 3 1/2 feet of water throughout its length.'[179]

Marden records what must have been one of the less serious weather-related events when: 'The BGC 19th Infantry Brigade had his boots sucked off by the mud and went round the trenches without them.'[180] On 11 December the trenches of the 1st West Yorkshires were 'suddenly flooded owing to the breakage of a dam', the men finding themselves up to their waists, this being first reported as being 'flooded by the enemy.'[181] Six days later, 17 Brigade noted: 'The communication trenches are now so wet as to be

175 Marden, op. cit. p.10.
176 War Diary, HQ 16 Infantry Brigade, 30 November 1914, TNA WO95/1605.
177 B.J. Brookes, Private Papers, IWM Docs 10825. As a result of wounding, Brookes would spend time in the Labour Corps in 1917.
178 War Diary, HQ 16 Infantry Brigade, 5 December 1914, TNA WO95/1605.
179 P.H. Jones, Private Papers, IWM Docs 12253.
180 Marden, op. cit. p.10.
181 War Diary, HQ 16 Infantry Brigade, 11 December 1914, TNA WO95/1605.

almost impassable.'[182] 1st Leicestershire went into line several days before Christmas. Water was 'knee-deep, numerous things were floating about' and C Company 'had to work continuously with tins baling out the water', the trenches 'almost as wide as a country lane in places.'[183] A similar flooding beset 1st East Yorkshire when they went back into the line on Boxing Day,[184] when there was a sudden thaw. Material for revetments was slow to appear, and 'parapets would not stand and were so flimsy that many men were shot through them.'[185] A Leicester officer noted the 'scarcity of sandbags, shovels or trench pumps.'[186] 16 Brigade, however, recorded at the end of November that 'short fascines are being laid along the trenches and bricks & in places macadam' in an attempt to master the mud.[187]

Whilst GHQ robustly declined to think about retirement on the grounds of weather difficulties in the front line, there was discussion within III Corps that it might not be possible to hold a continuous line, resorting to 'defence ... in some depth', utilising buildings and hence relying on 'the strength of defended posts and localities and on counter-attack, rather than on holding a continuous trench line.'[188] These proposals were rejected by 6th Division. In contemplating the 10,500 yards of his line, General Keir calculated that it was held by 1.25 men per yard, inclusive of reserves. 'The country is low-lying and dead flat; fields of view and of fire are limited; buildings along the firing line' (of the limited number which were still standing) 'are few; and there are no outstanding features, artificial or natural.' He thus concluded that there were no localities he could use as strong points, and that the 'close nature' of the country did not allow for the safe existence of gaps in the front-line, where 'the strength and nearness' of the enemy might make a sudden attack a very risky proposition. Based on the recommendations of his brigade commanders, he proposed to use high command trenches to the rear of the front line where weather made fire trenches uninhabitable, thus maintaining a front line which all regarded as more secure.[189] If defence was problematic, then offence was unthinkable. He was adamant that 'there are no objectives in front of my line which could justify the assumption of the local offensive on a small scale.'[190] The opposing armies thus dedicated themselves to mere survival.

182 War Diary, HQ 17 Infantry Brigade, 17 December 1914, TNA WO95/1612.
183 H.C. Wylly, *History of the 1st and 2nd Battalions The Leicestershire Regiment in the Great War*, p.14-5.
184 War Diary, HQ 18 Infantry Brigade, 7, 9 & 11 December 1914, TNA WO95/1614.
185 Marden, op. cit. p.10.
186 Wylly, op. cit. p.14.
187 War Diary, HQ 16 Infantry Brigade, 25 November 1914, TNA WO95/1605.
188 War Diary, HQ III Corps, G.60 22 December 1914, TNA WO95/668.
189 War Diary, HQ III Corps, G/16/4, 28 December 1914, TNA WO95/668.
190 War Diary, HQ III Corps, G/16/4 30, December 1914, TNA WO95/668.

Christmas 1914

The so-called 'Christmas Truce' of 1914 has become emblematic of the stuttering flame of the candle of gentlemanly warfare. It has also been a vehicle for myths. On Christmas Eve, 16 Brigade reported that the 'Germans appeared to be very jovial in their trenches. Two came over to our lines and were made prisoner.'[191] 1st Leicesters responded to German carols with 'a good old English carol.'[192] Lance-Corporal Charles Quayle of 1/16th London described how he and his fellows also embarked on carols, whereupon singing sprang up in the enemy trenches with 'a voice shouting "A merry Christmas", and "don't shoot & we won't".'[193] Private Percy Jones, also of the Westminsters, first noted 'about three large fires behind the enemy lines. This in a place where it is generally madness to strike a match.' Christingle was,[194] of course, a German tradition, and lights appeared on the top of the opposing trenches, 'followed by weird tunes on their peculiarly pitched bugles or horns.' Songs followed, and the British put their own lights out. The Saxon soldiers opposite sang a song to the tune of 'God Save the King', and the Westminsters replied with the 'Austrian Hymn', to 'terrific' applause.[195] CSM Conway of C Company, 1st North Staffordshire, observing what was beginning to happen, reported to Captain Arthur Conway; 'What am I to do, Sir? The Germans are sitting on their parapets, lighting candles and singing hymns!.' Conway, seeing one of his rankers talking to a German (who claimed to be a waiter from Brighton), went out and asked to be taken to meet his officers, who asked for a truce to bury their dead. Such was agreed for 10.00 on Christmas Day.[196] Lieutenant Vyvyan Pope noted how 'we fixed up how many men were to do it, and that otherwise both sides must remain in their trenches.'[197] A similar scene was played out elsewhere. Lieutenant Frederick Chandler, medical officer of 2nd Argyll and Sutherland Highlanders, 19 Brigade, described how: 'One of our sergeants got out of the trench and met one of the Germans half way. He lived in Scotland and spoke English with a Scotch accent! They shook hands and exchanged hats.' Between 2nd

191 War Diary, HQ 16 Infantry Brigade, 24 December 1914, TNA WO95/1605.
192 Wylly, op. cit. p.15.
193 C.P. Quayle, Private Papers, IWM Docs 1955. Quayle would be commissioned on the Oxfordshire and Buckinghamshire Light Infantry in August 1915 but was killed in action on 15 June 1916.
194 Christingle, symbolising Christ as the 'Light of the World', was a Moravian tradition which emerged in the mid-1700s.
195 Jones, op. cit.
196 Thornton, *Our War* <https://ourwar1915.wordpress.com/tag/north-staffordshire-regiment-christmas-truce-staffordshire-sentinel-tamworth-herald-armentieres-rue-du-bois-myths/> (Accessed 15 March 2019). Major Arthur Septimus Conway DSO would be killed in action on 17 June 1917.
197 Thornton, op. cit.

Royal Welsh Fusiliers 'and the Germans opposite them were passed greetings and words of bonhomie, and also intermittent fire.'[198]

As Charles Quayle and Percy Jones recorded, singing was clearly a significant part of the evening. In an era when spoken sentimentality was anathema, emotion was often expressed in song. Captain Reginald Armes recorded that: 'I got on top of the trench and talked German and asked them to sing a German Volkslied, which they did, then our men sang quite well and each side clapped and cheered the other. I asked a German who sang a solo to sing one of Schumann's songs, so he sang "The Two Grenadiers" splendidly. Our men were a good audience and really enjoyed his singing.'[199] Corporal Arthur Oakes offered more detail:

> A regular singing contest began our chaps giving 'Tipperary', 'Thora', 'Way Down De Swannee River' and several other well-known songs. The programme tendered by the "Grey-coated Pierrots" (Germans) was very good and included the Austrian and German National Anthems and 'The Watch on the Rhine.' A baritone singer gave 'Sailor Beware' in English, and several other songs. We learned that he was a well-known opera singer and he certainly did not disgrace opera. At 10 o'clock we sang 'The King,' bade them good-night and turned in.[200]

Christmas Day came cold, and foggy initially, and with a fall of snow, although the day brightened. There is little detailed reference to the truce in the formation war diaries, 6th Division simply noting: 'unofficial truce',[201] and 16 Brigade even recorded suffering more casualties than usual. It is clear that there was some attempt to obscure its occurrence. 17 Brigade recorded, however: 'There was an informal truce this day except on the left of the Leinsters, and both sides left their trenches and talked together.' 1st Leicesters recorded little fraternisation, rather waving and shouting, and the battalion, 'quick to take advantage of the opportunity, set to work repairing the trench parapet and collecting wood for fires.'[202] 1st North Staffordshire were most open in the official record, the war diarist recording: 'Not a shot fired. The Germans bury their dead, our men go and help. Baccy and cigars exchanged, and our men walk about in the open together!!'[203] During the work of burial, Captain Ferdinand Ewald

198 F.G. Chandler, Private Papers, IWM Docs 15460. Born in 18815, Frederick George Chandler had qualified from St. Barts in 1911. He served in a Field Ambulance and No. 2 General Hospital. 'He was a pioneer in chest surgery at a critical stage of its development and devised a useful single-puncture thoracoscope.' He died in 1942. http://munksroll.rcplondon.ac.uk/Biography/Details/813 (accessed 7 March 2018).

199 Thornton, op. cit.

200 Thornton, op. cit.

201 War Diary, HQ 6th Infantry Division, 25 December 1914, TNA WO95/1581.

202 Wylly, op. cit. p.15.

203 War Diary, 1st Battalion North Staffordshire Regiment, 25 December 1914, TNA WO95/1613.

attempted some reconnaissance of the enemy trenches, but was warned off.[204] Where fraternisation did occur, there was clearly some attempt at limiting the extent. Percy Jones noted, however, that: 'Both sides had the greatest difficulty in keeping their men away from each other's trenches.'[205] Lance-Corporal Kenneth Gaunt, 1/16th London, described how 'we walked over the top of the trenches and exchanged greetings.' The enemy, he found, were 'a very nice set of fellows … we exchanged souvenirs, and they gave us some very fine cigars. A party of theirs met one of ours halfway between the trenches, they all linked arms and had their photos taken by a German officer.'[206] John du Plessis Langrishe, medical officer of 38th Brigade RFA, walked up to where the Westminsters were fraternising and observed how: 'The Saxons (107th) came out and talked to our men of Q.W.R., had a sing-song & a game of football which the Saxons won 3-2! They even sang "God save the King"!! & gave our men some wine in which to drink his health.' In an act which must have caused the Westminsters' officers some anxiety, 'Some came into our trenches, a few remaining, saying they preferred to go to England! Their Col(onel) and Adj(utant) also came out and chatted.' Charles Quayle reported the exchange of 'buttons, cigars, cigarettes and cognac', concluding with hand shaking. He described the enemy 'playing footer', the match that Langrishe apparently observed, and in response he and his fellows climbed out the back of their trench and commenced at rounders 'with an entrenching tool haft and a jam tin.' There are thus two apparently contemporary eye-witness accounts of the occurrence of a football match. It must be noted, however, that the accounts differ somewhat, Langrishe giving a score-line, Quayle referring to the enemy playing the game. Langrishe's account has been challenged, if erroneously.[207] Chris Baker has concluded concerning truce football matches that 'the evidence in favour of a match suggests at least one such game took place at Wulverghem and no score was kept. It is quite likely there were other "informal" kick arounds elsewhere along the Western Front.'[208] Langrishe reminds us that the truce was not universal, concluding: 'Very different on the south of the Rue du Bac, where the German Reg(iment) fired on the Leicesters & refused to have any truck with them.'[209] Frederick Chandler, who also noted 'sniping going on on our right', recorded that the enemy 'brought a barrel of beer over to the

204 Thornton, op. cit.
205 Jones, op. cit.
206 K.M. Gaunt, Private Papers, IWM Docs 7490.
207 Mark Connelly has challenged the account based on Langrishe's letter which appeared in *The Times* in 1 January 1915. See Connelly, *Christmas Truce Football Match* <https://www.historyextra.com/period/first-world-war/world-war-one-christmas-truce-football-match-really-happen-facts-debate/> (Accessed 15 march 2019). The letter, however, accords with his diary in the Imperial War Museum.
208 Connelly, op. cit.
209 J. du P. Langrishe, Private Papers, IWM Docs 15014. Born in 1883, Langrishe had been commissioned in 1907 and served in India. He was transferred to 16 Field Ambulance, 16 Infantry Brigade in January 1915, and after a period in a staff role commanded 12 Field Ambulance in 4th Division until the end of the war.

reg(iment) on our left!'[210] The fact that the division faced Saxons was probably the key to the degree of fraternisation. Corporal Frederick Cornes recorded that: 'They were all Saxons from the 179th Regiment, 79th Regiment, 102nd Regiment and 132 Regiment. A good many of them came from London.' The Staffords were 'warned about the occupants of the trenches on their left, who were Prussians and described as 'Bosen Kerle' (surly ruffians).'[211]

Captain John Liddell, the machine gun officer of 2nd Argyll & Sutherland Highlanders, 19 Brigade, 'met the man from Glasgow, and gave him tobacco in exchange for cigars. Also newspapers. Talked to a lot of them in English.' He also reported, however, that 'they are all confident that the Russians are beaten, and that the Austrians are in Belgrade. Victory for them in 6 months.'[212] Percy Jones exchanged 'biscuits and matches' as well as collecting autographs from 'a very good class of fellows' who appeared to be 'students at Leipzig.' He noted one German officer clearing North Staffords away from his machine gun, saying: 'You shall not come so near.'[213] Others had more humour. Bernard Brookes of the Westminsters described the enemy wearing 'costumes which had been taken from the houses nearby, and one facetious fellow had a blouse, skirt, top hat and umbrella, which grotesque figure caused much merriment.'[214] The enemy was not alone in this. Lance-Corporal Arthur Lockett of 1st North Staffordshire described that: 'One of our fellows went across to the German trenches dressed in women's clothes.'[215] On Boxing Day, Arthur Conway met a German officer in No Man's Land and was told that his commanding officer had ordered that hostilities were to resume at mid-day.[216]

In 18 Brigade, Walter Congreve wrote to his wife on Christmas Day, noting that he had lunched with two of his battalions in a large factory and then visited the North Staffords at Rue du Bois, taking 'mother's gifts of toffee, sweets cigarettes, pencils, handkerchiefs, and writing paper.' On arrival, he 'found an astonishing state of affairs' – his soldiers and the enemy had 'been walking about all day giving each other cigars and singing songs.' Congreve himself clearly did not enter his trenches, relying on an informant who told him that he had 'smoked a cigar with the best shot in the German army, then not more than 18. They say he's killed more of our men than any other 12 together but I know now where he shoots from & I hope we down him tomorrow.'

210 Chandler, op. cit.
211 Thornton, op. cit.
212 J.A. Liddell, Private papers, IWM Docs 11126. John Aidan Liddell would train as a pilot and was awarded the Victoria Cross when he brought his aircraft and observer down safely despite suffering wounds which would prove fatal.
213 Jones, op. cit.
214 Brookes, op. cit.
215 Thornton, op. cit.
216 Thornton, op. cit.

Congreve continued: 'I was invited to go & see the Germans myself but refrained as I thought they might not be able to resist a General.'[217]

For Frederick Chandler it had been a glorious relief: 'You can't imagine how delicious was that silliness and calm.'[218] Kenneth Gaunt recorded a sense of incongruity: 'It seems most weird, talking and laughing with them one day and killing each other next.'[219] Private Ernest Morley, also of 1/16th London, similarly wrote of 'the curious pleasure of chatting with the men who had been doing their best to kill us & we them.'[220] Reginald Armes wrote: 'Try and imagine two lines of trenches in peace, only 50 yards apart, the men of either side have never seen each other except perhaps a head now and again, and have never been outside in front of their trenches. Then suddenly one day men stream out and nest in friendly talk in the middle.'[221] It would not happen again. It is recorded dourly on 1 January 1915: 'The commander Second Army orders that informal understandings with the enemy are not to take place.'[222]

Conclusion

By the close of 1914 combat 'had torn the heart' from the pre-war Regular British Army.[223] A quarter of the army's pre-war officer class had become casualties by 30 November 1914.[224] 6th Division, which was technically the strongest in the BEF with four brigades, had lost 239 officers by this point, or 49 percent of the number of officers the brigades had gone overseas with. Taking the example of 1st East Yorkshire, 18 Brigade (a unit not subject to either of the two enemy flanking manoeuvres which netted large numbers of prisoners), 83 percent of the infantry company officers who arrived in France with the battalion had become casualties, as Table 1.1 shows. However, having not been involved in the First Battle of Ypres, its units were by no means as depleted as many of those had fought there.[225] These seven divisions

217 https://www.theguardian.com/world/2014/dec/04/letter-british-general-1914-christmas-day-truce-walter-congreve#img-1 (accessed 17 November 2017).
218 Chandler, op. cit.
219 K.M. Gaunt, Private Papers, IWM Docs 7490.
220 E.G. Morley, Private Papers, IWM Docs 2450.
221 Thornton, op. cit. Lieutenant-Colonel Reginald John Armes *psc* would survive the war on the staff.
222 War Diary, HQ 6th Infantry Division, 1 January 1915, TNA WO95/1581.
223 S Jones, 'The British Army and the Problem of the Western Front,1915', in S. Jones (ed) *Courage without Glory*, p.38.
224 P. Hodgkinson, '"The Infantry Battalion Commanding Officers of the BEF', in S. Jones (ed), *Stemming the Tide*, p.305.
225 The 6th Division had suffered 789 fatal casualties in its three original brigades to 30 November 1914. In comparison, 1st Division had suffered 4,104, 2nd Division 2,608, 3rd Division 3,346, and 4th Division 1,924.

'had been reduced to virtual skeleton formations.'[226] 6th Division had experienced its desperate days, but these had been fewer than for many units in the Salient.

		KIA/DOW	Wounded	POW
Lt-Colonel	R.E. Benson	27/09/1914		
Major	W.H. Young			
Captain	B.W.Bogle		11/11/1914	
Captain	A.H. Wilson	18/10/1914		
Captain	E.L.P. Edwards	20/09/1914		
Captain	B. Lawrence	27/10/1914		
Captain	D.F. Anderson		20/09/1914	
Captain	F. Hind	29/10/1914		
Captain	P.B. Maxwell	24/09/1914		
Lieutenant	C.L. Leadley-Brown			
Lieutenant	V.E. Inglefield		20/09/1914	
Lieutenant	F.H. Sasse	(08/05/1915)	20/09/1914	
Lieutenant	J.A. Markham	(07/05/1915)	18/10/1914	
Lieutenant	B.S.C. Hutchinson			20/09/1914
Lieutenant	H.S.F. Cossens	27/10/1914		
Lieutenant	N.V. Blacker		27/10/1914	
Second-Lieutenant	G.R. Smallwood			
Second-Lieutenant	P. Clutterbuck	20/10/1914		
Second-Lieutenant	T.M. Robson		20/10/1914	
Second-Lieutenant	R.T.F. Scott	(16/03/1918)		
Second-Lieutenant	J.A. Hartcup		18/10/1914	
Second-Lieutenant	M.R. Pease	20/10/1914		
Second-Lieutenant	A.W. Meller	(29/01/1916)	20/10/1914	
Second-Lieutenant	T.R. Bottomley	23/09/1914		

Table 1.1: Officer casualties in 1st East Yorkshire, 18 Brigade 1914

From a positive point of view, during the month of October General Keir felt that his division was coming together with the experience of combat particularly in terms

226 Jones, op. cit. p.40.

of the co-ordination between infantry and artillery.[227] Such learning was hampered, however, by the reality of inadequate artillery supplies. In terms of the infantry, there is no indication that any units fought less than well. In considering 1st Buffs in particular, Mark Connelly describes the battalion during this period as a 'cohesive and dependable whole.' NCOs could step up in the absence of officers (indeed, seven were commissioned subalterns in the field during the first four months on active service), and 'officers were … capable of interpreting their role flexibly and authoritatively.' He downplays any impact on the battalion of the fact that half were reservists on embarkation. Others disagree – it has been suggested that the large number of surrenders in 1914 was related to the high levels of reservists, and two units of the division experienced large scale surrenders.[228] The Official Historian describes the new drafts into Regular units in the early part of 1915 as 'half-trained, only partially disciplined and new to battle' – they would show 'courage and fighting spirit', but not the same skill.[229] In addition, reservists had little time to readjust to army life and had been spirited out of their families without time to put their affairs in order. Connelly also takes the view that inter-unit cooperation within 16 Brigade was good, and echoing Keir, that 'communications with the supporting artillery appear to have been generally good.' He highlights, however, 'co-ordination with higher level formations was not as smooth', e.g. with flanking brigades, divisions, and (notably) the French cavalry. He picks an example of lack of communication between brigade and division leading to contradictory orders at Radinghem.[230] The fact that Keir clearly had confidence in his brigadiers meant that the 'man on the spot' had the lassitude to make decisions. This only held until the next higher level decided otherwise. At that point, contradictory orders might arise. This situation held across the BEF, of course, and was not peculiar to 6th Division. Despite the demonstrated courage, however, there was unevenness within the division. This sometimes showed itself in discipline, and at others points in inconsistent officering manifested in action, some COs making impetuous decisions. The latter was reflection of an army as yet unappreciative of firepower. The BEF had only begun to learn its craft in a new warfare.

227 See Chapter 12.
228 Peter Simkins – personal communication. See Chapter 3.
229 J.E. Edmonds & G.C. Wynne, *Military Operations France and Belgium 1915 Vol. 1*, p.325.
230 Connelly, op. cit. locations 969-975.

2

'Courage, Resolution and Decision of a High Order':[1] Commanders and Command 1914-15

John Bourne has described the key features of generalship in the First World War as: 'The capacity to take infinite care with planning and preparation; to respond effectively to battlefield emergencies; and to maintain the initiative by constant harassing of the enemy.' He claims that by 29 September 1918, when all the five British armies were in action, these qualities 'were widespread at battalion, brigade and divisional command levels throughout the BEF and were increasingly to be found at corps level.'[2] He thus describes a bottom-up progression of able men, evolving through infantry battalion command or staff roles, and honed by the experience of the new warfare.

In 1914, however, as General Sir Thomas Snow would note: 'We were one as bad, or should I say as ignorant, as the other', since 'none of us had the practice in handling such large bodies of troops.'[3] Neither was there the organisational framework. Bourne observes that 'few, if any, had contemplated a command structure for an army larger than six infantry divisions and one cavalry division … and no one had had any practical experience even of that.'[4] The army had perpetuated a 'neglect of the operational aspects of modern war; namely the planning and staff work required for operations on a continental scale.'[5] It was thus partly a matter of experience rather than competence. Yet, whilst Simon Robbins observes that 'it would … be mistaken to think that an outdated minority of incompetents represented the Old Army's best

1 J.M. Bourne, 'British Generals in the First World War', in G.D. Sheffield (ed.), *Leadership & Command*, p.96.
2 J.M. Bourne, 'The BEFs Generals on 29 September 1918', in P. Dennis & J. Grey (eds), *1918 Defining Victory*, p.113.
3 T. Snow, 'The Account of the Retreat of 1914', TNA CAB45/129, quoted in S. Robbins, *British Generalship on the Western Front 1914-18*, p.19. Lieutenant-General Sir Thomas D'Oyly 'Snowball' Snow (1858-1940) commanded 4th and 27th Infantry Divisions and VII Corps before being sent home in January 1918.
4 Bourne, op. cit. (1997), p.94.
5 Robbins, op. cit. p.35.

officers',[6] at the same time there was 'a drastic shortage of adequate officers for higher command at operational level.'[7]

In August 1914, the opportunity for 'good fun', as Bill Slim would have had it,[8] in commanding 6th Division lay at the door of Major-General John Lindesay Keir. Born on 6 July 1856 in Ceylon, the son of Scots-born John Lindesay and Helen Keir, his father was a merchant and estate proprietor in that country.[9] He was educated at Wimbledon School, and subsequently the Royal Military Academy, Woolwich. He was commissioned into the Royal Artillery in February 1876 as a lieutenant and was posted to a Royal Field Artillery battery in India, and after six years was able to transfer to the Royal Horse Artillery where he was promoted captain in October 1884. In addition to being a golf enthusiast, for a heavy man he had become a skilled rider and was a polo player, a point-to-point racer, and enjoyed the hunt. He attended and passed Staff College in 1892, and attained his majority on 9 November that year, commanding a field battery RFA. It was at this rank that he married Alice Mary Simpson in 1895 at the relatively older age of 39, as was often the case for army officers.[10] At the time of the outbreak of the Second Boer War in 1899 he was commanding an RHA battery. He was promoted lieutenant-colonel in March 1901 and offered command of the 1st Battalion of the Imperial Yeomanry, volunteer mounted infantry.[11] This switch of professional thread speaks to how he was perceived. He commanded this unit for several months along the Orange River, and in January 1902 was assigned to command the Royal Artillery Mounted Rifles, a force drawn from regular artillerymen, with which unit he remained until shortly before the end of the war.[12] Mentioned in despatches, he received the brevet rank of colonel in June 1902, a rank made substantive in September 1904 whilst serving back with the RHA in India, having been awarded the Royal Artillery Gold Medal for Prize Essay in 1903. Appointed Assistant Adjutant General (AAG) during 1904 to the 1st and later 2nd Divisions in India, he at last was able to put his *psc* qualification to good

6 Robbins, op. cit. p.40.
7 Robbins, op. cit. p.52.
8 W.J. Slim, *Defeat into Victory*, p. 14.
9 There was, however, a military history in the family. One ancestor, Sir William Keir Grant, had taken part in the famous charge of the 15th Light Dragoons at Villers-en-Cauchies during the Seven Years War.
10 The couple had no children.
11 This contained two squadrons of the Wiltshire, one of the Gloucestershire, and one of the Glamorganshire Yeomanry Regiments.
12 The RAMR were originally formed from two howitzer brigades. Commanded by a lieutenant-colonel, the brigades and batteries retained their own organisations and nomenclature. Each of the Corps, or Columns, as they were usually known, was self-contained, having its own pom-pom section, scouts and signallers. A column would usually have a strength of 750 men. From P. Jobson, *Royal Artillery Glossary*, posted by the author at <http://www.victorianwars.com/viewtopic.php?f=17&t=7429> (Accessed 1 December 2017).

use. In October 1907 he was given the command of a brigade at Allahabad, and in July 1909 was promoted to major-general, returning home in 1911. In July 1912 he was assigned to the (Territorial) South Midland Division, replacing Major-General Alexander Thorneycroft somewhat unexpectedly due to the latter's ill-health.[13] He was transferred to the helm of 6th Division in July 1914, only a month before the outbreak of war.

John Bourne suggests that what the senior British Army officers 'brought to command positions were the training, experience and instincts of regimental officers.' The latter 'emphasised personal courage, a high sense of duty, concern for the welfare of their men and professional attention to detail, not least in unit administration.'[14] Keir was apparently an intelligent and thoughtful soldier, who appeared to possess these qualities. He had experience of command of battalion size (if not of infantry) in war. As a Staff College graduate he had developed organisational abilities and put such to use in the post of AAG. He had experience of brigade and divisional command in peace and was thus in tune with the administration of a formation. In a Regular army of few divisions in August 1914, he had shone brightly enough to be promoted to the command of one (which would almost certainly have been the pinnacle of his career). Further evidence of the regard in which he was held was the fact that he had achieved this as an artilleryman, a breed which lagged in importance behind cavalry and infantry, and his star must thus have been sufficiently luminous to attract attention.[15] Unfortunately, when war broke out, he had had little time to build up relationships with either his staff officer or brigade commanders. Further, in the field in September 1914, Keir did not have the chance to command his division, his brigades being placed under the command of other formations. Unfortunately, the absence of the divisional war diary for October 1914 gives little opportunity to get any sense of his approach to command in that crucial month, yet an image appears of a man careful with his division, confident in his brigade commanders and defensive of their actions.

Keir would spend 11 months at the helm of his formation. On 1 June 1915, when VI Corps was formed, he was promoted temporary lieutenant-general and given its command. The third of the new corps to be formed, it took over 4th and 6th Divisions. Again, Keir must have been thought of sufficiently highly to have been given this role, even if the potential corps command pool was likely a small one. 6th Division's attack under VI Corps control on 9 August 1915 at Hooge was 'a model of its kind, took the enemy by surprise and was entirely successful.'[16] (Corps exerted a light hand in planning with the exception, as might be expected, of the artillery arrangements).

13 Alexander Whitelaw Thorneycroft (1859-1931), who had served in the Zulu and both Boer Wars, would not see service during the First World War.

14 Bourne, (1997), p.112.

15 Robbins, op. cit. p.52 – artillery officers provided only 15 percent of corps commanders during the war and 11 percent of divisional commanders.

16 J.E. Edmonds, *Military Operations France and Belgium 1915, Vol. 2*, p.106.

Similarly, Michael LoCicero draws attention to the operation at International Trench carried out 6-10 July 1915. Although 4th Division's War Diary does not leave a record of detailed preparation to compare with 6th Division's Hooge attack, it was a well-planned assault in which the artillery played a key part. LoCicero points out that the 'waspish' Major-General Aylmer Haldane, commanding 3rd Division, described Keir as 'a distinguished artillery officer and took care that neither guns or ammunition was stinted.'[17] Further, on 19 December 1915, the Corps front was the subject of the first phosgene gas attack. 'Standing measures against cloud gas attacks were in force', a special warning had been issued, and 'the measures named in the defence scheme were carried out', corps reserves being immediately deployed.'[18]

Balancing this seemingly positive picture, Major William Ironside, Keir's GSO3, had significant reservations about Keir. He wrote: 'Jack Keir was an extraordinary man, who hardly knew what was going on. He didn't bother himself about any detail and couldn't show the line on the map.' Keir, of course, would not be the only general who relied heavily on his staff officers for detail, which is what, after all, they were there for. Ironside, however, provided a rather startling example:

> He came into the J.S. Office just before the King's visit and I showed him where the line was and gave him all the details. When the King came, Keir showed him the 4th Division line as the one held by us and they discussed it for some time. Naturally the King didn't know, and the mistake was never discovered. I thought this pretty good for the commander of a Division.

These observations do not sit comfortably with the facts of Keir's pre-war career. Ironside also cast aspersions on Keir's temperament: 'He afterwards became very violent in temper … I think the strain of things was rapidly driving him off his head.' [19] In January 1915, Keir inspected every unit that was out of the trenches. His summarised comments were passed to the brigades and circulated. 'One of the most difficult problems before us is the supply of good officers and NCOs', he began. 'The platoon is a very good command for a young officer, but he must be taught to really command it … the company commander's chief duty is the training of his platoon commanders. The platoon commander's that of the training of his section commanders. The chain of responsibility must be maintained. It is the only system which gives permanency of efficiency.'[20] Whatever Ironside thought of him, Keir's remarks can be viewed as either banal or representing good basic principles.

17 M. LoCicero, '"A Coda to the Second Battle of Ypres": International Trench 6-10 July 1915', in *Courage without Glory*, S. Jones (ed), p.321.
18 J.E. Edmonds, *Military Operations France and Belgium 1916, Vol. 1*, pp.158-161.
19 E. Ironside, *Ironside: The Authorised Biography*, Kindle Edition location 113.
20 War Diary, HQ 18 Infantry Brigade, untitled memo, 13 February 1915, WO95/1614.

Adding less sensational weight to the negative view, in June 1915, a correspondence took place between Brigadier-General The Honourable William Lambton, Military Secretary at GHQ and King George V concerning the selection of new army commanders. Three were being considered, namely Pulteney, Keir and Charles Carmichael Monro (GOC I Corps).[21] Of these, Lambton viewed Pulteney as the best choice. In a letter dated 9 July to Kitchener, Secretary of State for War, Lambton expanded that 'reports on Keir both as a divisional and corps commander were not very good. He has only had a corps for about a month and is reported to be slow, rather obstructive and wanting in decision.' Considering Pulteney's merits undervalued, Lambton believed 'Keir has been given underserved credit.'[22]

On 5 February 1916, VI Corps was transferred to Third Army under General Edmund 'The Bull' Allenby. Allenby was 'to many a frightening and unpredictable creature', a man of toughness and discipline, with a 'violent temper', who was, frankly, a bully. Keir demonstrated a 'willingness to stand up to, and formally complain about, Allenby's bullying',[23] actions which earned him the nickname 'The Matador.' Ironside described the conflict as one with a 'man with a temper even more volcanic than his own.'[24] As John Bourne and Gary Sheffield note, however: 'The bull gored him fatally in the end.' Allenby was 'conspicuously loyal to Haig and would not permit his own subordinates to criticize G.H.Q.'.[25] Whilst Haig was never warm towards Allenby, it seems that he repaid the favour. Allenby, no doubt resenting Keir's challenges, reported to Haig that his 'defensive arrangements were unsatisfactory, and that he had no real plans worked out for offensive action.' As the Germans 'showed signs of activity near Arras where Keir's sector of defence was', Haig 'felt it would be highly dangerous to retain him in command, so I *at once* relieved him of his Command.' The performance of VI Corps under Keir in both offence and defence in 1915 had, of course, not been faulted. On 8 August 1916 Keir demanded to see Haig: 'Quite beside himself with rage against Allenby and said that he had been wronged. He meant to go home and make a row; he was not done with the Army yet, etc..' Haig added: 'I was sorry for the old man as he is over 60, but I felt I had done right in relieving of his Command … no one who is any good at all as a Commander is ever sent home by me.'[26] Whilst older corps commanders were indeed replaced as the war progressed, 'the difficulty of finding even half-competent corps commanders' meant that 'many were able to linger.'[27] Haig's remarks, on the surface, smack of something of the disingenuous, given the circumstances, but he would have been more than privy to the

21 Only Monro would achieve army command, that of First Army briefly in 1916.
22 Quoted in A. Leask, *Putty*, pp.300-1.
23 P. Simkins, 'Haig and the Army Commanders', in B. Bond & N. Cave, *Haig: A Re-appraisal 80 Years On*, pp.82-3.
24 Ironside op. cit. location 1113.
25 Simkins, op. cit. p.83.
26 Sheffield and Bourne, op. cit. p.217.
27 Robbins, op. cit. p.65.

observations reported by William Lambton. Aylmer Haldane,[28] who succeeded Keir, 'felt that there were firm military grounds for removing' him. This therefore suggests a change in his views on Keir as expressed a year earlier. Whilst it might be thought that that is exactly what he, as the replacement, might well say, he clearly shared Ironside's views. Whilst noting that Haldane was a man stringent in his criticism of others, even he, however, noted that 'the arbitrary way' in which the replacement was made 'caused friction and insecurity within the high command.'[29] Keir's obituary in *The Times* refers to the 'strain of active service.'[30] Trying to reconcile the various strands it is likely that Keir increasingly struggled with the wide range of demands of divisional and corps command in war, and, if Ironside is to be believed, he latterly failed to provide John Bourne's first test of generalship, 'infinite care with planning and preparation.' Successful command of a battalion in war and a formation in peacetime, was not an adequate test of higher command. If he both lacked ultimate competence at senior level, and was also tiring and stressed, his downfall was as a victim of rivalry. Proving that he was not a fool, Keir published *A 'Soldier's-Eye-View' of Our Armies* in 1919. On one hand, it contained many criticisms of the system that had ousted him: 'A profession in which a man can be condemned and then cast out from unheard without a chance of appeal is both unhealthy and unsuited to our justice-loving race.'[31] It also contained, however, radical proposals for a National Army including the Dominions. Keir would have known that his vision would never come to fruition, but he was determined to go down giving the impression of being a free-wheeling thinker. Awarded the CB in 1908 and KCB in 1915, he died in 1937.

Brigade Command

John Bourne offers the opinion that: 'Leadership at brigade level was not fundamentally different from that at battalion.'[32] It is true that the divisional commander, unlike the brigadier, had a responsibility for coordinating infantry, cavalry, artillery, engineers and logistical support. For the brigadier there was, however, a step up from coordinating company commanders to working with battalion commanders. Major-General Oliver Nugent reflects Bourne's view, advising Lieutenant-Colonel Frank Crozier on his elevation: 'Treat your new brigade as a big battalion',[33] but there was always the tension of wishing to interfere. Brigadier-General 'Bulgy' Thorne longed to command his troops 'as a Battalion Commander instead of as a Brigadier-General.

28 Sir James Aylmer Lowthorpe Haldane (1862-1950) commanded 10th Infantry Brigade, 3rd Division, and VI Corps until the Armistice.
29 Robbins, op. cit. p.60, based on Haldane's war diary, 7 August 1916, (National Library of Scotland).
30 Obituary, *The Times*, 4 May 1937.
31 J. Keir, *A 'Soldier's-Eye-View' of Our Armies*, p.225.
32 Bourne, (1997), p.99.
33 F.P. Crozier, *A Brass Hat in No Man's Land*, p.131.

One cannot get at them except through their COs and I feel I could run their show so much better than they could.'[34] Commanding a brigade required not only organisational competence, but a certain degree of trust and ability to work with some potentially powerful personalities.

The actions of the brigades of 6th Division in September and October 1914 show brigade command to be a very hands-on affair. This was as it should be, for as Bourne notes: 'A brigade commander's ability to influence operational and tactical planning was strictly limited.'[35] Brigadiers were close to the action and assumed a firm direction when they could. It is this that shapes Bourne's opinion that brigade command was both operationally and morally the most difficult level of senior command.[36] This 'hands-on' command would change with the advent of positional warfare and the great attritional battles of 1916-17. It would be 1918 before this situation would swing back to a greater hands-on approach.

In August 1914, as noted in Chapter One, the three brigade commanders were Brigadier-Generals Edward Charles Ingouville-Williams (16 Brigade); Walter Robert Butler Doran (17 Brigade); and Walter Norris Congreve (18 Brigade). Born on 15 December 1861, the son of General Sir John Doran, Walter Doran had been commissioned into the Royal Irish Rifles in May 1882. He served in the Anglo-Egyptian War of 1882 (being present at the battles of Kassassin and Tel-el-Kebir) and with the Sudan Expedition of 1884-85. His first staff experience was as a staff captain, March-August 1885. He was promoted captain in November 1888 and served with the 2nd Battalion of his regiment in the Hazara Expedition of that year. He passed Staff College in 1895. During attachment to the Egyptian Army (1897-1900), he took part in the Nile Expeditions of 1897 and 1898 (being present at the battles of Atbara and Khartoum), commanding an Egyptian battalion during the latter, and in the 1899 expedition he commanded the 9th Sudanese at Kordofan. Stationed in South Africa 1899-1902, he was a brigade-major and served in other staff posts. Achieving his majority in February 1901, he commanded a flying column from November 1901 to May 1902 and was awarded the DSO. Returning to England, from June 1903 to August 1904 he was employed as Deputy Assistant Adjutant General (DAAG), 4th Army Corps. He became a lieutenant-colonel in August 1904, commanding 2nd Battalion Leinster Regiment; and was promoted colonel four years later, serving as GSO1, 5th Division, Irish Command, from July 1909 to April, 1912.

Doran, therefore, was exactly the sort of successful regimental officer, a Staff College graduate with considerable war experience at battalion command level, who would likely be promoted to brigade command. Indeed, he took command of 17 Brigade on 8 April 1912. William Ironside described him as 'a gloomy individual,

34 D. Lindsay, *Forgotten General: A Life of Andrew Thorne*, p.74.
35 Bourne, (1997), p.101.
36 J. Bourne, 'British Generals on the Cusp of Victory, September 1918', paper presented at University of Wolverhampton, 3 March 2018.

always grousy.'[37] He was relieved of his post on 11 February 1915. Thomas Marden's history does not mention his departure, nor does the 6th Division war diary. The only record, not giving a reason, is in the 17 Brigade diary. His obituary in *The Times* refers to 'ill-health.'[38] Returning to Great Britain, he served as Inspector of Infantry from 12 April to 9 May 1915; but on 26 May 1915, he was assigned to command 88 Brigade, 29th Division, then in Gallipoli. He was invalided almost immediately on 7 June. Interestingly, this followed an attack by 88 Brigade in the Third Battle of Krithia, where the *Official History* notes: 'The good progress made by individual detachments was not realized at brigade headquarters, and the advanced troops … being unsupported, were forced to retire.'[39] If his health was not of the best, it seems unlikely he would have been sent to Gallipoli. Removal from post in Flanders, and again just after an unsuccessful operation in Gallipoli, points towards a perceived lack of competence at higher command in the field. Designated Brigadier-General General Staff (BGGS) in the Training Centre, Aldershot Command, from 25 September 1915, he retired in March 1919, and his health was good enough to sustain him until 1945. Like Keir, the transition to senior command in war apparently revealed fault lines in his abilities.

The other two brigade commanders had more stellar careers. Walter Norris 'Squibs' Congreve (also known as 'Old Concrete' to rankers) was born on 20 November 1862.[40] Educated at Harrow, he went up to Pembroke College, Oxford, but did not take his degree. 'His premature departure from the university appears to have been occasioned by his taking a pot shot at a senior member of Pembroke College with an air rifle.'[41] He was commissioned into the Rifle Brigade in February 1885, married Cecelia la Touche in 1890, and was promoted captain in December 1893. He served as Deputy Inspector of Musketry at Aldershot from January 1898 to October 1899 at which point, he went to South Africa with his regiment. In the campaign, he famously was awarded the Victoria Cross at Colenso, on 15 December 1899, attempting to save Colonel Long's guns.

> The detachments serving the guns of the 14th and 66th Batteries, Royal Field Artillery, had all been either killed, wounded, or driven from their guns by infantry fire at close range, and the guns were deserted. About 500 yards behind the guns was a donga, in which some of the few horses and drivers left alive were sheltered. The intervening space was swept with shell and rifle fire. Captain

37 Ironside op. cit. location 1158.
38 Obituary, *The Times*, 9 February 1945.
39 C.F. Aspinall-Oglander, *Military Operations Gallipoli, Vol. 2*, p.50.
40 His nickname was acquired as a result of an ancestor, William Congreve, who patented the Congreve Rocket used in the Napoleonic Wars. He was also related to the Restoration poet, William Congreve.
41 *Donkey Archive* <https://www.birmingham.ac.uk/research/activity/warstudies/research/projects/lionsdonkeys/c.aspx> Accessed 3 December 2017).

> Congreve, Rifle Brigade, who was in the donga, assisted to hook a team into a limber, went out and assisted to limber up a gun. Being wounded, he took shelter, but seeing Lieutenant Roberts fall badly wounded, he went out and brought him in. Captain Congreve was shot through the leg, the toe of his boot, grazed on the elbow and shoulder, and his horse shot in three places.[42]

After a period as adjutant with Kitchener's Horse, perhaps partly due to having brought back Lord Roberts' wounded son in the Colenso action but also to having previously served on the personal staff of Sir Redvers Buller, he was appointed to Roberts' staff as a brigade-major and DAAG.[43] He later served as Assistant Military Secretary (AMS) and private secretary to Lord Kitchener. Returning to England he further served as AMS and Aide-de-Camp (1902-04) to HRH Duke of Connaught, commanding III Corps and the forces in Ireland. He 'possessed personal charm of no ordinary kind' which no doubt assisted in these tasks.[44] Until April 1906 he was private secretary to the Inspector General of the Forces, and promoted colonel in July 1908, became commandant of the School of Musketry, Hythe, in September 1909, a post in which he served until promoted to command 18 Brigade on 6 September 1911.

Congreve thus had a totally different career path to Doran. He had held no unit commands in South Africa and had not commanded a battalion of his own regiment. Yet he had been at the shoulder of the army's best-known generals whilst they made their decisions. As observed in Chapter One, he was an active, responsive, and thoughtful brigade commander. He would go on to command 6th Division, and later XIII Corps. William Ironside would not have been the only individual to describe him as 'undoubtedly our best Brigadier.'[45] His son, Billy Congreve VC, encountered General Keir on 23 September on the Aisne, who 'said that Dads was having plenty of fighting and that he was doing very well.'[46] Bourne adds that 'Congreve never curbed his instincts to be in the front line or to see for himself. He constantly courted

42 *London Gazette*, 2 February 1900, p. 689.
43 Sir Redvers Henry Buller (1839-1908) commanded the British Army in South Africa until December 1899 when he was sacked and replaced by Frederick Sleigh Roberts (1832-1914). 'Bobs', who had served in the Indian Rebellion, the Expedition to Abyssinia and the Second Anglo-Afghan War, would prove a far more successful commander until he handed over to Lord Kitchener in December 1900.
44 Obituary, *The Times*, 1 March 1927.
45 Ironside, op. cit. location 1158.
46 B. Congreve (T. Norman ed.), *Armageddon Road*, p. 34. William la Touche Congreve VC DSO MC and his father were one of only three father/son Victoria Cross pairings. A lieutenant at the outbreak of war, Billy became a brigade-major in December 1915 with 76 Brigade but was killed by a sniper near Longueval on the Somme on 20 July 1916. At the funeral of a friend in February 1915, Walter Congreve wrote: 'Billy was splendid and quite collected. I felt like a baby.' (Congreve, op. cit. p.104.)

danger.'[47] Ferdinand Stanley, GOC 89 Brigade, recalled a visit to his frontline trenches by Congreve in March 1916.[48] The visit took place during a snow storm. 'He is a most adventurous man,' Stanley wrote in his diary, 'and infinitely preferred walking out in full view and quite close to the enemy than anything else. He simply asked for trouble.'[49] Private Percy Jones, 1/16th London, described Congreve and his staff on a trench visit on 7 January 1915. Six shells landed and Jones found 'three men down ... General Congreve was smothered in blood and brains, but cool as a cucumber. He made an enquiry about the men and went on.'[50] Congreve's determination to see for himself, however, was not confined to trench visits – he also carried out personal aerial reconnaissance. He replaced Keir as commander of 6th Division, showing the attention to detail in the Hooge attack of August 1915 that Ironside regarded as lacking in his predecessor, until 14 November that year. On his departure, Billy would write: 'I was filled with pride and then almost reduced to tears when hundreds and hundreds of men rushed out all along the road and cheered him – *real* cheering.' Emphasising his father's emotional side, he continued: 'I think he nearly wept – lieutenant-generals can weep!.'[51] When news reached Congreve of his son's death, however: 'He was absolutely calm to all outward appearance and, after a few seconds said quite calmly, "He was a good soldier"', and carried on with what he was doing. Brigadier-General Walter Greenly, the unfortunate informant, added: 'I shall never ... lose the admiration I felt for the marvellous self-suppression of the "man" in the capacity of the commander.'[52] Congreve proved a highly successful corps commander until June 1917, when he was invalided home after his left hand was blown off by an enemy shell. On top of asthma and bronchitis, not to mention a bout of typhoid in August 1916, he was not quite of the same stature when he returned in March 1918 to VII Corps. On 15 April 1918 Congreve was transferred to X Corps, then rested, and sent home the following month. The demands of command at this level were hard. He was appointed in August 1919 to the command of British forces in Syria and North Palestine, and then Egypt until 1923, returning to Great Britain as GOC Southern Command for a year, before proceeding as Governor and Commander-in-Chief to

47 https://www.birmingham.ac.uk/research/activity/warstudies/research/projects/lionsdonkeys/c.aspx (accessed 7 December 2017).
48 Ferdinand Charles Stanley, an officer of both the Kings Royal Rifle Corps and the Grenadier Guards, would command 17 King's Liverpool, and 89 Brigade for two periods between December 1914 and April 1918.
49 F.C. Stanley, *The History of the 89th Brigade 1914-1918*, pp. 112-13.
50 P.H. Jones, Private Papers, IWM Docs 12253.
51 Congreve, op. cit. p.175.
52 W.H. Greenly, quoted in Congreve, op. cit. p.194. Walter Howorth 'Bob' Greenly, an officer of the 19th Hussars, served variously as GOC 9 Cavalry Brigade (1915), BGGS XIII Corps (1916), and GOC 2nd Cavalry Division from November 1916 to March 1918, and which point he took command of 14th Light Division for five days before being invalided.

Malta in a difficult political climate.[53] His 1927 obituary in *The Times* noted: 'He did not attempt to pass through the Staff College, or even to qualify by means of study for high appointments.' This speaks to something significant in Congreve's nature. 'But he possessed the great gifts of imperturbability in the most trying circumstances, common sense and good judgement.' The obituary continued that Congreve 'would always think of the comfort of his troops' and 'was still at heart the thoughtful, sympathetic, company commander.' Indeed, Congreve never quite lost the protective instincts of the regimental officer, writing to his son and fellow VC winner, Billy, on 5 April 1916: 'I don't feel I can ever make a general, for I cannot face having men killed in the ruthless way generals must do.'[54]

Walter Norris Congreve (Open source).

53 He was made MVO in 1903, awarded the CB in 1911, and promoted to KCB in 1917.
54 Quoted in T. Norman, *The Hell They Called High Wood: The Somme, 1916*, p.33.

The third of the original 6th Division brigadiers, Edward Charles 'Inky Bill' Ingouville-Williams,[55] was born on 13 December 1861, son of General Sir John Williams.[56] He was commissioned into the Buffs from the Militia in April 1881, and served in the Sudan Expedition, 1884-85, as Staff Captain Special Officer for Boats. From 1898-9 was attached to the Egyptian Army as a Special Service Officer and took part in in the Nile Expedition of 1898. In the expedition of 1890 he served as DAAG to the Kordofan Field Force. In South Africa (1899-1902) he was on Sir Charles Warren's staff as provost-marshal and brigade major.[57] He therefore had the opportunity to witness failure of judgement, delay and indecision at first hand in the bungled second attempted relief of Ladysmith and at Spion Kop in January 1900. Between January 1901 (in which year his elder brother George was killed on active service) and September 1902 he commanded a Mounted Infantry Corps and a Mobile Column. Awarded the DSO, he transferred to the Worcestershire Regiment in April 1903; and commanded the 2nd Battalion (1904-8) in Ceylon and India. He then served as Commandant, School of Mounted Infantry, Longmoor Camp (1910-12) and was promoted to the command of 16 Brigade on 18 June 1912.

Ingouville-Williams therefore shared much the antecedents as his fellow general officers, particularly Keir and Doran, namely a rich tapestry of war, command in combat, and staff experience. William Ironside described him as 'a small nervous-looking man, always on springs.'[58] Thomas Grove, GSO3 with the division, dubbed him 'a very good little brigadier and officer and strenuous soldier.' Emphasising his high standards and decisiveness he stated that 'of the four battalion commanders he took out to France he had sent home three with three months of arrival there.' (The actual total was two).[59] Grove did not find him easy: 'The only way to get on with Inky was to stand up to him and not submit to be bullied.'[60] After his sound leadership of 16 Brigade, he was given command of the 34th Division in Great Britain in June 1915, which he trained and took to the Western Front in January 1916. In September 1915 he crashed his car into a traction engine and was in a coma for seven days. He was back at duty within two weeks, which demonstrates the determination of the man.[61] He bore the mark of the regimental officer – care of his men. An officer of the 11th Suffolks noted: 'He says he is going to save every life he can in his division. He

55 He changed his name by deed poll in 1902 to include Ingouville, his mother's maiden name.
56 Sir John William Collman Williams (1824-1911) was a general of the Royal Marines.
57 Sir Charles Warren (1840-1927) was of the Royal Engineers, but later served as an MP and was head of the Metropolitan Police during the Jack the Ripper murders. He had also excavated Jerusalem's Temple Mount. Returning to command 5th Division in the Second Boer War, he proved less than competent.
58 Ironside, op. cit. location 1158.
59 Lieutenant-Colonels Hill (1st Buffs) and Cobbold (2nd York & Lancaster).
60 T.T. Grove, 'It Happened by Chance', NAM 1963-08-14.
61 J. Costin, *Cambridgeshire Kitcheners*, p.60.

is going to improve any trenches we go into, to make them absolutely safe … he is a fine man. He was in command of a brigade at the beginning of the war, and saved his own brigade by his calmness and his bravery.'[62] As for bravery, at the front it is reputed that he led patrols himself.[63] In the final analysis, however, there was only so much he could do to protect his men – the Tyneside Scottish and Irish Brigades of his division suffered the highest casualties of any brigades on the Somme on 1 July 1916. On the 22nd, Ingouville-Williams went with his ADC to Mametz Wood to make a personal reconnaissance of the ground where he was to take his division into action the following week. Returning to his car he was caught in a barrage by the Queen's Nullah, hit by a piece of shell and killed instantly.

Edward Charles Ingouville-Williams (Open source).

Lastly, if 19 Brigade (which was attached to 6th Division from 12 October 1914 to 31 May 1915) is also considered, the career of Brigadier-General the Honourable Frederick Gordon must be taken into account. Born on 9 October 1861, the son of Lord Gordon of Drumearn,[64] Gordon was educated at the Edinburgh Academy and

62 A. Mack, quoted in Costin, op. cit. p.60.
63 Costin, op. cit. p.60.
64 His grandfather, Major John Gordon, had served in the 2nd Foot.

Sandhurst and commissioned into the 91st Foot (Argyllshire Highlanders), transferred to the 49th Foot (Royal Berkshire), and lastly into the Gordon Highlanders. He served in the Egyptian Expedition of 1882-4 (being present at Tel-el-Kebir and wounded in 1884) and with the Egyptian Army in 1889 in the Sudan. After a posting as brigade-major in Malta, he served throughout the Second Boer War as DAAG (Intelligence) and then at Army HQ. From 1903-4 he was DAQMG of 1st Division, and from 1908-11 served as CO of 1st Gordon Highlanders, leaving this post before his four-year term was up to become GSO1 with 1st Division at Aldershot. When 19 Infantry Brigade was formed on 22-3 August 1915, Gordon became its second GOC on 5 September 1914.[65] William Ironside viewed Gordon as 'a dour old bird, often very sarcastic to us on the Divisional Staff. A good fighting man and very good at heart.'[66] Gordon's Staff Captain, James Jack described him as possessing:

> A fine character, a spare frame and a very strong sense of duty; but I find him tryingly reserved and hard … His tastes are simple, even austere; he sleeps and eats little besides drinking less; he is always up at dawn and works or reads till bedtime. The table in his room is never without a Bible which I often observe him studying.[67]

On 2 January 1915, Jack described Gordon refusing to conduct a raid of least a battalion strength on the enemy trenches,[68] demonstrating the regimental officer's protectiveness of his men. Gordon would remain in charge until 16 June 1915 when he took up the command of the 22nd Division at Aldershot, carrying out its last intensive training. The division went to France in September 1915 but the following month was transferred to Salonika from whence Gordon was invalided on 7 May 1917, serving in staff posts in Great Britain from December that year.[69] Gordon, like the other brigadiers of 6th Division, had the crucial blend of war, staff and command experience.

In the expanding army, such men would move up the ladder of senior command rapidly. The army's task was, therefore, to find suitable replacements. Fortunately, the cupboard was not bare of talented individuals. Doran's replacement was Brigadier-General 'Uncle' George Montague Harper. A *psc*, he was 'an outstanding staff officer', who later 'turned the 51st (Highland) Division into one of the best divisions in the BEF', and who in 1918 became an 'outstanding commander' of IV Corps. Walter

65 Major-General L.G. Drummond lasted five days before being invalided, and Lieutenant-Colonel B.E. Ward acted until Gordon's appointment.
66 Ironside, op. cit. location 1158.
67 J. Terraine (ed), *General Jack's Diary*, p.58.
68 Terraine, op. cit. p.90.
69 He was an area commander for the RAF 1918-19, and in 1919 briefly enjoyed divisional command before retiring in 1920. Awarded the CB and promoted to KCB, he died in 1927.

Nicholson, a staff officer, described how '"Uncle" had a sparkling brain, alive to all the changing conditions, unperturbed by events' – a man 'sure of himself.'[70] Born on 12 January 1865, the son of a doctor and educated at Bath College and RMA Woolwich, Harper had been commissioned into the Royal Engineers in July 1884. He had been employed in the mobilisation department at Army HQ (1902-3) as a staff captain and DAQMG, and had then become GSO2 in the same location for three years, before going to the Staff College as a DAAG and GSO2 (1907-10). He was promoted GSO1 at the War Office in June 1911, at which point he became a substantive colonel. His organisational credentials were impeccable, even if he had never held battalion command, and he would state in 1918 that success in battle was 'largely dependent on the care and forethought exercised by Commanders in laying their initial plans' and that most battles were 'won or lost before zero hour.'[71] Harper had served in South Africa 1899-1900, being present at the Relief of Ladysmith, Spion Kop, Vall Kranz, Tugela Heights, and Pieter's Hill. Showing the good qualities of a regimental officer, he attracted 'the genuine affection of all ranks' by being 'in constant touch with his troops, both in and out of the line' and was 'known personally to many of them.'[72] Harper would demonstrate Bourne's first requirement of generalship, 'infinite care with planning and preparation' in the attack on l'Epinette in March 1915 (see Chapter 3). Ivor Maxse later described Harper's 'intimate up-to-date knowledge of infantry tactics' and 'masterly manner in active operations.'[73] On the Somme in 1916, Sir Douglas Haig thought that Harper 'knew his work.'[74]

The replacement for 'Inky Bill' was 49-year-old Cecil Lothian Nicholson. 'Johnny Nick' was one of three brothers who became major-generals. Yet another brother was an admiral, and the father of this remarkable quartet was General Sir Lothian Nicholson, Royal Engineers. Nicholson had been commissioned into the Yorkshire Regiment in August 1885, transferring to the Worcestershire Regiment. He had passed Staff College and served as ADC to the Governor and Commander-in-Chief of Gibraltar 1891-93, following which he went to India where he served as staff captain and DAQMG for mobilisation (1900-1). He then succeeded to a position as DAQMG at Bengal Eastern Command, later reprising his mobilisation role (1901-5). Returning to Great Britain he served as brigade major with both 15 and 16 Brigades in Ireland (1905-09), and then as a GSO2 in South Africa (1911-2). Commanding 2nd East Lancashire from February 1912, his only previous war experience was in the

70 W. N. Nicholson, *Behind the Lines*, p.140.
71 G.M. Harper, quoted in Robbins, op. cit. p.26.
72 N.G. Barron and F.W. Brewster, quoted in Robbins, op. cit. p.17.
73 I. Maxse, quoted in Robbins, op. cit. p.63. Sir Frederick Ivor Maxse (1862-1958) had commanded the 1st Coldstream Guards prior to the war, and commanded the 1st Guards Brigade, 18th Division, and XVIII Corps, lastly to become Inspector General of Training in 1918.
74 Sheffield & Bourne, op. cit. p. 210. Harper's car skidded and overturned in December 1922. As a result, he suffered a fractured skull and died, his wife being seriously injured.

Tirah operations 1897-98. He would serve as a brigade commander until July 1916 and would command 34th Division from that point until the Armistice. Like Harper, he was clearly a highly competent officer.[75]

18 Brigade had less success in replacing Congreve. Initially, 46-year-old Henry Sandys Ainslie was appointed. He had served as CO 1st Northumberland Fusiliers since February 1912 but had had no previous war experience and little staff experience, limited to serving as ADC to the Governor and Commander-in-Chief Straits Settlement, Malaya. He went 'sick' on 5 August. William Ironside stated that four days prior to the Hooge operation on 9 August, Ainslie 'came to Congreve and said that he couldn't carry on any more & that it would be murder to send the Brigade into action against the Enemy under him.'[76] Ainslie's brief promotion suggest a reliance on seniority during a period of limited choice, but also reminds us of the demands of such command. On 14 August 1915, 46-year-old Robert James Bridgford was appointed in his place. Bridgford had fought in South Africa 1899-1902, but had no staff experience. He had commanded 2nd King's Shropshire Light Infantry since February 1914. He served until 19 April 1916 when he fell during the night and broke several ribs, returning to command 141 Brigade (47th Division) from 5 July to 19 August 1916, at which point he was transferred back to 18 Brigade until 14 September 1917, when he was sent home. He returned to command 31st Division on 21 March 1918, was transferred to 32nd Division on 7 May and dismissed 24 days later.

The BEF thus had the luxury of replacing, in the case of 6th Division, one experienced brigade commander, who had apparently fallen short of expectations, and one experienced and successful commander with two skilled officers who would show their worth and promotability. Not all the replacements could have the depth of experience, as the careers of Ainslie and Bridgford showed. Bridgford clearly failed to make the transition from brigade to divisional command. It might be considered that these two men reflect some of the limitations of the group of senior officers of 1914. Some were less than competent in most respects, like the vulnerable Ainslie. Others struggled with the transition from peace to war, brigade to division or division to corps. Yet the careers of a number of the brigadiers of 6th Division serving during 1914-15 point to the abilities of many of the much-maligned senior officers of the British Army at the outbreak of war.

Battalion Command

The five months of warfare of 1914 were undoubtedly the most demanding of the war on regimental officers, and at unit command level the demand fell on men who lacked one thing in common, youth. The twelve COs of the battalions of the three original brigades had an average age of 48 years nine months, with a range of 47 to 52, being

75 See Chapter 6.
76 Ironside op. cit. location 1228.

just a little older than the average age across all the Regular COs of August 1914 of a fraction under 48 years.[77] Richard Erle Benson (1st East Yorkshire), killed in action on 20 September, was the oldest CO at 52. There was an inevitability to this age profile, as with Kier and his brigadiers – these men were near the end of the trajectory of an army career. A lieutenant-colonel at this point had taken 25 years to reach unit command level. To what extent, however, was age a problem in terms of operational demand? James Edmonds, the official historian, observed wisely that 'age is biological and should not be reckoned by the calendar. Each case should be judged for itself.' There is clearly a distinction between age and fitness, and Edmonds continued: 'Activity is the criterion; in 1914 some lieutenant-colonels could be seen running forward with the best of athletes; others collapsed because they were worn out by marching a few miles; not being able to ride their horses in battle.' He specifically referred to the St Quentin surrender COs, Elkington and Mainwaring, noting that 'two were tried by court martial for dereliction of duty, when bodily fatigue with consequent mental break-down was their offence.'[78] This certainly was the fate of Henry Ainslie, and as will be seen in Chapter Three, Frederick Towsey (if temporarily) at a crucial moment of the August 1915 Hooge operation.

The group had an average of 22 months of battalion command. Francis William Towsey (1st West Yorkshire), so sorely tested on his first day in action on the Aisne, had only been in command for five months, whilst Henry Cecil de la Montague Hill (1st Buffs) was due to have surrendered his command, his four year term having expired, on the day that war was declared. Indeed, it appears he was largely a 'passenger' in his battalion, brevet Colonel Julian Hasler exerting command in action, and he was 'invalided' on 15 November 1914, later posted commandant of the Machine Gun Corps Training School in October 1915. One of three COs aged 47, Cyril Randell Crofton-Atkins (2nd Sherwood Foresters) was similarly invalided on 7 October 1914. He achieved brigade commander rank in 1916 with a training brigade, and would never see active service again. Two out of twelve COs therefore had constitutions which would not see out three months of demanding warfare.

What of their experience? At a time when twelve percent of Regular COs had no experience of war, a similar proportion of 6th Division COs, two of the twelve, had none.[79] Whilst it has been popular to deride the 'small war' experience of the British Army in 1914, it must not be forgotten that the German Army would have been very pleased to have had this experience. Much of this had been acquired in South Africa in the Second Boer War. Thus, Henry Leycester Croker (1st Leicestershire) had been adjutant to the battalion he would later command over those three years, fighting at Talana, Lombards Kop, in the Defence of Ladysmith, at Laings Nek, and on the

77 P.E. Hodgkinson, *British Infantry Battalion Commanders in the First World War*, p. 12.
78 James E. Edmonds and R. Maxwell-Hyslop, *Military Operations France and Belgium 1918, Vol. 5*, p. 613.
79 Henry Hill (1st Buffs), and Richard Fowler-Butler (1st Royal Fusiliers).

Zululand Frontier. Similarly, Ernest Cazenove Cobbold (2nd York & Lancaster) had served during the same period, being present at the Relief of Ladysmith, Spion Kop, Vall Kranz, Tugela Heights, and Pieters Hill. Bernard William Lynedoch McMahon (2nd Durham Light Infantry) had also spent three years in South Africa as adjutant to 1st Durham Light Infantry, being present at the relief of Ladysmith, Colenso, Vaal Kranz, Tugela Heights, and Laings Nek. Cyril Crofton-Atkins had also been in South Africa for three years (and further had fought in Sierra Leone 1898-9), as had Cecil Pickford Higginson (1st Kings Shropshire Light Infantry) who had briefly served as adjutant to 2nd King's Shropshire Light Infantry. Reginald Alexander (3rd Rifle Brigade) had similarly spent three years in South Africa, being severely wounded. Vigant William de Falbe (1st North Staffordshire) had missed the disasters of 1899, but had served in South Africa 1900-02 as the adjutant of 2nd North Staffordshire. Richard Benson had also been adjutant to 4th East Surrey during the conflict in 1902. Although they did not serve in South Africa, William Tankerville Monypenny Reeve (2nd Leinster) had been in action in the 1900 Ashanti war, and Francis Towsey had fought in Lushai (1892) and Ashanti (1895-6). There was thus a rich tapestry of war into which these unit commanders were woven.

One area in which the unit COs of 6th Division at the outbreak of war were slightly less experienced than the whole group of Regular COs, was staff experience. Whereas 22 percent of the COs of the Regular army at the outbreak of war had passed the two-year Camberley Staff College course, only one of the 6th Division COs had the initials *psc* following their name, Cecil Higginson. Four of the 12 had significant extra-regimental staff service, which was also less than the near 50 percent across the Regular COs of August 1914 as a group. Henry Hill had served as Assistant Inspector at the School of Musketry (1892-97); Inspector (1898-1901); and Experimental Officer there (1901-04). He was lastly a brigade major attached to the General Staff Northern Command (1906-09). He was thus one of those responsible for the BEF's rifle fire prowess in 1914, and it was no accident that he was later sent to the Machine Gun Training School. Cecil Higginson had served as brigade major and DAAG in South Africa (1901), as brigade major to 2 Brigade (1903-06), Deputy Assistant Director General Medical Services (1906-09), and lastly as DAAQMG in China (1909-13). Cyril Crofton-Atkins had been assigned as a staff officer to a Mounted Infantry Corps in South Africa, as a recruiting staff officer, and as ADC to a General Officer Commanding in both South Africa and Great Britain. Lastly, Bernard McMahon had been a brigade major on the General Staff at Aldershot (1908-12). The remaining eight had all served as regimental adjutants. There was thus a reasonable level of organisational skill.

The 1914 campaign would sever these men from their posts sooner rather than later. As already noted, two would be invalided, never to return to active service. Two were killed in action or died of wounds. Indeed six, half the group, would be wounded in 1914, a testament if nothing else to the tradition of the unit commander leading from the front. One of these, Reginald Alexander, would be wounded a second time and die. A further two, Richard Fowler-Butler and William Reeve, were wounded so severely that they could not continue in active service, Fowler-Butler serving later as a Commandant on Lines of Communication. Yet not all proved adequate to the task of sustaining command of their units in combat, two being replaced. Bernard McMahon was sent home in January 1915, to serve as Chief Instructor and then Commandant of the School of Musketry, Hythe. Ernest Cobbold was also replaced that month, a quiet period in operations clearly allowing divisional reflection, to serve as CO of a Special Reserve battalion. Lastly, in addition to death, wounding and lack of sufficient sustained competence, there was a further reason for erosion of the CO group – the rapidly expanding BEF needed brigade commanders and staff officers. Thus, Henry Croker went to the command of 81 Brigade (March 1915 to May 1916); Vigant de Falbe commanded 185 Brigade (January 1916 to August 1917, when he was invalided); and Francis Towsey went to 122 Brigade (September 1915 to June 1918). Their length of service as brigade commanders indicates competence at this level. Lastly, Cecil Higginson, the only *psc* of the group, served after wounding as GSO2 then GSO 1 with the 67th (second-line Territorial) Division in Great Britain (June 1915 to May 1916), then as AAG and AQMG (May 1916 to March 1917), and finally as the GOC of 9th Training Reserve Brigade. It may well be that the nature of his wounds precluded active staff service. It has been calculated that the 'endurance and promotability' rate of the original Regular COs of 1914 was 64 percent.[80] The figure for the original COs of 6th Division is 75 percent. Eight of the original 12 were, however, no longer in post at the end of 1914.

Conclusion

John Bourne concludes that: 'The performance of the British Expeditionary Force in the late summer and autumn of 1914 proved the army's leadership qualities. Regimental officers displayed courage, resolution and decision of a high order.'[81] This is reflected in the performance of the senior officers within 6th Division. It had a richly experienced set of divisional and brigade commanders. This did not, however, guarantee success. With all his experience and achievements, Sir John Keir did not prove a competent commander at such senior level in war, and one of the original brigade commanders failed at his level. There was nothing wrong with Keir and Doran's credentials. Keir had no doubt shown verve and vigour dashing about the South African veldt on horseback but had not been tested by peacetime command in a way that would reveal his deficiencies. In contrast to a divisional commander like, say, Thompson Capper, there are no reports of him in the front line exhorting his troops in the desperate days of October 1914.[82] This does not cast aspersions on

80 Hodgkinson, op. cit. p.22.
81 Bourne, (1997), p.96.
82 Thompson Copeland Capper commanded 7th Division. His insistence on being with his men led to his death at Loos in 1915.

Keir's courage. It merely indicates that he did not place a premium on this aspect of command. More significantly, whilst the detailed planning needed for operations in positional warfare was beyond him, his handling of the October defensive battle does not attract criticism. Such shortcomings were likely the same for Doran, removed in a fallow period before further operations were undertaken.

It should not be underestimated how difficult a period this was for senior officers. As Michael LoCicero observes, the 1914 campaign 'compelled intermediate level British commanders to demonstrate acquired military skills and overt soldierly endurance during months of arduous fighting.' The majority of pre-war general officers had 'devoted considerable time and thought to their chosen vocation', Keir being an excellent example of this, 'and exhibited a consummate professionalism on active service.' Further, 'quiet confidence and imperturbability' were most desirable, and brigadier-generals like Congreve and Gordon had these qualities in spades.[83] Similarly, flexibility, initiative and cooperation were required. Congreve and Ingouville-Williams demonstrated this on 22 October, meeting together and walking the ground to agree a retirement to a safer defensive position. That Keir would accept their conclusions reflected perfect adherence to the *Field Service Regulations (Part1)* principle that no prescription should be made 'to a subordinate at a distance … that he should be better able to decide on the spot with a fuller knowledge of local conditions.'[84] Particularly at unit level, the 'command and control conundrum' in being the 'man on the spot' required the instincts of the regimental officer 'to risk their lives by being well forward at critical moments, almost wholly unavoidable during the opening moments of the western campaign.'[85] The fatal nature of this risk for many meant that many experienced and talented senior officers were prevented from going on to more senior leadership in the expanding army. But despite their training and experience, the nature of warfare was changing. 'Once positional warfare had been assumed, their store of experience, as for all officers, irrespective of nationality, no longer served them as well.'[86]

The period from October 1914 to February 1915 allowed little opportunity for the general officers of 6th Division to demonstrate several of John Bourne's key characteristics of generalship, notably 'infinite care with planning and preparation' and maintaining 'the initiative by constant harassing of the enemy.' Keir had responded to 'battlefield emergencies' in September-October 1914 by adopting caution in advance and husbanding his reserves carefully in defence. His brigadiers had done the same, keeping closely in touch with the action, and managing what reserves they possessed ably under enemy pressure. Until March 1915, as will be seen in Chapter

83 M. LoCicero, '"A Tower of Strength": Brigadier-General Edward Bulfin', in S. Jones (ed.), *Stemming the Tide*, p.236-7.
84 General Staff, *Field Service Regulations (Part 1)*, p.27.
85 LoCicero, op. cit. p.238.
86 Hodgkinson, op. cit. p.18.

Three, circumstances allowed little or no opportunity for planning and preparation, or harassing the enemy. The winter was such that 6th Division's major task was survival – managing its defences in the face of 'General Winter.' Only when spring had sprung, the trenches had stabilised with engineering assistance, and organisational structures had been developed to manage the routine of positional warfare, was the luxury of planning and harassment possible. The first carefully planned minor operation, carried out by 17 Brigade on 11/12 March under the direction of 'Uncle' Harper would begin to demonstrate the planning abilities of the general officers. It would be Walter Congreve who would show the full range of Bourne's key characteristics, beginning with his meticulous orchestration of the Hooge operation in August 1915. Sadly, however, '1914 had torn the heart from the pre-war British Army.' 1915 would prove a year of 'courage without glory.'[87] If 6th Division, by not being in line at Ypres, had escaped the very worst of the mauling, it too would have to take part in the process of regeneration, expansion, and learning, and its command personnel would undergo many changes. None of its original senior officers would remain in the post they occupied in August 1914 by the end of 1915.

87 S Jones, 'The British Army and the Problem of the Western Front, 1915' in S. Jones (ed.) *Courage Without Glory*, p.38.

3

'The Greatest Battleground of the British Race':[1] Operations at Ypres 1915-16

'The next few months were uneventful ones', noted Thomas Marden of the opening months of 1915.[2] Although the trenches were improved, the winter of 1914-15 remained very trying.

Morale and discipline 1914-1915

Lance-Corporal Kenneth Gaunt, 1/16th London, wrote to his aunt on 9 January: 'The weather is indescribable, and the trenches are in an appalling condition, but we still keep smiling.'[3] The River Lys rose seven feet during January. Writing for home consumption, the notion of 'smiling' was likely disingenuous. Private Ernest Buffey, 2nd York & Lancaster, described a comrade 'so very tired and weary he just couldn't make the pace.' He took shelter in a deserted barn but the battalion moved on that day. 'For seven long weary days he wandered about ... he became scruffy, a scarecrow of a man ... on the eighth day he was picked up by a provost ... later to be charged with a crime he never committed, "Desertion".' Condemned to death, General Smith-Dorrien apparently commuted his sentence. 'That unfortunate soldier should have been given a medal for endurance, not a Court Martial', Buffey opined. Private Ernest Morley, 1/16th London described coming out of the trenches and 'with the help of another rang the water out of my blanket and my overcoat, when dry, stood up by itself.'[4] Others took to cutting off the bottoms of their greatcoats which became caked with mud. Ernest Buffey continued how: 'We lost more men with frost-bite than we did through enemy action. We were bogged down in icy mud ... stood sometimes in trenches with water up to our thighs.' Probably revealing Kenneth

1 P. Gibbs, *Ypres Times*, October 1921.
2 T.O. Marden, *A Short History of the Sixth Division*, p.10.
3 K.M. Gaunt, Private Papers, IWM Docs 7490.
4 E.G. Morley, Private Papers, IWM Docs 2450.

Gaunt's true feelings he acknowledged: 'We were truly miserable, yet we had the fighting spirit to make the best of such conditions. Spirits boosted in the knowledge that things were no better for Jerry, and if he could stick it so could we.' He recalled an occasion when 'half my Company reported sick … one chap, a Londoner, pulled off his socks … when two of his toes came off with the sodden sock.'[5] III Corps noted of one of its brigades that 1,290 men were admitted to hospital between 1 November 1914 and 22 January 1915, and that between 20 and 29 January 1915, 6th Division had five cases of frostbite, 25 of feet problems, and 19 'effects of cold' pass through casualty clearing stations.[6] The division's 16th Field Ambulance established convalescent homes at Steenwerck and Bac St. Maur, where 50 percent of those who went sick at this time were sent. It was calculated that 25 percent 'only require rest and sleep' and would be back at duty within a week.[7] Yet, in terms of morale, James Jack (19 Brigade) would write of the 1st Scottish Rifles on 2 January that his battalion:

> Was in good form … the senior company commanders … all about 40 years old or more, have stood the strain and exposure … without a sign of breaking down … the only officers to 'crack up' mentally or in health have been a few youths like myself; the rest have become hardened soldiers. The other ranks maintain their imperturbable good humour. The War seems to have affected their spirits little more than uncomfortable manoeuvres in peace-time.[8]

General Pulteney himself noted several weeks later that: 'The men are truly wonderful, some of the North Stafford were playing football near Armentières yesterday afternoon, three shells pitched among them, killing one man and wounding nine, within 1/4 hour they were back playing football again.'[9] Morale was clearly dented temporarily by climatic conditions, but would soon rise again.

The relationship between morale and discipline is intimate and complex. Discipline is a product of morale, and morale is 'the product of discipline, training and organization.' 1914 was the BEF's real year of crisis in respect of discipline. 'Self-inflicted wounds were more prevalent in the autumn and winter of 1914 than at any other point during the war', whilst 'prosecutions for desertion rose rapidly from November 1914 and peaked in February 1915',[10] when it was three times the wartime

5 E. Buffey, Private Papers, IWM Docs 7104.
6 War Diary, DAQMG III Corps, 'Notes for Conference at 2nd Army Head Quarters, January 1915,' TNA WO95/683. The total of CCS cases was 77 for 4th Division as against 49 for the 6th.
7 War Diary, DAQMG III Corps, 'Temporary workshops and institutes 3rd Corps', January 1915, TNA WO95/683.
8 J. Terraine (ed.), *General Jack's Diary*, p.91.
9 A. Leask, *Putty*, p.258.
10 A. Watson, *Enduring the Great War*, p.142.

average. On 3 November it was noted that 16 ORs had been admitted to hospital with self-inflicted wounds, seven of these from 1st King's Shropshire Light Infantry and three from 2nd York & Lancaster.[11] Three days later a further 21 ORs were listed with self-inflicted wounds, eleven of these from 1st East Yorkshire, and five from 2nd Sherwood Foresters. Clearly a spate of self-inflicted wounds would occur in specific battalions in a matter of days. It was promulgated that such individuals would 'not be put on the Medal Roll or be entitled to War Gratuity unless recommended by their Commanding Officers for subsequent good work in the field.'[12] Another two were noted on 15 November,[13] and on 10 December all cases of self-inflicted injuries were directed to 17 Field Ambulance who reported the individual to a Court of Enquiry. Further, the surrender rate in 1914 was exceptionally high, nearly twice that of the March 1918 retreats.[14] The mass surrenders of 1st West Yorkshire on 20 September 1914, and 2nd Sherwood Foresters on 20 October clearly indicate no willingness to 'fight to the death.'

The reasons why 1914 was such a problematic year for discipline probably relate firstly to the bloodiness of the fighting of that year and the harshness of the winter endured into 1915. Secondly, the heavy reliance on reservists who had not had the chance to re-adapt to army life, and then those of the Special Reserve, who were undoubtedly under-trained, was a further weakness. Reservists might not have handled a rifle in several years and would not have had the required fitness for the strenuous efforts of 1914. On 3 October 1914 6th Division received reinforcements of 14 officers and 1,036 ORs, all who would have come within these reservations.[15] In February 1915 III Corps reported on the drafts that were arriving for its divisions: 'Discipline is not good and generally speaking the NCOs are below the standard', and that 'one battalion reports a lack of "Esprit de Corps" amongst its reinforcements.'[16]

11 War Diary, AAQMG 6th Division, Routine Order No.39, 3 November 1914, TNA WO95/1585.
12 War Diary, AAQMG 6th Division, Routine Order No.42, 6 November 1914, TNA WO95/1585.
13 Thereafter all personal details concerning discipline have been redacted from the AAQMG records.
14 Watson, op. cit. pp.142-3.
15 War Diary, AAQMG 6th Division, 3 October 1914, TNA WO95/1585.
16 War Diary, DAQMG III Corps, Memo 8 February 1918, TNA WO95/683.

RFA		40
RE		13
ASC		10
RAMC		7
Cyclists		4
16 Brigade	1st Buffs	7
	1st Leicester	21
	1st KSLI	18
	2nd York & Lancaster	27
17 Brigade	1st Royal Fusiliers	23
	2nd Leinster	57
	1st North Staffordshire	63
	3rd Rifle Brigade	33
18 Brigade	1st West Yorkshire	77
	1st East Yorkshire	22
	2nd Sherwood Foresters	27
	2nd DLI	102

Table 3.1: Court martials in 6th Division, January-April 1915

The first recorded court martial in the division took place on 13 November. Court martials do not, of course, reflect a full picture of discipline – 'crimes' would have been dealt with within units in different ways. III Corps did not begin to record Field General Court Martials until January 1915.[17] It is possible therefore to compare the discipline in 6th and 4th Divisions during the first four months of 1915. During that period, 551 men of 6th Division were court-martialled, whilst only 359 men of the 4th were.[18] Forty-five percent of 6th Division convictions were for drunkenness, whilst 40 percent of convictions in 4th Division were for this crime. 6th Division evidently had significantly greater discipline problems during this period. There were also differences between brigades. 18 Brigade had 228 FGCMs (51 percent drunkenness), 17 Brigade

17 There were four types of courts martial. Only two of them - the general court martial (GCM) and the field general court martial (FGCM) - were invested with the authority to sanction the death penalty. The district court martial and the regimental court martial tried minor offences and could only impose limited terms of punishment that excluded the death penalty.

18 This analysis involved only the three original brigades of 6th Division, to allow direct comparison.

176 (43 percent drunkenness), and 16 Brigade 83 (18 percent drunkenness). 19 Brigade, not part of the original division, had 86 FGCMs (48 percent drunkenness). 16 and 19 Brigades thus had a lower level of FGCMs than the average per brigade (120) in 4th Division. General Smith-Dorrien, commanding Second Army, referred to the discipline of 18 Brigade in February 1915 as 'the worst in the army' and that within 1st West Yorkshire as 'the worst in that brigade.'[19] General Keir noted in the same month of the West Yorkshires that 'the amount of crime in this battalion is excessive.'[20] Walter Congreve accepted that there was 'much drunkenness at the time.'[21] This reflects poorly on the officering of the unit, within which two death sentences had been carried out within the first seven months. Of the 346 military executions carried out during the First World War, twelve involved soldiers of 6th Division. Four took place within the first three months of 1915.[22] Table 3.1 demonstrates the significant differences in number of FGCMs between battalions. There were only seven in 1st Buffs of 16 Brigade during this period, whilst 2nd Durham Light Infantry topped the list with 102. As Timothy Bowman, in his study of discipline in Irish regiments has noted: 'There appears to be no easy explanation as to this marked difference between battalions in terms of courts martial.'[23] He found discipline issues to be unconnected to rural/urban recruitment, or even losses in action. Thus 1st West Yorkshire and 1st East Yorkshire both recruited from urban and rural areas of the same county yet have strikingly different FGCM figures. The one difference is that 1st West Yorkshire had to sustain a much earlier and larger influx of replacements due to the mass surrender of 20 September. The monthly figures are steady during the period January to March (141, 143 and 155), but drop in April to 112. With improvement of the weather at this point, it is possible that simple physical conditions played a significant part in this improvement.

The first 'model' attack – l'Epinette 11-12 March 1915

The composition of the division changed. At the end of 1914 the four brigades had each received a Territorial battalion. 1/16th London (Queen's Westminster Rifles) joined on the 11th November and were allotted to 18 Brigade. Londoner Lance-Corporal Charles Quayle wrote home on 21 December noting that he was in 'the famous division that has done the best work out here - we are honoured to be in it.'[24] The statement indicates a certain divisional *esprit de corps*. 1/5th Scottish Rifles joined 19 Brigade eight days later. 1/2nd London Regiment were attached to 17 Brigade in

19 Court martial record, Private A. Atkinson TNA WO71/402.
20 Court martial record, Private E. Kirk TNA WO71/403.
21 Court martial record, Private A. Atkinson TNA WO71/402.
22 See Appendix III.
23 T. Bowman, *Irish Regiments in the Great War: Discipline and Morale*, p.41.
24 C.P. Quayle, Private Papers, IWM Docs 1955.

February, and 1/5th Loyal North Lancashire Regiment to 16 Brigade on the 15th of that month.

Not only did the composition of the division change, it had a number of visitors, some celebrities, and some officers and units in training. 16 Brigade, for instance, noted a visit by Winston Churchill in January, and on 31 May they were graced by The Honourable Herbert Asquith, the Prime Minister. In January, three new army battalion COs, and two Canadian battalions were attached and went into the trenches. In May, 12 officers of each battalion of 27 Brigade, 9th Division arrived for two days acclimatisation, followed by the 11th Royal Scots, 6th King's Own Scottish Borderers and 8th Black Watch, each also attached for two days. On 4 October 200 men of 12th Royal Fusiliers were attached for two days, followed on 6 Oct by 300 men of 7th Northamptonshire and 100 of 12th Royal Fusiliers, and finally on 8 October by 400 more men of 12th Royal Fusiliers.[25] Thus the New Armies were inducted into the ways of trench warfare. Not every visit went well. On 18 January Brigadier-General Hugh Fitton of 34 Division, attached to 16 Brigade for instruction, was hit by a stray bullet and died two days later.[26]

Trench life developed further. Lieutenant Frederick Chandler, Medical Officer of 2nd Argyll & Sutherland Highlanders, fell into conversation in March 1915 with Lieutenant-Colonel Oliver de Lancey Williams,[27] CO of 2nd Royal Welsh Fusiliers, who had devised ' a system of "punishments"' in response to any over-enthusiasm on the part of the enemy. 'Every time they snipe, the Welsh snipe four times, every time they fire a burst of machine gun fire, they fire four bursts, every time a shell comes over, they have four shells back, and this has shut them up a bit.' Conversely, the enemy were 'cheerful and brave', playing musical instruments, and 'sometimes their patrols will creep along in the dark and shout out "Get back into your trench, Jock"', and when the Argylls went on patrol: 'We are just having a game of whist. Come and have a cup of tea, Jock.'[28]

During January 1915, enemy shellfire was the rule, and 6th Division's guns had little to respond with.[29] On 4 February a heavy bombardment opened against the second (Bois Grenier) line, lifting to the 19 Brigade front, whilst a half-hearted infantry attack was mounted against 16 Brigade at Rue du Bois, which was easily driven back. Over the weeks that followed the enemy shelling increased in intensity.

25 19 Brigade hosted Canadians in February, the 4th Canadian Battalion and the Canadian Scottish each spending a week with them. On 20 March 6th North Staffordshire were attached for five days.

26 Hugh Gregory Fitton, born in 1863 and commissioned in 1884 into the Royal West Kent Regiment was a colonel and Director of Recruitment and Organization at the War Office in August 1914.

27 Oliver de Lancey Williams would be promoted to command 92 Brigade in June 1916, a post he would hold until the Armistice.

28 F.G. Chandler, Private Papers, IWM Docs 25460.

29 Field artillery was limited to four rounds per day.

The British response remained limited – as Marden notes: 'We had practically no artillery ammunition with which to worry the enemy.'[30] The divisional war diary noted with excitement on 24 April, when the Second Battle of Ypres was underway: 'In view of the fighting in progress in the north the Corps Commander allotted an extra ten rounds of shrapnel per gun for 18-pounders with a view to making a demonstration by fire to hold the enemy in front of us.'[31] If the enemy action of 4 February had been an attempt to instil aggressive purpose to counter the corrosive torpor of positional warfare, then the British were planning a minor operation with a little more purpose.

Ernest Buffey described (no doubt with some relief) that 'the weather was improving with Spring in the offing, but it was still cold. The mire was drying up a little but the ice was still there.'[32] The BEF began to stir itself aggressively once more. As John Shea's order as GSO1 of 6th Division dated 9 March stated: 'The 1st and 2nd Armies will assume the offensive on March 10th and subsequent days.' What he was describing would become known as the Battle of Neuve Chapelle. 'The role of the 2nd Army will be to prevent the enemy from withdrawing from his front any troops for employment against the 1st Army.' 6th Division's artillery would harass the enemy, brigade commanders would organise 'fire attacks against the enemy's line by day and night', and sapping and mining would be pushed forward 'vigorously.'[33] The Neuve Chapelle operation itself was the first stage of an attempt to push on to the Aubers Ridge, 'thereby threatening the enemy's communications between La Bassée and Lille.'[34] Elements of 6th Division had, of course, struggled on to this ridge, if further north, in the fighting of October 1914, only to be pushed off again. The fighting at Neuve Chapelle, momentarily successful then grinding to a halt, is not of concern here. As part of their supporting action, 6th Division chalked up a minor success in line reorganisation (an activity that would at some points in the war be a costly and dubious activity).

At midnight on 11/12 March, 17 Brigade took action against l'Epinette. Lying directly to the east of Armentières, the village of l'Epinette, represented by a line of houses, lay in No Man's Land on a right-angled road, the enemy having wired out from their front line to include several of the houses which were fronted with short trenches. The brigade, following Brigadier-General Doran's removal a month

30 Marden, op. cit. p.11.
31 War Diary, HQ 6 Infantry Division, 24 April 1915, TNA WO95/1581. It was noted that day that the enemy retaliatory fire was directed at support positions where troops massing for an attack might be located, indicating that they truly believed an attack was possible, and hence the tactical aim of the fire was seemingly achieved. Further, 17 hostile batteries were located, but the success of any counterbattery fire is not recorded.
32 Buffey, op. cit.
33 War Diary, HQ 6th Infantry Division, Operation Order No. 22, 9 March 1915, TNA WO95/1581.
34 J.E. Edmonds & G.C. Wynne, *Military Operations France and Belgium 1915 Vol. 1*, p. 75. French cooperation was hoped for as part of a wider effort, but this did not materialise.

earlier, was now commanded by George Montague 'Uncle' Harper. The operation bears the stamp of a commander of his quality – 'To avoid confusion, every detail was as far as possible thought out beforehand and difficulties foreseen.'[35] It was planned in two stages. The first involved the rapid occupation of a line in the middle of No Man's Land to the right of two short German trenches. This involved the seizure of a series of five houses, one occupied as a sniper's position, although on the night in question it was unoccupied. 'Uncle' then withdrew his working parties fortifying the position at 11.45 to protect them against retaliatory fire, and the second phase was to take place. At midnight, the houses in the centre of the village, including two large farms, all occupied, wired and strongly fortified, would be attacked. These structures had been continually shelled but this had not rendered them untenable by the enemy. Harper decreed a night-time attack to seize the element of surprise and eschewed a preliminary bombardment to try further to ensure this. The endeavour was entrusted to 1st North Staffordshire, Lieutenant Vyvyan Pope commanding the company tasked with this second element. The CO, Lieutenant-Colonel Vigant de Falbe[36] had only returned from brigade the previous day with the scheme, and spent the rest of the day composing his detailed orders.[37] The first operation orders he had issued, they covered three sides of paper encompassing 19 points in great detail, and at least six different maps were prepared. It was intended to cut off the enemy by seizing the communication trenches, but the opposition, Saxons of the *135th* and *139th Regiments*, mounted a 'miserable resistance' and scuttled away whilst Pope's men were delayed cutting through the wire.[38] Pope sustained no casualties in the initial attack, but Lieutenant Cedric Gordon, attacking Water Wheel Farm to the right, was wounded in the knee by a bomb along with seven of his men.[39] Vyvyan Vavasour Pope was commended by his Army commander, Horace Smith-Dorrien, and by June 1917 would find himself commanding the battalion.

The operation involved the close coordination of engineers and artillery. The 12 Field Company RE was attached to the attacking columns and had fortified the position for defence by dawn, whilst the artillery had pre-ranged on its targets, and 'telephone arrangements were perfected with Forward Observation Officers in trenches' co-ordinating the 05.15 barrage that assisted in beating off three counter-attacks. The North Staffordshire casualties to midday on the 12th included four

35 War Diary, HQ 17 Infantry Brigade, 'Report on the Operations carried out 11th/12th March', TNA WO95/1612.

36 Vigant de Falbe, the son of a Danish navy captain, would command 185 Brigade for 18 months from January 1916.

37 War Diary, 1st Battalion North Staffordshire Regiment, 10 March 1915, TNA WO95/1613.

38 The unit had been supplied with 47 wire cutters for the attack, and each man carried 220 rounds.

39 Cedric Foskett Gordon would serve in staff roles, last as a brigade-major, and finished his war as a captain in the RFC.

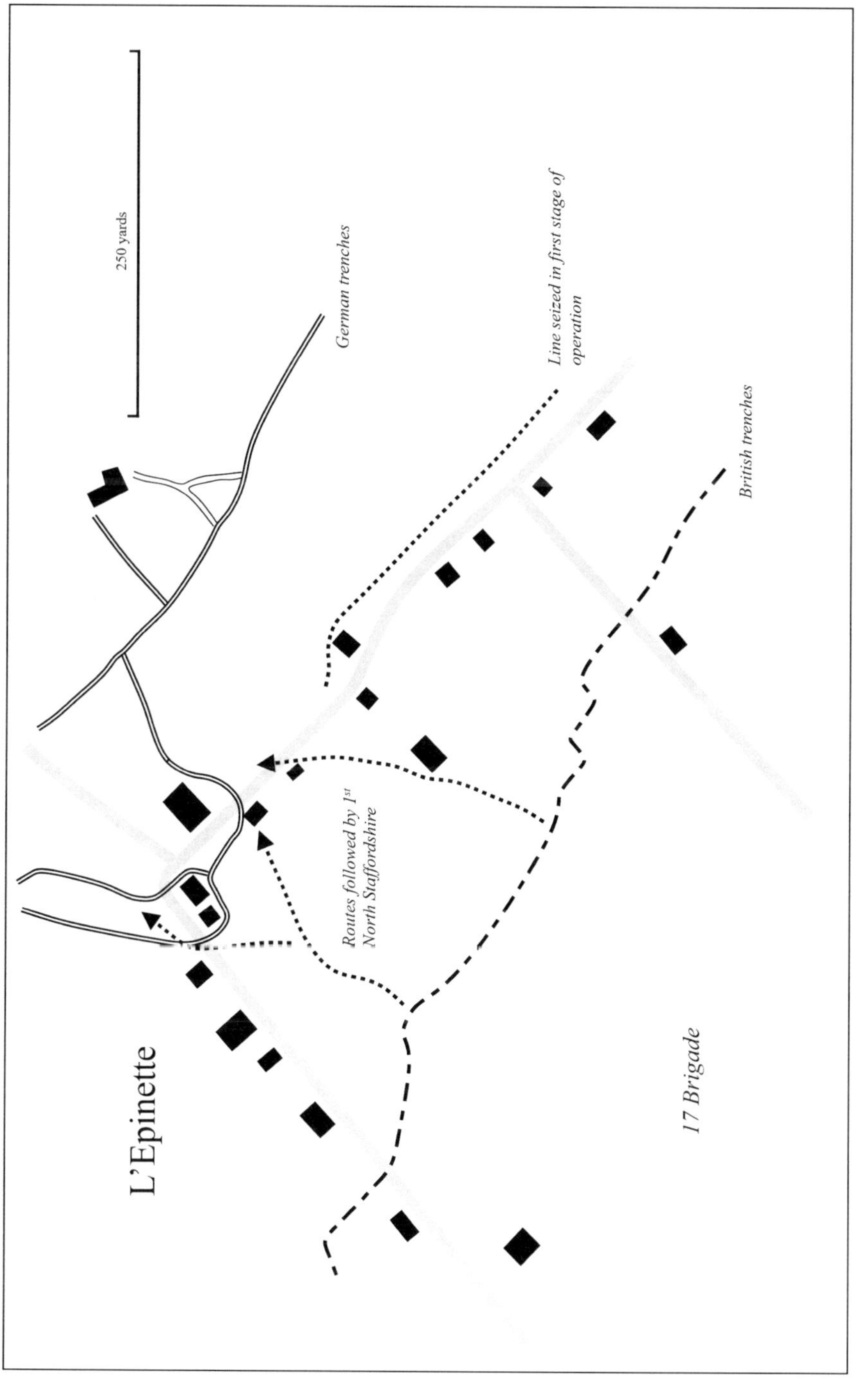

Map 3.1: l'Epinette 11-12 March 1915.

officers including one fatality, and 34 ORs, again with one dead. The little operation was a model of positional warfare, showing a brigade under a new commander raising its organisational game. The brigade front was advanced 200 to 300 yards across half a mile, if creating a salient.

Two days later, on 15 March, 16 Brigade was ordered to move north to V Corps. The latter corps had begun its life at the end of December 1914, under Lieutenant-General Sir Herbert Plumer and had taken over the 27th and 28th Divisions and the front opposite St. Eloi. The previous day, at 17.00, the enemy had fired two mines and taken the village, the 27th Division trenches, and 'The Mound' south of the village, an artificial heap which gave excellent observation. A counterattack mounted in the early hours of the 15th had recaptured the village and trenches, but not 'The Mound.' By 03.00 16 Brigade was entraining north, only to learn that the relatively successful counterattack had taken place, and any threat had receded. At 06.30, the brigade entrained once more for Armentières. The move and return had demonstrated two things. Firstly, the BEF's perception of its vulnerability; and secondly, effective management of lines of communication. After these alarms and excursions the month of March continued with reciprocal shelling and British patrols disrupting enemy activities. These latter activities increased during the month, indicating the division's more active approach to dominating No Man's Land.

The dawn of mining – Armentières, January-May 1915

The division's engineers had begun work in earnest after the line stabilised. In October 1914, the first priority was establishing the rear defence line and bridging across the Lys. The second priority, given the deteriorating weather, was the maintenance of the roads and improving the trenches, notably making fascines, hurdles and footboards, and improving drainage and building breastworks. This remained ongoing though the winter months. Civilians were employed on a number of these tasks, particularly on roads and in the rear defence line. From the middle of November, the engineers began a range of tasks specific to trench warfare. These included manufacturing steel loop-hole plates, making grenades, chevaux de frise, rifle rests, and periscopes; as well as building water heaters; and trialling equipment such as fuze lighters.

Another RE activity was tunnelling. The mining war began in the la Bassée area. The first German mine was a series of ten small charges blown under the Indian Sirhind Brigade at le Plantin near la Bassée on 20 December 1914, forcing the Indians back to their reserve line. The first British mine had been dug earlier in the month to assist an attack by the Dehra Dun Brigade near Festubert, but it had not been detonated. Another early attempt took place in January 1915 in 6th Division's area, by 20th Fortress Company, at Rue du Bois, where Second-Lieutenant Frederick Hyland noted the lines 'were only about 30 yards apart.' He had been sent:

> [T]o put in a mine to protect their trench against alleged mining. The infantry were up to their necks in water. It was a pretty gloomy business. We started

> sinking this shaft and it filled with water, so we pumped it out with hand pumps – lift and force. We got down about 10 feet or so. It was heart breaking – I hated it. But I had to keep my men going. The Boche saved us. We were making a lot of noise ... the Boche opposite us were Saxons, rather friendly, and they put up a notice on a blackboard 'No good your mining. We've tried. It can't be done.' The notice was in English. I reported this to my OC, and it went up to HQ and they stopped the mine.[40]

The CRE of 6th Division, Lieutenant-Colonel Geoffrey Kemp,[41] met with the Chief Engineer of Second Army, Major-General Arthur Sandbach[42] and Major John Norton-Griffiths on 6 March to discuss mining and the formation of a Tunnelling Company. These companies were the brain-child of 'Empire Jack' (as Norton-Griffiths was nick-named), a civil engineer who had served in South Africa, and who had gleaned his tunnelling experience in the sewers of Manchester and London. 174 Tunnelling Company RE was thus created, under the command of Major Bertram Danford.[43] The company started with 54 'clay kickers', ten men with an RE background, and 170 ordinary infantry drafted in, many from 6th and 4th Divisions. (Thus, on 28 March a party of miners from 2nd Leinster in 17 Brigade were released to work at l'Epinette, although in general regiments representing the Yorkshire coalfields provided many of the men, as to a lesser extent did the Durham and Midlands coalfields). The company immediately took over two mines at Rue du Bois from 20th Fortress, where two shafts were being dug, on the 11th. Geological information was obtained from the local mairie and well-sinkers.

40 F.G. Hyland, quoted in P. Barton, P. Doyle and J. Vandewalle, *Beneath Flanders Fields*, p.53. Frederick Gordon Hyland would end his war as Lieutenant-Colonel Controller of Mines, having previously acted as a staff officer to the Chief Engineer. After commanding an anti-aircraft group in the late 1930s he was promoted Major General just before the outbreak of the Second World War and served as Deputy Commander of Gibraltar.

41 Geoffrey Chicheley Kemp, b. 1868, had been commissioned into the Royal Engineers in 1886. In August 1915 he would be appointed to command 138 Brigade then 2 Brigade, until being wounded on 2 March 1918.

42 Arthur Edmund Sandbach, b. 1859, had been commissioned into the Royal Engineers in 1879. His role as chief engineer ended in May 1915, after which he served for six months as Inspector of Royal Engineers.

43 Forty-year-old Bertram William Young Danford, commissioned into the Royal Engineers in 1894, would reach the rank of Lieutenant-Colonel in December 1915, and finished the war in a staff role. Their first casualty of his unit would be Sapper T. Moore, 'accidentally shot in billets.' Danford was badly injured in a motorcar accident near the front on 3 May 1916 which left his arm broken in three places and required some 90 days of recuperation. He served as Assistant Quarter Master General and Assistant Inspector of Mines as a Lieutenant-Colonel in 1918. He was shot in the head and shoulders during the kidnap of General Cuthbert Lucas by the IRA in 1920 but recovered to end his military career as Chief Engineer, Egypt.

A further three mines were being constructed in the 18 Brigade area in the north near Houplines, and these were taken over on 15 March. A new shaft was started at Rue du Bois on the 21st. By the end of the month, tunnelling was underway at l'Epinette and Houplines, the tunnel at l'Epinette being abandoned during April due to collapse. The tunnellers were labouring within three separate areas in 6th Division's area.[44] The waterlogged ground caused numerous problems, thus by 18 April work stopped at Rue du Bois as the pumps could not handle the ingress of water. Despite this, eight days later the work was completed on No. 1 'shallow filling' at Rue du Bois and work on No. 3 began. On 27 April, the enemy were heard counter-mining at No. 6 tunnel, pushed out from near Houplines on the north-east outskirts of Armentières, towards Le Touquet and Frelinghien. Two days later the sounds were still approaching, and the shaft was packed with 550 pounds of gunpowder. By 2 May the situation at No. 6 was regarded as 'critical', 6th Division recording that the enemy gallery was only three feet away, and Lieutenant-Colonel Kemp ordered that the mine be fired the following morning, even though it was 40 feet short of its target, the 'Barricade' in le Touquet.

George Ashurst, a private in 2nd Lancashire Fusiliers (12 Brigade in adjacent 4th Division, in the Le Touquet area), did not need specialist listening equipment. In cottages in No Man's Land, 'as we lay on the floor we could hear the dull sounds as the German engineers dug away beneath us, never knowing the moment he might decide to blow us all to eternity.'[45] At 08.30 on the 3rd the first mine was fired on 6th Division's front. Ashurst described how: 'The ground shook and the trench seemed to rock, and with a muffled roar a blue flame shot up into the sky into the sky. Showers of bricks and dirt came hurtling over … pieces of cloth floated down through the clouds of dust.'[46] The result was that a 'large crater which was not regular had apparently opened up underground work – two lines of blinded saps or galleries',[47] the crater being between the 'Barricade' and the 'Chicken Run', a maze of trenches on the other side of the river from whence sniping was notorious. The enemy could be seen digging in the crater, and no attempt was made to occupy it. Re-occupying the cottages, Ashurst noted: 'One German had been blown clean onto an outhouse. Right under our noses, within ten yards of our rifle barrels, another German calmly placed a ladder against the outhouse, climbed it and, lifting his wounded comrade on to his shoulder, carried him to safety.'[48]

In an interesting diversion from the increased mining activity, III Corps were asked to make 'vigorous demonstrations' in association with First Army's assault at Aubers. Thus between 20.00 on 7 May and 02.00 on the 8th a train was run into Armentières

44 Also at Ploegsteert in the north.
45 G. Ashurst, *My Bit*, p.47.
46 Ashurst, op. cit. p.47.
47 War Diary, 174th Tunnelling Company Royal Engineers, 3 May 1915, TNA WO95/404.
48 Ashurst, op. cit. p.48.

station six times with a 30-minute stop. 'Bodies of troops' from 6th Division 'were collected quietly under cover of dark in the station and marched ostentatiously out in connection with the trains and marched through the town', in connection with the constant movement of motor vehicles.[49] On the 9th, 6th Division's artillery opened up a barrage with small arms fire from the trenches. Both demonstrations could do nothing to avert the catastrophe at Aubers, which resulted in over 11,500 casualties for no gain.

Mining activities continued. On the 8th the enemy had detonated one such close to the 'Chicken Run'. Their judgement of distance was out as the mine exploded nearer to their trenches than to those of 6th Division, and no damage was done. As part of their demonstrations of the 9th, 18 Brigade fired another mine near the le Touquet 'Barricade.' As with the enemy's mine of the previous day, it exploded short of the German trenches, merely rearranging the wire. Later that day, an incident occurred which demonstrated the growing sophistication of the division in trench warfare. The officer in charge of the snipers of 1st West Yorkshire, 18 Brigade, observed the enemy carrying out a relief. He estimated the range and got two machine guns trained with indirect fire on the location, dividing the fire of his platoon. 'Having arranged a code of whistle signals he returned to his look-out post.' When the enemy next appeared, he whistled, and fire was opened. The enemy selecting a new route, he re-laid his guns and now caught the Germans in a 'close column of fours.' Of 50 estimated casualties, 15 were observed to be fatal.[50]

On 13 May the enemy exploded another mine some 30-yards short of the British trenches at the 'Railway Fort' just north of Le Touquet. This blew in part of a British gallery killing two listeners of 174 Tunnelling Company. Six days later in the same location enemy mining was heard above a gallery in the same location, and at 21.00 a charge was detonated. Work resuming next day, the tunnellers were gassed. Rescue work was attempted by both fellow tunnellers and infantry contrary to orders, descending the shaft in breathing apparatus to repair the damaged pipe. Two men were found dead, and an officer and six men rescued. On 24 May the enemy exploded yet another small mine near the 'Chicken Run', and again two days later, this time occupying the crater.

As (literally) the ground beneath their feet was hotting up, the 6th Division would make a move to the even hotter Ypres Salient, leaving behind the divisional soubriquet 'The Mademoiselles.'[51] In their final months in the Armentières sector, the division's trench warfare practice had been developing. One of the brigades had

49 War Diary, HQ 6th Infantry Division, 8 May 1915, TNA WO95/1581.
50 War Diary, HQ 6th Infantry Division, 9 May 1915, TNA WO95/1581.
51 From the popular song 'Mademoiselle from Armentières.' The tune of the song is believed to have been popular in the French army in the 1830s, the original words telling of the encounter of an inn-keeper's daughter, named Mademoiselle de Bar le Duc, with two German officers. During the Franco-Prussian war of 1870, the tune was resurrected, and again in 1914 when the British Tommy encountered it.

mounted the division's first sophisticated operation in miniature at l'Epinette, and operational refinement was, hence, evident. The first attempts to dominate No Man's Land with patrols had been undertaken, and where munitions allowed, the enemy had been harassed. The division's individual officers were becoming attuned to taking opportunities, as the actions of the West Yorkshire sniper officer showed. The Ypres Salient would soon allow demonstration of what 6th Division had learnt on a wider canvas. Line holding at Armentières had been costly, however – Marden gives the casualty figures from 1 November to 31 May as 3,940.[52] This may be a underestimation as reported infantry brigade casualties during this period total 4,407.

Attack at Hooge – 9 August 1915

The headquarters of the newly established VI Corps (Second Army) began to form at the end of May, General Keir of 6th Division being promoted to its command. He took with him 6th Division, now commanded by Walter Congreve, earning deserved promotion, and 4th Division, whom he had fought alongside. The corps also received the newly formed 14th (Light) Division. 6th Division would remain in the Ypres salient until July 1916, occupying at some point all sections of the line between the Yser canal to the north, near Boesinghe, and Hooge to the east. The Second Battle of Ypres had petered out on 25 May with the last of the significant fighting on the Bellewaarde Ridge. The division took over a line just north of this feature, from approximately near Gully Farm adjacent to the Ypres-Roulers railway north to Wieltje.[53] (See Map 4 colour section). The infantry did not take part in any offensive action in this portion of the line. The artillery, however, supported neighbouring divisions on either flank. The first of these actions was on 16 June when 3rd Division attacked Bellewaarde Farm north-west of Hooge in a night operation. Private Frank Minter, 1/16th London, in the front line, described how the shelling began at 02.40. 'The row was terrific. Every kind of shell was going over, shrapnel from Indian batteries just behind, high explosives from around Ypres plus immense howitzer shells from right behind Ypres which came over with a noise like trams going round a curve.' The enemy, he observed, 'seemed quite resigned to defeat.'[54] The division's artillery broke up a number of counterattacks, successfully cut wire, and effectively placed barrages on the enemy's front line, lifting to their support trenches. On 22 June, 42 Brigade, 14th Division, unsuccessfully attempted a small evening operation, preceded by a half-hour barrage by 6th Division's guns, firing for 10 minutes, ceasing for 10 and the firing again for a further 10 minutes. Finally, on 6 July 4th Division were supported whilst carrying out a successful local operation near Pilckem. Entry into the salient ratcheted up

52 Marden, op. cit. p.81.
53 A graphic account of trench life June-August 1915 can be found in F.C. Hitchcock, *Stand To*, pp.32-60. Francis Clere Hitchcock was commissioned in January 1915.
54 F. Minter, Private Papers, IWM Docs 14360.

daily pressure on the division. Second-Lieutenant Francis Hitchcock, 2nd Leinster, reported a conversation between 'two old "toughs"': 'Faith, Mick, Armentières was cushy compared to this spot. The shells down there were only connecting files, but here, begad, there's battalions of them – and in column of route, too!.'[55]

The position in the Salient after the Second Battle of Ypres was that the 33 days fighting had cost the BEF 59,275 casualties and the Germans 34,933.[56] The ammunition situation for the British was 'most desperate', but 'apart from lack of ammunition, both sides were in need of rest', being 'thoroughly exhausted.' The divisions that fought, on both sides with no hope of reinforcement, had been 'engaged again and again until practically annihilated.' The enemy advance, however, 'supported by an overwhelming strength of artillery ... had achieved nothing decisive.'[57] The relatively fresh 6th Division arrived to face the tired *4th Army*, who from the canal in the north to the Menin Road, deployed (north to south), *XXVI Reserve Corps*, *XXVII Reserve Corps*, and *XV Corps*.

The fighting was by no means over, however. On 30 July 14th Division at Hooge were famously attacked by *flammenwerfer*, the first time flamethrowers had been employed in warfare. Hooge was the apex of an acute salient at the southern end of the Ypres Salient itself. Weakly held by V Corps, the ruined chateau and stables on the Menin Road had been taken by the enemy on 2 June after a heavy bombardment (although the stables were subsequently recovered). On 16 June 3rd Division made a carefully planned assault on the Bellewaarde Ridge that ran roughly north from Hooge and which gave the enemy good observation over much of the ground east of Ypres. Although the German front line was taken, the enemy remained firmly on top of the ridge itself. On 19 July the British had exploded one and a half tons of ammonal beneath a German strongpoint near the Hooge stables and consolidated the large crater torn in the German position. The *flammenwerfer* attack was the enemy's retaliation, and 8th Rifle Brigade, holding the line at the crater, were overrun. As the line held was at a rough right-angle facing north (the Rifle Brigade) and east (7th King's Royal Rifle Corps), the latter were attacked from the rear when the attack fell on the former. 14th Division was forced back to the edges of Zouave and Sanctuary Woods. It had been inevitable that the enemy would want to reverse the mining mishap, and it was equally inevitable that once they had succeeded there would be a response to restore British dominance yet again. Walter Congreve addressed 1st Buffs on the necessity of retaking the position: 'It was a case either of going forwards or of going backwards owing to the nature of the ground.'[58] The location was of considerable importance in relation to observation. To the west the ground fell away downhill giving a clear view along the Menin Road towards Ypres. The ground similarly fell away towards the new

55 Hitchcock, op. cit. p.34.
56 Probably higher as light casualties were often not listed.
57 Edmonds and Wynne, op. cit. pp.353-4.
58 War Diary, 1st Battalion Buffs, 5 August 1915, TNA WO95/1608.

British lines on the edges of the two woods, as well as to the east along the Menin Road. With lips fifteen feet above ground level the crater now provided the enemy with even better observation and dominance than the location itself had previously given. From the British point of view, as the ground fell away to the north, before rising to the Bellewaarde Ridge, to retake the position not only removed the enemy's dominance over their positions at the edges of the woods, but afforded good views of the Bellewaarde Ridge.

16 Brigade were moved up for a hasty counterattack. Thankfully for the brigade, they were not thrown in in such a fashion. Billy Congreve, a staff officer in 3rd Division, saw his father on the evening of 30 July, and wrote: 'I saw Dads tonight. He thinks he will have to go to Hooge. I bet *one* of us does and hope it's him!' Indeed, the following day orders were given that the whole division would be withdrawn from the line and would regain the Hooge position. Congreve junior wrote again: 'So Dads has a jolly little job on his hands. If anyone in the world can do it, I know it is he and the 6th Division.'[59] Whilst the faith of a son in his father is touching, no doubt both the new commander of Second Army, Sir Herbert Plumer, and Keir had faith in Congreve senior as well, although in using 6th Division, they were deploying the formation closest to the position and one that had not been tired by recent offensive or defensive action. On the 5th, the officers of 16th and 18th Brigades (the latter commanded by Brigadier-General Henry Ainslie[60] who would ask to be relieved of command that day) reconnoitered the position and it was decided that the attack would go in on the 9th rather than the 8th as previously planned. Proper preparation time would be allowed, and this is reflected in the collection of notes, orders and after-operation reports preserved, for the first time, in 6th Division's war diary. Second-Lieutenant Francis Hitchcock, 17 Brigade, reported that: 'The role for the Brigades in the attack was decided by the toss of a coin between the respective Brigadiers, and we lost.'[61] If not an apocryphal story, in terms of the casualties sustained, it was a good toss to lose.

On 2 August, Congreve and his GSO1, Lieutenant-Colonel Gerald Boyd, prepared 'Notes for Conference:- Matters to be settled by Brigadiers',[62] as well as notes on useful observation points over the enemy lines, and three pages of notes on the country and trenches around Hooge, with an additional two pages on Hooge itself. These two latter documents indicated in particular where the attacking troops might be exposed to enemy machine gun fire. It is worth listing the 27 points for consideration, as they

59 B. Congreve (T. Norman ed.), *Armageddon Road*, pp. 163-44.

60 Forty-year-old Henry Sandys Ainslie had been commanding 1st Northumberland Fusiliers at the outbreak of war. He had been promoted to command 18 Brigade on 29 May 1915. 'Unfortunately it was evident that the labours and anxieties of battalion command had undermined a constitution never too robust', and he never returned to active duty. (H.R. Sandilands, *The Fifth Division in the Great War*, p.110.)

61 Hitchcock, op. cit. p.60.

62 War Diary, HQ 6th Infantry Division, 'Notes for Conference', 2 August 1915, WO95/1581.

exemplify both the depth of preparation and the degree of learning achieved by 6th Division at this point in the war in terms of what made for a successful 'break-in' operation:

1. Position of Battle Station
2. Position of RE store advanced Depots. Wire Piquets. Sandbags. Trench covers. French wire.
3. Position of Bomb stores. Tool depots. Ammunition and Rifle Grenade Depots.
4. Evacuation trenches for wounded and down traffic. Sentries for the same. Sign boards.
5. Water. Petrol tins?
6. Storing of packs.
7. Flags. Number to be carried.
8. Carrying of shovels.
9. Reconnaissance of position.
10. Plan of attack.
11. Means of getting out of trenches. Ladders.
12. Communication trenches. Russian Saps. German barrage. Probably best to pack front trench.
13. CO's 'postes-de-commandement.'
14. Respirators.
15. Wire cutters.
16. What RE required?
17. Iron ration and first field dressing.
18. What rations to be carried?
19. Getting up Machine Guns.
20. Exact arrangements for occupation of captured position.
21. Lines of runners.
22. Visual signalling.
23. Carrying of sandbags by men attacking.
24. Dressing station and evacuation from.
25. Position of First Line Transport.
26. Very lights.

The degree of detail in this list demonstrates a variety of things. Firstly, the complexity of things to be taken into account in positional warfare, not least of all the importance of the Royal Engineers in putting the captured position into a defensible state. Secondly, it indicates Walter Congreve and his staff's grasp of these matters. Thirdly, it reflects his anxiety to get things right – in late December 1914 after a disastrous attack at Ploegsteert Wood he had written: 'These small isolated attacks seem to me deadly … horrid losses and nothing done with them.'[63] Later in the war division would be content to leave some of these minutiae to brigades.

The object of the attack was to secure the high ground to the north of the crater, the crater itself, ground beyond the chateau stables, and the trench that led back from the Menin Road at right-angles to Sanctuary Wood, restoring the original front. (See Map 5, colour section). The attack on the right would be carried out by 18 Brigade,[64] now commanded temporarily by Lieutenant-Colonel Towsey, debouching from the wood. On the left, 16 Brigade would capture the crater.[65] The action of the artillery was crucial to the operation. Eighteen batteries took part from four field artillery brigades and one howitzer brigade, with a siege battery and other heavy batteries from 14th and 46th Divisions, as well as two batteries of French 75mm guns firing phosphorous shells. The vast majority of the batteries fired high explosive. The bombardment began on the 3rd and the artillery orders ran to 18 pages, a final conference being held with the infantry on the 8th.

'Artillery subterfuge was used on a rather grander scale than previously.'[66] The fact that an attack was likely to be made could not be concealed, but the enemy could be misled concerning the timing. Each morning the enemy trenches were subject to bombardment in the early morning: '3 to 4 A.M., 2 to 3.30 A.M., etc. So, when the final and real bombardment was carried out the Germans assumed it was only the normal "hate", to which they had become accustomed, and retired to their dug-outs.'[67] Subterfuge was not limited to the artillery. Demonstrations were made across Second Army's front to mislead the enemy as to the point of attack. On the evening of the 8th, 49th Division made a feint against Pilckem with the French *XXXVI Corps* to the north; whilst 46th Division did the same against Hill 60 to the south. The 17th and 28th Divisions even further south simulated assault preparations and attracted artillery fire, heavy in the case of the 28th. The barrage, beginning at 02.45 on 9 August, as per the initially successful Neuve Chapelle attack would last for 30 minutes only, with a lift onto a second line after five minutes followed by a third lift. During the last ten minutes of the bombardment, the infantry were to 'deploy under the cover of the Artillery fire, and advance as near as possible to the enemy's position and lie down, our own wire being removed during the night.' The guns would lift at 03.15, and the assault was to 'push on as rapidly as possible.'[68] Trench mortars (such as were present) were placed under the command of infantry COs.

The attack was concentric, starting on a wider front (albeit only 1,000 yards), than it would hopefully conclude on. The attacking troops would therefore be bunching,

63 Congreve, op. cit. p.92.
64 Supported by 26th Trench Howitzer Battery and 1st London Field Company RE.
65 Supported by 38th Trench Howitzer Battery and 12th Field Company RE.
66 N. Cave, *Sanctuary Wood & Hooge*, p.60.
67 J.E. Edmonds, *Military Operations France and Belgium 1915, Vol. 2*, p. 107.
68 War Diary, HQ 6 Infantry Division, Operation Order No. 27, 5 August 1915, TNA WO95/1581.

hence Congreve stamped his tactical imprint on the operation: 'The GOC considers that our best chance of success is to reduce the men in the front line' once the position had been taken, and 'hold important points with machine guns, establish communications, and relieve men in the front line as opportunity offers.'[69] 18 Brigade might have viewed themselves as drawing the short straw, No Man's Land being 75 yards wide on the left but 500 yards wide on the right, the ground they were attacking over. 16 Brigade were assaulting over the shorter distance, albeit against the crater, and General Nicholson inspected the entirety of his front line the day before the assault. On the day itself, in his brigade 'Battle Station', dust and smoke completely obscured his vision, and telephone lines to both his assaulting battalions were cut. He received his first runner with news at 04.37, by which time the operation was already a success. He noted that the 'preliminary bombardment was all that could be desired. Only 3 or 4 men were hit by their own shells.' This speaks to accuracy. The failure of previous use of yellow flags to indicate to the artillery a captured trench amidst the smoke of battle led to the first employment of portable wireless sets between brigade and divisional HQs, although the experiment was unsuccessful. (In terms of other novelties, 'a few steel helmets also were tried',[70] but drew friendly fire in mistake for the enemy). The enemy artillery response during the bombardment was weak – taken in by the subterfuge, they failed to shell the British front position, and bombarded rear positions from where Nicholson had wisely cleared his men. Few of the enemy, who were the *126th* and *132nd Infantry Regiments* (*39th Division, XV Corps*), a competent division that would perform well on the Somme in 1916, were encountered in the front line, nor were machine guns.

1st King's Shropshire Light Infantry attacked on the brigade left. Preparation had even included the removal of their CO, Lieutenant-Colonel John Strick the day before 16 Brigade came into line.[71] The new CO, Major Edward Luard called all his officers together the previous night and 'thoroughly explained everything required, answering their questions' – he had suffered the misfortune of losing two company commanders and his adjutant to a shell that afternoon.[72] His bombers began their attack on the nearest enemy trench (Bond Street) five minutes before the barrage lifted and at 03.15 A and B Companies stormed into the crater, 'where much hand to hand fighting took place with bayonet & bombs took place.' The north side of the crater

69 War Diary, HQ 6 Infantry Division, 18 Infantry Brigade Operation Order No. 3, 6 August 1915, TNA WO95/1581.

70 Edmonds, op. cit. *1915 Vol.2*, p.109.

71 Forty-five-year-old John Arkwright Strick, commissioned in 1890, had served in staff posts between 1908 and 1912, and was moved into the role of AAQMG until May 1917, when he became a commandant on lines of communication, finishing the war as a major-general Inspector-General of Communications.

72 Edward Bourryau Luard, born 1870, the son of Major-General R.G.A. Luard, was major in the battalion in August 1914. Commissioned in 1891 he had been presented with a gold Albert medal in 1894 for gallant services during plague at Hong Kong.

The attack of 16 Brigade on Hooge Crater, 9 August 1915. The crater lay directly on the Menin Road. The attack was made from the edge of Zouave Wood, no longer in existence, but which extended to the back fence of the present Hooge Crater Cemetery, from where the image was taken.

was taken, and trenches dug 30 yards beyond, although these had to be evacuated due to retaliatory shelling.[73] Three officers were awarded the Military Cross (MC),[74] and six Distinguished Conduct Medals (DCM) went to the other ranks. One such was awarded to Private H. Langford, who attacked a party of the enemy who had been overlooked in a sap and were bombarding the Shropshires from the rear. Langford 'at once collected all the bombs he could find, and, standing fearlessly on the top of the parapet, bombed the enemy until they had all been killed or captured.'[75] Francis Hitchcock provided a description of the crater once the British had reoccupied it:

> What a sight we saw! At least two hundred German corpses in every imaginable shape and form; the place was one mass of torn flesh. The enemy had worked like ants in this vast mine crater since the 30th July … It resembled an amphitheatre,

73 War Diary, 1st Battalion King's Shropshire Light Infantry, 'Report 11 August 1915', TNA WO95/1609.
74 Second-Lieutenant R.H. Marriott; Lieutenant R. Bryans; and Lieutenant T.L. Ingram.
75 F.A. Mumby (ed.), *The Great World War, Vol. IV*, pp.89-90.

with its tiers of bomb proof shelters scooped out of the crumbling sides of the chasm and shored up with tree trunks.[76]

Hooge Crater employed as New Zealand Brigade HQ, 1917. (Ref: 1/2-013161-G. Alexander Turnbull Library, Wellington, New Zealand)

2nd York & Lancaster were the second front-line battalion, and 'careful preparation and reconnaissance' involved company commanders being 'taken over the ground and all details carefully explained to them.' They attacked with two companies advancing on 'two lines of platoons each', the second lines carrying ammunition, bombs, tools, and sandbags with instructions to start digging communication trenches back as soon as possible. Trench mortars and machine guns were to move forward into the captured trench immediately. Their assault took the enemy front line 'with practically no resistance.' The Germans were seen 'evacuating their 2nd line trenches and running back – these were caught by our artillery and also machine guns which had rushed up into first line and were quickly in position.' By 03.17 the attached engineers began wiring the position. Captain Arnold Turner, Royal Engineers, led two sections and six blocking parties through the front line under heavy fire and:

76 Hitchcock, op. cit. p.74.

> [I]mmediately put out wire in front of the captured position. When the senior Infantry Officers were killed or wounded, Captain Turner assumed command of the whole party in his vicinity, and proceeded to consolidate the position, continuing to do so after being wounded till incapacitated by loss of blood.[77]

For at least one man on the battlefield the assault on the senses generated by the intensity of the artillery fire created a surreal experience. Second-Lieutenant Ernest Smith of 1st Buffs, tasked with consolidating the line, wrote how: 'The taking over of that line seemed an unreal sort of dream to me … it seemed as though there was an infinity of time and space separating us from anything beautiful or desirable, and the weird effect was increased by the half-light and mist.'[78] The brigade captured approximately 200 prisoners, 'but many of these were killed or wounded before they got back to Ypres.' The enemy dead was estimated at 300 or more. The cost was significant, however – between 5 and 12 August the brigade lost 33 officers and 798 other ranks.[79]

On the right, 18 Brigade, as noted, had much further to go to achieve their objective. It would prove a feat of endurance and, in the end, partly impossible. 'The heavy bombardment by guns from the south and the very accurate fire of trench howitzers and machine guns … on the right flank, rendered the position untenable.' The 2nd Durham Light Infantry attacked from Sanctuary Wood across the open towards the Menin Road. Three machine guns accompanied their first line, and three the second. Bombers advanced with the leading companies, creeping out first to the edge of the bombardment, with orders to block communication trenches whilst a new line was being dug. Their advance was rapid and successful. About 300 German dead were later located around the stables, 'most of them bayonetted.'[80] They dug in, and no counter-attack developed. The support battalion, 2nd Sherwood Foresters, was tasked with the protection of the DLI's right flank by holding the line running from the Menin Road back to Sanctuary Wood, the old British front line. This would prove the most problematic task of the whole operation. The difficulty arose because of an aspect of positional warfare that would only be taken into consideration properly at the opening of the Battle of Arras in 1917. Essentially, the problem was that the destructive shoots of the artillery made the ground over which the infantry were to attack too difficult to traverse. Indeed, the trenches 18 Brigade were supposed to occupy were either blown in or full of the dead, and could not be held, especially as the absence of counter-battery work meant that they were exposed to constant unsuppressed enemy artillery fire. Calls for reinforcements by both the attacking units absorbed the whole of 1st

77 *Edinburgh Gazette*, 10 September 1915, p. 1378. Arnold Geoffrey Turner DSO had been commissioned in 1900 and would finish the war a lieutenant-colonel.
78 E.K. Smith, Private Papers, IWM Docs 2535.
79 War Diary, HQ 16 Infantry Brigade, August 1915, TNA WO95/1605.
80 War Diary, 2nd Battalion Durham Light Infantry, 'Report on Operations Near Hooge, 9th August [1915]', TNA WO95/1617.

East Yorkshire, and elements of 1/16th London. This caused the ruined trenches to be too thickly held (exactly as Congreve had not wanted), accounting for the higher level of casualties in the brigade, and the line had to be thinned. Private Frank Minter of the Westminsters was one of those sent forward. 'On reaching the fringe of the wood we were heavily fired upon from the right and almost from the rear where the line curves back and fellows began to fall.' Moving up what was the old British front line and negotiating mounds where the trench had been blown in, Minter was shot in the left thigh. His battalion being recalled, he lay in a dug-out. 'The Germans were shelling heavily', he recorded, and 'a few chaps came back with messages' and 'told me that we were losing heavily.' As the day turned into evening 'five chaps came along from the trench in front and their yarn gave me a nasty jar … they were the sole survivors of the holders of the trenches in front and … they were now going back to report.' With likely understatement, Minter reported feeling 'very insecure.' He eventually decided to try and drag himself back and found himself in a trench the enemy had subjected to liquid fire. 'The woodwork of the dugout was charred' and he could see 'burnt water bottles, straps, scorched hats.'[81]

As Minter indicated, by noon, 'under a hail of shells', the front-line trenches facing east and supposedly to be occupied by the Sherwoods 'were only held by isolated groups where they had not been blown in.'[82] The impossibility of digging new trenches under such an intensity of enemy fire had created an unsustainable position. 6th Division staff came up to Maple Copse, and it was decided to reconstruct Bond Street, roughly parallel to the west of the objective running from Zouave Wood towards the Stables, instead of attempting to hold the line further east as the Sherwoods had been tasked. This did not defeat the object of the operation, as it still restored observation to the east. That night, orders were issued for both the Sherwoods and the Durham Light Infantry to draw back,[83] although some of the DLI were left in isolated outposts which they occupied until the following day. Sergeant Plews, of one of the attacking DLI companies, noted in the initial rush which carried them to between the enemy's second and third lines: 'A general mix-up … we advanced too far, we were under our own artillery fire.'[84] Private Percy Jones, 1/16th London, described of the robust Durham men: 'There was no stopping them.' When his unit relieved them that night 'they were almost crazed with thirst, snatched our water-bottles from us, and seemed half demented.'[85] Four officers of the DLI were awarded the MC. The citation for Lieutenant Gerald Sopwith makes heroic reading:

81 Minter, op. cit.
82 War Diary, 2nd Battalion Sherwood Foresters, 9 August 1918, TNA WO95/1616.
83 Two MCs were awarded to officers, and five DCMs to the other ranks of the Sherwood Foresters.
84 Quoted in Cave, op. cit. p.72.
85 P.H. Jones, Private Papers, IWM Docs 12253.

> Although blown several yards by a large shell, wounded in the shoulder and slightly in the leg, he refused to leave the firing line, taking command of his Company when the Commander had been badly wounded, and another officer killed. At a critical moment he left the trenches under heavy fire, rallied and led back some men who were retiring owing to a misunderstanding. At 5 a.m., 10th August, he was again wounded, and his jaw broken. He had to lie down but continued to command and encourage his men till he was relieved.[86]

Seven DCMs were awarded to other ranks of the battalion. One went to Lance-Corporal J.G. Smith who was stranded in the stables whilst the battalion withdrew, and who held on until 19.30 the following day 'declining to yield, merely sending back, long after his party had been given up for lost, for more bombs and reinforcements, and only withdrawing when other troops relieved him.'[87] Two others of his party, Corporal J. Gott and Private R.D. Howse, also received the DCM. 18 Brigade suffered casualties (9-10 August) of 45 officers and 1,253 other ranks, reflecting their trials.

The attack of 18 Brigade from Sanctuary Wood and the final Bond Street line achieved, 9 August 1915. The picture is taken from the eastern tip of the crater.

86 *Edinburgh Gazette*, 10 September 1915, p.1380. Commissioned in the 3rd Battalion DLI on 4 September 1914, Sopwith would survive the war.
87 Mumby, op. cit. p.88-9.

According to Ironside, now 6th Division's GSO2, command of 18 Brigade did not run smoothly that morning. Communication became increasingly difficult with the brigade, and Congreve sent Ironside up to their HQ in a hut in Zouave Wood. There Ironside discovered that 'the whole show had collapsed with the exception of Morgan-Grenville the signal officer. The commander, Towsey, was sitting with his head in his hands and moaning. He could say nothing but "Oh those Guns" & I could get no sense out of him.' (Francis Towsey, it will be recalled, had suffered the decimation of his unit, 1st West Yorkshire, on the Aisne, when he had been wounded). Ironside claimed the other staff of brigade HQ were asleep and that 'no one had been down the line and no arrangements made to run the show.' After conferring with the GSO1, Gerald Boyd, Ironside 'went round the line and found everything in hopeless confusion.' He then 'personally got the men in position and thinned out the line & pushed the machine guns into the line.' Returning to 18 Brigade HQ he handed over to Lieutenant-Colonel Bartholomew Price of the 1st Royal Fusiliers of 17 Brigade.[88] Ironside concluded: 'The show was really too disgraceful. Towsey was quite incapable of command & should really have been court-martialled. As it was, he was sent off to get fit again.' It must be assumed that this was a momentary blip for Towsey, who would command 122 Brigade from 27 September 1915 until June 1918 (at which point he was sent home). Ironside concluded: 'Nothing was ever said of the whole episode nor known to no one except the immediate actors.'[89]

The total infantry casualties of 6th Division for the operation came to an appalling 2,129 (Marden underestimating these at 70 officers and 1,700 ORs). Lieutenant Murray Hill of 1st Royal Fusiliers, observed that 17 Brigade did not take part in the attack: 'Which is one of the reasons I am alive now.'[90] The operation was the first major test of the division's medical services. Planning had begun on 4 August, with the taking over of the Ypres asylum temporarily. On the 6th, the Assistant Director of Medical Services, Lieutenant-Colonel Bertal Scott 'went over the ground to be evacuated' by the two brigade field ambulances, and 'the site where a Collecting Station is to be formed, dug outs to be improved', and 'to see means of communication for getting walking cases back to Advanced Dressing Station at Asylum.'[91] On the following two days he

88 Bartholomew George Price, a major of the Royal Fusiliers in August 1914, would command the battalion until February 1916 when he was promoted to command 150 Infantry Brigade until February 1918. He was given the command of 157 Brigade the day before the Armistice.

89 Ironside, op. cit. location 1247.

90 M.V.B. Hill, Private Papers, IWM Docs 6370. Murray Victor Burrow Hill would command his battalion for two months in 1916, then 9th Sussex from November 1916 to the Armistice.

91 War Diary, ADMS 6th Division, 6 August 1915, TNA WO95/1592. Fifty-two-year-old Bertal Hopton Scott received his medical training at Trinity College, Toronto and the London Hospital. He was commissioned into the RAMC in 1887. He served in Chitral in 1895 and Sierra Leone 1898-9 where, at Karene, wounded in the chest and his thigh fractured, he continued to minister to his wounded comrades. He commanded No.9

went round the Field Ambulances. Captain John du Plessis Langrishe, Medical Officer with 16 Field Ambulance, 16 Brigade, had only 24 casualties admitted on the 9th. He then, however, described 'a busy night – hard at work from 11.30 till 10 this morning with only one hour off. 161 wounded admitted, (as) many as half being stretcher cases, a total of 434 passing through in 24 hours.' The most severely injured did not arrive at the Field Ambulances until night. This was followed by 'another night of it … 39 stretcher cases', but on the 12th 'only 15 stretcher cases but coming in by 3s and 4s at intervals of an hour.'[92] Richard Wilkinson, chaplain to 18th Field Ambulance, 18 Brigade suffering more casualties, recorded that: 'At 5.30 a.m. the wounded began to come in. The Ambulance had made extensive preparations. Three doctors had been sent up to organise dressing stations, cars had been requisitioned … for 24 hours we toiled and during that time over 600 cases had been dressed and evacuated.' He continued that 'few of these cases will be fatal. We have had to sleep in turns. My work has consisted of small ministrations. The men are wonderfully cheerful but they say it is hell out here.'[93] Overall, 'all worked well and efficiently; only a few wounded in (the) Crater Line were not got in within 24 hours.'[94]

Despite the terrible cost, all viewed the operation as a success. Second Army claimed, with wild disingenuousness, that it 'resulted in the whole of the works about Hooge recently captured … being retaken with small loss.'[95] 6th Division's war diary states: 'The whole affair was thoroughly successful due to the cooperation between the arms and the excellent artillery bombardment.'[96] The Official History trumpeted that: 'The attack was a model of its kind, took the enemy by surprise and was entirely successful: it marks further progress in the methods of minor operations.'[97] Marden, in his history of the division, conceded that it had been impossible to hold the ground on the right, but on the left: 'Not only was all the ground lost on the 30th July regained, but an important spur north of the Menin Road, which had hitherto been in German occupation, was included in the final position consolidated.' In terms of tactical development he observed that the attack 'was the first attempt made to follow the barrage really closely' (although it was not, of course, a creeping barrage). He concluded: 'The attack was looked upon for some time as a model of really close co-operation between infantry and artillery.'[98]

General Hospital at the outbreak of war, and after his stint with 6th Division, commanded No. 10 General Hospital.

92 J. du P. Langrishe, Private Papers, IWM Docs 15014.

93 R.B. Wilkinson, Private Papers, IWM Docs 5761. Richard Brindle Wilkinson, born 1886, had been ordained a Wesleyan minister in 1914. Commissioned into the Army Chaplain's Department in April 1915, and he served in France & Flanders until June 1919.

94 War Diary, ADMS 6th Division, 10 August 1915, TNA WO95/1592.

95 War Diary, HQ Second Army, '2nd Army Summary of Operations' 8-14 August 1915, TNA WO95/271.

96 War Diary, HQ 6th Infantry Division, 9 August 1915, TNA WO95/1581.

97 Edmonds, op. cit. *1915 Vol.2*, p.196.

98 Marden, op. cit. p.15.

From 11-17 August 2nd Leinster occupied the trenches around the crater. The positions to the left were enfiladed from high ground, and at its most extreme point, the British line was 'up in the air', the Leinsters and the enemy sharing the same original German front trench, separated by a sandbagged bombing stop. Second-Lieutenant Francis Hitchcock left a detailed account that perfectly exemplifies the cost of retaining a position. At 05.00 on the 12th a 'dozen shells ... traversed our line from left to right, ranging shots for a pukka bombardment.' Within 15 minutes a steady bombardment opened. The skill of the German gunners was evident. 'They fired by a grouping system of five shells to a limited area, under 12 yards. They burst shrapnel over this area ... three out of the five shells hit our trench, obliterating it.' The shelling stopped at 12.30, and recommenced at 15.00. The Leinsters were enfiladed on both sides, shells from Bellewaarde blowing in the traverses, and firing from Hill 60 destroying the parados. Casualties mounted rapidly – of the three platoons in the front line in Hitchcock's company, 65 out of 120 were casualties. It was 'exasperating, sitting there getting crumped to blazes, while our own guns kept silent.' Only late in the afternoon did British guns retaliate, Hitchcock presuming the intention being to break up a counter-attack, for which he surmised the artillery had been saving their shells. 'This retaliation was perfect, and cheered us immensely.' The British shelling was directed at infantry, and the enemy shelling did not cease, ending only at 17.30. In describing the desolation at Hooge, Hitchcock recorded the gloomy observation: 'I never saw anything like it again during my service at the front.'[99]

4th Division had made their representations to Keir at VI Corps HQ exactly a month earlier about precisely this issue, the necessity of support in holding a captured position, after the operations at International Trench had resulted in 1,026 casualties, 325 fatal:

> The losses during the actual attack were very small, but as is usually the case in the small enterprises, heavy casualties have been suffered by the units who held the captured trenches afterwards. It is, I think, worth consideration whether such enterprises should be undertaken unless to gain some very important tactical point which materially affects the remainder of the line, or unless a methodical progress from tactical point to tactical point is intended. If undertaken they must be well supported with artillery afterwards, and the consolidation of the captured position continued under cover of severe daily bombardments by our own heavy guns and howitzers, otherwise the advantage gained will not compensate for the losses suffered by our infantry.[100]

99 Hitchcock, op. cit. pp.64-70.
100 War Diary, 11 Infantry Brigade, 4/Div. No. GGG.316, 13 July 1915, TNA WO95/1489. Michael LoCicero notes that 'Although bearing the signature of BGRA Brigadier-General R.F. Fox, temporary GOC 4th Division in Major-General Wilson's absence, the observations and sentiments expressed in this document were no doubt those of the latter.' M. LoCicero, '"A Coda to the Second Battle of Ypres": International Trench 6-10 July 1915', in S. Jones (ed.) *Courage without Glory*, p. 355.

The divisional artillery War Diary is missing for this period, and hence it is difficult to identify whether the absence of 'severe daily bombardments' to protect 2nd Leinster on the 12th represented a failure of learning or the conservation of ammunition. However, that the comments of 4th Division lacked specificity is evident from Hitchcock's observation that the British bombardment, when it eventually happened, discomfited the enemy infantry, but did not silence their guns.

The Hooge operation is notable for the first appearance in 6th Division's records of after-action reports that contained learning points. Cecil Nicholson, commenting on 16 Brigade's behalf, wrote of the importance of keeping support troops away from retaliatory fire (which he had achieved). Given the difficulties of transmission of information, he advocated more extensive preparation of communication trenches, and greater numbers of runners. He noted the profligate use of bombs, sometimes without a proper target, and that supplies of them thus ran low. He suggested a better carrying apparatus for bombs, and the regular sending up of supplies. He also recommended a larger supply of water held ready to send up; and was concerned about the care of casualties, despite Bertal Scott's good preparations, advocating special dug-outs for the wounded, and more medical officers. The DSO awarded to Captain Kingsmill Jones (RAMC, attached 1st Buffs) bore testimony to this need:

> During the entire night of 9th-10th August 1915 and the whole of the following day and night, he was attending to and evacuating wounded from the front trenches, time after time exposing himself to shell and rifle fire. He was twice slightly wounded but stuck to his work with unflagging energy. It was entirely owing to Captain Jones that the crater was successfully evacuated of wounded.[101]

Nicholson also stressed the importance of the removal of the dead.[102] Walter Congreve would have agreed. He visited the crater the day after the assault, writing: 'It is a bad place altogether. Everywhere dead men, some days old and some blown to bits. You step over them in the trenches and see them wherever you look out over the trenches.'[103]

Brigadier-General Bridgford, replacing Lieutenant-Colonel Towsey, wrote a report specifically on the subject of machine-guns. He advocated strong dug-outs for machine gun teams (noting that the enemy had many machine-guns smashed through having not brought them in at night), with a small team of bombers attached to each gun, to defend it from enemy bombers. He encouraged greater provision of ammunition carriers and noted the inadequate numbers of Lewis gun magazines.[104] No unit COs submitted recommendations in their operation reports. Walter Congreve submitted a

101 *Edinburgh Gazette*, 10 September 1915, p.12849.
102 War Diary, HQ 6th Infantry Division, '16th Infantry Brigade – Report on the Operations at Hooge', 13 August 1915, TNA WO95/1581.
103 W. Congreve quoted in Cave, op. cit. p.74.
104 War Diary, HQ 6th Infantry Division, 'Machine Guns', 17 August 1915, TNA WO95/1581.

series of ten points for the consideration of corps.[105] These largely reflect his brigadier's observations, with points of his own concerning the inadvisability of wiring before nightfall as 'it is costly in men, it marks our position', and 'it advertises the fact that we do not mean further advance.' Showing his aggressive tendencies, he noted that whilst he had set a definite line so his troops should not be led into low ground, 'I am convinced that more ground could have been gained.' This would have required greater concentration of artillery for wider wire cutting on each flank, and initiative on the ground. In essence he was arguing against a narrow-fronted attack. These reports produced a two-way process – Congreve's observations went up to Second Army, and they, in turn asked questions of him, namely: (i) Where were the Forward Observation Officers (FOO) placed?, and (ii) What arrangements were made for the bombing parties? Congreve's responses were forthright, that the notion of a FOO was a 'misnomer', as none could see fall of shell, but that more valuable work was done in liaison with battalion HQs in discovering where the infantry actually were, which, although he did not make it explicit, would decrease the risk of friendly fire casualties, and increase the likelihood of suppressing the enemy. His response to the latter reiterated the issue of the desirability of greater numbers of ammunition carriers and the need to teach bombers to use German grenades.[106]

In many ways, the details of these recommendations are of less interest. What is of note is that 6th Division, which had no doubt previously had processed learning verbally (otherwise the minor l'Epinette operation would not have been the success it was), was now committing it to paper. This gave the possibility of wider promulgation, and division, corps and army were engaging in a formal tactical dialogue. The results were passed across armies. Thus 47th (2nd London) Division in First Army produced edited highlights of the notes on the Hooge operations for its infantry brigades, artillery, engineers and 'Q' functions.[107]

Alarms and excursions – Gas! Gas! Gas![108]

Following the successful attack at Hooge, 6th Division returned to holding the line in the Salient. The next major action to be taken by the BEF would be the Battle of Loos, the reluctant British contribution to the Third Battle of Artois, whose main combatants would be the French *Tenth Army* and the German *6th Army*, the French successfully forcing themselves onto Vimy Ridge. 6th Division would take

105 War Diary, HQ 6th Infantry Division, 6th Div. No. 6/6/22, 18 August 1915, TNA WO95/1581.
106 War Diary, HQ 6th Infantry Division, 'Reply to Questions Asked by 2nd Army' (undated), TNA WO95/1581.
107 War Diary, HQ 6th Infantry Division, G/435/1 47th Infantry Division, 2 September 1915, TNA WO95/1581.
108 16 Brigade were first subject to a gas attack from both shells and cylinder discharge on 19 June 1915, but no infantry attack was made.

part in a diversionary exercise on 25 September, the day the British First Army at Loos attacked. The divisional artillery bombarded the enemy's line at certain points, cutting wire, and a gas attack was to be simulated, gas genuinely being deployed to mixed effect at Loos itself. This was effected by 'Paynes smoke candles,[109] 18-pounder grenades, Threlfallite No. 1,[110] and Red Mixture grenades.'[111] The grenades would make the eyes smart, but were not poisonous. Several thousand were thrown, the throwers standing carefully 30 yards apart. The 'gas bombs proved very effective and created a great deal of alarm and despondency along the whole front".[112] Any alarm and despondency almost certainly had little impact on the events at Loos that day.

Towards the end of October the weather began to close in again. Second-Lieutenant Ernest Smith wrote on 24 October: 'Previously I had always looked upon rain and mud as things you can get away from if you want to, but not so here, for the last two days nothing has been really clean or dry ... at times the mud has permeated everything.'[113] By 2 November the trenches were yet again described as 'in a dreadful state.' Two days later, it was recorded: 'Both Germans and ourselves indulging in baling.' Smith, who had requested an oilskin from his parents on 2 November and miraculously received it by the 12th, added that 'it would not matter so much if it were ordinary water, but unfortunately it has passed a good many corpses on the way and stinks most horribly!'[114] By 7 November, when the weather had cleared, both sides were repairing their parapets. Writing of a 16-day stint in the trenches, Private George Clifthill, 2nd York & Lancaster, claimed that 'over three hundred of our chaps were admitted into hospital during that time.'[115] By the 11th, the rain had returned and the trenches were falling in once more.[116] Private Percy Jones, 1/16th London wrote of the line near the St Julien Road on 16 November 1917: 'We have to keep three pumps going all the time or we should be waist deep. As it is we are up to our knees, and poor old Frost, acting orderly-corporal, has just been fished out of a "sump-hole" six feet deep.' The trenches 'refuse to stick up, and constantly fall in, dug-outs and all. We dig down about two feet and strike water, this being the actual depth of the trench. Cover is got by building up a wall of sandbags, wire barricades, and piling earth against them.'[117]

109 James Pain & Sons of London were firework manufacturers.
110 Threlfallite No. 1 Grenade, a 5-inch tin canister, filled with red phosphorous, detonator and fuze configuration.
111 This produced coloured smoke.
112 War Diary, HQ 6th Infantry Division, 25 September 1915, TNA WO95/1581.
113 Smith, op. cit.
114 Smith, op. cit. Ernest Kennedy Smith died of wounds on 22 December 1915. 'A piece of shell had penetrated the abdomen and another piece had fractured his skull.' Captain H.F. Vellacott, RAMC, noted that: 'While I was closing the abdomen, after having repaired a hole in the intestine, he suddenly developed signs of bleeding into the brain ... although his pulse continued to beat for three hours, he never regained consciousness.'
115 G. Clifthill, Private Papers, IWM Docs 2611.
116 War Diary, HQ 6th Infantry Division, November 1915, TNA WO95/1581.
117 Jones, op. cit.

Fortunately, on 20 November, the division was withdrawn from the line to Houtkerque and Poperinghe.[118] By this point changes had been afoot. On 14 October, the original composition of the division altered. 17 Brigade was transferred to 24th Infantry Division, and 71 Brigade, commanded by Brigadier-General Mansell Shewen,[119] was transferred from the 24th to the 6th.[120] This occurred in the aftermath of the Loos offensive, when New Army brigades were transferred to Regular divisions and Regular and New Army units interchanged to achieve a mix of experience. There would follow another significant change. On 14 November Major-General Walter Congreve left to assume command of XIII Corps, and was replaced by Major-General Charles Ross[121] who would be at the helm of the division for nearly 22 months.

On the night of 15 December, 18 and 71 brigades went into the line between the Roulers railway and the Wieltje salient, 16 Brigade following the next night, extending to the Forward Cottage salient to the north. All three brigades were thus in line when a gas attack was delivered by the opposing *XXVI Reserve Corps* at 05.15 on the morning of the 19th,[122] on a front of about two and three-quarter miles. The attack was not unheralded – one captured officer from the relevant corps and yet another source gave warning of an attack after 10 December. 6th Division had been warned and was thus prepared, a 'Gas Alert' being issued each time the weather appeared favourable to the enemy.[123] The 16 Brigade were the first to become aware of what was happening. At 05.15, several unusual red lights were fired, and slow rifle fire accompanied the emission of gas. This appeared as a 'thick white cloud' (reaching some fifty feet high), emitted with a 'loud hissing' from cylinders at intervals along the enemy front line. Fifteen minutes later a bombardment opened along the division's front on the support line and lines of communication, lasting about four hours. A party of 12 enemy under a single officer advanced (and a further party of 30 got into trenches to the north,

118 This was the first of three rest periods. although working parties were supplied to the 49th and 14th Divisions.

119 Mansell Travers Shewen, b. 1862, a retired Indian Army officer of the 97th Deccan Infantry, would command the brigade until May 1916.

120 There was an accompanying redistribution of battalions to brigades. 1st Leicestershire (16 Brigade) and 2nd Sherwood Foresters (18 Brigade) were transferred to 71 Brigade in exchange for 8th Bedfordshire and 11th Essex respectively. This achieved a balance of Regular and New Army units in brigades. On 1 April 1916, 11th Leicestershire joined as pioneers.

121 See Chapter 6.

122 This corps held the front between the Roulers and Staden railways.

123 J.E. Edmonds, *Military Operations France and Belgium 1916 Vol. 1,* p. 158. A 'Gas Alert' meant that 'a sentry was posted near each alarm horn or gong, at every dug-out holding ten men or more, on every group of small dug-outs, and at each signal office; that gas helmets and gas alarms were inspected once every 12 hours; that all ranks wore the helmet outside the great coat, or rolled up on the head, and had the top button of the great coat left undone, so that the helmet might be tucked in; and that special precautions were taken to lubricate the working parts of all rifles, machine guns and guns in forward positions.'

held by 49th Division). The gas cleared by 06.35. 2nd York & Lancaster moved up to the canal bank, and the battalions in the front line were reinforced. The German officer's body was recovered and he was noted to be of '235th Regiment 51st Division 26th Reserve Corps and had in his possession a valuable map showing accurately various items of importance opposite Mortaldje and Forward Cottage. Schemes were arranged whereby full advantage was taken of information thus gained.'[124]

Captain Edward Simeons was with 8th Bedfordshire at Forward Cottage. He received news of the possible impending attack at 02.00 on the 18th.[125] He inspected his company's gas helmets immediately. He recorded seeing four red and two green rockets at 05.20 and could hear the gas being released. At the sound of multiple gas gongs his first response was a brief prayer. 'Within a few seconds every man had his gas helmet properly adjusted', and 'our machine gun & rifle fire which was very well controlled swept the enemy's parapets.' The gas was 'so strong that it turned all our buttons olive green and stopped our wrist watches.' Masses of rats appeared. The gas cloud soon passed, but half an hour later a very accurate bombardment dropped on the front-line. The bottom of his trench was soon 'covered with wounded & dead,' casualties of artillery rather than gas. He was not relieved until midnight and made the relieving officer 'stop with me as I am sure I would have gone mad being by myself all this time.'[126] The brigade had 63 gas casualties, with an additional five gas deaths. Forty-nine were killed, 133 wounded, and three were missing as a result of the enemy bombardment.

At 05.20, 71 Brigade in the centre of the division's line were aware of two red lights going up, and gas appeared to be emanating from amongst trees in the salient to the south of the Wieltje-'s Gravenstafel road. 1st Leicestershire actually witnessed the enemy within 100 yards of their trench apparently turning on a tap.[127] 2nd Sherwood Foresters came up to the canal bank north of Ypres, and 9th Norfolk moved to Burgomaster's Farm, just east of Dickebush to the south-west of the town. Two companies of the 9th Suffolks came up to the support line. On the right, gas was detected by 18 Brigade at 05.30, drifting down from in front of the other brigades. The battalions in line, as with the two brigades to the north, opened up heavy rifle and machine gun fire. The 14th Durham Light Infantry on the brigade's left (who were in the gas cloud for about 45 minutes) were reinforced by companies of 1/16th London and 1st West Yorkshire, whilst 11th Essex were brought up by train from Poperinghe to defensive works just behind Ypres. Six dead Germans were counted in

124 War Diary, HQ 16 Infantry Brigade, 'Summary – December 1915', TNA WO95/1605.
125 18 Brigade records warnings as received daily from 13 December. (War Diary, HQ 16 Infantry Brigade, 16 December 1915, TNA WO95/1605).
126 E.E. Simeons, Private Papers, IWM Docs 2808. Edward Emil Simeons died of wounds on 17 February 1916. His CO wrote: 'He was a splendid Company Commander, keen, bold and self-reliant.' http://www.worldwar1luton.com/individual/captain-edward-emil-simeons (accessed 6 March 2018).
127 War Diary, 1st Battalion Leicestershire Regiment, 19 December 1915, TNA WO95/1621.

front of the DLI positions, and it was here that there were the only reports of cut wire. Lachrymatory shells followed at 06.15, but 'gas helmets were adjusted and proved efficient.'[128] Yet it was far from the case that gas casualties had been avoided in the front line. 14th DLI suffered 149 casualties in the ranks with two officers gassed and two wounded, a total which 'would have been lighter if there had not been so many defective gas helmets',[129] (although, as will be seen, it was not exactly the case that the helmets were defective). 1st Leicestershire noted that the effects of the gas appeared to be delayed in some. Those who could not get their helmets on or who had lost them were overcome within five minutes and died within two to three hours. By noon, three had died and eight were suffering, but by 18.00 over 100 men from the front line were suffering 'very severely', and 'men who attempted to come to the dressing station in St Jean fell on the way and were picked up insensible.'[130]

Lieutenant John Gamble of 14th DLI described his experiences. He was woken by a gas-helmeted sentry at 05.30 with a 'choking feeling', aware that his dug-out was 'already full of gas.' At first, he could not find his helmet, and 'began to splutter and choke.' At last accoutred, he ventured outside. Here, 'the gas was rolling across towards us in thick whiteish yellow clouds; men were running about with their weird-looking gas helmets on, and shells were bursting all around.' Ordered to man the reserve trench, he became aware that 'a number of men were already gassed' whilst others 'began to stifle and choke.' The enemy barrage was 'doing a great deal of damage amongst our troops, but they stuck it wonderfully.' The noise 'was appalling and nerve-racking and there was no cessation for 3 hours', whereupon 'the gas began to thin.' He concluded: 'The gas is … past description! Of course our Battalion only got a part of the attack … but we got just about the worst part … I wouldn't have thought it possible that humanity could stand it.' In terms of the rats that appeared, 'one good thing the gas did was to kill a lot of the little beasts.' The effect of his brief exposure persisted. On New Year's Eve he wrote home complaining of 'throat trouble – not much – brought on by the gas.' Five days later he described a 'hacking cough.' In hospital a week later and on a diet of milk, he met another officer of his battalion who had been gassed that morning. 'This gas is awful stuff. It seems to do a lasting and prolonged harm to one; not like an ordinary wound which one gets and recovers from.' He described how the officer, Second-Lieutenant Lawrence Hickson, 'was pretty bad when in England, and when he got back, he gave way again, and is now in hospital with very bad lungs, chest etc. He'll probably not be fit for any further active service.'[131]

128 War Diary, HQ 6th Infantry Division, 19 December 1915, TNA WO95/1581.
129 W. Miles, *The Durham Forces in the Field 1914-18*, p.35.
130 War Diary, 1st Battalion Leicestershire Regiment 19 December 1915, TNA WO95/1621.
131 J.W. Gamble, Private Papers, IWM Docs 12003. Lawrence Newby Hickson, b. 1895, would live until 1970. John Walcote Gamble was shot on 21 May 1916, a bullet passing through his left arm and entering his side, and departing through the middle of his back,

6th Division's defensive arrangements were thorough in terms of the moving up of units from reserve. Divisional staff mused that night on the nature of the venture. They observed that 'no attack appears to have been intended' but believed that the enemy trenches had been manned to take advantage of any serendipitous collapse in the British positions, deterred by the stout rifle fire. They reflected that the sudden change in the wind to the north (such changes always being a threat to the success of gas released in such a way), may have led to the cancellation of an infantry attack. Yet at the same time they noted that the enemy wire did not appear prepared, nor was the British wire cut by artillery. Another explanation, it was thought, might be that the ratcheting up of the British artillery harassment of the previous week, intended on destroying the suspected cylinders, had simply led to retaliation. Alternatively, the enemy had realised that the British knew about the presence of the cylinders, the gas being released before the cylinders could be blown up in their home trenches. Lastly, 6th Division concluded that: 'It may have been a test of a new gas, patrols being sent to see effect' (an observation balloon was sent up and German aircraft overflew the British positions). 'Gas is believed to be chlorine & prussic acid', it was added.[132]

It was the last speculations that proved in most part correct. The division had experienced the first phosgene gas attack (chlorine mixed with 20 percent phosgene).[133] In the following years the *Reichsarchiv* put forth the following explanation:

> No infantry attack was intended ... the object of the gas attack, which had been ordered and prepared months before ... was solely to damage the enemy by losses and destruction of his positions; in addition, experience in the release of gas would be perfected. At the end of the discharge, twenty patrols went forward ... they were to discover the effect of the discharge, and also bring in prisoners and make booty, but only two of the patrols reached the British trenches. The rest could not advance under the heavy fire, and some suffered severe losses.[134]

The effort therefore was in many respects tactically unsuccessful, although the total British casualties amounted to 1,069 with 120 deaths. Many of these, of course, were victims of the bombardment. Three-quarters of these occurred in 49th Division's area, where, in terms of the effects of the gas, No Man's Land was particularly narrow, only

leaving a serious abdominal wound. He died in No. 10 Casualty Clearing Station the following day.

132 War Diary, HQ 6th Infantry Division, 19 December 1915, TNA WO95/1581. It was not prussic acid (hydrogen cyanide), however.

133 Eighty-eight tons of the gas was released. Chlorine helped spread the heavier phosgene. It was later used in a 50-50 mix, the Allies referring to it as 'White Star' when delivered by shells. Phosgene was the deadliest of the gasses employed during the First World War, accounting for 85 percent of approximately 100,000 gas deaths. Its use had been considered by the British as early as June 1915, and it would become their gas of choice.

134 Edmonds, op. cit. *1916 Vol. 1*, p. 162.

twenty yards in two places, (the distance being 300 yards in 6th Division's area). In some respects the British were fortunate in the front line, as the P helmet in use at the time was only partly effective against phosgene, which had led to the assertion by troops that they were defective.[135] The effect of the gas had been mitigated by its rapid passage. Despite the fact that it had spread from a front of under three miles to a width of eight miles and a depth of ten, the enemy concluded: 'The general impression was that in spite of the relatively very favourable conditions, the gas had not had the expected effect, and that a break-through of the enemy position solely as the result of the gas discharge would not be possible.'[136] 6th Division had weathered yet another escalation of the increasing technological war.[137]

The early months of 1916 were marked by regular German shelling and retaliation, occasional bombing by aeroplanes, and the presence of Zeppelins over Ypres. A careful eye was kept on wind conditions given the events of 19 December 1916. On 26 February it was recorded: '6th Div(ision) line is now held in three sectors, each in charge of a Brigadier.' There was only one battalion in divisional reserve. 'The line extends from where the Beelewarde [*sic*] Beek crosses the front line on the right to the communication trench Pratt Street just 200 yards north of the salient at Wieltje.'[138] On 1 March the front line was 3,700 yards in length,[139] but the division was 'considerably below strength.' On 2 March, V Corps to the south attacked and retook the Bluff. This was a man-made mound on the north bank of the Ypres-Comines canal, created by spoil during its excavation. It had been taken in a surprise attack by the enemy on 14 February, and counter-attacks over the next two days failed to recapture it. A set-piece attack was prepared and delivered on 2 March. 6th Division contributed by making a demonstration with rifle fire along its whole front, with 24, 42 and 53 Brigades RFA firing 100 rounds.

135 'The Phenate Helmet (or 'P' Helmet, or the Tube Helmet, as it was officially known) was adopted from mid-November 1915 and featured the more durable glass goggles set on a hood made of multi-layered linen. Normal exhalation of carbon dioxide reduced the ability to combat hydrogen cyanide gas therefore a tube-shaped valve was fitted so that the man would breathe out through his mouth. Each soldier carried one Hypo Helmet as a reserve and one P Helmet until stocks could be replaced by a second P Helmet. A further development followed the realization that when the P Helmet was exposed to greater concentrations of phosgene it lost its capacity to protect the wearer. From January 1916 all such helmets were to be dipped in a phenate-hexamine solution; thus the PH Helmet came into being and it was this type that was commonly used by all British troops in France by July 1916.' See *Imperial War Museum* <https://www.iwm.org.uk/collections/item/object/30110811> (Accessed 5 March 2018).
136 Edmonds, op. cit. *1916 Vol. 1*, p. 162.
137 Another cloud of gas followed by smoke passed across the divisional front on 12 February 1916, but no infantry effort followed.
138 War Diary, HQ 6th Infantry Division, 26 February 1916, TNA WO95/1581.
139 16 Brigade on the right, 18 Brigade in the centre, and 71 Brigade to the left.

Following a period out of the line, the division returned to the trenches between 15-18 April, its left abutting the French on the canal bank near Boesinghe to Cross Roads Farm, 400 yards north-east of Wieltje. No doubt appreciating that a relief had taken place, the *52nd Reserve Division, XXVI Reserve Corps* (regarded as a good division, but one which had lost heavily during Second Ypres) carried out another surprise attack between Morteldje Estaminet and Turco Farm, where the High Command Redoubt, 150 yards from the British line, held a dominating position. After a day of heavy shellfire on 16 Brigade's line on the 19th, Willow Walk, held by one company of 8th Bedfordshire, who had had the misfortune to lose their CO Lieutenant-Colonel Henry Jackson two days previously, hit in the leg by a spare bullet, were seized.[140] One company of the Bedfords and two of 2nd York & Lancaster mounted a counterattack at 01.30 on the 20th, and by 04.15 16 Brigade reported the trenches retaken. In the daylight it became clear that this was not the case – the right portion of the attack, unfamiliar with a ground badly smashed, had not proceeded far enough, the left portion had simply been destroyed. It was only at 21.00, however, that a clear picture emerged, by which time the enemy had consolidated, wiring the position and bringing up five machine guns. Artillery preparation was clearly required, and on the fine morning of the 21st aeroplane observation was undertaken, and photographs printed. At 12.00 accurate fire based on carefully prepared artillery orders drove two parties of the enemy back to their own lines. They were seen returning, however, at dusk. At 20.00 a new bombardment opened and at 22.00 an infantry attack went in, made by three companies of 1st King's Shropshire Light Infantry. The late start was decided upon to decrease the likelihood that the enemy could effectively reinforce and to allow maximum time for preparation for counter-attack. The position was taken in difficult conditions across appalling ground, men falling and suffocating in the mud, the attack comprising three separate assaults, not all of which were able to be launched at the same time due to the conditions. Enemy counter-attacks were broken up by artillery supported by Forward Observation Officers, with Lieutenant-Colonel Oldfield, commanding 2 Brigade RFA, attaching himself to 16 Brigade HQ. The infantry attack was carefully planned by Lieutenant-Colonel Edward Luard,[141] who would lose his life as a result of the operation. He was hit in the head by shrapnel by the last enemy shell fired in retaliation. Tactically, a hastily organised immediate counter-attack had failed. A carefully planned counter-attack with detailed artillery support based on aerial photographs and close liaison with FOOs had succeeded despite horrendous conditions on the ground. The cost, however, had been terrible. During the month of April, 16 Brigade suffered 23 officer casualties (seven fatal and

140 His second occasion of wounding, Henry Cholmondeley 'Jacko' Jackson, a captain of the Bedfordshire Regiment in August 1914, would not return. He would command 175 Brigade from August 1916, and 50th Division from March 1918.

141 He died of wounds on 24 April. All officers except one and 200 ORs attended his funeral at No. 10 casualty Clearing Station.

two missing) and 528 casualties in the other ranks (93 fatalities and 113 missing). All bar three of the Shropshires' 166 casualties for the month were sustained in this operation, 8th Bedfordshire suffered 221 casualties, and 2nd York & Lancaster 97.

In the tit-for-tat that was trench warfare, on the night of 3/4 June 1st West Yorkshire, 18 Brigade, in the northernmost sector held by 6th Division adjacent to the canal, seized back the 'Old British Front Line', evacuated by another division previously, from the *239th Regiment, 52nd Reserve Division.* In some parts, this was 450 yards from the brigade trenches. Reconnaissance was carried out over four nights, each platoon commander reconnoitring his specific ground. The attack itself was made with 200 troops, with an additional 40 wiring and 25 filling sandbags over the two preceding nights. After an afternoon bombardment by III Corps heavy and divisional artillery, the operation was carried out successfully at 21.30 (although one section of the line could not be occupied or wired as it had been flattened). Second-Lieutenant Charles Newton,[142] five sergeants,[143] and five ORs were killed, two sergeants and 24 ORs being wounded. The battalion observed of the seven sergeant casualties that this was 'a very heavy percentage and one we could ill afford.' Losing experienced NCOs was a serious matter – 'At the beginning of the war all these sergeants were privates and had worked their way up by hard work and merit.'[144] Even a well-thought out operation could be costly.

	Casualties		Sick		Reinforcements	
	Officers	ORs	Officers	ORs	Officers	ORs
February 1916	16	438	20	500	28	808
March 1916	4	440	34	699	20	1017
April 1916	40	901	26	544	33	976
May 1916	41	727	27	237	82	1532
June 1916	13	329	17	234	52	1090
July 1916	16	176	16	366	56	160
TOTALS	130	3011	140	2580	271	5583

Table 3.2: Casualties, sickness and reinforcements, February-July 1916

142 Charles Thomas Kemp Newton was commissioned from the Cape Town Highlanders in April 1915.

143 Sergeant John Hunter (aged 33), Sergeant James H. Tyson, Sergeant John Frith DCM (aged 30), Sergeant Maurice W. Lamb, and Lance-Sergeant Thomas Queenan (aged 21).

144 War Diary, 1st Battalion West Yorkshire Regiment, TNA WO95/1618.

Whilst experience could not be replaced, simple numbers could. Whilst 6th Division was with XIV Corps in the Salient in 1916, as Table 3.1 shows, 3,141 casualties were almost matched by 2,720 cases of sickness, and replacements were found to exactly match losses.[145]

Rise of the Trench Raid

The Official History suggests that the first recorded trench raid was carried out on the night of 3/4 February 1915 by Lieutenant F.C. Roberts and 25 men of 1st Worcestershire (24 Brigade, 8th Division).[146] The first such raid, however, aimed at the seizure and demolition of an enemy held trench on the Aisne, was in fact carried out by 1st Coldstream Guards on the night of 4/5 October 1914. GHQ formally ordered raiding as a tactic in February 1915. Lieutenant-General William Robertson,[147] Chief of the General Staff, issued an order on the 5th,[148] asserting that 'enterprises of this nature constitute the most effective form of defence.' They would 'relieve monotony and improve the moral (sic) of our own troops', whilst downgrading that of the enemy. Raids should, however, have 'a specific object, have a reasonable chance of success, and be commensurate with the losses likely to be entailed.' They should also be 'methodically initiated' and 'well thought out beforehand.'

Patrolling was by now a regular occurrence in No Man's Land. James Jack observed on 30 January 1915: 'When the nights are suitable the company sends a small patrol into No Man's land, always with a definite, even if unimportant mission.' His view of the main purpose, echoing Robertson, was 'to prevent morale deteriorating through our remaining always behind parapets and so leaving the Germans in undisputed possession of No Man's Land.'[149] One objective was to take a prisoner for identification purposes, although such were more often made from the dead in front of the British trenches. Typical of a 'definite mission' was that of a patrol on the night of 27/28 January 1916 when 16 Brigade occupied the Canadian Dugouts in the middle of No Man's Land between Mouse Trap Farm and Cross Roads Farm with 30 men, checking to see what the enemy were doing therein (the dugouts were empty). As Brigadier-General Nicholson stated, echoing 'Wully' Robertson: 'Apart from the information obtained I think the chief value of the enterprise is to impress upon the enemy that

145 War Diary, AQMG XIV Corps, February-July 1916, TNA WO95/914.
146 Edmonds & Wynne, op. cit. p.32.
147 Sir William Robert 'Wully' Robertson (1860-1933) famously rose from private to field-marshal. After serving as Chief of Staff to the BEF he was appointed Chief of the Imperial General Staff.
148 O.A. 447, reproduced in Edmonds & Wynne, op. cit. p.33-4.
149 Terraine, op. cit. p.98.

NO MAN'S LAND is really ours and that and that we can interfere with anything he is doing.'[150]

The brigades of 6th Division did not begin to compile detailed reports on raids until early 1916. Thus on the night of 23/24 January two parties of 11th Essex, each with officers and five ORs 'attempted to rush the Mound' at Verlorenhoek, the aim being to establish identifications. Crossing the enemy wire with the aid of a mat, they could not enter their trenches, but 'ascended the parapet and fired down into (the) trench', killing five and wounding more, and returned without casualties. The object of the enterprise was not achieved, but 'the plan was nevertheless well conceived' and 'boldly carried out.' The 'whole performance had been rehearsed, details arranged, and the whole scheme cut and dried.' The men had blackened faces, and tapes were laid to assist return.[151] The mat had been used in an enterprise undertaken by 8th Somerset Light Infantry (50th Division) on 15/16 December 1915 in the Armentières sector, the methodology of which had been clearly well publicised. 18 Brigade's war diary entry for January 1916 contains the report of a raid by 62 Brigade, 21st Division, which listed eight 'lessons', confirming that such learning points were circulating widely. On the night of 9/10 March 1st Buffs of 16 Brigade carried out a bombing raid on the enemy crater at Bellewaarde, largely for the purpose of close reconnaissance, supported by an artillery barrage, trench mortars and machine-guns. Thus the pattern of raids supported by a range of arms developed.

On 9 June, 'The Admiral', an individual strongly associated with the development of 6th Division's patrolling and raiding, was reported missing in an enterprise with 9th Norfolk. Lieutenant Cyril Aldin Smith, born in 1877, the son of a jeweller, was the director of an antique and fine art business. He had been commissioned into the Royal Marines as an honorary second-lieutenant on 26 September 1914, and when his commission was terminated, he obtained commissioned again into the Royal Naval Volunteer Reserve on 7 August 1915 as a sub-lieutenant, promoted lieutenant the following month. He had accompanied the Royal Naval Division in its ill-fated expedition to Antwerp (4-10 October 1914) as a 'motor owner driver' in charge of a convoy of London busses.[152] After the withdrawal he reached France, and driving an officer to the front line succeeded in getting himself attached to 6th Division's HQ at Fleurbaix in October 1914. He was formally seconded to 6th Division on 14 September 1915. For a portion of his time he was attached to the 6th Divisional Bombing School, and it was here that the soubriquet 'The Admiral' was acquired, a promotion from the nickname 'Bos'n', which he rejected.[153] He 'interested himself in various experiments in trench warfare engines, moveable shields on wheels, crocodiles

150 War Diary, HQ 6th Infantry Division, Appendix III 10 March 1916, TNA WO95/1581. See Chapter 5 for further discussion.
151 War Diary, HQ 18 Infantry Brigade, 'Report on Minor Enterprise', January 1916, TNA WO95/1614.
152 Smith was paid £1 a day with 6d per mile allowance.
153 V.W. Andrews, 'The Legend of the Admiral', *The Ypres Times*, pp.70-1.

etc and later had been engaged on experiments with torpedoes for blowing up wire … a party of 24 men had recently assembled under Lt. Smith as specialist in their work and scouting.'[154] This collective was known as the '6th Division Shield Party.'

He was wounded on 21 July 1915 at Forward Cottage, receiving a shell splinter in the neck preceding the shield by several yards to give directions, (which seemed to defeat the purpose of the mechanism). The road in front of the position was thereafter known as 'Admiral's Road.' He was repatriated to England two days later. This was the point (at Blandford Camp) that his RNVR commission was substituted for his Marines commission, and his secondment to 6th Division formalised. His experiments with crocodiles are (likely) immortalised under the name of Nolan in a fictional account of Second-Lieutenant Ralph Hale Mottram: 'He had produced an apparatus called "Nolan's Armadillo" – a flat plank on little wheels, actuated by clockwork, which was supposed to travel across No Man's Land until the trigger on its back caught in the Boche wire and ignited the charge.'[155] Such was the triumph of hope over the actual state of No Man's Land. Smith was subsequently awarded the DSO for his actions:

> For excellent work on the nights of the 13th-14th and 14th-15th March 1916, in connection with enterprises against the enemy's trenches south of Verlorenhoek. This officer on two successive nights went forward to the enemy's wire, superintended the laying of torpedoes and blew gaps in the enemy's wire. His conduct and gallantry were conspicuous on both occasions.[156]

On the first of these March nights, a strong patrol of two officers and 23 ORs of 11th Essex and two officers and 54 other ranks of 2nd Durham Light Infantry attempted 'to effect a footing' in the enemy trenches beyond Verlorenhoek mound. The DLI were delayed and had to abandon the attempt, but Smith blew a gap of about 15 feet in the enemy's wire with his torpedoes. The DLI returned the following night, protected by a barrage on the enemy's communication trenches, Smith preceding them with more torpedoes. Unfortunately, in the dark, the party could not find the hole blown, but got into the German trenches all the same, spending 6-7 minutes there, taking a prisoner, and returning with two wounded raiders. General Bridgford noted of Smith that he conducted 'excellent work … it was no fault of his that the gaps so made were not utilised.'[157]

His father recorded how 'he came home to England to receive his decoration from the King in early June 1916 and returned about the 7th June.'[158] Two days later he

154 War Diary, HQ 6th Infantry Division, 1 June 1916, TNA WO95/1581.
155 R.H. Mottram, *Ten Years Ago*, p. 93, quoted in C. Taylor, 'One Man and his Car (and Dog).'
156 *London Gazette*, 7 April 1916, p. 3691.
157 War Diary, HQ 6th Infantry Division, 'Report on Enterprise by Party of 2nd Durham Lt. Infantry, Night 14/15th March' 1916, TNA WO95/1614.
158 *The VC & DSO Book, Vol. 3 1916-1923*, p.342.

would be dead. At 21.00 on 9 June Smith, with two other officers and 23 ORs left their trench and headed for the Canadian Dugouts near Mouse Trap Farm. They were challenged by an enemy sentry and Smith ordered the firing of rifle grenades. After examining the (empty) dugouts they withdrew but were subject to rifle and grenade fire and were followed. Smith shot one of the pursuers with his revolver, but by the time the party had brought their eight wounded back, Smith and another OR were missing. Private Brooman reported that a bomb fell between Smith and Private Porter, and that he believed both were killed.[159] Three search parties failed to find them.[160] William Ironside wrote in a letter dated 9 April 1916: 'I can assure you that he has earned his distinction several times over. Always jolly, he was welcomed by everybody. The dangerous work which he was daily carrying out with explosives was just suited to his temperament. I used to tell him that I should have to chain him down.'[161] After Smith's death an undignified squabble took place over his car. The first car he had taken to France was borrowed, and he had replaced this with his own Straker-Squire. This had become worn out, and he was provided a third vehicle. The Admiralty reneged on an initial agreement on delapidations and repairs, but Smith's Straker-Squire was eventually repaired in 1917. He also left a black spaniel dog which eight months after his death was in the care of the Transport Officer of 2nd York & Lancaster.[162] The image of Smith bowling along the roads to the west of Ypres in the open-top Straker-Squire with the black spaniel sitting in the passenger seat is a delightful representation of a lost era. The man represents the spirit of enterprise that was required in development of the new warfare.

Engineering in the Salient

The Royal Engineers, on moving into the Ypres Salient, had to attend to domestic matters such as water supply and hutting. On 17 July 1915 the CRE, Colonel Geoffrey Kemp, attended a demonstration of the 'Schneider Crocodile', or (as it was designed by the French), the 'Torpille Terrestre.'[163] It was a mechanised device for carrying a 40-kilogramme charge under enemy wire. Kemp did not record his thoughts, but unsurprisingly given the damaged terrain of the Western Front, its operational trials were lacklustre. 'Nolan's Armadillo' no doubt met the same fate. Less lacklustre was the performance of the field companies in the Hooge operations, the wiring of the

159 Officers' Services, Lieutenant C.A. Smith, TNA WO 9339/78698.
160 War Diary, 9th Battalion Norfolk Regiment, 9 June 1916, TNA WO95/1623.
161 *The VC & DSO Book, Vol. 3,* p.342.
162 Officers' Services, Lieutenant C.A. Smith, TNA WO 9339/78698.
163 Geoffrey Chicheley Kemp, commissioned into the Royal Engineers in 1886, was a soldier of ability. He was promoted to the command of 128 Infantry Brigade in August 1915, a post which he only left in April 1917 due to sickness. He then commanded 12 Brigade from July 1917 until wounding in March 1918.

positions having been the subject of 'specially prepared drill.'[164] Kemp issued his own observations on the deployment of the Engineers in the attack, which were circulated around brigades. Two RE officers were wounded, two were missing, with 37 sappers wounded, 11 killed, and 14 missing. For the demonstration to coincide with the opening of the Battle of Loos, the divisional Engineers manufactured 670 smoke bombs in 18-pounder cartridge cases.[165] This was so successful that they were requested to manufacture 20,000 such bombs for use by II Corps. Whilst the onset of winter brought attention on mundane matters such as drainage schemes and hutment, in December they attended a demonstration of an Inglis Bridge.[166] A tool that would come into its own in the Hundred Days advance of 1918, it is another reminder that the war was forcing technological development. Otherwise, engineering in the Salient proved dull, and the movement in and out of different parts of the line meant that the closer connections with the work of the Tunnelling Companies that had been achieved in the more static Armentières sector was not so intimate. Indeed, the geological nature of the northern part of the Salient meant that no mining operations were carried out north of the Hooge area, where 6th Division spent most of their time.

Conclusion

6th Division furthered its learning process in the Salient. The first carefully planned, but very minor operation at l'Epinette, at a brigade level involving infantry, artillery and engineers, was replicated in even more meticulous detail at Hooge at divisional level. The second operation involved much more complex and sophisticated artillery arrangements, which represented tactical advance. More of the elements of the 'complete orchestra of war' had had to become involved in the planning, specifically engineering and medical services. And in the small 'Willow Walk' operation, the Royal Flying Corps had been used in photographic reconnaissance for artillery planning. The elements of the 'weapons system' were demonstrably beginning to work in closer harmony. Gaining experience, however, came at cost. Marden states that 6th Division suffered 'nearly 11,000' casualties in that blighted area which would be

164 War Diary, Commander Royal Engineers 6th Division, 9 August 1915, TNA WO95/1594.

165 War Diary, Commander Royal Engineers 6th Division, 24 September 1915, TNA WO95/1594.

166 The Inglis Portable Military Bridge - Light Type was designed in 1913 by Charles Inglis whilst he was a lecturer at Cambridge University. On the outbreak of war he was accepted for a commission in the Royal Engineers. The Light Type, which was undoubtedly the version inspected by 6th Division, was principally intended as a footbridge with a central gangway supported by transoms within the triangular structure. Because of the triangular shape of the structure it was found generally unsuitable for transport. This led to Inglis designing the Inglis Bridge Mark 1 which was rectangular in cross section and had pierced RSJ's for overhead bracing whilst still retaining the tubular construction of the original bridge. This was used to good effect in the advances of the Hundred Days.

forever immortalised in the history of the British Army.[167] On 29 July, 6th Division commenced its withdrawal from the line in the Salient. They were now bound for another cradle of slaughter, legend and learning – the Somme.

167 Marden, op. cit. p. 20. The sum of those reported by the infantry brigades totalled 10,021.

4

'The World Grew Mad': The Somme September-October 1916

'Before the world grew mad, the Somme was a placid steam of Picardy', wrote Arthur Gristwood in 1927.[1] The great offensive of 1916, due north of that serene waterway, so strategically ill-conceived as a breakthrough battle, yet so grimly effective as a great attritional battle, had opened on 1 July. The artillery barrage, spread over 20 miles of front and stretched in depth to cover both the first and second lines of the German defences, failed in its destructive intent, and had given insufficient attention to counterbattery fire. Ambition outstripped tactical reality. Yet there had been success in the southern part of the battlefield. In the period 2-13 July, 86 battalions of Fourth Army launched a further 46 assaults, 'poorly planned and uncoordinated',[2] yet gaining ground, which increased the casualty bill of nearly 57,000 from the first day to some 85,000. 14 July saw the far more successful Battle of the Bazentin Ridge. This attempt to pursue the southern success involved a night attack, with artillery massed on a much more constricted front. A section of the German second line was taken. Yet the reminder of July was spent in a costly and unproductive series of further larger and smaller scale attacks attempting to push the gains made in every direction possible against a stiffening German defence.

The German *2nd Army*, commanded by General von Below,[3] had met the British and French assaults. However the perception that it had given too much ground let to the appointment of Fritz von Lossberg as Chief of Staff on 2 July,[4] and Lossberg

1 A.D. Gristwood, *The Somme*, p.27. Gristwood served with the London Rifle Brigade on the Somme.
2 P. Prior & T. Wilson, *The Somme*, pp.127-9.
3 Fritz Theodor Carl von Below (1853-1918) had commanded *XXI Corps* and took over *2nd Army* just prior to the Somme offensive. He was appointed to command *9th Army* in June 1918, but contracted pneumonia, and died just after the Armistice.
4 Regarded as the German's supreme defensive tactician, Friedrich Karl 'Fritz' von Lossberg (1868–1942) had become a staff officer in 1911, and after serving as chief of staff to *XIII Corps*, was transferred to *OHL* in early 1915, serving thereafter as chief of staff to *3rd*, *2nd*, *6th* and *4th Armies*.

would essentially conduct the rest of the battle. Whilst ordering defenders not to cede ground, he began to develop a more mobile defence in depth. The front line was to be held lightly, with defenders moving forward into shell holes as soon as a bombardment began. Enemy penetrations would be driven back by counter-attacks supported by well-positioned artillery, and counter-attack divisions were stationed behind the front. On 19 July *1st Army* was reformed from the right wing of the *2nd*, and General von Gallwitz[5] took command of the reduced *2nd Army* that 6th Division would mount its attacks against. Despite the new tactics, which came slowly into effect, the enemy, who fought tenaciously, was progressively exhausted as the battle developed.

Prelude on the Ancre

6th Division had been within the newly formed XIV Corps since 4 February 1916, and this formation took over the Beaumont Hamel front on 30 July. The division's translation to the Somme was complete by 6 August and it entered the line on the 7th, from the River Ancre northwards to just south of the Hawthorn Ridge. By the 15th a front of 4,000 yards was being held. Extensive preparations were made for an attack to be made by the division in conjunction with 49th Division operations south of the Ancre. This was postponed, however, taking place (unsuccessfully), on 3 September. The division's attempts to sap the line forward to facilitate the assault proved impossible, but advanced brigade and battalion HQs, dressing stations and dumps were constructed. General Ross's three pages of notes on the planned operation show both an emphasis on preparation and tactical grasp balanced by 'bite-and-hold' caution.[6] The division was relieved on 27 August, and after a brief period of training went south into the new area of XIV Corps, taken over on 16/17 August, and inserted into the line Leuze Wood to Ginchy on the night of 11/12 September. On 26 August, the intelligence branch of the German supreme command (*OHL*) assessed the combat worthiness of 6th Division as 'good.'[7] This assessment would now be put to the test.

The Quadrilateral, Ginchy

August 1916 in the south of the Somme battlefield had been a bloody and frustrating month. Whilst no progress could be made to the east against High Wood and the Switch Line, the ANZAC Corps ground its way north towards Mouquet Farm approaching the Thiepval fortress from an alternative direction to that attempted on 1 July. In a month where no major coordinated offensive action would take place, Sir

5 Max Karl Wilhelm von Gallwitz (1852-1937) had commanded the *Guards Reserve Corps*, the *12th and 11th Armies* on the Eastern front, and the *2nd and 5th Armies* on the Western Front.

6 War Diary, HQ 6th Infantry Division, '6th Division Tactical Scheme', G/85/2 August 1916, WO95/1582.

7 Crown Prince Rupprecht of Bavaria, *Mein Kriegstagbuch*, *Vol. III*, pp. 90-1.

Douglas Haig urged his army commanders to pursue operations that would further the 'wearing-out battle' whilst a major offensive in September was prepared. On the right of Fourth Army, Haig referred on the 11 August to the 'main effort … to capture Guillemont and Ginchy and assist the French to come up into line.' In fact, it was more that the French advance necessitated the British to push forward 'to overrun the German positions that threatened the French left flank in any projected joint advance.'[8] The taking of the spur of ground above Combles was deemed necessary to achieve a good starting position for the mid-September offensive. This involved breaching the German second line at Guillemont. The village was finally taken on 3 September by 20th Division, but Ginchy, 500 yards to the north-east, did not fall. Six days later, the 16th Irish Division took Ginchy, and the 56th Division secured Leuze Wood, 1,000 yards to the south-east. The spur, however, was not reached.

At the end of this last action the German position beyond Ginchy and Leuze Wood represented a salient. (See Map 6 in colour section). Thomas Marden summed up the geographical situation concisely. 'The Germans were holding very strongly the high ground which lies in the form of a horseshoe.' This ground was the spur whose capture was desired, a feature 'which dominates the country for some distance to the south.' Whilst Marden's use of the phrase 'high ground' perhaps seems over-complimentary to the position to the modern eye, these matters are relative. The ground certainly gave observational advantage and prevented British observation of what was beyond. The enemy trenches roughly followed the shape of the spur, but along the bowed base of the salient i.e. 'the back end of the horseshoe', lay a further trench line, on the north-east end of which reposed the Quadrilateral (*Sydow Hohe*), some 1,000 yards to the east of Ginchy. This was 'a four-sided trench in the form of a parallelogram of some 300 yards by 150 yards.'[9] Unfortunately for the British, the ground at the back of the horseshoe fell away into a ravine, and the Quadrilateral could not be directly observed. A railway ran from Guillemont north-east to pass through the corner of the Quadrilateral.

Taking over the line on the night of 11/12 September 6th Division were ordered, according to Marden, to straighten the line by capturing the enemy trenches on the 13th. Not only did 6th Division have no knowledge of the ground, neither did anyone else. Marden observes that 'the situation within the horseshoe was undefined, and the exact positions of the Quadrilateral and other trenches were not known, owing to the bad flying weather.' Aerial photographs appear to have been taken on the 12th but were clearly not available to the division. The map in 71 Brigade's war diary barely warrants description as a rough sketch, and that in 16 Brigade's war diary dates from air photographs taken on the 15th (i.e. the day of the major offensive itself), and later reconnaissance on the ground. Marden added grimly, 'even our own positions were

8 P. Hart, *The Somme*, p. 328.
9 T. O. Marden, *A Short History of the Sixth Division*, p.20.

The defences at the 'horseshoe' and the Quadrilateral, Ginchy, September 1916.

in doubt.'[10] Thus, even the map based on the photographs of 15 September notes that the positions of the forward 56th Division trenches were uncertain, and that certain German positions were also 'doubtful.' The auguries for the attack on the 13th were poor.

In fact, the division was not initially asked to capture the Quadrilateral. Rather, the orders as issued by the division (which mirror those issued by XIV Corps) state that the final objective was a line joining with the Guards Division at Ginchy Telegraph, about half-way between Ginchy and the Quadrilateral, and across to 16 Brigade in an advanced trench north of Leuze Wood.[11] This involved occupying most of the raised horseshoe of ground. In the assault of 71 Brigade, 2nd Sherwood Foresters were to attack north of the railway and 9th Suffolk to the south, with 8th Bedfordshire bombing up a trench from Leuze Wood. The enemy was represented by the *5th Bavarian Division*. This, 'although not among the best Bavarian divisions ... was a good combat unit.'[12] The German division had taken over the trenches on the same night as 6th Division, with the *7th* and *21st Bavarians* (and the *161st Regiment, 185th Division*) around the Quadrilateral. At Zero there would be a three-minute shrapnel barrage on the enemy's forward positions, with the infantry advancing to rush them at Zero +3 when the barrage would lift 100 yards and 'roll forward at the rate of 50 yards per minute.' The orders have, added in pencil to the typed document, a note that the barrage would halt on the road running from Ginchy to Leuze Wood, and that the infantry would consolidate this line.[13] This barrage halt certainly involved overrunning the enemy forward positions as a sketch map in the divisional war diary indicates, referring to 'orders to clear up the space in the horseshoe.'[14] The road on which orders indicated that the barrage would halt, however, was short of the Quadrilateral and was not even the final objective. The *Official History* states that 'patrols had discovered no live Germans in the trenches immediately south-east of Ginchy',[15] but this is not mentioned in contemporary accounts and was certainly not the situation encountered on the ground by the attacking battalions.

The 2nd Sherwood Foresters made their attack at 06.00 on the 13th. After much confusion it appeared that B & C companies had advanced about 500 yards. 9th Suffolk attacked at 06.20 with three companies and the war diary records that the first two lines of enemy trenches were captured, the regimental history referring to the outpost

10 Marden, op. cit. p.21.
11 War Diary, HQ 6th Infantry Division, Operation Order No. 83 12 September 1916, TNA WO95/1582.
12 *Histories of Two Hundred and Fifty-One Divisions of the German Army which Participated in the war (1914-1918)*, p. 122. It comprised Bavarian Regiments Nos. 7, 14, 19 & 21.
13 War Diary, HQ 71 Infantry Brigade, Operation Order No. 85 12 September 1916, TNA WO95/1612.
14 War Diary, HQ 6th Infantry Division, 12 September 1916, TNA WO95/1582.
15 W. Miles, *Military Operations France and Belgium 1916, Vol. 2*, p. 277.

line being breached 'quite easily.'[16] (If they did indeed attack at 06.20, as their war diary indicates, the barrage would have lifted 20 minutes earlier and they would have been bereft of its benefit). Beyond this were 400 yards of open ground to the enemy wire, dominated by artillery fire and the machine guns of the Quadrilateral, which caused heavy casualties. The attack ground to a halt. At 16.15 orders were received by the Sherwood Foresters to attack again at 18.00. The artillery orders issued for the second attack, after an hour's barrage before the new Zero, now refer to attacking the Quadrilateral, a rolling barrage finishing well beyond the Quadrilateral.[17] 71 Brigade's orders give a trench map reference which corresponds to the Quadrilateral, specifying that the entirety of both battalions should renew the attack. It is curious, therefore, that the division's operational report states that: 'On the afternoon of the 13th, the Division was ordered not to attack the QUADRILATERAL before the 15th, when the general advance was to take place.'[18]

Time did not allow the Sherwoods to deploy both support companies that evening, and hence the depleted companies of the morning attack were detailed to repeat their efforts with the assistance of D Company. B and C did not, however, receive their orders and the attack was made by D Company alone, who advanced to meet uncut wire and heavy machine gun fire yet again – 'very few got back.' Three officers were killed, six wounded and 'casualties other ranks – about 50%.'[19] The war diary of 9th Suffolk describes a further attack made at 19.30 by A Company on the Quadrilateral which could not be reached – why the timings between the two battalions were not synchronized is unclear. Two officers were killed and ten wounded, whilst there were 15 OR fatalities with 185 wounded.[20] That nothing would go right that day extended to 71st Trench Mortar Battery. They had assigned two Stokes guns to each of the attacking battalions and joined in the preliminary bombardment in the early morning attack, delivering rapid fire at Zero for three minutes, then proceeding with the ammunition carrying wave. They had organised carrying parties for shells within each battalion, but these failed to turn up. The Stokes guns advanced but 'without shells and having suffered heavy casualties, took no further part.'[21]

The *Official History* lists 'a total loss of 21 officers and 500 other ranks in these gallant but unfortunate affairs.'[22] The whole episode demonstrates the problems generated by

16 C.C.R. Murphy, *The History of the Suffolk Regiment 1914-1927*, p. 195.
17 War Diary, CRA Royal Artillery 6th Division, Centre Divisional Artilleries, XIV Corps Operation Order No. 2, 13 September 1916. TNA WO95/1589. The daily war diary for the month does not remain.
18 War Diary, HQ 6th Infantry Division, 'Operations of the 6th Division between the 12-18th September 1916, at the Quadrilateral', TNA WO95/1582.
19 War Diary, 2nd Battalion Sherwood Foresters, 13 September 1916, TNA WO95/1624.
20 War Diary, 9th Battalion Suffolk Regiment, 13 September 1916, TNA WO95/1625. Murphy, op. cit. p.195.
21 War Diary, HQ 71 Infantry Brigade, 'Report on 71st TM Battery' 17 September 1916, TNA WO95/1619.
22 Miles, op. cit. p.278.

orders issued at short notice, to attack ground which had not been reconnoitered, and over which the dispositions and defences of both enemy and friendly forces were not clear. All the experience of Congreve's carefully planned attack at Hooge was dispensed with in the urgency of the moment. 71 Brigade's hastily issued orders with pencil clarifications for the first attack were contradictory in terms of final objective and termination of barrage. The orders for the second attack indicated a different, more distant, and stronger objective (the Quadrilateral) to be achieved through uncut wire, an assault which was undeliverable in appropriate strength. Further, the gunners had not played their part effectively, Marden noting that the 'artillery cooperation was weak.'[23] Whilst some responsibility for confusion lay with 6th Division and 71 Brigade, the real problem lay with the pressure of the deadline for the upcoming major attack of 15 September, generated downwards from GHQ to Fourth Army to XIV Corps. During the Somme offensive, Fourth Army had also proved over-fond of 'line straightening' operations, of which this was essentially one. The casualty bills for these minor operations, it might be thought, were out of balance from the human standpoint with the tactical value of ensuring the shortest line to assault from and a straight line from which to commence an artillery barrage. Somme operations up to this time had also been marred by mounting a swift second attack, if the first had failed, generally with a weaker force (and often the same one) that had made the initial failed attack. 6th Division was drawn into exactly this pattern on the 13th, and their experiences absolutely echoed Sir Douglas Haig's observation after the attacks on Guillemont that 'something is wanting in the methods employed.'[24]

The attack of 15 September, which would become known as the Battle of Flers-Courcelette, had its conceptual origin on 19 August, and had been the subject of planning since the start of September. Detailed orders were issued on the 11th, as 6th Division came into the line. The main thrust of the attack would take place further north towards Flers, where it was hoped that three lines of enemy positions would be taken (the third of which could not be reached by British artillery, however), and breakthrough achieved. The aims on the XIV Corps front were marginally more modest. On the right, the first objective involved taking the forward slopes of the high ground north-west of Combles, an advance of about 600 yards on the 6th Division front. The corps would hold a defensive flank, 56th Division taking Bouleaux Wood on 6th Division's right, whilst the French advanced to their south, Combles being pinched out. The advance would continue in a north-easterly direction, the second objective being the German second position. The final objective for XIV Corps (6th and Guards Divisions) would involve the capture of Morval and Lesboeufs. 71 Brigade, on the division's left, would take the southerly portion of Lesboeufs, 16 Brigade occupying Morval.

23 Marden, op. cit. p.21.
24 GHQ to Fourth Army (OAD 123), 24 August 1916, IWM Docs 29537, Fourth Army Papers, Vol. 5.

The attacks of 6th Division 13 & 15 September 1916, as seen from the front of the Quadrilateral. The attacking brigades were pinned down midway across the picture.

6th Division's operation orders for the attack cover five pages.[25] The bombardment by heavy artillery had already begun by the time 6th Division had made its failed initial attack on the Quadrilateral. Prior and Wilson estimate that the weight of the bombardment, 280 pounds of shell for every yard of German defences, was twice that employed on 1 July, but less than half that for the highly successful bite-and-hold operation on the Bazentin Ridge of 14 July. This was 'not of such an intensity as to ensure the attack a reasonable chance of success.'[26] The bombardment would continue with no escalation of fire before Zero (06.20). A creeping barrage, advancing at the rate of 50 yards per minute, would then be fired. 6th Division, although it had been directed to follow a creeping barrage on the 12th, had yet to attempt this. This barrage in front of the division had a lane of 'about 100 yards width'[27] (some sources say 'about 200 yards'),[28] left open to allow the progress of the battle's novel introduction

25 War Diary, HQ 6th Infantry Division, Operation Order No. 84, 13 September 1916, TNA WO95/1582.
26 R. Prior & T. Wilson, *Command on the Western Front*, p.233.
27 War Diary, HQ 18 Infantry Brigade, 'Employment of Tanks', Appendix C, September 1916, TNA WO95/1614.
28 Marden, op. cit. p.22.

– tanks. For the attack on the second and third objectives there would, however, be no creeping barrage. The divisional artillery came into line only on the night of the 13th/14th and carried out its registration on the 14th. The position from the point of view of guns, however, seemed one of riches. With the artillery of the Guards and 56th Division, 6th Division had 'the equivalent of 2 div(isional) artilleries less one brigade.'[29] However, the failure to 'carry the high ground between Ginchy and Leuze Wood … prevented the moving up of guns to within effective range for wire cutting' in front of the second objective.[30] Weight of guns would not, in the final analysis, compensate for lack of accuracy.

Three tanks were allotted to 6th Division, and of nine assigned to the Guards Division three were to move into 6th Division's area to assist in taking the second and third objectives. The division noted that 'reliance was placed on the three tanks to carry the line of trench in front of the 1st objective', i.e. Straight Trench running north from the Quadrilateral. They would start (proceeding along the train line) at a time that would allow them to reach the first objective five minutes before the infantry. 6th Division's War Diary states that they would arrive at and take the Quadrilateral '25 to 30 minutes in front of the infantry.'[31] These two cited time-frames seem confusing until it is understood that the first objective, the Green Line, lay *beyond* the Quadrilateral. The stationary barrage of heavy and field artillery on the Green Line would lift 'some minutes' before the arrival of the tanks. This estimated time frame did not allow for the inevitable friction of war. Crucially for 6th Division, corps orders stated that 'the line for the Creeping Barrage to start on will … be 100 yards beyond the QUADRILATERAL.' This in effect meant that the division would be attacking this strongpoint without artillery cover. General Ross was able to alter this along the right half of his front, starting the creeper short of the Quadrilateral, but not on the left-hand side. Tanks and infantry would then 'advance together under the creeping barrage.' To add complication, 6th Division had one less objective than the Guards to their left, who had a creeping barrage for the first two objectives, and hence tanks and infantry would be advancing beyond the Green Line again without the protection of a creeper. The tactical role of the tanks was specified, i.e. to 'crush wire and keep down hostile rifle fire and machine gun fire.' In the absence of any experience of tank/infantry cooperation, the infantry were merely instructed to advance at tank pace, '30-50 yards per minute', and 'on no account to wait for them' if they were delayed.[32] 6th Division was not only 'largely dependent' on the tanks to carry the Quadrilateral, but also to destroy the wire in front of the second objective.[33]

29 War Diary, HQ 6th Infantry Division, 15 September 1916, TNA WO95/1582.
30 War Diary, HQ 6th Infantry Division, 15 September 1916, TNA WO95/1582.
31 War Diary, HQ 6th Infantry Division, 15 September 1916, TNA WO95/1582.
32 War Diary, HQ 6th Infantry Division, 'Instructions for the Employment of "Tanks"', 229/17(G) 11 September 1916, TNA WO95/1582.
33 War Diary, HQ 6th Infantry Division, 15 September 1916, TNA WO95/1582.

The news received during the night was therefore alarming. Two of the three tanks had broken down. The tanks allotted to 6th Division were from No. 4 Section C Company, Heavy Section, Machine Gun Corps. One was a male tank, C19 *Clan Leslie*, commanded by Captain Archie Holford-Walker,[34] armed with two 6-pounder guns and three Hotchkiss machine guns. Two were female, armed with four Vickers and one Hotchkiss machine guns. C20 was commanded by Lieutenant George Macpherson,[35] C22 by Lieutenant Basil Henriques.[36] They had started their journey at 17.00 on the 13th, travelling all night, then spent the 14th in maintenance in Chimpanzee Valley just west of Maltz Horn Farm, setting off again at 19.00. Expecting written orders from 6th Division, Holford-Walker had understood he would be using the Quadrilateral as a starting point for the advance on Morval, but learnt at 17.00 on the 14th, by word of mouth and only two hours before departure, that his three machines would have to take the Quadrilateral first.[37] Gunner William Dawson of C20 described how: 'The briefing and instructions regarding objectives were quite inadequate and there was little or no cooperation between the infantry and the tanks.'[38] It had been left to Brigadier-General Osborn of 16 Brigade 'to issue the orders for attack. In answer to my protests that I could not make a plan of any worth. I was told to get on with it as GHQ had issued orders for the tanks to move in this way.'[39] Setting off towards the action, Macpherson's C20 broke down twice with engine trouble, and was abandoned. Holford-Walker's *Clan Leslie*, descending a steep slope, broke its tail, namely the stub axle or hydraulic stabilizer. Believing that this was essential to steering (it was not), Holford-Walker dropped out as well. C22 proceeded alone to reach the front line at 05.45.[40] In response to these mechanical failures, one tank was directed from 56th Division's area to assist with the wire on the second objective, but this would obviously only be of help if 6th Division got that far. The *Official History* states that Major-General Ross, on learning the ill news of the breakdowns, requested that the tank lane in the barrage be closed. XIV Corps allegedly agreed, and issued appropriate orders,

34 The son of Brigadier-General Edgar Holford-Walker, Archie had been commissioned into the 3rd Shropshire Light Infantry in September 1914. Archies' brother, Major Allen Holford-Walker, had overseen tank training at Bisley and Elveden, commanding C Company. On 26 July 1916, King George V inspected the tanks at Elveden and rode in the tank commanded by Archie. At his request, the driver allegedly gave the King a bumpy ride.

35 Born in 1896, George Mcpherson attended Winchester College, and had been commissioned in the Buffs.

36 Sir Basil Lucas Quixano 'The Gaffer' Henriques (1890-1961) was the son of a wealthy Manchester merchant, and educated at Harrow and University College, Oxford. He devoted his life to working with Jewish youth in the East End of London.

37 C. Hardy, 'Rewriting History – An Alternative Account of the Death of Lieutenant George Macpherson', pp. 30-2.

38 Gunner W. Dawson, quoted in Hart, op. cit. p. 403.

39 W.L. Osborn to Official Historian, 28 January 1936, TNA CAB45/136.

40 D. Fletcher, 'The First Tank Action in History.'

but the commander of 6th Division's artillery seemingly did not act upon them, if he received them.[41] C22 started on time and advanced up the north-west side of the railway line, reaching the enemy front line. The *21st Bavarian Regiment* reported three machines, only one of which went into action. (In fact Macpherson had got his tank going and, with another tank commanded by Second-Lieutenant Thomas Murphy which had broken down supporting the Guards Division, advanced for a further attack at 13.30. This was cancelled but both machines came under fire).[42] They were thought at first by the enemy 'to be ambulances of some kind, on account of the red and white crosses painted on them.'[43] Henriques in C22 'immediately opened fire with his machine guns enfilading the German trench on either side',[44] but met heavy fire. All the machine's periscopes were broken and it was pierced by bullets. Henriques had glass in his eyes, the driver was wounded, and he could see two of his gunners (who claimed to have shot 30 or 40 of the enemy) on the floor and believed them dead.[45] Henriques, who later described his crew as in a 'blue funk',[46] retired through the advancing infantry, having discovered, much to his surprise, that his machine was not bulletproof. 'How we got back, I shall never understand. We dodged shells from the artillery, and it was just a preserving hand which saved us.' He concluded: 'The way we got over the ground was marvellous; every moment we were going to stick, but we didn't.' No preserving hand would save the infantry. Henriques described, sadly, how 'the sight of thousands of men dying, and wounded was ghastly. I hate to think of it all.'[47] Despite his efforts, the division concluded in disgust: 'The three tanks might have sufficed to carry the position. The one tank interfered with the arrangements for the artillery barrage (and) drew attention to our attack and a heavy fire on the infantry.'[48]

Although the *21st Bavarian Regiment* described the British as 'cool and determined lads' they 'responded with fury – our machine guns with prolonged bursts of fire and our troops by rapid rife fire … the ground was covered with hundreds of dead or badly wounded British.'[49] 'By 9 a.m. it was apparent that the 6 Div(ision) attack had failed', the division recorded dismally.[50] 16 Brigade had assaulted the Quadrilateral from the south. 8th Bedfordshire attacked both across the open and up a trench

41 Miles, op. cit. pp. 309-10. The war diary for CRA 6th Division for September is, interestingly, missing.
42 Hardy, op. cit. Macpherson died later that day. Debate has lasted on whether he committed suicide, fearing being accused of cowardice, or was struck by shrapnel.
43 C. Duffy, *Through German Eyes: The British and the Somme 1916*, p.228.
44 War Diary, 1st Battalion Leicestershire Regiment, 15 September 1916, TNA95/1621. This was Straight Trench.
45 Fletcher, op. cit.
46 Hardy, op. cit.
47 Quoted in L.L. Loewe, *Basil Henriques*, p.44.
48 War Diary, HQ 6th Infantry Division, 15 September 1916, TNA WO95/1582.
49 Cited in Duffy, op. cit., pp. 228-9.
50 War Diary, HQ 6th Infantry Division, 15 September 1916, TNA WO95/1582.

running south-east from the Quadrilateral with bombers. The barrage, which opened at 06.20, unfortunately fell short upon the three companies drawn up in shell holes, causing many casualties. The Quadrilateral, according to the unit, 'was not heavily shelled previous to the attack', the wire was uncut, and the enemy's machine guns were unsuppressed. The execution they wrought resulted in five officers killed and six wounded, with 53 ORs killed, 143 wounded and 97 missing. 1st Buffs advanced at 06.35, but intense machine gun fire similarly made progress impossible and as many as could, who were not trapped in shell holes in front of the enemy position, occupied the Bedfords' original front trench. About 40 Buffs, 100 Bedfords and 2-300 men of the 2nd York & Lancasters, who had followed the Buffs, gathered there. Second-Lieutenant Malcolm Hills of the Buffs was trapped 200 yards from the enemy line with 12 men.[51] He sent a message back concerning the inadequacy of the artillery fire: 'Our shells fell 1st right beyond German line, 2nd just short, 3rd very short. People in valley on left have just returned on account of our shell fire.' His battalion suffered the heaviest casualties of the brigade that day – four officers and 53 ORs were killed, four officers and 58 ORs were missing, whilst three officers and 183 ORs were wounded. Brigadier-General Osborn put forward a proposal to division at 10.25 for a second attack, likely somewhat out of touch with how thoroughly his units were pinned down. He was instructed to make his own arrangements for artillery support. The York & Lancasters were ordered to attack again at 13.30, seemingly without any advice on what artillery preparation would be made – whether Osborn had made progress in his lonely quest for support from the artillery is not clear. The battalion's (correct) response was to ask for exactly this. The attack, mercifully, was then postponed, as it was clearly realised that more time was needed for a proper bombardment. The casualties in the York & Lancasters totalled two officers wounded, with 18 ORs killed, 106 wounded, and six missing.

The 71 Brigade assaulted from the north-west with 1st Leicestershire and 9th Norfolk, passing through 9th Suffolk and 2nd Sherwood Foresters. Private Dennis Douglas of 9th Norfolk described the forming up at 01.00. 'Eventually we made it to the line of trenches held by the Suffolks. The chaos was total and it took our senior officers an age to get some sort of order. At 5.50am a strange mechanical thing ground its way through our line. Like some mobile pill box.'[52] Manifestly, Douglas's preparation for battle included no concept of advancing with this machine. The *Official History* states that the Norfolks, on the brigade right, suffered as this lone tank, that of Henriques, 'by mistake, opened fire on the waiting troops.' Captain Arthur Crosse allegedly 'approached the tank under heavy fire and pointed out its

51 Malcolm Arthur Hills, commissioned in August 1915, would be killed on 15 September 1916.

52 Diary of Private D. Douglas, http://www.cawstonheritage.co.uk/files/original/09c26d6a35353a850a2864d82550fb95.pdf (accessed 21 April 2018).

true direction.'[53] The regimental history does not mention this, nor does the unit war diary or the account of Private Douglas. Basil Henriques did not. Neither General Osborn, who was exceeding fed up with the tanks that day, or 16 Brigade mentioned such an incident. There is thus grounds for considerable scepticism that this in fact occurred. The Norfolks 'advanced up the glacis-like slope with insufficient artillery support', the latter due to the tank lane left in the barrage.[54] Marden states that this lane 'unfortunately coincided with the strongest point of the Quadrilateral', adding that by the time the infantry advanced, the barrage had 'passed over the German trenches.'[55] Private Douglas set off into unsuppressed fire: 'My heart was pounding fit to burst, and I was feeling light headed. I ... just kept heading forward in a low, stumbling stoop. All around me was the whizzing of bullets and the crash of shell fire. The churned-up earth felt more like a porridge mixture.' He caught sight of his brother George 'in a group of men being led by Major Bradshaw. As I tried to reach them, I felt a sting in my right leg and was spun round and fell to the ground. For a moment I looked up into the sky and wondered if this was my lot.' Douglas believed that 'I must have passed out, as the next thing I remember, two privates from the Suffolks were dragging me towards their trench.[56] The front line of the advance found the wire in front of them uncut, and the party of 40 survivors spotted by Dennis Douglas dug in in front of it (Lieutenant-Colonel Frederick Bradshaw being wounded),[57] the remainder being scattered in shell holes back to the start line. The Norfolks' casualties totalled an appalling 431 ORs, with five officers killed and 12 wounded.

The 1st Leicestershire advanced in mist and smoke which was 'terribly thick.' Although the enemy counter barrage fell behind them, after taking some outposts easily, the battalion suffered 'very heavily' from machine gun fire, similarly encountering uncut wire in front of the Quadrilateral, which the unit war diary curiously refers to as 'a strong point hitherto unknown.' The regimental history repeats this assertion. Given that 71 Brigade had been involved in the attack of the 12th, not to have briefed the Leicesters properly (if that was the case) would have been a gross error. Like the Norfolks, the battalion dug in. Six officers had been killed, whilst seven were wounded. 108 ORs were fatalities, whilst 221 had been wounded and 32 missing. The Suffolks and Sherwood Foresters, who had been leapfrogged, moved up in support. They met the same fate. 9th Suffolk lost four officers (including the

53 Miles, op. cit. p.310. Arthur John Green Crosse, son of the vicar of Hickling, Norfolk, was commissioned in September 1914. He was awarded the MC and bar. A rubber planter in Malaya after the war he was captured at fall of Singapore in 1942 and put to work by the Japanese on the Burma railway.

54 F.L. Petrie, *The History of the Norfolk Regiment*, p.255.

55 Marden, op. cit. p.22.

56 Douglas, op. cit.

57 Frederick Ewart Bradshaw, a retired Indian Army major, would return in October to command 2nd Sherwood Foresters for a year. George Douglas died that day.

CO, Lieutenant-Colonel Arthur Mack) killed,[58] seven wounded and two missing, whilst 35 ORs were dead, 99 were wounded and 93 missing. 2nd Sherwood Foresters advanced until they saw the helmets of the 1st Leicesters stalled 150 yards in front and entrenched as well. Lieutenant-Colonel Charles Hobbs went forward to find the Leicesters' CO, Reginald Gillespie,[59] who declined help, which would clearly have been futile.[60] Two officers of the Sherwoods had been killed and five wounded (including Colonel Hobbs, who remained at duty), with probably around 200 OR casualties.[61]

It is possible to contrast the infantry tactics in terms of formation for attack used by several battalions that day. Sir Henry Rawlinson's Army had issued 'Fourth Army Tactical Notes' in May 1916, prior to the division's arrival on the Somme.[62] In the four days of training at the start of September, the division would most likely have considered these, and their method of attack on the 15th certainly suggests so. The September training, however, was largely to do with breakthrough. In 16 Brigade, whilst General Osborn and Captain Denison-Pender, his brigade-major, went to see 'experiments with "TANKS"',[63] (no other brigades mentioning this), and there was basic training with the bayonet and on the rifle range, the main excitement concerned live exercises in contact with aeroplanes (mentioned by 16 and 18 Brigades) and practice 'attacking over 1½ miles and forming a defensive flank.'[64] From the point of view of formation for assault, depth of attack and control were seen as the key issues. SS109, *Training of Divisions for Offensive Action*, also issued in May 1916, stated: 'It is impossible to lay down any definite rules as to the strength of assaulting columns, the number of lines of which they consist, or the distance apart of these lines.' Fourth Army's 'Notes' did just this, however. A two company, two platoon front with two platoons as a second line, followed by the remaining two companies; or a four-company front in four successive lines of platoons were regarded as 'probably the best two formations.' In case of multiple lines of resistance, four successive platoon lines per company on a two-company front were recommended or a one company,

58 Arthur Paston Mack had retired as a captain of the Suffolk Militia in 1886, and after exploring the Egyptian desert and working as a liquidator in London, had been commissioned at the age of 51 in September 1914. He had commanded the battalion from 14 May 1916.
59 Lieutenant-Colonel Reginald Henry Gillespie had been a Regular captain of the Leicestershire Regiment in August 1914. He would command the battalion until July 1917.
60 Charles James Willoughby Hobbs was a captain with 2nd Sherwood Foresters in August 1914.
61 2nd Sherwood Foresters listed their casualties up to 19 September as five officers killed and 12 wounded, with 421 OR casualties, a good two-thirds of the unit's strength.
62 Anon. *Military Operations France and Belgium, 1916 – Appendices*, Appendix 18, p.131.
63 War Diary, HQ 16 Infantry Brigade, 1 September 1916, TNA WO95/1605. These were carried out near St Requier.
64 War Diary, HQ 16 Infantry Brigade, 4 September 1916, TNA WO95/1605.

two-platoon front, there being two lines of platoons, with the remaining three companies following. 'The leading lines should not be more than 100 yards apart', the 'Notes' stated. The division's battalions demonstrated familiarity with these concepts. In 16 Brigade, 2nd York & Lancaster advanced on a two-company front, each company on a two-platoon front, in artillery formation. The distance between the lines was 100 yards, the frontage of each company being 250 yards. Battalion HQ was in the centre of the first line. 1st Buffs attacked on a similar two company/two platoon front, but advanced in waves, one section of the 16th Machine Gun Company with the third wave and battalion HQ in the rear. 8th Bedfordshire attacked in three waves, formed from three companies (one company being employed in a bombing operation). In 71 Brigade, 2nd Sherwood Foresters used the two company/two platoon model in front, two companies on a one platoon front following. 150 yards was maintained between the two sets of companies. 9th Norfolk left no record, whilst 1st Leicesters set down considerable detail. The battalion commander's role in choosing the formation for attack is clear: 'The CO decided to attack' on a two-company front, two to the rear. Two Lewis guns accompanied each company, and two bombing squads of ten men had been formed in each company (although each ranker carried two Mills bombs). The companies advanced 'at a walk' in four lines, the two following companies 300 yards behind. Battalion HQ brought up the rear. When the two leading companies diverged in the mist during the advance, the support companies moved up into the centre, which demonstrated effective command and control. There was thus variability on the Fourth Army suggested model. The attack of 1st Buffs, with Vickers guns in the third wave, went in the face of the recommendation in the 'Notes' that machine guns should be 'kept in hand under the Brigadier', to be sent forward once positions had been prepared. It was assumed Stokes mortars would go forward with the attacking troops and rifles were to be sacrificed for ammunition carrying. The woeful experience of 71st Trench Mortar Battery on the 13th bore testimony to the sagacity of this. 6th Division's infantry demonstrated that they were up to date with current principles – in the event, however, no alternative tactics would have made any difference to the fate of these units that morning.

Why had the taking of the Quadrilateral proved such a problem? The division summarised:

> Owing to the extreme difficulty of observation on the enemy's lines, the dull weather which made it impossible to get air photos, and the short time for reconnaissance and selection of O.P.s, the enemy's trenches were inadequately shelled on the 14th. It was, however, impossible to defer the attack, which was to take place on a wide front and to be executed by several Corps.[65]

65 War Diary, HQ 6th Infantry Division, 'Operations of the 6th Division between the 12th-18th September, 1916, at the Quadrilateral', TNA WO95/1582.

Whilst there is no evidence that the division sought to defer the operation, it was clear its senior officers were convinced that the failure of the artillery had been at the root of the misfortunes of their infantry. The reason for the failure of the artillery to achieve its aims partly lay in topography. This 'centre of resistance' was 'situated close behind the crest of the high ground east of Ginchy [and] was protected by wire which lay in a depression, concealed by grass and weeds.' Observation of fire was nearly impossible from the positions reached, and, as stated, air reconnaissance had not been thorough due to adverse weather. This does not explain the friendly shelling of the attacking troops as they left their front lines, on ground which was well observed. This was simply the result of inaccuracy. There was also a failure of infantry-artillery tactical cooperation resulting at least in part from the expectancy that the tanks would achieve much, and the gap in time before the infantry left their trenches to allow this to be accomplished. This meant that the infantry were advancing when the barrage had departed.

6th Division was indeed conscious of its failure. General Ross ordered 18 Brigade to move up to Ginchy and position itself both north (in the Guards Division area) and south of the Quadrilateral. In doing so, he pre-empted the orders of XIV Corps by one and a half hours. Marden suggests that with reports coming in of the success of the Guards Division in taking Lesboeufs, 'it appeared' to General Ross 'that the prospect of a break-through on a large scale was prejudiced solely by the repulse of the 6th Division.'[66] He gives the impression that it was Ross who ordered the attack of 18 Brigade that evening in an act of *mea culpa*. Whilst Ross may have been planning exactly what took place, it was, in fact, XIV Corps who ordered the evening attack. It was an assault that could, and should, have been postponed, as there was no threat to the stalled progress or the flank of the Guards Division that night. At 15.10 the picture on the front had become clear through aircraft observation. 6th Division was held up by the Quadrilateral and the trench running north from it. On the left, however, although the Guards had advanced more successfully, Morval and Lesboeufs was still strongly held by the enemy.

18 Brigade were ordered to assault at 19.30, after a bombardment commencing at 18.30. 2nd Durham Light Infantry would attack from the north, taking Straight Trench that ran north from the Quadrilateral, 11th Essex from the south, attacking the Quadrilateral itself. 18 Brigade would be the only formation of XIV Corps attacking that evening, and viewed the prospect grimly: 'The attack has very little chance of success as the position and exact situation is most obscure – the ground is new and only the very shortest time is available for reconnaissance work.'[67] But attack they did. 2nd DLI captured about 500 yards of a trench that did not in fact lead to the Quadrilateral, rather being a position that lay 40 to 70 yards in front of the objective, Straight Trench. This did not become clear to division until late the

66 Marden, op. cit. p.23.
67 War Diary, HQ 18 Infantry Brigade, 15 September 1916, TNA WO96/1615.

following morning. The battalion lost four officers killed and six wounded, with 30 OR fatalities, 99 wounded and 34 missing in this futile effort. To the south, the CO of 11th Essex and his officers managed reconnaissance of the ground but as the battalion got into position they were observed by an enemy aircraft and heavily shelled. Two companies were detailed for the attack – two companies where three battalions had failed earlier that day. The division was being forced to clutch at straws. Under machine-gun fire from both front and rear (Bouleaux Wood) the Essex unit lost direction and the assault collapsed. Two officers were killed and two wounded, with about 20 ORs killed and 80 wounded. 6th Division's war diary concluded the day with pathos: 'All did their best in difficult circumstances.'[68]

On the night of 16/17 September 18 Brigade relieved 71 Brigade, and preparations were begun for a fresh assault on the Quadrilateral on the 18th. The line was withdrawn, on the orders of corps, to allow for a bombardment by heavy guns. 14th DLI and 1st West Yorkshire took up positions about 250 yards from the enemy front line. In 16 Brigade, a similar withdrawal was made, and 2nd York & Lancaster and 1st King's Shropshire Light Infantry stationed themselves a comparable distance back. The heavy guns opened at 11.00 on the 17th, 2nd York & Lancaster helping direct their fire and with artillery Forward Observation Officers in a specially dug forward trench in front of 18 Brigade. Although the weather continued unsettled, air observation assisted the bombardment. The onlookers could see that the shooting appeared accurate in the northern area, but only eventually got to grips with the southern portion of the Quadrilateral at 18.00, the bombardment ceasing at 20.00. Meanwhile, General Ross met with the commanders of 16 and 18 Brigades that morning and arranged the details of the attack. Three tanks were made available but, perhaps unsurprisingly, both brigadiers were 'greatly adverse to employing them.'[69] At last, however, proper preparation had been granted to the division.

Zero was at 05.50 on a damp and slippery morning, and 'the guns opened exactly to time.'[70] 1st King's Shropshire Light Infantry attacked with their left on the railway, supported by two Stokes mortars and machine guns, and 2nd York & Lancaster began bombing up the trench leading to the southern end of the Quadrilateral. The Shropshires attacked in three lines, each having an objective, the first line meeting little resistance 'except from machine guns.' Many German dead were encountered, but a party of about 40, armed with a machine gun, held out in the southern corner, becoming sandwiched between the bombers of 2nd York & Lancaster, and those of the third line of Shropshires. They duly surrendered. By 06.15, the Quadrilateral had fallen, and the third line pressed on, bombing dugouts on the sunken road en route to digging in 500 yards beyond, in the direction of the original objective of the 15th,

68 War Diary, HQ 6th Infantry Division, 15 September 1916, TNA WO95/1582.
69 War Diary, HQ 6th Infantry Division, 17 September 1916, TNA WO95/1582. No operation orders have survived for this attack.
70 War Diary, HQ 16 Infantry Brigade, 18 September 1916, TNA WO95/1605.

Lesboeufs and Morval, now some half mile away. Whilst 2nd York & Lancaster had only sustained 18 casualties in the other ranks (seven fatal), 1st KSLI lost eight officers (one killed) with 19 ORs killed, 124 wounded and 14 missing. In the attack of 18 Brigade on the left, 14th Durham Light Infantry assaulted with their right on the railway to enter the northern tip of the Quadrilateral. They advanced 'under heavy artillery creeping and stationary barrage', using rifle grenades against machine gun positions. Progressing beyond, their casualties totalled two officer and 31 OR fatalities, with five officers and 161 ORs wounded, with 32 of the latter missing. 1st West Yorkshire's attack on the left on Straight Trench did not go so well initially, meeting heavy machine gun and rifle fire, and they had to withdraw to their start line. Reorganising, their attack was now successful, carried forward by bombers and a party enveloping the enemy trench to the left and attacking it from the rear, albeit at a cost of three officers and ten ORs killed, and four officers and 93 ORs wounded. Two officers and 38 ORs were missing. Marden concludes: 'This redoubtable strong point was at last captured with comparatively small loss after what must be conceded as a magnificent defence.'[71] The 'comparatively small loss' amounted to 550 men. One hundred and sixty unwounded Germans were captured from the *21st* and *7th Bavarian Regiments*. The *3rd Battalion* of the *21st*, which described how 'a dense row of figures emerged running from the curtain of mist', reported 'a wild and desperate close quarter combat', the battalion losing 175 in killed alone.[72] The defenders responded to the report in *The Times* describing the taking of the Quadrilateral as 'a triumphal storming of a fortress-like stronghold' with contempt:

> It was no fortress at all, this position of the *21st*. In what did it consist? In rifle trenches which were repeatedly ploughed into heaps of rubble … and in shell-holes, where thirsty men with hollow cheeks, blackened with dust, crouched with burning eyes … determined to defend the position entrusted the them with the last breath.[73]

Christopher Duffy agrees that the British exaggerated the defences of the Quadrilateral, which on German trench maps was 'nothing beyond an ordinary trench with a couple of pieces of fragmentary trench behind.' This, however, probably underplays its significance as aerial photographs suggest more to it. However, as Duffy notes, 'the strength of the position derived from the lie of the ground and the front', as it 'was located in an enfilading position and commanded an excellent filed of grazing fire.'[74] The success on the 18th was undoubtedly down to the carefully observed, and hence successful, bombardment of the Quadrilateral for nine hours on the previous day.

71 Marden, op. cit. p.24.
72 Quoted in Duffy, op. cit. p.235.
73 Quoted in Duffy, op. cit. p.235.
74 Duffy, op. cit. p.228.

The wire had now effectively been destroyed, and many of the defenders annihilated. Proper preparation was the key.

Marden stated that the attacks on the Quadrilateral over the five days had cost the division 'upwards of 3,500 casualties', (the infantry casualties as calculated from unit and brigade war diaries total just under 3,200). Either way, the division had, in effect, lost a quarter of its nominal infantry strength. The number of casualties that would pass through the division's Field Ambulances during the Quadrilateral attacks were far greater than that which the division's medical arrangements had previously had to cope with. In the August 1915 attack at Hooge, there had been time for detailed preparation for the reception of casualties. For the first attack on the Quadrilateral on the 13th there was no preparation out of the ordinary, organisational thinking being focussed on the upcoming Flers-Coucelette offensive.

The normal evacuation chain led from the regimental aid posts where each battalion fielded a Medical Officer, orderlies and bearers, to the Field Ambulances. These provided bearer posts but also Main and Advanced Dressing Stations where a casualty could receive further treatment. In the case of the 15th, there was also a Corps Main Dressing Station. Triaged, a casualty would be prepared for evacuation, if necessary, to a Casualty Clearing Station. These might try to stabilise severe injuries which could not be moved on, evacuate others to Base Hospitals, or treat and return men to their units.

The Assistant Director of Medical Services was still Lieutenant-Colonel Bertal Scott. For the attack of the 15th, he held a conference with his Field Ambulances on the 14th, having been in the area five days. 16 Field Ambulance, commanded by Lieutenant-Colonel John Nightingale,[75] had its HQ at Maltz Horn Farm. He was acting as Divisional Collecting Officer and was situated near 16 Brigade HQ. Each brigade had been ordered to form a Brigade Aid Post. The lines of evacuation would be from Guillemont or Leuze Wood through Maltz Horn. The total number of bearers under Nightingale's command that morning, a 'Divisional Bearer Division' having been formed for this attack, were 10 officers, 16 NCOs and 297 privates, the divisional band, salvage company and sanitary section having been mobilised. There were two Aid Posts left and right. The attack having begun at 06.20, at 07.50 the first walking wounded appeared. A reserve of bearers was kept at Maltz Horn, distributed according to need. The horse ambulances were brought up to the same location at noon to shorten carries, and after 16.00 'Ford cars' were also required. Messages kept arriving concerning the weight of casualties, and by 16.50 the Medical Officer of 9th Norfolks, himself wounded, had only two bearers left and 'over 100 wounded still lying out.' The division had gone into action short of three MOs, three were now wounded, and one sick.[76] The slowness of bringing casualties in initially deceived Bertal Scott,

75 John Nightingale was a Territorial officer who prior to the war had been surgeon-major with the 1st West Riding Brigade RFA and had assumed command in April 1916.
76 War Diary, ADMS 6th Division, 15 September 1916, TNA WO95/1592.

who was informed during the afternoon that only 16 officers and 126 ORs had been admitted to the Corps Main Dressing Station at Bronfray Farm, Bray. By 17.00, going up to advanced Divisional HQ, he learnt that the situation was grimmer than this. At 18.35 the left sector aid post had 150 cases lying out, and Captain Scott there required 'every available bearer.' At 20.15 16 Brigade requested bearers to assist the 1st KSLI to clear a trench of wounded for 'tactical reasons.' At that moment, however, Nightingale had none to send. During the evening the DAQMG gave orders for a range of rear echelon units to provide more bearers, but only 70 reported. 'Many of (the) F(ield) A(mbulance) bearers have been working nearly 48 hours with only short rests and require rest and sleep', Scott noted.[77] Operations continued into the night and at 06.45 on the 16th, Captain Scott still required 100 more bearers. Nightingale visited this post himself at 08.30 and found the 'situation not so bad as represented.' Fewer wounded were lying out than he expected, and by late afternoon, most cases had been dealt with.[78] This, of course, did not include the wounded who were unreachable, lying in shell holes before the Quadrilateral. Meanwhile, 17 Field Ambulance, commanded by Major Reginald Collins,[79] had its two sector aid posts in trenches north-east and south-east of Guillemont. Collins was in charge of the Advanced Dressing Station at Dublin Post, near the briqueterie, 500 yards south of Bernafay Wood, and was responsible for evacuation to the Corps Main Dressing Station. The evacuation of stretcher cases was largely undertaken at night, horse ambulances coming up to the quarry on the western edge of Guillemont.[80] 18 Field Ambulance did not record its location, and simply recorded: 'Bearers work continuously all day and night', with 'wounded walking cases being taken to one post, and serious lying cases to Bronfray Farm.'[81] Scott's orders for the 15th, which run to two and a half pages,[82] are much concerned with advancing the medical facilities as the attack progressed. In the event, whilst the chain of evacuation worked, it is clear that the lessons of heavy casualties earlier in the Somme operations (which the division had not, of course, been part of), had not quite been absorbed. Given the very real problem that the attack had failed completely, and the wounded were lying in No Man's Land and not in ground that lay behind advancing troops, the very front end of the operations were undermanned.

77 War Diary, ADMS 6th Division, 16 September 1916, TNA WO95/1592.
78 War Diary, 16 Field Ambulance, 15-16 September 1916, TNA WO95/1602.
79 Reginald Thomas Collins DSO had arrived on the Western Front with the RAMC in August 1914. Educated at Dulwich College and Guy's Hospital, he had been commissioned in the RAMC in 1903. He joined 17 Field Ambulance on 10 September 1916 and would be killed with this unit on 18 September 1918.
80 War Diary, 17 Field Ambulance, 15-16 September 1916, TNA WO95/1602.
81 War Diary, 18 Field Ambulance, 15-16 September 1916, TNA WO95/1603.
82 War Diary, ADMS 6th Division, Operation Order No. 17, 13 September 196, TNA WO95/1592.

The Quadrilateral – Recriminations

The battered 6th Division came out of line with General Ross clearly fuming at his division's ordeal, one he evidently thought was unnecessary. The Earl of Cavan,[83] commanding XIV Corps and a competent soldier, would also have been seething on receipt of Ross's secret memo dated 20 September. Ross started by indicating that he had already gone over Cavan's head in his complaints. On the 15th 'Liaison Officers of the Fourth Army and G.H.Q. came to see me and I told them that our failure was due to inadequate artillery preparation and support', and further, 'that our artillery had on more than one occasion fired on our infantry.' This statement, preceding the bulk of his comments, was undoubtedly a careful tactical move. In terms of the 'certainly ineffectual' artillery preparation, he acknowledged that 'there is every excuse for it' due to observation problems. He had more to say about the 'inadequate' support during the attack. The first objective, the Green Line was, he claimed 'an arbitrary line drawn across country some hundreds of yards behind the enemy's trenches instead of along the enemy's trench itself.' The stationary barrage was therefore put on a line 'where there was probably not one single German', instead of on the front line full of the enemy. This was absolutely true. In the original corps plans for the 15th, the Quadrilateral was to be subject to no artillery fire at all at Zero. The standing barrage would be put down beyond it, and the creeping barrage 'also started beyond the German trenches', and could therefore have no suppressant effect. This was an egregious error in planning. Ross asserted: 'I was not permitted to alter either the objective or the barrages, being told the tanks were to flabbergast the enemy.' On the failure of two, the remaining machine 'merely served to attract the enemy's attention.' He acknowledged: 'I nevertheless did, on my own authority, start a portion of the creeping barrage short of the enemy's trenches' but could do no more for fear of uncovering the Guards Division's right flank. He accepted that episodes of friendly fire 'are bound to occur', but qualified this critically as happening when observation has been poor, i.e. as a result of poor preparation. In this case, he continued, matters were compounded by haste: 'O.P's should be carefully selected' and the artillery 'given every opportunity to register carefully.' The situation was further complicated, Ross went on, by the fact that 'a large portion of our supporting artillery was only brought up into the line on the 14th' and registered hastily. Further, 'the whole Field Artillery supporting the Division appears to have been changed with new Liaison Officers, Group Commanders and F.O.O.s – an ample explanation of the failure of the artillery co-operation.' This, palpably, was down to XIV Corps.

83 Frederick Rudolph Lambart, 10th Earl of Cavan (1865-1946), had commanded 2nd Grenadier Guards, 4th (Guards) Brigade, 50th Division, the Guards Division, and had taken command of XIV Corps in January 1916. In July 1918 David Lloyd-George would 'vet' him as a potential successor to Sir Douglas Haig.

Ross continued angrily: 'The organisation of the artillery was most unsatisfactory from a Divisional Commander's point of view, who appears to have no control even over the Divisional Artillery supporting his Division.' He claimed he could not fulfil 'my obvious duty to co-ordinate the action of the artillery' when part was under the orders of both Guards and 56th Divisions. On the 18th, he had worked out a scheme to take the trench west of Morval, but was told the artillery would rest on the 19th. He gave further example that during the bombardment of the 17th, he had learnt at 16.30 that fire was passing over the enemy trenches. He told the Liaison Officer attached to get the range shortened and continue the bombardment. This officer returned with the information that the bombardment was ordered to cease at 18.00, which would not allow time for sufficient destruction. Ross then rang the BGGS, Brigadier-General Gathorne-Hardy,[84] who agreed to get the bombardment prolonged, but to no avail, and Ross had to ring the CRA XIV Corps, Brigadier-General Alexander Wardrop,[85] to extend the firing. 'It should be quite unnecessary for a divisional commander himself to labour at the telephone in this fashion to get the necessary artillery work done.' He continued with the remark: 'I venture to suggest that the responsibility of the Corps and the Divisional Commander requires to be clearly defined' and that the divisional artillery and several batteries of 6-inch howitzers should be under divisional control during preparation as well as attack, and that the divisional general should have 'a deciding voice.' Ross concluded that: 'I hope it will be made quite clear that no blame attaches to the 6th Division' for the failure of the 15th, as he had heard that 'a wounded Guards officer of high rank has already said that "the Guards were let down by the 6th Division".'[86] He continued: 'If any blame attaches to any officer in the Division, it is to me for not having protested most strongly against the inadequacy of the artillery preparation and support. I should have assuredly have done so had I had

84 John Francis Gathorne-Hardy *psc* had been commissioned in the Grenadier Guards in 1894, and had served as a staff officer at the War Office before the war. He had served as GSO2, GSO1 and then BGGS on the Western Front from January 1916 and would become MGGS in October 1918. Cavan knew and trusted him.

85 Alexander Ernest Wardrop had been commissioned in the Royal Artillery in 1892, and had become a BGRA in September 1915, promoted MGRA in August 1918.

86 Ross would have been unhappy to read the XIV Corps report for 15 September, which concluded that 6th Division's 'failure to advance here seriously impeded the Guards Division in their advance on the Second Objective, having their right flank exposed, were forced to form a defensive flank.' (War Diary, HQ XIV Corps, 'Narrative of Operations' 15 September 1916, TNA WO95/911). Indeed, as 2 Guards Brigade topped the Ginchy ridge, they were hit in the right flank by fire from the Quadrilateral. The battalion on the right, 3rd Grenadier Guards, reported suffering from many of the same problems as 6th Division, poor artillery support, failure of the tanks, and uncut wire. The officer Ross referred to was Lieutenant-Colonel Bertram Norman Sergison-Brooke, who was on his unit's right and undoubtedly was personally a victim of fire from the Quadrilateral. He returned to command the brigade in 1917.

more time to study the situation.'[87] Having at the start cleverly pointed out that he had already complained over Cavan's head, he thus silently dared Cavan to sack him, having set out such a well-constructed argument that the failures that were not his. It was an assault on haste in planning, poor preparation, and unresponsive staff officers.

On the day of the incendiary memo, Cavan 'held a conference at Corps H.Q. G.O.C. Divisions, B.G.G.S., B.G.R.A., and Senior Staff Officers attended.'[88] After this, he wrote a swingeing response to Ross, which thrusted the problem back to the divisional general. He had spoken to all the divisional BGRA, his own CRA (Wardrop), and his staff. Corps orders, he set out, only stated that there would be a creeping barrage and a fixed barrage for each objective, and 'The Division orders exactly where these barrages are to be put down.' This was simply not true – the XIV Corps orders were very clear where 6th Division's creeper would start.[89] Cavan continued: 'But – in the event of a Divisional Commander wanting fire on any one point, he can at once ask for it through his Liaison Officer direct to Heavy Artillery and it will be given.' Cavan's counterthrust was, thus, that it was 6th Division's fault not only for failing to specify where the barrage line should be, but also for not demanding the action of 6-inch howitzers which would be available after Zero. This latter point ignored the fact that getting information back from the infantry to divisional HQ took so long that such a request could likely only be made long after the point where it was needed. Rubbing it in, Cavan continued: 'Your Artillery Commander' (Brigadier-General Egerton Cleeve),[90] 'informs me he was and is fully aware of the above', and that the Green, Brown and Blue Lines of the 15th were infantry objectives and not barrage lines. This latter point was untrue as well. Cavan clearly had not read his own corps artillery orders before replying or was badly briefed. He reminded Ross that 'the procedure invariably followed is that the Corps Artillery Commander goes round and sees all Divisional Commanders before a battle and asks if they have any complaints or suggestions and are they satisfied.' However, 'On the 14th Wardrop did not see you as you were out, but did see Rennie,[91] and Gathorne-Hardy was there at the time.'[92]

Ross would not let the matter lie. He replied to Cavan's letter stating that he complained about the location of the Green Line at the corps conference on the 13th to be told that 'the barrages and objectives had been laid down by the Army and could not be altered' (thus suggesting that Cavan was not telling truth that he could request changes as he thought appropriate), and that the 'whole thing was a gamble in tanks.'

87 War Diary, HQ 6th Infantry Division, Memo G/18/17, 20 September 1916, TNA WO95/1582.
88 War Diary, HQ XIV Corps, 20 September 1916, TNA WO95/911.
89 War Diary, HQ 6th Infantry Division, Order No. B.M. 921/6. 14 September 1916, TNA WO95/1582.
90 Egerton Stewart Cleeve served as CRA only between 22 June and 24 October 1916.
91 Lieutenant-Colonel L.F. Renny, GSO1 of 6th Division.
92 War Diary, HQ 6th Infantry Division, Memo from Earl of Cavan to General Ross, 20 September 1916, TNA WO95/1582.

He continued that if Wardrop was aware that the Green Line was merely an infantry objective, and not the barrage line, then 'he must also have been aware of the horrible misconception under which I, and my GSO1 laboured and of the consequences which would result if the tanks failed. Yet he gave me no warning.' If it was his mistake concerning the Green Line, Ross concluded, 'then I alone am fully responsible for the repulse of the Div(ision) on the 15th.' Knowing full well that he was *not* in error, he attached the corps artillery order that showed the Green Line to be both the first infantry objective and the line of the first stationary barrage. 'In that case, I hope I may be removed from command without delay.'[93] He knew that he would not be.

Wardrop made the final observations. He began, naturally enough, by stating: 'I can guarantee that every effort was made to cut wire.' He sought, however, to push responsibility away, stating that: 'I told CRAs that they were entirely responsible for their barrage.' He had asked both Cleeve's brigade major and Renny on the 14th if the barrage was satisfactory, and claimed that he had been assured that it was (even though the lack of observation meant that no-one could see whether the barrage had had the desired effect of cutting wire to give this assurance). He both questioned some of Ross's observations, but at the same time acknowledged some truth in them. Yet in pointing out that divisions often had 6-inch howitzers attached he was indicating that Ross was out of touch with practice. Indeed, it was over a year since 6th Division had undertaken a major attack, and Ross had not commanded one such. 'I regret exceedingly any shooting of our infantry. I cannot say this too strongly. I fear the fire was British', he finished.[94]

The entire episode could not but sour the relations between those concerned. The matters highlight some of the less than adequate staff work at the time, and the terrible human consequences thereof. The problems lay at the confluence of a number of different issues. Some of these rested with 6th Division. As observed, they had no experience of a major trench-to-trench attack in conjunction with other divisions – Congreve's well planned attack on Hooge had been a solo operation. Hustled into action on 13 September, the division's and brigades' own staff work was confused. Yet these problems were comparatively minor in the final analysis. The overarching problem on the 13th lay with haste, and this was not the division's fault. Ross was correct that the orders XIV Corps presented for the division's attack on the 15th in terms of the Green Line and artillery support were profoundly flawed. This was a far more serious problem. The location of the first objective was predicated on the Quadrilateral having been taken, and it had not been. There was seemingly no flexibility or will to take this into account in new artillery orders. The nexus of the failure on the 15th, thus lay with the artillery. If it was hoped that the preliminary bombardment would

93 War Diary, HQ 6th Infantry Division, G/18/17/1 20 September 1918, TNA WO95/1582.

94 War Diary, HQ 6th Infantry Division, 'RE. paper of G.O.C. 6th Division', undated, September 1918, TNA WO95/1582.

nullify the Quadrilateral, then this hope was misplaced. As previously observed, the artillery of the whole army was stretched too thin to achieve the desired result. And without proper observation, no amount of artillery at this point in the war could hope to be successful. A number of matters, weather included, made observation of the effectiveness of the preliminary bombardment of the Quadrilateral nearly impossible. Clearly, however, lack of sufficient effort by artillery observation officers, no doubt stretched too thin, was also to blame. In addition, the corps and massed divisional artilleries were inaccurate in their fire on the day in shelling positions occupied by infantry whose locations they should have been aware of in order to avoid. It is interesting to note that Cleeve, the commander of 6th Division's artillery, was sent home on 24 October. The plan of XIV Corps for 6th Division smacked more of hope rather than careful thought. Lastly, too much weight was lazily placed on the new weapon, the tank. Lack of any experience of co-ordinating artillery and infantry with this tool left gaping holes (literally) in timing and tactics. The division had succumbed to both imperatives emanating from way above it, inadequate planning, as well as the 'fog' and 'friction' of war, in a savage way. Their next experience would, however, be redemptive.

Battle of Morval, 25 September 1916

6th Division came out of the line on 19 September and on the 21st 16 and 18 Brigades took over a front of about 700 yards, right and left respectively, from 1st Guards Brigade in preparation for a renewed attack on Lesboeufs and Morval. They were, uncomfortably, taking over a line which the enemy still held on both flanks, being, in fact, part of the third objective of the 15th. Marden notes that 'considerable excitement and amusement were caused by the occasional arrival of German ration parties at our part of the trench … uttering many guttural oaths these fled for their lives, speeded up by our machine and Lewis guns.'[95] At 06.45 on the 24th the enemy attacked both flanks, and although they entered the trenches at one point the assault was otherwise easily repelled.

The major attack ordered on the 20th, known as the Battle of Morval, was finally scheduled for 25 September, 6th Division's objective being the ground between the north end of Morval and the road which passed through the centre of Lesboufs. (See Map 7, colour section). The attack was redemptive not just for 6th Division but for Fourth Army itself, in that Marden concludes: 'This was one of the most successful battles on the Somme – thanks to good weather and observation, a carefully arranged creeping barrage, and a sound preliminary bombardment.'[96] XIV Corps had four divisions in line on a 2,000 yard front, Cavan 'being of the opinion that a narrower

95 Marden, op. cit. p. 24.

96 Marden, op. cit. p. 25. The *Official History* suggests, however, that 'bad visibility hampered the artillery preparation', (Miles, op. cit. p.372).

frontage would give each division greater penetrative power by facilitating the forward flow of supports and reserves.'[97] Postponement from the 23rd to the 25th had allowed all formations to dig better assembly trenches. Things were not quite as easy as Marden implied, however. 6th Division's position was anomalous – it held what was essentially a square salient, established on the forward slope of the ridge on which Morval stood. The gap between Lesboeufs and Morval was obscured on the divisional frontage by the ridge, but observation could be obtained from near the Quadrilateral. Aerial photographs, reassuringly, revealed 'no very formidable works', but realistically, in terms of very recent experience, 'we felt some anxiety about wire.'[98] The peculiar position of 6th Division meant that the adjacent divisions, the 5th to the right and the Guards to the left, would have to first take the trench on either side of section 6th Division occupied before all formations could move forward together. This, of course, had implications for the barrage. Bombardment began on the morning of the 24th with a Zero of 12.35 on the 25th, timed to suit the French who were also attacking. On the day, the heavy artillery fired at a normal rate until Zero, when an intense field artillery barrage opened on either flank of 6th Division, on whose front it was placed 200 yards to the east, whilst the line on either side was assaulted. General von Gallwitz, commanding *2nd Army,* had warned his formations that the British would attack 'early in the morning … after a heavy *Trommelfeuer*.'[99] He was proved wrong on the first count by accident, and on the second by intent. On each flank 6th Division employed Stokes mortars, Vickers guns and rifle grenades to support the neighbouring attacks by enfilading the adjoining trenches. A senior RFA officer was placed at each brigade HQ on the day, and a Field Artillery Liaison officer with each battalion in the front line.

16 Brigade assaulted with 1st Buffs, 2nd York & Lancaster passing through on the corps second objective (the division's first). 18 Brigade assaulted with 2nd Durham Light Infantry and 11th Essex, 1st West Yorkshire being in support. There were two objectives (technically the second and third as 6th Division were already established on the first objective for the neighbouring formations). The first was essentially the road lying parallel to the two villages to their west, the distance to reach this position being a 'cause for anxiety.'[100] The second (to be attacked at Zero + two hours) was the far side of the villages to the east, including the further point of Morval Mill. The attack began at Zero + one hour, the infantry following a creeping barrage moving at 50 yards a minute, against *52nd Reserve Division, XXVI Reserve Corps*, whom Marden noted as 'our old opponents at Ypres' (having occupied the northern part of the Salient,

97 Miles, op. cit. p. 370.
98 War Diary, HQ 6th Infantry Division, 25 September 1916, TNA WO95/1582.
99 Cited in Duffy, op. cit. p. 237.
100 War Diary, HQ 6th Infantry Division, 25 September 1916, TNA WO95/1582.

adjacent to the canal), 'where the ground was all in their favour and where they had proved troublesome antagonists.'[101]

Battle of Morval, 25 September 1916

In 16 Brigade, at Zero + nine minutes, 1st Buffs attacked the enemy to their right despite the British barrage. During the night they had been out in No Man's Land and cut all the wire in front of them and as far as possible in front of 15 Brigade, 5th Division. Two squads of 10 men each, one under the redoubtable Sergeant Edward Dowman, who had already led a reconnaissance on the German bombing post the two squads were now attacking two nights previously, took 50 prisoners. Dowman was killed and recommended by the brigade for a posthumous Victoria Cross, which he did not receive.[102] At 13.35 the battalion advanced in three waves to reach the objective. Captain William Corrall found the enemy were in position a short distance in front, and advanced further, his company (D) consequently suffering casualties from the stationary barrage.[103] Nineteen ORs had been killed, four were missing and

101 Although they lost heavily in this attack, in 1917 they 'acted like a good division.' *Histories* p.506.

102 Thirty-five-year-old Edward Dowman, a cement works labourer, volunteered as a private in August 1914.

103 William Rousall Corrall was a regular sergeant at the outbreak of war and was commissioned on 1 October 1914. He would command 9th Sussex and 11th Sherwood Foresters in 1918.

73, along with four officers, wounded. 18 Brigade described the enemy as 'completely demoralised by our bombardment', and that 'except at a few stoutly contested points' they did not 'offer a great deal of resistance.'[104] Indeed, Christopher Duffy describes the 'scattered units and feeble positions of the German *XXVI Corps* ... crumbling' in the face of the British attack.[105] Those of the enemy who had survived the bombardment 'were caught before they were prepared for resistance, some even fled unarmed.'[106] Their defensive barrage fell too late to significantly disrupt the British advance. The 2nd DLI were the central battalion of the division's attack, and secured the corps second objective with few casualties taking 'about 200 prisoners, including 3 officers, 3 machine guns and much artillery ammunition.'[107] On the left, 11th Essex suffered 'practically no casualties going across the open owing to the men keeping very close up to our own barrage.' In contrast to the experience of the Quadrilateral, 'the artillery work was very good indeed', a view shared by all the attacking units. The Essex battalion captured about 200 of the enemy and 12 trench mortars including three *Minenwerfers*.[108]

The division would now carry out a leapfrog – the first time they had attempted such a manoeuvre. 2nd York & Lancaster set off at 14.29 in artillery formation and leapfrogged the Buffs at 14.35, securing the final objective by 15.00. One officer had been killed and two wounded, including the CO, Lieutenant-Colonel Allan St. J. Blunt, wounded whilst returning at night from an inspection of the forward line.[109] In 18 Brigade, the two attacking battalions were leapfrogged by 1st West Yorkshire. Arriving on the corps second objective at 14.30, five minutes before the creeping barrage, they 'found Germans still coming out of dug-outs and surrendering, but very little fighting.' The unit advanced on a two-company front, one company in support, and entered Lesboeufs. Little opposition was met with. 'The village had been very heavily bombarded and the entrances to most of the cellars were blown in', A and D companies advancing to the far side whilst C company systematically searched the

104 War Diary, HQ 18 Infantry Brigade, 25 September 1916, TNA WO95/1614.
105 Duffy, op. cit. p. 237.
106 Miles, op. cit. p. 373.
107 War Diary 2nd Battalion Durham Light Infantry, 25 September 1916 TNA WO95/1617. At the end of the month the unit had a total strength of 28 officers and 792 ORS, with 21 and 545 available for trench duty. During the month casualties totalled three officers killed and nine wounded, with 38 ORs killed, 19 missing, and 190 wounded.
108 War Diary, 11th Battalion Essex Regiment, 25 September 1916, TNA WO95/1616.
109 The battalion did not record the number of OR casualties in this action, but during the month suffered 43 killed 279 wounded, 23 missing and eight invalided with shell shock. (War Diary, 2nd Battalion York & Lancaster Regiment, September 1916, TNA WO95/1610). Allan St. John Blunt had been a captain of the 1st Battalion York & Lancasters in August 1914. The 1st King's Shropshire Light Infantry followed the York & Lancasters and suffered two officers wounded but failed to list casualties in the other ranks.

remaining houses and cellars.[110] One officer and 18 ORs had been killed, with four officers and 77 ORs wounded. The enemy artillery retaliated later in the afternoon, and *52nd Reserve Division* ordered the *239th* and *240th Regiments* to recapture Morval but their short advance merely served to cover the withdrawal of artillery.[111]

The division received the following from XIV Corps: 'Hearty thanks, sincere congratulations to you all. A very fine achievement, splendidly executed. CAVAN.' Perhaps some of the bitterness of the experience at the Quadrilateral evaporated. And perhaps 6th Division regained some of its confidence in the protective power of the artillery. The division summarised: 'Excellent air photos had been taken of the enemy's trenches – observation across the valley was easy' (any worry about the area between Lesboeufs and Morval having been shaken off), and 'the weather was fine and aeroplane observation was easy – time was available for reconnaissance ... the enemy's positions were heavily and accurately bombarded.' Everything the reverse of the experience at the Quadrilateral, in fact. The division's 'lessons to be learnt' memorandum at the end of September solely concerned the artillery. General Ross (with the Quadrilateral clearly still in his mind) observed that if heavy artillery 'hammered' a defensive position, a barrage was put on the trench to be assaulted, and troops advanced under a creeping barrage, then 'our infantry can capture any trench, or succession of trenches, but with little loss.' If these three conditions were not fulfilled, 'our losses will be heavy, and our attack will probably fail.' 'The whole thing', he continued, 'depends on careful and accurate observation.' If aeroplanes could not fulfil this function, then 'the reconnaissance must be carried out by infantry and artillery F.O.O.s.' In underlining the word 'must', Ross was describing what *had not* happened on the 13th and 15th, and what *had* happened before the 25th. 'Every particle of information obtained will save us hundreds of good men', he stated. To ensure success, Ross opined, location and observation of the enemy trenches and wire, perhaps from a flank, keeping down snipers by counter-sniping, and machine-gun, Stokes mortar and artillery fire, was essential. The infantry should dig in 250 yards in from of the enemy wire, with a support trench 100 yards to the rear and 'plenty of deep communication trenches.' From here they should push forward and dig in OPs, and the infantry should participate in observation for artillery.[112] It was an argument for careful preparation over haste.

As 6th Division consolidated its position, on the following day at the far right of the XIV Corps line 56th Division captured Combles, and to the left XV Corps captured Guedecourt. By the 28th the fighting died down, whilst the fighting on the Thiepval ridge raged to the north. The attack of the 25th had been the most successful day on

110 War Diary, 1st Battalion West Yorkshire Regiment, 25 September 1916, TNA WO95/1618.

111 Miles, op. cit. p. 377.

112 War Diary, HQ 6th Infantry Division, 'Lessons to be Learnt from these Operations', September 1916, TNA WO95/1582.

the Somme since the attack on the Bazentin Ridge on 14 July, but yet again, any fond hopes of a breakthrough had to be abandoned. The Official Historian described the enemy as 'badly shaken, unable for the moment to present a continuous front, obliged to extemporize new field defences', yet having offered sufficient fight to hold up the French on the British right, and frustrate the capture of Guedecourt that day. 'Fourth Army, with no fresh divisions available, and the troops in the line all very tired, could do little more than regain contact with the enemy.'[113] This portion of the Army would now have to muster itself to attack the German positions on the Transloy Ridges.

Battle of the Transloy Ridges, 7-20 October 1916

6th Division was relieved on 30 September. The weather deteriorated, then improved from 4 October, although low cloud continued a problem for air observation. In front of the enemy's defences before Beaulencourt and Le Transloy there were known to be trenches and gun pits, but their location was unclear. Indeed, 'the position of the British front was only approximately known at corps and Army headquarters.'[114] In contrast to 25 September, auspices were less than promising and distinctly reminiscent of the position on 13 September as far as 6th Division were concerned. On 7 October, the 20th and 56th Divisions of XIV Corps made only limited progress, and 6th Division was brought back into the line on the night of 8/9 October, taking over about 1,500 yards of the ridge east of Guedecourt and Lesboeufs. 20th Division had made the most progress just beyond Guedecourt, but 56th Division at Lesboeufs and 12th Division north of Guedecourt had been largely thrown back. Once again, the division found itself in a salient.

The renewed attack was scheduled for 12 October, its objective being to secure good observation of, and an advantageous position to attack the Le Transloy line. (See Map 8 in colour section). Aerial photographs taken on the 10th revealed that the enemy had dug new trenches about 100 yards from the division's front line at places on both flanks of the salient, but in each case they were difficult to observe. The bombardment commenced the following day, a 'Chinese attack' being carried out by the artillery. A high wind further made accurate shooting difficult. The division noted anxiously on the 11th: 'Time was short.' The position for the attack was the same as on the 25th. At Zero (14.05) 4th Division would advance into line on the right of the 6th, taking the parts of the trench system (Spectrum etc. trenches) that were not as yet occupied, 12th Division on the left advancing similarly. At Zero + 20 minutes, all three divisions would advance in unison, 6th Division having all three brigades in the line. On the right, 16 Brigade were attacking a trench that was only believed to be in existence. The ground is bleak, flat and featureless, except on the right of the divisional attack where it drops down into a declivity north east of Lesboeufs. On the left, 18 Brigade

113 Miles, op. cit. p.389.
114 Miles, op. cit. p.434.

were to attack Rainbow Trench. In the centre of the salient, 71 Brigade were to stand still, assisting the others on their flanks as they could. In terms of the defenders, the *19th Reserve Division*, fresh from rest in the Argonne after heavy (79 percent) losses at Verdun, a division which showed 'energetic and intelligent leadership',[115] had just come into line. It would offer strong resistance.

16 Brigade record that 'within 45 seconds of the commencement of the attack the Germans had got their barrage on behind [*sic*] our front lines and a barrage of machine guns on our parapet.'[116] The fire faced by the assaulting battalion, 2nd York & Lancaster, the brigade stated, was 'murderous … nothing could stand against it.' The battalion's fighting strength had only totalled 350. Soon, three officers were dead and five wounded, whilst in the other ranks 57 were dead, 33 missing, and 130 wounded – 65 percent casualties. The battalion had suffered many of these in leaving its jumping-off position, where it remained at the end of the day. On the left, 18 Brigade made slightly more progress. 14th Durham Light Infantry advanced through the enemy barrage and took Rainbow Trench and pushed on up a sunken road, the bombing and rifle grenade sections clearing dug-outs. They advanced further towards Mild Trench, with their Lewis guns and rifle grenadiers at the front, A and C Companies leading in artillery formation, but casualties mounted. 'A large number of untouched machine guns came into action and further advance became perfectly impossible without further artillery preparation.'[117] 1st West Yorkshire suffered the misery of their trenches being shelled by their own artillery before Zero, 'and in spite of repeated messages this could not be stopped.' The enemy, 'quite untouched' by the bombardment, met the battalion with machine gun and rifle fire, and with reports of 12th Division's failure on its left, the battalion returned to its trenches. Two officers and 71 ORs had been wounded, whilst 24 ORs were dead and 10 missing.[118] The DLI left flank was 400 yards in air, and the battalion formed a defensive flank, one officer and seven ORs being dead, four officers and 80 ORs wounded, with 19 ORs missing.

The *Official History* noted that the enemy was 'ready and alert', warned by the bombardment and now accustomed to early afternoon attacks. They were attacked by weakened units (with many half-trained newcomers), such as the paltry numbers constituting 2nd York & Lancaster. Indeed, 'at this time few battalions in the Fourth Army could muster more than 400 men for an attack.' The enemy positions were uncertain, and 'many German machine guns now appeared to be sited further back in well concealed positions from which they swept with deadly effect the zone of the assault.'[119] The limitations of the artillery were exposed again. Nothing could substitute for effective destructive fire on well-observed positions whose machine guns

115 *Histories*, pp.301-2.
116 War Diary, HQ 16 Infantry Brigade, 12 October 1916 TNA WO95/1605.
117 War Diary, HQ 18 Infantry Brigade, 12 October 1916, TNA WO95/1614.
118 War Diary, 1st Battalion West Yorkshire Regiment, 12 October 1916, TNA WO95/1618.
119 Miles, op. cit. pp.442-3.

6th Division's attack between Lesboeufs and Guedecourt, October 1916. The view is from the Guedecourt Caribou, on the site of Grease Trench.

could otherwise wreak havoc, before the suppressant effect of the creeping barrage could achieve its purpose. Aeroplane observation had been rendered impossible by continuing bad weather, and no observation post could be found which would allow a line of sight for purposeful shelling of the German positions. Patrols that went out were met in strength. Artillery efforts were concentrated only on what could be observed, and the new enemy trench opposite the centre of the division's position could indeed be seen to be destroyed. Knowing that Fourth Army would attack again, the enemy had busied themselves consolidating their positions under the crest of the ridge in front of 6th Division, and under von Lossberg's edicts, had made adjustment to their defensive tactics.

The attack was renewed on the 15th. Zero was altered to 05.35 and the attack was made by 18 Brigade on the left and 71 Brigade in the centre, to assist 12th Division forward. In 71 Brigade, 2nd Sherwood Foresters were to take gun pits 200 yards in front of their position and then a new German trench to the left of these. They reached the gun pits, but the new trench was further away than believed, and the battalion was bombed out of it. Lieutenant-Colonel Charles Hobbs was severely wounded going up to the gun pits (which were being joined together and communication trenches dug back) to assess the situation, and died soon after. Three officers had been killed and three wounded, whilst during the month 40 ORs were killed, six were missing and 144 wounded. In its time on the Somme, 2nd Sherwood Foresters lost 12 officers and 152 other ranks killed, with 16 officers and 625 ORs wounded. The total of 805 casualties was thus four-fifths of its nominal strength in a little over a month's fighting.[120] In 18 Brigade, 2nd Durham Light Infantry on the right were to capture parts of Cloudy and Mild Trenches. They were faced with 'a large number of untouched machine guns' and fell back to their jumping off position. Two officers were dead, one was missing and five wounded. In the other ranks, 18 were dead, 28 missing and 93 wounded. 11th Essex occupied part of Mild Trench but with the failure of the DLI were machine-gunned from their right rear and then bombed back to their original line. Three officers had been killed, two were missing and four wounded. Thirteen ORs were dead, 76 wounded, and 75 missing, a number of the latter surrounded by the enemy having advanced to the second objective. The brigade concluded: 'The cause of the failure was (i) insufficiently accurate artillery preparation by the heavy artillery, (ii) the attacking battalions did not follow sufficiently close up to the creeping barrage.'[121] In a misjudged effort (as they were not adjacent) 9th Norfolk of 71 Brigade attacked Mild Trench again in conjunction with an assault by 12th Division at 04.30 on the 18th. The weather was bad, and the ground a 'quagmire.' Lieutenant-Colonel Prior had

120 H.C. Wylly, *1st and 2nd Battalions the Sherwood Foresters in the Great War*, Kindle edition location 5280.
121 War Diary, HQ 18 Infantry Brigade, 15 October 1916, TNA WO95/1614.

instructed steps to be cut in the parapet for easy egress,[122] but the clay was so saturated that 'it was most difficult to get out of the trench.' Prior followed in the second wave to find each shell hole 'a slimy sticky obstacle.' The advance could not keep up with the barrage. Under heavy machine gun fire direction was lost. Prior received only one message from his front the whole day. Some parties advanced beyond their first objective and were cut off, others retired to the first objective where they were twice subjected to friendly bombardment, not to mention three enemy counter-attacks. In his after-action report, Prior outlined the consequences of the heavy losses suffered earlier in September. The battalion had lost 20 officers, including its adjutant, at the Quadrilateral. Of the five survivors, 'three were badly shaken.' The 470 OR casualties had been made up with 'drafts, many of whom were little trained', particularly in 'the value of the rifle.' Thirteen days before the attack, nine officers had arrived and more followed. All bar one were subalterns, and Prior therefore had to pick three company commanders from their number – 'they had not sufficient training or experience to at once assume command of Companies in the field.'[123]

Major-General Ross provided an overview of the failure of the operations. First, poor weather allowed only two 'fleeting occasions' for aerial photography, and the photos of the trenches 6th Division assaulted 'were failures.' Preparatory artillery fire could therefore not achieve accurate results. Second, the weather affected assembly. The assembly trenches were poor, and, as Lieutenant-Colonel Prior had observed, egress from them was difficult. The attacking troops were thus delayed and could not follow the barrage closely. Third, there was, as ever, the independent will of the enemy – counterattack drove the attackers back. Despite the emphasis paced during the summer by the division on training,[124] Ross blamed 'the large number of practically untrained officers and men in the battalions' – a result of the Quadrilateral attacks. Thus, a whole night had been wasted 'in digging an assembly trench in the wrong place', sited on a forward slope under constant fire of all sorts. Similarly, Ross blamed the failure to jump-off with alacrity on inexperience as well as weather. He concluded:

> I am satisfied that if our battalions had been as well trained as they were when we came down to the SOMME, or if we had had longer time in which to train the new entry, we should have captured and held our objectives at the first attempt in spite of the difficulty of observation. The officers who we receive to replace casualties are complete strangers to the rank and file who come out. I suppose it

122 Bernard Henry Leathes Prior was the CO of 6th Norfolk (Cyclist) Battalion in August 1914.
123 War Diary, 9th Battalion Norfolk Regiment, 'Report on Operations on 18th October', TNA WO95/1623.
124 See Chapter 9.

> is not possible to train them together, but if it could be managed it would greatly facilitate and expedite the training of the new entry.[125]

It might have been expected that Ross would seek to provide excuses for the failure of his division, but his points were well made. His observations about training in the setting of his other comments can be seen as reaching the following conclusion – a division cannot be repeatedly thrown completely unprepared at a largely unknown objective to sustain massive casualties, and a month later, with reinforcements barely integrated, at a similarly unknown objective and be expected to succeed. Yet again, the undertow of his remarks contained serious criticism of the British way of war on the Somme.

Two days after these failures 6th Division was relieved and, moving north, was placed in reserve to I Corps, First Army.[126]

Engineering on the Somme

In the preparations for the Somme operations, the Royal Engineers trained, as did the infantry in the early part of the month. Indeed, General Ross inspected the divisional Pioneers, 11th Leicestershire on 3 September, and they carried out 'a small tactical scheme.'[127] For the operations 15-18 September, a field company Royal Engineers was attached to each brigade, the 12th to 18 Brigade, the 509th (1/1st London) to 16 Brigade, and the 459th (2/2nd West Riding) to 71 Brigade. In the failure of the attacks their efforts were directed to road repair, and in this activity four men of the 12th Field Company were wounded by a bomb on the road south of Guillemont on the 16th. Such work was therefore never safe, and might perhaps seem mundane, but as 2/2nd West Riding pointed out, it was essential to 'enable rations, stores etc. and ammunition to be taken to attacking troops.'[128] Little information is available concerning the logistical work of 6th Divisional train during this period. 11th Leicestershire participated in road repair and track creation, but during 16-17 September a company was detailed as stretcher bearers, and on 18-20 September they were working on clearing the battlefield, sustaining 12 casualties over these days.[129] When the attack was successful on the 18th, the Engineers were involved in wiring

125 War Diary, 9th Battalion Norfolk Regiment, Memo of Major-General C. Ross 'XIV Corps', 31 October 1916, TNA WO95/1623.
126 On 25 November the division went into the line in the La Bassée area, and by the 30th was holding a 4,000-yard front from Auchy to Givenchy. Here they remained for a number of weeks in unremarkable trench holding.
127 War Diary, 11th Battalion Leicestershire Regiment, 3 September 1916, TNA WO95/1601.
128 War Diary, 459 Field Company Royal Engineers, 15 September 1918, TNA WO95/1600.
129 War Diary, 11th Battalion Leicestershire Regiment, 318-20 September 1916, TNA WO95/1601.

and constructing strong points, 1/1st London noting that this was completed 'in spite of heavy shelling.' Each strong point of three fire bays and two fire and machine-gun bays with wire on both front and flank required the effort of 15 engineers and 35 infantry.[130] In the Battle of Morval, the Pioneers constructed assembly trenches on the 24th, whilst the Engineers' activities on the 25th largely involved constructing strong points in captured positions. 1/1st London lost one officer and six ORs in the attempted construction of three such positions, only one of which was successfully completed due to shellfire and casualties suffered en route. On the 26th they were wiring at night, working on strong points and new trenches, and building new brigade HQs.[131] 11th Leicestershire continued work on tracks. In the days prior to the Battle of the Transloy Ridges, the Pioneers were again set to two days of battlefield clearance, whilst in terms of the Engineers as the battle opened, 12th Company were largely engaged constructing dug-outs, as were 1/1st London, also working on strongpoints and trench mortar emplacements. 2/2nd West Riding were working on strong points at night and consolidating captured ground. The work of 11th Leicestershire in laying footboard tracks was even more essential given the deterioration in the weather, but again, on 12-13 and 16-18 October they were acting as stretcher bearers. Without such work the battles could not have been fought.

Conclusion

Prior to their arrival on the Somme, 6th Division had, since their exertions as the line settled around Armentières in October 1914, only taken part in one major offensive action, at Hooge in August 1915, and that without the need to cooperate with flanking divisions. Whilst the division had defended the line in conjunction with other formations, it had never taken the offensive. Although Hooge had been a masterpiece of organisation, a year had passed since that major action. The crucible of the Somme cost the division, according to Marden, 277 officer and 6,440 other rank casualties. This is an underestimate – the infantry brigades actually reported losses of 267 officers and 6,843 ORs. Nearly half of these resulted from the attacks on the Quadrilateral. The division had taken part in three major planned attacks and carried out three subordinate operations. The learning concerning major multi-corps offensives was swift and brutal. There is nothing to suggest from their performance in the Salient that the division's infantry came to the Somme with any particular inadequacies in their tactical performance (although they had to learn to follow a creeping barrage and to leapfrog). The disasters at the Quadrilateral represented no failure in respect of infantry tactics.

130 War Diary, 509 Field Company Royal Engineers, 18 September 1918, TNA WO95/1600.
131 War Diary, 509 Field Company Royal Engineers, 25-6 September 1918, TNA WO95/1600.

If any reasons are needed to understand why BEF progress was never a smooth improvement curve, the experiences of 6th Division on the Somme exemplify these. Firstly, problems lay at the top, with GHQ and Fourth Army. The massive scale of operations between 1 July and 18 November revealed deficiencies in planning and staff work. The objectives passed from Fourth Army to its corps for the grand attack of 15 September reflect this deficiency. The chain of command that operationalised Sir Douglas Haig's orders for the 15th, through Fourth Army and XIV Corps, allowed no wriggle room to take into account local tactical situations such as that which faced 6th Division. Fourth Army HQ had no understanding of the nature of the problem that the Quadrilateral would present. Indeed, they perhaps did not know it existed – it was too small in their scheme of things. Even at corps level it was simply too late to fine tune the motion of the juggernaut on 15 September. The start date of the Hooge operation had been adjusted to suit the pace of preparation. This was not possible in an attack as large as Flers-Courcelette. Planning on the Somme was sometimes a matter of hope. The attack on the 13th reflected the haste that had characterised a number of Fourth Army's subsidiary operations on the Somme to this point. Rawlinson's forces had repeatedly been drawn into hurried operations, in which attacks would be repeated with diminished forces in the hope that the enemy was sufficiently damaged to crumble. The division fell victim to this pattern of operations when it was thrust at the Quadrilateral, and again at Le Transloy.

Second, problems lay within XIV Corps. The corps had had less than a month in the area, drawn in necessarily to replace exhausted formations, and the operations it conducted were its first within Fourth Army – indeed, they were its first operations since its formation in January 1916. In that month it took part in the struggle to take Guillemont, which it finally achieved, and then Ginchy. Well though it had performed in securing these locations, corps HQ did not truly grasp the problem that the Quadrilateral would present on the 15th. Despite the failure of the 13th, whatever might have been learnt (or not as the case might be) could not be factored into the plan for the 15th, and the corps staff work deficiencies manifested themselves in a less than full mastery of the corps artillery orders for the day. The exertions of the other divisions of the corps had required the insertion of 6th Division into a strange line, and to take part in a major attack the next day, blind to both the dispositions of friend and foe alike. This was poor practice, but the organisational requirements of the impending major operations demanded it. If Ross is correct that there had been wholesale re-organisation of corps artillery personnel, however, then that was an unnecessary own goal at a time of external pressure to succeed. Thirdly, as noted, 6th Division contributed its own poor staff work on the 13th, in its confused orders for the first attack on the Quadrilateral. This, too, was a result of haste and of working without necessary intelligence. But it was also a reflection of lack of familiarity with swift moving major operations. The GSO1, Renny, was also the least sharp the division would be endowed with.[132] Fourthly, the three major attacks carried out by the division emphasised the crucial role of artillery in destructive fire on points of likely strong resistance, in counterbattery fire suppressing the enemy's artillery, and in the protection of the infantry with the creeping barrage, the pace of which would remain an issue for the rest of the war. 6th Division rarely benefitted from effective counterbattery fire – indeed, in two of their three operations they experienced a healthy counter-barrage from the enemy. The learning process was as much about firepower and its technical development and tactical deployment as about anything else. Lastly, however, many of the problems encountered were simply down to the 'friction' of war – a competent force and a good plan could always fall foul of both the independent will of the enemy and the unexpected. The division suffered from friendly fire, but this would remain a risk throughout the war. It was weather-related problems in observation that led to ineffective gunnery on 15 September and 12 October. On 25 September, when good observation was achieved, fire was accurate, and objectives were reached with relatively few casualties. Topography and weather were nothing that the BEF could control. Good generalship, however, required the friction of war to be considered.

If the Somme was a great attritional campaign, it had the same effect on both sides. 6th Division lost 50 percent of its nominal infantry strength in a little over five weeks and had increasingly to attack with understrength units which were forced of necessity to field novice infantry and officers, as Bernard Prior so clearly set out. It is difficult to assess the effect these costly operations on morale. As set out in the previous chapter, 'most indicators suggest that not 1916 or 1918 but rather 1914 was the British Army's year of crisis.'[133] 6th Division had sustained a significant level of attrition in the Ypres salient, and was no doubt now beginning to receive those with no military experience prior to August 1914. These men, as Alexander Watson suggests, 'comprised the best fed, best educated, probably most intelligent and therefore most resilient members of British society.'[134] There is every reason to suggest that they arrived on the Somme in good form in all respects. Major Henry Dillon, second-in-command of 1st West Yorkshire, 18 Brigade (and a pre-war Regular), could write in August 1916 of the Somme offensive: 'This battle is being run on the right lines I am sure, i.e. for every man we lose we out more than one German.'[135] This was, however, written before 6th Division became engaged at the Quadrilateral. Overall, however, there is little evidence to suggest that the British army's morale was significantly dented by the Somme, except perhaps in the latter stages of the battle, noticeably in the mud of the Transloy Ridges, when some senior commanders began to resist the impetus to continue battle

132 See Chapter 7.
133 A. Watson, *Enduring the Great War*, p. 142.
134 Watson, op. cit. p.149.
135 Cited in Watson, op. cit. p.150. Henry Mountifort Dillon (born 1881) would die in January 1918 of illness, having had two periods of battalion command.

in such conditions. The Earl of Cavan protested to Sir Henry Rawlinson that his men could not be expected to attack again there in November (although by this point, of course, 6th Division had left the line). At this point 'battle fatigue was starting to take its toll, and Rawlinson recommended that Fourth Army's tired divisions really needed rest.'[136] It was of course just before this point that Lieutenant-Colonel Prior was reporting on fall-off in effectiveness with the advent of replacements. Rest (and training) was what 6th Division would get in December. And as the following chapter will show, there was no diminution of the tenacity with which 6th Division's troops would fight in the Loos sector in April 1917. Indeed, if September and October on the Somme had proved major exertion, 1917 would offer only partial relief.

136 W. Philpott, *Bloody Victory*, p.403.

5

'A heavy demand on the endurance of the troops'[1] Operations Loos Sector 1917

The year 1917 opened to find 6th Division holding a front of 5,700 yards in the Cambrin-Hohenzollern Quarries area. The trenches were in bad condition, but as Marden notes, despite the fact that 'all this front had a most evil repute', the four-month period from moving into the sector at the end of November 1916 'proved the quietest the division ever experienced.'[2] On 1 March the division moved south to relieve the 37th Division and a brigade front of 21st Division. Their front, from the Double Crassier south of Loos to the Hohenzollern Redoubt, nearly doubled to 11,000 yards, and all three brigades were in line, with a brigade of 21st Division attached.

Trench Raiding

The early months of the year, after the coldest winter in living memory, were marked by trench raids. During January and February the Germans carried out two such raids, and 6th Division mounted six (see Table 5.1). The division had, of course, learnt its craft in trench raiding in the Ypres Salient.[3] In positional warfare in which 'break-in' could often be successfully achieved, but 'breakthrough' and 'break-out' were condemned to failure, the trench raid was an ideal vehicle for practicing 'break-in' tactics. It was one that both sides used. Although the argument that German tactics were more sophisticated than those of the British rings a little hollow in the face of modern scholarship, the German *Sturmabteilung* tactics developed from October 1915 were certainly practiced in trench raiding.[4] The British were always more enthusiastic

1 Lieutenant-General Holland to Major-General Marden on the performance of 6th Division during April 1917 at Hill 70. War Diary 18 Infantry Brigade, G0/9/64, 25 April 1917, TNA WO95/1615.
2 T.O. Marden, *A Short History of the Sixth Division*, p.28.
3 See Chapter 3.
4 M. Samuels, *Doctrine and Dogma*, p.19.

trench raiders than their enemy, and the sophistication of the early 1917 raids by 6th Division represents a step-up in organisation in comparison to their 1915-16 counterparts. The very earliest raids were simple and uncoordinated with other arms, and it was noted in Chapter Three that the division only began to produce reports on raids in early 1916 as greater sophistication developed.

26/01 03.00	1st West Yorkshire	Madagascar Trench, Auchy	160 men in six parties	Box barrage. Demonstration by 16 & 71 Brigades. 15 dugouts bombed. Five prisoners. Five killed, 40 wounded.
26/01 23.00	14th Durham Light Infantry	Madagascar Trench	18 men in two parties	Front line & box barrage. Two enemy killed, identifications made. Eight wounded.
29/01 03.30	8th Bedfordshire	Little Willie & Hindenburg Trenches	150 men	Barrage. Demonstration by 18 & 71 Brigades. Six dug-outs bombed, two prisoners. One killed, five wounded.
09/02 07.00	2nd Sherwood Foresters	Hulluch Quarries	100 men	Smoke barrage. 20 dugouts destroyed & 60 enemy casualties. Eight prisoners. Ten killed, 31 wounded.
10/02 20.00	2nd Durham Light Infantry	Mad Point Sap	41 men	Barrage. Dugouts destroyed. 30 enemy dead. One prisoner. 13 wounded.
12/02 23.20	Mixed party 71 Brigade	Hulluch Road	94 men	Barrage. Five dugouts bombed & four enemy killed. Five killed & 13 wounded.

Table 5.1: Raids carried out by 6th Division January/February 1917.

John Pratt has described the trench raid as the 'battle in miniature.'[5] He notes the description in the 33rd Division history that planning for a raid could include:

> The study of the ground; compilation and issue of maps; siting of mortar and machine guns; digging of mine galleries; cutting of wire; placing of barrage; getting up bombs, gas cylinders, medical stores, signalling apparatus; deductions by the intelligence branch of the General Staff from aeroplane photographs; and not least, the rehearsal on similar ground behind the line.[6]

Patrolling success and domination of No Man's Land was the necessary precursor to a successful raid. Patrolling had been a constant feature of battalion work since early

5 J. Pratt, 'The BEF and the Art of Trench Raiding 1916', in S. Jones (ed.), *At All Costs*, p. 180.
6 G. S. Hutchinson, *The Thirty-Third Division in France and Flanders 1915-1919*, p. 6.

1915. Churn of troops meant constant induction into this work. Lieutenant-Colonel Allan St John Blunt of 2nd York & Lancaster, wrote in his diary on 31 March 1917 at the Double Crassier: 'Am making Co(mpan)ys do a lot of patrolling to get used to walking about in No Man's land. At present they think a visit to our wire is quite an adventure.'[7] Carried out mostly in the dark, Paddy Griffiths has described raids as 'fiendish and deadly.'[8] That they were deadly, 'The Admiral' (amongst others) had found out to his cost in the Salient. They were reputedly unpopular with troops because of this. Edmund Blunden, writing in the aftermath of the Somme offensive, stated that 'our greatest distress at this period was due to that short and dry word "raid"', describing them as 'nightly suicide operations.' There is some suggestion that the incidence of raids accelerated during this period. The 5th Division historian noted that during the winter of 1916-17: 'The Higher Authorities ordained that all through the Winter the Germans were to be harassed in every possible way. Constant patrolling in No Man's land and at least two raids in each Division every week was the order.'[9] A division that did not contribute to the mounting total of raids was, it was claimed, viewed as 'showing slackness and want of zeal.'[10] Tony Ashworth's summary of the statistics on raiding do not quite bear this supposed emphasis out. In the first six months of 1916, there were 106 raids across the BEF, during the Somme offensive there were 310, and during 1917 there were about 270.[11] The dubious Blunden summarised the reasons given for raiding as 'the lowering of the enemy's spirits, the raising of our own, the identification of some supposedly new troops opposite, (and) the damaging of the German trenches.'[12] The General Staff, a year earlier, had opined that: 'Minor local enterprises … in the trenches furnish the best means of maintaining the efficiency of the troops.'[13] 'Efficiency' likely meant both honed fighting skill and offensive spirit. Tactically, at this time, it was certainly reasonable to attempt to reinforce the negative impact that the Somme had impressed on the enemy. Raiding was, in part, supposedly an aspect of attrition – it was hoped it would encourage the enemy to keep more troops in the front line who would hence be more vulnerable in a major attack.

As Ashworth observes: 'The raid was a complex tactic involving diverse skills as well as the coordination of weapon groups from several arms, and it comprised two successive parts: the preparation and the performance.'[14] A highly successful raid by the Canadian Corps on the night of 16/17 November 1915 on the Douve River, with the intent of securing prisoners for identification, drawing reserves forward to be shelled, and lowering enemy morale, had given indications of the template. Firstly,

7 A. St. J. Blunt, Private Papers, IWM Docs 16149.
8 P. Griffith, *Battle Tactics of the Western Front*, p.60.
9 A.H. Hussey & D.S. Inman, *The Fifth Division in the Great War*, p.142.
10 A. H. Atteridge, *History of the 17th (Northern) Division*, p.69.
11 T. Ashworth, *Trench Warfare 1914-1918*, p.185.
12 E. Blunden, *Undertones of War*, p.125.
13 General Staff, *Notes for Infantry Officers on Trench Warfare*, p.8.
14 Ashworth, op. cit. p.73.

'careful training and rehearsal over similar ground'; secondly, careful selection of raiders with specialist skills; thirdly, use of artillery to cut off the enemy front line; and fourthly, carefully ensuring wire was cut.'[15] Thomas Grove, the division's GSO1 in 1917 described how 'great ingenuity was employed' in the planning of raids with 'much care devoted to their preparation.' He noted how 'it was common practice to lay out from aeroplane photographs a trace of the position of enemy front forming the objective and to drill the raiding party over this.' And whereas an attack coordinated with other formations imposed a deadline for being ready or not (as the situation at the Quadrilateral had demonstrated), 'time was rarely an important consideration' in raid planning – 'the week after next would do as well as next week.'[16]

The raid carried out by 71 Brigade at 23.20 on 12 February can be taken as an example of the degree of complexity. The brigade had a raiding company (also known as the Brigade Scouting Party), led by Captain Samuel Blackwell, 9th Norfolk.[17] He was well chosen having been awarded the DSO in November 1916 for his actions at Mild Trench on the Transloy Ridges:

> He led a reinforcement party over the open under very heavy fire, bombing back the enemy and maintaining his position against three enemy counter-attacks for 36 hours. Later, he led a daring patrol, and proceeded over 100 yards along the enemy line and obtained valuable information.[18]

The brigade orders for the 12th run into two pages and an addendum.[19] The raid was at least five days in the planning. The object was to 'destroy a suspected T.M. emplacement … to obtain identifications, to kill Germans and to destroy deep dugouts.' A Forward Observation Officer of divisional artillery was to accompany Blackwell, running out a telephone wire. The divisional artillery was comprised of three groups, and two – Hohenzollern and Quarries – fired a total of 934 shells in the accompanying barrage. A Bangalore torpedo was used against the enemy wire, which the frontline battalions, 9th Norfolk and 9th Suffolk, went out to cut. The barrage was supplemented by the 71st Trench Mortar Battery, four mortars located in two places and in position by 06.00 that morning. They barraged the enemy trenches and cut wire, keeping up fire throughout the raid. The 71st Machine Gun Company

15 B. Rawling, *Surviving Trench Warfare*, pp. 48-50.
16 T.T. Grove, 'It Happened by Chance', NAM 1963-08-14.
17 Samuel Frederick Baker Blackwell would be killed at Cambrai in 20 November 1918, aged 29, commanding D Company 9th Norfolk. A Warwickshire farmer, he had volunteered in August 1914 and served with the RE Motor Cyclist Section as a corporal before being commissioned into the East Kent Yeomanry in May 1915, serving on Gallipoli and later attached to the Tank Corps.
18 *Edinburgh Gazette*, 27 November 1916, p. 2191.
19 War Diary, HQ 71 Infantry Brigade, Operation Order No. 139, 7 February 1917, TNA WO95/1619.

similarly fired on the enemy's front line on either side of the area raided (using 25,00 rounds) but also on the reserve line and communication trenches. Both front line battalions kept up rifle, Lewis gun and rifle grenade fire throughout. A dummy attack was carried out at Zero by 16 Infantry Brigade and the adjacent 24th Division. (The raid carried out by 2nd Sherwood Foresters three days earlier had added a smoke barrage fired from mortars by No. 4 Special Company RE at a dummy location, and lachrymatory shells surrounding the area to be raided).

On the day, the brigade noted 'our artillery cooperation was good', but not all matters ran smoothly, the friction of war asserting itself in the face of detailed planning. The enemy was on the alert, active with machine guns and Very lights up to Zero, and the Bangalore torpedo only blew a hole wide enough to allow one man at a time through, and the enemy's wire on knife rests fell back into place after the explosion. Further, Second-Lieutenant George King of the 9th Suffolks was killed by a mobile charge which went off prematurely at the mouth of an enemy dugout before he had thrown it. Despite this, the raid demonstrates the use of specialists, careful planning, artillery barrage with trench mortar and machine gun integration, and deception in the form of dummy attacks. It will also be noticed (Table 5.1) that raids were never mounted at a standard time.

During March and April the division mounted eleven raids (see Table 5.2), and the enemy in turn replied with four. That on 25 March took place between 04.30 and 05.00 against 71 Brigade. Under a heavy barrage of *minenwerfers*, aerial darts (often recorded as used by the enemy both on raiders whilst in the German trenches and more generally) and rifle grenades along the whole front, 'a strong body of specially trained raiding troops of *72nd IR*',[20] split into two parties, and attacked the junction of 2nd Sherwood Foresters and 9th Norfolk. At this location there was a gap of 150 yards, which indicates good intelligence on the part of the enemy. In the front line the Germans destroyed a bombing post and one party penetrated as far as the support line where they were stopped by another bombing post. They bombed a dugout and took nine Sherwood Foresters prisoner. They left four dead behind, and 71 Brigade suffered 26 casualties. Colonel Bernard Prior of the 9th Norfolks left an animated description:

> The Bosche made a very determined night raid, broke into the trenches of the Sherwood Foresters on our right, and part of the enemy, led by a sergeant-major, swinging round, came up between the front and support lines of my right company. They got into the dug-out of the front-line platoon and captured the sergeant who was portioning out the rations, and at the moment unarmed. They brought him up to the trench and ordered him to get out, which he promptly obeyed, kicking his nearest captor in the mouth as he did so, and bolted to the front line, yelling to the men to line the parados as the Bosches were behind him. Although, in making his escape, he was severely wounded, his prompt

20 War Diary, HQ 6th Infantry Division, 25 March 1917, TNA WO95/1583.

> action saved the situation. The majority of the enemy doubled back, leaving the sergeant-major (badly wounded) and one unwounded prisoner in our hands, and several dead in our lines and in No Man's Land.[21]

The enemy followed the raid with increased aircraft activity. Interestingly, 9th Norfolk failed to mention the penetration to the support line in their diary, and the Sherwood Foresters failed to mention the loss of nine prisoners in theirs. 71 Brigade tried to shrug matters off by suggesting that if the isolated bombing post had not been taken 'the raid would have been a complete failure.'[22] In reality, given that five days previously the Brigade had issued a three-page order on a defence scheme, the enemy raid could justly be viewed a success. A successful British raid was talked up, a successful German raid talked down. General Ross, however, descended upon 2nd Sherwood Foresters on 26 March 'to discuss the German raid and whether any better system of holding the line could be devised.' He suggested 'concentrated platoon posts' rather than isolated sentry groups.' Lieutenant-Colonel Bradshaw was sympathetic, but pointed out that the system in place 'was due to (the) fact that Stokes Guns etc. could not be left in the air & must be guarded.'[23] In reality, 6th Division were holding an overextended front, and enemy penetration in a raid was always a risk. Lieutenant-Colonel Prior of 9th Norfolk spelt out the defensive principles to his officers on 3 April. 'Companies in the line now are in some respects outposts only & in other respects the fixed garrisons of definite positions.' In addition to the outposts protecting troops in the rear, they had to hold 'the exits to the tunnel communications' and be able to break up enemy attempts at penetration by cross-fire. Whilst sentry groups had to be posted to avoid surprise, 'no unnecessary groups are to be posted' as this reduced the concentration of rifle fire: 'The fatal thing is dissemination. If you attempt to meet with sentry groups or small detachments at every possible contingency, you will have no force in hand with which to fight, which is your real job.' These outpost defensive positions needed to be 'made & kept strong.' The 'rule of 1 man in three' in defence no longer applied. And reminding his officers of the tenets of SS143, Prior continued, underlining for emphasis: 'The platoon is now the unit.'[24] This was the same in both defence as well as in attack. The Norfolks' War Diary for August 1917 shows its front line with five Vickers gun positions and six Lewis gun positions with their fields of fire coving the whole of the enemy front. The notes reflect well on Prior as CO, and on 6th Division's willingness to consider problems and take effective solutions. And whilst historiography focusses on the German reorganisation of defensive tactics, it is a reminder that the BEF devoted thought to this problem as well.

21 F.L. Petre, *The History of the Norfolk Regiment, Vol II*, p.264.
22 War Diary, HQ 71 Infantry Brigade, 25 March 1917, TNA WO95/1619.
23 War Diary, 2nd Battalion Sherwood Foresters, 26 March 1917, TNA WO95/1624.
24 War Diary, 9th Battalion Norfolk Regiment, 'Circular Letter to all Officers by Commanding Officer', 3 April 1917, TNA WO95/1623.

The relatively peaceful period was now to come to an end, however. The raid by 2nd York & Lancaster at the Double Crassier on 12 April was prescient. The following day the division received information that the enemy was about to withdraw on a front running from the Double Crassier to the Souchez River.

16/03 05.00	110 Bde (attached)	Salient, The Dump	Two parties	Barrage. Adjacent feint raid. Only one party penetrated. Four positions bombed. 5 prisoners. 16 casualties.
24/03 19.00	11th Essex	Posen Crater	328 men, two waves	Raid practiced on facsimile trenches. Barrage and box barrage. 10 prisoners taken, 20 dugouts/emplacements destroyed. 66 casualties.
30/03 22.00	1st Buffs	Natal Trench	3 parties 4 officers 100 ORs	Barrage, box barrage & dummy barrage. 1 prisoner. Seven dugouts destroyed. 44 casualties.
09/04 02.00	2nd Durham Light Infantry	Opposite Loos	Three columns	Barrage. Adjacent feint raid. Failure – guides missed gaps in wire. 22 casualties.
10/04 23.40	9th Suffolk	Lookout Crater	One company	No identifications. One dugout destroyed. 10 casualties.
12/04 22.00	2nd York & Lancs	Triangle, Double Crassier	Two officers, 80 ORs	16 enemy killed, dugouts and shafts destroyed. No identifications. Casualties 'slight'.
16/04 04.00	1st West Yorkshire	Hill 70	3 officers 65 ORs	Barrage – enemy counterbarrage heavy. Failure. One officer, one OR killed; 2 officers 38 ORs wounded; one officer 7 ORs missing.
16/04	2nd Sherwoods		Several patrols	Unprepared raid for identifications. Failed.
18/04 02.00	1st Leicester	Hulluch	C Company Two waves	Dugouts blown in. One prisoner taken. Casualties: One officer & 21 ORs wounded, one officer & 3 ORs missing.
28/04 23.00	9th Norfolk	Dynamite Magazine	One platoon	Enemy encountered in strength. One OR wounded & one killed.
29/04 02.00	1st West Yorkshire	Hill 70	50 men	Held up by strong wire and machine-gun fire. Three killed.

Table 5.2: Raids carried out by 6th Division March-April 1917

German withdrawal of 13 April and the push towards Hill 70

First Army, in its position north of Arras, had been unaffected by the German withdrawal to the *Siegfriedstellung*, or Hindenburg Line, that took place between 25 February and 5 April 1917. Although I Corps, to whom 6th Division were now attached, played a part (utilising 24th Division) in the Battle of Arras, the BEF's contribution to the doomed Nivelle offensive, which in the British sector opened on 9 April to such seeming success, 6th Division itself would have no involvement. However, 'influenced in part by the successes … at the Pimple', on the northern end of Vimy Ridge, 'and the Bois en Hache, on either side of the Souchez river', a mile to the north, 'the Germans fell back under cover of small rear guards from the ground immediately commanded by Vimy Ridge.'[25] Crown Prince Rupprecht, writing on the day following the first day of the Battle of Arras, had observed that: 'No one could have foreseen that the expected offensive would gain ground so quickly.'[26] On the 11th, on the advice of the newly arrived 'Fritz' von Lossberg as Chief of Staff of the *Sixth Army,* the order was given for withdrawal to the German Third Position, which in the area that concerned I Corps, was to the Avion Switch, which encircled the western suburbs of Lens. This move deprived the BEF of much of the direct observation opportunities afforded by the capture of Vimy Ridge.

The withdrawal would lead to a period of ten days of continuous fighting on the part of 6th Division. At the outset, 16 Brigade held the line from the northern side of the Double Crassier to Hill 70, 18 Brigade from thence to Hulluch, with 71 Brigade in the rest of the line to the Hohenzollern Redoubt. 16 Brigade faced a junction in the German order of battle, between *IV Army Corps Gruppe Loos* (Saxon troops) and *VIII Reserve Corps Gruppe Souchez*. These corps were part of the *Sixth Army*, 6th Division's old opponents at Armentières in 1914-15, but now commanded by General von Falkenhausen.[27] Von Falkenhausen would be sacked by Ludendorff for failing to deploy defence-in-depth principles effectively (although von Lossberg would blame Crown Prince Rupprecht for allowing reinforcement too late),[28] on 23 April. The fighting against 6th Division that month was borne by *8th Division*, *IV Army Corps*, which in 1917 'always defended itself well in attacks and held its positions with tenacity' and whose 'morale was good.'[29] The British assaults would fall on *153rd*

25 C. Falls, *Military Operations France and Belgium 1917, Vol. 1*, pp. 287-8.
26 Crown Prince Rupprecht, *Mein Kriegstagebuch II*, p. 138.
27 Ludwig von Falkenhausen (1844-1936) was a veteran of the Franco-Prussian War and was retired in 1914. He was given command of the *Ersatz Corps* of *6th Army*, and *6th Army* itself in September 1916.
28 F. von Lossberg (D.T. Zabecki & D.J. Biedekarkne, eds), *Lossberg's War*, Kindle edition location 6029.
29 *Histories of Two Hundred and Fifty-one Divisions of the German Army which Participated in the War (1914-1918)*, p.159.

Infantry Regiment (*16 Brigade*) to the left of the 6th Division push and *93rd Infantry Regiment* (*16 Brigade*) to the right.

The advance of 24th and 6th Divisions (the dividing line between whom was the Double Crassier) in response to the German pull-back was strictly controlled by I Corps, commanded by Lieutenant-General Arthur Holland.[30] Modest objectives were given, and it was laid down that 'divisions will not become seriously engaged', reaching their objectives whereupon 'posts will be established at tactical points along this line and reconnoitring patrols sent forward.'[31] On 13 April, 2nd York & Lancaster, the most southerly unit of the division and adjacent to the Double Crassier, heard explosions from the German lines all day, which they believed to be dugouts being blown up. At 16.30 they were informed by 24th Division that the enemy had evacuated their front line, and Lieutenant-Colonel Blunt pushed patrols from his three front-line companies on his own initiative into the Triangle,[32] which they had raided only the day before. This triangular salient jutted out northwards from the Double Crassier.[33] The unit, meeting slight opposition, advanced to the tip of the Double Crassier and the line of the east-west railway there, which ran to the rear of the enemy support trenches to the north. Their advance that day amounted to a distance of about 500 yards.[34] General Osborn, who expected the enemy only to withdraw to the end of the Double Crassier, and was evidently following matters closely, ordered both a company of 8th Bedfordshire from brigade reserve and 1st Buffs (in line on the left of 2nd York & Lancasters) to conform to the advance. The Buffs pushed out one company and occupied the enemy front and support lines, before running into more stout machine gun opposition. The Buff's advance did not progress further the following day due to heavy shellfire. The York & Lancasters, whom Osborn had reinforced with subsections of 16th Machine Gun Company and another company of 8th Bedfords, made some progress under heavy shelling, although 24th Division to their right was not able to get forward.

30 Arthur Edward Aveling Holland, an artillery officer, had served as CRA 8th Division and VII Corps, had commanded 1st Division, and had been GOCRA Third Army, before assuming command of I Corps in February 1917, a post he held until the Armistice. A highly able officer he had proposed a hurricane 48-hour bombardment prior to the Battle of Arras, a plan accepted by GOC Third Army, but vetoed by subordinate commanders, whereupon Holland was transferred to corps command.

31 War Diary, HQ I Corps, Order No. 1117/19 (G.a) 13 April 1917, TNA WO95/594.

32 Allan St. John Blunt had been a captain of the 1st Battalion York and Lancaster in August 1914. He had commanded the 2nd Battalion since June 1916, and although wounded in September that year would continue in command until April 1918. Captain John Horlington appears to have been the first to set off across No Man's Land under his own initiative, an act for which he would be awarded the MC (*London Gazette*, 18 June 1917, p. 5992). Blunt was therefore conforming to Horlington's initiative with his right-hand company.

33 Marden incorrectly refers to this as the 'Railway Triangle'.

.34 War Diary, 2nd Battalion York & Lancaster, 13 April 1917, WO95/1610.

The enemy withdrawal was essentially a swinging door pivoting on Hill 70 towards Lens, the hinge at the north-east (left) of 16 Brigade's frontage. The brigade was pushing directly against this hinge and meeting resistance and would essentially be attempting to roll up the German front and support lines in a north-easterly direction. (See Map 10, colour section). This posed an entirely different problem to a frontal attack on a trench. I Corps noted: 'Every sign that the enemy left in a hurry as roads are not blown up. Good artillery instruments, two truckloads and dumps of timber are amongst material abandoned by him.'[35] Marden asserts that '16th Infantry Brigade pressed the enemy with such vigour, within the limits allowed to it, that he was evidently rushed rather farther back than had been his intention, and began to become apprehensive as to his hold on Hill 70.'[36] Given the comparative lack of movement on the 14th, this claim of the enemy being 'rushed' is overenthusiastic. The German positions as they existed on the ground converged from Lens towards the southern tip of the Loos Crassier (3,000 yards to the north-east of the Double Crassier), and it is here that resistance would stiffen. I Corps did not know how far the enemy was intending to retire, but the parameters of what was likely to be held on to were self-evident. Hill 70 to the north was crucial, and the enemy had been noted to be siting many new artillery positions there on the 13th. They held their original front from there northwards strongly, even raiding 18 Brigade's trenches to the west of the hill on the 14th.

The advance of 16 Brigade, Loos, April 1917, as seen from atop the Double Crassier. The Triangle has disappeared under the modern spoil heap.

35 War Diary, HQ I Corps, 14 April 1917, TNA WO95/594.
36 Marden, op. cit. p.29.

I Corps issued orders on the 14th that Fosse 12, a mine with housing immediately to the south, and which lay where the Loos Crassier railway met the east-west railway, was to be taken as soon as possible. General Ross's detailed orders set out that the position would be bombarded by the divisional and corps heavy artillery until 03.00 on the 15th, whereupon patrols would seize it. Patrols of 18 Brigade, facing the enemy front-line to the north of Hill 70, would also move forward to seize their opposing trenches following artillery preparation. (This part of the operation seemingly downplayed the reality that the raid of the previous day indicated that the enemy intended to hold this front, and this part of the order was later cancelled). 16 Brigade would then work round to the south of Hill 70. In essence, Ross's intention was to position forces with the potential to pinch Hill 70 out, and in this he anticipated General Holland's orders by 24 hours. Ross intended to proceed with vigour: 'In the advance of the 16th I.B. immediately the infantry are held up, the Brigadier, acting through his group, will concentrate all available artillery, including H.A. on the point that is stopping the advance.' (Brigadiers had been instructed the previous day to 'call without hesitation' on corps heavy artillery).[37] At a time fixed by General Osborn, the barrage would cease, and the heavy artillery would resume wire-cutting. Ross was delegating artillery command for speed of results.[38] That night, there was a bombardment from 21.00 to midnight, an hour's pause for patrolling, resumption between 01.00-02.00, with a further hour's pause followed by another hour of artillery work. The plan was not unsophisticated. Patrols on the night of 14/15 April certainly found that the enemy had given up more ground, and at 04.30 an advance was made to the Loos Crassier and Railway Triangle at Fosse 12 of about 400 yards, the ground being held in the face of two 'vigorous counter attacks.' The Buffs then probed towards a sunken road to the east in the afternoon. Their casualties were significant, three officers and 11 ORs killed and four officers and 65 ORs wounded to this point.[39] Meanwhile the corps heavy artillery bombarded Fosse 12 which was holding up the advance of 24th Division to 16 Brigade's left.

On 15 April I Corps sent out an order stating: 'On the night of April 15/16th, the Corps Commander intends to capture HILL 70 without committing himself to a serious infantry attack and desires the G.O.C. 6th Division to make the necessary arrangements.' This operation required rolling up three parallel trenches (Natal, Netley & Nero/Nelson) and the capture of the Dynamite Magazine strongpoint (in Nash Alley which connected Netley and the junction between Nero and Nelson). For an hour all available firepower would be directed on Hill 70, which 'if found unoccupied by the enemy, will be taken possession of by the 6th Division.'[40] This plan

37 War Diary, HQ 6th Infantry Division, 13 April 1917, WO95/1582.
38 The division's artillery at this point had been split into three Groups, that supporting 16 Brigade, comprising three batteries of six 18-pounder guns and 1 battery of six 4.5-inch howitzers.
39 War Diary, 1st Battalion Buffs, 13-14 April 1917, WO95/1608.
40 War Diary, HQ I Corps, Order No. 1117/19/2, 15 April 1917, TNA WO95/594.

was doomed to failure. It was grandiose in that it embodied the belief that the enemy might evacuate Hill 70 without a fight, made light of their resistance to date, and ignored the strengthening of that position with artillery.

Hill 70 was 'a treeless expanse of chalk downland standing at the end of one of the many spurs which reached north-eastward from the Artois plateau.' It 'dominated Lens and gave a commanding view of the Douai plain beyond.'[41] To its south-west, from which direction 6th Division were advancing, it was covered with the shattered ruins of houses, which gave considerable advantages to the enemy who had carefully organised its defence. Not only was it a crucial point for the Germans in terms of observation, it was the king pin both of the right of their withdrawal and any subsequent line. They were bound to defend it with tenacity. General Ross must have recognised the contradictory nature of the order that the hill could be taken without 'serious infantry attack' as the enemy had begun heavy shelling of the advancing 16 Brigade, the back areas and Loos in particular, and were mounting counter-attacks. Topography did not assist. The original British front line lay at about 50 metres above sea level. The direction of their advance was along a spur (along which lay Natal, Netley and Nelson trenches) at 65 metres leading directly to the 70-metre high hilltop. The British advance was under close observation and directly under the newly positioned enemy guns. Lieutenant-Colonel Prior of 9th Norfolk summarised: 'The enemy was fighting very fiercely; he had altogether the best of the ground, he knew exactly where every dug-out was placed, and altogether had every means at his disposal to give us a most unpleasant time. He certainly succeeded.'[42] I Corps was, however, correct in considering trying to take the hill at a time of flux on the front if it could be done. In reality, taking the hill would require much preparation and a very carefully orchestrated assault by two fresh divisions.

6th Division pushed on regardless. At the end of the 15th, General Osborn, with the permission of both corps and division 'put in another battalion (to) harass the enemy's rearguard posts on their withdrawal,'[43] this being 1st Kings Shropshire Light Infantry. More force was being drawn in as resistance mounted. On the 16th, the start of three days of heavy rain which made progress even more difficult, 16 Brigade began their advance under the slow bombardment Ross had ordered. The day would be a frustrating one – 1st Buffs were pushed back, whilst 2nd York & Lancaster made only very limited progess. At the end of the day the 1st Buffs held a right-angled position consisting of part of the north-east running British front line and in a south-easterly direction down the Loos Crassier railway, intermixed with the 2nd York & Lancasters, whilst 8th Bedfords held a forward position in advance of the two other battalions at the southernmost extent, with a flank to Fosse 12. On the 17th, after a British release of 450 gas cylinders north of Hill 70, 8th Bedfords were strongly

41 G.W.L. Nicholson, *Canadian Expeditionary Force 1914-1919*, p. 286.
42 Petre, op. cit. p.265.
43 War Diary, HQ 16 Infantry Brigade, 15 April 1917, WO95/1606.

attacked, and shelling by enemy heavy artillery increased markedly. 1st KSLI, the fourth unit now involved, sent out a force to reach the sunken road that ran parallel to and about 200 yards from the Loos Crassier railway, whose capture had eluded 1st Buffs, but this was repulsed. Osborn 'now ordered no more operations to take place without an artillery bombardment first',[44] indicating the battalions' attempts to advance had become somewhat uncoordinated. After a bombardment from 16.00 to 05.45 on the 17-18th, the Shropshires and the Bedfords took the sunken road, thus reaching the western end of two of the three trenches (Natal and Netley) whose capture had been ordered two days before, and which could now be enfiladed, some limited penetration along their length having been achieved. Osborn now increased the number of Vickers guns attached to the attacking units. The degree of the difficulty in communication is indicated by the fact that the remainder of the day was spent in establishing the exact positions of the infantry for a barrage to help them forward on the 19th. On that day 1st KSLI made limited progress into Natal Trench, the more northerly of the parallel pair Natal/Netley, but the 8th Bedfords could not advance, although the two units were now linked by Novel Alley which connected the two. Osborn reorganised his brigade front that night, the Bedfords being relieved by 14th Durham Light Infantry, and 11th Essex relieving the exhausted 1st Buffs (both these new units from neighbouring 18 Brigade). 46th Division simultaneously took over the line in 6th Division's right from the 24th. The latter's progress had continued to be stalled, which had exposed the flank of 16 Brigade to enfilade fire.

April 20th was spent with the brigade's Stokes mortars attempting to destroy enemy strongpoints but failing. On the 21st the infantry drew back and 14th DLI attacked after an early morning barrage by heavy artillery, holding their gains (the extension of Novel Alley to the south to Nero Trench) against counterattack. On the following day, the 14th DLI and 11th Essex (with the support of companies from 2nd York & Lancaster and 1st KSLI) again attacked under a creeping and stationary bombardment of three minutes at Zero (08.00). It had been planned to use gas once more, but the weather was unfavourable. The DLI captured a portion of Nash Alley (parallel to Novel) to the Dynamite Magazine, but were bombed out of Nash, retreating to Nero Trench where they beat off three counterattacks. To their north 11th Essex were driven back out of Nash Alley with repeated counterattacks. That night, 1st Leicestershire relieved the 14th DLI, and offensive action ceased. The line at noon on the 22nd was in the shape of a figure '5.' The top of the figure was the original British front line and the bulge at the bottom of the figure was the gain of Nash Alley, looping back to the 46th Division on the east side of Fosse 12, who had made no progress. At the end of the day the bulge at the bottom of the figure '5' was much thinner, Novel Alley now being the front line to the enemy-held Nash Alley. No more progress would be attempted.

44 War Diary, HQ 16 Infantry Brigade, 15 April 1917, WO95/1606.

Site of Netley Trench from the slopes of Hill 70.

In assessing this period of fighting, most of the documentation prepared in terms of reports by both 6th Division and 16 Infantry Brigade is missing from their respective war diaries. Marden viewed the demands on the division as very hard:

> Four battalions from other brigades, in addition to its own four, had passed through the hands of 16th Infantry Brigade … Battalions relieved from the fighting front one night were put straight into the line elsewhere on the following night, and battalions which had already done a long continuous tour in the trenches were relieved one night, put into the fighting front on the following night, and twenty-four hours later had to deliver an attack.[45]

16 Brigade added that:

> The battalions could not have done better, they went into the offensive after 5 ½ months (except for ten days) continuous trench warfare, one battalion not having been even in Reserve for 22 days and fought with the highest morale and courage imaginable but was very tired at the finish.[46]

45 Marden, op. cit. p.31.
46 War Diary, HQ 16 Infantry Brigade, 'Note on Operations of 16th Inf Bde from April 13th to April 23rd', April 1917, TNA WO95/1606.

The other two infantry brigades were holding a front of 7,000 yards, and Marden reinforces the perception that the line was severely stretched by pointing out that not only had one German raid passed through both front and support lines without being noticed and was only located in the reserve line, but that in another place the enemy had set up a bomb and ration store in the British front line at a point where only two posts were being garrisoned.

16 Infantry Brigade concluded that they believed that the enemy 'had never intended us to gain the line of the Loos Crassier railway.' At this point 'he resisted to his utmost, the *153rd Infantry Regiment* opposite out left flank fighting most especially well and very much better than the *93rd Infantry Regiment* opposite our right flank.'[47] In describing the advance beyond the railway to Nash Alley, the brigade noted that it was 'a most important switch trench ... which all prisoners called their 3rd Line.' If so, then this was the line to which withdrawal had been ordered (although British trench maps do not even note it as wired). Lossberg is clear in his memoirs that he ordered a withdrawal to 'east of Loos.'[48] This corresponds well to Nash Alley. If the line of the Loos Crassier railway had been held to the south, an impossible salient would have been created in the German position. 16 Brigade was therefore in some respects incorrect in its assumptions. Lossberg was also attempting to put in place his new defensive principles: 'Our active defence required lightly manned forward lines, with the mass of the infantry deeply echeloned farther in the rear.' He continued that: 'It was obvious to me, then, that we would have to abandon the techniques of rigidly defending every piece of ground to the last man.'[49] He ordered forward positions to be lightly held with machine guns and wired, to be given up under attack. This is the defensive organisation that the Canadians would encounter when they attacked Hill 70 in August. The very strong resistance to 16 Brigade's advance represented an absolute determination to retain Nash Alley as the German front, and to keep an area to the west of this as No Man's Land. In the service of retaining this defensive position it is no surprise that 16 Brigade reported that 'the artillery barrage was heavier both in calibre, number of guns & rate of fire than the 16th Inf(antry) B(riga)de have ever yet encountered even in the fighting on the Somme ... and it was partly the weight of the artillery which drove our men out.'[50]

One set of battalion orders survive from these ten days, those for 14th Durham Light Infantry, who came into line on the 20th and attacked the following day. The orders shed light on the tactical progress the division had made since its attacks on the Somme the previous September. The battalion was commanded by 27-year-old Lieutenant-Colonel John Brenchley Rosher. Rosher, the son of barrister, had been

47 War Diary, HQ 16 Infantry Brigade, 'Note on Operations of 16th Inf Bde from April 13th to April 23rd', April 1917, TNA WO95/1606.
48 Von Lossberg, op. cit. location 5993.
49 Von Lossberg, op. cit. locations 5904-5911.
50 War Diary, HQ 16 Infantry Brigade, 'Note on Operations of 16th Inf Bde from April 13th to April 23rd', April 1917, TNA WO95/1606.

educated at Charterhouse and studied law at Trinity College, Cambridge, obtaining a first in both parts of the Law Tripos. A rowing Blue, he had also been president of Cambridge University Boat Club, 1910-11. He was a solicitor with Rashleigh, Turner, Mann & Rosher, London, having entered the firm in July 1914. Enlisting as private in the Artists Rifles (28th Battalion London Regiment) on 6 August 1914, he was commissioned into the 10th DLI on 26 September 1914. Wounded in September 1915 at Ypres (a shrapnel bullet in the right shoulder) and August 1916 on the Somme (when his left eye was injured by a shell), he took over the command of the battalion on 28 September 1916 and remained CO as a major until 5 August 1917, when he was gazetted acting lieutenant-colonel. Any civilian who took command of an infantry battalion in 1916 would have been an exceptional individual who must have been perceived as possessing organisational skills, an acute military mind, and a strong ability for leadership. That he served in this role as a major for 10 months suggests resistance within the army to acknowledging that a civilian could make a better CO than available Regular officers (although initially during this period the original CO, Lieutenant-Colonel G.F. Menzies, made occasional guest appearances).[51] Rosher was manifestly a man of intelligence, military ability and courage. His preparation for the Loos attack reflects the first two characteristics. The award of the MC in January 1917 for his services at Ypres, the DSO in December that year for his capture of Marcoing and a bar for its defence, during the Battle of Cambrai, reflects the latter. In March 1918 he would be given command of the 6th Division Machine Gun Battalion.[52]

On the 20th, as his unit began to move into the line (a relief that was only complete at 03.45 on the 21st), Rosher issued two pages of orders. He had clearly studied the potential problems at 16 Brigade HQ, likely with outgoing COs. He identified a strong point containing four machine guns where the railway touched Nero Trench in front of the Dynamite Magazine, which would hold up progress. 'It will have to be outflanked', he observed, detailing a bombing attack up Nero Trench while a platoon of B Company 'will get round south of Fosse 12' using the cover of houses and 'attack the strong point from (the) South.' The officer commanding the platoon, Lieutenant Charles Gold, was instructed to take 'a strong patrol' and reconnoitre the ground overnight. He advised that the commander of B Company (carrying out this manoeuvre) had the freedom to site the supporting machine guns as he saw fit to command the strong point and added that he had command of three Stokes and one medium mortar which could be deployed as required. 'Superiority in sniping must be

51 Rosher returned to practice as a solicitor with his pre-war firm, served as a staff officer during the Second World War, and died in 1965. He was a man with a sense of humour. Summonsed for riding his bicycle on the pavement whilst at Cambridge and fined, he sent 2/6 to the court as a joke and was fined £1 and costs for his pains.

52 In October 1918 he was sent on a staff course at Camberley – the military career of a highly able citizen was being mapped out. (Officers' Service, J.B. Rosher, TNA WO339/18477).

obtained at all cost', he stated.[53] Rosher thus demonstrated tactical finesse, with a grip on SS143 infantry tactics, an appreciation of the crucial nature of understanding the ground over which the attack would take place, and was prepared to delegate to junior officers. His formal operation orders, covering three pages, concentrated further tactically on suppression: 'Lewis Gun fire must be brought to bear on the trenches in front of the bombing parties to keep down the heads of the enemy', and 'the utmost use must be made of Rifle Grenadiers to cover the advance of the bombing parties.'[54] The orders show the very close cooperation of divisional artillery, corps heavy artillery, with brigade machine-guns firing directly down the railway in the five minutes prior to Zero, and Stokes mortars targeting key points in the ten minutes before Zero. Rosher's plan, showing such a keen grip on the tactics of trench warfare, worked well. In terms of the outflanking manoeuvre, at 17.00 Lieutenant Gold, Sergeant (15667) W. Simpson, Corporal (6121) S. Cable, Lance-Corporal (15469) T. Pearson and Private (18/467) N. Colwell rushed the strong point from the rear (the remaining 14 from the platoon providing cover), this gallant band of five killing 20 of the enemy and capturing 22 men and two machine guns, arriving as they emerged from their dug-outs.[55] Careful planning and reconnaissance had demonstrated their worth. For the attack on the Dynamite Magazine on the 22nd, Rosher issued a further three pages of orders. Again, the emphasis on suppressive fire was effective, 'our men getting over just as the German machine guns opened fire', and after 'a sharp fight for about 5 minutes', resistance ceased.[56] That the Dynamite Magazine could not be held was due to a relentless series of four counterattacks, enemy artillery, and sniping from the ruins of houses which provided observation over positions that barrage had largely flattened. This, the independent will of the enemy, could not be dealt with in orders.

The casualties for the month of April for 16 Brigade comprised nine officers killed and 27 wounded, with 160 other ranks killed, 746 wounded and 24 missing, a total of 967. 8th Bedfordshire had suffered 294 casualties, 2nd York & Lancaster 230, 1st KSLI 294, and 1st Buffs 202.[57] 14th DLI incurred losses of one officer and 34 ORs killed, with ten officers and 173 ORs wounded and 24 missing. 11th Essex lost one officer killed and 11 wounded with 44 ORs killed, 174 wounded and 20 missing. The total infantry casualties were therefore at the very most 1,459, just less than half the 3,200 at the Quadrilateral. The problems of evacuating these casualties was not

53 War Diary, 14th Battalion Durham Light Infantry, Appendix A, 20 April 1917, TNA WO95/1617.
54 War Diary, 14th Battalion Durham Light Infantry, Operation Orders No.23, 21 April 1917, TNA WO95/1617.
55 Charles René Gold had joined the Honourable Artillery Company, moved to the Derbyshire Yeomanry, and finally to the DLI, arriving on the Western Front in October 1916. He would be killed at Cambrai on 21 November 1917. He was awarded the DSO for this action. His four fellows were all awarded the Distinguished Conduct Medal.
56 War Diary, 14th Battalion Durham Light Infantry, 22 April 1917, TNA WO95/1617.
57 16 MGC suffered 25 casualties, 16 Trench Mortar battery three.

problematic as it had been at the Quadrilateral in 1916. Bertal Scott had been sent to command No. 10 General Hospital at the end of March, and was replaced by Lieutenant-Colonel Henry Grattan, who appeared to be a very active new broom.[58] Prior to Scott's departure the medical services had been reorganised and a system of grouping cases adopted. On 5 April 1917, under Grattan, there was a series of medical conferences with further new procedures introduced. Unlike all three actions on the Somme, the Field Ambulances had been in their chosen positions for some time and casualty evacuation routes well-practiced. Thus in the first 13 days of April 447 cases of sickness and 358 wounded were evacuated. Evacuation was made easier by the fact that 'Boche has retired over the crest of the ridge and movement in daylight is possible to LOOS.'[59] The casualties of 2nd York & Lancaster were thus the first able to be evacuated through the town, followed by evacuations from the regimental aid posts of 1st Buffs and 1st KSLI when on the 15th 'cases are being evacuated by car during daylight', and 'walking wounded can pass down the main road.'[60] Both the DDMS of I Corps visited (to review evacuation) as well as the DMS of First Army (to the main St Patrick's Aid Post) on the 16th. This attention stemmed from the luxury of the whole Corps and Army not being involved in a major offensive. During the first four days the daily evacuations did not exceed normal evacuations by a significant amount, but on the 17th 109 wounded were evacuated with 53 sick. However, there was no shortage of stretcher bearers and cars were available in sufficient number. On the 19th it was possible to consider a new ADS 400 yards west of Loos Crassier with:

> 35 feet of head cover … a long sloping gallery 150 feet, then a tunnel 150 feet long, 4 feet wide, 6 f(oo)t high. Cars can come within 300 yards. 3rd Australian Tunn(elling) Co(mpan)y will work on it, make a chamber for dressing cases and a 2nd exit. Position is hidden from BOSCHE.

It is an interesting reflection of the conditions that the RAMC were working under, but matters were different at a regimental level – on 19 April the medical officer of 8th Bedfordshire, James Black, was killed in action.[61] His CO, Lord Ampthill wrote how 'he established his Aid post as near the fighting line as possible, and there he worked with unremitting zeal and devotion without a thought of danger till the end.'[62] On

58 Henry William Grattan had been commissioned into the RAMC in 1895 and was a major at the outbreak of war. He would be promoted Deputy Director of Medical Services on 1 November 1918.
59 War Diary, ADMS 6th Division, 14 April 1917, TNA WO95/1593.
60 War Diary, ADMS 6th Division, 15 April 1917, TNA WO95/1593.
61 James Elliot Black MB was thirty when he died. He had studied at Glasgow University and University College, London, as well as Cambridge University. He had volunteered and was commissioned in September 1914. He had been awarded the Military Cross for tending the wounded under machine-gun and shellfire.
62 http://www.ramc-ww1.com/profile.php?profile_id=9459 (accessed 7 January 2019).

the day he died it was recorded that 'evacuation from LOOS (was) working smoothly', with cases wounded in the morning being at the Philosophe ADC by mid-day.[63] That day 120 wounded and 41 sick were evacuated, and on the 20th 171 wounded and 42 sick. On the 22nd, as the result of the enemy counter-attacks, it was noted 'casualties anticipated 500-700', and a company of the divisional pioneers were drafted in to collect the wounded. Only 70 wounded and 38 sick were evacuated however, although on the 23rd, 316 wounded and 27 sick were removed. This day was a grim one for the RAMC. Captain Robert Home of 17th Field Ambulance was killed and Lieutenant-Colonel David Chiles-Evans, commanding 18th Field Ambulance was gravely wounded in the head and died.[64] By the following day, however, the push having come to an end, the casualties decreased.

The nature of the Loos fighting was exceptionally difficult – much of the attack was made in enfilade along trenches under close observation rather than the normal frontal attack. Indeed, along the whole of 6th Division's front during this month life in the line was hard. On 30 April the commander of A Company, 2nd Sherwood Foresters in 71 Brigade to the north requested that his company be relieved 'as his men are terribly shaken with the strain of the last 30 days in the trenches & with the continuous heavy shelling they have been through during the last 3 days.'[65] Bernard Prior, commanding 9th Norfolk, described the position in front of Hill 70 as a 'bestial place.' It was 'impossible to move along the communication trenches by day without being observed by the enemy', the German trenches taken over being relatively shallow with sloping sides. In addition, the battalion was shelled by their own heavy guns. Prior had 'not minced my words in reporting it' and the artillery liaison officer 'had reported the language I had used to him and generally the fat was in the fire.' He continued:

> General Ross had evidently been ordered by the Corps Commander to tell us off for our want of confidence in our artillery. It was obvious that he was just as sick as we were on the way the gunners had let us down but he made a very good speech pointing out that if there were constant complaints of this sort the heavies would be afraid to fire at all and ended up by saying that even if we were shelled we must grin and bear it as this was all 'part and parcel of war.'

In the face of this less than sympathetic pronouncement, Prior noted the 'unholy joy' of the infantry when enemy shells were landing to the rear. He described how his opposite number in 9th Suffolk, Lieutenant-Colonel Latham, had had a rest made

63 War Diary, ADMS 6th Division, 19 April 1917, TNA WO95/1593.
64 Robert Home (born Toronto 1890) had qualified in 1913 and had arrived on the Western Front in January 1916. David Brynmor Chiles-Evans DSO (b. 1877) had previously been the MO of 1st West Yorkshire and had been wounded at Ginchy on 17 September 1916.
65 War Diary, 2nd Battalion Sherwood Foresters, 30 April 1917, TNA WO95/1624.

on the parados behind his battalion HQ where 'he found it the greatest joy of his trench life to rest there on a nice sunny day and watch Brigade Headquarters being bumped.'[66]

If the fighting had been as hard, if in slightly different ways, at both Loos and the Quadrilateral, the whole operational atmosphere was entirely different. Firstly, General Holland was not operating under the cosh of a timetable for a major offensive as the Earl of Cavan had been. If Cavan might be thought reckless in throwing the division at the Quadrilateral with no preparation to meet a deadline, Holland had demonstrated admirable caution over the first days, attempting to avoid major infantry engagement. General Ross and his brigade commanders, operating in the dark at the Quadrilateral, understood their front, if not the enemy's intentions, and were able to issue clear orders. Secondly, Brigadier-General William Osborn,[67] commanding 16 Brigade, was clearly a competent officer who kept very closely in touch with both Ross and the action and managed his reserves and brigade resources well, in close liaison downwards with his COs and upwards with divisional and corps artillery. Thirdly, even if John Rosher was an exceptional unit CO, it is clear that sophisticated infantry tactics within a combined arms approach was now a firm element of the division's repertoire. Lastly, devolved command was evident at a number of points in the chain of responsibility. The 6th Division had raised its game. General Holland concluded: 'The work done by the division on Hill 70 is worthy of the highest praise.'[68]

The one question that hangs over the fighting is the thrust towards Hill 70. Holland, as previously noted, had hoped to take this position on 15/16 April. In this aim, he was in good company: 'The capture of the summit had been the constant pre-occupation of those responsible for the sector ever since the Battle of Loos on the 25th September 1915, when it had been overrun, but not held.'[69] If Holland was over-hopeful in thinking that the enemy might withdraw from it spontaneously, he certainly did not make the mistake of throwing more elements of 6th Division hurriedly at it, which would have undoubtedly, given the massing of enemy artillery, have resulted in a multiplicity of casualties. As an objective, Hill 70 would rear its head again for I Corps in June, an attack which would be postponed, and then again

66 War Diary, 9th Battalion Norfolk Regiment, 'Diary of Lieutenant-Colonel B.H.L. Prior', WO95/1623.

67 Forty-six-year-old William Lushington Osborn had been commissioned in 1890 into the Sussex Regiment. He had fought on the North-West Frontier and Tirah, 1897-8, had served as a brigade-major, and had commanded 1st Sussex in India before the war. A depot major at the outbreak of war he was given command of 7th Sussex which he commanded until July 1916. Likely subject to the six-month rest rule in October 1917 he left 16 Brigade, returning to command 5 Brigade in April 1918, in command of whom he was wounded by a shell in October 1918.

68 Wat Diary, HQ 16 Infantry Brigade, GO/9/64, 25 April 1917, WO95/1606.

69 J.E. Edmonds, *Military Operations France and Belgium 1917, Vol 2*, p.221.

for the Canadian Corps on 15 August, when a meticulously rehearsed attack by the 1st and 2nd Canadian Divisions would carry it.

Engineering in the Loos Sector

Reference to the CRE's war diary for March 1917 shows the engineers and pioneers engaged on familiar tasks, providing water supply, maintaining keeps and roads, digging communication trenches, and providing camouflage. However, there was return to an activity not indulged in since Armentières – mining. Thus there were discussions with 173 Tunnelling Company about reconstructing the Wrexham Tunnel through the Double Crassier,[70] and at least two tunnellers conferences. However, the emergence of 'doctrine' in early 1917 involved the engineers as well as infantry. Thus, on 6 April 1917 there was a 'conference at CRE's mess' the primary subject being the role of the Royal Engineers and pioneers 'before & during an offensive',[71] as specified by *SS145 Notes on R.E. Preparations for, and the Employment of the R.E. in Offensive Operations* (February 1917),and *SS135 Instructions for the Training of Divisions for Offensive Action* (December 1916). The latter specified their role as:

i. The location and construction of strong points.
ii. The opening up of communication trenches from our jumping off trench to the objective.
iii. Arrangements for bridging … to enable the Field Artillery to get forward.
iv. Construction of a track for pack transport.
v. Searching for and opening up water supply in the captured position.
vi. Providing and fixing signboards and markers in the captured trenches.
vii. Formation of dumps of RE stores near the objective.
viii. Repairing and improving dugouts in the captured position for use as Command Posts.
ix. Extension of the tramway system.
x. Repairing roads … to take MT and heavy guns.
xi. Extension of piped water supply.

Thus on 14 April 11th Leicestershire (Pioneers) commenced work on roads in Loos, and RE companies began work on tracks for the artillery and bridging trenches. As with the medical services, the Chief Engineer of I Corps descended to review progress with roads.[72] It was, however, not possible to fulfil more than three of the tasks specified by *SS135* due to the limited progress, and during the last days of the

70 Constructed by the 4th Royal Welsh Fusiliers (the Pioneers of the 47th London Division) in January 1916.
71 War Diary CRE 6th Infantry Division, 6 April 1917, TNA WO95/1594.
72 Brigadier-General E.H. de V. Atkinson.

fighting shelling forced the engineers to reduce their presence at the front whilst 11th Leicestershire had to provide men as stretcher bearers.

Holding the Line May-October 1917

Returning to holding the line, the Division returned to raiding. Indeed, this period following the German withdrawal saw an increase in the harassment both sides offered to each other. The new ground in the south, still under observation from Hill 70, was in a terrible state. When General Ross inspected 2nd Sherwood Foresters' trenches by the Loos Crassier on 28 April, they were noted in many places to be 'filled in with debris, just the bayonets on the rifles being visible. Doubtless the owners of the rifles are underneath.'[73] In addition to the usual artillery strafes, there were several random heavy machine-gun barrages conducted across the whole of 6th Division's front, and new techniques of 'hate' were deployed. At midnight on 27 April, three Special Companies, Royal Engineers, launched gas attacks. Opposite the Bois Hugo and Puits 14 Bis, E Company launched 150 large and 70 small cylinders of phosgene (CG) using Livens projectors. No. 2 Company, using Stokes mortars fired 150 PS shells (chloropicrin, an irritant to skin, eyes and upper respiratory tract) and 108 SK shells (ethyl iodoacetate, a lachrymatory agent). D Company fired 150 cylinders of CG from Livens projectors into Cité St Elie. The enemy retaliated with a barrage at Zero+15, and on 4 May attacked 2nd DLI with gas shells at 03.30, causing 29 casualties. C Special Company carried out a successful gas release south of Hulluch on 15 May at 01.00. The wind was good and the 'cloud kept low and travelled well, being evenly distributed, and lasted 15 minutes.' Livens projectors were utilised on either side of the attack. The enemy artillery retaliated more quickly on this occasion, at Zero+5, and fired gas shells that evening on a column of 800 men in marching order, 'causing panic and casualties.'[74] On 30 May at 01.15 E Special Company fired 450 projectors on targets around Puits No 13, and a retaliatory barrage began 13 minutes later. Similarly, on 9 June 200 projectors were fired, '100 on target.'[75] A month later, on 9 July 1,036 gas cylinders were discharged opposite Bois Hugo and to its north, with 240 drums of gas fired from 100 Livens projectors at Puits 14 Bis and north of Hulluch. The British were, at this point, more enthusiastic purveyors of gas than their enemy.

Towards the end of May, General Ross interested himself tactically in the matter of raiding. SS107 *Notes on Minor Enterprises*, issued in March 1916, had not been prescriptive, stating 'no definite rules for the conduct of such operations can be laid down.'[76] It was, however, clear that surprise was key, aided by ruses and deception.

73 War Diary, 2nd Battalion Sherwood Foresters, 28 April 1917, TNA WO95/1624.
74 War Diary, HQ 6th Infantry Division, 15 May 1917, TNA WO95/1583.
75 War Diary, HQ 6th Infantry Division, 9 June 1917, TNA WO95/1583.
76 General Staff, *SS107 Notes on Minor Enterprises*, March 1916.

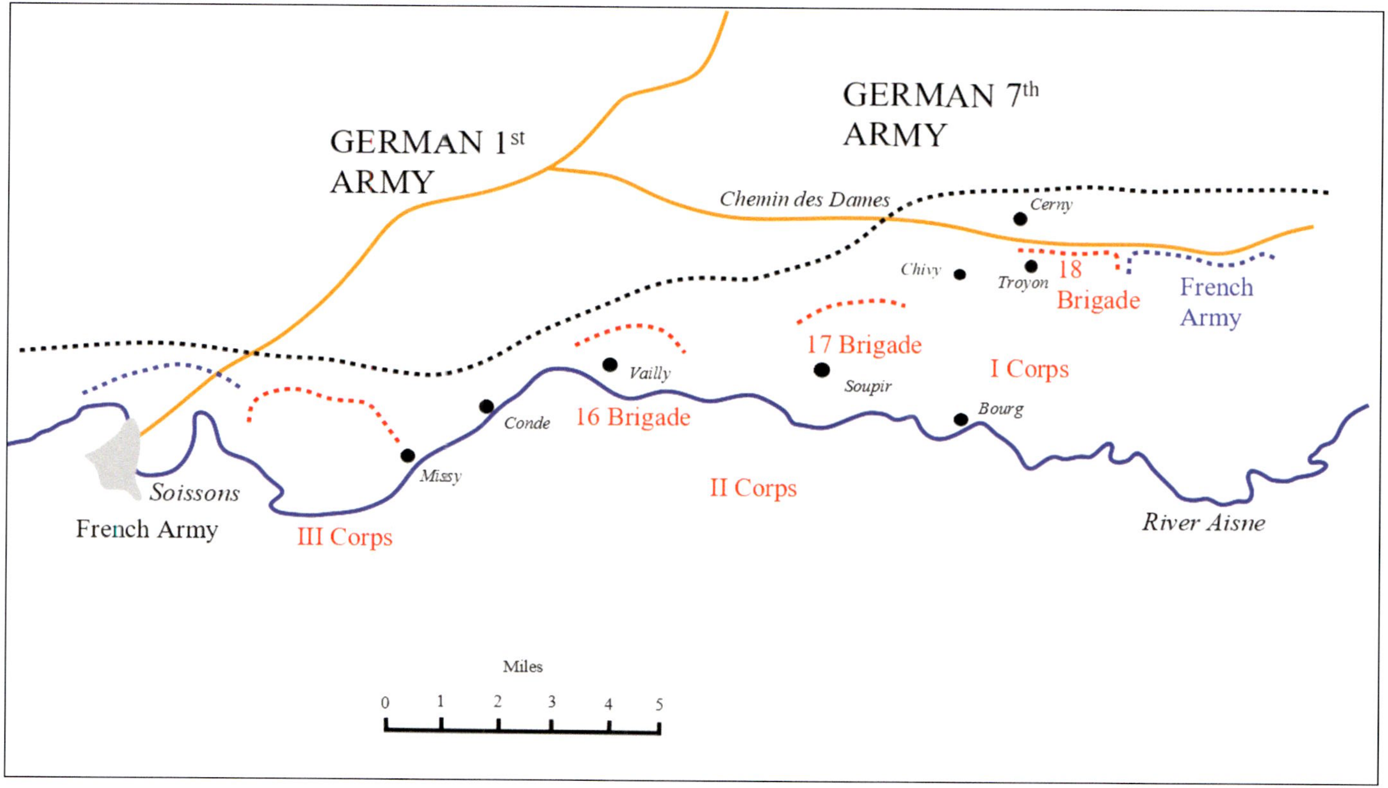

Map 1: River Aisne, September 1914.

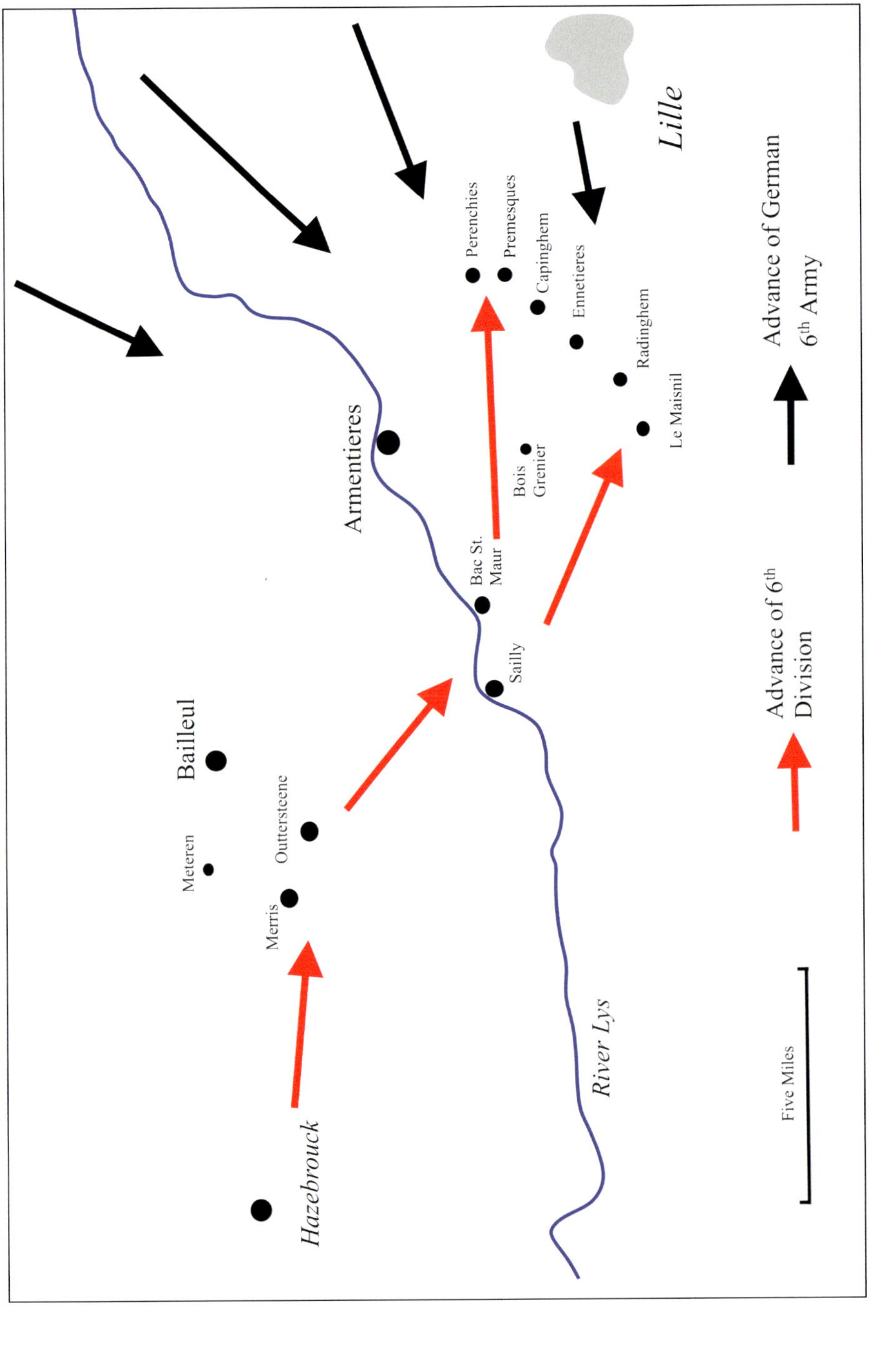

Map 2: Advance from Hazebrouck, October 1914.

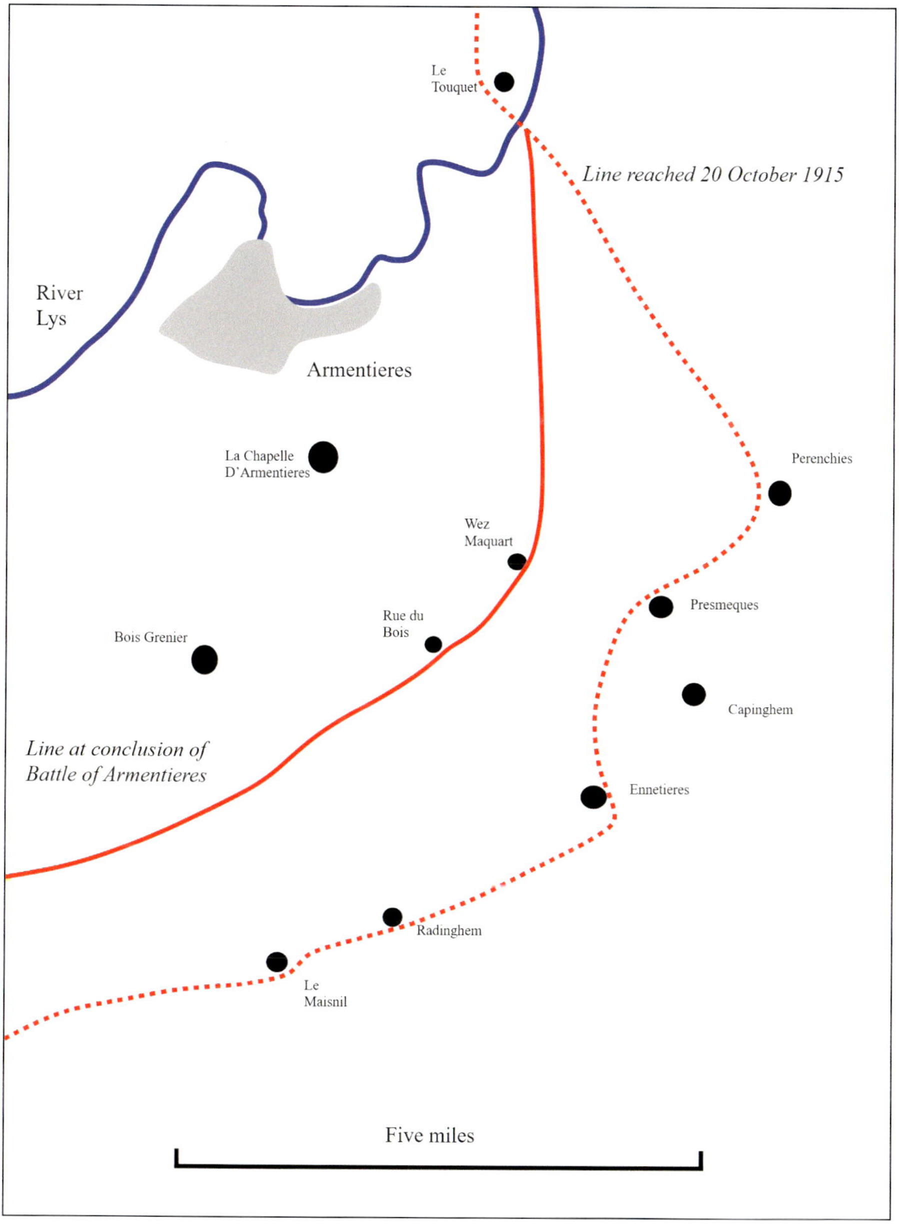

Map 3: Armentières Sector, 1914.

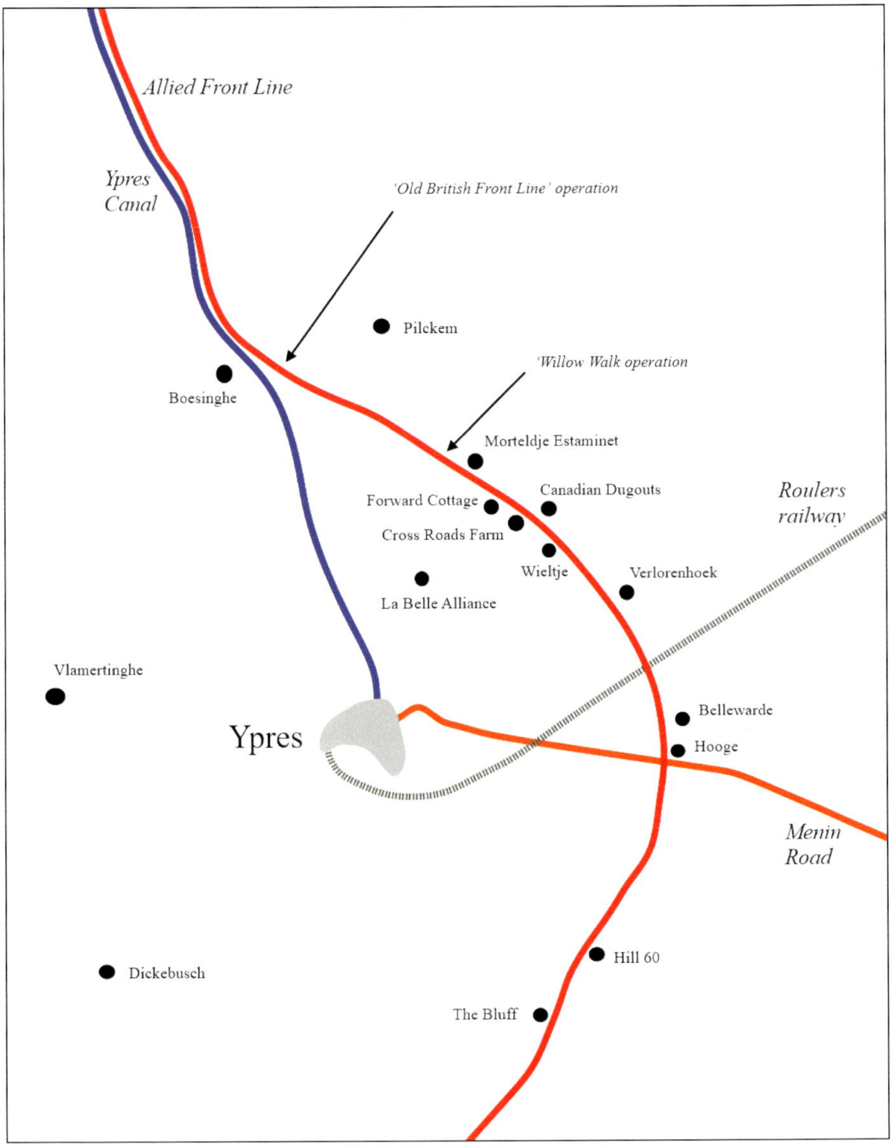

Map 4: Ypres Sector, 1915.

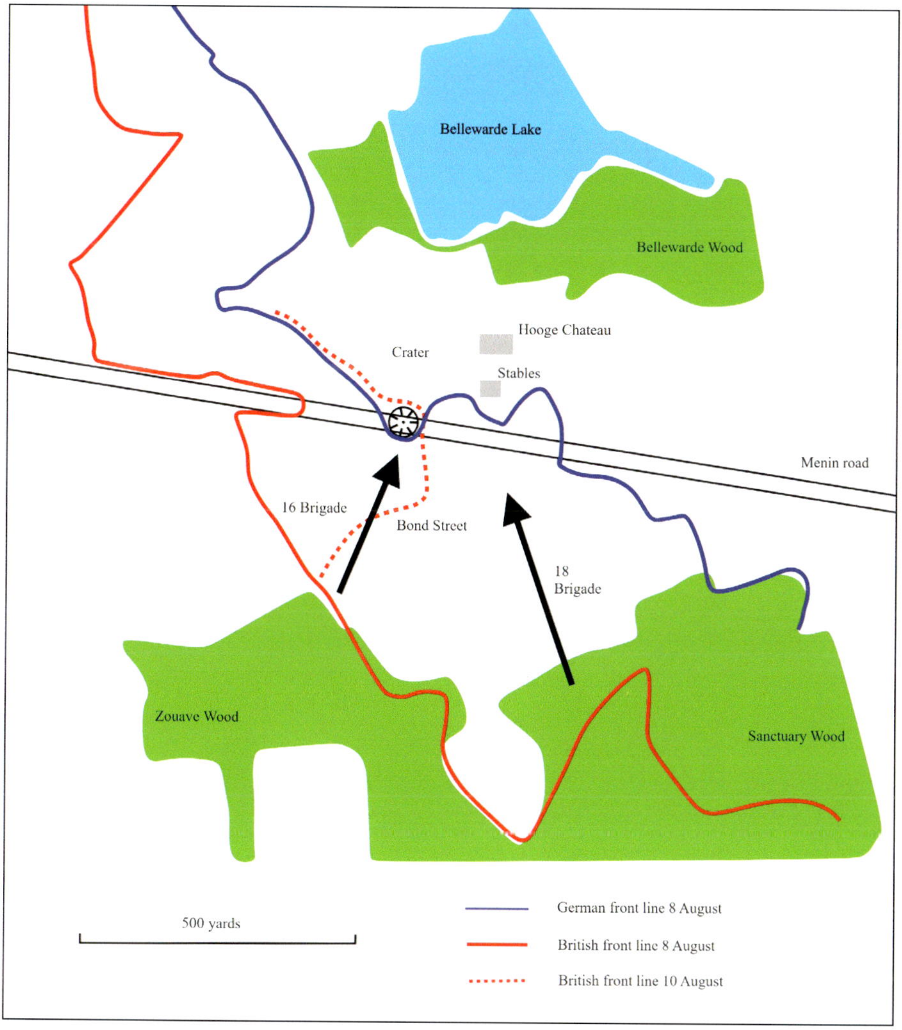

Map 5: Hooge, 9 August 1915.

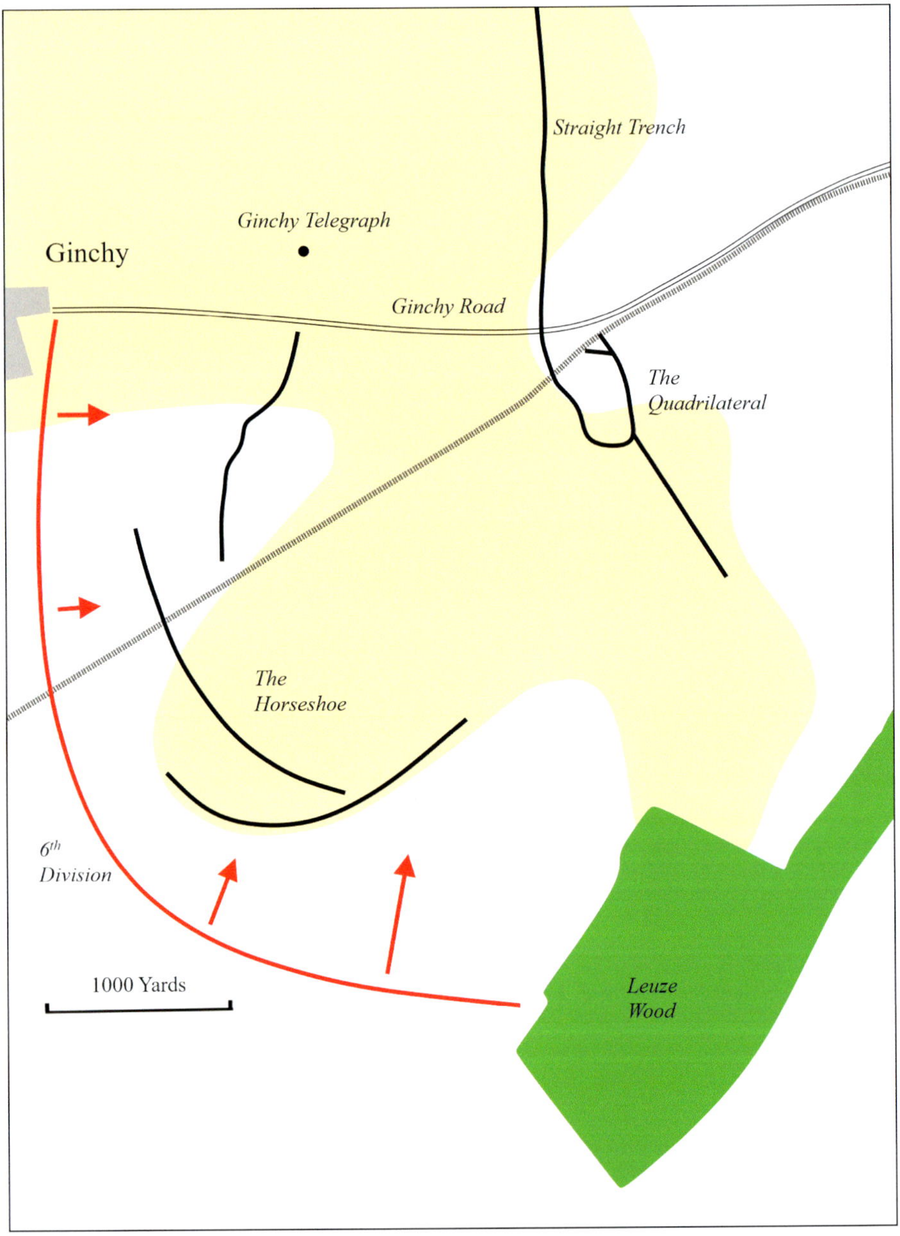

Map 6: Quadrilateral, Ginchy, September 1916.

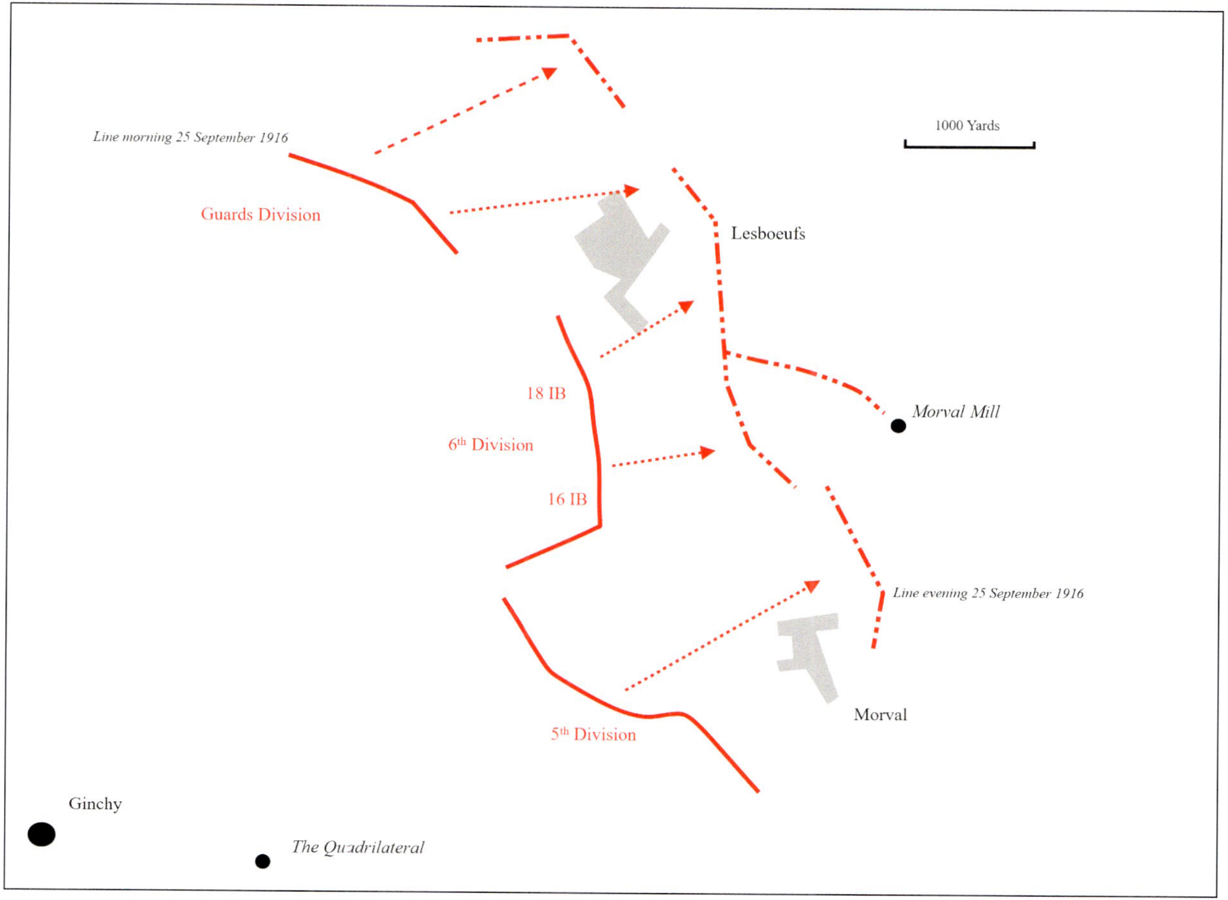

Map 7: Battle of Morval, September 1916.

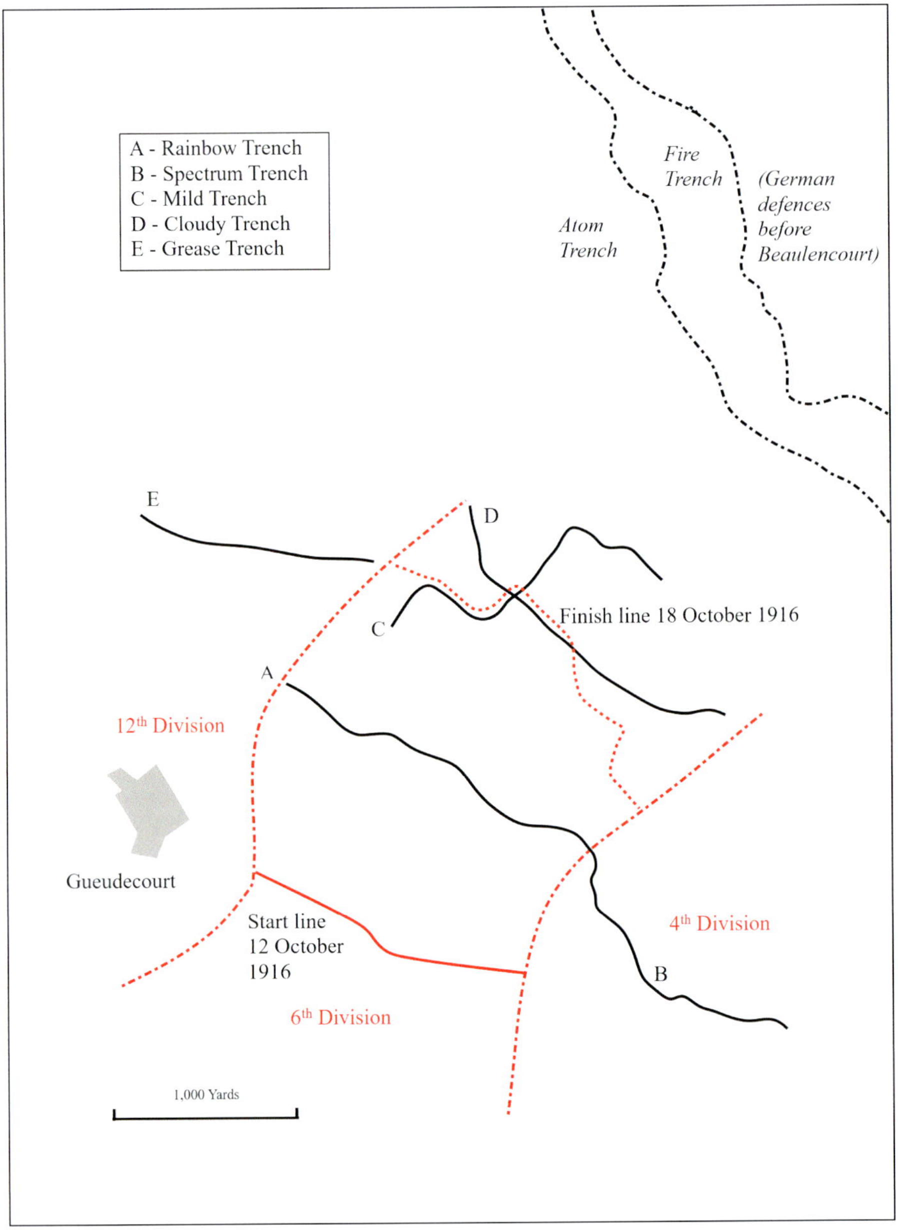

Map 8: Transloy Ridges, October 1916.

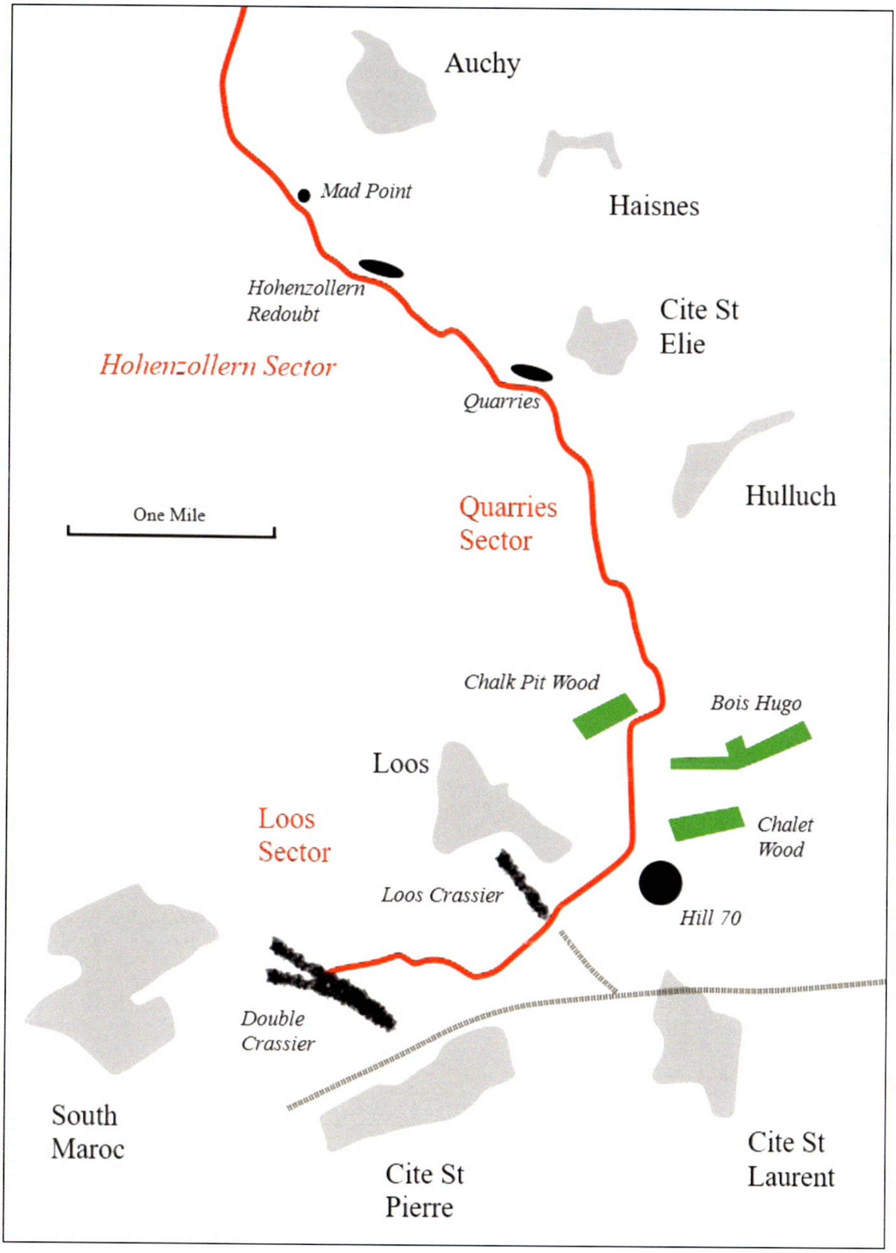

Map 9: Loos, Quarries and Hohenzollern Sectors, 1917.

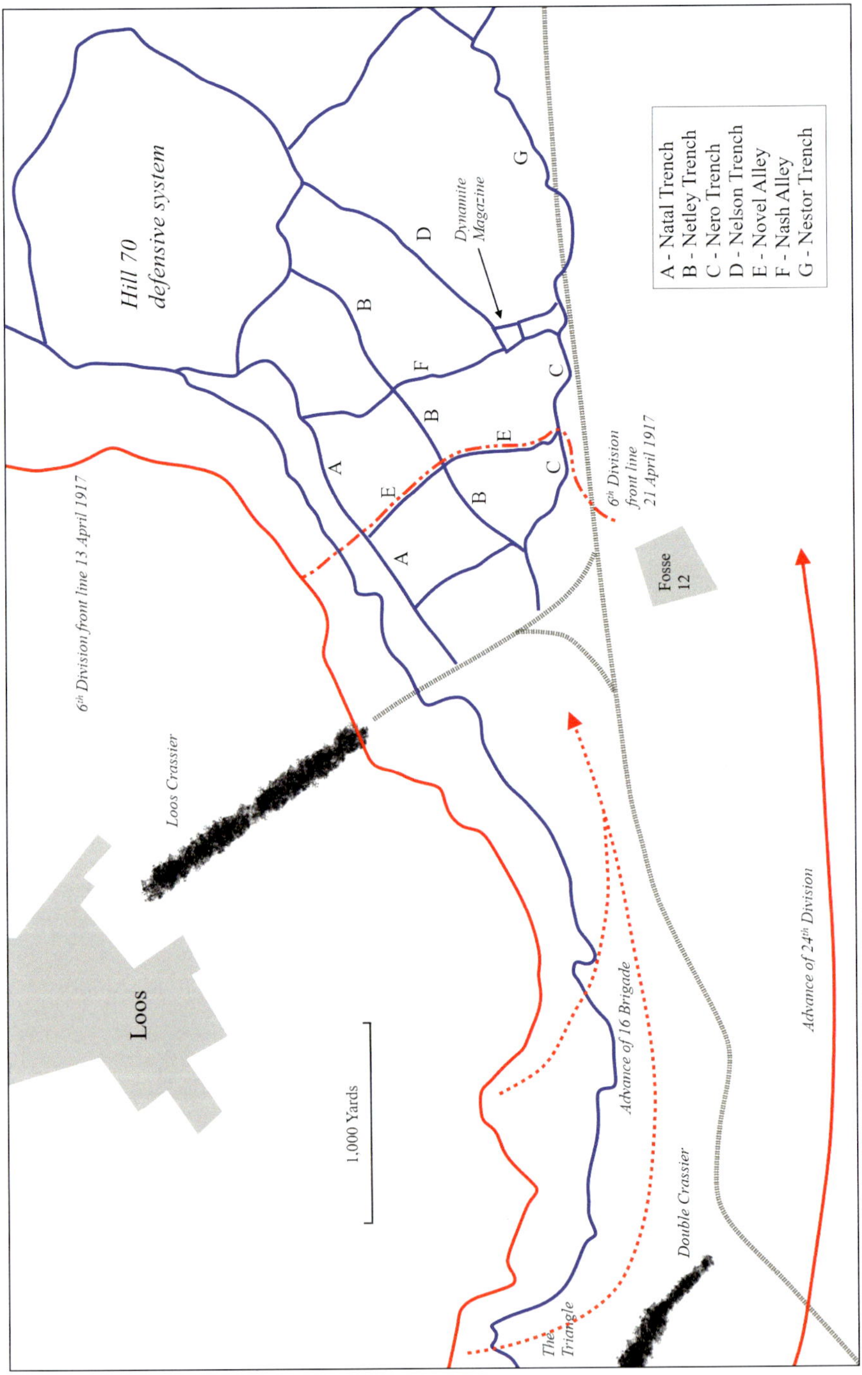

Map 10: 6th Division operations at Hill 70, April 1917.

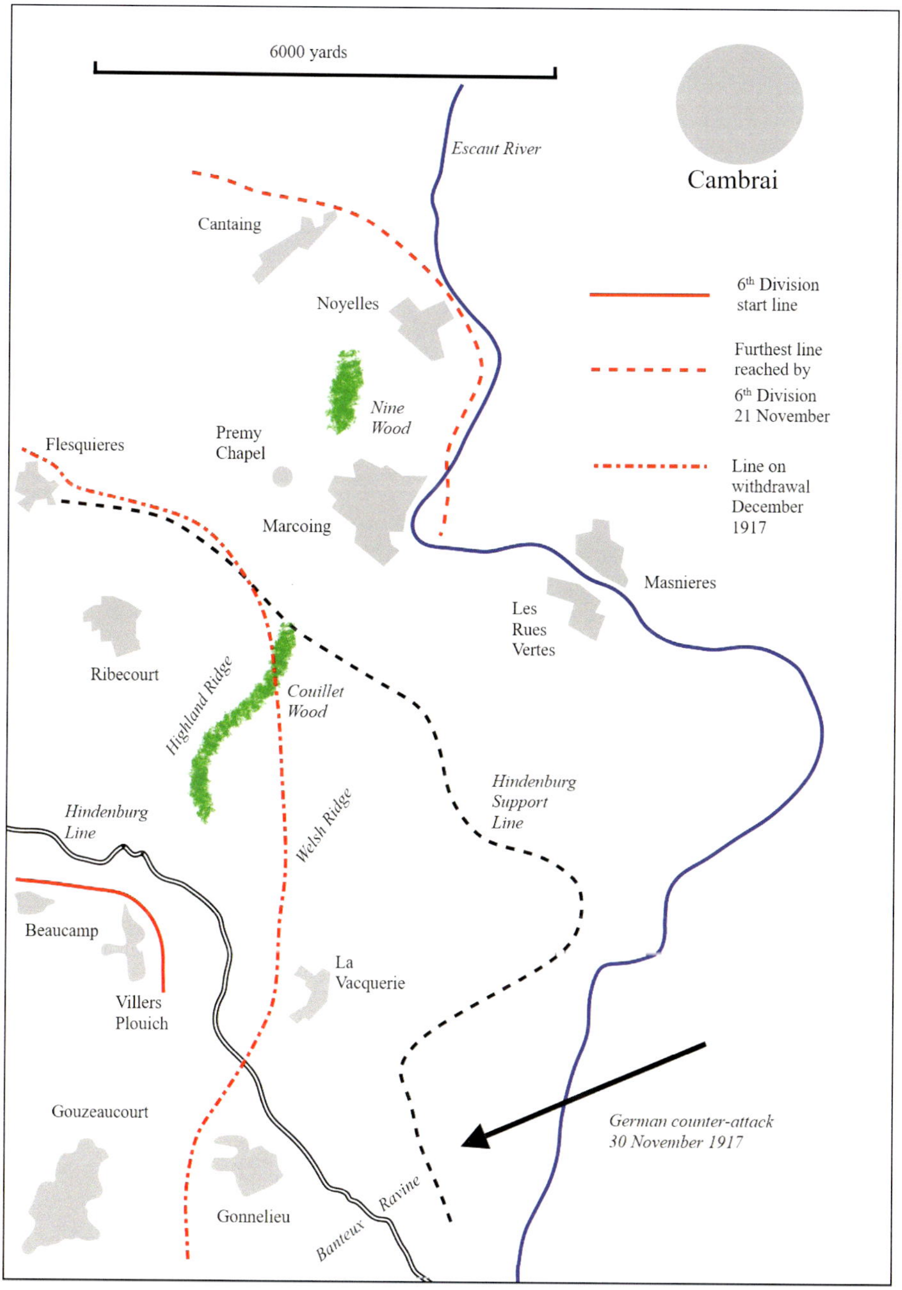

Map 11: Battle of Cambrai, November-December 1917.

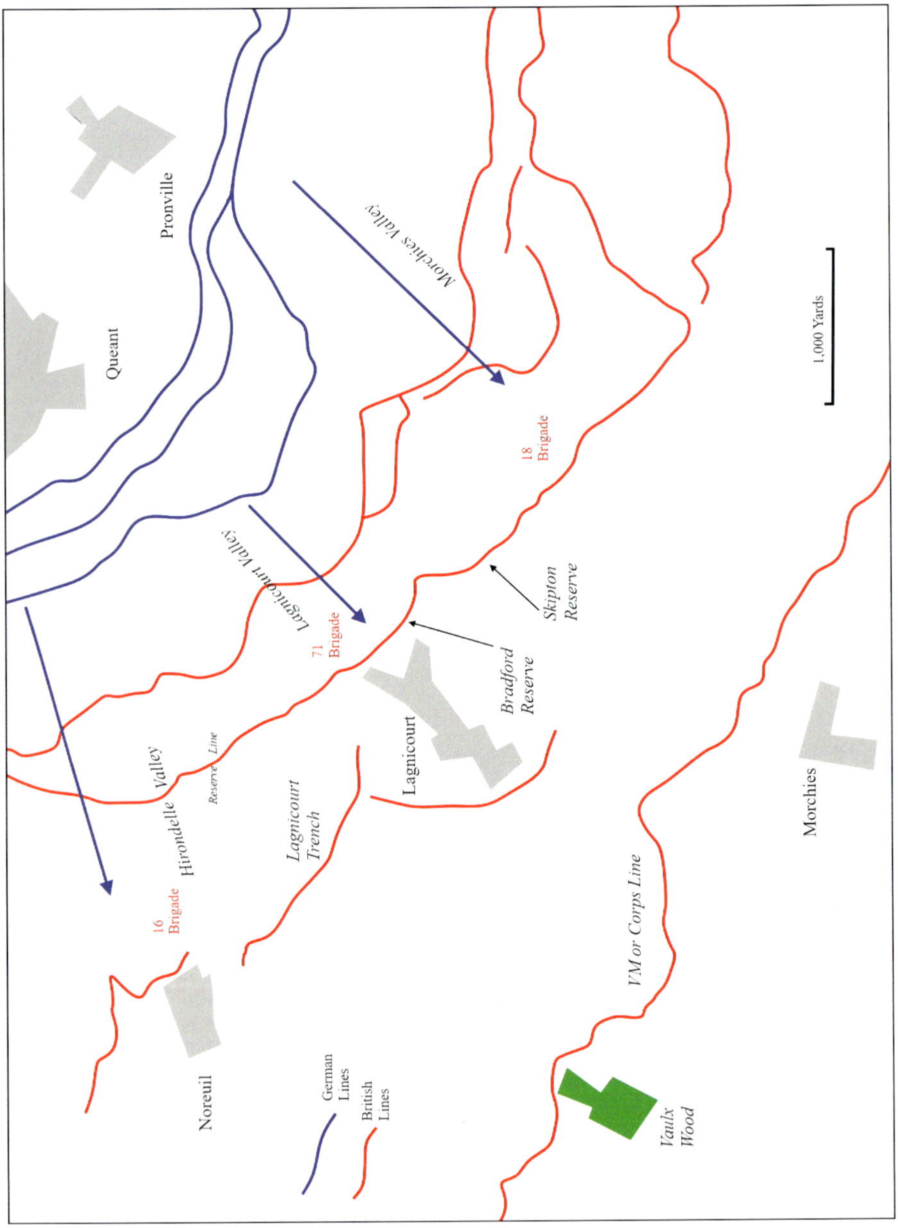

Map 12: *Kaiserschlacht*, 21 March 1918.

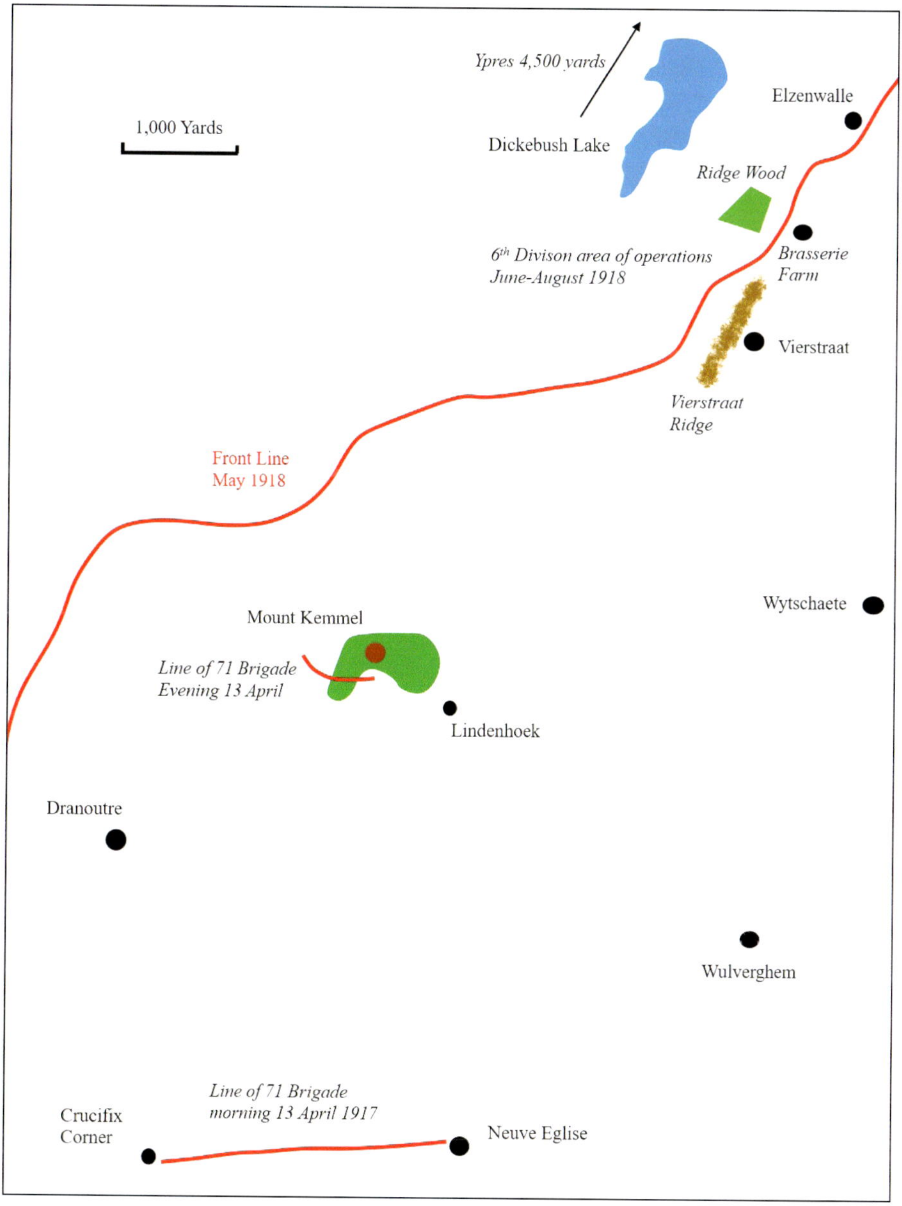

Map 13: Kemmel Sector, Ypres, April-August 1918.

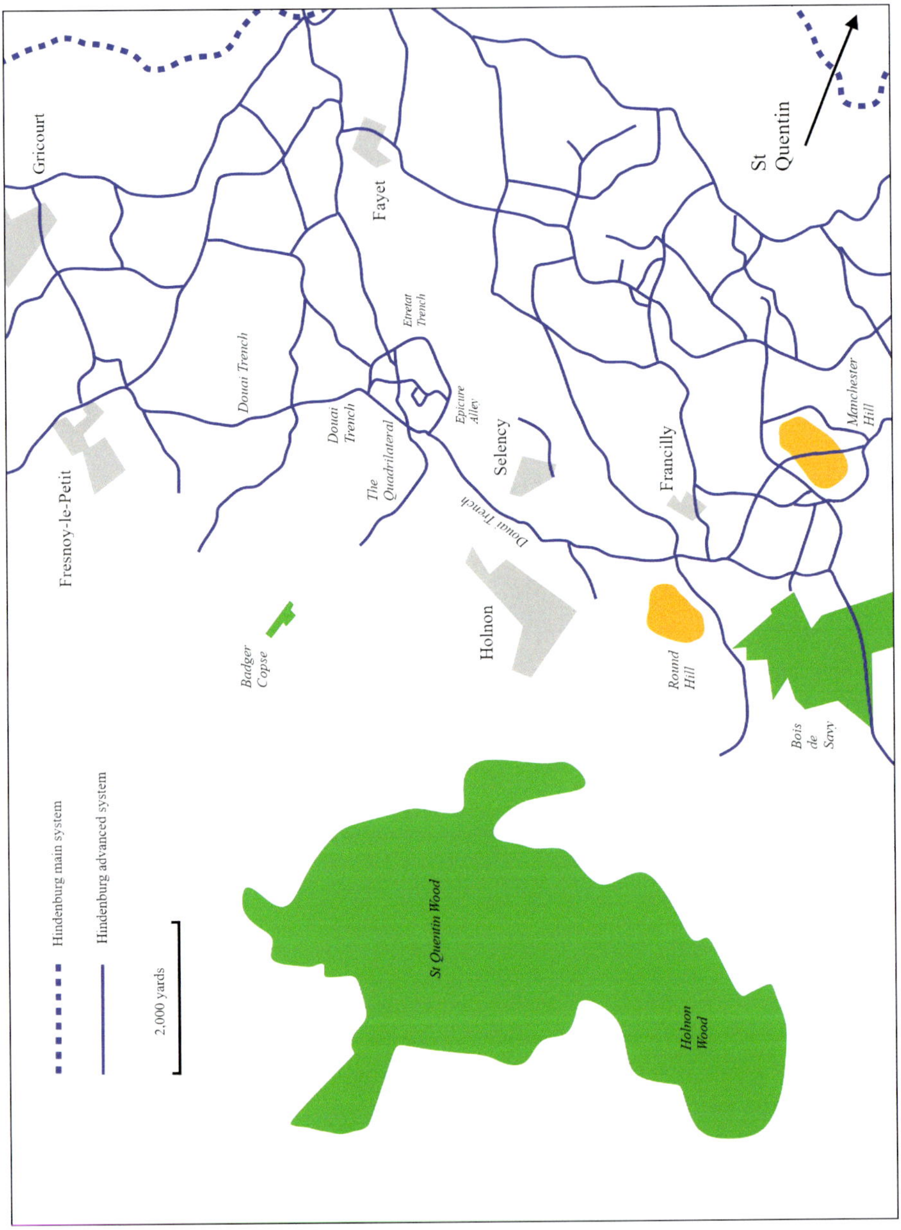

Map 14: Hindenburg Outpost System, Holnon, September 1918.

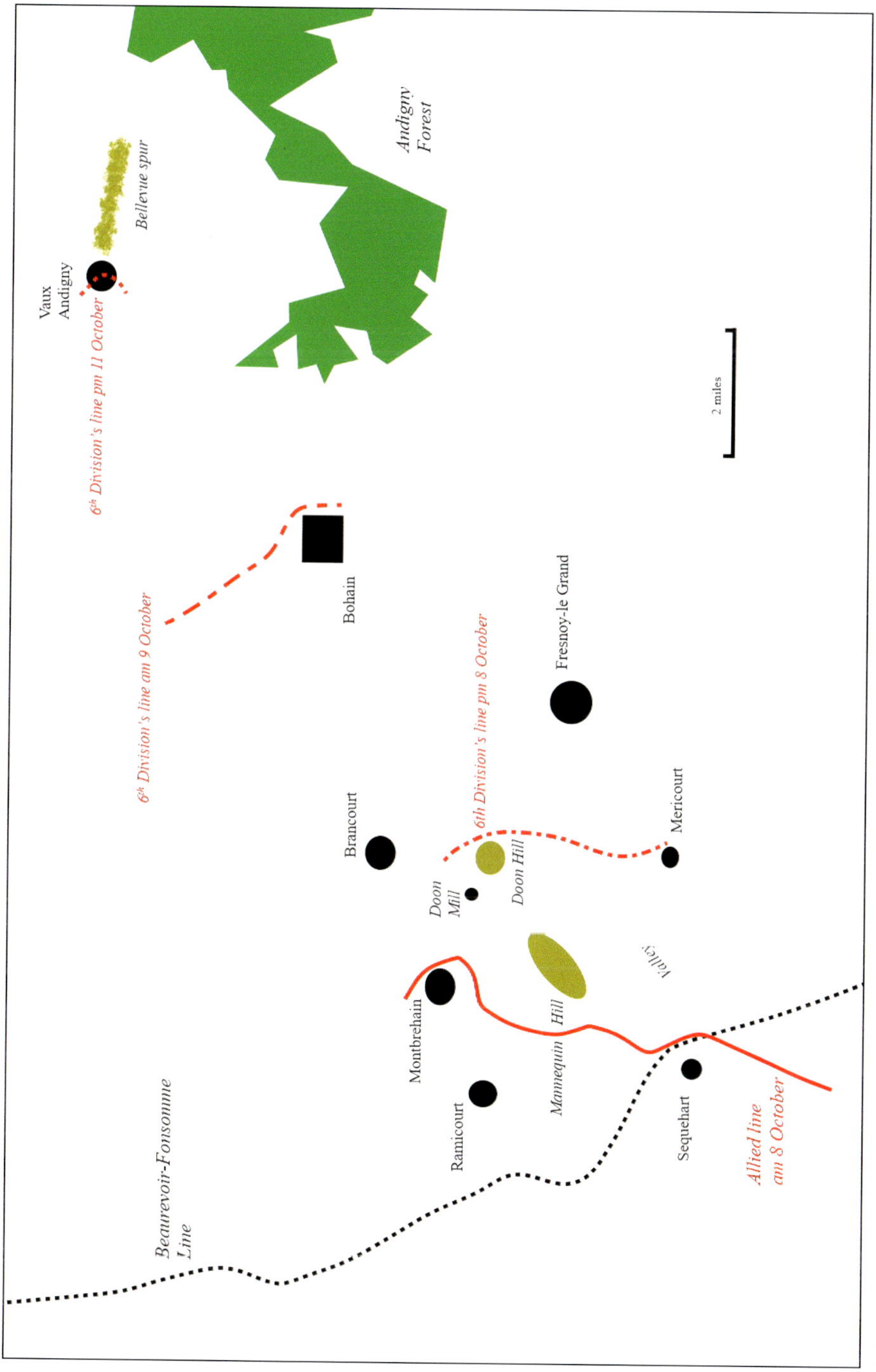

Map 15: Pursuit to the Selle, October 1918.

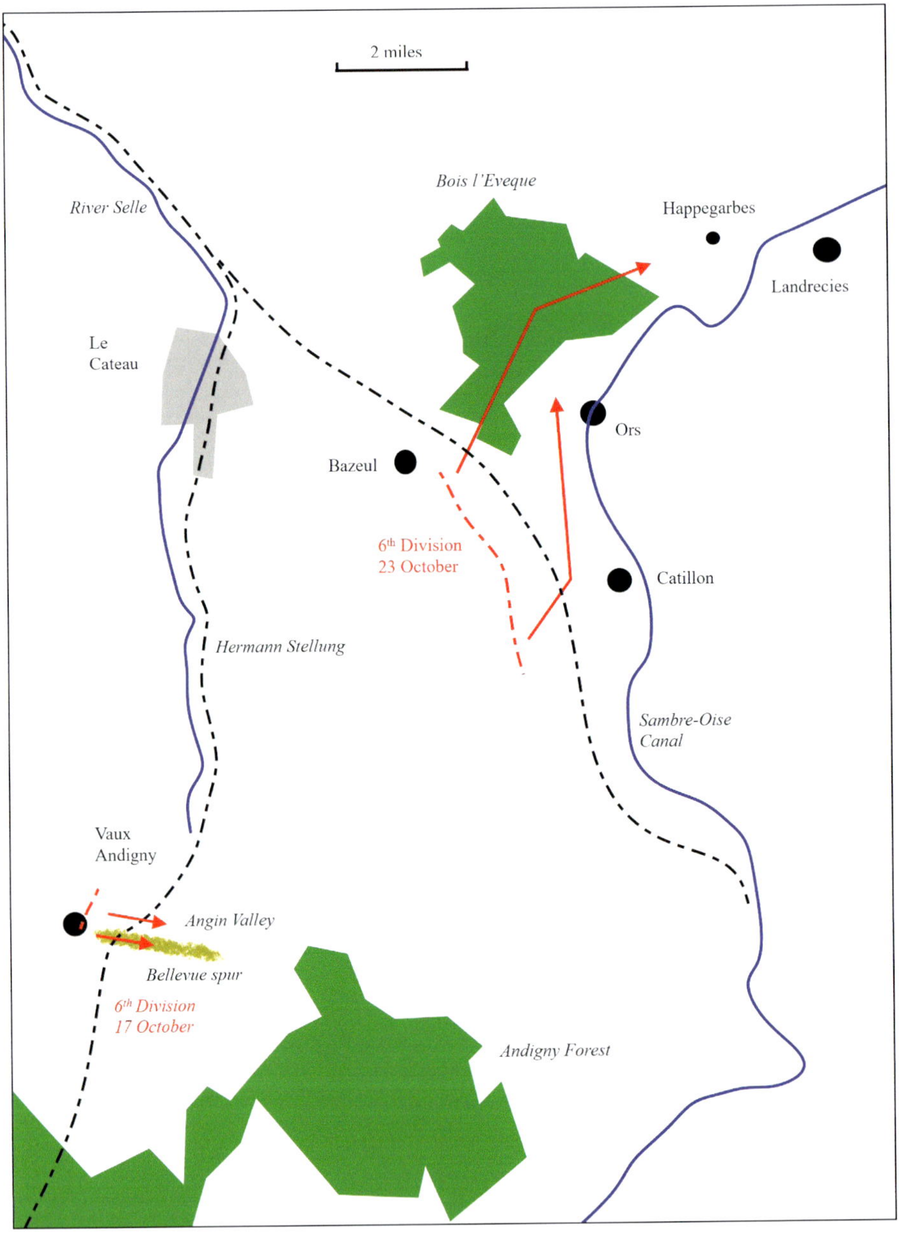

Map 16: Battle of the Selle 17-24 October 1918.

Ross viewed the raid of 1st West Yorkshire on 21 May (see Table 5.3) as 'admirably executed.' The reality that no prisoners were taken was a result of the fact that, alerted by the activity of artillery and trench mortars in cutting wire to create 'more gaps', the enemy 'evacuated his front trench in expectation of the raid.' He observed that in small raids, Bangalore torpedoes should be used to cut wire, i.e. preserving surprise as much as possible. Ross similarly admired the 1st Leicesters' daytime raid of 22 May. 'This raid proved once more that with proper arrangements, it is as easy to cross No Man's Land by day as by night, or indeed easier.' However, he came down hard on the matter of achievement of objectives. 'We want to make certain of getting hold of the enemy, killing a number of them and bring in such prisoners as we require. The methods adopted in these two raids' – neither of which had succeeded in netting prisoners – 'do not give the desired results.' Bombing dug outs did not figure in Ross's valued goals.

21/05 12.30	1st West Yorkshire	Hill 70	2 parties – total two officers, 45 ORs	Barrage. No dug outs found, no prisoners taken. Casualties – 1 officer & 1 OR wounded, 2 ORs missing.
22/05 12.00	1st Leicesters	Quarries	4 officers, 132 ORs in two waves	Smoke box barrage – dummy smoke barrage elsewhere. 15 dugouts destroyed, no prisoners. Casualties – 9 ORs wounded.
28/05 05.00	2nd Sherwoods	Quarries	6 officers, 133 ORs	Smoke barrage – dummy smoke barrage elsewhere. Two prisoners – dug outs/MG emplacement/tunnels destroyed. Casualties – 9 ORs killed, 1 officer and 27 ORs wounded.

Table 5.3: Raids carried out by 6th Division, May 1917

He went on to suggest that 'bigger raids, which penetrate more deeply, offer far greater chances of success while not increasing the proportion of casualties.' Success depended, he continued, on the artillery available 'to get the enemy wire into a ragged condition on wide stretches' and that 'now our 4.5-inch How(itzer)s can co-operate with our T.M.s we shall be able to do it … we shall then have greater chances of surprising the enemy.' Although Ross did not seemingly recognise it, he had restated the conundrum. A bombardment ruined surprise, alerted the enemy to a potential raid, and led to them evacuating their trenches. Yet what Ross was advocating was a heavy bombardment to ensure wire was cut. What sophistication was to be applied to the artillery technique was not made clear – Ross's document does not inspire. It was perhaps in response to the point that surprise was so difficult to obtain that he went on next to draw attention to 'a method which was tried by the Buffs near the Loos Crassier.' Two raiding parties were involved. The first behaved as if it was a normal raid, the second lay 'in ambush behind the enemy's parapet or parados' in order to 'catch the enemy when they came up out of their dug-outs in the belief that the raid had finished.' (Ross added, however, that the ruse had failed – the second party had been drawn into the fight resulting from the severe resistance the first party had met). He also suggested that a low flying aircraft could be used a distraction, and that an enemy drilled into taking cover in response to a trench mortar attack could be surprised by a rush across No Man's Land under the cover of 'duds.' These were ruses that probably had a very limited shelf life. He spent more time on what was clearly a preferred option:

> To enter the enemy's trenches about dusk and remain about two or three hours. To let the box barrage stop about Zero+30 minutes as if the raid had finished, arrangements being made however to bring the box barrage down again at a moment's notice. Enemy infantry would certainly come forward to reoccupy the front trench the moment he believed the raid had finished, or to counter-attack if he knew that we still held his trench. In either case if the arrangements with the artillery had been well thought out the first enemy counter-attack should be easily repulsed, the enemy counter-attacking troops isolated and attacked in their turn. It would be necessary however for the 'mopping up' arrangements to be thoroughly carried out.

Ross concluded: 'It is necessary to display ingenuity and constantly to change our methods if we are to execute successful raids; and all battalion and Company Commanders should devote much thought to the subject.'[77] Lieutenant-Colonel St. John Blunt of 2nd York & Lancaster did just that. He noted in his diary on 7 June: 'There has to be such a lot of preparation before we can bring off a raid' that the enemy 'knows one is coming – the only way is to confuse him as much as possible. This I am trying to do by daily arranged shoots & demonstrations combined with wire cutting.'[78] Cecil Nicholson, his brigade commander, described him as 'smart and capable.'[79] Blunt was, however, stating the only answer to the problem Ross posed. Barrages and wire cutting always indicated that the attacker was coming. The only thing that could be done was to confuse the defender as to when.

77 War Diary, HQ 6th Infantry Division, No. GO/2/5, 25 May 1917, TNA WO95/1593.
78 A. St. J. Blunt, op. cit.
79 C.L. Nicholson, Private Papers, IWM Docs 9975, 8 July 1916.

01/06 01.30	1st KSLI	Hulluch	4 officers, 132 ORs	Barrage. 16 Germans killed, dugouts and one MG emplacement blown in. Identifications made. Three ORs killed, one officer & 12 ORs wounded.
04/06 02.45	1st KSLI	Hulluch	2 officers, 40 ORs in 2 parties	Barrage. No prisoners/identifications. Casualties – two ORs killed & one missing; both officers and 12 ORs wounded.
07/06 12.15	2nd DLI	Hill 70	2 officers, 50 ORs	Barrage. Dummy raid by 16 Brigade. Failure due to enemy counterbarrage. Casualties – 9 killed, 10 wounded.
08/06 01.30	1st KSLI		Fighting patrol	Under cover of raids by 46th & 66th Divisions. Failure.
11/06 12.30	1st KSLI 9th Suffolk	Cité St Elie	3 officers, 94 ORs	Barrage. Cooperation by 16 Brigade, using smoke. 1st KSLI failed. 4 dugouts blown in. No prisoners. Casualties – 11 ORs wounded, 10 missing.
12/06 11.30	9th Norfolk	Quarries	2 officers, 33 ORs	'Silent' raid. Failed due to enemy machine-guns and bombing.
13/06 04.00	16 Brigade			Dummy raid with artillery and trench mortar barrage.
15/06 06.30	14th DLI	Hill 70	3 officers, 78 ORs	Practiced over facsimile trenches. Barrage. Dummy raid by 16 Brigade. 50 enemy killed by snipers, dugouts bombed 7 prisoners taken. Casualties – two ORs killed & 26 wounded.
24/06 21.00	1st Buffs	Hulluch	12 officers 314 ORs in three waves	Artillery & machine-gun barrage & smoke barrage. Dummy raid at 14 Bis. One prisoner taken. Casualties – one officer & 8 ORs killed, one officer & 18 ORs missing, four officers & 64 ORs wounded.
28/06 19.10	2nd DLI 11th Essex	Hill 70	One company per unit	Two prior dummy barrages. At least one prisoner taken, dug-outs destroyed. Casualties – 2nd DLI: One officer killed 16 ORs wounded & 12 missing. 11th Essex: 'Severe'.

Table 5.4: Raids carried out by 6th Division, June 1917

Whatever Ross's interest from the tactical point of view, and his memorandum concerning raiding was an obvious statement to the division that he viewed this activity as important, there were wider operational considerations that influenced both 6th Division's raiding and their deployment in the coming months. Following the Inter-Allied Conference in Paris on 4/5 May 1917, the Ypres offensive that would start on 31 July (Sir Douglas Haig's long desired location for operations), became the BEF's focus. In conjunction with this, Haig needed Lieutenant-General Henry Horne's First Army to keep its pressure on the German *Sixth Army*, whilst the battle proceeded against *Fourth Army* to the north.[80] 'Haig's intention was that the Arras battle', which would judder to a halt on 16 May, 'should be continued with Lens being taken as the basis for persuading the Germans that there would be further attacks towards Lille.'[81] As early as 30 April, a week after 6th Division's advance ground to a conclusion on the slopes to the south of Hill 70, Haig had given First Army objectives including the taking of the hill, Lens itself and Sallaumines Hill and the Sallaumines-Méricourt ridge to the south of Lens. First Army subsequently underwent a process of being deprived of tanks and losing guns to Fifth Army's offensive against the Messines Ridge and the Salient, and its power to fulfil Haig's wishes were thus diminished.

They were, however, able to keep raiding. On 8-9 June the 46th Division, on 6th Division's right, together with the 3rd and 4th Canadian Divisions carried out a large raid on the enemy positions in front of Lens. After this, much smaller scale raiding continued, Trevor Harvey noting that I, XI and the Canadian Corps carried out 14, 12 and nine raids respectively during June. 6th Division's total raids in June trebled over those in May, and they thus carried out two-thirds of the I Corps raids (see Table 5.4). It is not at all obvious that Ross's tactical suggestions were taken up. The June raids were no bigger than May, and the one real attempt at surprise, the 'silent' raid (the wire already being cut) carried out by 9th Norfolk on 12 June, failed. The one tactical change made to attempt to deceive the enemy was the increased use and sophistication of the use of dummy raids, involving both heavy artillery, trench mortars, and the Special Brigade in releasing smoke. As St. John Blunt had stated, the only real option was to confuse the enemy as to when, but also where.

An attack on Hill 70 was postponed, but on 28-29 June operations by 46th Division and the Canadian Corps captured Hill 65 south of Lens, a textbook 'bite-and-hold' attack. General Arthur Currie, commanding the Canadian Corps, after consulting various of his subordinate commanders, put it to General Horne that the next focus of operations should be Hill 70, rather than a direct attack on Lens, and Horne, an intelligent general whose consultative style encouraged suggestions, agreed.[82] This

80 Henry Sinclair Horne (1861-1929), a distinguished artillery officer, had commanded 2nd Division and XV Corps, taking command of First Army on 30 September 1916. History now views him as a competent army commander.

81 T. Harvey, 'The Battle of Hill 70 – 15-25 August 1917', p.31.

82 See Harvey, op. cit. for a wider discussion.

decision, the attack finally taking place on 15 August, would dominate the rest of 6th Division's time in the Loos sector, and during July they would keep pressure on the enemy by raiding. In addition, on 1 July two companies of 2nd Sherwood Foresters were attached to 139 Brigade of 46th Division in an attack that was intended to capture the last line of enemy defences to the west of Lens. This attack was to be made across a ruined urban landscape at night, and predictably was very difficult. The Sherwood companies had a series of organisational mishaps, and D Company attacked prematurely to be caught by the British barrage. Seven officers and 179 ORs became casualties.

The start of the month was otherwise marked by a series of reliefs in 6th Division's line, and there were four German raids during the period 2-7 July. Until they were relieved on 25 July, the division noted a further five raids. Marden summarises the period January to July 1917 and reaches a total of 30 raids 'of which 13 were successful in obtaining their objective and securing prisoners (total for the 13 raids: 54)' while '11 secured their objective but failed to yield any prisoners, and only six definitely failed.'[83] In fact, careful comparison of unit diaries reveals 34 raids (see Tables 5.1 to 5.5). If Ashworth's statistics are correct, 6th Division accounted for nearly 13 percent of the BEF's raids in 1917 in the first six months alone. They were thus prolific raiders. Marden attributed the low average of prisoners taken to three sources. Firstly, the growing enemy tendency to evacuate trenches or retreat to dugouts; and secondly bloodthirstiness on the part of the raiders. Lastly, the enemy might suffer significant casualties to the barrage and accurate trench mortaring. In other words, the means necessary to enter the enemy trenches sometimes defeated the purpose of taking prisoners. The friction of war is no better illustrated, however, than in the raid carried out by 9th Norfolk on 16 July. No preliminary bombardment was ordered 'and no precise zero hour fixed.' The barrage commenced on Very light signals from the raiders. Every attempt was being made to achieve surprise, but, 'owing to some mistake, the smoke barrage began whilst they were still crawling over.' To increase the raiders' woes, a British machine gun was firing on the gap in the wire that they intended to use, and they had to locate another. Not all the raiders made it into the German trenches, and the enemy thus alerted, resistance was strong. The raiders had to withdraw without securing a prisoner.[84]

Thomas Grove recalled that 'some units were habitually rough by nature and up-bringing. Such a one was our 14th DLI.' It is easy to imagine the hackles of the Cambridge first, John Rosher, the unit's CO, rising had he read this. 'They did many raids but never produced a prisoner.' Grove described how: 'Eventually General Ross addressed a party of them, detailed to carry out a raid, explained the value of prisoners

83 General Ross visited 2nd Sherwood Foresters on 26 March to discuss the enemy raid the previous day which had penetrated between the Norfolks and Sherwoods, to discuss how the line was being held.

84 Petre, op. cit. p.270.

for Intelligence purposes and said that he must have three prisoners. That party brought back just that number and no more.' This does not quite tally with the evidence, 14th DLI's raid of 15 June bringing back seven prisoners, but the insight no doubt has some basis. He continued: 'Other units normally less brutal might be rendered vindictive by circumstances.' At the risk of evoking a north-south divide, he described 1st Buffs as 'by nature clean fighters.' However, their raid of 24 June occurred 'just after a home mail had contained accounts of a bombing raid on Folkestone' (obviously a Buffs recruiting area and a town that made a sizeable contribution to the Territorial 4th Battalion). 'A number of the prisoners sent back by the first wave were killed when they reached the supporting wave on the front line.'

Marden clearly viewed the taking of prisoners as the prime purpose of raiding. The report of the raid carried out by 1st West Yorkshire on the night of 20/21 May lists three objectives: '(a) To ascertain the strength in which the enemy was holding his trenches. (b) To secure prisoners. (c) To kill as many of the enemy and to do as much damage as possible.'[85] That carried out by 1st Buffs on 24 June had the added purpose of distracting enemy attention away from an attack by 4th Division. Marden (correctly) calculated the number of enemy raids during the period as 21, 'of which only 4 succeeded in taking prisoners, 5 entered our trenches without securing prisoners, and 12 were entire failures.' Three of the enemy raids left prisoners behind, and four identifications were thus achieved.[86]

85 War Diary, HQ 6th Infantry Division, No. GO/2/61, TNA WO95/1593.
86 Marden, op. cit. pp.31-2.

09/07 06.00	14th DLI	Hill 70	3 officers 30 ORs	Two minute barrage lifting to box barrage. Dummy & smoke bombardment elsewehere. Dugouts bombed, no identifications. Casualties. Two ORs killed, four wounded.
12/07 23.30	8th Bedfords	Hulluch	3 parties of 12 ORs	Artillery/mortar/machine-gun barrage. Two dugouts destroyed, one prisoner. Casualties: three ORs wounded, three missing.
16/07 14.46	9th Norfolks	Quarries	2 officers 36 ORs	No preliminary barrage, dummy smoke barrage elsewhere. 15 enemy casualties. Casualties: one OR missing, two wounded.
20/07 22.30	2nd York & Lancaster	Hulluch	3 parties 3 officers 55 ORs	Heavy barrage & dummy raid . No identifications. Casualties: two officers killed, one officer and 'several' ORs wounded, one missing.
23/07 21.15	1st Leicester	Quarries	9 officers 302 ORs 2 companies each in 4 waves	Heavy artillery/machine-gun/mortgar barrage. Oil drums projected at zero. Dummy artillery smoke barrage elsewhere. 14 dugouts/4 LTMs/1 MG destroyed. One prisoner taken. Two officers wounded & one missing. Two ORs killed, 16 wounded and two missing.

Table 5.5: Raids carried out by 6th Division, July 1917

1st Leicestershire, after their raid on 22 May claimed that 'the experience was valuable for the junior officers and NCOs, and the morale and offensive spirit of the Company engaged was increased.[87] Pratt observes that 'the military value of raiding to the BEF remains difficult to quantify.'[88] The opinion of history has come down, on balance, against the raid. If the view of those who were tasked with carrying them out was often negative, historians have argued that the British raided too often, and raids caused the enemy (contrary to Marden's observation) to man their trenches more heavily which in turn led to higher casualties in major attacks. Further, despite the Leicester unit's comments, there is no evidence that they increased aggressive spirit and some historians maintain that the reverse occurred.[89] The debate on raiding will no doubt continue, but Pratt makes the plea that it should 'not be seen in isolation,

87 War Diary, HQ 6th Infantry Division, No. GO/2/62, TNA WO95/1593.
88 Pratt, op. cit. p.193.
89 See Ashworth, op. cit. pp.185-203 for a fuller discussion.

but instead as part of wider British efforts to wear down and ultimately defeat the German army.'[90]

After relief on 24-5 July, the division went into rest in the Monchy-Breton area for a month. From November 1916 to the end of July 1917, the Division had suffered 5,617 infantry casualties. Forty-seven officers had been killed, 179 had been wounded, and nine were missing. Amongst the other ranks there had been 952 fatalities, 4,233 had been wounded, and 197 were missing.

Hill 70 Reprise

The Third Battle of Ypres having opened on 31 July, the 1st and 2nd Canadian Divisions assaulted Hill 70 at 04.25 on 15 August and by the following morning the German third position on the reverse (eastern) slope of the hill had been won, the enemy mounting repeated counter-attacks. The cost to the Canadians was over 8,400 casualties. On 24 August, the division (now commanded by Major-General Thomas Marden),[91] began to relieve the 3rd Canadian Division on the forward slopes of Hill 70 above Cité St Auguste, and north past Bois Hugo. 'In all this forward area the dead were still lying thick, both Canadians and the enemy', and in the Chalk Pit 'where there had evidently been a hand to hand fight there were many corpses and the stench in some places was appalling.' One particular trench near Cité St. Pierre 'had been the scene of desperate fighting, attack and counter-attack until it became so choked with dead that neither side could hold it.'[92] Marden notes that the month in this position 'was one of hard work for all ranks consolidating the newly won position.'[93] Noting that the old German positions were in a very poor condition, Lieutenant-Colonel St. John Blunt of 2nd York & Lancaster (near the Hill 70 chalk pit) noted on 1 September that 'the new bit of line is getting on nicely and should be quite strong soon.' On the 4th he noted that the enemy launched their first bombardment with aerial darts 'which shows he is getting settled.'[94] Sited on a forward slope, unfortunately, it was very difficult to get supplies to the front line. This period was marked by two further raids by the division, the enemy mounting a similar number.

The division was not to remain in this line for long, however. On 24 September it sidestepped south to take over a front to the north-west of Lens, this move intended to allow involvement in the upcoming operation against Sallaumines Hill. This was General Currie's proposed second step in dominating Lens, and plans had been fine tuned at a conference on 26 September. However, on 3 October General Horne informed Currie of a change of plans. The Canadian Corps was to be sent north to

90 Pratt, op. cit. p.193.
91 See Chapter 6.
92 War Diary, 9th Battalion Norfolk Regiment, 'Diary of Lieutenant-Colonel B.H.L. Prior', TNA WO95/1623.
93 Marden, op. cit. p.33.
94 A. St. J. Blunt, op. cit.

participate in the battle for the Passchendaele Ridge.[95] 6th Division occupied this line until 23 October, when it was withdrawn. The divisional war diary notes no raiding during this period, but records that the enemy made one raid and an attempt to seize an outpost after a day's bombardment against the whole divisional front. The day after they had moved into the new line, 16 Infantry Brigade were raided on 29 September. Colonel Blunt noted dismally: 'Men behaved very badly & bolted in some places & did not fight in others ... This partly the result of Pratt & Waller's slackness with Coys & partly the rotten material one gets nowadays for junior officers and men.'[96] Blunt had, of course, noted in April the tentativeness his men had in patrolling. These remarks in relation to two of his company commanders, however, betray lack of acknowledgement of his own responsibility in grasping the problem of supposedly slack officers. His observations, however, reflect a matter that would continue to be an issue for the BEF in the latter stages of the war, namely the unevenness of reinforcements in terms of training.

The two months of trench holding, from the end of August to the end of October, had cost a further 1,090 casualties. Withdrawing from the line, after six days the division moved south. It was to take part in the Battle of Cambrai.

Conclusion

The April fighting in front of Loos had been savage and taxing. The weather had been vile – snow, wind and rain – in some respects resembling the foul conditions at the Transloy Ridges. Yet the division had shown a distinct advancement in its performance on the Somme. There had been demonstrations of good generalship, and the introduction of *SS143* was reflected in the infantry tactics employed, despite the constrained nature of the battle. But perhaps nowhere was tactical improvement better reflected than in the division's raiding. Here there were real indications of skilled integration of mobile weaponry, machine guns and trench mortars, in conjunction with artillery, and this was woven into the Loos fighting.

95 It was not until 3 September 1918 that Lens fell into the BEF's hands when it was evacuated by the Germans.

96 A. St. J. Blunt, op. cit. The officers were Captain Francis Norton Pratt (Reserve of Officers) and Captain Hardress Edmund Waller (commissioned 7 August 1914). The former had been on the Western Front since January 1915, the latter since September 1914. Pratt would be killed in action on 18 September 1918, Waller on 22 November 1917.

6

Technocrats of War: Commanders and Command 1915-18

It was concluded in Chapter Two that whilst the divisional and brigade commanders at the helm of 6th Division in August 1914 reflected the wealth of experience that many of the senior officers of the Regular Army possessed, this, in the cases of Sir John Keir and Walter Doran, did not guarantee success in formation command at war. The careers of two of the brigadiers, Walter Congreve and Edward Ingouville-Williams, however, demonstrated the opportunities for promotion available in the rapidly expanding army for a senior soldier of both experience and ability. Sir Douglas Haig wrote in his diary on 25 June 1915 that progress, 'even if ample guns etc. provided', would be achieved only when 'young capable commanders are brought to the front. Captains to command Battalions; Majors Brigades etc.'[1] His words bear close scrutiny – Haig's early view was that youth and ability were the key to command and would be the mainspring of success.

Divisional Command

The command of 6th Division changed hand four times during the war. This was par for the course. Of the six Regular divisions of August 1914, 1st Division had five commanders, as did 5th Division; 2nd Division had four, as did 3rd Division; whilst 4th Division had seven (although it suffered two commanders incapacitated and one killed).[2] The second commander, Congreve, like his ancestor's invention, rocketed to corps command and left the division on 14 November 1915 to be replaced by Sir Charles Ross.

1 National Library of Scotland, Acc. 3155, Field-Marshal Sir Douglas Haig, Manuscript Diary, 25 June 1915.
2 These totals ignore temporary or acting commanders. 1st Division lost one major-general through wounds, 3rd Division having one killed and one invalided.

Sir Charles Ross (born 10 March 1864) was the third son (of 10 siblings) of General Sir Campbell Claye Grant Ross KCB.[3] His elder brother Ronald, a doctor, was the first to prove that malaria was transmitted by mosquito in 1897. He was born in India, his father being in the Bengal Staff Corps. Schooled at Stubbington (for a youth aiming at the army it was actually known as 'The Cradle of the Navy'), Ross was commissioned as a lieutenant in August 1884 in the Norfolk Regiment, and attached to the Egyptian Army 1893-1904. Having passed Staff College (where he attended 1897-99), he served on the staff in South Africa 1900-2, first as a Staff Captain at Headquarters, then, after a few months in the Mounted Infantry, as Deputy Assistant Adjutant General for Intelligence. He was present at the relief of Kimberley and was awarded the DSO. He married Clara Marion Horton (née Schreiber, the widow of an army officer) in 1905 at the age of 41, the couple having no children. After his return from the Boer War, at which point he had been a captain for nine years (and the fifth senior at that), Ross might well have thought that battalion command within his regiment would elude him. He thus obtained a post as an instructor at RMA Woolwich and subsequently at RMC Sandhurst for three years before finally becoming a lieutenant-colonel in 1908 and an instructor (GSO2) at the Staff College. It was said that 'Ross was a remarkably good lecturer, and during the war many of his old pupils sought him out to tell him how valuable they had found his teaching at the front.' At the Staff College reunion of 1930 'two of his pupils, now occupying high positions, said that they owed all their success to him.'[4]

During his early years as an instructor, Ross wrote *Representative Government and War* (1903). The review in *The Spectator* remarked that:

> A great fear of the future is responsible for this very readable and very wrong-headed book. Captain Ross believes that Germany since the accession of the present Emperor has been steadily developing a policy of 'peace strategy' intended to lead to a war which will utterly crush Great Britain and leave Germany the master of the Continent. He thinks that this war is inevitable, and that unless we 'prepare for war' – and this phrase has a definite and technical meaning in his mind – we shall inevitably succumb in the conflict. The Boer War and all that happened before it through the century have convinced Captain Ross that we are totally unprepared.[5]

History, of course, might be thought as proving Ross far more right than 'wrong-headed.' Undaunted, he continued the same theme in *The Problem of National Defence*, (1907); and followed this with the likely less controversial *An Outline of the Russo-Japanese War, 1904 and 1905* (1912). By the standards of the time, he was an educated

3 There was a military lineage, Campbell Ross's father was Lieutenant Colonel Hugh Ross.
4 Obituary, *The Times*, 30 December 1930.
5 *The Spectator*, 5 March 1904, p.16.

and thoughtful soldier. Becoming a substantive colonel in October 1911, he was placed on half-pay in January 1912 and then on retired pay in July that year. Ross came out of retirement on 5 August 1914 when he was appointed GSO1 GHQ Central Force (i.e. Home Forces), and on 29 December 1914 he was appointed GSO1 in place of Major J.W.H. Pollard of Eastern Command Coastal Defences. Dug out again from this rather remote post, he became GOC 61 Brigade in 20th (Light) Division on 6 July 1915 and embarked with his new command for France on the 20th. On immediate arrival in France, Ross was very active, visiting his units regularly and going to investigate various training schools. His tactical notes issued early in the brigade's active service show thoughtfulness. Under his command, the brigade took place in the attack towards Fromelles on 25 September 1915. Due to heavy enemy shelling, it was unable to take any meaningful offensive action, although no fault whatsoever accrued. Ross therefore came to the command of 6th Division on 13 November with a mere three and a half months' experience on the Western Front under his belt. He had never commanded a unit, and his previous experience of the teeth end of war was a few months assigned to the mounted infantry. He must have been reasonably well thought of, however, to have been promoted from a New Army division when there were other well-qualified officers in France and Flanders who had experience within Regular divisions. His appointment underlines the reliance on dug-outs in these opening years of the war.

Ross remains a shadowy figure during the next nine months in the Salient, the division being required to undertake no offensive. This does not mean he was inactive. Brigadier-General Cecil Nicholson, commanding 16 Brigade, noted in his diary a major divisional conference on a scheme of defence on 22 July, and that on 8 December he was summoned to Divisional HQ as Ross 'wanted to talk about system of holding the line when we go back to it.'[6] Ross's HQ handled the phosgene gas attack on 19 December by bringing up divisional reserves promptly. Moving to the Somme, his general outline for the projected attack north of the Ancre in August 1916 was as sensible as might be expected from a divisional commander at that point in the war, although it was not tested. Being pitched into the attack on the Quadrilateral in September would have been an unfair test of any officer's generalship, and any division would have failed due to circumstances entirely beyond their control. This does not mean that the division's staff work was adequate on 13 September. As previously observed, it was confused and misleading and there was clearly less than adequate communication with unit commanders. Ross, however, was not in a strong position to alter the course of events. Evidence suggests that he and his staff perceived problems, but the friction of war prevented his interventions from being entirely effective. In the aftermath he stood up to the Earl of Cavan, whose own corps staff work had been less than flawless, daring him to fire him (albeit from a position of comparative safety). Given the prescriptiveness of Corps at the time, Ross can earn no particular credit for

6 C.L. Nicholson, Private Papers, IWM Docs 9975.

the success of the Battle of Morval on 25 September, and no particular blame for the terrible confusion at the Battle of the Transloy Ridges in October, when, again, his division found itself fighting blind in respect of the situation of the ground.

Ross appears on paper at his best in the enemy retreat at Loos on 13 April. He seemingly worked reasonably well between his corps commander and brigadiers, maintaining Holland's initial caution, yet allowing what appeared to be devolved command to his brigadiers to allow them to take advantage of any opportunity that was offered. Ross's GSO1, Lieutenant-Colonel Thomas Grove, put another slant on matters, stating that 'the situation was competently handled by General Osborn', and that 'for the most part all that was required of Div(isional) HQ was to arrange for the succession of battalions from the brigade on his left to pass temporarily under his command.' He added that 'only once did Div(isional) HQ have to take a more active hand', when an attack had to be coordinated with 46th Division on Osborne's right, 'and then Ross's system of command nearly resulted in what would have been a very unfortunate situation.' Grove arrived at 46th Division HQ with the 16 Brigade orders only to find he had a page missing. When the despatch rider returned with the errant document, Grove then discovered 'that the order did not conform to the agreed plan.' Ross had changed it in his absence, and 'it was then too late to put things right.'[7] It was fortunate that 46th Division could not advance as the wire was uncut.

Ross's 'system of command' becomes clear through extant accounts. Lieutenant-Colonel Alan St John Blunt, 2nd York & Lancaster, recorded a number of encounters with Ross in his diary. The first was at a meeting with all brigade commanders and COs on 22 February concerning the reorganisation of platoons that followed the adoption of the principles of SS143. Blunt noted: 'Couldn't get much out of him as to what was wanted.' He then recorded that on 20 May that: 'Gen. Ross came round in morning while I was at breakfast to talk over schemes for straefing [*sic*] Bosch.' This was no doubt a consultative enterprise in conjunction with Ross's memo of 25 May concerning raiding. (From Blunt's point of view the visit was hopefully more profitable than the lecture he attended two days later 'on scouting by some idiot who had a tame music hall ju-jitsu professor with him to show how to kill Bosches.') On 19 August he finally noted: 'Gen. Ross is going home to take over a new Division, sorry in some ways to lose him.' This last comment is a case of damning with faint praise. What is most clarifying is his observation on Ross's successor, General Marden who 'seems a rather meddlesome person & goes in for centralisation of command.'[8] What Blunt would miss, therefore, was a divisional commander who let his subordinate commanders get on with things. Thomas Grove went farther. He correctly summarised Ross as having 'very little experience of regimental soldiering or command', and that he 'made practically no attempt to exercise any command over his division, giving his brigadiers

7 T.T. Grove, 'It Happened by Chance', NAM 1963-08-14.
8 A. St. J. Blunt, Private Papers, IWM Docs 16149.

a free hand to go their own way.'[9] If there 'was any divergence between them and Div(isional) HQ then, to Ross, the division must be wrong.' Whilst this would not have been an entirely accurate description of the way Ross stood up to be counted after the Quadrilateral debacle, this behaviour must have made it hard to be on his staff team in terms of being undermined. He was not always soft with his brigadiers, however. Cecil Nicholson noted that on 4 March 1916 Ross had made a visit 'which was rather a stormy one.'[10] Exactly why it was stormy is not clear, but an enterprise was to have happened the following day which Nicholson had to cancel on the day of Ross's visit. Ross could, perhaps, assert himself when he chose.

Ross was relieved of command on 21 August 1917. There is no eulogy in the divisional war diary. He had commanded for 20 months and was being replaced not by a particularly younger man (Thomas Marden was only two years his junior, even if he was a decade younger than Sir John Keir), but by a different sort of man. Given Blunt and Grove's observations, what appeared to be devolved command was a lack of ability to give direction. This was a profound inadequacy in a divisional commander. He was placed in command of 69th (2nd East Anglian) Division, a second-line Territorial home division on 8 September 1917, and remained in post until 4 November 1918. This could hardly be called a challenging job and was one in which his command deficits would not prove a problem. Brigadier-General Philip Howell criticised 'old "dug out" generals' who conducted attacks which 'just throw men's lives away.' Ross, dug-out though he was, could not be accused of this. Howell continued that such individuals possessed 'no imagination, or no first-hand knowledge, & with minds far too "set" ever to learn new things.'[11] Even this would not be an entirely fair description of Ross. He was not removed for any particular single failure on the battlefield. But as Simon Robbins observes, it was the rapid expansion of the army that led to the appointment of 'officers of modest accomplishment.'[12] Ross was certainly one of this ilk.

A golf and tennis enthusiast in his younger days, Ross devoted his (second) retirement to writing lurid fiction, publishing five mystery novels: *The Fly-By-Nights* (1921), where a teetotal Britain is threatened by the illegal importation of drink and drugs and liquor by communists flying advanced airships; *The Haunted Seventh* (1922), a golf murder mystery; *Every Man's Hand* (1923); *When the Devil Was Sick* (1924), a horror tale about evil lurking underground in a Cornish mine where worshippers of Moloch reinstitute human sacrifice (1924); and *The Castle Fenham Case* (1927). A fertile imagination (lacking on the battlefield) is in evidence, although he was assisted by his wife, reportedly also an accomplished writer. Ross died in 1930.

9 Grove, op. cit.
10 Nicholson op. cit. 4 March 1916. Ross visited again the next day 'but there was no strafe this time.'
11 P. Howell, quoted in S. Robbins, *British Generalship on the Western Front 1914-18*, p.55.
12 Robbins, *British Generalship*, p.55.

The new divisional commander, Thomas Owen Marden, was born on 15 September 1866 in Kodaikanal, Tamil Nadu, in Southern India, son of Thomas and Ellen Marden, his father being HM Inspector of Schools in India. He was sent back to England for schooling at Berkhamsted Grammar School from 1879, where he was captain of cricket and football. He passed tenth into RMC Sandhurst and was fourth on the passing-out list with prize for Fortification. He was commissioned in the Cheshire Regiment in 1886. His younger brother Arthur William Marden also joined the army, being commissioned in the Manchester Regiment in 1888.[13] Thomas saw action with his regiment in the Burmese Expedition 1887-99 and then served as a Special Service Officer in South Africa in 1899-1900. His roles included Commandant Worcester, Railway Staff Officer, Staff Officer to Commandant Colesberg and Naaupoort Districts, Staff Officer to an Assistant Inspector General Lines of Communication, and latterly Commandant Colesberg. Thomas likely had more ambition than his brother. He returned from South Africa to pass Staff College in 1902 and was posted to India as DAAG for Instruction. He had married Mabel Marianne Nesbitt in 1901, the first of his two sons, Paul, being christened in Poona in 1902. He soon returned to Great Britain as a Staff Captain in the Directorate of Military Training at the War Office, afterwards serving as GSO3 and GSO2 at Army HQ. He was then sent as DAAQMG to the Orange River Colony and Orange Free State Districts. In a further indication of his ambition he moved to the Northumberland Fusiliers to attain his majority, transferring again to the Welsh Regiment as a major. He was clearly manoeuvring for battalion command and achieved this in the 1st Battalion in December 1912. He divorced the following year, which must have been an embarrassing matter for a senior officer. The battalion was at the military cantonment of Chakrata in Northern India in August 1914 and arrived at Plymouth on 22 December. Marden landed in France with his unit on 18 January 1915. On 25 May the battalion was involved in the Battle of the Bellewarde Ridge, when Marden 'who had gone forward to Brigade HQ in the railway cutting just south-west of Hellfire Corner, to get orders, was severely wounded by shrapnel.'[14] He never returned to his regiment, being appointed on recovery to command 114 Brigade 38th Welsh Division on 10 November 1915,[15] the division finally concentrating in France on 6 December. Despite its torrid time at Mametz Wood in July 1916, Marden rebuilt his brigade only to suffer heavy casualties again on the Pilckem Ridge on the opening day of the Third Battle of Ypres. Neither of these two difficult actions prevented his elevation to divisional command. Marden rose to such a level, as did other officers at

13 Arthur Marden retired in 1911 with the rank of major. He was recalled during the war to serve as a Railway Transport Officer and an Assistant (later full) Embarkation Commandant.

14 T.O. Marden, *The History of the Welch Regiment, Vol. 2, 1914-1918*, p.349.

15 One of two brigade commanders put in place immediately before the division was sent to the Western Front.

this stage of the war, 'having undergone the most rigorous on-the-job training at the front during 1915-16, a crucible which burned away all but the most able.'[16]

Marden's appointment was a reflection of the growing professionalisation of the BEF. When Lieutenant Charles Clayton met him in March 1915 he noted: 'His face is an arresting one. It is of an intellectual type, and his eyes, incisive yet quick to twinkle, give the impression that they miss nothing.'[17] He correctly identified that Marden was an intelligent officer. When Sir Henry Rawlinson met him on 9 September 1918 he noted, if less effusively: 'He is all right – I rather liked the look of him.'[18] Marden's 648 days of brigade and 416 days of divisional command speak to a man who steadily grew in competence and stature. Lieutenant-Colonel Blunt, who had dubbed Marden 'meddlesome', described his insistence on centralised command. In the latter stages of the war when corps would increasingly devolve responsibility for organisation in attacks to division, a sure grip on the part of the divisional commander was essential. This was not necessarily to the taste to some of his other senior commanders. Thus Blunt noted on 13 October that his brigadier, the competent General Osborn, was 'leaving us shortly – going home – fed up with new regime.' Contrasting him with Ross, Thomas Grove observed that 'two more different men for the position would be hard to imagine.' He summed up the new professionalism in describing Marden as 'a man of restless energy and a first class regimental officer, with an exceptional knowledge of detail' and that 'no one could ever be in any doubt who commanded the division.' At the same time he found Marden 'not an easy man to serve under – very ready with criticism and grudging of praise.'[19] Grove noted that 'in trench warfare there were periods when there was little for a divisional commander to do but to see that his front was being satisfactorily maintained', a matter normally entrusted to brigade commanders. This inactivity did not suit Marden – 'the more there was requiring action by him … the better he became. When his command was engaged in active fighting, he was first-class.' Importantly, Grove noted: 'He always had a thorough grasp of the situation and I never saw him ruffled.' Grove felt trusted by Marden and they got on well. 'The only peevish word I can remember to have had from him', Grove recalled, was when he 'issued an order without previous submission to him', a matter he thought too trivial. Marden asked 'whether I commanded the division or him.'[20]

Following the war, Marden commanded a brigade on the Rhine, and then, after marrying Edith Minshull-Ford (another military widow of whom there was a tragic abundance), was sent to command the 28th Division in the allied occupying force at the Dardanelles in the early 1920s, in place whilst the Treaty of Sèvres was being

16 S. Robbins, 'Henry Horne as Divisional Commander during 1915', in S. Jones (ed.), *Courage Without Glory*, p.105.
17 C. P. Clayton, *The Hungry One*, p.14.
18 Sir H. Rawlinson, War Journal, 9 September 1918, Churchill College RWLN 1/11.
19 Grove, op. cit.
20 Grove, op. cit.

negotiated. 'His tactful handling of the situation of the deadlock of Chanak, when he was placed in command by Sir Charles Harrington ... brought him further recognition',[21] and he was awarded the KBE in addition to his CMG (1915) and CB (1918). The Turks, in an attempt to push the Greek army (and Allies) out of their homeland, had marched on the Dardanelles forces. Renewed war seemed a possibility, but Marden refused to relay an ultimatum to the Turks, counting on a negotiated settlement, which was achieved just in time, in the form of Armistice of Mudanya. He returned home to take command of the 53rd Welsh (Territorial Division) and retired in 1927, having found time to write a brief history of 6th Division (1920) and, later, the history of the Welch Regiment in the Great War (1932). His restless energy remained. These works likely flew off the shelves less swiftly than Ross's, but unlike his predecessor's, have not been forgotten. Marden died in 1951.

Brigade Command

A divisional commander in 1918 was a decade younger than his counterpart of 1914 (although Marden, at 52, was well above the BEF's average age of 45.6 years for divisional commanders on 29 September 1918).[22] How far, however, was Haig's desired shift to youth achieved within the brigade commanders of 6th Division?

The average age of the division's three brigade commanders of 1914 was a little over 52 years. The second round of brigadiers was scarcely less, at 50.5 years. They were, of course, fished from the same senior pool. The third tranche showed a further slight decline with an average age of 48 years. The fourth round of promotees showed a reverse trend of 51.3 years, the fifth an average age of 45.6 years. In such a small group, an average was easily distorted. Thus in the group of third appointees, FitzJames Maine 'Tabasco Jim' Edwards was appointed to 71 Brigade at the age of 55 years,[23] and in the fourth group, William Kerr McClintoch was appointed at 18 Brigade at the yet more senior age of 58. There was a start-to-finish overall decrease in age of seven and a half years, but the average age of a brigade commander in 6th Division at the end of the war was still over three years above the average for the BEF on 29 September 1918 of 42.2 years.[24] Six of the 16 replacements for the original brigadiers were in fact majors at the outbreak of war, but this was not a guarantee of youth, as their average age in August 1914 was 45.6 years. Only one was a captain in August 1914, Percy Wilson Brown starting the war at this rank, assuming command of 71 Brigade in August 1917 at the age of 41.

21 Obituary, *The Times*, 12 September 1951.
22 J.M. Bourne, 'The BEF's Generals on 29 September 1918', in P. Dennis & J. Grey, *1918 Defining Victory*, p.111.
23 J.F. Edwards is incorrectly listed as the commander of 71 Brigade in both Marden's history and A.F. Becke *Order of Battle of Divisions*, Part 1.
24 Bourne, 'BEF's Generals', p.111.

In terms of source, predictably, all of 6th Division's brigade commanders were professional soldiers. Most were Regulars with the exception of 'Tabasco Jim' and Mansel Travers Shewen, Edwards' predecessor, both Indian Army officers.[25] The pair were gone by October 1916, reflecting the progressive lack of use of Indian officers at general officer level (by 29 September 1918, only nine held such rank).[26] 'Tabasco Jim' was the odd one out in another way, being a cavalryman (23rd Light Cavalry). The remainder were infantry officers and, indeed, 86 percent of the BEF's brigadiers on 29 September 1918 were infantry officers, figures which John Bourne notes are 'broadly in line with the proportion of cavalry to infantry officers in the pre-war Regular Army,[27] scotching any myth that Sir Douglas Haig favoured cavalry officers. In terms of all-round organisational ability, 37 percent had passed Staff College. Two of the three original brigadiers had done so, the exception being Walter Congreve, this form of studying not being in his nature. The man, however, had organisational skill in spades, and not possessing the *psc* initials was, clearly, no bar to brigade command in the pre-war army. Two of the five second tranche commanders (taking 19 and 71 Brigades into account) were *psc*, whilst none of the third tranche were so qualified, yet one of each of the third, fourth and fifth tranches had achieved this. Whilst this reflects the war's erosion of the *psc* group, in terms of later appointees some of those who had passed staff college were upcycled into brigade command after serving on the staff.

Excluding those who served first and last, the second tranche served for 250 days, the third for 280, and the fourth for 240 days. There was therefore a degree of stability during the bulk of the war. But where had the replacements for those who commanded brigades at the war's outset come from? Unsurprisingly, given the dominance of infantry officers, sixty-nine percent had come from infantry battalion command. Moreover, these were mainly Regular units. Thus, Cecil Nicholson (16 Brigade) had commanded 2nd East Lancashire, Henry Ainslie (18 Brigade) 1st Northumberland Fusiliers, Robert Bridgford (18 Brigade) 2nd Shropshire, and Edward Feetham (71 Brigade) 2nd Royal Berkshire, and all had been in command of these units at the outbreak of war. In terms of New Army battalions, John Carroll (a depot major in August 1914) had commanded 7th Norfolk before commanding 17 Brigade, and William Osborn (also a 1914 depot major) had been CO of 7th Sussex before commanding 16 Brigade. Percy Brown, a captain in 1914, had had string of unit commands from April 1915, 1st then 1/6th Gordon Highlanders, 15th then 2nd Argyll and Sutherland, and lastly 2nd Gordon Highlanders. He had thus been a battalion commander for 28 months (with a five-month break) before assuming command of 71 Brigade in August 1917, a post

25 This is not surprising as only one citizen of August 1914 and eleven TF officers held the post of infantry brigade commander on 29 September 1918.
26 Bourne, 'BEF's Generals', p.101.
27 Bourne, 'BEF's Generals', p.105.

he held until the Armistice, demonstrating stamina on the back of rich experience. He might be thought the perfectly 'evolved' model that Sir Douglas Haig was seeking.

Four had already commanded brigades. 'Tabasco Jim' was originally commissioned into the Royal West Surrey Regiment, had transferred to the Indian Army and, having passed staff college, served in a series of staff posts in peace and war.[28] From September 1913 he had been brigadier-general commanding the Meerut Cavalry, but was transferred out of this post immediately on arrival in France to that of BGGS, from whence he was sent to 71 Brigade. He had, of course, only commanded a brigade in peace. William McClintock had commanded the Territorial 145 Brigade (48th Division) from 1911 to 12 December 1915 (on which day he proceeded, likely exhausted, to the Divisional Rest Station),[29] for eight months on the Western Front. He was placed on half-pay in early 1916, but presumably believed to be rejuvenated, assumed command of 18 Brigade at the end of April 1916. Edward Feetham had commanded 137 Brigade from April 1915 to March 1916 and was invalided for four months before returning to command 71 Brigade for ten months. Lastly, George Craufurd had commanded 3 Brigade from November 1916 to March 1917 and then had six months rest before assuming command of 18 Brigade in September 1917.

On the other hand, four had come from staff posts. Harry Walker (16 Brigade) had been GSO1 of 65th Division (having started the war as brigade-major of the Dehra Dun Brigade), and Frederick Gordon (19 Brigade) had served as GSO1 of 2nd Division (a post he had held at the outbreak of war). Walker had never commanded a battalion, but Gordon had been a CO in the pre-war period. Walter Braithwaite (16 Brigade) had being serving as GSO3 with the New Zealand forces in August 1914 and then went as GSO1 to Australian and New Zealand Army Corps HQ before serving as Brigadier-General General Staff (BGGS) with XXIII Corps. George Harper (17 Brigade) had had similarly served as GSO1 and BGGS at GHQ. Neither had been battalion commanders.

Two of 6th Division's brigadiers would go on to corps command, as noted in Chapter Two, Congreve to XIII and later VII Corps, and Harper to IV Corps, both proving effective in those roles. Seven would go on to divisional command. Congreve and Harper rose through 6th and 51st Divisions respectively. Of the remaining five, Cecil Nicholson (16 Brigade) stepped into 'Inky Bill's' shoes in 34th Division and remained there until the Armistice. He was clearly a soldier of skill, and it is indicative of the bottleneck at corps level that he did not get a chance at corps command. Robert Bridgford had commanded 18 Brigade from August 1915 until he fell and broke ribs on 19 April 1916, recovering to command 141 Brigade from 5 July to 19 August 1918, whereupon he was restored to the helm of 18 Brigade until 14 September 1917.

28 His staff postings were all in India. ADC (1895-96), DAAG (1896-1900); DAQMG Mohmand Field Force (1897); DAQMG Tirah (1897-98); GSO1 (1911-13). He was the author of *The Defence and Defensive Positions* (1902).

29 He had spent three weeks in command of the division in May 1915.

Referred to by old hands of 1st West Yorkshire as 'the Brigade Major', due to their esteem for Walter Congreve whom he had replaced,[30] he thus had 683 days of brigade command under his belt, and hence regarded to this point as a safe pair of hands, before he was given six months rest. He returned to commanded 31st Division (45 days) moving to 32nd Division where he spent 24 days before being dismissed. The Hon. Frederick Gordon (19 Brigade) commanded 22 Division in Salonika for nearly two years (June 1915 to May 1917) before being invalided. Lastly, Edward Feetham (71 Brigade) commanded 39th Division from August 1917 to 29 March 1918, when he was killed near Villers-Bretonneux by a shell fragment to the neck. As a brigadier Feetham was described as 'a very stern & strict disciplinarian and was held in awe by his brigade.' He was energetic. 'Few Brigadiers, certainly none of his years' (he was 54) 'could have undertaken the daily complete round of his Brigade front that he invariably carried out.' He was noted for a 'complete disregard of danger.' Amusingly, 'his luncheon always consisted of a few gingerbreads and would generally consume these standing on the fire step of a frontline trench accentuating his remarks by waving a partly consumed gingerbread.'[31]

Half of the brigadiers of 6th Division therefore received promotion. Six out of seven were promoted to divisional command and proved competent, Bridgford's case indicating that being a successful brigade commander was not an absolute guarantee of proficiency at divisional level. This leaves eight officers whose careers as brigadiers ended prior to the armistice. Trevor Harvey, in his study of turnover of brigade commanders in 1917,[32] identifies seven methods of turnover: (i) killed/died of wounds (eight percent), (ii) wounded/gassed (five percent), (iii) sick (eight percent), (iv) promoted (eleven percent), (v) dismissed (six percent), (vi) rested and reappointed (40 percent), and (vii) relieved and not reappointed (22 percent). No general officer lost their life whilst within 6th Division, and only one succumbed to wounds, Harry Walker losing an arm commanding 16 Brigade at the Selle in October 1918. It is interesting that the largest category in Harvey's classification is those who returned after the application of the 'six-month rest rule', which he dates to mid-1917 (although the practice of rest had been used informally before that point). Only one such case appears in 6th Division, William Osborn evidently being rested for six months before appointment to 5 Brigade.

There are four brigadiers whose careers were particularly short. 'Tabasco Jim' Edwards only served 55 days in command of 71 Brigade to be 'invalided' on 6 October 1916. His experiences on the Somme revealed a different sort of limitation to Ainslie, presumably bulk. He 'had to be relieved of his command because he found it beyond

30 War Diary, 1st Battalion West Yorkshire Regiment, 'Diary of Colonel W.T.C. Huffam', TNA WO95/1618.
31 War Diary, 9th Battalion Norfolk Regiment, 'Diary of Lieutenant-Colonel B.H.L. Prior', TNA WO95/1623.
32 T. Harvey, 'Turnover Amongst Brigade Commanders, 1917 – The Real Reasons?.'

his physical powers to go round his front line.'[33] He served, however, from 9 November 1916 to January 1918 as GOC 179 Brigade, 60th Division, appointed just as it was sent to Salonika. It is not clear why the front line at Salonika was any easier for a fat man to visit. His appointment in 1916 was undoubtedly due to seniority rather than merit, and uninspired leadership may have weighed in the scales as heavily as bulk. Of the three whose careers were particularly short, Henry Ainslie, who spent 65 days in command of 18 Division in 1915, was in the 'relieved and not reappointed' group but was relieved (see Chapter 3) at his own request. No doubt seniority played a role in his appointment in the face of a known weak psychological constitution. William McClintock, the oldest of the brigadiers was relieved and not reappointed. He had left 145 Brigade exhausted in December 1915 returning to command 18 Brigade for only 44 days, from whence he was placed on half-pay, although several months later he resumed full pay if not on active service. His history is indicative that brigade command was hard on older officers. Mansell Shewen, a 54-year-old Indian Army officer was also clearly relieved and not reappointed after 267 days in command, serving briefly as a staff captain before fully retiring (again) in June 1917. Cecil Nicholson described him as 'broken down' and clearly believed him an essentially good brigadier as he continued: 'A great loss to me.'[34] William McClintock had been a replacement for the incapacitated Bridgford, as was his successor, Harold Tew. Tew was relieved of command on 16 August 1916 and Bridgford returned three days later. Tew returned to England and having taken up his brigade command from being CO 1st East Surrey, was sent to command 9th East Surrey on 5 September 1916. Some officers who were clearly able at battalion level, being 'good fighting COs', could not make the leap to formation command. Tew was likely one such. He was not the only brigadier to return to battalion command. John Carroll of 17 Brigade commanded for 472 days and would therefore be considered having a track record indicating a competent brigadier, but was allegedly relieved of command 'sick' on 16 January 1917 (although the brigade war diary does not mention it), reappearing in command of his old battalion, 1st Norfolk, sometime during March. 'Sick' in his case appears to be euphemism for 'relieved.' Four out of 19 brigadiers (21 percent) were therefore relieved of command in short order, clearly not up to the job. If Carroll and Shewen are added, which may not be entirely fair in the latter's case, the total rises to 31 percent, which is a somewhat higher than Harvey's 1917 figure of 22 percent either dismissed or relieved and not reappointed. 6th Division might be thought of as, on balance, reasonably average in terms of the overall competence of its brigadiers by this yardstick.

33 Grove, op. cit.
34 Nicholson, op. cit. 26 May 1916.

John Bourne, noting the high level of awards for valour possessed by brigadier-generals, observes that 'courage retained its currency in appointments to brigade command.'[35] He offered the opinion that:

> Tactical innovation and original thought were not essential for competent brigade, division or even corps commanders. What was absolutely necessary was careful (preferably personal) reconnaissance, thorough preparation and an awareness of the 'friction of war.' Anything less invited disaster at the hands of a formidable enemy.[36]

There were, however, clearly innovators and original thinkers in the brigadiers of 6th Division, Congreve and Harper amongst them. Trevor Harvey, in reviewing brigade command at the Battle of Arras, describes brigadier commanders at this point in the war as 'promoted on the basis of merit and … had the virtue of having been tried and tested. Their experience was practical and relevant. Their performance, both in their preceding roles and in command of their brigades, generated confidence amongst their superiors.'[37] This would be a reasonable summary across the bulk of the BEF, and would include in 6th Division, William Osborn, Robert Bridgford and Edward Feetham, in post during the Arras period being all very competent brigadiers. Harvey views their roles at this stage of the war as having 'flexibility … to develop their own operational styles and emphases whilst all fulfilled their common "administration and training" responsibilities.'[38] Indeed, in contrast to Bourne's comments which relate largely to the operational role, Harvey asserts that 'the most significant contribution of brigadier-generals was not on the field.' Rather, their role was in preparation, being 'on a treadmill to recreate the capability of their brigades to fight.'[39] John Gellibrand, who would serve as a long-standing brigadier (and latterly major-general) in the ANZAC Corps, would remark that: 'The Brigadier had little scope beyond oiling the works and using his eyes.'[40] Lest this might be considered to sell the role short, a summary of Peter Simkins' view of the responsibilities of a brigadier includes 'training, administration and man management with a central focus on efficiency.'[41] A brigadier would and could dismiss unit COs if he thought them lacking in

35 J. Bourne, 'British Generals in the First World War', in G.D. Sheffield (ed.), *Leadership and Command*, p.99.
36 J. Bourne, 'BEF's Generals', p.112.
37 T. Harvey, 'An Army of Brigadiers', p.336.
38 Harvey, op. cit. p.335.
39 Harvey, op. cit. p.336.
40 Quoted in P. Simkins, '"Building Blocks": Aspects of Command and Control at Brigade level in the BEF's Offensive Operations, 1916-1918', in G. Sheffield and D. Todman (eds) *Command and Control on the Western Front*, p.145.
41 M. LoCicero, '"A Tower of Strength": Brigadier-General Edward Bulfin', in S. Jones (ed.), *Stemming the Tide*, p.237.

competence, as will be seen in the next section on Cecil Nicholson's command of 16 Brigade. (There is, however, no evidence of widespread 'new broom' dismissals in the division). Organisational skills were therefore at a premium. As Bourne observes, and Cecil Nicholson's routine bears out: 'A brigade commander's relationships with his subordinates were essentially face-to-face and day-to-day. Brigade commanders were not isolated from the front line. They were often in the trenches and sometimes beyond them.'[42] In terms of operations, the brigadier would interpret the divisional orders for his units, making sure the right number of battalions were deployed in the right place at the right time; attempt to make adjustments in action; and would decide when and where to commit his reserves. As Peter Simkins notes: 'He could therefore exert some influence on the course and outcome of the battle', and 'provided he had sited his headquarters or command post wisely, was able to keep in touch with his subordinates and could consequently judge what was happening in the front line', even if this was often limited by communication problems.[43] This was exactly what General Osborn was able to do in his handling of the fighting at Loos in April 1917. In March 1918, Simkins considers that brigadiers learnt that 'improvisation at a local level could still retrieve the situation',[44] and during the Hundred Days campaign 'the BEF required, and got, effective local control of the battle by its brigade commanders.'[45] Whilst there is truth in this statement, the experience of 6th Division in the Battle of the Selle on 17 October 1918 would demonstrate the limitations.[46] The difficulties of the brigade command role should not be underestimated. As Simkins observes: 'Even the most dedicated, gifted or experienced' of brigadiers 'were rarely able to meet all these criteria at the same time and the unremitting pressure inevitably undermined the physical or mental resilience of many.'[47]

A Year in the Life – Cecil Nicholson's command of 16 Brigade, 1915-16

Cecil Lothian 'Johnny Nick' Nicholson arrived to take up command of 16 Brigade from 'Inky Bill' on 16 June 1915. At the start of July the war diary noted that: 'Health of the men remains good and their morale excellent.' Captain Hugh Headlam,[48] the brigade-major, added that comparing the sick returns of the division's brigades 'it appears that during last 12 weeks the sickness in this brigade is very considerably less.'[49] 'Inky Bill' had left Nicholson a formation in good shape. During three days of initial visits to units in the line between Wieltje and the Ypres-Roulers railway, he reported

42 Bourne, 'British Generals', p.101.
43 Simkins, op. cit. p.145.
44 Simkins, op. cit. p.162.
45 Simkins, op. cit. p.165.
46 See Chapter 12.
47 Simkins, p.146.
48 See Chapter 7.
49 War Diary, 16 Infantry Brigade, July 1915, WO95/1605.

himself 'not much impressed with the trenches or the way they were held.' He 'came to the conclusion that it was no good putting all four Battalions into trenches' from the point of view of overcrowding.[50] On the fourth day he ventured out into the advanced post, Stink Houses, on the Verlorenhoek Road, which he found 'quite the worst place in the way of fortifications that I have seen yet.'[51] Nicholson's first activities involved, therefore, stamping his mark on the brigade, reorganising the way it defended its trenches. His actions also demonstrated the concerns of a regimental officer – reducing the overcrowding in the trenches meant less casualties to regular shelling. On the last day of the month he went round the brigade's trenches, 'and took COs with me. Each over his own lot to make certain that they knew the communication trenches.' He was clearly taking a firm hand with his unit commanders. His concern was also directed at understanding his front line, personally reconnoitring (without useful result) 'a mound in the German lines which is a source of mystery to us.'[52] On 6 July, when out of line, he assembled 1st King's Shropshire Light Infantry in Poperinghe, for inspection by Lord Kitchener and Herbert Asquith. He met with General Ross to inspect the first line transport and found 'none of it very good.' As a new broom he clearly had an eye to that which needed sweeping. Kitchener arrived half an hour early and 'walked up and down the ranks and told me to express his satisfaction.'[53]

Returning to the line on the left of the division's front, Nicholson had to repeat the process of familiarising himself with his line. After his first trench tour on 12 July 'there was a constant procession of RE and RA to see me and talk things over, generally the case on taking over a fresh set of lines.'[54] This demonstrates how the various elements within the division were coordinating in trench warfare. On the following two days he went round the trenches with the CRE Lieutenant-Colonel Kemp, reconnoitring sites for new trenches. On the 15th and the 16th he spent time selecting artillery positions and sites for machine-guns. Given that no offensive was planned, he was very active in establishing an adequate defence. On the 18th a revolver shot by a member of working party at Forward Cottage 'started trouble', and after retaliation the working party 'retired quite unnecessarily. Bad business.'[55] The following day Nicholson went to the HQ of 1st Buffs and saw Lieutenant-Colonels Finch-Hatton and Murray (1st KSLI) to identify what had happened and 'made arrangements to carry it out properly tonight.'[56] He was going to let no slip-ups pass by on his watch. Similarly, after finding 'trench discipline generally indifferent' at

50 Nicholson, op. cit. 18 June 1915.
51 Nicholson, op. cit. 19 June 1915.
52 Nicholson, op. cit. 2 July 1915.
53 Nicholson, op. cit. 7 July 1915.
54 Nicholson, op. cit. 12 July 1915.
55 Nicholson, op. cit. 18 July 1915.
56 Nicholson, op. cit. 19 July 1915.

Cross Roads Farm on the 23rd, Nicholson went straight to battalion HQ 'but missed the CO and had to write to him afterwards.'[57]

On coming out of line on 27 July, Nicholson's brigade was soon warned to support 14 Division who had lost the trenches at Hooge. Walter Congreve was being pressured to retake the trenches on the morning of 1 August, and to Nicholson's view 'he propounded a plan I did not at all like.' Reconnoitering, Nicholson came under whizz-bang and field artillery fire and Lieutenant-Colonel Arthur Sargeaunt, CRE 14th Division, was killed 'close to me and we must all have had extraordinary narrow escapes.'[58] In general, he 'did not like the job at all', and telephoned Sir John Keir from 41 Brigade's HQ (thus bypassing Congreve) stating that the attack had to be postponed. Keir assented, but no doubt Nicholson's was not the only voice.[59] He was, however, confident to assert his opinion. Clearly finding Congreve's properly considered plans more acceptable, Nicholson then relieved Lieutenant-Colonel John Strick from command of 1st KSLI, clearly having no confidence in him for the coming attack.[60] In terms of the planning the operation, he noted: 'There is such a lot to do and think about that one hardly knows where to begin.'[61] The brigade operation orders stretch to four pages, reflecting Congreve's detail. Nicholson added: 'The Brigadier expects that lightly wounded men will stick at their posts.'[62] He was setting standards for tenacity. On the day of the attack he went up to an observation post with Hugh Headlam. The assault went in at 03.15, but Nicholson was effectively blind. He could see little, the telephone wires were all cut, and he only heard at 05.00 that the attack had been successful. On the way back a shrapnel ball grazed his head, cutting his eyebrow. He was still essentially unclear as to the situation at 07.00 the following day, but 'Headlam did a very gallant reconnaissance' under an enemy barrage 'and brought back a clear report of the situation.'[63] His experience at Hooge is a salutary reminder that in trench warfare, with communication so problematic, a brigadier was mostly impotent during an assault. The only way the course of the fighting could be influenced was through proper planning. This was in the major part a matter of reconnaissance, and Nicholson had experienced a close shave in this activity. Despite success, Congreve was disappointed with the performance of 1st Buffs, and on the

57 Nicholson, op. cit. 23 July 1915.

58 Arthur Frederick 'Sally' Sargeaunt had been commissioned into the Royal Engineers in 1890 and had spent two years as an instructor at the School of Military Engineering. He had served in South Africa 1899-1902. Thomas Grove described him as 'the most genuinely fearless man I ever knew' and noted that he died choosing not to walk in the mud at the bottom of a communication trench. (Grove, op. cit.).

59 Nicholson, op. cit. 31 July 1915.

60 John Arkwright Strick had been a major of 2nd KSLI in August 1914 and had commanded the 1st Battalion since December 1914. He would serve in staff posts for the rest of the war.

61 Nicholson, op. cit. 5 August 1915.

62 War Diary, 16 Infantry Brigade, Operation Order No. 2, 6 August 1915, WO95/1605.

63 Nicholson, op. cit. 10 August 1915.

12th Nicholson met Finch-Hatton but 'did not get much out of him as to what his battalion had done, and I am afraid it was not much.' Nicholson's words suggested he pedalled softly with a man who had been in action, in contrast with his approach to the same CO after the Forward Cottage patrol debacle. Finch-Hatton would remain in post, despite Congreve's threat that 'he would get relieved if he didn't look out',[64] and would be promoted to brigade command ten months later.

Following five days leave, Nicholson returned to find the brigade in the familiar Wieltje sector, and he began his routine of examining the trenches. Yet again, he was not satisfied. He criticised the TF and New Army units that had been holding the line. 'They don't seem to grasp the necessity of thick parapets, or of building up blown up parapets and communication trenches.'[65] In this he indicates one reason why the army used a preponderance of Regular officers in senior posts – there was an all-round approach to soldiering bestowed by training and experience. Indeed, there were no support trenches, which he ordered dug. Inspecting these six days later, with a view to drawing up a defence scheme, Nicholson considered the principles 'laid down by the Corps, with which I did not agree at all.' He was a thinking soldier. Examining trenches in the old Wieltje-Roulers railway section in September 1915 he recorded: 'Heartbreaking work for us here, as I could not see a single thing I had asked the 17th Brigade to do had been done.'[66] He was directly criticising Brigadier-General Carroll, a fellow Regular, and as noted previously, Carroll was eventually relieved and returned to battalion command. Condemning the state in which a previous unit/formation had left a location was, however, a time-honoured ritual.

Nicholson was a brigadier relentless in his visits to the trenches. From taking up to command to the end of the year, he visited the forward trenches on 69 percent of days when the brigade was in line. He must have been a very recognisable figure to the other ranks. But it was a tiring activity for the older man. In late August 1915 he wrote: 'Four days running – in the trenches for long hours – is about as much as I can manage.'[67] He also ventured beyond the trenches. On 21 September he went out into No Man's Land to reconnoitre German sap heads about 100 yards from the British trenches with four others. He and Major Richard Wood of 2nd York & Lancaster had to stop half-way across as 'the crawling was too much for me.'[68] Indeed, there was an exchange of fire and to Nicholson's chagrin, Captain Henry Colville, the 16 Brigade Machine Gun Officer, was killed.[69] As the weather deteriorated towards the

64 Nicholson, op. cit. 13 August 1915.
65 Nicholson, op. cit. 25 August 1915.
66 Nicholson, op. cit. 18 September 1915.
67 Nicholson, op. cit. 26 August 1915.
68 Nicholson, op. cit. 21 September 1915. Richard Poingdestre was a Regular lieutenant of the York and Lancasters in August 1914 and would command the battalion briefly from the end of September 1916 until he was killed on 9 October 1916.
69 Nicholson was remorseful: 'I blame myself very much for allowing the reconnaissance for what was perhaps an insufficient object.' He wrote to Colville's wife that evening.

end of the year, visits became more demanding. On 14 November Nicholson visited the Morteldje Estaminet trenches. He summarised: 'Trenches in an awful state. Almost impossible to move except over the top. Had rather a perilous walk back as communication trenches were impassable and it was rather light.'[70] On Christmas Eve 1915 he described himself as 'very beat. The labour of walking in the mud is very great.'[71] He made sure, however, that he personally understood the front-line conditions. Resorting to a different type of reconnaissance, on 7 February 1916 he climbed the water tower in Ypres to observe the German line, the only place from which the Pilckem Ridge could be observed, 'but owing to difficulty of ascent could not manage much observation.' Achieving a better view from the attic of another house he observed (perhaps mindfully) that the water tower was brought down by enemy shellfire two days later.[72] When he did not visit the trenches he was generally visiting battalion HQs. There were few days when he stayed in his brigade HQ and did not go out. Amongst these were a handful of occasions when he described feeling unwell, and hence was without the energy to venture out.[73] He needed to preserve his health and, indeed, had no time off sick in his 13 months. His pattern earlier on was to visit trenches in the morning, return to his HQ in the afternoon and do paperwork into the evening. In the winter, when weather resulted in him visiting the trenches slightly less, he sometimes reversed his schedule and went out to the trenches in the late afternoon. In May and June 1916, when he was visiting forward positions much less regularly, he would go most days to La Belle Alliance, about 500 yards behind the centre of his front-line.

Nicholson only conducted two offensive operations, namely the Hooge attack and the Willow Walk attack of April 1916 (when there is a 29-day gap in his diary). The historiography of the Great War tends to concentrate on attack, neglecting routine British defence (yet paying disproportionately more attention to German defensive principles). Defence was no less important to the BEF – indeed, battalion COs were sometimes degummed after a successful enemy raid had entered their trenches, and one of the reasons put forward by Allenby for Sir John Keir's dismissal was inadequate defensive arrangements. Nicholson's trench visits served his preoccupation with the best defence of his sector – he certainly fulfilled Bourne's criteria for 'reconnaissance' and 'preparedness.' Outside of his involvement in organising his brigade's reliefs, not a matter he left entirely to his brigade-majors (again demonstrating the protective care of a regimental officer, as such moments represented threat), he most often describes writing defence schemes, particularly when his brigade took over a new section of line.

(Nicholson, op. cit. 22 September 1915). Henry George Coulson Colville had been commissioned in the Shropshire Light Infantry in 1906.

70 Nicholson, op. cit. 14 November 1915.

71 Nicholson, op. cit. 24 December 1915.

72 Nicholson, op. cit. 7 January 1915.

73 Outside of his 28 days leave to Great Britain, his main relaxation seems to have been riding his horses.

Although he fairly regularly encountered his two divisional commanders and their staff officers he only records attending twelve divisional conferences in 13 months, and only four of these in eight months under Sir Charles Ross's command, which indirectly confirms the picture of Ross's *liassez-faire* management. Nicholson also rarely had conferences of all his battalion commanders, describing only four such, appearing to deal with them on an individual basis.

In terms of the picture of the role of the brigade commander given by Trevor Harvey for the period including the Battle of Arras, evolution is demonstrated from the year of Nicholson's tenure at 16 Brigade. Not being on the treadmill of constant operations, Nicholson had a reduced need to 'recreate the capability' of his brigade to fight. Indeed, in his diaries he makes virtually no reference to training. On four occasions he recorded riding out on his horse to view potential training grounds, and on 3 April he described writing a brigade tactical exercise. During the period of his command, the brigade war diary makes reference to only eleven days training. This is unsurprising as the brigade held the line for very long periods. However there is no reference to training in his diary during the period 21 June to 17 July 1916, when the brigade enjoyed nearly a month out of the line, yet unit diaries indicate considerable training during this period (1st Buffs 14 days; 2nd York & Lancaster 20 days; 8th Bedfordshire 18 days). It is difficult to think that Nicholson, as a Regular soldier, did not believe in the importance of training – he likely simply left it, correct in terms of *Field Service Regulations*, to the unit COs. Simon Robbins observes that 'poor training was probably the single most serious weakness of the British Army in 1915-17', poor leadership 'starting a cycle of poor training and poor fighting efficiency.'[74] Nicholson was very far from a poor leader, yet in this pre-Somme period, long before the advent of Arthur Solly-Flood and the Training Directorate, when the opportunity for training arose, he appeared largely content to leave this responsibility to others.

Battalion Commanders

One hundred and two officers commanded the 24 units that were at one time or another attached to 6th Division at the rank of lieutenant-colonel. The seven Regular battalions that served all their time with the division had an average eight COs each. The overall average for Regular units during the war was seven COs,[75] and hence 6th Division was more or less typical in turnover. Even though it was a Regular division, it is notable that 88 percent were professional soldiers (including one Indian Army officer)[76]. During the war, the Regular officer corps of 1914 provided 43 percent of

74 Robbins, *British Generalship*, p.136.
75 With a range of two to fourteen. P.E. Hodgkinson, *British Infantry Battalion Commanders in the First World War*, p. 50.
76 Frederick Ewart Bradshaw had retired in December 1904 as a major in the Indian Army. As a Persian and Pashtu speaker he seems to have spent a number of years working with the civil authorities.

infantry battalion commanders, professional soldiers in all providing 60 percent of active battalion commands.[77] In terms of Regular battalions, however, 93 percent of COs throughout the war were professional soldiers. The figure for the seven units permanently with 6th Division is 98 percent, only seven percent of whom were dug-outs. Given that only one was Indian Army, these seven units retained a slightly higher than average number of Regular COs, and the whole division had a higher preponderance of Regular unit commanders than many.

Otherwise, of the 102 COs, four were from the Special Reserve, six were Territorials, and three were citizens in August 1914. Three of the six Territorials were commanding TF units temporarily attached. Of the other three, Lyndon Henry Morris, a pre-war solicitor's articled clerk and 29 years old in 1918, must have been highly thought of (given the prejudice against Territorial officers in terms of promotion) to be given command of 1st King's Shropshire Light Infantry on 10 October 1918 (having been a captain of 4th KSLI in August 1914), and his subsequent career in the Prison Service and police indicates strong organisational abilities.[78] Similarly, Hubert Tylden-Wright, a captain of the Territorial Nottinghamshire and Derby Mounted Brigade in August 1914 commanded 2nd Sherwood Foresters for two spells of several weeks in late 1917 and early 1918. The third Territorial officer finding command outside a Territorial unit was the remarkable Bernard Henry Leathes Prior, the Haileybury-educated son of a solicitor who had followed his father's profession. He had served in South Africa 1900-1, and was commanding 6th Norfolk (cyclist) at the outbreak of war, aged 37. Prior was transferred in mid-1916 to the 7th Battalion on the Western Front, and again at the end of September to command 9th Norfolk, a post he held until August 1918. He alleged that before he took command of the unit General Ross summoned him and declaimed: 'I don't know why you have been sent to this Division. This is a regular Division. We have no Territorial commanding officers here and to be quite frank we don't want you.' On discovering that Prior had served in Ross's old battalion, 2nd Norfolk, in South Africa, the general's attitude softened. Prior remined convinced that if there had not been this fortunate confluence of regimental identity: 'I should have been relegated forthwith to the limbo of lost hopes and an Area Commandant's, Town Major's, or R.T.O.'s job.'[79] Prior was wounded on four occasions. Firstly in October and again in December 1916, the latter occasion providing an insight into the nature of his leadership, as he was shot through the right forearm by a sniper in No Man's Land whilst returning from a reconnaissance for a raid; again in January 1918, when he was gassed; and finally on 22 March during the German spring offensive. In

77 Hodgkinson, op. cit. p.52.

78 After fruit farming in Florida immediately after the war, Morris returned to Great Britain, entered the Prison Service, where he was highly thought of, latterly being governor of Dartmoor Prison. In 1931 he was appointed Chief Constable of Devon out of 133 candidates. He died in 1946, having been the county ARP controller in WW2.

79 War Diary, 9th Battalion Norfolk Regiment, 'Diary of Lieutenant-Colonel B.H.L. Prior', TNA WO95/1623.

August, 'shattered by wounds and gas', he was finally invalided.[80] He was seven times mentioned in dispatches, and awarded the DSO and bar as CO. The citation for his bar, related to the German spring offensive of 21-2 March 1918, reads:

> Throughout two days of an enemy advance, and until wounded, he set a splendid example of coolness and courage under the most trying conditions, personally supervising the readjustments which had to be made to meet the enemy attacks, and the gallant resistance offered by his battalion was largely due to his magnificent example of fearless determination.[81]

Three COs were citizens of August 1914. John Brenchley Rosher of 14th Durham Light Infantry has already been encountered. William James Spurrell (9th Norfolk), a chemist, commanded between January and March 1918. Wounded at the Quadrilateral in 1916, he was awarded the DSO whilst commanding the battalion:

> He personally made a reconnaissance of the ground for a counter-attack, giving orders for the disposition of the men under a very heavy shell and machine-gun fire. Although wounded, he insisted on carrying on, and gathering every man from battalion headquarters, until he received a second wound. Throughout the whole time he commanded the battalion his example and gallantry were of a very fine order.[82]

Thirdly, 26-year-old Charles Edward Hudson (2nd Sherwood Foresters) was a tea planter in Ceylon in August 1914, and had already commanded 11th Sherwood Foresters from November 1917 to June 1918 before taking command of the 2nd Battalion on 15 September 1918. A citizen commanding a Regular unit (he had attended RMC Sandhurst for a year before dropping out due to the death of his father and going to Ceylon as a tea planter), Hudson had won a DSO at Arras as a major, reorganising his battalion and taking the objective, showing 'capacity of the highest military value';[83] and a bar to this award in holding his line against attack, displaying 'splendid leadership and great energy and courage.'[84] A man who at Sherborne School was 'terribly conscious of being a coward on the football field',[85] he won the Victoria Cross in June 1918 on the Asiago Plateau in Italy.[86] Hudson would command 2

80 F. L. Petre, *The History of the Norfolk Regiment 1914-1918,* p.292.
81 *London Gazette*, 26 July 1918. Despite his wounds, he only died in 1953, aged 76.
82 *London Gazette*, 13 September 1918, p. 10873.
83 *Edinburgh Gazette*, 20 August 1917, p. 1645.
84 *London Gazette*, 6 April 1918, p. 4196.
85 M.M.L. Hudson, *Two Lives.*
86 *London Gazette*, 6 April 1918. The citation reads: 'His battalion was holding the right front sector during an attack on the British front. The shelling had been very heavy on the right, the trench destroyed, and considerable casualties had occurred, and all the officers

Brigade in France in 1940, and 46th Infantry Division for five months, demoted after a dispute with his corps commander, later commanding 159 and 182 Brigades.

The bulk of the division's COs were Regulars, however. In terms of Haig's desire for the rise of junior officers and hence youth, 18 percent were lieutenant-colonels in August 1914, 36 percent were majors, 37 percent were captains and eight percent lieutenants. One was a ranker. Forty-seven-year-old James Hall Martin, who took command of 1st Leicestershire on 26 October 1918, had been in the ranks for 17 years, and was a Warrant Officer Class 1 of 1st Royal Scots before he was commissioned second-lieutenant in that regiment in March 1915. His rise was then meteoric, promoted temporary lieutenant-colonel commanding 1/8th Durham Light Infantry from May 1917 to 26 March 1918 when he was wounded at Pozières. He re-joined on 20 September and was transferred to 1st Leicestershire. He was clearly a soldier of stature.

Across the 24 units the average length of a COs tenure was 220 days, but as might be imagined, this hides an extraordinary variability. In the seven Regular units that served their whole period of the war in 6th Division the average was 177 days, or roughly six months. Interestingly, during the Second World War, Lieutenant-General G. Simonds, commanding II Canadian Corps, sent a memo to Canadian Military Headquarters in 1944 in which he stated: 'It has been amply demonstrated both in North Africa and Italy that when active operations are continuous, the Commanding Officer of an infantry battalion is good for about four to six months.'[87] Many commanded beyond such a timespan. Reginald Gillespie, a captain of the Leicestershire Regiment 1914, commanded 1st Leicestershire between February 1916 and January 1918 in three chunks, twice having been invalided. Francis Latham, another Leicestershire captain at the outbreak of war, commanded for 592 days, 163 with 1st Leicestershire and 429 with 9th Suffolk. Cyril Winterscale, a lieutenant of the King's Shropshire

on the spot were killed or wounded. This enabled the enemy to penetrate our front line. The enemy pushed their advance as far as the support line which was the key to our right flank. The situation demanded immediate action. Lt.-Col. Hudson, recognising its gravity, at once collected various headquarter details, such as orderlies, servants, runners, etc., and, together with some Allies, personally led them up the hill. Driving the enemy down the hill towards our front, line, he again led a party of about five up the trench, where there were about 200 enemy, in order to attack them from the flank. He then with, two men got out of the trench and rushed the position, shouting to the enemy to surrender, some of whom did. He was then severely wounded by a bomb which exploded on his foot. Although in great pain, he gave directions for the counter-attack to be continued, and this was done successfully, about 100 prisoners and six machine-guns being taken. Without doubt the high courage and determination displayed by Lt.-Col. Hudson saved a serious situation, and had it not been for his quick determination in organising the counter-attack a large number of the enemy would have dribbled through, and counter-attack on a larger scale would have been necessary to restore the situation.'

87 *Battlefront* <http://www.battlefront.com/community/showthread.php?t=32644> (Accessed 5 June 2018).

Light Infantry in August 1914 commanded the 1st Battalion for 486 days, and Alan St John Blunt, a captain of the York & Lancaster Regiment at the onset of hostilities commanded the 2nd Battalion for 487 days. Never promoted to brigade command (although Blunt and Latham frequently acted up in the absence of their brigadiers), these officers were clearly 'good fighting battalion commanders.' Possibly the shortest command was recorded by Cecil Nicholson. He noted on Christmas Eve 1915:

> A Col(onel) Kennedy came to command the 8th Bedfords on the afternoon of the 23rd and reported himself this morning as medically unfit to command a battalion. As I had already heard a good deal about him of a very unfavourable nature, I got a medical board on him at once and by the morning of the 25th, he was evacuated to base.[88]

Kennedy's brief appearance was not even noted in the war diary, and it is difficult to identify him with clarity. Nicholson was successful in his replacement with Lieutenant-Colonel Henry Jackson 'who I got out of the Corps staff – a very good man.'[89] Jackson was indeed good, ending the war commanding 50th Division.[90]

What were the causes of change of command? Twenty-five (30 percent taking into account those who could not progress their careers due to being killed or wounded), left their posts as battalion COs because they were promoted. Ten percent of active COs across the British armies were promoted to brigade command during the war, and over 93 percent of these were active or retired professional soldiers.[91] Before the idea is formed that 6th Division was an exceptional creche for general officers, the fact that it had an exceptionally high number of Regular COs must be taken into account. Promotion to brigadier was, of course, often at the expense of the battalion and brigade left behind. Cecil Nicholson regarded William Clemson, 2nd York & Lancaster, appointed to a brigade command in Great Britain as 'a great loss – a first rate CO and had a first-rate Battalion.'[92] Eight COs were killed in action or died of wounds. Of promising careers cut short, Richard Poingdestre Wood might be considered. A Regular Lieutenant of the York and Lancasters in August 1915, he had lain out in No Man's Land, it will be remembered, with Cecil Nicholson. Promoted to command his battalion on 25 September 1916, he was killed visiting his front line at night 14 days later. He was exactly the sort of officer Sir Douglas Haig envisaged

88 Nicholson, op. cit. 24 December 1915.
89 Nicholson, op. cit. 14 January 1916.
90 Henry Cholmondeley Jackson was a captain of the Bedfordshire Regiment in August 1914 and appointed to divisional command in March 1918 would prove a more than able GOC at the Battle of the Selle on 18 October 1918, inventively restructuring his command in the face of battlefield chaos.
91 Hodgkinson, op. cit. p. 105.
92 Nicholson, op. cit. 17 September 1915. William Fletcher Clemson was a major in August 1914 and would command 124 Brigade for three years.

rising to unit command. At eight percent, the attrition rate of COs through death is lower than the BEF average of 11 percent,[93] which likely reflects the avoidance of major offensives during the period holding the line at Ypres 1915-16, and a later arrival on the Somme.

What of those who could not make the grade? A poor CO could do damage to his unit. Cecil Nicholson described Lieutenant-Colonel Edward Thomson of 2nd York & Lancaster as 'very indifferent CO' and when he inspected the unit on 24 June found they looked 'not so good', attributing this entirely to Thomson,[94] describing him as 'the drunkard and the fool.' He lasted 19 days at the helm of his battalion. Thirty officers were replaced as CO and their careers did not progress. This represents 33 percent of total COs (leaving out those who were still in post at the Armistice) and compares favourably with the 38 percent estimate for the BEF as a whole and the Canadian Corps.[95] Six COS were invalided, this not being a euphemism for removal. Amongst these was Lieutenant-Colonel Henry Delme-Radcliffe, who was invalided from command of the 2nd Royal Welsh Fusiliers (19 Brigade) in October 1914 with a 'nervous breakdown' according to Private Frank Richards, whose amateur diagnosis was confirmed by the medical officer of 19th Field Ambulance with the hardly more professional words: 'A bit of a nervous wreck.'[96] Life at the front was hard for regimental officers in 1914.

Did the COs of 6th Division represent a progression towards youth and competence tempered by experience? On 1 July 1916, the first day of the Battle of the Somme, the average age of COs across the BEF was 42 years one month, and in 6th Division 41 years 10 months. On 31 July 1917, the opening day of the Third Battle of Ypres, the average age across the BEF was 36 years seven months, but 37 years two months in 6th Division. On 29 September 1918, when all the BEF's five armies were in action together for the first time in the Hundred Days campaign, the average across the BEF was 34 years 11 months, whilst in 6th Division the gap had widened a little further, the average being 36 years nine months. Thus, whilst the division followed the general trend towards younger unit COs, it lagged behind the rest of the army. This was due to its greater use of Regular officers of August 1914. On the 29th, the day the Hindenburg Line was penetrated, of the nine COs in post, seven had been Regulars

93 Hodgkinson, op. cit. p.108.

94 Nicholson, op. cit. 24 June 1916.Edward Lionel Thomson had retired from the Norfolk Regiment and was a Special Reserve captain with the York & Lancasters in August 1914. Surprisingly, given Nicholson's comments, he was given a further 18 days in charge of 12th West Yorkshire several weeks after removal, and then, briefly, command of a battalion of the Northumberland Fusiliers after the armistice.

95 Hodgkinson, op. cit. p.117. P.H. Brennan, 'Good Men for a Hard Job: Infantry Battalion Commanders in the Canadian Expeditionary Force', *Canadian Army Journal*, 9/1 (2006) pp.9-28.

96 F. Richards, *Old Soldiers Never Die* (London: Faber, 1965), p.55. T. Hampson, *A Medical Officer's Diary and Narrative of the First World War*, http://myweb.tiscali.co.uk/philsnet/T%20Hampson%20WW1%20Diary%20100.htm (accessed 9 June 2018).

in August 1914, one a major and six captains. Two, however, were civilians. One was the extraordinary Lieutenant-Colonel Charles Hudson, the other was commanding 11th Essex at the rank of major. Born in 1891, the son of the director of a distilling company, Alistair Grant Saunders had just left Cambridge University in August 1914, and had been commissioned into the London Regiment in October 1914. Of the seven Regulars, by the Armistice the major of 1914, Godfrey Meynell of 1st KSLI, had been promoted to the command of 171 Brigade and had been replaced by Lyndon Morris, a Territorial captain of August 1914. One of the captains (Francis Latham, 1st Leicestershire) had been transferred to command of another battalion and replaced by that veteran ranker, James Hall Martin. Even in the short period of time between the breaking of the *Siegfried Stellung* and the Armistice, battalion command in 6th Division had become a slightly more diverse environment, with no lessening of the depth of experience. All the division's COs at the conflict's end, clearly, had been very well tempered by war.

A Year in the Life – Allan St John Blunt's command of 2nd York & Lancaster 1917

Allan St John Blunt was a well-respected officer and able battalion commander. Born on 27 October 1880, he came from a military family, being the third son of Colonel Arthur Blunt RHA. Commissioned in 1899 he was sent straight to South Africa, where he served 1899-1902, being present at the relief of Ladysmith and Spion Kop. He had served as adjutant, and in August 1914 was a captain of 1st York & Lancaster, although he was not with his regiment in India at the outbreak of war and went to the Western Front attached to 1st Gloucestershire. He served as the brigade-major of 60 Brigade from September 1915 to June 1916, demonstrating organisational efficiency, when he was appointed to the command of the 2nd Battalion of his regiment on 30 June 1916. Wounded in September 1916 at Morval, 16 February 1917 found him on a post lorry heading back to his battalion at Le Robeq.[97] The unit was in divisional rest and he spent his first day going round all four companies. The next day he 'made out scheme for attack under the new organisation which seems sound',[98] referring here to the specialist organisation of platoons and accompanying tactics set out in the new *SS143* pamphlet, and the next morning he watched the companies practising attack. On the 23rd he inspected C and B companies and 'saw work on the range.'[99] The following day there was a 'brigade scheme in conjunction with an aeroplane',[100] which after technical problems was repeated successfully on the 26th. Immediately on return, therefore, he was involved in one of the CO's most important functions – ensuring the

97 His diary begins on 15 February 1917.
98 A. St. J. Blunt, Private papers, IWM Docs 16149, 18 February 1917.
99 Blunt op. cit. 23 February 1917.
100 Blunt op. cit. 24 February 1917.

technical competence of his unit. If Cecil Nicholson found it unnecessary to refer to training in his diary, it was clearly one of Blunt's primary concerns. As his battalion prepared to go back into the line on 28 February, he carried out another important function of a battalion commander, reconnaissance: 'Co(mpan)y C(ommande)rs & I went by bus to see line, Loos sector. Trenches bad & very muddy. 37th Div(ision) do not seem to have done any work.'[101] On the following day he gave a 'Lecture to Co(mpan)y C(ommande)rs re. new line. Shall have a lot of work to do.'[102] On the 3rd he began what would be a familiar routine – leaving his HQ at 04.45 he went round his line at 'stand to', and again in the evening. Of the 110 days the unit was in line, Blunt recorded touring his front line companies on 40 days, and this is no doubt a significant underestimate of his intentions and effort as on the first and last days of a spell in the trenches he was too busy with the relief to do so, and towards the end of the year he tended to record routine matters less. He was always determined to keep his eye on things, and like Nicholson, took the defence of his part of the line very seriously. (When the battalion went back into line in May, Blunt noted: 'Huns have been coming into this bit of line but I think we shall stop their games.')[103] Even in support positions he took as much care in understanding the defensive position of both trenches and keeps in his area as he did his front line.

The battalion came out of the line on 8 March and on the 10th began training again. Of the 138 days that the battalion was out of line and Blunt could be engaged with their activities, not being on leave or acting-up, he was involved with them in training on 38 days. The BEF was now putting a higher premium on training than during Nicholson's tenure. On 12 March he received instructions 'for daylight raid on a large scale in the Triangle.'[104] Training for this upcoming event began on 3 April, nine days before it would take place (there being 31 days between conception and execution), Blunt personally taking a hand on the 7th. When the battalion went back into line the raiding party stayed out, continuing their preparation. On the 8th Blunt again fulfilled his duty of reconnaissance, firstly observing the wire-cutting and the Triangle itself from the forward observation post and then going up onto the Double Crassier to inspect closely the state of the wire where the raid would take place from above. His next two days were spent in further preparations, and the raid came to fruition successfully on the 12th (although no identifications were achieved). He noted: 'I think we rather surprised them.' On the 13th the enemy began to withdraw, as described in the previous chapter. Engaged for four days, it is difficult to get a picture of Blunt's actions in this trench-to-trench fighting, but these would have been limited. When all four of his companies were attached to other units in the fighting

101 Blunt, op. cit. 28 February 1917.
102 Blunt, op. cit. 1 March 1917.
103 Blunt, op. cit. 12 May 1917.
104 Blunt, op. cit. 12 March 1917.

on subsequent days he wrote ruefully: 'I was left with nothing.'[105] The central role of a CO in trench operations was, however, in preparing his men for battle, both in training and in attending divisional or brigade conferences, translating orders for an attack into battalion orders, and briefing his company commanders. The enemy withdrawal was so sudden that Blunt issued no written orders during these four days, unlike John Rosher who came into line on the 20th and who was able to issue detailed and tactically aware orders. The second thing that a CO had to achieve in action was a flow of information back from the front line to brigade HQ, and liaison with adjacent units. A unit commander's ability to influence the course of actual combat was limited, although personal reconnaissance and minor tactical adjustment was a possibility, if dangerous. Of the 301 days covered by his diary, Blunt spent only eight in action. His operation orders for the Cambrai attack on 20 November do not survive, but as will be seen later, he was heavily engaged in preparing his unit for action. It appears he spent the day itself in the transport lines. From the day of the German counter-attack, 30th November, he conducted a fighting retreat over several days, forming defensive flanks, but ordered to counterattack himself these actions were frustrated, either being abandoned due to lack of support, or the unit being beaten back by greater firepower. For Blunt, the experience of a fighting retreat would be repeated on 21 March 1918.

Another possible activity for a CO was acting-up in the absence of his brigadier. That Blunt did this not just within his own brigade indicates that he must have been regarded as virtually the safest pair of hands in the division. But it was a significant step up in responsibility. Thus, on 1 June he had to take over from General Osborn, who had gone on leave for two weeks, and noted ruefully: 'I don't think there is going to be much rest at this job.'[106] On 18 August he took over the brigade again whilst Osborn went on a course. During this period 6th Division was ordered to relieve 3rd Canadian Division, a task which Blunt likely found unwelcome, as clearly even the able Nicholson found arranging a brigade relief taxing. Osborn conveniently arrived back on 26 August as the relief was complete. On 3 October Blunt found himself required to act up again as commander of 71 Brigade as 'Gen(eral) on leave & trouble about acting brigadier.'[107] The 8th found him arranging a relief within 18 Brigade. He noted that the 'Sherwoods got lost as usual' and on the 10th: 'Strafed Sherwoods & gingered everybody up about working parties.' How Lieutenant-Colonel Bradshaw felt about the 'strafing' he received from a peer is unknown, but any injury to his dignity was overtaken by a shrapnel wound to his leg nine days later. Blunt was clearly taking his role seriously and likely hoped that such would be noticed, as he wrote on 13 October: 'Getting rather fed up myself waiting for a B(riga)de.'[108] As any ambitious CO might, he hoped for promotion. When his new Brigadier, Harry Walker, arrived on the 27th,

105 Blunt, op. cit. 22 April 1917.
106 Blunt, op. cit. 2 June 1917.
107 Blunt, op. cit. 4 Oct 1917.
108 Blunt, op. cit. 13 October 1917.

having had a good relationship with his predecessor Osborn, Blunt noted sniffily: 'Not much impressed with him – may be alright.'[109] Perhaps he had entertained hopes of succeeding to 16 Brigade himself. Lieutenant-colonels were, however, more likely to be promoted brigadier into another division rather than one their battalion was serving with – the within-division promotion rate was only 17 percent.[110]

Out of the line in the middle of July, on the 12th Blunt was warned that his battalion would be asked to conduct another raid on the 19th. On the 15th he was advised that the scheme would be modified, and on the following day spent the morning with General Osborn on the revision. On the 17th he and Osborn went to watch A & D companies performing the original scheme on a training ground at Allouagne, and then gave them (likely to their dismay), the revised scheme. After two days of wire-cutting, the battalion raided on 20 July. Blunt grumbled: 'Our barrage was not effective – just over the trench. Right and centre parties did not get in but ought to have.'[111] He must have been disappointed. The battalion was relieved two days later, Blunt writing: 'We go out for, I hope, a month & not before it was needed.'[112] It was not to be a matter of pure rest, however. On the 23rd Blunt 'rode about to look for a training ground unsuccessfully.'[113] He found one two days later and afterwards attended a conference at brigade HQ, clearly about training, as he noted: 'Devil of a training programme.' He recorded in his diary over the following days extensive range practice and an 'officers tactical scheme', carried out three times (receiving five new officers between the first and second occasions), and personally conducting a map reading exercise with them.[114] On the 28th he recorded: 'Lots of work. Studying all the latest training pamphlets and fitting things in.'[115] One of his last acts with Osborn was to ride around on 25 October looking for a suitable training ground for a brigade scheme. He was clearly personally involving himself heavily with training at the time as the following day he carried out a scheme with his company commanders and on the 27th recorded 'a good morning's training.'[116]

At the end of October, Blunt's unit began to move south. He obviously had not been informed prior to this of the reason for the move as he wrote: 'Don't know what is happening as we were expecting to go north to Ypres.'[117] The battalion was, of course, moving south to Cambrai. Again, he was heavily involved in training and preparation. On 4th November he watched a tank demonstration near Arras, and three days later seems to have taken part of the battalion on a similar mission, others the following

109 Blunt, op. cit. 27 October 1917.
110 Hodgkinson, op. cit. p.106.
111 Blunt, op. cit. 20 July 1917.
112 Blunt, op. cit. 21 July 1917.
113 Blunt, op. cit. 23 July 1917.
114 Blunt, op. cit. 26 July 1917.
115 Blunt, op. cit. 28 July 1917.
116 Blunt, op. cit. 27 October 1917.
117 Blunt op. cit. 28 October 1918.

day. On the 9th he 'put each company through a special exercise.'[118] On the 12th there was a skeleton brigade scheme, followed by a full brigade scheme the next day, Blunt noting: 'Working all day these days.'[119] On the 18th the battalion had moved south to Cambrai itself and was practising assembly with tanks. The training for this attack had been the most intensive that Blunt had experienced and as CO he clearly found it tiring.

Despite the competence that his length of tenure indicates, Allan St John Blunt would never be promoted to command a brigade. He was relieved of command in April 1918, the war diary not recording his departure, and in July was placed in a staff post. He was likely simply exhausted. After the war he set up a petrol station and fruit farm on the Oxford road at Beedon, West Berkshire, with his wife Doris who he had married in March 1914 in Karachi, and his two small daughters. They did not enjoy their father for long as he died in 1931 following an operation.

Conclusion

Sir John Smythe observed that in the First World War: 'Leadership, above a battalion command, had never been more difficult, and was never to be so again.'[120] The commanders of 6th Division at the rank of major-general who had to meet this challenge fell roughly into two types, and transition through the four years of war represented no smooth evolution. Command passed from the seemingly well qualified yet inadequate hands of Sir John Keir, a man who had no eye for detail, to the hands of an aggressive soldier who was able to plan with a wide understanding of the new warfare in all its particulars, Walter Congreve. There was then a step backwards under the command of Sir John Ross, an underqualified dug-out, again with no eye for detail and even less of a concept of leadership. Finally, there was a giant step forward with the appointment of a true technocrat of war, Thomas Marden, a man of fizzing energy, a marked concept of co-ordination and control, and a fine eye for mastery of the minutiae of Western Front warfare. As Simon Robbins observes, 1916-18 saw the replacement of 'tired and mediocre commanders, paving the way for a new generation of professional soldiers', and that 'by 1917-18 a cadre of officers led divisions with a level of competence that allowed them to compete with their German counterparts.'[121] Thomas Marden exemplifies this, one of a group of 'more energetic men who had learnt many harsh lessons during the war.'[122] These men had had to 'learn how to run large-scale operations the hard way under combat conditions.'[123] John Lee observes that by the end of 1917, when Marden was exerting his organisational grip on the

118 Blunt, op. cit. 9 November 1917.
119 Blunt, op. cit. 12 November 1917.
120 J. Smyth, *Leadership in Battle*, p.55.
121 Robbins, *British Generalship*, p.59.
122 Robbins, *British Generalship*, p.133.
123 Robbins, *British Generalship*, p.135.

division, 'the executive conduct of the battle was firmly in the hands of the Divisional Commander', and that all 'conformed to a standard operational procedure in the planning and preparation of their battles.'[124] This was exactly what Marden and his staff mastered. It was the sole way to operate in the only war ever fought without 'voice control', and where, once troops left the frontline trench, they 'entered a void.'[125]

Major-General Sir Cameron Shute, who had commanded 32nd Division, lectured at the Staff College in 1920: 'COMMAND. Efficiency of every Formation or Unit from Div(ision) downwards is a reflection of PERSONALITY OF COMMANDER.'[126] By this criteria it can be surmised that Keir and Ross made little such impact on the brigades and units of 6th Division, whilst Congreve's example of courage and aggression reached down to the private in the front-line, and Marden's centralised management made a very clear impact on his brigadiers. Sir Douglas Haig believed that 'much … depends on the fighting spirit of the GOC division', who needed to be 'able to inspire the unit with their own personal energy and fighting spirit.'[127] Yet is there evidence that Marden's ruthless efficiency impacted positively on the performance of the division? To say so would be to step too far. Marden in fact had had little operational success as a brigadier, and only the division's performance at Cambrai in November 1917 demonstrated unalloyed success. Yet, as Jonathan Krause has observed in his study of the French Army in 1915: 'It is one of the essential hurdles for students of military history to surpass: the recognition that a particular force can do everything "right" and still suffer defeat.'[128] Marden repeatedly met the independent will of the enemy. His time as a CO demonstrated the hands-on courage of the regimental officer, his time as a divisional general demonstrated determination and optimism, important leadership characteristics. Whilst having a firm vision, he consulted widely and frequently with his brigadiers, yet his opportunities for facilitating devolved command were few, and most freely only during the Pursuit to the Selle 9-12 October 1918 (see Chapter 13). Whilst Marden undoubtedly understood the importance of deference to the 'man on the spot', the tension between this principle and his preference for centralised control was not truly tested. As has been noted, however, 'the decentralised approach rested upon the foundations of well-planned actions.'[129] Decentralisation and delegation were not a panacea for successful warfare in the Hundred Days. Moreover, as Jonathan Boff has observed, in terms of delegation, 'paradoxically, the more fluid the situation, the

124 J. Lee, 'Command and Control in Battle: British Divisions on the Menin Road Ridge, 20 September 1917', in Sheffield & Todman, op. cit. p.139.
125 Bourne, 'British Generals', p.105. The point about 'voice control' is John Terraine's.
126 Cited in S.B.T. Mitchell, 'An Inter-Disciplinary Study of Learning in the 32nd Division on the Western Front, 1916-1918', p.201.
127 Quoted in S. Robbins, *British Generalship*, p.57.
128 Jonathan Krause, *Early Trench Tactics in the French Army: The Second Battle of Artois, May-June 1915*, p. 1.
129 Mitchell, op. cit. p.230.

less impact it had' – GHQ found it necessary to chide infantry for advancing too slowly and pausing on intermediate objectives for too long.[130]

During the reigns of Keir and particularly Ross, brigade command may have assumed a more important role due to the want of firm leadership. Under Marden they assumed a more directed role. The three brigadiers in post at the Armistice represent a slightly uneven mix in terms of development. Percy Brown clearly reflected Sir Douglas Haig's aspirations for evolution – a captain in August 1914, passing through five battalion commands before reaching the rank of brigadier. William Braithwaite (the last arrival) also demonstrated progression, if of a different sort. A major in August 1914 and never having commanded a battalion, he had experienced a series of staff posts. These two appointees demonstrate opposed evolutionary routes to brigade command, and undoubtedly fit the description of the evolved professionalism set out by Robbins. George Craufurd demonstrated a mixed route, rising though a GSO2 post, unit command and previous brigade command. He may, however, have been worn out by the process. Walter Guinness, a staff officer, stated on 21 March 1918 that Craufurd was 'a nice little man, an oriental scholar and linguist', but 'by this time was very tired.'[131] If Craufurd was tired in March 1918, then his energy can only have been more depleted nearer the Armistice, and at the Battle of the Selle in October 1918 his brigade struggled. Yet both Brown and Craufurd had been in post for over a year in a climate where replacement was an ever-present possibility.

The community of COs in 6th Division at the end of the war do not represent a meritocracy in terms of a modern definition as a group 'selected competitively according to merit.'[132] Selection was always at the mercy of personal recommendation, which could be influenced by a variety of factors, not least of all the bias towards the Regular officer, particularly marked in 6th Division, and the army's general bias against the amateur (particularly the Territorial). Despite being so heavily endowed with Regular senior officers, the division, however, sported amongst the ranks of its nine unit commanders at the Armistice one Territorial officer and two civilians of August 1914. In the honed and tempered army of the Hundred Days, 'the unstructured assessment of merit always and increasingly played apart, and, in a temporary sea-change for the British army, seniority did not.'[133] This was a central part of the BEF's nurture of 'professional men of war.'[134]

130 J. Boff, 'Command Culture and Complexity', in G. Sheffield and P. Gray (eds), *Changing War*, pp. 26-31.
131 B. Bond & S. Robbins, *Staff Officer: The Diaries of Walter Guinness*, p.191.
132 *Oxford English Reference Dictionary*.
133 Hodgkinson, op. cit. p.206.
134 A phrase used by a senior officer of the Australian army in World War Two to citizen soldiers, quoted in: G. Pratten, *Australian Battalion Commanders in the Second World War*, p.235.

7

'Friends and Servants of the Troops':[1] The Staff of 6th Division

A cursory reading of memoirs would suggest that regimental personnel thought of staff officers as remote and out of touch with the realities of the front line, and their 'chateau' life as comfortable and untroubled by a particularly heavy workload. Captain Gerald Burgoyne's view of the red tabs of the staff was that they were the 'insignia of hopeless inefficiency.'[2] Gordon Corrigan has suggested, however, that such opprobrium 'was rarely directed at brigade or divisional staffs', rather corps or army staff, of whom the front-line officer often had no personal knowledge. 'Regimental officers got to know the brigade and divisional staff officers, and with personal knowledge antipathy – often artificial anyway – disappeared.'[3] Major Walter Guinness at least partly confirmed this view, noting: 'I haven't the same contempt for Brigade Staff Officers as for those of higher units.'[4] Staff officers, of course, were crucial to the success or failure of a division's varied activities – a divisional general would have been unable to function without his staff team (despite the fact that three out of four of 6th Division's commanders were *psc*, and the one who was not, Walter Congreve, had an exceptional grasp of organisation). As the British Army rapidly increased in size, the demand for experienced officers in staff positions only revealed the paucity thereof in the small pre-war professional army. However effectively reformed was the course at the Staff College at Camberley, it only admitted 32 students a year. This led to the situation after August 1914 where in terms of all levels of staff work 'the most competent officers were working on a scale and in conditions of which they had

1 The Staff Manual of 1912 (p.7) stated that: 'Staff Officers must regard themselves as the friends and servants of the troops; always unsparing in their efforts to help them by every possible means in carrying out their difficult task.'
2 G. A. Burgoyne (C. Davidson ed.), *The Burgoyne Diaries*, p.281.
3 G. Corrigan, *Mud, Blood and Poppycock*, p.210.
4 B. Bond & S. Robbins (eds), *Staff Officer: The Diaries of Walter Guinness*, Kindle edition location 1339.

no experience, and they had to learn their jobs.'[5] Even trained pre-war staff officers had little concept and even less practice at work above divisional level. Further, as the war progressed, their work was constantly evolving, encompassing new battlefield technological developments (aerial photography, for instance, was a significant boon to staff planning). As so-called 'revisionist' historians such as Gary Sheffield have argued, the work of the staff evolved positively, in line with that of the whole army, in the last two years of the war.[6]

The staff of an infantry division at war comprised officers within a 'trinity' of 'G' (General Staff), 'A' (Adjutant General) and 'Q' (Quartermaster General) functions.[7] The General Staff, the most prestigious branch, were responsible for intelligence and planning and implementing of operations, and comprised General Staff Officers 1st, 2nd and 3rd grade. There was then an Assistant Adjutant & Quartermaster General overseeing both 'A' and 'Q' branches. The Adjutant General function dealt with personnel, casualties, medical matters and discipline, and was run by an Deputy Assistant Adjutant General (DAAG). The Quartermaster General function was responsible for supplies and transport and was headed by a Deputy Assistant Quartermaster General (DAQMG). This chapter will be concerned largely with those who fulfilled General Staff functions at divisional and brigade level.

Divisional General Staff

Infantry divisions only boasted a single GSO1 at the outbreak of war, and in 6th Division this was Colonel William Thomas Furse *psc*. 'Bill' Furse was commissioned into the Royal Artillery in 1884. He initially served as ADC to Lord Roberts in India, returning home to pass Staff College in 1897. He then served as a Staff Captain and DAAG at Army HQ. In South Africa he held the various roles of DAAG, then the same role responsible for mobilisation at Army HQ, AAG for transport and then DAQMG (mobilisation). He was further posted to India as DAQMG I Indian Army Corps and DAQMG (Intelligence) at Army HQ. Furse was subsequently GSO2 at Army HQ, moving to the posts of DAAG and GSO2 at the Staff College for four years 1908-11. On 1 October 1913 he was posted as GSO1 6th Division, and at the outbreak of war was, manifestly, a highly experienced staff officer. Much of his time, however, had been devoted to 'A' and 'Q' functions, 23 months only having been spent as GSO2 at Army level. If the Staff College might be accused of never quite being sure whether it thought it ought to be producing trained staff officers or commanders with

5 Captain P. Choate, cited in S. Robbins, *British Generalship on the Western Front 1914-18*, p.34.
6 G. Sheffield, *Forgotten Victory*, pp.258-63.
7 The GOC would also have two ADCs; there would be an Assistant and Deputy Assistant Director of Medical Services; an Assistant Director of Veterinary Services; a Deputy Assistant Director of Ordnance Services; and an Assistant Provost Marshall. Theoretically, Divisional HQ comprised 15 Officers and 67 ORs.

staff experience, then Furse would soon be required to fulfil the second proposition. The demands of the expanding army were such that on 1 January 1915 he mounted the next rung on the staff ladder, becoming Brigadier General General Staff (BGGS) at II Corps, and was subsequently promoted to the command of 9th (Scottish) Division from September 1915 to December 1916, a role he achieved with a record that did not include either unit or brigade command. He was finally transferred to the War Office as Master General of the Ordnance, responsible for all artillery, engineers, fortifications etc.

The division had to absorb two more 'G' officers, a GSO2 and a GSO3 on mobilisation. The new GSO2 was Lieutenant-Colonel John Burnett-Stuart, and the GSO3 was Captain Alan Paley. To take the most junior first, 38-year-old Alan Thomas Paley had been commissioned into the Rifle Brigade, and after being seriously wounded in South Africa became regimental adjutant. After service at Sandhurst he obtained his *psc* in 1912, and at the outbreak of war was a GSO3 at the War Office. He would not remain in this role on 6th Division's staff for long, moving on to be Brigade Major of 18 Brigade on 29 October 1914. For Paley, the new job would have been far more interesting than his GSO3 function, and he remained in it until 14 July 1915 when he was promoted GSO2 of VII Corps, and then GSO1 of 21st Division on 7 March 1916.[8] As GSO2, 39 year-old John Theodosius 'Jock' Burnett-Stuart had been commissioned into the Rifle Brigade two years earlier than Paley, in 1895. After seeing active service on the North-West Frontier in 1897-98, he was a signalling officer throughout the Second Boer War. He passed Staff College in 1904 and served as a Staff Captain and both GSO3 and GSO2 at Army HQ, when in 1910 he became Director of Military Operations with the New Zealand forces, returning to Great Britain where the opening of the war found him GSO2 at the Staff College. He served as GSO2 with 6th Division until 18 February 1915 and thereafter pursued a stellar staff career, including posts as GSO1 15th Division and then GHQ, and BGGS at GHQ and subsequently XIX and VII Corps, ending the war as Deputy Adjutant General at GHQ. These latter posts would have been a contrast to his description of the unglamorous activities in 6th Division's Armentières sector prior to Christmas 1914 when the 'G' officers 'spent most of their time plodding around muddy trenches, laying out reserve lines, fixing boundaries and keeping in touch with divisions on the flanks.'[9]

The 6th Division thus began the war with a talented and highly experienced staff team, albeit with no history of working together. They probably counted themselves lucky in not having been involved in the retreat from Mons, a strenuous test of the staff, deprived of sleep and exhausted.[10] In what was a less hectic moment they ably managed

8 In October 1917 he became Assistant Commandant RMC Sandhurst.
9 J. Burnett-Stuart, cited in P.M. Harris, 'The Men who Planned the War', p.83.
10 Colonel F.R.F. Boileau, GSO1 of 3rd Division, suffered a psychological breakdown after the battle of Le Cateau and shot himself in the head with a revolver on 27 August.

the task of 6th Division's translation to the Aisne and from there to Flanders. These unglamorous activities were no mean feats. The pre-war staff officer had been trained in producing correspondence, orders (if not within the rapid timescale required in wartime), intelligence reports, fields messages, communications of all sorts, routes for marches, and establishing billets.[11] The three GSOs had distinct roles. The all-important GSO1 had responsibility for operations, the GSO2 had an additional responsibility for training, whilst the GSO3's patch was intelligence. When Edmund Ironside replaced Paley as GSO3 at the end of October 1914 'there were times when there was little for him to do, with only a few prisoners … to interrogate.'[12] (As he spoke seven languages he was entirely suited to this role, however). Intelligence, of course, was crucial. As the war progressed, GSO3s would produce a daily divisional intelligence summary. Few survive as they were marked: 'To be destroyed when finished with.' No.278, covering 4 October 1917, is one of a handful of survivors in the divisional war diary, complied by the GSO3, Captain Michael Bell. It describes 'Our Operations' (artillery operations on the day in question); 'Enemy Operations' (artillery activity and, on the 4th, a series of simultaneous raids); and 'Intelligence' (the enemy's use of a light railway and work on roads, a suspected German bomb block, and a hostile post in a forward trench). The GSO3's efforts were directed at keeping the whole division informed.[13] One rung up the chain, Bernard Montgomery described in 1916 that in his role as GSO2: 'I have no fixed work like the GSO3; the GSO1 and myself divide the work between us and I am now responsible that it is done and nothing is forgotten.'[14] At the top of the tree, the central role of the GSO1 was providing the divisional commander with all available information necessary to formulate his plans, and then turning those plans into orders. The relationship between the two was manifestly crucial, and in terms of the differing natures of 6th Division's GOCs, as set out in Chapters Two and Six, it does not stretch the imagination to comprehend how the nature of the efforts of the GSO1 of 6th Division varied over time.[15]

As the careers of the first trio of 'G' staff show, in the expanding army the movement of staff officers was the norm. Paul Harris notes that amongst the 31 'G' officers of the first six divisions the average time in post was four months, the longest serving lasting nine.[16] Furse was in post for 141 days, Burnett-Stuart for 167, and Paley for 86. Furse was one of a number of officers who passed from staff to command roles. Edmund Ironside was almost desperate for command and pestered Furse when he

11 The duties of the staff officer were set out in the Staff Manual of 1912.
12 E. Ironside, *Ironside: The Authorised Biography*, Kindle Edition location 1175.
13 War Diary, 6th Infantry Division, 'Summary of Operations and Intelligence – No. 278', TNA WO95/1583.
14 B. Montgomery cited in Harris, op. cit. p.29.
15 'G' officers also had to include in their planning artillery and engineering staff officers. At divisional level the CRA had a Brigade Major, Staff Captain and reconnaissance staff officer.
16 Harris, op. cit. pp.83-4.

was a divisional general and Ironside a GSO2. He recorded how: 'He offered me the command of the 7th Seaforths, if he could get me & I jumped at it. He very nearly got me but was defeated by Wigram on the Staff who refused to let me go.'[17] Ironside found himself 'tied to the wheel of the staff' where he somewhat cynically suggested that 'the best officers in the Army were kept to bolster up the incompetents.'[18] Of the five GSO1s of 6th Division three would go on to command divisions, one via brigade command (John Shea – the only one who would move directly from GSO1 to a command role). Only one GSO2 (and no GSO3) would go on to command a brigade, this being the eager Ironside. The transfer of trained staff officers to command roles was controversial. Sir Launcelot Kiggell, Chief of the General Staff at GHQ, would send a formal communiqué to army commanders in November 1916 stating that 'the majority, if not all' of those at GSO1 and BGGS level would be brigade commanders if they had not been retained as staff officers 'for the good of the Service.'[19] Ironside certainly fell foul of this, only achieving brigade command in 1918.

Furse's replacement as GSO1 was 45-year-old John Stuart Mackenzie Shea. An Indian cavalry officer, he had seen active service during the Second Boer War, and after passing Staff College in 1905 served as a professor at the Quetta Staff College 1906-10. His appointment as GSO2 in August 1914 was his first 'G' post. Joining 6th Division was something of a family affair as he was Walter Congreve's brother-in-law. Thomas Grove, who served as GSO3 to 'Jimmy' was of the opinion that 'we were fortunate in our G1 … I cannot remember to have met many, if any, men with a quicker brain than his.' Serving for a little over six months, Shea was promoted to the command of 151 Brigade in July 1915 and subsequently elevated as GOC 30th and 60th Divisions. He was not involved in planning any major operations with 6th Division and would not be in post for the Hooge attack of August 1915, having been promoted a month beforehand. This would fall to Lieutenant-Colonel Gerald Farrell Boyd. Failing entry to RMA Woolwich, Boyd had served in the ranks for over four years and was commissioned from the rank of sergeant during the Second Boer War, during which conflict he was awarded both DCM and DSO. His staff college qualification was from Quetta, and the outbreak of war found him Brigade Major of 11 Infantry Brigade. His 1913 Confidential Report described him as:

> Loyal, cool, self-reliant. He possesses in a marked degree the valuable characteristic of a good staff-officer in dealing with many minor matters on his own initiative without giving offence, and at the same time keeping me informed where necessary. He is very quick, thorough and active in mind and body … he

17 Clive Wigram was assistant military secretary to the commander-in-chief.
18 Ironside, op. cit. location 1299.
19 Cited in Harris, op. cit. p.205.

> has considerable professional knowledge, which he is able to apply very quickly and accurately in the form of orders.[20]

Severely wounded in the shoulder at Le Cateau he had returned to serve as GSO2 of 1st Division from whence he was promoted to 6th Division. Boyd was elevated to BGGS V Corps in June 1916, and after brief command of 170 Brigade he was given the command of 46th Division in early September 1918, proving a more than capable commander in the Hundred Days campaign. General Cecil Nicholson, GOC 16 Brigade wrote after a misunderstanding on the telephone with Boyd in September 1915: 'Boyd is not a satisfactory GSO1.' He corrected himself in retrospect: 'This opinion was an entirely erroneous one. He was the best I have ever met.'[21]

Whilst Walter Congreve was a highly capable officer, it was a team effort to plan the Hooge operation. In addition to Boyd, with his 'brain like lightning and an imagination as vivid',[22] the GSO2 was the redoubtable 35-year-old William Edmund Ironside. An artilleryman, Ironside has served as a Staff Captain and Brigade Major in South Africa and was awarded his *psc* on the outbreak of war. After a brief spell as a mobilisation Staff Captain at No. 3 base, Boulogne, he became GSO3 with 6th Division, rising to GSO2 on the departure of Burnett-Stuart. The GSO3 was Thomas Thackeray Grove, who would have a longstanding connection with the staff of 6th Division, returning as GSO1 in 1917. Of the team that planned the attack of 9 August, Boyd had been in post 33 days, and both Ironside and Grove 174 days, none being familiar with the ground over which the action would be fought. It was perhaps fortunate that all three were highly capable individuals. The Official History describes their preparatory planning as 'particularly thorough and complete', continuing that (as observed in Chapter Three): 'The instructions for the assault took up many typewritten sheets. This was a complete change from the short attack orders of the first days of the war.'[23] Planned over a period of eight days, the operation involved arranging deception activities across three other divisions, a complex artillery plan, and integrating both Royal Flying Corps activity and French artillery support. None of these officers would ever have planned such a complex operation. Tom Grove wrote home to his wife five days later: 'The Commander-in-Chief actually described it as one of the best planned & best carried out of the smaller operations of the war.' He added: 'I had quite a lot of examining of prisoners to do & managed to get on pretty well with my German, rusty as it is.' Due to leave the division five days after the attack he expressed sorrow, describing 'many friends' and an environment 'where we are all like a happy family.' He added that 'Gerry' Boyd 'asked me to dine in his mess with him as a farewell', and

20 *Donkey Archive* <https://www.birmingham.ac.uk/research/activity/warstudies/research/projects/lionsdonkeys/b.aspx> (Accessed 5 May 2018).
21 C.L. Nicholson, Private Papers, IWM Docs 9975, 16 September 1915.
22 https://www.birmingham.ac.uk/research/activity/warstudies/research/projects/lionsdonkeys/b.aspx (accessed 5 May 2018), citing the history of 1/4th Leicestershire.
23 J.E. Edmonds, *Military Operations France and Belgium 1915, Vol 2*, p.107.

that 'I also dined out two nights before, a farewell dinner with one of our Brigade HQ.'[24] This latter comment weighs against any idea that divisional staff officers were unpopular. The notion of the 'happy family' suggests a very good atmosphere at 6th Divisional HQ, which can only have helped the planning process. Paul Harris compares the detailed organisation of this attack to that carried out on 24 April at St Julien, another operation ordered to seize back a front very recently taken by the enemy. Costing over 2,000 casualties, Brigadier-General Hull of 10 Brigade recorded 'no opportunity for any previous reconnaissance' and how 'I had to issue my orders off the map.'[25] The Official History observed that 'nothing, however, but a carefully prepared offensive requiring much time to organise, could … possibly dislodge the Germans.'[26] Captain Alistair Macdougall of 3rd Cavalry Brigade was more forthright: 'There were enormous losses in this attack and simply through bad staff work. Most of the staff in this salient want stellenbosching badly.'[27] This highlights the imperatives within the relationships between army, corps and division. 10 Brigade (4th Division) had been pushed into the attack by II Corps (commanded by Sir Hubert Plumer) no doubt under the cosh of General Smith-Dorrien commanding Second Army and Sir John French in turn. In contrast, at Hooge, 6th Division had been able to secure postponement of the attack until they were entirely ready, and VI Corps had no difficulty in agreeing this, giving Congreve 'an absolutely free hand to make his own plan.'[28] The new commander of Second Army, Plumer,[29] had no doubt learnt from his experience of 24 April. 6th Division would, of course, fall victim to similar rushing and poor staff work at both corps and divisional level at the Quadrilateral 13 months later.

'Tiny' Ironside, who by his own account had played a very active role at Hooge (see Chapter 3), had hoped to be Boyd's successor, but was posted back to the UK as GSO1 of the newly formed 4th Canadian Division, with whom he remained until January 1918. A man who was 'supremely self-confident, forceful and opinionated',[30] Ironside (demonstrating the crucial nature of the relationship between GOC and GSO1) overshadowed the divisional commander, Major-General David Watson, and 'the general opinion was that Ironside was the real commander of the division.'[31] This was decidedly not the position that Thomas Grove would enjoy as Thomas Marden's GSO1.

24 T.T. Grove, 'It Happened by Chance', NAM 1963-08-14.
25 C.P.A. Hull, cited in Harris, op. cit. p.98.
26 J.E. Edmonds and C.G. Wynne, *Military Operations France and Belgium 1915, Vol 1*, p.270.
27 A. MacDougall cited in Harris, op. cit. pp.97-8.
28 Grove, op. cit. letter of 14 August 1915.
29 Herbert Charles Onslow Plumer was commissioned in the York & Lancaster Regiment in 1876, had served in Egypt and South Africa, and took command of V Corps in April 1915, and Second Army in May. A popular and methodical officer, he would remain in command until the Armistice.
30 B. Bond, 'Ironside', in *Churchill's Generals*, ed. J. Keegan, p.18.
31 H. M. Urquhart, *Arthur Currie: The Biography of a Great Canadian*, pp.145-6.

Ironside was far from faultless, as his insistence on persevering with the disastrous Canadian gas raid at Vimy Ridge in March 1917 demonstrated, thus emphasising the importance of the partiality of the advice a GSO1 offered to his general.[32]

The generals and staff of the First World War became enshrined in myth for their 'chateau' lifestyle. Whilst some formations, largely above divisional level, lived comfortably, many divisional staff did not. From 8 June 1915 and into 1916, the 6th Division HQ was at Valmertinghe Chateau. When the division moved there, it described being 'billeted or bivouacked in or around' it.[33] There was clearly not room for all. The village was just off the road between Ypres and Poperinghe, and when the division was holding the northern part of the salient, was approximately 3,000 yards behind the front line. It was not necessarily a safe place. The enemy were well aware what buildings British staff would likely use and Poperinghe, 3,500 yards to the west was regularly shelled. Indeed, on 2 May 1916, divisional HQ was compelled to move further west from Vlamertinghe 'on account of enemy shell fire directed in the neighbourhood of HQ during the past three weeks.'[34] Outside of periods of operations, the working life of staff was very far from 'one long loaf.'[35] One GSO2 at divisional level described a typical day involving working from 07.30 to 09.00, when he would 'then go out & study the line we are holding', in order to make plans for better defence, getting back before 16.00 and then working until 22.30 or 23.00.[36] As implied by this account, staff were no strangers to the front. The *Official History* offers the opinion in 1917 that 'complaints that staff officers did not regularly visit junior commanders and see the situation for themselves are so numerous that they cannot all be unfounded.'[37] This may have been a side effect of the importation of untrained staff officers as the army expanded, and may have been more apparent at brigade level. Cecil Nicholson (see Chapter 6) regularly noted encountering divisional staff on his own visits to the front line, support or reserve positions in 1915-16.

Lewis Frederick Renny was the replacement for Gerry Boyd. He was very probably the least sparkling officer to serve as GSO1 of the division, which he did for nine months. Commissioned into the 2nd Royal Dublin Fusiliers he was the battalion's transport officer in South Africa before becoming ADC to a major-general. He passed Staff College in 1910 and was sent as a Brigade Major to an infantry brigade stationed in Malta. After war broke out, he served as Brigade Major of 23 Brigade and GSO2 of 4th Division before coming to 6th Division as GSO1. When he was replaced by Tom Grove he was sent as Superintendent of Training to the Machine Gun Corps

32 After a brief spell as Commandant of the Small Arms School was elevated to GOC 99 Brigade, moving to Russia in September 1918, promoted major-general.
33 War Diary, 6th Infantry Division, 8 June 1915, TNA WO95/1581.
34 War Diary, 6th Infantry Division, 2 May 1916, TNA WO95/1582.
35 There was a popular musical hall joke of the period: 'If bread is the staff of life, what is the life of the staff? One long loaf!', R. Holmes, *Tommy*, p. 224.
36 C. Bonham-Carter, GSO2 50th Division, February 1916, cited in Harris, op. cit. p.124.
37 C. Falls, *Military Operations France and Belgium 1917, Vol 1*, p.552.

Training Centre, later promoted brigade commander of 28 Training Reserve Brigade, and lastly Inspector of Machine Gun Units at GHQ. Given that he did not progress to BGGS or active command, it is likely that he was judged mediocre, and he clearly never possessed the promotional potential of his peers at the rank of GSO1.

Renny had been in post for some two and a half months when the 'G' team was faced with the attack on the Quadrilateral in September 1916. That team included Major Lewis Evans as GSO2 and Captain Mark Wardle as GSO3. Lewis Pugh Evans, 6th Division's third GSO2, had been interrupted in his Staff College course by the war three-quarters way through, but like the other attendees, had been awarded his *psc*. He had previously served as a GSO3 and Brigade Major, and would go on to command 1st Lincolnshire, at the helm of which unit he would win the Victoria Cross at Third Ypres (he also was awarded the DSO and bar).[38] He was promoted to command 14 Brigade for the last five months of the war. He was clearly an exceptional officer. Mark Kingsley Wardle was a lieutenant of the Leicestershire Regiment in August 1914, and would be 6th Division's longest-serving GSO3 at over a year before moving to a Brigade Major post.[39] Wardle, responsible for intelligence, must have had a deeply frustrating experience at the Quadrilateral as there was none to be had. As discussed at length in Chapter Four, there was little knowledge of where the British lines were, let alone the German. It is no wonder that the orders for the first attack were confused and confusing. On 13 August, Renny had been in post 52 days, Evans for 162 days, and Wardle for 49 days. Gerry Boyd had been in post for two-thirds of the time that Renny had when he orchestrated the Hooge operation, but even the most competent staff team could have done little in the face of a rushed attack with little or no intelligence. It was therefore unfortunate that the nature of the operations coincided with an unremarkable divisional commander and GSO1. Whether a Congreve and a Boyd would have achieved a different result is both counterfactual and, perhaps, debateable.

38 The VC citation reads: 'For most conspicuous bravery and leadership. Lt.-Col. Evans took his battalion in perfect order through a terrific enemy barrage, personally formed up all units, and led them to the assault. While a strong machine gun emplacement was causing casualties, and the troops were working round the flank, Lt.-Col. Evans rushed at it himself and by firing his revolver through the loophole forced the garrison to capitulate. After capturing the first objective he was severely wounded in the shoulder, but refused to be bandaged, and re-formed the troops, pointed out all future objectives, and again led his battalion forward. Again badly wounded, he nevertheless continued to command until the second objective was won, and, after consolidation, collapsed from loss of blood. As there were numerous casualties, he refused assistance, and by his own efforts ultimately reached the Dressing Station. His example of cool bravery stimulated in all ranks the highest valour and determination to win.' *London Gazette*, 23 November 1917, p.12327.

39 A thoughtful soldier, Wardle would write *Foundations of Soldiering. A New Study of Regimental Soldiering in the British Army* (1936), although he produced the less than academic *An Alphabet from the Trenches – Rhymes by Capt. M. K. Wardle and Lt.-Col. A. Buchanan-Dunlop – Sketches by the Last-Named*, in 1916.

Tom Grove was Renny's replacement and the division's last GSO1. He had entered the Royal Engineers, and at 'The Shop' at Woolwich described himself as 'fundamentally idle.' The boredom of submarine mining in Mauritius kindled a desire for education, and he returned to England to undertake the 'Advanced Course' at Chatham, where he 'worked really hard' and decided to aim for Staff College, entering which required three attempts without the benefit of a crammer. Starting in 1914 he described the course as 'strenuous.' The outbreak of war projected Grove (with a hastily awarded *psc*) into a different strenuousness. He was attached to 12th Field Company RE, regarding himself as in luck as the remainder of his Camberley cohort were sent as assistant embarkation officers or assistant military landing officers (much the fate befalling Ironside, who was in the year above him). From GSO3 he had moved to the post of GSO2 in the Cavalry Corps in August 1915 and noted of this period: 'The life … was all very pleasant but I was not really happy. I felt something like shame that with a war on I was doing nothing in it.' His life in 6th Division 'had got hold of me.'[40] He approached Walter Congreve in terms of a vacant COs post but although Congreve was encouraging, this transfer did not work out. Grove mused in later life that if he had survived the Somme as a CO he might have gone on to divisional command. Instead, he went to 17th Division as GSO2, returning to 6th Division on 24 March 1917, and served as GSO1 until the Armistice. He was undoubtedly a talented staff officer. Lieutenant-Colonel Jack Collins, GSO1 of 17th Division, said of him: 'You should see him at a conference. While I am sweating blood the cursed fellow will either be reading a French novel or sleeping peacefully. Yet he never misses anything that matters. I don't know how the hell he does it.' Walter Nicholson added: 'Tom Grove was a mighty clever fellow, which most of us are not.'[41]

Outside of the heat of battle, divisional reliefs were a major test of staff efficiency, and a move of corps was generally very unwelcome as 'every one of these and armies had a completely different method of office work. They all demanded different "Returns."'[42] Staff work was a matter of detail, and organising operations was the acid test. Lack of clear and informed detail in the orders relating to the first attack on the Quadrilateral was not entirely responsible for the failure of the attack, but it was painfully evident. And staff clearly felt a pressure not to fail. In conversation with Thomas Marden after the Armistice, Grove recorded how:

> I was saying what a relief it was to feel that if one did make a small mistake or forget some little thing no serious consequences would come of it and that the feeling, whilst we were fighting, that something dreadful might happen if one overlooked anything was a constant strain even when one didn't realize it. He said, 'Well you have the satisfaction of knowing anyhow that you never did.'

40 Grove, op. cit.
41 W.N. Nicholson, *Behind the Lines*, p.189.
42 W.N. Nicholson, op. cit. p.22.

In relating this to his wife, Grove added: 'Rather sweet of him, wasn't it?'[43] Undoubtedly, given Grove's description of Marden's character (see Chapter 6), a compliment was a rarity, and sweetness not a notable aspect of his personality.

For divisional staff an important feature was the growing importance of corps in planning operations. Having begun the war in post-box mode, i.e. a place where army sent orders for dissemination to divisions, corps became an increasingly important determinant of the nature of operations, certainly in terms of the artillery plan, as corps controlled heavy guns. Andy Simpson notes that by the time of the battle of Arras, 'since staffs were now more experienced, corps were less prescriptive in their dealings with divisions',[44] and as 1917 progressed 'corps permitted divisions more latitude in the handling of their artillery.'[45] This may well have stemmed from not just the increased experience of staff, but the fact that the way attacks were conducted was now well understood within the guidelines of *SS135 Instructions for the Training of Divisions for Offensive Action* and other manuals. The picture is one of increasing maturity of the part of divisions and their staff, who were clearly taking more and more responsibility. Grove was dismissive, however, of the staff demands of the operations at Lens in April 1917, implying that this was far more demanding for the staff of 16 Brigade than it was for division. During this period, Mark Wardle remained as GSO3, but the GSO2 was now Major Miles Beevor, who had replaced Major Evans. Beevor was a captain of the Buffs in August 1914 with no pre-war staff experience, although he had been a Brigade Major since June 1916. Beevor was the division's first GSO2 not to have attended Staff College, but his track record of unit command was, and would be, impressive. He commanded 2nd Buffs from September 1915 to May 1916 and would afterwards command 1/9th London from November 1917 to January 1918, and 1/7th Middlesex from February 1918 to the Armistice. His experience of battalion command meant that he certainly had experience of translating brigade orders into unit orders.

The year 1918 would be a different experience again for the staff. Walter Nicholson quoted a staff officer whose view no doubt reflected the experience of most staff officers during *Kaiserschlacht*:

> During the worst of the German offensive in the Spring of 1918 Staff officers toiled from 8.30 am to midnight, with half-hour intervals for meals. I have seen a Staff officer faint at table from sheer pressure of work, and dozens of men, come fresh from regimental work, wilt away under the fierce pressure.[46]

43 Grove, op. cit. letter November 1918.
44 A. Simpson, 'The Operational Role of British Corps Command on the Western Front, 1914-1918', p.97.
45 Simpson, op. cit. p.109.
46 W.N. Nicholson, op. cit. p. xi.

Grove's team during this difficult period included Major Wilfrid Harris St John as GSO2 and Major Arthur Wright as GSO3, neither of whom were qualified staff officers. St John had been commissioned into the Royal Welsh Fusiliers in 1898, and had begun his staff service in December 1915, first as a GSO3 and then as a Brigade Major. Arthur Stanley Wright was born in Ottawa and had served in the Royal Canadian Artillery for over nine years by August 1914. He had arrived on the Western Front as an artillery Staff Captain, promoted GSO3 and then GSO2 in June 1916. Both had good track records. The War Diary for the two days 21-2 March gives a picture of frenetic phone calls representing attempts to gain a picture of an ever-changing situation, and order and counter-order. No doubt Grove and his fellow officers got little sleep. It is clear, however, that despite loss of initiative and major communication difficulties, command and control was never relinquished during these difficult two days.

St John was replaced as GSO2 on 16 June by Major Reginald Walter Barnett, who represents a new breed of staff officer in the evolving BEF. A citizen soldier, having just graduated from Pembroke College, Cambridge in 1914, he had served as the Brigade Major of 189 Brigade, Royal Naval Division, and had been gassed in March 1918. Restored and promoted, he would demonstrate the life of a staff officer was not free of risk, becoming the only member of divisional level 'G' staff to be killed in action, shot by a sniper whilst escorting a sergeant of the American 27th Division at an advanced post at Hooge on 12 August 1918. He was one of 37 'G' staff deaths during the war (3.4 percent of the total number of 'G' officers).[47] A critical issue in 'G' staff casualties was that a disproportionate number of officers qualified *psc* were killed or wounded in 1914.[48] The whole of 6th Division only suffered two 'G' staff fatalities during the war, but one of these indeed happened in 1914. The Brigade Major of 17 Brigade, Major Arthur Green *psc*,[49] was shot through the left breast by a sniper on 28 September on the Aisne. All the GSO1s of the division possessed, however, the *psc* initials, even if Tom Grove had only attended a quarter of his course in 1914. Three out of eight of the GSO2s had attended Staff College. Miles Beevor, appointed in March 1917, was the first of a series of five GSO2s who had not. The supply of GSO3s who had obtained their *psc* ran out earlier. Of the nine who served at this grade, Arthur Lawson, appointed the fourth GSO3 in August 1915, was the first of a series of six who had not been to Camberley. The division's 45 percent of 'G' staff officers with the *psc* qualification compares well the 'G' staff average for the war across the BEF of

47 Harris op. cit. p.231.
48 Harris, op. cit. p.153.
49 Major Arthur Dowson Green *psc*, aged 40, had been commissioned into the Essex Regiment in June 1894, moving as captain to the Worcestershire Regiment in June 1900. He had served in Sierra Leone 1898-9; South Africa 1899-1902, where he had been awarded the DSO; and Nigeria 1906, having served with the West Africa Frontier Force 1903-1912. He had passed Staff College in 1910 and became Brigade Major with 17 Brigade on 28 June 1911.

31 percent.[50] This does not mean that officers without the qualification had no staff training. The first staff schools were opened in France in the winter of 1915 with a six-week course (Camberley having shut its doors to staff training), and later moved to Great Britain. From late 1915 a 'staff learner' scheme operated, attaching regimental officers to staff teams for a month. Whatever a brief course could teach, as the Official History observed, these new staff officers had to 'learn their skills in the heat of battle.'[51] All of 6th Division's non-*psc* GSO2s would have attended such training and attachment, and of the GSO3s, only Arthur Lawson and Henry Denison-Pender (both the only cavalry officers who served on the division's staff) likely did not. These two officers were simply available at the time, given their branch of the army, and must have been deemed suitable, Lawson having served as an adjutant and ADC. Denison-Pender, however, had served in no administrative role at all. Lieutenant-Colonel Arthur Richardson, who commanded three battalions between August 1914 and December 1916, cynically suggested that 'all the shell shocked idiots of the British Empire were put to do staff work.'[52] There is some evidence that wounded officers appeared in the ranks of the 'G' staff of 6th Division. There are at least three cases at GSO2 and GSO3 level. Wilfrid Harris St John had been wounded in October 1914 and had not returned to his battalion, and Mark Kinglsey Wardle was in the same position having been wounded twice. Reginald Barnett, as noted, was gassed in early 1918. All would have been recommended for staff posts, received training, and have passed their courses. It is unlikely that shell-shock would have been compatible with the concentration required for staff work and the mental and physical exhaustion often reported.

Having noted the two cavalry officers and adding John Shea from the Indian cavalry to their number, all bar four of 6th Division's 20 'G' officers were professional soldiers, and 13 were from the infantry. Furse and Ironside were artillerymen and Grove an engineer. In terms of professional status, Leonard Taylor, the last GSO2, was a Territorial officer and Arthur Wright (GSO3) was a pre-war Canadian 'territorial equivalent'; whilst John Horlington, the division's last GSO3, had been in the Special Reserve. Given that only 12 percent of GSO2s and 22 percent of GSO3s were non-regulars, this was a lower figure than the 17 percent and 42 percent for the BEF as a whole, particularly in respect of GSO3s.[53] Reginald Barnett was the only citizen of August 1914 who would break into the division's 'G' staff ranks, but more would serve at Brigade Major level, the next step up from GSO3.

The Hundred Days brought more change and more responsibility for the staff of divisions in operations. The 1918 revision of *SS135* laid down that 'Divisional Artillery

50 Harris, op. cit. p.198. This at army, corps and divisional level.
51 W. Miles, *Military Operations France and Belgium 1916, Vol 2*, p. 570. The training system was so successful that in 1917 it was suspended for a couple of months due to a surfeit of graduates. (Harris, op. cit. p.157).
52 A.J. Richardson, cited in Harris, op. cit. p.13.
53 Harris, op. cit. p.211.

barrages are worked out by C.R.A.s of divisions in accordance with the directions of their Divisional Commanders.'[54] Divisions were therefore 'gaining more influence in the planning of the attack',[55] with an formal emphasis towards decentralisation, which, as Andy Simpson observes, potentially increased tempo in more open warfare. This was part of a reassertion of a principle of pre-war Field Service Regulations, that of the authority of the 'man on the spot.' Decentralisation was variable, however. IX Corps were very prescriptive in their orders for the attack on the Hindenburg outpost system, yet devolved command of the artillery back to 6th Division for the penetration of the Beaurevoir-Fonsomme line on 8 October, and corps orders for the attack at the Selle on 17 October were brief, there being wider delegation back to divisions. The artillery plan was always central, and in respect of this it was up to divisions to state their requirements to corps in respect of heavy artillery. Whilst in non-set-piece operations divisions had greater freedom in planning, even in set-piece operations there was more solicitation of the views of divisions.[56] Marden's concern for fine detail and Tom Grove's efficiency were therefore in their element.

Grove had the blessing of a settled team during the Hundred Days campaign. From 24 August his GSO2 was Major Leonard Taylor and the GSO3 Captain John Horlington. Leonard Mainwaring Taylor was commissioned a Territorial officer in 1904, a solicitor by profession and a captain of 4th Yorkshire Light Infantry in August 1914. He had been appointed a Staff Captain in November 1915 and a Brigade Major in August 1916. He must have been exceptional to be appointed GSO2 to a Regular Division as a Territorial. John Horlington had been commissioned as a second-lieutenant into the Special Reserve of the York & Lancaster Regiment in 1913. He had risen to the rank of acting major in the 2nd Battalion at the end of 1916, yet his GSO3 post in May 1918 must have felt like a downwards move as he had served for a month as Brigade Major to 18 Brigade. Given that he gone overseas with the division in September 1914 he was, however, very much a known quantity. During the forward movement of the Hundred Days, his work in reconnaissance and intelligence would have been very active. The Official History observes that: 'The staffs of all formations great and small, had been trained in the trench warfare period and, except for a very few old hands, had no experience of the difficulties of communication in, and the speed of open warfare.'[57] Paul Harris suggests that this 'made their achievements all the more impressive.'[58] Indeed Grove's team must have been very efficient in terms of the swiftly organised attacks of late 1918, gathering information and issuing short, succinct orders. This was despite both their comparative youth – Taylor was 35 and Horlington 28, the pair not possessing the supposed all-round ability that pre-war

54 *SS135 Instructions for the Training of Divisions for Offensive Action,* (1918) pp.12-13.
55 Simpson, op. cit. p.190.
56 Simpson, op. cit. p.218.
57 J.E. Edmonds, *Military Operations France and Belgium 1918 Vol. IV*, p.157.
58 Harris, op. cit. p.271.

professional training granted. Both had essentially mastered their trade in trench warfare, and seemed to adapt to the demands of open warfare well – their learning process in positional conflict was not as intellectually confining as might have been imagined. Grove (aged 39), the professional, clearly found his senior job demanding during this period, however. He wrote how: 'Towards the end of the war when I was feeling the strain my responsibilities put on me, I applied for a transfer home.' This was approved, but Grove withdrew the application: 'As the time came nearer, I liked less and less the prospect of being out of it.' It was perhaps fortunate in sustaining his stresses that Grove was noted as having a good sense of humour, possessing a 'quick wit and loud voice.'[59]

Brigade Staff

At brigade level, the Brigade Major fulfilled 'G' functions, and a Staff Captain the 'A' and 'Q' functions. Captain Alexander Johnston experienced 'intense disgust' on being made GSO3, and hoped it would only be 'stepping stone to becoming a Brigade Major, which is the job I had hoped to get.'[60] Major Walter Guinness reflected two sides of the coin. On one hand he noted: 'Although Brigade Majors get more pay than 3rd grade General Staff Officers … many soldiers are said to prefer Divisional to Brigade work.'[61] Personally, however, he agreed with Johnston – 'there's no doubt that a Brigade Major's job is the most attractive to my taste.'[62] When his brigadier was promoted to divisional command, he grumbled: 'I hate the idea of being a GSO2, as to my mind it is nothing like such interesting work as Brigade Major.'[63] The Brigade Major was responsible for: 'The preparation of orders and maps, their distribution, the gathering and reporting of intelligence information, liaison with divisional staff and adjacent brigades and the preparation of reports and diaries.'[64] He provided 'the essential link between the world of grand tactics and that of minor tactics.'[65] His ability in shaping minor tactics, in the view of Peter Simkins, was 'a crucial factor in shaping a brigade's battle performance.'[66] One Brigade Major dourly pictured his role in a much less exotic way. 'I am now a sort of glorified policemen, adjutant and sgt.-major

59 W.N. Nicholson, op. cit. p.124.
60 E. Astill (ed.), *The Great War Diaries of Brigadier General Alexander Johnston 1914-1917*, p.133.
61 Bond & Robbins, op. cit. location 1507.
62 Bond & Robbins, op. cit. location 2140.
63 Bond & Robbins, op. cit. location 3531.
64 T.G. Harvey, 'An Army of Brigadiers', p.28.
65 P. Griffith, *Battle Tactics of the Western Front*, p. 23.
66 P. Simkins, '"Building Blocks": Aspects of Command and Control at Brigade level in the BEF's Operations, 1916-1918', in G. Sheffield & D. Todman (eds), *Command and Control on the Western Front*, p.147.

rolled into one.'[67] The role of the Staff Captain in A & Q 'was to ensure that the brigade was suitably equipped and supplied. His wide remit included the supervision of transport, sanitation, billets, dumps and salvage, courts martial, spiritual welfare and leave.'[68] Interchangeability was, however, expected.

The functional relationship between Brigade Major and brigadier was essentially the same as GSO1 and divisional commander, but in a smaller team environment. As observed in Chapter Five, Cecil Nicholson was full of exceptional praise for Hugh Headlam on 10 August 1915 at Hooge, Headlam disappearing into the shellfire of early dawn to relieve his brigadier's blindness to the situation. When Headlam departed to (very briefly) take up a battalion command, Nicholson wrote that it was 'a great loss to me.'[69] Andrew Noble Pope turned up as replacement and Nicholson took an instant dislike to him. Walter Congreve shifted Pope to 17 Brigade, where he lasted only 37 days before being replaced. Nicholson described Headlam's replacement, Captain Charles Barry Costin, as 'mooney [*sic*] and absent-minded.'[70] On 19 October, Nicholson told Congreve that 'I could not do with Costin as BM any more',[71] and after Costin failed to redirect a relief on 23 October, Nicholson wrote: 'Staff very trying all the evening, and I turned in a furious temper.'[72] After 82 days, Costin was sent as Machine Gun Officer to 18 Brigade, a very clear demotion. Indeed in 1915, Major-General Sir Ivor Maxse (18th Division) would express his dissatisfaction that 'the Brigade Majors are inexperienced in staff work' and this led to a greater centralisation of control in the brigadier.[73] Nicholson was therefore fortunate that after coming back from leave in early December 1915 he found his new Brigade Major, Captain Bertie Christopher Butler Tower 'going very strong.'[74] Tower would remain in post for 215 days, but after a period as a GSO2 would return to his regiment and be mortally wounded commanding 4th Royal Fusiliers on 21 August 1918. Clearly, personalities would rub up against each other and faults become swiftly apparent in the comparatively small brigade team.

Gerald Burgoyne was scathing in claiming that he only ever once saw a member of brigade staff in the trenches.[75] Indeed, there may have been some limited truth in this during the first two years of the war, and *SS135* (1916) addressed the issue of 'the problem of command and control in battle, placing greater emphasis on the role

67 War Diary, 149 Infantry Brigade, letter from Captain H. W. Jackson to Brigadier-General E. P. A. Riddell, 26 October 1918, TNA WO95/2872.
68 Harvey, op. cit. p.29.
69 C.L. Nicholson, op. cit. 1 September 1915.
70 C.L. Nicholson, op. cit. 30 September 1915.
71 C.L. Nicholson, op. cit. 19 October 1915.
72 C.L. Nicholson, op. cit. 23 October 1915.
73 A. Fox-Godden, '"Hopeless Inefficiency?" The Transformation and Operational Performance of Brigade Staff, 1916-1918', in M. LoCicero, R. Mahoney & S. Mitchell, *A Military Transformed?*, p.142.
74 C.L. Nicholson, op. cit. 3 December 1915.
75 Burgoyne, op. cit. p.142.

of staff officers within the forward areas', and including 'the active encouragement of personal reconnaissance by staff officers and the positioning of a brigade staff officer at the Advance Report Station.'[76] Whilst Hugh Headlam had done just this at Hooge, being a *psc* who understood perfectly the need for accurate intelligence, decline in brigade staff performance during 1915-16 is attributed to the deskilling of the BEF by an influx of untrained staff officers – as Ivor Maxse observed. Peter Simkins notes that 'it is small wonder that the fiery furnace of the Somme quickly exposed the inexperience of a large number' of brigade staff officers.[77] As has been observed, staff function in 6th Division at the Quadrilateral in September 1916 was poor, lack of experience of offensive operations colliding painfully with a hasty attack. *Notes on Recent Fighting – No. 4* (dealing with staff duties, and issued in April 1918), incorporating lessons learnt from the mobile fighting of the March retreats, emphasised even more strongly 'the need for frequent, personal reconnaissance by staff',[78] stating that 'It is the duty of Staff officers to use every means at their disposal to ascertain the truth by immediate investigation.'

Twenty-eight Brigade Majors served with the five brigades that were attached to 6th Division. Of the two brigades that spent all their time with the division, 16 Brigade had ten, and 18 Brigade only six. A number of Brigade Majors served for long periods. Captain Bernard Burbury served for 559 days under three brigadiers with 71 Brigade before being promoted to GSO2;[79] Captain Thomas Morgan-Gavin-Grenville served under four brigadiers for 475 days with 18 Brigade before being similarly elevated;[80] and Captain Robert Leslie served for 383 days under the competent Brigadier-General Osborn in 16 Brigade (notably during the fighting at Loos in April 1917) before moving to another post at the same grade.[81] These officers provided stability and continuity to both to new GOCs and battalion COs, being on the receiving end of countless field telephone calls from the latter in terms of correcting inaccurate artillery fire. In terms of stability overall, Brigade Majors served for an average 259 days in 18 Brigade, 210 days in 71 Brigade, and 153 days in 16 Brigade.

At the outbreak of war, the Brigade Majors of the three original brigades were all Staff College graduates. Arthur Green had been Brigade Major of 17 Brigade since June 1911 but, as observed, his wartime career was terminated by a sniper on the Aisne. Roland Henry Mangles of 16 Brigade had passed Staff College in 1909 and had taken up the Brigade Major post in 16 Brigade in March 1912. In addition to being an England rugby international, he was an extraordinarily competent staff officer, who

76 Fox-Godden, op. cit. pp.149-150.
77 Simkins, op. cit. p.147.
78 Fox-Godden, op. cit. p.152.
79 Bernard Thornley Burbury had been commissioned into the Royal Warwickshire Regiment in 1904 and transferred to the Yorkshire Regiment.
80 Thomas George Bredalbane Morgan-Gavin-Grenville had been commissioned into the Rifle Brigade in 1912.
81 Robert Burton Leslie had been commissioned into the Lincolnshire Regiment in 1912.

would be promoted to serve as GSO1 with both 58th and 34th Divisions, and then BGGS V Corps from July 1918. Robert Francis Hurter Wallace of 18 Brigade (33rd chief of the clan Wallace) had obtained his *psc* in 1910 and had been with 18 Brigade since October 1913. He would leave the battlefield and rise through War Office posts to GSO1 and Assistant Director of Staff Duties. The three replacements, Hugh Roger Headlam (16 Brigade), William Henry Erik Segrave (17 Brigade) and Alan Thomas Paley (18 Brigade), were also Staff College graduates. Headlam went on to command 64 Brigade, becoming the longest serving brigade commander of 21st Division during the war. Segrave would become GSO1 of 4th Division, and finally GOC 152 Brigade. Paley would serve as GSO2 VII Corps and GSO1 of 21st Division. There were riches indeed amongst Brigade Majors for the division in these early months of the war.

Regulars kept a close grip on the Brigade Major role, filling 82 percent of posts. John Horlington (16 Brigade), was from the Special Reserve, as was Bernard Ewart Davies (the last Brigade Major of 71 Brigade). Davies's two predecessors in 71 Brigade from July 1918 onward were civilians in August 1914. Claude Allerton (a bootmaker) was commissioned in December 1914, and James Frederick Tamblyn (a bank clerk) was commissioned in the same month. Allerton only lasted eight days in post but would be appointed GSO3 in October 1918. The third citizen at the outbreak of war was Nelson Frederick Wellington (who would have three spells with 16 Brigade), who was a wounded officer from the Australian Imperial Force and had been an assistant town clerk. Aimée Fox-Godden offers the opinion that 'the "civilianization" of brigade staff during the First World War represented a meritocratic approach to promotion.'[82] At the rank of Brigade Major there is less evidence of promotion and more evidence of replacement, six individuals meeting this fate and not serving again in staff posts. This suggests rigour in assessing competence at this level.

The Junior Staff School was established in Hesdin in November 1916, and Brigade Majors were amongst attendees. Staff Captains at this point attracted no formal training, but were supposed to gain their craft by being a staff learner at brigade or division.[83] By mid-1918, 'all potential staff officers were required to undertake a Probationary Course', including 'at least three weeks mandatory attachment to the staff of an infantry brigade', and if they were 'deemed suitable for further training, they were permitted to attend the Staff Course.' On successful completion, such officers were deemed eligible for appointment as GSO3 or Staff Captain.[84] Thus the BEF increased its professionalism, and the army of the Hundred Days was able to operate with competence. Fox-Godden believes that this improvement in brigade staff performance was evident in 1917, operations during this year revealing 'a growing confidence at the tactical level with commanders and staff demonstrating outstanding

82 Fox-Godden, op. cit. p.156.
83 Fox-Godden, op. cit. p.145.
84 Fox-Godden, op. cit. pp.146-7.

leadership and initiative.'[85] The fluidity of the fighting of the Hundred Days required proactive decision making at battalion and brigade level, and placed an even heavier burden on brigade staff and 'the decisive emphasis on flexibility and going forward led to … a high level of exhaustion among staff.'[86] One expenditure of energy was saved, however – the lengthy orders of 1916 became much shorter and even non-existent.

In the Hundred Days, when brigade commanders had resumed a role closer to their front line and were enjoying more devolved command, 16 Brigade enjoyed the services of 21 year-old Captain Eric Dryden (from 5 June 1918 to the Armistice); 18 Brigade 25 year-old Captain Hubert Charles Edward Hull (from 1 April 1918 to the Armistice); and 71 Brigade the previously-mentioned 24 year-old Captain James Frederick Tamblyn (from 12 July to 4 November 1918). Brigades therefore benefitted from stability in their principal staff officer during this period. Eric Dryden had been commissioned in the Regular army from the TF in May 1915 and had served as adjutant and GSO3; Hubert Hull had been commissioned as a Regular in March 1911 and had served as a GSO3. No previous staff service can be identified for James Tamblyn, but it is unlikely that he would have achieved the role of Brigade Major without. He received the OBE in 1951 for his service with the Ministry of Food – administration was clearly his metier. That these men had uninterrupted service during this key period indicates their quality.

'Q' and 'A' Staff

Major Walter Nicholson, a 'Q' staff officer himself, readily acknowledged that 'the best of our staff officers were on the general staff', and he took the view that 'Q' and 'G' staff did not work sufficiently closely together.[87] The Adjutant General personnel function, though seemingly dull, was important. A sound knowledge of a division's officers was key in promotion. Supplies and transport were obviously similarly crucial to a division's functioning, but the QMG function of a division was dependant to a large extent on a logistics system to its rear. And despite training, these administrative staff were learning on the job. Nicholson, as DAAQMG with 17th Division, succinctly described how in the period 1915-17: 'We learnt by real practical experience how to handle transport.' Within transport he included 'the combinations and permutations of first and second line wagons, pack transport, train, corps and army echelons, bus companies', adding light and broad-gauge railways. All these systems had to be 'brought into use to transport troops, ammunition, supplies and all the unforeseen requirements of war at the shortest notice in any direction.' Further, transport was deployed 'over roads that had been cratered, were under shell fire, or in

85 Fox-Godden, op. cit. p.151.
86 Fox-Godden, op. cit. p.153.
87 W.N. Nicholson, op. cit. p.170.

bad condition; roads that had to be traffic circuited and timed to avoid congestion and to allow of repairs.'[88]

The Assistant Adjutant and Quartermaster General assigned to the division on the outbreak of war was Colonel Walter Campbell. Fifty years-old and a Staff College graduate, he had served as a Brigade Major and then DAAG at Army HQ in South Africa. He had then been posted DAAG III Corps and DAQMG at Army HQ in the post-war period. He was subsequently Deputy Assistant Director of Movements, GSO2 at Aldershot, and lastly AQMG Scottish Command. An officer of his experience would not last long at divisional level, and on 6 October 1914, before the move to Flanders, he was promoted DAQMG III Corps and then Third Army. In October 1915 he left the Western Front to be DAQMG to the Egyptian Expeditionary Force. After a month reducing confusion in the supply of the Gallipoli operations, he concentrated on Egypt itself, 'where he transformed the EEF's logistical infrastructure, building railways and pipelines … and rapidly reorganising captured ports.' Sir Charles Monro, GOC Third Army, declared: 'I wish I could feel that I had done half as much for the world as Walter Campbell.'[89] Campbell displays the extraordinary talent available to the pre-war British Army.

Cambell's replacement was Colonel Robert Wanless-O'Gowan. His *curriculum vitae* was less impressive than Campbell's, having served as a railway officer in South Africa, moving to be AQMG Eastern Command only in April 1914. Not having passed Staff College, he had gone to war as AAG Lines of Communication and would only last until 7 February with 6th Division before moving on to command 13 Brigade in 5th Division, then taking the reins at 31 Division from August 1915 to March 1918. The division clearly needed a period of stability in 'Q' function, and this was provided by Lieutenant-Colonel Reginald Seaburne May. A 1906 Staff College graduate, his experience was in a range of GSO2 posts, at which grade he went to war. Serving for a year with 6th Division he was promoted in February 1916 to AQMG Fourth Army and in December that year to DAQMG Second Army, moving in November 1917 to DQMG at GHQ. His administrative career was therefore distinguished.

In the place of the illustrious May came Lieutenant-Colonel Mainwaring Ravell Walsh, who had obtained his *psc* in 1912. He had no pe-war 'Q' experience, but served his whole war in either DAAG, DAAQMG, AAQMG and AAG posts, finally being AAG to the Army of the Rhine.[90] He was clearly a talented administrator. Serving for a year and a half, and notably during the division's operations on the Somme, Walsh was replaced by Lieutenant-Colonel Morris Boscawen Savage, who had not attended Staff College. Indeed, he was a regimental officer severely wounded at Pilckem on 23 October 1914. He returned as a Staff Captain in April 1915 with 110 Brigade, and

88 W.N. Nicholson, op. cit. p.213.
89 J. Bourne, *Who's Who in World War 1*, p.50.
90 He died on 15 May 1940 serving as King's Messenger with the rank of Brigadier-General as a result of enemy bombing of the Hotel L'Univers, Arras.

from October that year served as DAAQMG 9th Scottish Division, DAAG XIX Corps, AAQMG with 6th Division and AAG Scottish Command. Serving for only three and a half months before passing on to other staff posts, he was replaced from the start of 1918 by Lieutenant-Colonel Percy Hudson. Hudson also had not attended Staff College and began his career as a Staff Captain in February 1915, having been wounded as adjutant of 1st Liverpool near Zonnebeke the day after his predecessor, Savage. He would face the challenge of logistics in the Hundred Days campaign.

It is worth considering the 'Q' tasks during September on the Somme, which Walsh had to coordinate through his DAQMG, Major Herbert Street, an Indian Army officer who had transferred to the Devonshire Regiment and who had previously served as a Staff Captain (and who would be promoted AAQMG of 4th Division). Street provided continuity serving with 6th Division for 460 days. In relation to the failed attack on the Quadrilateral on 15 September:

> A forward SAA (small arms ammunition) dump was formed at BRIQUETTERIE. Each brigade had a reserve of 2000 iron rations and a forward dump of water in petrol tins was formed. Each brigade was supplied with 16 additional pack saddles, also 24 improvised ration sacks. Each company of the battalions attacking were furnished with improvised ration packs and crates to carry (petrol) water tins. Each company had five horses for pack work apart from ammunition – three for rations and two for water. It was found impossible to get up rations otherwise than by pack animals and with the assistance of train horses. A brigade section of 40 pack horses was formed in each brigade.[91]

In preparation for the successful Battle of Morval, on 25 September, 'as the division was pushed in as an extra division, no dumps of water, rations or small arms ammunition and bombs were available to be taken over and new dumps had to be hurriedly formed. This was commenced on the 21st and ongoing by the 22nd.' Owing to shelling the small arms dump at Briquetterie had to be moved, and water dumps were transferred there. Brigades were 'supplied during the night 21st/22nd with stores for their own forward dumps.' It was noted with likely pride that 'as events proved the special efforts put forward during the 21st and 22nd enabled the division to form dumps with practically all that was required for the contemplated attack.' The assault being postponed from the 23rd to the 25th allowed '"Q" to completely equip all dumps.'[92] Following the attack, it was noted sombrely that 11th Leicestershire (the divisional pioneers) 'were chiefly engaged in burying dead and did remarkably good work.' This took place over three days. It was also recorded that 'the salvage company

91 War Diary AAQMG 6th Infantry Division, 'Operations from 15th to 30th September 1916', TNA WO95/1586.
92 War Diary AQMG 6th Infantry Division, 22-24 September 1916, TNA WO95/1586.

was most successful in their efforts, some 3000 rifles and a large quantity of war material including machine guns, Lewis guns and mortars being salved.'[93]

Such were the varied tasks of the 'Q' branch. It would appear that local logistics ran smoothly during the division's operations on the Somme. The Hundred Days campaign and a war of greater movement would present different challenges (see Chapter 12). There is, however, no evidence that 6th Division possessed anything other than competent officers at the head of its 'Q' functions. Indeed, the whole BEF in 1918 showed more appreciation of the crucial relationship of logistics to tempo than the enemy had done in their spring offensives.

Conclusion

Simon Robbins has suggested that during the war 'staff functions became more responsive and multi-faceted than ever before, demanding a high degree of teamwork, efficiency and knowledge.'[94] The 'G' staff of 6th Division showed a clear evolution with the seemingly efficient team of the Hundred Days campaign comprising a Regular, a Territorial and an officer of the Special Reserve, whereas in August 1914 all three posts had been held by Regular officers who had passed Staff College. This transformation was achieved with no evident drop in efficiency. Indeed, in the Selle operations, General Braithwaite met with General Marden first on 13 October 1918, with the attack taking place on 17 October. That 6th Division's staff could orchestrate such a complex set-piece operation (see Chapter 13) in four days is remarkable. It is certainly the case that the formation was blessed throughout the war with highly competent GSO1s, with one probable exception. In respect of turnover, on the divisional staff team there were 5 GSO1s, eight GSO2s and nine GSO3s, and 94 percent of the turnover was due to promotion. This indicates able officers, and only the GSO1 Lewis Renny was sidelined into a non-active staff role. The division appears to have had an able staff team at all GSO levels throughout the war. Robbins notes that 'to achieve a "staff Culture" of greater flexibility and effectiveness, the British high command were required to improve its staff training, procedures and techniques.'[95] And if that training did not produce the all-weather staff officer that Camberley achieved, then the blend of learning both in the class room and on the job provided 6th Division with a nearly consistently competent team.

The situation at brigade level was more complex. The same evolution was apparent. All three original brigades each had *psc* holders as their first two Brigade Majors, and during the Hundred Days had two Regular officers and a New Army captain in post who had only acquired staff experience from mid-1917. Overall, 48 percent

93 War Diary AQMG 6th Infantry Division, 30 September 1916 TNA WO95/1586.
94 S. Robbins, *British Generalship on the Western Front 1914-18*, (Abingdon: Frank Cass, 2005), p.50.
95 Robbins, *British Generalship*, p.50.

were promoted and 30 percent were replaced (with two taking a downward step to GSO3). The lower promotion rate than for division level 'G' officers is not indicative of lack of competence, rather of a bottleneck. The next staff rank up for a Brigade Major was GSO2, at which level there obviously fewer posts, although nine of the 23 Brigade Majors who could have been promoted obtained this level. The seemingly high replacement rate, however, indicates variability in quality. The replaced include four individuals who had held no previous staff post, and three who had been Staff Captains. In these cases the step up apparently proved one too far.

The overall picture of the staff of 6th Division stands good comparison with Paul Harris's summary of the performance of the BEF's staff during the war: 'They performed fairly well during the first few months, struggled during the middle years and evolved into a highly competent organization by the end of hostilities.'[96]

96 Harris, op. cit. p.290.

8

'Tomorrow a New Page in the History of the War will be Turned':[1] The Battle of Cambrai November 1917

The Battle of Cambrai opened on 20 November 1917. Bryn Hammond describes this as 'a day that can legitimately be seen as marking the commencement of a 'Modern Style of Warfare',[2] but not, as myth would have it, because it was the occasion of the first massed use of tanks. It was, rather, a step towards the development of 'deep battle' through advanced artillery technique. Although the BEF had contemplated an attack on the enemy defences south-west of the town since May 1917, the plan that finally matured had its seeds in the thinking of Brigadier-General Hugh Tudor,[3] commanding the artillery of 9th Division. He put forward through IV Corps the idea of an assault using the 'silent registration' of carefully calibrated guns to neutralise both defensive positions and enemy artillery, whilst forgoing a preliminary bombardment to cut wire, leaving this obstacle to be flattened by tanks. Meanwhile, Lieutenant-Colonel John Fuller,[4] the chief staff officer of the Tank Corps, in conjunction with the corps commander, Brigadier-General Hugh Elles,[5] had formulated a scheme for a 'tank raid' in the Cambrai area, supported by low-flying aircraft. Lieutenant-General Julian Byng[6] and his Third Army staff constructed a plan based on both of these

1 War Diary, 6th Infantry Division, General Marden's 'Special Order of the Day', 19 November 1917, TNA WO95/1583.
2 B. Hammond, *Cambrai 1917*, p.435.
3 Henry Hugh Tudor rose during the war from the rank of captain in charge of an artillery battery in 1914 to the rank of major-general commanding the 9th (Scottish) Division.
4 John Frederick Charles 'Boney' Fuller served in staff roles during the war, notably with the Tank Corps. An enthusiastic proponent of mechanized warfare through his writings, he rose to the rank of major-general in the post-war period. His leanings towards fascism prevented his recall during WW2.
5 Hugh Jamieson Elles was a staff officer with 4th Division in 1914-15 who was appointed to head what would become the Tank Corps in September 1916.
6 Julian Hedworth George Byng had begun the war in the Cavalry Corps, and in 1915 was sent to Gallipoli to IX Corps to supervise the withdrawal. He returned to the Western Front to command the Canadian Corps, and commanded Third Army from June 1917.

concepts, adding the use of cavalry to support a breakthrough. Sir Douglas Haig, conscious that the Third Battle of Ypres was grinding to a muddy halt, approved, and from 26 October Byng and his corps commanders (VII Corps under Lieutenant-General Sir Thomas Snow, III Corps under Lieutenant-General Sir William Pulteney, and IV Corps under Lieutenant-General Sir Charles Woolcombe),[7] expanded their plans. The battle was to achieve surprise based on absolute secrecy in preparation. Three hundred and seventy eight fighting tanks would be deployed (with a further 98 tanks to be used for supply, wire pulling etc.). The Royal Flying Corps had produced detailed photographs of the Hindenburg System, and practiced ground attack for strikes against German airfields, gun positions, and the hampering of deployment of reserves, supplies and communications. The successful work of the RE Field Survey Companies with sound-ranging equipment allowed the identification of enemy batteries so that there would be no counter-battery struggle. This allowed the BEF's artillery 'to be placed far forward in "silent" positions close to the front line from which they could fire deep into the German defences.'[8] The massive British superiority in artillery would fire a lifting rather than a creeping barrage, a barrage Hammond describes as 'jumping.'[9] The lifts would be onto successive enemy defensive positions, an accurate creeper being questionable due to lack of registration. The attack would proceed in three stages. Firstly the main Hindenburg Position would be overrun, the canal crossings at Masnières and Marcoing would be seized and the German Second Position (the Masnières–Beaurevoir line) would be captured. The cavalry would then pass through to seize the crossings of the Sensée River and capture Bourlon Wood which, on a ridge, overlooked Cambrai. Finally, Cambrai would be taken, and the enemy forces trapped between the St Quentin Canal, the Canal du Nord and the river would be destroyed. The enemy position represented a salient, but Marden notes that the plan involved the BEF creating its own salient, extending its line from 7,000 to 15,000 yards. This afforded 'the enemy a chance of a blow at the sides and hinges of the salient, of which he availed himself to good purpose ten days after our initial attack.'[10] The least risky option was to ensure that all the key tactical points were seized within 48 hours, the earliest point at which it was estimated enemy reinforcements could arrive. They were not.

For the infantry, a major issue would be the cooperation of advancing in conjunction with tanks. This had gone badly for 6th Division on 15 September 1916 at the Quadrilateral, where absolutely no preparation had been undertaken. At the start of November the battalions of the Tank Corps were mostly in the countryside around Arras, with Wailly as their main training ground, and 6th Division underwent nearly

7 Sir Charles Louis Woolcombe served as GOC Eastern Command 1914-15, moving to another home command, GOC 2nd Army, Central Force, before taking over IV Corps in 1916.

8 Hammond, op. cit. p.113.

9 Hammond, op. cit. p.114. Nine major 'jumps' are described in IV Corps.

10 T. O. Marden, *A Short History of the 6th Division*, p.36.

two weeks of training. 71 Brigade recorded that from 1-5 November there was platoon and company training in 'open warfare.' This included: 'Platoons advancing under a barrage, the company in attack, wood fighting, platoons attacking strong points, fire control and direction.' Attention was given to the training of 'young officers and junior NCOs.' There was also 'special training as regards advancing to the attack with TANKS.'[11] Third Army had circulated documents concerning tank warfare, notably *Notes on Infantry and Tank Operations*, giving detailed instructions on how tanks and infantry were to work together, and this was no doubt the document 6th Division were using. On 4 November the senior officers of all brigades viewed a demonstration at Mercatel of an infantry attack with tanks over a system of trenches. These demonstrations continued from the 7th for three days (71 Brigade on the 7th, 16 Brigade on the 8th, and 18 Brigade on the 9th, all with H Tank Battalion), one company of infantry operating with a section of tanks in a trench-to-trench attack. The conditions of the Hindenburg System were recreated: 'The wire was very thick indeed, and the trench system very deep and wide.' There were two demonstrations a day, 'the entire brigade watching.'[12] On the 9th, 18 Brigade described companies of 1st West Yorkshire and 11th Essex carrying out 'attacks in cooperation with a section of tanks, the remainder watching', General Marden observing.[13] From the 10th to the 14th 71 Brigade practiced attacks with imaginary tanks, Sir Douglas Haig watching on the 13th when 1st Leicestershire and 9th Suffolk carried out a trench-to-trench attack 'over a flag course' tanks being represented 'by 3 men carrying flags.'[14] Lieutenant-Colonel Prior of 9th Norfolk recorded that the training 'largely consisted in trying all kinds of alternative methods of how we could best get through the passage' of wire 'with the least casualties.'[15] His battalion's War Diary recorded that 'Lt. G.H.G. Dye mapped out with flags and sawdust the full-sized plan of the village of RIBECOURT and its approaches' (this the unit's main objective).[16] Further, the brigade had 'marked out on the ground the trench system of the frontage of attack allotted to the Brigade', and had also constructed 'a small relief model of the frontage and this was invaluable.'[17] 18 Brigade carried out a tactical exercise in the presence of General Byng on 12 November with 14th Durham Light Infantry as the enemy, 1st West Yorkshire attacking with 11th Essex, and 2nd DLI in support, who 'were used to form a defensive flank later in the operation.' A contact aircraft 'succeeded in dropping

11 War Diary, HQ 71 Infantry Brigade, 1-5 November 1917, TNA WO95/1619.
12 War Diary, HQ 71 Infantry Brigade, 7-9 November 1917, TNA WO95/1619.
13 War Diary, HQ 18 Infantry Brigade, 9 November 1917, TNA WO95/1615.
14 War Diary, HQ 71 Infantry Brigade, 13 November 1917, TNA WO95/1619.
15 War Diary, 9th Battalion Norfolk Regiment, 'Diary of Lieutenant-Colonel B.H.L. Prior', TNA WO95/1623.
16 George Harry Gordon Dye, the battalion intelligence officer, a pre-war school teacher, had risen to the rank of corporal with 20th Royal Fusiliers, and had been commissioned in 9th Norfolks in November 1916. He would die of wounds on 21 November 1917.
17 War Diary, 9th Battalion Norfolk Regiment, 1-15 November 1917, TNA WO95/1623.

a map of the situation … at B(riga)de report centre.'[18] Battalions practiced musketry, and the machine gun companies their barrage. Marden describes officers and men going 'through the operation on a carefully made ground model without being aware what ground it represented.'[19] At one level, the training was intense and varied. At another, practice alongside a real tank was limited, although this likely mattered little in practice. 9th Norfolk noted the problem that the training with actual tanks brought out – the tanks moved slowly and this caused the infantry to bunch when moving through wire.[20] Sir Douglas Haig visited on the 13th, and 'explained to Divisional and subordinate Commanders' the cavalry breakthrough nature of the operation. He impressed on them that 'this requires bold and determined action on the part of the subordinate Infantry Commanders. This was not, I thought, fully realised in all units I saw today, especially in the 6th Division.'[21] One suspects that with Marden's keen eye realistic observations were made concerning whether all objectives were achievable.

6th Division came under Lieutenant-General William Pulteney's III Corps, to whom they had been attached at Armentières in 1914-15. III was the southernmost corps involved in the attack, and had to hold the southern flank of the salient that would be created for trapping the enemy forces, this being the responsibility of 12 Division on the corps right. 6th Division, on the left, would attack on the front Villers Plouich to Beaucamps, 71 Brigade (with one battalion from 18 Brigade) would go forward on the left, abutting 51st Division, 16 Brigade on the right, both brigades attacking in three waves. The first objective involved an advance of 3,000 yards to Ribécourt, which lay between the main line of resistance of the Hindenburg Position and the Hindenburg Support System, then advancing a further 1,000 yards to take the support system itself, the second objective. The Hindenburg System was a formidable exposition of defence in depth. The main line of resistance was dug in on a reverse slope, but forward positions extended some five hundred yards in front, with four belts of barbed wire some 50 feet deep and three feet high with 20 feet between them, gaps funnelling attackers into killing zones covered by machine guns. (6th Division would have a second experience of assaulting these forward positions in September 1918). The brigades were to leave specially trained mopping up troops in the main lines of resistance. Once the support system had been overcome, 18 Brigade would then advance through 71 Brigade at three hours 20 minutes after Zero, which was set at 06.20, and secure the third objective a further 1,000 yards on, the Premy Chapel Ridge, on the right shoulder of which Marcoing stretched down to the St Quentin Canal. In doing so, they would throw back a defensive flank towards Flesquières where 51st Division were advancing. The 29th Division would then pass through to secure the crossings at Marcoing and Masnières. Two battalions of tanks were allotted

18 War Diary, 18 Infantry Brigade, 12 November 1917, TNA WO95/1615.
19 Marden, op. cit. p.36.
20 War Diary, 9th Battalion Norfolk Regiment, 7 November 1917, TNA WO95/1623.
21 G. Sheffield and J. Bourne (eds), *Douglas Haig: War Diaries and Letters 1914-1918*, p.341.

to 6th Division. B Battalion (Lieutenant-Colonel Edward Bryce),[22] would operate with 16 Brigade; H Battalion (Lieutenant-Colonel Hon. Claud Willoughby)[23] with 71 Brigade. Hugh Elles, the Tank Corps commander would accompany H Battalion in 'Hilda' (allegedly the name of a favourite aunt), flying the improvised brown, red and green battle-standard, these colours signifying 'from mud through blood to green fields beyond.' The tanks attacked in three waves. 1st Cavalry Division was to pass through 6th Division's area, Ribécourt and Marcoing, and 2nd and 5th Cavalry Divisions were to cross at Masnières and Marcoing, accompanied by 12 tanks. It was an ambitious plan.

The 6th Division's war diary for the month of November has not survived, but the operational orders have. The main set of orders (issued on the 13th) runs to five pages,[24] and on the 14th an addendum was issued, almost certainly in response to Haig's chidings, that in order to take advantage of likely any enemy disorganisation, 16 and 71 Brigades should each send a company on from Premy Chapel to Marcoing to secure the bridge, without waiting for 18 Brigade. (In the original orders tanks alone had been detailed to proceed to Marcoing). With typical Marden thoroughness there were detailed instructions for reorganising and establishing defensive positions, given the German propensity to immediate counter-attack. A two-page document concerning the preservation of secrecy was sent out on the following day.[25] Three further addenda on this topic were issued, emphasising how crucial secrecy was to success. Instructions for the machine-gun barrage (provided by 36 guns, eight going forward with each brigade) and the subsequent movement of guns ran to three pages.[26] There was a further order relating to anti-aircraft defence,[27] and a two page order concerning Royal Engineer and Pioneer activities (the establishment of strongpoints, communication trenches and road maintenance to get field guns forward).[28] The

22 Edward Daniel Bryce was a rubber planter in India in 1914, and joined what would become the Tank Corps in October 1916.
23 The Hon. Claud Heathcote-Drummond-Willoughby was a retired officer of the Coldstream Guards, promoted lieutenant-colonel from the Cheshire Regiment in what would become the Tank Corps in November 1916.
24 War Diary, HQ 6th Infantry Division, No. G. 22/2 (271), 13 November 1917, TNA WO95/1583.
25 War Diary, HQ 6th Infantry Division, No. G. 22/2/4 (283), 14 November 1917, TNA WO95/1583.
26 War Diary, HQ 6th Infantry Division, No. G. 22/2/5, 15 November 1917, TNA WO95/1583.
27 War Diary, HQ 6th Infantry Division, Appendix B to order no. 164, November 1917, TNA WO95/1583.
28 War Diary, HQ 6th Infantry Division, No. G.22/2/7 (313), 17 November 1917, TNA WO95/1583.

signals order ran to eight pages,[29] and the intelligence orders to two.[30] A two-page order concerning 'Exploitation of Success' was issued on the 19th, concerning assisting 29th Division forward on the following day.[31] The divisional artillery orders have not survived, but the supporting guns included twelve 13-pounders, seventy-two 18-pounders, and twenty-four 4.5-inch howitzers,[32] and it is stated (contrary to other general reviews of artillery that day) that they fired a creeping barrage, also with smoke at various points. It was noted afterwards that 'the action of the hostile artillery ... was almost negligible', and that 'no counter-battery work was undertaken by the enemy.'[33] It was a well prepared operation, and 6th Division's orders reflect this.

The Cambrai sector was held by the German *Second Army*, commanded by Georg von der Marwitz.[34] A good deal of intelligence had been obtained on the enemy, and 6th Division was opposed by *54th Division*. It was later noted of this formation that it had 'held the most active sectors on the Western Front' and had 'everywhere given proof of great energy in its resistance, especially at Cambrai in November 1917', although it was added that prior to Cambrai 'rather frequent desertions proved that the losses incurred at Ypres' in August 1917 'had weakened the morale of the troops.' It would lose 2,789 men on 20 November taken prisoner.[35] Anthony Leask describes that it had 'almost been destroyed with 5,785 officers and men reported missing at the end of the day.'[36] In addition, the enemy were weak in artillery and low on ammunition. In front of 6th Division, *90th* and *27th Reserve Infantry Regiments* were known to have three battalions in line, and the total enemy forces available immediately for defence and counter-attack on the corps front was estimated at 15 battalions.

29 War Diary, HQ 6th Infantry Division, No. G.22/2/8 (316), 17 November 1917, TNA WO95/1583.
30 War Diary, HQ 6th Infantry Division, No. G.22/2/9 (335), 17 November 1917, TNA WO95/1583.
31 War Diary, HQ 6th Infantry Division, No. G.22/2/12 (363), 17 November 1917, TNA WO95/1583.
32 Reinforced by 17 Brigade RFA of 29th Division and 181 Brigade of 40th Division as well as two Brigades RHA.
33 War Diary, CRA 6th Infantry Division, 'Report on Operations carried out on November 20th and 21st 1917', TNA WO95/1591.
34 Marwitz began the war as commander of *II Cavalry Corps* and was transferred to the Eastern Front to command *XXXVIII Reserve Corps*. He commanded *VI Corps* on the Western Front, was sent back to to the Eastern Front and finally returned to the west to command Second Army in December 1916.
35 *Histories of the Two Hundred and Fifty-One Divisions of the German Army Which Participated in the war (1914-1918)*, p.513.
36 A. Leask, *Putty*, p.630.

The Attack – 20 November 1917

In front of 71 Brigade, the enemy outpost line (Plush Trench) was 750 yards distant but only 250 yards away in front of 16 Brigade. The position was 'out of sight of our front trenches by reason of the curve of the ground.'[37] The ground rises from both Beaucamps and Villers Plouch, onto a ridge, the Hindenburg Line lying some way down the reverse slope. Beyond a series of machine gun nests, the main Hindenburg Line (Unseen Trench) lay at varying distances to the west, with a second line just to its rear. From left to right on 6th Division's front this trench was called Unseen Support, Valley Support and Ridge Support, which accurately reflected the topography – in the centre of the division's attack was a valley leading from Villers Plouch, and on 16 Brigade's right was a ridge, on which lay Couillet Wood, in which tanks could not operate. This wood and Ribécourt village were the only causes of concern in terms of resistance. Between 1,000 and 1,500 yards further on lay the two lines of the support system. (See Map 11, colour section).

The attack on Ribécourt from Villers-Plouich, 20 November 1917.

With a Zero of 06.20, 16 Brigade's tanks were not in position until 05.30, and the infantry 'did not wait in every case for the tanks to arrive.' As the barrage opened, they

37 Marden, op. cit. p.38.

attacked in 'both columns and waves … according to ground.'[38] There was only one occasion of difficulty with wire and this was swiftly dealt with by a tank, the machines also dealing with strong points. A special brigade sniper party worked successfully through Couillet Wood. Both advancing machine gun sections and trench mortars had difficulty in keeping up with the pace of advance, however. The brigade noted that the bombardment of the second objective was 'unnecessarily long and held up this advance some 35 minutes.'[39] 2nd York & Lancaster attacked on the right, and took the main Hindenburg position for the loss of three killed and 19 wounded. On the left 8 Bedfordshire's tanks reached Plush Trench at 06.29, the infantry passing six minutes later. The atmosphere was such that the men were 'lighting pipes and cigarettes on the way',[40] arriving at Unseen Trench at 06.45. The main Hindenburg Position was taken for the loss of eleven dead and 40 wounded. The second wave consisted of one company each of 1st Buffs and 1st King's Shropshire Light Infantry, right and left, the third wave consisting of the remaining companies of those units. 1st Buffs consolidated a line from Nine Wood to the Escault River, several hundred yards north of Marcoing, for the loss of eight killed and 33 wounded. Passing the main Hindenburg Position, the second wave company of 1st KSLI were subjected to machine-gun fire from Ribécourt, sustaining 40 casualties, as were the companies advancing in the third wave, suffering 23 casualties. Outside of this machine-gun fire, little resistance was encountered. The situation of the defenders was very difficult. Arthur Pries of *90th Reserve Infantry Regiment* described how:

> Suddenly all of the enemy's artillery began to fire madly right along our division's sector. The incendiary shells illuminated the whole front, left and right, as far as the eye could see, as if the entire area was on fire. We barely had time to instruct this battalion to follow our orders, when our own position and likewise the other commands in our rear were covered in a hailstorm of shells of every imaginable calibre. Our telephone lines were shot to pieces straight away and could not be restored despite the utter fearlessness of our radio operators and engineers.[41]

In 71 Brigade, 9th Suffolk attacked on the right, 1st Leicestershire on the left. The infantry attacked in 'worms', and in No Man's land 'the "worms" then extended into waves and kept this formation until within a short distance of the Hindenburg main line.' The waves advanced 50 yards behind the main body of tanks. In 9th Suffolk the tanks lost direction and bunched in, as did the following infantry, and this led to increased casualties under shellfire. Two of these tanks were out of action soon after

38 War Diary, HQ 16 Infantry Brigade, 'Account of part taken by 16th Infantry Brigade in action before Cambrai November 20/21st 1917', TNA WO95/1607.
39 War Diary, HQ 16 Infantry Brigade, 'Account of part taken by 16th Infantry Brigade in action before Cambrai November 20/21st 1917', TNA WO95/1607.
40 War Diary, 8th Battalion Bedfordshire Regiment, 20 November 1917, TNA WO95/1611.
41 A. Pries, quoted in Leask, op. cit. p.620.

Zero, and one of the Suffolk's companies had to riskily use the gaps created by the enemy through their own wire. The Suffolks pushed on into Marcoing with the loss of eight killed and 59 wounded, capturing the bridge there. The tanks leading 1st Leicestershire breached the wire with ease, the battalion's casualties in taking the main Hindenburg position amounting to five killed and 48 wounded. The second wave of infantry, half of 2nd Sherwood Foresters on the right and 9th Norfolk on the left, advanced in artillery formation until the main Hindenburg position was reached, suffering some casualties on the downward slope into the Grand Ravine, 9th Norfolk going ahead of the tanks which were delayed on the Grand Ravine bridges. The third wave, the remainder of the Sherwood Foresters and 11th Essex of 18 Brigade 'advanced with their tanks in the formation practised during training and were soon in possession of the Hindenburg support line.[42]

The Sherwood Foresters of both waves achieved their objectives with relative ease, at the cost of nine dead and 30 wounded. C Company took the second objective, the Hindenburg support position, without the aid of their tanks who found the going too difficult, and D Company 'charged home' on the second objective 'with the bayonet, killing about 12 Germans & taking prisoner a similar number.'[43] Advancing with 9th Norfolk, Lieutenant-Colonel Prior bemoaned: 'Oh the slowness of those tanks. It is at these moments that one itches for quickness and rapidity and the slow deliberate action of these monsters was exasperating.' In front of Unseen Trench Prior was faced with 'the most colossal belt of barbed wire that I have ever seen.' Following the tanks through this obstacle the battalion could see Ribécourt ahead and came under both machine-gun and shell fire. The tanks made swifter progress downhill, and Prior watched A Company 'make a beautiful attack on the line of houses on the left of the village supported by a male tank whose gun was in action.' 11th Essex then passed through at 09.45 to seize the Hindenburg support position.[44] Remaining in Ribécourt, Prior noted the arrival of the cavalry, who 'remained there all day without moving.' He was particularly frustrated that on the left flank, where 51st (Highland) Division had failed to take the Flesquières Ridge, 'there seemed to be a splendid opportunity for them to work round the flank of Flesquières Village and so cut off the enemy garrison.' This inaction led to 'very uncomplimentary remarks' from the infantry, and 'at one time there was very nearly a free fight between some of the Leicesters and a troop of cavalry.' 1st West Yorkshire referred to the horsemen as 'sticky and windy.'[45] Marden noted that the cavalry claimed at 15.15 that 'they could not advance owing to snipers in Ribécourt', but added (without the obvious comment) that the village had been in 6th Division's hands since 10.00 and two units had passed through it. The cavalry

42 War Diary, HQ 71 Infantry Brigade, 'Operations of 20th November', TNA WO95/1619.
43 War Diary, 2nd Battalion Sherwood Foresters, 20 November 1917, TNA WO95/1624.
44 11th Essex suffered casualties amounting to six killed and 42 wounded with four missing.
45 War Diary, 1st Battalion West Yorkshire Regiment, 20 November 1917, TNA WO95/1618.

were not the sum of Prior's frustrations as Brigadier-General Feetham 'offered no word of congratulation or praise to the Battalion, nor I believe any other unit in the Brigade for its work that day.' 9th Norfolk were about 400 strong going into action and killed 80 of the enemy and took 600 prisoners, and a 'runner of D company, without assistance, took over seventy men prisoners, including a staff officer.'[46] The unit suffered casualties totalling 32 killed and 61 wounded.

18 Brigade, tasked with passing through the other two, advanced with 1st West Yorkshire as advanced guard, 14th Durham Light Infantry on the right and 2nd DLI on the left. The brigade was in something of an information vacuum, but at 09.50 tanks could be seen advancing up Premy Chapel Ridge, 'and it was evident that if success was to be exploited, no time was to be lost.'[47] By 12.15 1st West Yorkshire were holding the ridge, B Company having 'very gallantly rushed at the point of the bayonet a battery of 4.2-inch howitzers and 1.77mm field guns which continued firing into them at point blank range.'[48] Major Hugh Boxer, of 14th DLI but temporarily commanding 2nd DLI, believed Flésquieres to have been captured, but when Premy Ridge 'hove in sight … I was speedily undeceived by a hail of machine gun bullets from it, but the shooting was high & they did not hit.' He described 'capturing 11 Hun guns & killing or capturing all the gunners.'[49] 14th DLI achieved their objectives easily, suffering only seven wounded, and by 12.00 were to the west of Marcoing. 2nd DLI made easy progress until leaving Ribécourt when they came under the heavy but ill-aimed machine-gun fire noted by Major Boxer. They entered the Hindenburg Support system at various points; C Company on the left, closest to Flesquières, 'was met by fire at close range from a battery of five field guns' and forced back.

> Captain Fawcett, commanding the company, immediately formed two parties, one under Captain Fillingham and the other which he took, and working round the right flank of the battery, charged the guns … he was covered in this operation by the fire of the co(mpan)y Lewis guns.[50]

46 War Diary, 9th Battalion Norfolk Regiment, 'Diary of Lieutenant-Colonel B.H.L. Prior', TNA WO95/1623.
47 War Diary, HQ 18 Infantry Brigade, 'Narrative of Sequence of Events, November 20th & 21st', TNA WO95/1615.
48 War Diary, 1st Battalion West Yorkshire Regiment, 20 November 1917, TNA WO95/1618. The unit suffered one killed and 13 wounded.
49 H.C. Boxer, Private Papers, letter 10 December 1917, IWM Docs 4891. Hugh Caldwell Boxer had been commissioned in 1903, and was in India during 1915, only reaching the Western Front in 1917. He would later serve in the Tank Corps.
50 War Diary, 2nd Battalion Durham Light Infantry, 20 November 1917, TNA WO95/1617. The battalion lost 4 killed, 18 wounded and two missing. Captain Edward Fawcett had been commissioned on 2 July 1914 into the Special Reserve of the DLI, Captain George Sidney Fillingham, commissioned on 11 August 1015, had also served with the Royal Flying Corps.

The company was faithfully following the infantry tactics of *SS143*. The battalion reached the Premy Chapel Ridge with 'some good shooting at the enemy.' 1st West Yorkshire, to their right, pushed into Nine Wood beyond. 29th Division passed through and got troops across the canal at both Masnières and Marcoing but failed to make any impression on the Masnières-Beaurevoir Line.

Flesquières from the Premy Chapel Ridge, with the exposed flank of 71 Brigade, p.m. 20 November 1917.

By the afternoon, 6th Division's left flank 'was in the air', and the situation was 'very obscure.'[51] At about 15.30 Marden ordered an attempt to turn the flank of the enemy holding Flesquières, in conjunction with tanks. H Tank Battalion could not get machines into position before dusk, and although there was 'little doubt that the village could have been entered with small loss',[52] an attack in conjunction with 152 Brigade (51st Division) was called off at the latter's request. Flesquières was found to be empty of the enemy when it was attacked under a bombardment at 06.15 the following morning. Brigadier-General Craufurd was clearly frustrated by what had happened latterly and his first recommendation was that: 'In operations where a

51 War Diary, HQ 18 Infantry Brigade, 'Narrative of Sequence of Events, November 20th & 21st', TNA WO95/1615.
52 War Diary, HQ 18 Infantry Brigade, 'Narrative of Sequence of Events, November 20th & 21st', TNA WO95/1615.

possible gap may be contemplated, wide latitude of discretion should be allowed to subordinate Commanders.'[53] There was thus a tension between a highly detailed and meticulously planned operation and the possibility of room for initiative. Sir Douglas Haig had wanted huroosh and exploitation, but the balance between prescriptive detail and more devolved command would only be achieved in the Hundred Days campaign.

Marden summarised: 'The Division had a most successful day, with very light casualties (about 650), capturing 28 officers and 1,227 other ranks prisoners, 23 guns, and between 40 and 50 machine-guns and many trench-mortars.'[54] It had indeed secured all its objectives. Overall, however, the problems faced by III Corps revealed inadequacies in planning. There were no infantry reserves to give 29th Division impetus forward, for instance. Further, insufficient thought had been given to getting tanks and cavalry across the canal – there were simply not enough (surviving) bridges. The tanks, which had been so successful in breaching the main Hindenburg position, had also proved vulnerable as they progressed. Thus, at Flesquières, all had been knocked out by gunfire, and the weight of the infantry attack was insufficient to carry the second position. By the end of the day, German resistance had stiffened, recovering from the initial shock, and the Masnières-Beaurevoir Line had not been taken (this being a further reason for the failure of the cavalry to advance). As Bryn Hammond notes: 'Guns, tanks and aircraft could not provide an adequate substitute for the presence of sufficient numbers of infantry.'[55]

In comparison with the limited movement at Loos, the Royal Engineers were able to fulfil more of the functions that *SS135* set out. 12 Field Company was attached to 18 Brigade, Major Williamson RE being located at brigade HQ with one section. No. 2 section went forward with five pack animals loaded with wire, but sustained casualties, Lieutenant Arthur Newland commanding dying of wounds.[56] Three wagons and two tool carts moved up to Ribécourt at midday loaded with picks, shovels, sandbags, and more wire, where they were no doubt delighted to discover three enemy pioneer dumps. Three strongpoints were constructed on the Premy Chapel Ridge. 459 Company was involved in trench bridging, two sections taking part in the assault whilst one section prepared a road for 24 Brigade RFA to get forward to Ribécourt and the other a track for pack animals. 509 Company had one section working on a mule transport track, and another on consolidation, whilst the 11th Leicesters worked on roads.

53 War Diary, HQ 18 Infantry Brigade, 'Narrative of Sequence of Events, November 20th & 21st', TNA WO95/1615.
54 Marden, op. cit. p.39.
55 Hammond, op. cit. p.194.
56 Twenty-five year-old Arthur Kenyon Newland had obtained a first-class degree in Civil and Mechanical Engineering and was working on building destroyers for Thorneycroft at Southampton before the war. He volunteered into the Honourable Artillery Company in December 1914, and was commissioned into the South Staffords in July 1915, transferring to the Royal Engineers in February 1916.

The following day, as Flesquières was occupied, 14th DLI pushed on with a squadron of the Queen's Bays to occupy Cantaing, and 1st Buffs cleared Noyelles. As the Guards fought to secure Fontaine, on the division's left, a half mile of the front was handed over to 29th Division. As Marden described, the division 'now held a rectangular strip, 2,500 yards by 7,000 yards, with the head at Cantaing and Noyelles, and the rear in the Hindenburg Main Line.' To the division's right, the 29th Division still head bridgeheads across the canal. Marden's description of the situation cannot be bettered:

> Comparing the position with the back of a man's left hand, the 6th Division occupied the third finger, the 29th Division the main finger, the 20th Division the index finger, the 12th Division the portion below the index finger down to the lower portion of the thumb when fully extended, the 55th Division occupied the thumb.[57]

Such was the position when the enemy hammer blow fell on 30th November.

German Counterattack – 30 November 1917

As the British brought their Cambrai offensive to a close after the failure to master the whole of the Bourlon Ridge, they had punched their way into a salient 'some nine miles wide and four miles deep, which was by no means easy to defend.'[58] Given the somewhat insecure tenure of the Bourlon position, 6th Division's possession of Cantaing and Noyelles was important in protecting the right flank of the formations there. However much German defensive practice had been modified on the Somme, and experimented with at Third Ypres, counter-attack to regain lost ground (which had already accounted for much costly self-inflicted attrition) was still a key part of German military doctrine. Therefore, on the morning of 24 November, the enemy began their planning for a counter-offensive, starting with a reorganisation and reinforcement of their forces, increasing the number of 'groups.' Ludendorff and Crown Prince Rupprecht met at the *Second Army* HQ at Le Cateau on the 27th and issued orders that the 'Eastern Groups' (Busigny and Caudry – seven divisions) would attack to capture Flesquières and Havrincourt Wood 'from the south in order to take the British in flank and rear.'[59] This would be followed by an attack by the 'Arras Group' from Bourlon Wood southwards.

It was not the case that the German attack was unexpected. Those on the ground were to varying degrees aware of preparations. As Lieutenant-Colonel Prior of the 9th Norfolks noted: 'Signs were not wanting that a more serious hostile attack was

57 Marden, op. cit. p.40.
58 W. Miles, *Military Operations France and Belgium 1917 – The Battle of Cambrai*, p.164.
59 Miles, op. cit. p.174.

pending.'[60] VII Corps, to the south of III Corps, and 55th Division in particular, were particularly clear on the matter, and had discussed this with Byng's HQ. As damning a statement as any in the Official History is the brief summary that: 'The Third Army issued no warning order, ordered no movement of reserves, took no steps to ensure that troops in the rear areas should be readily available.' It continued: 'On two occasions the III Corps, without result, had appealed to the Army for the relief of its tired divisions.'[61] Yet III Corps itself also issued no warning order. It was left to the divisional commanders to make do.

The blow fell first at 05.30 on VII Corps, and in particular 55th Division, the 'Busigny Group'[62] making particular inroads up the Banteux Ravine to take Villers Guislain, and for a while the plan to cut off the base of the salient looked very realisable, with the prospect of driving deep into the rear of III Corps. III Corps faced the 'Caudry Group', from the enemy left to right represented by *28th Division*, *220th Division*, *30th Division*, and *107th Division*. 12th Division lost Gonnelieu above the Banteux Ravine and Gouzeaucourt to its west, although the enemy were held up at the latter and the village was eventually retaken on the arrival of the Guards Division. 20th Division to the north of the 12th had a particular unfortunate day, being thrown back onto the slopes of Welsh Ridge. Marden, persisting with his left hand analogy described the German assault as 'driving the 20th and 12th Divisions on to the main finger except for a few posts, and occupying the thumb.'[63] Unfortunately, any significant reversal to the 20th put the 29th Division to its north in peril. The two brigades of 29th Division had their backs to water, being across the canal, and were in a particularly vulnerable position, but in a display of extraordinary resistance, the enemy were held. 'By gallant and vigorous leadership and the admirable fighting qualities of the troops the 29th Division had saved itself and in doing so had saved the 6th Division and the right of the IV Corps from a dangerous penetration of their right flank.'[64]

On 30 November 6th Division had 71 and 18 Brigades in line, 16 Brigade in reserve. 71 Brigade held a series of outposts in Noyelles, with a line of resistance in Nine Wood to the rear. 1st Leicestershire were on the right, 9th Suffolk on the left and 9th Norfolk in support, 2nd Sherwood Foresters being in reserve. 'The battle could be watched with great facility for observation from our Brigade H.Q. on the Premy Chapel Ridge.'[65] Lieutenant-Colonel Prior, who had woken 'very early sneezing violently and with … eyes streaming' from gas described how: 'Marcoing lies in a valley and', from his HQ in a sand pit in Nine Wood 'on the slopes on the

60 War Diary, 9th Battalion Norfolk Regiment, 'Diary of Lieutenant-Colonel B.H.L. Prior', TNA WO95/1623.
61 Miles, op. cit. p.169.
62 *XIII Reserve Corps.*
63 Marden, op. cit. p.40.
64 Miles, op. cit. p.210.
65 War Diary, HQ 71 Infantry Brigade, 30 November 1917, TNA WO95/1619.

other side we could see line after line of troops advancing.'[66] Brigade were aware of the simultaneous attack on Bourlon Wood and the line south of Masnières. The Suffolks could see the enemy advancing towards Fontaine, south-east of Bourlon Wood, whilst Prior and the Sherwood Foresters observed the advance toward Marcoing in their rear. 'We were being unmercifully shelled but the air was alive with enemy aircraft who were swooping down using their machine guns as well as directing their artillery fire.'[67] Marcoing, however, was not taken, and 'an attack by … *107th Infantry Division* against Noyelles … ground to a halt in the face of determined defence.'[68] This division, which had arrived from the Eastern Front only two days before the British attack, had been in line since 20 November and was 'very worn down.'[69] 18 Brigade's front at Cantaing was shelled, but similarly received no direct attack. The enemy intention had been for *107th Division* to surround Cantaing, but as it could make no progress, 6th Division remained safe. To the rear, 14th Durham Light Infantry were directed to take up a position where the main Hindenburg Line crossed Welsh Ridge, north-east of Villers Plouich, positioned to hold any further enemy penetration beyond the Banteux ravine and Masnières. The able Lieutenant-Colonel Rosher found himself in command of 2/5th and 2/6th Sherwood Foresters and two companies of Royal Engineers, in addition to his own battalion, but the mixed force was not called upon to fight that day.

Curiously, the most important action of 6th Division that day was fought by the 18 Brigade transport. They were actually in Gouzeaucourt when units of the *28th Division* entered and had been unaware of the extent of the enemy advance. Also present were the HQ and C Company, 11th Durham Light Infantry, the pioneers of 20th Division. The Durhams pulled back to the 'Brown Line', on a ridge 500 yards to the west of the village. Here they were joined by the assorted 18 Brigade party. Captain William Paul, adjutant of 1st West Yorkshire together with Captain Joseph Shea, the quartermaster of 2nd Durham Light Infantry and Captain Henry Roberts, quartermaster of 11th Essex, set about organising their 120 ORs, including mess sergeants, 'tailors and shoemakers.'[70] They formed the left of the makeshift defensive position, and held off the enemy until the Guards Division arrived and retook the village. Their resistance was at cost, however – Paul and Shea died of their wounds.

William Paul, who had been commissioned from quartermaster sergeant in December 1915 and who already been awarded the MC, was awarded the DSO for his part in this action. The citation reads:

66 War Diary, 9th Battalion Norfolk Regiment, 'Diary of Lieutenant-Colonel B.H.L. Prior', TNA WO95/1623.
67 War Diary, 9th Battalion Norfolk Regiment, 'Diary of Lieutenant-Colonel B.H.L. Prior', TNA WO95/1623.
68 J. Sheldon, *The German Army at Cambrai*, Kindle edition location 5593.
69 Sheldon, op. cit. location 5578.
70 War Diary, 2nd Battalion Durham Light Infantry, 30 November 1918, TNA WO95/1617.

> When the enemy was seen from the battalion transport lines to be advancing about 400 yards away, he at once collected all battalion details, held back the enemy at close range, and held the position for four hours until relieved, thus enabling the units in rear to reform. He was severely wounded but refused to withdraw until relieved. He showed splendid courage and determination.[71]

In the early part of 1916 the Prince of Wales had shown interest in the battalion's transport lines and had marked out Paul as 'a grand type of man.' He was right – 'In this case, the "Royal Boy" showed wonderful judgement of men.'[72] Joseph Patrick Lambert Shea, MC and bar, had fought in the Boer War and was awarded the Distinguished Conduct Medal 'as Colour Sergeant of K Company, when he was the first man up Vaal Krantz during the attack on 5 February 1900.'[73] The citation for the bar to his MC reads:

> The enemy were seen from the transport lines to be suddenly advancing, and many men from various units were withdrawing through the lines. Having got the transport away, he led all available men of his battalion forward in support and command until the arrival of reinforcements. He fearlessly exposed himself in pointing out the situation to the officer commanding the relieving troops and was severely wounded in so doing.

By the time he was relieved 'Joey' had allegedly accounted for 19 of the enemy with his revolver.

The last of the trio of officers, Henry Shred Roberts, was also awarded the MC. His citation reads:

> When the enemy were seen from the brigade transport lines to be advancing about 400 yards away and many scattered parties of different units passed through the lines, after seeing his transport moved off in good order under heavy shelling, he assembled all available details and reinforced the remainder of the brigade details. He captured six prisoners, and after holding the Ridge for four hours, the two senior officers being wounded, he took command, and with his party offered a strong resistance to the enemy.[74]

This motley crew of heroes performed one of the most valuable services on the 30th. A group of several hundred men fought for a number of hours, supported on neither

71 *London Gazette*, 5 July 1918.
72 War Diary, 1st Battalion West Yorkshire Regiment, Diary of Colonel W.T.C. Huffam, TNA WO95/1618.
73 *DLI Medal Collection* <dlicollection.durham.gov.uk/pgFullBiography.aspx?&Theme=Default&BioId=10978> (Accessed 3 September 2018).
74 *Edinburgh Gazette*, 8 July 1918, p.2393.

flank, and held up the enemy advance which, fortunately, had become somewhat disorganized and had sustained significant casualties, particularly amongst officers. 'It seemed', according to the British Official Historian, 'that a priceless opportunity was lost by the Germans.'[75]

16 Brigade, meanwhile, was in reserve in the Hindenburg main and support lines. A staff officer from 29th Division reported to 6th Division's HQ at 09.00 that their divisional headquarters north-east of Gouzeaucourt had been captured. As this was two miles to the right rear of 6th Division's HQ this news was alarming. Marden therefore ordered 16 Brigade onto the ridge between Beaucamps and Gouzeaucourt at Dead Man's Corner, and General Walker to report to the GOC 29th Division. Walker must have regarded this with trepidation, the divisional HQ in question having been captured, and, indeed, he and his brigade-major, Captain Wellington, were nearly taken prisoner. Such was the degree of confusion – all the telephone lines to III Corps had by now been cut. Further orders arrived for the brigade to retake Gouzeaucourt and Walker, locating tanks at Beaucamps, asked for their help. They were about to advance when patrols reported that the Irish Guards had beaten them to it. Walker, now having telephonic communication with his divisional HQ, was ordered to advance on Cemetery (or Quentin) Ridge between Gonnelieu and La Vaquerie, 1,000 yards to the east of Gouzeaucourt and Villers Plouich to the north. The advance faltered as dark fell, tanks being unable to cross a sunken road, and the brigade paused to consolidate. Marden now proposed 'a surprise attack by moonlight' to seize the ridge before the enemy could reinforce it.[76] The attack was launched at 01.00 on the 1 December without artillery support (all guns having been captured), in conjunction with 20th Division, but failed. Lieutenant-Colonel Blunt of 2nd York & Lancaster noted laconically: 'Buffs lost their way, KSLI did not push home.' In lamenting his 61 casualties he added: 'We got hung up by M.G. fire.'[77] The Guards and the tanks took the position at 06.30 under a barrage, one of a series of rather uncoordinated attacks across the whole front that disrupted the German *Second Army*'s plans for a renewed assault on the 1st, which in themselves were confused, as might be expected on the day after a major attack.

Later, on the 1st, in the north of the division's area, the enemy launched an assault as part of these uncoordinated efforts on the very left of 18 Brigade's front, falling on 2nd Durham Light Infantry at Cantaing and 59th Division to the left, south of Fontaine. The enemy were caught debouching from La Folie Wood in front of Cantaing at 13.45, and the attack was broken up by both artillery and machine-gun and rifle fire. 71 Brigade at Noyelles, Nine Wood and Marcoing were subject to a five hour bombardment and, more alarmingly, were informed that the enemy had broken through 29th Division's defensive flank south of Marcoing. Whilst this was not

75 Miles, op. cit. p.188.
76 Marden, op. cit. p.41.
77 A. St. J. Blunt, Private Papers, 1 December 1917, IWM Docs 16149.

correct, again reflecting how good quality intelligence was sometimes hard to obtain in the confusion, on the 2nd 16 Brigade were moved from Highland Ridge, and took over the line of 87 Brigade, 29th Division, which had been under considerable pressure on the eastern side of the canal at Marcoing. 14th DLI, who had been attached from 18 Brigade, were to hold the southern loop across the canal, 1st King's Shropshire Light taking over the northern part. Whilst the enemy had been unable to renew their attacks on the 2nd, it was an unhealthy position, exposed to fire from every direction bar the west. Defences were sketchy and not wired.

At 10.30 on the 3rd, after a heavy bombardment, the *107th Division* attacked in conjunction with *28th Division's* attempt to take La Vaquerie to the south. It was to be virtually the last of the enemy set-piece attacks. After asking for artillery support, the DLI found all communication with brigade cut. Their right company was driven out of its trenches but retook them. On the left 1st KSLI repulsed the attack. At 11.30, after another heavy bombardment, the right was driven in again, and Captain Arthur Lascelles,[78] who had led the first counterattack, was taken prisoner. He would be awarded the Victoria Cross for his efforts that day. His VC citation reads:

> For most conspicuous bravery, initiative and devotion to duty when in command of his company in a very exposed position. After a very heavy bombardment during which Capt. Lascelles was wounded, the enemy attacked in strong force but was driven off, success being due in great degree to the fine example set by this officer, who, refusing to allow his wound to be dressed, continue to encourage his men and organised the defence. Shortly afterwards the enemy again attacked and captured the trench, taking several of his men prisoners. Capt. Lascelles at once jumped on to the parapet and followed by the remainder of his company, 12 men only, rushed across under very heavy machine-gun fire and drove over 60 of the enemy back, thereby saving a most critical situation. He was untiring in reorganising the position, but shortly afterwards the enemy again attacked and captured the trench and Capt. Lascelles, who escaped later. The remarkable determination and gallantry of this officer in the course of operations, during which he received two further wounds, afforded an inspiring example to all.[79]

78 Arthur Moore Lascelles (1880-1918) VC MC was educated at Malvern and Uppingham Schools, and Bangor College, before going to Edinburgh University to study medicine. He abandoned his studies in 1902 and emigrated to South Africa where he enlisted in the Cape Mounted Rifles, with whom he fought during the first months of the war against Boer rebels, and in German South West Africa. He returned to England with his wife and son and was commissioned in 3rd Durham Light Infantry in December 1915. He was wounded on the Somme and was awarded the Military Cross in June 1917 leading a daylight trench raid near Loos. Following his wounding at Cambrai, despite his right arm still suffering disability, he re-joined the 15th DLI to be killed on 7 November 1918, crossing the River Sambre.

79 *London Gazette*, 11 January 1918, p.723.

Lascelles later described how at the time of the 10.30 attack 'the position had become so precarious that had my company given way it would have meant that the whole of the battalion would have been enfiladed and the Boches enabled to get round to the rear.' When the enemy renewed the attack 'there was no question of retiring – it could not be done. Very soon the Boche smashed my right bombing post, which enabled him to enfilade the whole trench occupied by my company. Two machine guns were in action, and ... the trench for a distance on the right of 250 yards was non-existent.' Lascelles was now in a difficult position, attacked both from the front whilst 'about 50 yards to my rear I saw a number of Germans advancing.' It was at this point that he jumped on the parapet and made his frontal charge. During this he was badly wounded in the elbow and weak from loss of blood was taken prisoner. 'When I recovered consciousness ... a big Hun took possession of my glasses and all I had, struck me with his fist and kicked me.'[80] When the Germans were driven back once more, this despite the inability of 6th Division to summon more artillery assistance, Lascelles escaped in the confusion. 1st KSLI's trenches had now been penetrated, and fierce hand-to-hand fighting was taking place. Further attacks at 12.15 and 12.45 were made. SOS rifle grenades from 14th DLI again received no response from the artillery. At 12.15, the DLI's right flank was held only by a bomb block, but with no bombs to defend it. By 12.45, when the enemy could be seen emerging from Masnières, the battalion was 'practically surrounded.' Lieutenant-Colonel Rosher stated that he liaised with Lieutenant-Colonel Cyril Winterscale, of the KSLI and 'we decided that the position was untenable', and without support, the only solution was to evacuate across the damaged Marcoing railway bridge.[81] This they achieved, the KSLI reporting 'desperate fighting' in the retreat,[82] some of their number having to swim the canal. At 16.00, however, reinforced by two companies of 8th Bedfords, and under the orders of 88 Brigade (which was temporarily under the command of 6th Division), 14th DLI crossed the canal once more, to meet the enemy manning their old positions. Out of bombs, there was little that could be done, and at 22.15, Rosher received orders to return once more to the west bank, and after they had withdrawn, the bridges were blown. 14th DLI had suffered 6 officers killed, one missing believed killed and seven wounded. The other ranks had suffered 33 killed, 109 wounded, three missing and wounded, 45 missing believed killed, and 72 others missing. The final casualty total of 276 was out of a fighting strength of 450 – over 60 percent casualties. The war diary noted: 'The number of missing does not represent prisoners. Nearly all these men were killed and buried during the severe fighting and heavy bombardments,

80 Interview with the *Western Mail* quoted at http://www.lightinfantry.me.uk/vcamlasclles.htm, (accessed 10 September 2018).

81 39 year-old Cyril Francis Barroneau Winterscale DSO had been a lieutenant with 2nd Battalion King's Shropshire Light Infantry in August 1914 and commanded the 1st Battalion between October 1916 and February 1918.

82 War Diary, 1st Battalion King's Shropshire Light Infantry, 3 December 1917, TNA WO95/1609.

but owing to the continuance of the fighting it was not possible to identify them.'[83] Hugh Boxer, still with 2nd DLI, reflected with some truth that had he still been with his unit, 'I might well be na-poo by now.' [84] 1st KSLI's casualties were much lighter. One officer had been killed and one was missing, whilst two officers were admitted to the Field Ambulance with 'shock.' Approximately, 20 ORs had been killed, 30 wounded, and 40 missing. It had been a titanic struggle in miniature.

Marden represented the concern as to the untenability of his position to III Corps but learnt that during the day General Byng had selected a rear line which corresponded roughly with the Hindenburg support system and included the defences of Flesquières. At 09.30 on the 4th the withdrawal of 6th Division from Cantaing, Noyelles, Nine Wood and Marcoing began, being complete on the morning of the 5th. On the 10th, the division was withdrawn from the line to rest in the Basseux area south-west of Arras. The rest was welcome. Lieutenant-Colonel Prior painted a picture of exhaustion: 'A dirtier looking crowd than the 9th Norfolk Regiment were on the night they came out of line would have been hard to find. Just four weeks without a change, living and sleeping anywhere and anyhow, fighting, marching & digging without respite.'[85]

Conclusion

On 20 November 1917, the well prepared 6th Division had performed as effectively as any other that day, achieving all its objectives. During the counterattacks of 30 November to 2 December, it had mainly escaped the brunt of the fighting, as the main enemy thrust had fallen to the north and south. The division had held an increasingly narrow salient, and worryingly so – any collapse on either side risked their being surrounded. Marden recorded that divisional HQ was 'three times shelled out of its Headquarters between 30th November and 9th December.'[86] The most frantic and desperate fighting of the whole German counterattack suffered by the division was that experienced by the transport on 30 November and 1st King's Shropshire Light Infantry and 14th Durham Light Infantry on 3 December. Both were triumphs of doggedness rather than tactical sophistication.

There was inevitably an intense sense of British disappointment – Lieutenant-Colonel Prior described how 'it is a hateful thing to have to give up hard won ground.'[87] The enemy attempt to encircle the Third Army in their newly-won salient

83 War Diary, 14th Battalion Durham Light Infantry, 'Report on Operations of 3rd December 1917', TNA WO95/1617.
84 Boxer, op. cit.
85 War Diary, 9th Battalion Norfolk Regiment, 'Diary of Lieutenant-Colonel B.H.L. Prior', TNA WO95/1623.
86 Marden, op. cit. p.43.
87 War Diary, 9th Battalion Norfolk Regiment, 'Diary of Lieutenant-Colonel B.H.L. Prior', TNA WO95/1623.

had, however, had failed. This reflected 'the near impossibility in practice of achieving a smooth transition from defence to counter-attack.'[88] Impetus had been quickly lost, and as with the British plans for 20 November, detailed consideration for exploitation was flawed, particularly from the logistical point of view. It was, yet again, a reminder that 'break in' could be achieved, whist 'breakthrough' could not. A template had been laid for both the initial success and later failure of the opening German Spring Offensive of 21 March 1918, in the frustration of which 6th Division would play a heroic part.

88 Sheldon, op. cit. location 6709.

9

'The Skill to go Forward':[1] Training in 6th Division

Out of the line, the troops of 6th Division spent their time cleaning and re-fitting, undergoing inspections, and resting. Sometimes they were at play. Private Percy Jones, 1/16th London, recorded on 14 November 1915, whilst the division was in the Ypres Salient:

> We adjourned to the 'Fancies' ... an institution in Poperinghe ... they give a good variety entertainment, the party consisting of two men from our battalion, an ex-Carl Rosa man from the RFA and four others ... they picked up two girl artistes at Armentières and brought them along. The show is given in a disused picture palace, and a jolly good show it is too ... The audience is naturally not very critical, but the show is really bright and breezy, some of the original numbers being very clever. There is a delightful scene featuring a chant in praise of the rum ration set to the music of Amy-Woodford-Findon's 'Love Lyrics.' Our man Dick Horne is a great comedian his speciality being the renowned Westminsters' song of 'Old Roger Rum.' The two girls sing sweetly enough in quite intelligible English.[2]

Jones further described that there was a 6th Division cinema in Poperinghe and a 6th Division Club. Away from the serious business of war, the division thus provided a range of opportunities for recreation. Recreation, of course, was about maintaining morale. Often when out of the line the division was involved in labour, but it was also engaged in the crucial activity of training.

Simon Robbins has claimed that 'Throughout the war the comparative low level of training achieved by the troops and their junior leadership was a serious problem.'

1 General Staff, *SS135, The Division in Attack,* November 1918.
2 P.H. Jones, Private Papers, IWM Docs 12253. The original Carl Rosa Opera Company operated from 1873 to 1960. The 'Fancies' were formed during the period the division were in line at Armentières.

He quotes General Sir Reginald Stephens (5th Division) complaining in October 1917 that 'most of our troubles have come from our lack of training.' General Sir Ivor Maxse blamed the reverse at Cambrai as due to 'lack of battle training'; and that old 6th Division stalwart, General Sir George Harper (IV Corps) was still grousing in September 1918 that problems in mobile warfare reflected the troops having 'not reached a sufficiently high standard.' This touches upon the whole notion of the 'deskilling' of the army, the large scale of the casualties suffered by the Regular Army in 1914 stripping out experience. Further, General Sir Aylmer Haldane (3rd Division) took the view in April 1916 that, due to rapid promotion, 'most of the brigadiers and COs now are not competent to teach.'[3] Indeed, within units, the quality of junior leadership resulting from attrition (and, indeed, skill levels in general) would remain an issue with which battalions were playing catch-up with throughout the war. The issue was casualties, consequent churn, and the quality of reinforcements.

As noted in Chapter One, the delayed departure of the division for the Western Front allowed for training in Great Britain, which brought the reservists up to scratch – indeed, 2nd Leinster recorded 18 days of training before they embarked for France.[4] The realities of movement and then trench holding for the overstretched BEF in 1914 and a good deal of 1915 were such, however, that little or no time was available for this activity. On 4 December 1915, 71 Brigade bemoaned the restrictions on training: 'No men being available for any training excepting the machine gun sections and the battalion grenadiers. Nothing in the way of training can be attempted. There is no ground available for training the snipers in the use of telescopic sights.'[5] This was the result of 'heavy working parties.'[6] Undoubtedly, overall, battalions spent more time in labouring than they did in training during the war. 71 Brigade, for instance, on 20 June 1916 recorded '1600 men on working parties every 24 hours', approximately half its infantry strength.[7] On 6 November 1916, in the midst of 8 days of brigade training, it was noted 'about 1800 men taken for working parties under 21st & 24th Divisions.'[8] As Robbins notes, 'as late as October 1918 a common complaint by Divisional and Corps Commanders was the lack of time and opportunity to train their men.'[9] In the early part of 1915, however, working on the age-old principle of experience being the best teacher, the division was 'training' other units, Territorial, New Army and Dominion, in terms of inducting them into the ways of trench warfare.[10]

3 S. Robbins, *British Generalship on the Western Front 1914-18*, p.85.
4 War Diary, 2nd Battalion Leinster Regiment, August-September 1914, TNA WO95/1612.
5 War Diary, HQ 71 Infantry Brigade, 4 December 1915, TNA WO95/1619.
6 War Diary, HQ 71 Infantry Brigade, 7 December 1915, TNA WO95/1619.
7 War Diary, HQ 71 Infantry Brigade, 20 June 1916, WO95/1619.
8 War Diary, HQ 71 Infantry Brigade, 6 December 1916, WO95/1619.
9 Robbins, op. cit. p.89.
10 See Chapter 3.

Unit Training

Most training took place at platoon, company, and battalion level. In June 1917, GHQ issued *SS152 Instructions for the Training of the British Armies in France.*[11] This reminded COs that they were (as they always had been) responsible for the training of all officers, NCOs and troops in their units, and that no form of training which COs could carry out was to be relegated to a school. Robbins states that by the time this pamphlet appeared, every battalion 'was required … to retain a permanent Instructional Staff, which did not go into battle', these being men who had trained at the Corps and Army schools.[12] *SS152* recommended that in the 24 days of a four week training period for a battalion, sequentially, four days should be devoted to section, platoon and company training, five days in platoon and company training, and two days in company training, with seven devoted to battalion training, and four days 'at disposal of Brigadier', with one 'at disposal of Divisional or Brigade Commander.'[13] Whether this ideal was ever lived up to in practice is impossible to know.

Unfortunately, very few battalion training programmes survive. 2nd Sherwood Foresters are unique in leaving the details of a three day training programme, 23-25 November 1915.[14] The programme for Tuesday 23rd was set out as follows:

7.30 to 8am	Physical Training, Running Drill, Rapid Marching etc.
9.30 – 10.15	Squad Drill under Section Com(mande)rs.
10.15 – 11am	Platoon and Co(mpan)y Drill.
11 – 11.30	Musketry under Sect(ion) Com(mander)s. Fire Control, rapid loading & firing.
11.30 to 12.30	Route march.
2 – 2.30	Physical Training.
2.30 – 3.30	Squad Drill & Musketry.

Such a programme reflected the training of any recruit in 1914, including physical training, route marching, squad drill, and musketry. It is, however, a recurrent theme of the historiography of the 'deskilling' of the BEF that the cult of the bomb asserted itself in 1916 at the expense of skill in musketry.[15] It is therefore of note that a Regular unit in 1915 was putting such effort into musketry practice as 1916 dawned. Rifle practice would remain an important feature of the division's training activities.

14th DLI left an example of a day's training for 10 January 1916 that not only demonstrates this, but emphasises skills training in new weaponry:

11 General Staff, *SS152 Instructions for the Training of the British Armies in France*, June 1917.
12 Robbins, op. cit. p.91.
13 *SS152*, p.59.
14 War Diary, 2nd Battalion Sherwood Foresters, November 1915, TNA WO95/1624.
15 See Robbins, op. cit. pp.91-2.

Morning	Before Breakfast – Physical Drill 20 minutes.
	After Breakfast – Kit inspection by CO. Musketry Drill, special attention being paid to rapid aiming and firing. Gas helmet drill.
Afternoon	Route Marching.
	6 men and 1 officer per Company who had no experience in the Maxim and Lewis guns instructed in the Machine Gun by the MG Officer who attached 2 men of the Machine Gunners to the six men from each Company.[16]

Reflecting both *SS152*'s assertion that training should be about building morale as well as developing skill, 9th Norfolk gave a broad description of a period of training in August 1917:

> The scheme of training was of the following general character. Three days were allotted for the inspection of kit, rifles, equipment, clothing etc. Then came training proper. During the morning all men trained with their own platoons in general company work, such as close and extended order drill, musketry, bayonet fighting & physical training & tactical handling of platoons. By this means, it was hoped to create an 'esprit de platoon' & and 'esprit de company' & to enable platoon officers & NCOs to arrive at a thorough knowledge of the capabilities & the limitations of the men under them. As the training progressed one or two mornings a week were to be devoted to battalion exercises in semi-open warfare. The afternoons were devoted to specialist training under either battalion or company officers & NCOs. The time allotted for this work was probably inadequate. Wednesday & Saturday afternoons & Sunday were observed as holidays. Much time was devoted to recreation. A football league was inaugurated, Brigade sports, a Divisional gymkhana & a Divisional rifle meeting & a Divisional tactical competition were held. Inter-platoon & company football & cricket matches were played. Possibly the men would have derived more pleasure & benefit if the less pretentious games last mentioned had been more numerous & the others less.[17]

The battalion diarist also recorded training activities 14-31 December 1917, when the unit came out of line from Cambrai:

> As a rule, the mornings were devoted to company work and the afternoons to specialists. Drill, physical training and bayonet fighting, musketry and the elementary practices of open warfare comprised the morning work. One company was on the range each day and an attempt was made to allow each man

16 War Diary, 14th Battalion Durham Light Infantry, 10 January 1916, TNA WO95/1617.
17 War Diary, 9th Battalion Norfolk Regiment, August 1917, TNA WO95/1623.

> to fire a few rounds with the Lewis Gun. In the afternoon at first all the NCOs and later a few of the junior NCOs received special instruction under the RSM. The officers in the earlier half of the period attended demonstrations and lectures in the afternoon and in the latter half supervised the afternoon training of their companies. Each company detailed a special party of 1 officer, 1 NCO and 9 men for wiring. The party practiced the construction of the double-apron pattern of wire entanglements in the afternoons.[18]

Not only was there thus the emphasis on training in the rifle and Lewis gun, 1917 and 1918 (and even the period just prior to its debut on the Somme in September 1916) saw the division training for open warfare. It is a further trope of the historiography that the BEF became too 'trench-minded' in its mentality, and it is clear that 6th Division never lost sight of this.

The descriptive comments in war diaries reflect the increasing sophistication in training over time. There was, however, always a strong emphasis on musketry which, despite the proliferation of automatic weaponry, intensified as the war progressed. 14th Durham Light Infantry had 60 snipers trained as early as December 1915. In July 1916 11th Essex recorded training with Lewis gun, signalling, bombing classes, young NCOs under the Regimental Sergeant Major, and practice in consolidating a crater.[19] On 5 October 1916, 2nd Durham Light Infantry noted that 'the battalion was trained by companies–physical training, drill, companies in attack, training of NCOs & specialists',[20] thus indicating the growing awareness of the need for good junior leadership and the growth of specialism. Fourth Army's Tactical Schemes were issued by GHQ as *SS159* in May 1917,[21] 'setting realistic exercises for Company, Platoon and Section commanders to discuss, undertake and solve both indoors and outdoors.'[22] In terms of practising attack, lessons from other divisions were also being circulated. Thus on 4 August 1916 in 8th Bedfords, 'Lt E. R. W. Draisey lectured to all officers and NCOs on lessons learned and methods used in the attack by 4th Division.'[23]

There had been much tactical experimentation undertaken by the Army during the Somme offensive. After-action reports passed upwards through brigade, division and corps to army led to a bottom-up distillation of wisdom. As a result, the winter of 1916-17 saw the production of new military manuals that would change the offensive tactics of the BEF's infantry. *SS143, Instructions for the Training of Platoons for Offensive*

18 War Diary, 9th Battalion Norfolk Regiment, 14-31 December 1917, TNA WO95/1623.
19 War Diary, 11th Battalion Essex Regiment, July 1916, TNA WO95/1616.
20 War Diary, 2nd Battalion Durham Light Infantry, 5 October 1916, TNA WO95/1617.
21 General Staff, *SS159, Notes on Tactical Schemes Compiled by Fourth Army*, May 1917.
22 Robbins, op. cit. p.93.
23 War Diary, 8th Battalion Bedfordshire Regiment, 4 August 1916, TNA WO95/1611. Edwin Roland Watts Draisey, the 21 year-old battalion Machine Gun Officer, would be dead a month later. Commissioned on 24 December 1914, he was killed on 15 September 1916 at the Quadrilateral, Ginchy.

Action 1917, laid the foundations for the way the infantry would fight until the end of the war – it, and allied documents, would be the closest the Army came to long-shunned doctrine.[24] Emphasis was placed upon infantry being able to fight its way forward independently of artillery support as a battle developed, bringing to bear the new range of infantry weapons on the enemy in conjunction with each other. At the outbreak of war, the infantry had been represented by riflemen. *SS143* promoted the self-contained platoon comprising a small HQ and four sections of specialists. The attack was to be led by bomb and rifle sections, with the rifle grenade and Lewis gun sections following close behind. Upon contact with the enemy, the rifles and the bombers were to seek out the enemy flank and attack with fire, bayonet and bomb. The rifle grenadiers and Lewis gun teams were to attempt to suppress enemy fire, allowing the other sections to press home their attack. This small unit flexible use of arms placed emphasis on the initiative of junior officers. Emphasising confidence in the use of and co-operation of weapons, *SS143* stated: 'The matter of control by even Company leaders on the battlefield is now so difficult that the smaller formations i.e. platoon, and section commanders must be trained to take the initiative, without waiting for orders.'

Coming out of the line on 18 February 1917, 6th Division recorded 'reorganisation of battalions, companies and platoons carried out', in accordance with the new strictures. Platoons were to be organized in four sections: 'No. 1 and 4 sections, riflemen sections each with 2 rifle grenades. No. 2, the Lewis gun section consisting of NCO, 6 Lewis gunners and 2 snipers. No. 3, the Bombing section, 1 NCO and 9 OR, 2 of whom to be Rifle grenadiers.' From 18 to 27 February, the division carried out training in the new formations.[25] On 22 February 2nd York & Lancaster 'executed a small scheme in front of GOC 6th Division and all the battalion commanders in the brigade to show and discuss the new reorganisation.'[26] The 8th Bedfordshire recorded on 19 March: 'Companies practicing by platoon new formation for attack laid down in SS144' (the diarist having failed to get his numbering right), and 'Companies practising attack (SS144) using Lewis gun fire and using rifle grenades.'[27] 11th Essex decided on this reorganisation that: '4th platoon in each company to consist of the untrained men now at 6th Division training area at CHOCQUES', having in January formed a 5th 'Training Company', with three officers and three NCOs from each company.[28]

24 Modified in 1918.
25 War Diary, HQ 6th Infantry Division, 18-27 February 1917, TNA WO95/1583.
26 War Diary, HQ 6th Infantry Division, 22 February 1917, TNA WO95/1581.
27 War Diary, 8th Battalion Bedfordshire Regiment, 19 March 1917, TNA WO95/1611.
28 War Diary 11th Battalion Essex Regiment, January and February 1917, TNA WO95/1614.

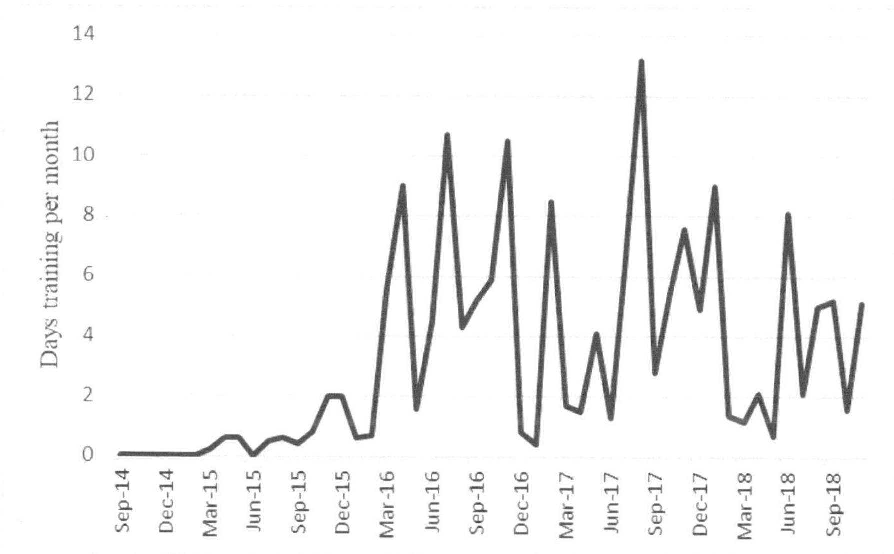

Table 9.1: Average days training per month of units in 6th Division.

Excluding route marching, from September 1914 to the Armistice, 18 Brigade spent 12 percent of its time in training.[29] 16 Brigade spent 9 percent of its time thus engaged, and 18 and 71 Brigade spent 11 percent of their time training. These should be taken as minimum figures, and the differences between the brigades are likely not significant – the war diarists of 1st Buffs of 16 Brigade almost certainly under-recorded training, and 9th Suffolk of 71 Brigade were omitted from the analysis as their diarists almost never recorded this activity.[30] Table 9.1 Shows seven peaks in training activities. April and June 1916, October 1916, March and August 1917, November/December 1917 and early 1918, and June 1918. The period of training in June through to September 1916 reflects the Division's likely then actual engagement in the Somme offensive. Thus on 14 June 14th Durham Light Infantry pursued brigade exercises in 'attack on trenches', including four to six Lewis guns;[31] and on 9 September (the division never have done this in action), 1st Shropshire Light Infantry recorded: 'Battalion practises attacking behind a "creeping barrage" which lifts 50 yards every minute.'[32]

29 Based on days in the war diaries in which training was recorded.
30 Figures are pro-rated to take account of this.
31 War Diary, 14th Battalion Durham Light Infantry, June 1916, TNA WO95/1617.
32 War Diary, 1st Battalion Shropshire Light Infantry, 9 September 1916, TNA WO95/1609.

8th Bedfordshire similarly noted on 9 September: 'Battalion training in the attack on trenches, moving closely under the artillery barrage'; and the following day: 'Battalion training in the attack in open warfare – moving over the open in extended lines, thickening the front line under cover of Stokes mortar barrage and then pressing home the assault.'[33] The fact that there was further peak of training in October 1916 reflects the large number of replacements that the division had been forced to absorb in terms of its losses in mid-September. This would always be the case, however – there would be constant rounds of basic training due to churn, underpinning specialist training. 9th Norfolk noted in the period between 2 and 10 May 1917: 'Chief attention was paid to specialists as, owing to heavy casualties, the battalion was in them much under establishment.'[34] Musketry remained very important, and in July 1917 11th Essex recorded: 'Each company having 8 targets on range for 4 hours', every man firing 80 rounds.[35] The period of training in August 1917 reflects the fact that the division was out of the line. The activities at this juncture included contact aeroplane schemes and attacks under mortar and machine gun barrages. The last big peak of training in November 1917 indicates, of course, the preparation for the Battle of Cambrai. 2nd Sherwood Foresters, however, enjoyed a good period of training in December 1917 and January 1918. Between 22 and 31 December: 'The training of the battalion has been more intense than in the preceding one. Every company has fired a course on the range with rifles & Lewis Guns. During the latter part of the week special emphasis has been put on wiring, each company having told off a special wiring squad.' Between 12 and 19 January 1918 it was noted: 'During this week rather more advanced training was carried out, the counter stroke especially being practised.'[36] There are smaller peaks at the end of March 1916 (when the division was out of line) and September 1918, prior to the division's involvement in the Hundred Days campaign. 1st Leicestershire recorded between 3 and 10 September 1918 five days 'open warfare' training, then 'attack practice ... taking a line of trenches under a barrage, advancing in open warfare formation, enveloping and capturing a strong point.' There was also a 'tactical scheme for officers & NCOs: "Attack on a Village" ... demonstration by 1 company, envelopment by 1 company on each flank, 1 company in reserve.'[37]

33 War Diary 8th Battalion Bedfordshire Regiment, 9-10 September 1916, TNA WO95/1611.
34 War Diary, 9th Battalion Norfolk Regiment, 2-10 May 1917, TNA WO95/1623.
35 War Diary, 11th Battalion Essex Regiment, July 1917, TNA WO95/1614.
36 War Diary 2nd Battalion Sherwood Foresters, December 1917 & January 1918, TNA WO95/1624.
37 War Diary 1st Battalion Leicestershire Regiment, 3-10 September 1918, TNA WO95/1621.

Brigade Schemes

As GHQ's projected pattern for battalion training indicates, brigadiers were expected to have a weekly input. Severe limitations were placed on training above unit level by line holding. 18 Brigade managed nine days training as a brigade during the war, these during 1916 and 1917. It carried out its first brigade scheme on 10 April 1916. This was essentially a scheme for officers, and it is the only scheme for 18 Brigade for which details survive. The general idea was that the enemy, having been defeated, were withdrawing. The brigade was to advance to clear a wood, lightly held, well wired and with opposing machine guns. Officers had to compose orders to reconnoitre and decide on formations for the attack. There were to be two battalions, one comprised of 1st West Yorkshire and 14th Durham Light Infantry, the other 2nd DLI and 11th Essex. Interestingly, the wood was to be assaulted directly, rather than pinched out, as future learning would dictate.[38] The second brigade scheme took place on a prepared training ground in June. Between the 24th and the 27th, the units of the brigade successively practiced platoons and companies in attack, and then attack as battalions as a complete unit. During the following three days the brigade practiced the attack as a whole. On 29 July a brigade tactical scheme was held for 'all COs and 2nd-in-commands and they in turn hold schemes for all their officers.'[39] This was undoubtedly a preparation for moving south to take part in the Somme offensive. In the period between the weeks on the Ancre and the move to Ginchy, two further days of brigade schemes were carried out, one involving practising contact patrol work with an aeroplane. The next brigade 'field day' was 9 December 1916, consisting of 'attack practice', when it was noted 'the work of the battalions is good.'[40] The brigade carried out another tactical exercise on 6th August 1917, and on 15 October practiced over a taped course for further operations against Lens. The last brigade exercise was carried out in preparation for the Battle of Cambrai on 12 November 1917 when:

> The brigade carried out a tactical exercise between BEAUFORT and LIGNEREUIL. The 14th DLI acted as enemy, 1st W. Yorks attacked on the right, 11th Essex on the left & 2nd DLI were in support. The latter were used to form a defensive left flank later in the operation. A contact aeroplane succeeded in dropping a map of the situation … at B[riga]de report centre.[41]

16 Infantry Brigade managed five days of brigade schemes. The brigade-major summarised at the end of April 1916 (again reflecting the training needs generated by churn): 'The early part of the month was spent in rest during which tactical exercises,

38 War Diary, HQ 18 Infantry Brigade, April 1916, TNA WO95/1614.
39 War Diary, HQ 18 Infantry Brigade, 29 July 1916, TNA WO95/1614.
40 War Diary, HQ 18 Infantry Brigade, 9 December 1916, TNA WO95/1614.
41 War Diary, HQ 18 Infantry Brigade, 12 November 1917, TNA WO95/1615.

physical training and the instruction of recruit officers and drafts was carried out.'[42] The nature of their first brigade scheme was different to that of 18 Brigade, carried out during the same period. The first purpose of the exercise carried out on 7 and 8 April 1916 was to 'give Officers practice in reconnoitring a position for defence' in relation to a hostile force, strength unknown, carried out by officers of each battalion and the Machine Gun Companies. Brigadier-General Nicholson went along the line receiving reconnaissance reports. The units of the brigade were to arrive on this line the following day, moving by different routes and taking up defensive positions.[43] It can only be observed that this was an exercise that had little bearing on the reality that faced the brigade, in that it represented an advance to contact, the last opportunities for which had disappeared in October 1914. When the division was out of line in June/July, perhaps because 18 Brigade were utilising the training area, there were no brigade schemes. However, on 2 September, on the Somme, the whole brigade carried out the aeroplane contact exercise 'with flares, discs, visual periscopes & calico sheets. Communication was easily established and messages brought back and dropped at B(riga)de HQ.'[44] On the 5th there was a further seven hour brigade scheme of 'attacking over 1½ miles & forming a defensive flank in conjunction with casualty clearing scheme.'[45] (This indicates a clear emphasis on mobile warfare, the training taking place in the same month that Major-General R.B. Stephens was addressing the Fourth Army School for Officers on the subject that 'men are inclined to be trench bound', and having taken an enemy position were 'quite satisfied to sit in it.')[46] A brigade scheme was mooted for 25 July 1917, but the brigade went into line instead, and, rather bizarrely, a brigade 'paper chase' took place on the 22nd instead. As the division prepared for the Battle of Cambrai, on 13 November there was a further brigade attack scheme.

Trevor Harvey, in his study of brigadier-generals at the Battle of Arras suggests that: 'Their greatest contribution was their perpetual struggle to ensure that the officers and ORs of their battalions were adequate in numbers and possessed of individual skills, tactical acuity and strength of morale sufficient to meet the next challenge of the battlefield.' Churn meant that 'their task was repeatedly to recreate the capability of their brigades to fight.' Brigades were supposed to have classes constantly in progress for musketry; Lewis gunnery; signalling; scouting, observation and sniping; dug-out making; bombing; and 3-inch Stokes mortar gunnery. The challenge for brigadiers, however, 'was not simply a matter of ensuring that adequate and appropriate training schemes were put in place and implemented for their battalions.' It was also to

42 War Diary, HQ 6th Infantry Division, April 1916, TNA WO95/1581.
43 War Diary, HQ 6th Infantry Division, April 1916, Memorandum No. 33, TNA WO95/1581.
44 War Diary, HQ 6th Infantry Division, 2 September 1916, TNA WO95/1581.
45 War Diary, HQ 6th Infantry Division, 5 September 1916, TNA WO95/1581.
46 Quoted in S. Bidwell & D. Graham, *Fire-Power*, pp. 120-1.

ensure the best blend of manpower.[47] As Harvey emphasises, in the absence of a job description, individual brigadiers had different styles and preoccupations (and under Sir Charles Ross, were left very much to their own devices). Thus Generals Bridgford (18 Brigade) and Nicholson (16 Brigade) could produce such different schemes.

71 Brigade left no details of any brigade schemes, yet the war diary faithfully records when units were training. The final brigade commander, General Brown, certainly kept himself up to date. Thus on 14 February 1918, he and his brigade-major attended a tank demonstration at Bray, observing somewhat dismissively that 'the Infantry tactics were just the same as those practiced by this Brigade and carried (out) in the CAMBRAI battle.' The following day found the pair at No. 59 Squadron RFC for a one day course. 'The course consisted of a lecture on organisation and work of a flying squadron.' There were 'demonstrations of aeroplanes at various heights', as well as aircraft armament and methods of photography. More crucially for the infantry, a 'lecture on contact patrol work' was given. A wireless officer explained wireless signalling flash spotting. Clearly the brigadier was expected to cascade knowledge. The day finished with Brown and Captain Weyman having the excitement of a short flight to give them the experience of signalling and picking targets from the air.[48] In 1918, however, there were no brigade schemes within 6th Division, and training was conducted entirely at battalion level.

Divisional Schools

SS152 was prescriptive that 'the training of each Division must be carried out under the personal guidance of its Divisional Commander.'[49] This would largely mean ensuring the division had the right structure of schools and adequate instructors. Third Army had been the first to establish a school in the autumn of 1915, at Flixécourt, for the training of officers and NCOs. The idea was quickly adopted by other formations, and by the winter of 1916-17, schools existed at GHQ, Army, corps and divisional level. 6th Division were no exception, noting on 31 March 1916:

> Classes of Instruction had been formed at Wormhoudt in grenade work, training trench mortar personnel. Training detachments from each B(attalion) in Torpedo work for wire cutting and in training instruction for physical training. In B(riga)de areas classes were started in gas defence and revetting.[50]

47 T. Harvey, 'An Army of Brigadiers', pp.335-6.
48 War Diary, HQ 71 Brigade 14-15 February 1918, TNA WO95/1620.
49 *SS152*, p.8.
50 War Diary, HQ 6th Infantry Division, 31 March 1916, TNA WO95/1582.

9th Norfolk noted as early as November 1915: '4 young NCOs for School of Instruction for young NCOs, & one NCO to Army Grenade School.'[51] And, as lacklustre as he may have been, 16 Brigade recorded at the end of October 1916 that General Ross visited the brigade HQ 'and talked about training' and 'about the system of Divisional Schools he proposed to introduce, also the system of training in battalions and brigades.'[52] One of the early creations was a 6th Divisional Training Company. Reinforcements would arrive at battalions from the base at Étaples and then proceed to the training company for a period. Similarly, a Divisional Officers School of Instruction was established. On 21 December 1917 the War Diary of 71 Brigade recorded: 'Bombing and Lewis Gun Schools opened' (not for the first time but merely in a new location) 'under the Brigade Bombing and Lewis Gun Officers.'[53] 16 Brigade refers to its own Grenade School in January 1917. The importance of training was clearly understood – in his observations on the relationship of the failure of undertrained troops at Cloudy and Mild Trenches in October 1917 on the Somme, General Ross observed:

> The Divisional and Brigade Schools had to be closed down when we went to the SOMME owing to the difficulty of finding accommodation for them – yet it is just at this very time, when the Division is suffering severe casualties, that these Schools should be working at the highest pressure.[54]

1st King's Own Shropshire Light Infantry recorded a constant traffic of officers from battalion to divisional (bombing and Lewis gun) schools; corps (Lewis gun, sniping and officer's) schools; and Army schools. The establishment of the GHQ Training Directorate under Brigadier-General Arthur Solly-Flood in January 1917 led to a standardisation of the system of schools,[55] divisional schools being abolished in 1917, training continuing in divisions and brigades in the form of 'Classes of Instruction.' Corps infantry schools were created, emphasising the growing importance of this level of army organisation. This, of course, took officers and men away from their units. In January 1917 1st West Yorkshire noted that five officers and 144 mean were away for three days training;[56] in August and October 1917 2nd Durham Light Infantry

51 War Diary, 9th Battalion Norfolk Regiment. 22 November 1915, TNA WO95/1623.
52 War Diary, HQ 6th Infantry Division, 31 October 1916, TNA WO95/1581.
53 War Diary, HQ 71 Infantry Brigade, 20 December 1917, TNA WO95/1619. These officers were relatively Junior. Lieutenant John Skidmore Cooke (9th Norfolk), who had been on the Western Front since August 1916 was the Brigade Bombing Officer, Second-Lieutenant James Vernon Tailby (9th Suffolk), commissioned in September 1916, was the Brigade Lewis gun Officer.
54 War Diary, 9th Battalion Norfolk Regiment, Memo of Major-General C. Ross 'XIV Corps', 31 October 1916, TNA WO95/1623.
55 Arthur Solly-Flood commanded 4th Dragoon Guards between November 1914 and November 1915, and was Brigadier-General 35 Brigade, 12th Division, before and during the Somme offensive in 1916. He later commanded 42nd Infantry Division.
56 War Diary, 1st Battalion West Yorkshire Regiment, January 1917, TNA WO95/1614.

recorded that five officers on each occasion and 46 and 31 ORs respectively were away on courses.[57] Repetition of the number '5' indicates a ceiling on the number of officers to be away at any one time. Demand went beyond this, however. On 2 July 1916, 1st King's Shropshire Light Infantry recorded (without complaint) that they became the 'training Battalion for the Second Army Central School at Wisques.'[58]

The structure within which training was delivered thus evolved. As Alistair Geddes has noted:

> The policy of training in France was based upon two main thoughts: that the responsibility for the training and efficiency of all officers and men in a unit belonged to the commanding officer; and that special instructors were to be trained at schools to assist them in that task. The schools themselves also had a dual objective: to train company and platoon officers and NCOs to command, and to produce a sufficient number of instructors to train individual fighting units in the multiplicity of general and specialist skills that trench warfare required. The numbers were substantial: by 1918 the system was designed to train 72 company and platoon officers and NCOs, and 111 officer and NCO instructors *per battalion*, every year. Schools also needed to be adapted to meet the demands of the new platoon organisation and tactics created by SS143.[59]

Conclusion

During the war the development of training went hand-in-hand in with tactical and technological development. The British army began the war from a position of eschewing a 'doctrine' of fighting yet during the war moved towards embracing such. The learning needs generated by the increasing sophistication of warfare required the development of a Directorate of Training and the production of a multiplicity of training manuals. 6th Division demonstrated itself committed, as did the whole BEF, to learning. Basic tactical training was recycled again and again as on a wheel, to respond to churn resulting from sickness, wounding and death. The basic skill of musketry remained prominent, whilst specialist training diversified and achieved a heavy emphasis as the war progressed. Similarly, the focus on junior leadership skills remained a prominent focus. The division and its brigades developed their own structures for skill-based training, first as schools and then as 'classes.' The division clearly welcomed the introduction of the *SS143* company restructuring as eminently sensible. Yet this is the only *SS* manual referred to in divisional records. These

57 War Diary 2nd Battalion Durham Light Infantry, 25 August & 1 October 1917, TNA WO95/1617.
58 War Diary, 1st Battalion King's Shropshire Light Infantry, TNA WO95/1609.
59 A Geddes, 'Solly-Flood, GHQ, and Tactical Training in the BEF, 1916-1918', pp.19-20.

manuals had multiplied in number yet remain under the radar as far as these records concern. This, perhaps, indicates that their assumption was so commonplace with training running automatically along the new, more prescriptive lines that there was no reason to refer to their use. Yet, in mid-1918, Charles Bonham-Carter, Brigadier General Staff (Training) at GHQ 1917-18 still thought that 'the progress in obtaining uniformity of training was not rapid enough.'[60] In June 1918 Sir Ivor Maxse was appointed Inspector-General of Training, and his deputy, Major-General Herbert Uniacke would remark the following month that the Training Branch at GHQ had 'generally neglected the somewhat important matter of instruction' (an observation that perhaps fails to recognise Solly-Flood's efforts), but also questioned 'whether instruction once given was ever properly applied.'[61] The BEF's application of training may have been patchy (Archibald Montgomery, MGGS Fourth Army, suggesting at the end of the war that the application of training only worked well in two out of the five Armies),[62] but whether this was due to lack of application or simple intrusion of events is a matter for discussion. The pressures on 6th Division in 1918 demonstrate the quandry. Shattered by the *Kaiserschalcht* in March 1918,[63] the defensive demands of an understrength army meant that is was in line for long periods with a raft of incomers who no doubt ideally required more training input than they received. To what extent this impacted on their performance at the Hindenburg outpost system in September 1918 is an open question.[64] Peter Simkins has observed of the Hundred Days that 'the doggedness and resilience of the British front-line soldier remained as important – and perhaps even more important – than the methods he employed.'[65] Determination mattered as well as tactical infantry skill. Both were essential to victory.

60 Cited in Robbins, op. cit. p.96.
61 Cited in Robbins, op. cit. p.96.
62 Cited in Robbins, op. cit. p.96.
63 See Chapter 11.
64 See Chapter 12.
65 P. Simkins, *From the Somme to Victory*, p. 205.

10

Firepower

The firepower of the whole BEF expanded exponentially as the war progressed, in terms of increased numbers of guns, development of new weapons, and increased sophistication in their tactical deployment. An infantry division possessed its field artillery, radically increased its possession of heavy machine guns, and acquired trench mortars and highly mobile automated weaponry.

Field Artillery 1914-16

In August 1914 the division's field artillery comprised three brigades of Royal Field Artillery, the 2nd,[1] 24th[2] and 38th[3] Brigades. These were arranged into three six-gun batteries of 18-pounder field guns, 54 pieces in all. This weapon had been adopted in 1904, had a range of 6,500 yards, and could fire up to twenty shrapnel rounds a minute. There was also the 12th Howitzer Brigade,[4] which comprised three batteries of six 4.5-inch howitzers. Adopted in 1908, it fired four high-explosive 35 pound shells

1 Commanded by Colonel William Arthur Murray Thompson. Born in 1866 and commissioned in 1885, with a *psc* and an impressive history of staff posts, Thompson would be CRA 38th and 39th Divisions, the latter until the Armistice. The brigade comprised the 21st, 42nd and 53rd batteries.

2 Commanded by Lieutenant-Colonel Charles Edward Lawrie. Born in 1864 and commissioned in 1884, Lawrie would serve as BGRA II Corps, and would then command the Royal Naval Division from February 1917 to August 1918. The brigade comprised 110th, 111th and 112th batteries.

3 Commanded by Lieutenant-Colonel Robert Fanshawe Fox. Born in 1862 and commissioned in 1882, Fox would be CRA 4th Division and BGRA VII Corps until June 1916, when he would become Inspector of Horse and Field Artillery. The brigade comprised 43rd, 86th and 87th batteries.

4 Commanded by Lieutenant-Colonel Gardiner Humphreys. Born in 1865 and commissioned in 1884, Humphreys would take over as CRA 6th Division in May 1915 and move to BGRA IX Corps in June 1916 until the Armistice. The brigade comprised 43rd, 86th and 87th batteries.

every minute some 7,300 yards, and with its elevation of 45 degrees it could lob shells almost vertically into enemy positions. Lastly, there was 24 Heavy Battery,[5] which comprised four 60-pounder guns. Dating from 1904, this weapon fired high-explosive or shrapnel shells 10,300 yards. The division would not keep these heavy guns for long, as they were removed and placed under Army control in April 1915. Before leaving England, the division rearranged its artillery, breaking up the howitzer batteries and distributing them amongst the three 18-pounder brigades. One 18-pounder battery was taken away from each brigade to form a fourth. On arrival in France, therefore, the divisional artillery comprised one 18-pounder brigade, three mixed brigades, and the heavy battery. It was commanded by Wellesley Lynedoch Henry 'Rajah' Paget. Born in 1858 and commissioned 20 years later, Paget had served in the Second Boer War, and had taken command of 6th Division's artillery in September 1910. In May 1915 he would be promoted BGRA VI Corps, a post he would hold until August 1916, when he was placed on half-pay, retiring in February 1917. The fact that he died in June 1918 suggests that his retirement was related more to health than competence.

The division's artillery first came into action on 17 September on the Aisne, the Heavy Battery and 12 Brigade supporting 4th Division. The field guns were short of range, and only the guns of the heavy battery could reach the enemy's artillery. Consequently, the German artillery had pounded the British trenches, and effective support (in the British view and contrary to the German experience), was limited. However, as Jack Sheldon has noted, at this point in the war: 'Both sides … claimed that the artillery fire of the opposition was extremely heavy and that their own was relatively ineffective.' Translated to the north, the gunners supported the division's advance on Outtersteene on 14 October with mixed success, there being problems coordinating fire with the advancing infantry's progress. The front would soon become static, however, and on 20 October, the major enemy assault began.[6]

Given that artillery would be crucial in maintaining the line, there were worrying matters. 38 Brigade RFA, who had played a crucial role in preventing the collapse at Ennetières, when 2nd Sherwood Foresters were nearly enveloped, reported at 13.40 on the 20th that there was no howitzer or 18-pounder ammunition left in the brigade ammunition column and 2 Brigade RFA were ordered to hand over any available ammunition. The Divisional Ammunition Column reported that only about 700 rounds 4.5-inch high explosive remained, adding ominously: 'Supply from England having ceased temporarily.'[7] On 26 October, General Keir received the following from III Corps: 'Instructions have been received from G.H.Q. limiting the expenditure

5 Commanded by Major Herbert Edward John Brake. Commissioned into the RA in 1886 Brake had spent ten years in Africa and the West Indies. He would be promoted BGRA in 1917, CRA XVIII Corps.

6 See Chapter 1.

7 War Diary, CRA 6th Infantry Division, 20 October 1914, TNA WO95/1588). A problem was also developing with rifles – the cartridges issued were slightly too big and were jamming in the breeches when the rifles became hot.

of 18 pr. Q.F. ammunition in this Corps to a "maximum daily average expenditure of 30 rounds per gun".' A warning was given (along with the observation that daily expenditure over the previous eight days had been 48 rounds): 'If this expenditure is exceeded it will not be made good from the railhead.' Significantly, the situation concerning 4.5 inch ammunition was becoming 'much more serious, and the expenditure of Lyddite especially must be reduced to an absolute minimum and reserved for special occasions.'[8] Three days later the ration for 18-pounders was reduced to 20 rounds per day, and a ceiling for the 4.5 inch howitzers was put at 10 rounds. The statistics offered by III Corps concerning average shell usage hid important variations. In the defensive battle of 20 October the six guns of 34 Battery RFA, for instance, had fired over 2,100 rounds, i.e. 350 rounds per gun. This compares to the 1,202 rounds fired by 24 Brigade RFA that day. This brigade recorded that 'reports from the infantry all said that the support given to them was very satisfactory.' If artillery was to become the dominating feature of the battlefield, then it was already making its presence felt. But the work had not been easy that day: 'The F.O.O's wires were frequently cut by the enemy's shells, but the work of repairing them and quickly re-establishing communication was always well carried out by men along the line.'[9] 12 Brigade noted sending out Forward Observation Officers from each battery and commended the work of 'Lieut Mansfield 86th Battery who remained forward all day only returning after dark.'[10] The FOO of 86th Battery of 12 Brigade RFA had a rough day on the 22nd, 'shelled out first house he occupied which was set on fire – and was later on, in another farm house, obliged to temporarily seek refuge in the cellar, owing to the heavy shell fire.'[11] The FOO of the heavy battery, Lieutenant Euan Rabagliati,[12] spent the whole afternoon of 27 October 'heavily fired upon by infantry

8 The situation for 60-pounder and 6 inch howitzer ammunition did not cause concern. War Diary III Corps, October 1914, Order G.156, TNA WO95/668.

9 War Diary, CRA 6th Division Artillery, 'Report on work of 24th Bde RFA', 20 October 1914, TNA WO95/1588.

10 War Diary, CRA 6th Division Artillery, Appendix VI October 1914, TNA WO95/1588. Geoffrey Edward Mansfield MC, born in 1891 and commissioned in 1913, would survive the war as a major. He was, however, wounded whilst acting as FOO on 16 November 1914.

11 War Diary, CRA 6th Division Artillery, '12th Brigade R.F.A., Report on Operations 22/10/15', WO95/1588.

12 Cuthbert Euan Charles Rabagliati MC, born 1892, had been commissioned into the Yorkshire Light Infantry in 1912, and was serving with the RFC in August 1914. How he came to be doing observation work on the ground is unknown. He is credited as being the first RFC pilot to shoot down an enemy aircraft on 25 August 1914. After the war he worked in aviation insurance, and pursued a career as a racing driver, although in the Double Twelve Hour race at Brooklands in 1930 he skidded whilst overtaking, another car crashed into him and he span off the track into the crowd killing one spectator and injuring 20 others, many seriously. His own serious head injuries required a silver plate in his skull and on emerging from his coma, his first words were to ask for a bottle of champagne. During World War II he served as head of MI6's Dutch section, and after the

and artillery (apparently howitzers)' but 'continued to carry on his observations with a total disregard of the enemy's fire … and his observations were most accurate.'[13]

The first report of aerial reconnaissance identifying hostile guns is recorded on 21 October. The threat posed by enemy aircraft is indicated by the arrival of the first anti-aircraft gun on 18 October.[14] From 28 October, siege and heavy batteries were in operation daily with aeroplanes. The heavy battery was engaged in counter-battery fire, the howitzers bombarding the enemy trenches, aircraft used to spot fall of shells. On 25 October, for instance, the heavy battery engaged seven enemy gun batteries.[15] Sir Geoffrey Salmond, later Air Chief Marshal, but then a captain on the staff of Royal Flying Corps HQ sent out an order on 3 November that every evening an officer would attend Divisional Artillery and arrange with the CRA what the targets were for the morrow for the heavy guns, whose fall of shell was much easier for fliers to spot. A reconnaissance of the enemy's gun positions was to be carried out every morning. Only four machines were, however, available each day to work with artillery across III Corps.[16] Diminishing stocks of ammunition was not the artillery's only issue. During November, an 'Inspector of Ordnance machinery' looked at some of the division's guns. Wear and tear, a matter so important to accuracy, was reported to be 'satisfactory', with 'some buffer springs broken' and a 'good deal of play in 18 p(ounde) r carriages.' The average number of rounds fired per gun since the opening of the campaign was estimated at 4,000.[17]

From a positive point of view, during the month of October General Keir clearly felt that his division was coming together with the experience of combat:

> The reports I receive daily from the artillery accentuate two points: (1) That the action of the infantry with that of the artillery is becoming daily more interwoven; (2) That splendid work is being done by a number of young artillery officers who in the most gallant fashion press forward into the vicinity of the firing line in order that their guns might be able to shoot at the right targets at the right moment.

Keir, an artilleryman, had an obvious interest in the progress of the gunners. The artillery of 6th Division were indeed furthering their craft, having 'quickly learnt

war as British vice-consul in San Francisco. He died in 1978 at Cannes, whence he had retired.

13 War Diary, CRA 6th Division Artillery, 'Report of Operations', 27/8 October 1914, TNA WO95/1588.
14 Attached to 28 Brigade RFA.
15 War Diary, CRA 6th Division Artillery, 'Report on Operations', 24 October 1914, TNA WO95/1588.
16 War Diary, HQ III Corps, Order G/135 HQRFC, 3 November 1914, TNA WO95/668.
17 War Diary, CRA 6th Infantry Division, November 1914, TNA WO95/1588.

from the French the great value of keeping the enemy's communications under fire at night.'[18]

By January 1915, the increased wiring of the front had given cause for experimentation as to how this obstacle should be addressed. This took place at St Omer on the 5th. The CRA's war diary noted that one 18-pounder gun at a time fired at a two barbed wire entanglements 30 yards deep with trous de loup (a pit with a stake in the centre) between, but that '50 rounds of HE low burst had practically no effect.' A hundred rounds of HE percussion only 'cut a passage through both lots of entanglement wide enough for two men to pass through abreast', the trous de loup not being damaged. '150 rounds low burst shrapnel cleared a passage about 4 yards wide', whilst 13,000 rounds fired from four machine guns at 200 yards 'cut a passage through the wire, but left the wire lying loose on the ground.'[19] 34th Battery carried out its own experiments in wire-cutting on 3 February, and although it did not note what type of shell was used, after 85 shells 'the obstacle was severed for some 15 yards as regards height but there was no clear path cut through.' It was noted that 'the fuzes even when carefully set by officers are erratic', and that wear meant the battery's guns 'cannot shoot either for elevation or deflection really accurately.'[20] 112th Battery carried out a test firing on enemy wire at La Houssoie on 16 May 1915, 150 shells being delivered on a hundred yards of front at a range of 2,700 yards. The wire was described as 'well knocked about' and that 'the infantry think they could get through on the frontage.'[21] The problems, at various levels, would not be solved in terms of wire-cutting by the time the Army made its attack on 1 July 1916 on the Somme.

On 5 February the divisional artillery received a curious addition with the arrival of HMAT *Churchill* into the goods station at Armentières. This armoured train, under the command of the RNAS, carried a 4.7-inch and a 6-inch gun.[22] On the 6th, *Churchill* demolished the tower of Ennetières church, used for observation, and tried the same feat against Wez Macquart church. It tried again on the 15th but 'failed to entirely destroy the tower.'[23] It ranged on batteries, cross roads, and various buildings, 6th Division noting with amusement after premature bursts of shells: 'The ammunition is dated 1893!'[24]

On the move to the Ypres Salient a different level of organisation was apparently applied. This move was accompanied by the elevation of Gardiner Humphreys to

18 War Diary, HQ III Corps, October 1914, TNA WO95/668.
19 War Diary, CRA 6th Division Artillery, 5 January 1915, TNA WO95/1588.
20 War Diary, CRA 6th Division Artillery, Appendix II February 1915, TNA WO95/1588.
21 War Diary, CRA 6th Division Artillery, 'Report on Wire Cutting', 17 May 1915, TNA WO95/1588.
22 Used initially to cover the Royal Naval Division's retirement from Antwerp, the train, one of three, was withdrawn from service in March 1916, ceasing work with the division on the 7th.
23 War Diary, CRA 6th Division Artillery, 15 February 1915, TNA WO95/1588.
24 War Diary, CRA 6th Division Artillery, 18 February 1915, TNA WO95/1588.

command of the divisional artillery. Whereas at Armentières there had been a great deal of movement of batteries, from 14 June the concepts of centre, left and right groups of field artillery with an attached howitzer battery began to be used, and it was recorded that 'at the end of June, batteries had full registration of their zones, also overlapping both on divisional flanks and flanks of brigade zones.'[25] Humphreys was clearly a competent artilleryman as he would serve as BGRA IX Corps until the Armistice, and it is possible the revamped organisation was 'new broom' related. August would, of course, prove the artillery's first test in terms of support of a major set-piece operation in the retaking of Hooge. Although the carefully planned attack on l'Epinette had involved the integration of artillery proactively, rather than reactively (as had all the artillery work to date been, the division being on the defensive), the Hooge operation would represent a major step forward in tactical and operational sophistication.

The artillery under divisional control for this operation was divided into six groups. 'A' comprised 2 Brigade RFA with a battery of 48 Brigade RFA from 14th Division; 'B' comprised 24 Brigade with a battery of 47 Brigade RFA, again from 14th Division. 'C' was 38 Brigade, 'D' the division's 4.5-inch howitzer brigade; and 'E' was made up of 49 Brigade RFA of the 14th Division with 6 Siege Battery (6-inch howitzers). Lastly, 'F' comprised 2 batteries of 23 Brigade RFA. Two batteries of French 75mm guns fired phosphorous shells (one attached to 'A' and one to 'B') and two mountain guns from 46th Division were grouped with 'F.' As observed in Chapter Three, the fact that an attack was in preparation could not be concealed, but the enemy could be misled concerning the timing. It is this emphasis on deception that represents the step up in tactical finesse. Each morning the enemy trenches were subject to bombardment in the early morning: '3 to 4 A.M., 2 to 3.30 A.M., etc. So, when the final and real bombardment was carried out the Germans assumed it was only the normal "hate", to which they had become accustomed, and retired to their dug-outs.'[26] A half hour bombardment lasted from 02.45 to 03.15, with a first lift at 03.15 and a second at 03.20. The targets for each battery were set out in detail. Marden observed that 'the attack was looked upon for some time as a model of really close co-operation between infantry and artillery',[27] especially in terms of following a barrage closely. The only (and major) failure of the artillery that day was in the realm of counter-battery fire, the only measure that would have reduced the butcher's bill, and meant that not all the ground desired to be held to the east of Hooge crater was taken. *Artillery Notes on Counter Battery Work*, published much later in the war summarised the situation concisely: 'Unless the enemy's batteries are discovered and destroyed, not only may his barrage fire render the capture of an objective difficult and costly, but his subsequent

25 War Diary, CRA 6th Division Artillery, Summary June 1915, TNA WO95/1588.
26 J.E. Edmonds, *Military Operations France and Belgium 1915, Vol. 2*, p.107.
27 Marden, op. cit. p.15.

bombardments may make its retention impossible.'[28] This was not, however, a specific failure of 6th Division's artillery. Even if it had been possible to register the enemy guns, the 6-inch howitzer was the weapon of choice for effective counter-battery work, and they were thin on the ground. Effective counter-battery fire would only come much later in the war.

The divisional artillery war diaries do not exist for the last five months of 1915, but until the middle of 1916, the division remained trench-holding in the salient, until it moved to the Somme in August 1916. When the war diary resumes in January 1916, one addition to firepower is notable, in that No. 21 Anti-Aircraft Battery was operating with the division.[29] The division had gone to war with No. 2 Pom-Pom Section attached, but the 1-pounder Maxim pom-pom was of limited use, and was replaced in 1915 by a 13-pounder gun mounted on a lorry chassis. In October 1915 these were grouped into four-gun batteries. In January 1916 the battery was in action on 13 days, engaging 144 aircraft and firing 3,043 shells. At an average of about 21 shells per aircraft, the battery believed they had brought down one Albatross on 16 January, witnessing it spinning down, any crash not being observable. Their most active day was 24 January 1916, when they spotted 47 aircraft and fired 801 shells. Their power was probably in deterrence, and indeed, anti-aircraft gunnery is a complex science.[30]

By this time the command of the division's artillery had changed once more. On Gardiner Humphrey's promotion, Brigadier-General Egerton Stewart Cleeve took his place. Born in 1864, Cleeve had been commissioned into the Royal Artillery in 1884 and had served in South Africa in 1902. At the outbreak of was he was in command of 10 Brigade RFA in Kirkee, India, and his active service had begun in Mesopotamia in November 1914. He was wounded at the Battle of Shaiba on 14 April 1915, coming under fire when the batteries of the brigade were advancing. He returned to duty, but on 24 October 1915 was 'ordered home.' He thus avoided being besieged in Kut with his brigade.[31] Translated to the Western Front, he served as BGRA only between 22 June and 24 October 1916.

During its time on the Somme, Marden records that the divisional artillery 'was grouped and re-grouped in accordance with the requirements of the situation, but never as a whole covered the operations of the division.'[32] XIV Corps organised its artillery into right, centre and left division groups for the bombardment and barrage for the battle of Flers-Courcelette which began on 12 September. Only one of the division's brigades were under the command of CRA 6th Division, whilst two were under the command of the Guards. The centre artillery was, however, under the control of 6th

28 GHQ, *Artillery Notes No.9 No.3 Counter Battery Work, 1918*, p.7.
29 It was replaced in March by No. 35 Anti-Aircraft Section.
30 See P. Hodgkinson, *The Resourceful Gunner*.
31 War Diary, 10 Brigade RFA, 25 October 1915, TNA WO95/5117.
32 Marden, op. cit. p.26.

Division. As implied, the artillery support for the division was split across groups. In respect of the attack on 13 September, the GOCs of 16 and 71 Brigades, who would undertake the attacks, were left to liaise with their supporting artilleries, 16 Brigade being supported by two brigades of 56th Divisional Artillery and 71 Brigade by two brigades of 6th Divisional Artillery and two of the Guards artillery. This enforced surrender of authority by divisional HQ obviously arose from fragmented command and control and relied on relationships between infantry and artillery commanders who were not familiar with working with each other. The corps heavy artillery shelled the Quadrilateral on the 12th, but there is no evidence of any special participation by corps in support of the division on the morning of the 13th outside of the continuing bombardment for the upcoming Flers-Courcelette operations. Not only were the artillery and infantry subject to all the intelligence problems concerning the exact location of the Quadrilateral as recounted in Chapter Four, the division had been subjected to command and control relationships with which they were completely unfamiliar.

The barrage fired by the field artillery on 15 September involved half firing a creeping barrage and half a stationary barrage. The creeping barrage advanced at a rate of 50 yards a minute – relatively quick in relation to later barrages. The artillery experimented in 1916 with lifts of this nature but later settled on 100 yards in three minutes, an artillery officer claiming that: 'There was no doubt that a barrage at this rate fired by shrapnel was effective. The machine gunners were killed in their shell holes.'[33] At Hooge, 6th Division had followed a lifting barrage over a relatively short distance, but their artillery had never fired and their infantry had never followed a creeper in action. Paul Strong and Sanders Marble credit the French with the introduction of the creeping barrage in General Robert Nivelle's Champagne offensive of September 1915, employed again in the early stages of the Verdun battle of 1916 to cover counter-attacks. On 1 July 1916, on the Somme, these authors claim that Major Alan Brooke 'adapted a French template for the creeping barrage' for the assault of 18th Division.[34] Shelford Bidwell and Dominick Graham refer to Brigadier Ernest Alexander, BGRA of XV Corps,[35] who claimed to have 'used a form of it at Loos' i.e. in September 1915, not 'in close conjunction with advancing infantry but to sweep the area behind the German front.' If both sources are right, then it appears the creeping barrage emerged at exactly the same time in both French and British armies, but that the French used it tactically to cover infantry advance first. Shelford Bidwell sees it as 'a natural development from the linear concentrations of fire that had been placed on objectives before they were attacked'[36] – it was therefore

33 A.F. Becke, 'The Coming of the Creeping Barrage.'
34 P. Strong and S. Marble, *Artillery in the Great War*, p.93.
35 Ernest Wright Alexander served as CRA 15th (Scottish Division), BGRA XV & XI Corps, and GOCRA First Army, this last post from April 1918 to the Armistice.
36 S. Bidwell & D. Graham, *Fire-Power*, p.83.

a gradual evolution rather than a light-bulb moment for artillery tacticians. Tactically the creeping shrapnel barrage suppressed the enemy by making them keep their heads down. As Shelford Bidwell notes, following artillery officers of the time such as Noel Birch,[37] the creeping barrage had potential negative effects on infantry tactics – they encouraged pursuit of linear targets and hindered fire and movement flexibility.[38]

In the event, no better command integration or barrage sophistication would have assisted 6th Division on either the 13th or the 15th of September. Whatever the flaws of the corps artillery plan, as discussed in Chapter Four, if the artillery could not register on its target, then all other gunnery sophistication failed. The Battle of Morval, on 25 September, showed what could be achieved by the same tactics if good observation was obtained. For this attack XIV Corps had four artillery groups, left, left-centre, right-centre and right, CRA 6th Division being responsible for the right-centre group, but its three brigades split over three groups. There followed the muddy confusion of the Battle of the Transloy Ridges, and on 24 October Egerton Cleeve was relieved of command. That this was a sacking is reflected in the fact that he was placed on half-pay on 30 November.[39] His replacement was Brigadier-General Edwin Francis Delaforce. Commissioned in 1890, Delaforce had commanded 1st East Lancashire Brigade RFA from 1911-13. At the outbreak of war he was Major OC 66th Battery RFA, part of the (Meerut) Division, Indian Army. Promoted lieutenant-colonel in January 1915, he rose from battery commander to divisional artillery commander in 24 months. Delaforce was clearly a competent artillery officer, who would remain CRA until the Armistice.

Trench Mortars

The mortar was an ancient weapon given a new lease of life by the Russo-Japanese war of 1904-5. Seeing a use for such a weapon against French fortifications, the Germans had developed light, medium and heavy trench mortars (the later the infamous *minenwerfer*) by 1914. The British army had none. Playing swift game of catch-up, a 4-inch mortar was introduced before the end of 1914, firing an 8.5-pound bomb; a 3.7-inch mortar was improvised in the field at about the same time, proving highly inaccurate, whilst the Vickers 1.57-inch trench mortar was introduced in March 1915 accompanied by the 2-inch mortar. It was, however, the Stokes 3-inch mortar (developed in January 1915 to a simple design but rejected initially because it did not use standard munitions), which would come to be the light weapon of choice. The 2-inch mortar was replaced by the 6-inch Newton mortar in 1917, and a heavy 9.45

37 Sir James Frederick Noel 'Curly' Birch served as BGGS Cavalry Corps, CRA 7th Division, BGRA I Corps, and MGRA GHQ BEF from May 1916 to the Armistice.

38 Bidwell & Graham, op. cit. p.112.

39 At the end of the war Cleeve would be found attached to 2a Reserve Brigade RFA at Preston. He had been well and truly side-lined.

inch mortar, the 'Flying Pig', had come into service by the end of 1916. The 4-inch Stokes mortar and the Livens projector[40] would be operated solely by the Special Brigade, Royal Engineers.

Organisation of trench mortar batteries was haphazard at first, but by the end of 1915 it had been ordained that light mortars would be under the control of the infantry whilst medium and heavy guns would be the remit of the Royal Field Artillery. The mortar was thus a weapon unavailable to the division for its attack at Hooge in August 1915. The divisional Trench Mortar Batteries have a war diary starting on 15 December 1915 which appears to be their date of formation. When 6th Division recorded the officers serving with the Divisional Artillery on 1 January 1916, it listed the 26th TMB which deployed 1.5-inch mortars,[41] the 38th TMB deploying the same,[42] and 52nd TMB deploying '4-pounder' mortars,[43] (these being 3.7-inch weapons) all under the command of Captain John Newell of the West Yorkshire Regiment.[44] This notes that 'the only firing done was retaliation at the request of the infantry' and that the 'only mortars in possession were 1 ½ in. and 3.7, both with very limited range.'[45] On 10 March the 300th TMB was formed with four 2-inch mortars, and on the 22nd of the month a class of instruction was set up for detachments of each brigade, and three light batteries, the 16th, 17th and 18th formed, the 26th, 38th and 300th TMBs becoming X/6, Y/6 and Z/6 (medium) and 52nd TMB becoming 16th TMB (light). On 1 May eight 2-inch mortars replaced the 1.5-inch weapons, and over the next six weeks 'organised shoots in cooperation with the Corps and Divisional Artillery were carried out with success.'[46] However, only 90 rounds were fired, and the batteries' positions were easily spotted and shelled by the enemy accordingly. The operation orders and accounts of the successful attack to retake Willow Walk on 21 April 1916 make no mention of trench mortars, and although they had certainly come into action in December, it seems that it was only in May that the newly-organised batteries began regular firing. On 20 July, W/6 heavy trench mortar battery arrived.

Medium and heavy mortars fired from an emplacement (another construction task for the Royal Engineers), whilst Stokes mortars could be deployed in a fire trench.

40 The Livens Projector was invented by Captain William H. Livens of the Royal Engineers. It consisted of a simple metal pipe that was set in a ground at a 45-degree angle which could throw large drums filled with flammable or toxic chemicals. Initially with a barrel based on 12-inch oil drums, it had its debut on 25 July 1916 at Ovillers, but an 8-inch barrel was settled upon with a range of 1,600 yards.
41 Under the command of Lieutenant J. Longbourne RFA.
42 Under the command of Lieutenant B. Bellew 4th Royal Irish Regiment.
43 Under the command of Second-Lieutenant C. Leigh, 3rd Buffs.
44 War Diary, CRA 6th Division, 1 January 1916, TNA WO95/1588. John Geoffrey Newell MC had been commissioned in January 1912.
45 War Diary, Trench Mortar Batteries, 6th Division, January 1916, TNA WO95/1598.
46 War Diary, Trench Mortar Batteries, 6th Division, 1 May 1916, TNA WO95/1598.

Eventually, three tactical roles evolved for the Stokes mortar.[47] Firstly, it was used for fire suppression during an assault, targeting machine-gun positions and strongpoints after the main artillery barrage had lifted. They were thus 'a part of the artillery programme and did not act independently.'[48] It was also a mobile weapon, moving forward with the infantry, dealing with obstacles the infantry met during their advance, although the problem of carrying forward sufficient ammunition was always a significant one. Close cooperation between the infantry and the Stokes detachment was obviously essential. Finally, it was used for interdiction to help prevent counter-attacks. The attacks against the Quadrilateral, as noted in Chapter Four, involved the taking forward of Stokes guns in action, and this was undoubtedly the first time the division had deployed the weapon in this way, and as has been seen, organisationally this was not successful. Further, it does not appear that the medium or heavy batteries were used in the Somme actions, and the mortar teams appear either to have been labouring or working with RFA batteries. They began reporting daily firing again when the division took over a new line in December.

Machine Guns

In August 1914 the British Army possessed 1,963 machine guns, and each infantry battalion boasted two. Nearly all were old Maxim and converted Maxim guns. Vickers had purchased the Maxim company in 1896 and had improved the design, the new version, the Vickers Gun .303-inch Mark 1 being adopted at the end of 1912, and of the total number of machine guns, 105 were of this new pattern at the outbreak of war. Production increased, and by July 1915, 1,022 Vickers had been delivered.[49] The Machine Gun Corps was created in October 1915, and machine guns were withdrawn from infantry battalions (to be replaced by the Lewis gun) and grouped at brigade level, being increasingly re-equipped with the new weapon. 6th Division from this point therefore contained the 16th, 18th and 71st Machine Gun Companies. The 192nd Company was added in December 1916, and from April 1917 came under divisional command. In March 1918 the companies would be amalgamated into the 6th Machine Gun Battalion.

It was certainly not the case that the machine was viewed as a front-line weapon at the outbreak of war. A book on machine-gun tactics had been written by Captain Reginald Applin DSO, 14th Hussars, in 1910. He observed that:

47 *SS135* 'The Training and Employment of Divisions', (January 1918), was an updated version of *SS135* 'Instructions for the Training of Divisions for Offensive Action', (December 1916), which immediately preceded the publication of *SS143*.
48 A.J. Saunders, 'A Muse of Fire', p.247.
49 J.E. Edmonds and G.C. Wynne, *Military Operations, France and Belgium 1915 Vol 1*, p.58.

> Machine guns will often be used to cover the advance of infantry from 'long' to 'effective' range when the artillery is still occupied in the artillery duel and the infantry first come under effective rifle fire from the enemy. The ease with which they can instantly open and cease fire, concentrate on a particular spot, or sweep a line of trenches, renders them particularly suited for this purpose, and the Japanese constantly used them to keep down the enemy's rifle fire in this manner during the late war. The narrow beaten zone enables them to fire safely over the heads of advancing infantry from all ranges beyond 800 yards.

Applin stated that 'the best method of using covering fire in the early stages of the attack is by indirect fire from the reverse slopes of a hill or from behind a ridge or other feature.'[50] It is thus wrong to assert that the British Army went to war lacking sophistication in machine gun tactics. The first recorded use of a machine gun barrage (as distinct from indirect fire) in the war was by 33rd Division on 24 August 1916 at High Wood, on the Somme, 100th MGC firing, allegedly, just short of a million rounds.

The various machine gun company war diaries survive (or perhaps begin) from mid-1916. Thus, 16 Brigade MGC recorded the positions of its nine guns on 31 May in the Salient, there being five open emplacements, four covered emplacements, one loophole emplacement, and two concrete emplacements on the canal, each with specific fields of fire. Three guns were in reserve on the canal bank and four guns at rest in camp.[51] On 28 June the company noted that it 'fired in cooperation with field artillery on hostile guns' for an hour and 25 minutes, using four guns and 7,000 rounds.[52] On 1 July, the company dispositions were recorded in right, centre and rear sectors, deploying four guns each, (the rear sector three). They had been inspected by the Corps Commander on 12 July and a surprise order had arrived to go into action. The Earl of Cavan was 'particularly pleased' to watch this, and noted that: 'The guns were brought into action very rapidly, every man thoroughly knew his job, and the transport was cleared in a very short space of time through a narrow gate and formed up under cover without confusion of any kind.'[53]

50 R.V.K. Applin, *Machine-Gun Tactics*, pp.46-7. Reginald Vincent Kempenfeldt Applin transferred from the Lancashire Fusiliers to the Royal Garrison Artillery to the 14th (King's) Hussars. He had served as DAAG Musketry in Malta, and during the Great War was attached to the Machine Gun Training Centre, later commanding the machine-guns of II Anzac Corps at Messines and Third Ypres.

51 War Diary, 16 Infantry Brigade Machine Gun Company, 31 May 1916, TNA WO95/1611.

52 War Diary, 16 Infantry Brigade Machine Gun Company, 28 June 1916, TNA WO95/1611.

53 War Diary, 16 Infantry Brigade Machine Gun Company, 6th Divn. No. A/6226/9, 12 July 1916, TNA WO95/1611.

The machine gun companies faced their first major engagements on the Somme in September 1916. In terms of 71 Brigade's attack on the Quadrilateral, 71st MGC placed No. 2 section under the command of the CO of 2nd Sherwood Foresters and No. 3 section under the CO of 9th Suffolk, half of each of section going forward with the attacking battalions.[54] This was to prove the principal usage of the MGCs in these engagements. On the 15th, the Battle of Flers-Courcelette, 16th MGC had No. 1 Section attached to 1st Buffs, No. 2 to 8th Bedfordshire and No. 4 to 2nd York & Lancaster.[55] 'During the attack the guns followed behind the support waves of the regiments', and after the attack failed, two guns were placed in the support line and two in the front line, and when 11th Essex attacked later, again unsuccessfully, the guns supported this attack.[56] 71st MGC sent two guns of No. 1 Section forward with the attacking waves, two guns following. Of the two leading, one team was completely knocked out with gun and tripod blown up, whilst the other was reduced to an NCO and two men. No. 2 section sent two guns up with the 2nd Sherwood Foresters. One had to be dumped due to casualties. No. 3 section followed 9th Suffolks with two guns, each team being reduced to three in number, the main ammunition dump being blown up. No. 4 section sent two guns forward with the attacking waves and two followed. The officer commanding and all NCOs were rendered casualties. Taking heavy machine guns forward into unsuppressed enemy fire, was courageous but foolhardy. Some guns were, however, able to deploy more tactically. During the action, two guns from No.1 section were moved to provide enfilade fire to cover the retreating brigade right, two guns of No. 2 section deployed indirect fire on the Quadrilateral, and two guns of No. 3 section used traversing fire on the ridge in front of the Quadrilateral in case of counterattack. 'It speaks well for the morale of the company that in spite of intense machine gun fire & very heavy shelling, it was found possible to re-organise and re-equip so many gun teams.'[57]

The 16 MGC refers to a machine gun barrage for the final successful attack on the Quadrilateral on the 18th, but it was clearly not integrated into the overall fire-plan. Three of 16 MGC's guns fired into the enemy trench and 'made the enemy keep down, as he was standing up and sniping at the bombers', one gun followed thirty yards behind the bombers.[58] 18 MGC (18 Brigade having come into line), do not refer to a barrage, and attached two guns of No. 4 Section to 1st West Yorkshire, and two guns of No. 2 section to 14th DLI, the enemy being more successfully suppressed on this

54 Sections 1 and 4 remained in reserve.
55 No. 3 Section was held in reserve.
56 War Diary, 16 Infantry Brigade Machine Gun Company, 15 September 1916, TNA WO95/1611.
57 War Diary, 71 Infantry Brigade Machine Gun Company, 15 September 1916, TNA WO95/1625.
58 War Diary, 16 Infantry Brigade Machine Gun Company, 18 September 1916, TNA WO95/1611.

occasion. They set up in in the captured trenches and fired on the retreating Germans, estimating that they accounted for about 50 of their number.[59]

The change in role of the Vickers gun was in part due to the increased availability of automated firepower to the infantry in the form of the Lewis gun. Although, strictly speaking, an automated rifle, this weapon became increasingly central to the infantry attack, as seen in the previous chapter, as indicated by the revision of *SS143* in early 1918.

Integrating Firepower 1917-18

On the Somme in 1916, the divisional artillery had learnt and practiced its barrage techniques, but it had not operated as a whole, nor had it tactically integrated its heavy trench mortars. Similarly the machine gun companies had yet to work in tandem with the guns, adopting barrage fire. On translation to the Loos sector, and a resumption of raiding in earnest, integration would at last be achieved. In this area of line, the divisional artillery was divided into three groups, north to south, Cambrin, Hohenzollern and Quarries. When 8th Bedfordshire of 16 Brigade raided trenches at the Hohenzollern Quarries on 29 January 1917, seven areas were selected and communicated to corps heavy artillery for bombardments with the divisional 4.5-inch howitzers also targeting these, with 18-pounders cutting wire and raking the front-line. These targets were selected by the infantry based on observation, and artillery tasks were to be completed by the 25th, three days before the raid.[60] An artillery barrage was arranged for the raid itself, both of heavy guns and a creeping barrage of 18-pounders beginning seven minutes after the heavy bombardment opened, with which medium and Stokes mortars were to co-operate. 16th MGC was to traverse the enemy parapet north of the area raided.[61] Similarly, when 2nd Sherwood Foresters raided the Hairpin Craters, Hulluch sector, on 9 February 1917, a FOO of the artillery was attached, and a 52 minute barrage from Zero delivered. Simultaneously, 71st MGC brought a barrage down on the enemy's reserve and communication trenches for 15 minutes from zero. Stokes mortars carried out a smoke barrage under No. 2 Special Company RE for the duration of the artillery barrage, whilst 71st LTM Battery brought fire to bear on enemy trenches, and X6 Medium Trench Mortar Battery bombarded alternative locations 'with the object of confusing the enemy and damaging his front trench and wire, the battalion to the right bringing rife, Lewis

59 War Diary, 18 Infantry Brigade Machine Gun Company, 18 September 1916, TNA WO95/1618.

60 War Diary, 16 Infantry Brigade, 'Hohenzollern Sector – Artillery work desired to be carried out before 25.1.17', January 1917, TNA WO95/1606.

61 War Diary, 16 Infantry Brigade, Operation Order No. 129, 26 January 1917, TNA WO95/1606.

Gun and rifle grenades to bear.'[62] If only on a small scale, the division was thus able to synchronise all its firepower, and it was as if with each raid the integration of firepower became more sophisticated.

The large raid carried out by 11th Essex on 24 March 1917 near Bois Hugo was even more complex in its coordination of firepower. The heavy artillery bombarded the enemy front and support lines and communications from Zero minus 45 to Zero minus two minutes, lifting to the rear communications and specially selected localities. At Zero the divisional 18-pounders placed a barrage on the front and support lines, lifting to the support and reserve lines at Zero plus 16, and lifting ten minutes later to form a box barrage. Two-inch trench mortars cut wire with the 18-pounders in the days beforehand, and then joined the heavy artillery bombardment. 18th MGC swept the rear of the enemy trenches during the attack with 'bursts' of fire. And it was more than fire-power that was co-ordinated. A trench tramway was placed at the disposal of the brigade, 18th Field Ambulance formed an advanced dressing station at Loos, and OC Signals and OC 12th Company RE were co-opted with specific tasks.[63] Whatever cynicism might be directed at raiding, 6th Division in these early months of 1917 built a much greater competence in orchestrating its firepower through these vehicles.

In the first week of April 1917,[64] the division's artillery, assisted by I Corps heavy artillery, carried out bombardments on several days in association with the opening of the Battle of Arras to the south on the 9th. After the German withdrawal on the 13th, two bombardments were organised in relation to the proposed push onto Hill 70. These (on the 16th and 18th) involved coordination with Corps heavy artillery and Nos. 2 and 10 Squadrons RFC. On the 18th, the divisional trench mortars were included, and on this occasion the bombardment was particularly well coordinated with the infantry, lifting at 05.00 for patrols to go forward, with a further lift at 05.15. The bombardment ceased at 05.45 at which point the GOC 16 Brigade was to arrange barrages to allow consolidation of any line reached.[65] During the advance the Vickers guns of 16 Machine Gun Company were constantly advanced providing covering fire for the advancing units. In comparison with the Somme operations, even though barrages were planned with only 24 hours' notice, there was a much more effective cooperation with the infantry, trench mortars were incorporated on at least one occasion, and the machine guns, whilst not included in the overall barrages, had devoted themselves to providing covering fire rather than moving forward with the infantry.

62 War Diary, 71 Infantry Brigade, Operation Order No. 137, 4 February 1917, TNA WO95/1619.

63 War Diary 18 Infantry Brigade, Operation Order No.149, 21 March 1917, TNA WO95/1615.

64 The Divisional artillery war diary is absent for the first three weeks of April.

65 War Diary, CRA 6th Division, Operation Order No.70, 17 April 1917, TNA WO95/1589.

As Chapter Eight set out, the artillery plan of 20 November at the Battle of Cambrai represented a major step forward in the BEF's artillery tactics, involving 'silent registration' neutralising both defensive positions and enemy artillery, forgoing preliminary bombardment, and firing a lifting barrage on successive enemy positions. The artillery plan was of course the child of army and corps. 6th Division's artillery on the day boasted 24 4.5-inch howitzers, 72 18-pounders (17th and 181st Brigades RFA being attached), and 18 13-pounders (16th Brigade RHA being attached). The artillery was split into right (16th Infantry Brigade) and left (71st Infantry Brigade) groups. Despite Hammond's assertion concerning the barrage being of a 'jumping' nature,[66] the 13 and 18-pounders fired a creeping barrage, with a delayed barrage on the Couillet Wood Valley. Smoke barrages were formed at various places on the corps front where the enemy had good observation, fired by 4.5-inch howitzers. Twelve 6-inch Newton mortars were allotted to the division and six placed with each group,[67] and their fire (370 rounds) was directed on known enemy machine-guns, trench mortars and strongpoints. The division's own medium trench mortars, 12 guns, were placed in two groups and fired 370 rounds on selected targets.[68] Both artillery group commanders integrated their HQs into the infantry brigade HQs, where wireless sets were installed, and parties of FOOs pushed forward as the attack progressed. An aeroplane was in the air continuously from daylight with its sole mission to detect hostile counter-attacks. A smoke bomb would be dropped at the location, and artillery and machine-gun barrages would open on such a spot.[69] The division's machine guns were partly concentrated in two groups. No. 2 Group consisted of one battery of three sections of 192nd Company MGC (12 guns), the other comprising 8 guns of 71st MGC. These fired in barrage, and then moved forward behind the infantry to a new position where they put down a defensive barrage and engaged the enemy with harassing fire. They were in constant telephone communication with the Divisional Machine Gun Officer's advanced HQ.[70] The remainder of the brigade machine gun companies supported the infantry, sending guns forward with battalions, but 18th MGC refer on the 21st to the 'barrage guns' moving up behind Ribecourt to put a barrage into Marcoing.[71] The division's integration of its firepower had come of age, and was growing in complexity all the time.

66 B. Hammond, *Cambrai 1917*, p.114.

67 The Stokes-Newton 6-inch mortar replaced the 2-inch medium mortar in February 1917 and became the principal British trench mortar during the last eighteen months of the First World War. It could fire a 50lb bomb up to 1950 yards at a rate of 8 rounds per minute.

68 War Diary 6th Division Trench Mortar Batteries, 19-20 November 1917, TNA WO95/1598.

69 War Diary, CRA 6th Division, '6th Divisional Artillery Report on Operation Carried out on November 20th and 21st 1917', TNA WO95/1591.

70 War Diary, 192 Machine Gun Company, 'Report on the Action of Machine Guns of No. 2 MG Group, 6th Division, on Nov 20th & 22nd', November 1917, TNA WO95/1601.

71 War Diary, 18th Machine Gun Company, 21 November 1917, TNA WO95/1618.

Gas

As Albert Palazzo has observed, the British became enthusiastic deployers of gas in the First World War.[72] After its use as a primary weapon at Loos, gas was used extensively in the run up to and at the opening of the Somme offensive on 1 July 1916. The first reference to 6th Division's artillery using gas is at the Battle of Flers-Courcelette on 15 September, when the 4.5-inch howitzers were to 'fire Poison Shell into Morval' on road junctions for two nights running, for half-an-hour at two different points in time.[73] As became a significant element of British practice, gas was being used in an inhibitory and morale-degrading fashion rather than as a lethal weapon. The division did not use gas at the Battle of Morval (there is no reference to gas in the corps heavy artillery records either, although smoke was used), and the same situation pertained during the division's attacks at the Transloy Ridges.

On 17 April 1917, the first cylinder attacks that are recorded by the division took place to support the efforts against Hill 70. (Cylinder discharges had been ongoing since the Battle of Loos and were favoured by Major-General Charles Foulkes of the Special Brigade but were diminishing in frequency as gas shells took the ascendancy). Similarly (see Chapter 7) on 27 April three companies of the Special Brigade launched another gas attack. One company hurled 150 large and 70 small cylinders of phosgene (CG) using Livens projectors. Another used Stokes mortars to fire 150 PS shells (the irritant chloropicrin), and 108 SK shells (the lachrymatory ethyl iodoacetate). The third fired 150 cylinders of phosgene from Livens projectors. This demonstrates several things. Firstly, the division was clearly more sophisticated, moving from describing 'poison shells' to being specific about the agents used. Secondly, there had been evolution in gas delivery techniques. Gas shells for Stokes mortars had only begun to arrive in September 1916, and the Livens projector was still in a phase of experimentation at this point. Early 1917 was therefore a point at which both weaponry and munitions were more plentifully available. The division's 4.5-inch howitzers did not fire gas on 20 November 1917 at Cambrai, rather smoke instead, reflecting increased sophistication in getting infantry across the fire-swept area of No Man's Land. (III Corps' 60-pounders fired lachrymatory shells in counter-battery fire). The Divisional Ammunition Column only begins to record the issue of smoke shells in October 1917. An issue of chemical shells was made in December 1917, and again to 4.5-inch howitzers in May and June 1918, but at no other time. On 27 May the division fired 'gas concentrations during night',[74] and clearly used it at other times, noting at the end of May '4.5 Howrs. have used gas shells for harassing fire

72 A. Palazzo, *Seeking Victory on the Western Front*.
73 War Diary, CRA 6th Infantry Division, Centre Divisional Artilleries, XIV Corps, Operation Order No. 3, TNA WO95/1589.
74 War Diary, CRA 6th Infantry Division, Summary of Intelligence & Operations 26-27 May 1918, TNA WO95/1591.

when conditions have been favourable. In addition they have co-operated with Heavy Artillery in gas concentrations on hostile batteries on several occasions.' In June, chemical shells were specifically noted as fired on 2-4 and 7-8 of the month. At the Battle of Epéhy on 18 September 1918, elements of the division's 4.5-inch howitzers and 18-pounders fired smoke, the same practice being followed at the Battle of the Selle on 17 October. By this time corps heavy artillery was firing mustard gas (BB) in counter-battery work. Mustard gas shells were now just becoming available for 18-pounder guns but arrived too late for the division's field artillery to fire them. 6th Division's howitzers indeed fired gas, but on very few occasions.

Firepower in Defence

So far, the discussion has centred on fire-power as deployed in attack. The German Spring offensive of 21 March 1918, to be discussed in the following chapter, allows consideration of the use of fire-power in defence. The artillery was split into a left and right group,[75] and 'both Group Commanders were living with their respective infantry brigadiers, and there was an Artillery Liaison Officer at the HQ of each battalion in the line.'[76] (The location of group commanders in this fashion was later thought to limit command and control of their guns). At about midnight there was warning of the impending attack, and all observation posts and signalling stations were manned, gunners were standing to, guns and mortars were laid on their SOS points and harassing fire was intensified. SOS lines were pre-determined lines that artillery fired on if the infantry was suddenly attacked. The lines were normally areas in No Man's Land or in the German front lines where attacks might start from. It was noted that communications were fragile from the start as there were few buried cables. Fog and smoke rendered visual communication impossible, and runners had long distances to cover. The enemy barrage opened at 05.00 most heavily on artillery positions, shifting somewhat onto the infantry positions. The divisional and heavy artillery fired until 10.00, when the degree of enemy penetration became clear, and when it was learnt at 11.40 that the enemy were establishing gun positions in the old British front line, fire from heavy artillery was directed thither. Although the position was obscure during the afternoon, reinforced by three further field artillery brigades, the artillery withdrew and established new SOS lines in front of the VM (corps) line to the rear, anticipating withdrawal thereto. On the following day, firing commenced at 05.00, the enemy's bombardment opening at 07.00. At 11.00, the most forward

75 The right group, commanded by Lieutenant-Colonel W.H.F. Webb, covered 18 Brigade and consisted of 2 Brigade RFA (less 21st Battery), with 87th Battery (4.5-inch howitzers). The left group, covering 18 and 71 Brigades, commanded by Lieutenant-Colonel J.A.C. Forsyth, comprised 24 Brigade RFA, 21st Battery, and 93rd Army Brigade RFA (three 18-pounder batteries), and 43 Battery (4.5-inch howitzers).

76 War Diary, CRA 6th Infantry Division, 'Operations March 21st to 24th 1918', TNA WO95/1591.

batteries were withdrawn again. It was noted that: 'Up till the present time batteries on withdrawal had been able to fall back on prepared and reconnoitered positions with ammunition already at hand. Henceforth all withdrawals were to unprepared and generally unreconnoitered positions.'[77] There were further withdrawals in the afternoon, both in daylight and during the night, and although the division was taken out of line on the 23rd, the guns remained in position for two more days. The divisional artillery, who had suffered no casualties on 20/21 November 1917 at Cambrai, suffered losses totalling 264.[78] Thirteen 18-pounders were lost, as were three 4.5-inch howitzers, and four 15-pounders. All trench mortars in action were lost. At the start of the attack there were 18 6-inch Newton mortars and two 9.45-inch Heavy Trench Mortars in position. 2 Brigade RFA could not be sure if half of its trench mortars had fired – 'probably they did', was the only conclusion. Two were noted as firing at the request of the left infantry battalion, but, it was sadly noted: 'None of the TM Officers (4 in all) have returned.'[79] W/6 Heavy Trench Mortar battery reported having to put a number of its guns out of action in retreating. Most were lost.

Marden describes the divisional artillery as performing 'magnificent services', particularly on 21 March.[80] Lieutenant-Colonel Weber of 2 Brigade RFA thought that 'the barrage may well have seemed very ineffective to the infantry though the magnificent fight put up by each battery on its own doubtless caused the enemy heavy losses and delay.'[81] Those whose guns were not destroyed, 'enjoyed the novel experience of firing over open sights' (the forward gun of 11th Battery fired nearly all its 500 rounds over open sights), fighting until all ammunition was gone, and then with small arms, inflicting 'very heavy casualties.'[82] The forward section of 87th Howitzer Battery continued firing until the enemy rushed them. This battery lost all of it nine officers as casualties on the 21st and was commanded by a corporal until a replacement officer arrived. At 12.40 the time came to withdraw the guns:

> The teams came up and there ensued a most dramatic scene. The battery was by this time under heavy machine gun fire from the old infantry brigade headquarters … Captain ARNOLD was killed and Major SHAW wounded. The wheel driver of one team was hit and several others, but as each driver was

77 War Diary, CRA 6th Infantry Division, 'Operations March 21st to 24th 1918', TNA WO95/1591.
78 Five officers were known to have been killed, 15 wounded and 13 missing. Twenty-seven ORs were known fatalities, 135 had been wounded and 69 missing.
79 War Diary, CRA 6th Infantry Division, 'History of 2nd Brigade RFA, March 21-27, 1918', TNA WO95/1591.
80 Marden, op. cit. pp.50-1.
81 War Diary, CRA 6th Infantry Division, 'History of 2nd Brigade RFA, March 21-27, 1918', TNA WO95/1591. William Hermann Frank Weber DSO *psc* had been commissioned in 1894 and had served in GSO2 & 1 posts before the war.
82 Marden, op. cit. pp.50.

> hit another man got in his place, teams going short of a driver each. It provided a most exciting moment on a day already full of incident.[83]

42nd Battery, 'having kept their three guns in action after our infantry had fallen back, succeeded in bringing (back) the two that were not destroyed', this though a heavy barrage. The forward section of 53rd Battery had one gun destroyed, but 'Lieut(enant) Reeves got the other into the open, and, after firing 850 rounds with it over open sights and having exhausted his ammunition',[84] withdrew his gun team and the breech-block. In 24 Brigade RFA, the 110th Battery fired for seven hours at ranges from 1,200 to 600 yards, loosing off 2,450 rounds, its gunners working in gas masks for four hours. All the gun pits were hit except one, but the guns were dug out and placed in the open. A forward gun of the battery was fought until its ammunition was used up and the breech-block was removed 'with the enemy almost on top of the gun.'[85] The 111th Battery fired 2,100 rounds. Sergeant A. Pengelly of 112th Battery, who was commanding an anti-tank 15-pounder destroyed in the initial bombardment, found himself now commanding a platoon of infantry, 'and did great execution himself with a pickaxe.'[86] He was awarded the DCM:

> The gun early received a direct hit and this NCO the led his detachment to reinforce neighbouring infantry. He also took part in a bombing attack. Later he organised a party to take a wounded officer to the dressing station. Finally he took command of a platoon of infantry and held position for two days.[87]

There were four 18-pounder and four 15-pounder anti-tank guns in position on the front, a number of which were knocked out before coming into action, and, being forward, all were lost. 112th Battery was in front of the VM (corps) line and was withdrawing its wounded and breech-blocks 'the enemy being by this time actually on the wire of the corps line.' 43rd Howitzer Battery had all its howitzers buried but dug them out again. 'Major Dyott was wounded in the head later on by rifle fire and as the enemy advanced they were engaged with open sights and fuze 106 till all

83 War Diary, CRA 6th Infantry Division, 'History of 2nd Brigade RFA, March 21-27, 1918', TNA WO95/1591. Twenty-eight year old Sir Robert de Vere Shaw MC and bar had been commissioned in 1910. Bernard William Arnold, an officer of the Special Reserve had arrived on the Western Front in February 1915 and had served with the Divisional Ammunition Column. He would die as a result of his wounds.

84 Robert Reeves, who arrived on the Western Front in November 1914, had been commissioned from sergeant in the Royal Horse Artillery in August 1915. Reeves was missing but survived.

85 Marden, op. cit. p.51.

86 Marden, op. cit. p.51.

87 *London Gazette*, 29 August 1918, p. 10131.

ammunition was expended.'[88] All the guns were saved. Major Claude Lyon of 53rd Battery was killed before daylight.[89] 21st Battery had lost two of its guns forward, had two of its surviving trio 'smashed and buried' and in early afternoon had 'enemy infantry streaming up on both sides.' With one remaining gun in action, a Lewis gun (and two rifles), they fought until the 1st Buffs came up, and 'it is very likely that it was the action of these two weapons that enabled them to do so.'[90] The remaining gun was then hit, and the survivors retired on the wagon lines to retrieve their sixth gun.

The four divisional machine gun companies had been amalgamated into 6th Battalion Machine Gun Corps on 1 March 1918. The disposition of the guns on the morning of 21 March reflects the development of a machine gun doctrine. Fourteen guns were in isolated positions away from the trenches (the early loss of the anti-tank guns was attributed to them being placed too far forward and close to trenches) 'forming bands of fire across the front of the second line and especially in front of selected strong points.' Lance-Corporal Thomas Brookbank described how he had 'two guns sited near a crossroad, one on each side of the road, a stone's throw apart and connected by means of a tunnel under the road; the sap heads at road level, each containing a machine gun.'[91] Behind these were four batteries – 'these batteries and the guns in front of them had two tasks: firstly, to put down a barrage in front of No Man's Land on the SOS going up.' On the day, 'all arrangements about SOS were useless as no SOS signals went up – in fact a quantity of ammunition was wasted by firing on SOS lines when the enemy was not actually attacking.' (Given that the bombardment opened at around 05.00 and the enemy did not attack for another three or so hours, the same must have been true for the artillery). The second task was 'to engage the enemy by direct fire should he break through the front line.' Between 500 and 700 yards behind the batteries were five pairs of guns in strong points, and behind these again, in the VM line 800 yards to the rear were four more pairs of guns. Sixty-four guns were distributed in depth over 2,000 yards.[92]

Rosher lost all communication with his guns within half an hour of the enemy bombardment opening. The experiences of the single guns in the front and the batteries to their rear gives a flavour of the action and what was achievable. Of the guns in the front, No. 1 fired 15 belts (the feed system of a Vickers gun was a 250 round canvas

88 War Diary, CRA 6th Infantry Division, 'A short report on the doing of 24th Brigade RFA on 21st March 1918', TNA WO95/1591. Thirty-seven year-old Richard Archibald Dyott was an American by birth, a barrister and a Territorial officer. He survived his wound to die in 1965.

89 Thirty-seven year-old Claude Stuart Lyon MC and bar had arrived on the Western Front as a gunner in December 1914 and had been commissioned in April 1916.

90 War Diary, CRA 6th Infantry Division, 'History of 2nd Brigade RFA, March 21-27 1918', TNA WO95/1591.

91 T. & M. Brookbank, *A Soldier of the 6th Division*, p.23.

92 War Diary, 6th Battalion Machine Gun Corps, '6. Bn. MGC 21-22 March 1918', TNA WO95/1601.

belt) when 'the enemy appeared in mass coming up the valley to the left front' and retired when 51st Division on the right fell back. No. 2 gun fired only three or four belts before being blown up. No. 3 gun was soon destroyed, as was its replacement, and No. 4 gun lost nearly all its crew. No. 10 gun 'had some very fine shooting at the enemy crossing the open. It fired 16 belts causing heavy casualties until the gun was put out of action.' No. 12 gun observed the enemy on a road by the Hirondelle River in parties of 30 to 50 whereupon 'fire was brought to bear … heavy casualties (were) inflicted and the enemy's advance at that spot stopped.' Of the line of batteries, A (four guns) found the enemy 'advancing in rather thick formation', and for an hour and a half held up their advance. Two guns were knocked out at 16.00, at which point the enemy advanced again 'over the open in mass', the remaining two guns 'doing great damage.' Eventually the enemy overwhelmed them, the battery fired off all its ammunition and retired with its sole remaining gun. D Battery again refers to the enemy advancing 'thickly.' Losing three guns in succession, the last gun could not be got away, and the enemy swept over the battery. F2 Battery was able to see the enemy working round its flanks and withdrew its remaining gun 'to a position where it got some good targets.' J Battery, further back, had no good targets until 18.00, when it halted the enemy advance. 'During this time the infantry were retiring past the battery covered by its fire and eventually the battery was left entirely unsupported.' Three guns were withdrawn to the VM line covered by the fourth gun which withdrew under the cover of rifle fire. By the end of 22 March, 60 out of 64 guns had been lost and 295 casualties sustained.[93]

The accounts of the Machine Gun Battalion put paid to the notion that the enemy infantry tactics were all of the 'stormtrooper infiltration' type. Whilst they indeed tried to pass up the valleys, much of the attack was made by massed troops who could be held up for a period by determined use of firepower. But it is also clear that the early breakdown of communications meant than the only integration of firepower achievable was in the plan, and that beyond this, guns or batteries were fighting on their own. And effectively so.

Firepower during the Hundred Days

Corporal Thomas Brookbank, of the 6th Machine Gun Battalion described how, on withdrawal from Ypres in May, they went to the Machine Gun Training Centre at Camiers for eight days and 'took part in developing barrage fire with 64 guns in the line for the purpose of covering advancing troops.'[94] Returning to static positions in the line in August 1918, they would carry out night-time harassment of enemy

93 War Diary, 6th Battalion Machine Gun Corps, '6. Bn. MGC 21-22 March 1918', TNA WO95/1601. Three officers were dead, six wounded and five missing. Eleven ORs were dead, 76 wounded and 194 missing.

94 Brookbank, op. cit. pp.33-4.

'assembly points, ration collecting points, groups of light field guns' and back roads where horse-drawn trucks were carrying supplies to the front line. 'Guns would be set up in position at dusk completely enclosed in sacking ... the direction would be laid out on a compass bearing and the elevation, to give the distance on a clinometer.' Just like all artillery, in fact. 'The one or, perhaps several points laid out would be checked by setting up siting, or ranging, poles at the top of which would be held a lighted cigarette so that we could switch points easily and quickly.' Several thousand rounds would be fired at intervals, switching quickly 'all though holes no bigger than a modern two penny piece.' Crews would take turns throughout the night, and 'all those participating in the firing would have black faces from the smoke of the cordite not being able to readily escape though the canvas.'[95]

This little vignette describes a small part of what, by this time in the war, Robin Prior and Trevor Wilson have described as the 'weapons system':

> At last the British army was employing a true weapons system, with interlocking roles assigned to tanks, aeroplanes, a variety of forms of communication, artillery, infantry, and even horse soldiers. Only with the most thorough co-operation between the various elements would the attack achieve its maximum effect' and 'a serious failure in interaction – particularly between the more vital elements – might imperil the whole undertaking.

This system 'stood a substantial chance of subduing' at a 'tolerable cost' to the infantry 'whatever defences the enemy placed in their path.'[96] This 'weapons system' was unleashed, achieving the zenith of its success, on 8 August 1918, at the Battle of Amiens. Although most historians attribute the success of the British Army in the Hundred Days campaign to the 'weapons system', there are many signs that it was never able to achieve that 'thorough co-operation' again. Nowhere was this more true for 6th Division than at the Battle of the Selle on 17 October 1918 (see Chapter 12).

The key feature of the Hundred Days campaign is that in terms of firepower, the BEF was fighting a rich man's war. Each British army had an abundance of heavy guns, and there were no delays switching the focus of attack from army to army occasioned by moving heavy artillery. Despite the greater devolution of planning to divisions, army and corps kept a firm control of the fire plan. Yet, as 6th Division's operations at the Hindenburg outpost system demonstrate (see Chapter 11) this weight of artillery could still have difficulties in getting the infantry forward. On the day before the Battle of Epéhy (18 September), Fourth Army's attack on this system, 6th Division were tasked with taking a jump-off line. They advanced behind a creeping barrage but were held up by machine guns in two woods. These were bombarded by the divisional 4.5-inch howitzers and corps heavy artillery, with 6-inch howitzers

95 Brookbank, op. cit. pp.41-2.
96 R. Prior & T. Wilson, *Command on the Western Front*, p.309.

cutting wire. Even this weight of fire did not enable further advance. On the 18th, there was no preliminary bombardment, Fourth Army's infantry advancing behind a creeping barrage (including 10 percent smoke) provided by 750 18-pound field guns and 228 4.5-inch howitzers to the first objective, with a further barrage from the first objective. 6th Division itself was covered by 16 18-pounder batteries (96 guns) and four 4.5-inch howitzer batteries (24 guns). In addition there was 21 Heavy Artillery Brigade with two 6-inch howitzer batteries (12 guns) and one 60-pounder battery (six guns), spread across two groups.[97] The sophistication of artillery at this point in the war is indicated by the plan for the division's 18-pounders:

Zero to +5 minutes	Rapid fire
+5 to +72 minutes	Normal
+72 to +87 minutes	Slow
+87 to +190 minutes	Burst of fire searching forward 500 yards 1/2 round per gun per minute
+190 to +194 minutes	Rapid
+194 to +269 minutes	Normal

Up to 4,500 yards, shrapnel was fired, and beyond this distance and when crossing trenches or wire, HE 106 fuze was fired. In the creeper one in six guns fired smoke, in the protective barrage one in three did so. The 4.5-inch howitzer barrage proceeded 200 yards beyond that of the field guns, and particular locations were identified for attention.[98] Perhaps surprisingly, the trench mortar batteries were not integrated into this attack, although two companies of 6th Battalion Machine Gun Corps participated (suffering 65 casualties).

Once more, despite these riches and fined-tuned planning, little progress was made, particularly against a well-sited defensive position ominously named the Quadrilateral. It was clear that (as with the same-named location on the Somme) there would need to be special artillery preparation on this location. Thus on the 21st, 21 and 14 Brigades RGA (affiliated to 6th Division) bombarded the Quadrilateral for three hours. The 6-inch howitzers fired 1,100 rounds at the north-westerly and south-westerly faces; and 1,000 6-inch, 360 9-inch and 300 8-inch rounds fell on the north-easterly and south-easterly faces. This was followed by the division's field artillery bombardment on the following day. On the 24th, when the Quadrilateral was finally taken, the infantry attacked again under a creeping barrage. The trench mortars

97 Two second-lieutenants were detained per brigade as Forward Observation and Intelligence Officers, leaving a signaller and horseman at selected points on a known route, the FIO being attended by four runners. (War Diary, CRA 6th Infantry Division, BM: 2165/4 16 September 1918, TNA WO95/1591).

98 War Diary, CRA 6th Infantry Division, Order No. 151, 17 September 1918, TNA WO95/1591.

were now integrated, firing a barrage (297 rounds),[99] whilst all four companies of 6th Battalion MGC were in action though their role is not clear. In terms of success, as at the Ginchy Quadrilateral, a very thorough preparation with heavy artillery had been necessary – such local problems, difficult to assess in advance given the time frames involved, could not be taken into account in a wider corps fire plan, where even ample heavy artillery had to be stretched across a wide front.

The advance through the Beaurevoir Line on 8 October saw a new development for the divisional artillery, the pushing forward of field artillery brigades behind the infantry. Marden recorded that 'the weight of artillery for the operations of the 8th October was immense',[100] with a complexity surpassing the attack of 18 September. In addition to the divisional artillery, nine further brigades of Field and Horse Artillery were in support,[101] although not all fired the creeping barrage. Notably, the 6th Divisional artillery and two further brigades[102] moved forward behind the infantry to support exploitation and ward off counter-attack. Five siege batteries were also allocated, each division attacking with one mobile brigade RGA. 2 Brigade RFA was put at the disposal of GOC 16 Infantry Brigade and 24 Brigade RFA under GOC 71 Brigade. Surviving records do not allow analysis of their actions but 2 Brigade RFA were certainly able to come into action to support 1st West Yorkshire take a wood heavily defended by machine guns. This pattern persisted in the three days of the Pursuit to the Selle (9-11 October 1918). After firing a completely unnecessary barrage, given that there were essentially no enemy within three and a half miles, one battery of each of the six artillery brigades RFA firing the creeper were to move forward to the infantry assembly line, and the brigades moved forward in consultation with the GOCs of the infantry brigades. There is no record of them being used on the move, although on both 10 and 11 October they fired on specific locations prior to the infantry setting off. The divisional Trench Mortar Batteries did not participate in the pursuit, although the 6th Battalion MGC attached a company to each attacking brigade.

The artillery operations at the Battle of the Selle, mounted to break the *Hermann Stellung*, involved some of the most complex arrangements yet attempted. Both the 6th and 1st Divisions were to attack from the same narrow area, the 1st passing through the 6th. In the artillery plan, 6th Division were to command the guns of 1st, 6th, & 32nd Divisions (24 batteries of 18-pounder guns, and 8 of 4.5-inch howitzers), whilst 80 machine-guns would complete the barrage. These guns were from 2nd Life Guards Machine Gun Battalion (two companies) and 6th Battalion Machine Gun Corps (three companies). The guns were to go forward if opposition was met. The latter split its guns up over five locations to fire the barrage, using new barrels to

99 War Diary, 6th Division Trench Mortar Batteries, 24 September 1918, TNA WO95/1598.
100 Marden, op. cit. p.66.
101 5th and 16th Brigades RHA; 161st, 168th, 230th, 231st and 232nd Brigades RFA.
102 5th Brigade RHA and 232nd Brigade RFA.

enhance accuracy. The guns fired 250 rounds per minute for the first five minutes, then one minute's rapid fire every two or four minutes, finishing with two minutes' rapid fire, and it was noted that 'if atmospheric conditions are such as to shorten the trajectory, allowances must be made.'[103] It is another indication how tactically sophisticated machine-gun barrages had become, and how the science of gunnery influenced practice as much as it did the artillery. No information is available for the deployment of the division's trench mortars, but it was practice at the time to push Stokes guns out along the flanks of the divisional advance. The composition of the heavy artillery was 36 60-pounder guns, 74 6-inch howitzers, 24 8-inch and 18 9.2-inch howitzers, and eight 6-inch guns. The firepower was immense. Divisions were given the responsibility for the siting of the guns and preparing barrage maps, but it was specified that as 1st Division passed through the 6th, CRA 1st Division would assume command of the artillery, three brigades being detailed to move forward in close support of their advance. The plans thus involved a very complex assembly of both artillery and forming-up of troops.

Limitations on firepower during the Hundred Days

As will be seen in Chapter Twelve, 6th Division, as with the whole of Fourth Army, met with uncut wire on the 17 October, and despite their lack of cover the enemy infantry had survived the two-day artillery preparation remarkably well, and fought back ably. Further, the progress of the barrage manifestly had its limitations. On 17 October the time spent overcoming enemy outposts, resistance in fortified positions, and dealing with uncut wire meant that, proceeding at a standard 100 yards every three minutes, the barrage was almost invariably lost by the troops whose advance supposed to be protecting.

The reality was that barrages that seemed very complex on paper may not have been so sophisticated in practice. On the first day of the Pursuit to the Selle Major Frederick Rice of 82 Brigade RFA described his brigade's artillery support for 25th Division as 'short and simple.' They 'merely fired concentrations on three small areas, beginning with the nearest, at a certain time and for a certain definite period. This was to save ammunition.' (The BEF had plenty of ammunition, but when guns were constantly moving forward, in addition to logistical issues shells often had to be left at abandoned gun positions for collection later). He confessed that the exact position of the enemy's 'forward troops was not known accurately, so the most likely spots were selected.'[104] It is highly likely that the same problems existed for 6th Division's field artillery. Indeed, there are further question marks which hang over the artillery's performance in respect of the complex barrage plans that had been drawn up for the set-piece attacks.

103 War Diary, 6th Battalion Machine Gun Corps, Order M.G. No. 0.0.92/1, TNA WO95/1601.

104 F.J. Rice, Diary (author's collection).

Thus on 17 October, when the guns of 1st Division were superimposed on those of the 6th, the artillery warned that due to 'hastily occupied positions an accurate creeping barrage will not be possible.' Rather, a 'heavy area shoot' was promised, the front edge of which might be 'somewhat irregular.' The assaulting infantry were warned not to 'follow too closely.'[105] Thus what looked an impressive creeping barrage on paper was more ragged in practice. In reviewing the days of the Pursuit 16 Brigade noted: 'The Artillery barrages were not up to the high standard to which we have been accustomed.'[106]

The survival of so much wire encountered on the morning of 17 October indicates either lack of knowledge, inaccuracy, or both. The frequent moves of artillery into new positions were undoubtedly highly disruptive to providing swift and accurate indirect fire in bombardment, barrage and counter-battery work, predicted fire being based on accurate map locations of both friendly artillery and infantry, and enemy artillery and positions. Further, the maps on which the divisions were relying were inaccurate. During the Pursuit to the Selle, Lieutenant George Grossmith advancing beyond Bohain on 10 October described how 'the ground was so totally unlike the map that the latter was useless.'[107] The geographical issue, the artillery being in hastily occupied positions and the intelligence problems of knowing exactly where the relevant guns/infantry were (and coupled with the issue of inaccurate maps), interacted with a third and uncontrollable factor, the weather. The weather was probably the dominant factor in many of the artillery problems as the Hundred Days progressed and at the Selle in particular. There appears to have been a minimum of effective counter-battery work, another matter related to the weather. By this stage in the war, 90 percent of counter-battery observation was achieved by aircraft. Hence, 'the success of the artillery battle had come to depend on the weather being suitable for flying.'[108] Given the importance of the artillery/air-power axis in the new warfare, the October weather was a considerable handicap, rendering the RAF ineffective in terms of observation for a significant part of the time. This meant that Fourth Army had limited knowledge of the enemy positions and artillery locations. The guns were reduced to shelling areas where it was *likely* that enemy artillery might be, rather than where they were *known* to be. The reports of the German units noted by Mark Whisler indicates that in a number of cases they got the locations right, but were insufficiently effective.[109] The enemy artillery was thus often able to maintain effective harassing fire on the BEF's rear areas, and in 6th Division's attacks on 17 and 23 October, it was noted how sophisticated the enemy's use of counter-barrage was. Fourth Army concluded that

105 War Diary, HQ 1st Infantry Division, 1st Division Battle Instructions Series D No. 8, 19 Oct 1918, TNA WO95/1234.
106 War Diary, HQ 16 Infantry Brigade, G.O. 530, 14 October 1918, TNA WO95/1607.
107 G.W. Grossmith, Private Papers, IWM Docs 11013.
108 Bidwell & Graham, op. cit. p.143.
109 M. Whisler, 'Der Tommy Kommt', p.32.

'this counter-preparation was undoubtedly the result of insufficient counter-battery work.'

Conclusions

The BEF's firepower during the war diversified. The number and types of artillery weapons increased as the conflict developed, and the finesse in their accurate use through flash-spotting and sound ranging outstripped that of the enemy. If the Royal Field Artillery who manned the division's guns were not scientific gunners like their Royal Garrison Artillery counterparts, then they learnt quickly. The Hooge operations in August 1915 were certainly not lacking in tactical sophistication. As the war developed, the divisional artillery became increasingly integrated into wider schemes, namely corps artillery schemes. This would remain the case for the rest of the war. From the Battle of Cambrai onwards, whilst corps remined central in artillery planning, increasing latitude would be given to division in terms of local artillery schemes. Beyond the artillery, whilst the Vickers gun itself did not develop, its use did, and the arrival of the automatic rifle, the Lewis gun, allowed it to be used in different ways. Far more technical development occurred in the area of mortars. The infantry themselves acquired their own pocket artillery, the grenade. The No. 5 Mills bomb arrived in quantity in 1916 and was adapted that year for rifle launching. Tactical development therefore went hand-in-hand with technical development and consequently was uneven. From 1916 onwards, and in particular during 1917, 6th Division learnt to integrate its firepower. Whilst raiding may have been detested by the infantry, it allowed the division to practice the integrated local deployment of trench mortars and heavy machine guns (as well as gas) in conjunction with artillery. They thus were potentially allowed to utilise *SS143* tactics to practice 'break in' with the wider components of the 'weapons system.' 6th Division demonstrated that it had learnt this at Cambrai in November 1917. Whilst the 'weapons system' may indeed have been the key to success in the advances of the Hundred Days, however, the ability of firepower to get the infantry forward proved fallible at times. This, of course, was down to the friction of war. The BEF could not control the enemy's choice of defensive positions, their will to defend them, and the weather, which hampered the crucial axis of air reconnaissance and artillery accuracy. 6th Division learnt this to their cost in the Hundred Days campaign.

11

Kaiserschlacht 1918: 'Michael' and 'Georgette'

After the Battle of Cambrai, 6th Division had a month's rest in the Basseux area, south-west of Arras. 'Rest' was always a euphemism, and training continued whilst 16 and 18 Brigades spent several days assisting 3rd Division relieve two of their brigades at Bullecourt. On 17 January the division began to take over the line of 51st Division on Third Army's front between Hermies and Boursies to the south of the Bapaume-Cambrai road. During this period, in response to manpower issues, the BEF's brigades shrank to three battalions each, 8th Bedfordshire (16 Brigade), 14th Durham Light Infantry (18 Brigade), and 9th Suffolk (71 Brigade) being disbanded. Further, as observed, the four Machine Gun Companies were formed into the 6th Machine Gun Battalion, and Lieutenant-Colonel Rosher, displaced from 14th DLI, was given command.[1] In mid-February the division moved north of the road into the Lagnicourt sector. Here they worked steadily on the defences for very good reasons. An enemy offensive, bolstered by divisions released from the Russian front, was expected.

The first signs of preparation for the coming attack had become evident on 26 February. As March opened, anticipation accelerated. At the Army Commanders' conference on 2 March, the intelligence statement read out concluded (correctly) that: 'There are strong indications that the enemy intends to attack on the Third and Fifth Army fronts, with the object of cutting off the Cambrai salient and drawing in our reserves.'[2] The salient lay just to the south of 6th Division's new position. 18 Brigade recorded on the day of the conference that 'a new army HQ & a new corps HQ, new hospitals and new aerodromes had made their appearance', with 'many new heavy gun positions prepared in front of us.'[3] On the 5th the division's artillery and corps heavies carried out 'intense bombardments' aimed at breaking up enemy preparations for

1 Rosher had been sent on a course to Great Britain for three weeks during the last two weeks of February. It seems likely that this was a machine-gun course, as he had no previous relevant experience.

2 J.E. Edmonds, *Military Operations France and Belgium 1918, Vol 1,* p.105.

3 War Diary, HQ 18 Infantry Brigade, 2 March 1918, TNA WO95/1615.

the attack, and this continued over the following two days.[4] On the 7th, 71 Brigade reported: 'Expecting enemy to attack in a few days. The utmost vigilance is being kept in patrolling … stores, SAA etc. are being put into strong points as quickly as possible and strong points strengthened.'[5]

In these first three weeks of March, the Royal Engineers and pioneers were engaged in a flurry of labour. The 459 Field Company had half of their men working on the Vaulx-Morchies (VM) line at the start of March, this also known as the 'Corps Line', i.e. a defensive backstop. They dug new trenches, strongpoints and carried out wiring.[6] 12 Field Company erected 20 splinter proof shelters in the VM line and 17 in the support line. The constructed 11 dugouts, two deep and large enough to hold 100 troops, and fitted all with gas blankets. Thirty-five firebays were inserted into the VM line and 12 in the support line. Brigade HQs were constructed.[7] 509 Field Company concentrated on gun positions and strong points.[8] The pioneers, 11th Leicestershire, worked on dugouts, trenches and wiring. The frenetic activity was matched by that of the CRE, Lieutenant-Colonel Goldney,[9] who seemed to be everywhere at once on the divisional front. He was particularly preoccupied with corps orders concerning the construction of the minefield. Anti-tank mines were so novel that he attended a demonstration of them at Albert on 10 March, and work began on the 11th, 900 mines being laid 100 yards in front of the British wire. This required carrying parties of 1,200 men from 25th Division.[10] On the 15th, 16 Brigade recorded: 'At night the protective anti-tank minefield was completed by the placing of 300 more bombs, making a total of 1179 laid and fused at a cost of only 7 casualties.'[11] These time-consuming preparations were based on false intelligence – the *Reichsarchiv* later confirmed to the Official Historian that only nine tanks were sent into action on the 21st, four of the cumbersome German make and five captured British Mark IV.[12]

The following day General Marden toured his line, inspecting defences, and called a conference of his brigade commanders. Raids on the enemy lines took place over the following days, unfruitful in terms of identifications. On the 10th, 71 Brigade noted: 'Enemy attack on a big scale expected at dawn', this with tanks, but 'nothing happened.' During that day, 59 Division acquired an Alsatian deserter who informed them a six division attack would begin at dawn on 13 March.[13] Marden called another

4 War Diary, HQ 16 Infantry Brigade, 5 March 1918, TNA WO95/1607.
5 War Diary, HQ 71 Infantry Brigade, 7 March 1918, TNA WO95/1620.
6 War Diary 459 Field Company RE, 1-20 March 1918, TNA WO95/1599.
7 War Diary 12 Field Company RE, 1-20 March 1918, TNA WO95/1599.
8 War Diary 509 Field Company RE, 1-20 March 1918, TNA WO95/1600.
9 George Francis Bennett Goldney DSO was 39 and had been commissioned in 1898. He was only an acting lieutenant-colonel.
10 War Diary, CRE 6th Infantry Division, 1-20 March 1918, TNA WO95/1594.
11 War Diary, HQ 16 Infantry Brigade, 15 March 1918, TNA WO95/1607.
12 Edmonds, op. cit. p.172.
13 War Diary, HQ 71 Infantry Brigade, 10 March 1918, TNA WO95/1620.

conference on the 11th and 'further measures of defence and preparation were decided upon',[14] afterwards touring his line once more. 'Great preparations' were made, patrols were constantly sent out, and all troops and reserves were in 'battle positions',[15] but the enemy stubbornly remained in their own trenches. Marden visited individual battalion commanders on the 12th, again on the 13th discussing the best ways to form defensive flanks, and yet again the following day with 6th Division's ex-brigadier, Lieutenant-General Harper, who had taken command of the parent formation, IV Corps, three days earlier. Defensive preparations continued unabated. Three days later, 59th Division came into possession of another deserter, who 'stated that (the) enemy were going to attack at 4.30 a.m. preceded by a heavy gas bombardment.'[16] Yet again no attack materialised, and Marden toured the front line once more on the 18th, Harper visiting the following day 'with a view to the construction of further flank defence switch trenches.'[17] Shortly before midnight on the 20th, a day when 'aeroplane photos disclosed ammunition pits for seventy extra batteries' opposite 6th Division,[18] the order was given that all battle and alarm posts were to be manned before dawn. The onslaught was about to begin.

It is clear that General Marden was attempting to keep a firm grip on 6th Division's response to the impending attack. The debate on British defensive preparations has been extensive. The *Official History* began its consideration by stating that in general 'defensive arrangements had to some extent been neglected' on the British side, in the Allied emphasis on the offensive.[19] 6th Division would possibly not have agreed as their records of their time at Loos are full of defensive schemes. What is correct to say is that the BEF did not possess a defensive doctrine. On 14 December, GHQ attempted to amend this deficit, issuing instructions that defences were to be organised (supposedly) on German 'defence in depth' principles, with Forward, Battle and Rear Zones. The Forward Zone 'was to coincide generally with the existing front system, duly strengthened.' There had been some debate as to naming this the 'Outpost Zone' but this was abandoned in the fear that troops manning it might fall back without offering serious resistance. The troops of the Forward Zone were to 'do all in their power to maintain their ground against every attack', the backbone of the defence being automatic fire. The Battle Zone, 2-3,000 yards in depth, was to be the location of the ground over which a counter-attack by reserves would be made. The Rear Zone, four to eight miles to the west, was, essentially a second position.[20] The problem was that in adopting the model, the German concept of elasticity had not

14 War Diary, HQ 16 Infantry Brigade, 11 March 1918, TNA WO95/1607.
15 War Diary, HQ 71 Infantry Brigade, 12 March 1918, TNA WO95/1620. Elements of 25 Division also moved up.
16 War Diary, HQ 71 Infantry Brigade, 18 March 1918, TNA WO95/1620.
17 War Diary, HQ 16 Infantry Brigade, 19 March 1918, TNA WO95/1607.
18 T. O. Marden, *A Short History of the Sixth Division*, p. 46.
19 Edmonds, op. cit. p.38.
20 Edmonds, op. cit. pp.41-2.

been truly grasped, and as Martin Kitchen notes: 'There was considerable confusion as to whether the forward zone was designed merely to hold up the enemy advance or to be held at all costs.'[21] The *Official History* puts the dilemma thus: 'The object of the Forward Zone was … to delay the advance of the enemy and oblige him to deploy in force', but notes the contradiction that 'it was in fact an Outpost Zone, but not to be given up without a struggle.'[22] In the final analysis the argument is academic – the weight of the German attack would likely have broken either system given available British manpower.

IV Corps issued principles of defence on 14 February. Firstly, it was stated clearly that: 'Work on the battle Zone is of paramount importance. (More so than the Front Line).' The 'front line' was to be 'held as thinly as possible commensurate with safety (chiefly by Lewis Guns).' The old-fashioned terminology of 'front line' will be noted, but there is no inference that it should be held all cost, and indeed, it is clear that the corps viewed the Battle Zone as where the main struggle would take place.' The phrase 'Defence in depth' was both used and underlined, instructing 'M.G.s in groups where possible and in great depth. M.G's must make up for weak artillery barrage.' Barrage would be weakened because of 'Artillery in depth. It is better to weaken the barrage than not have sufficient guns back to check a break through.'[23] It is clear that it was understood that the battle would be fought in depth in terms of geographical extent of defensive positions and tactical deployment of firepower to cover this area, without any acknowledgement of elasticity.

In Third and Fifth armies (on which the attack would fall, the latter being immediately to the south of the Third), 'the state of the Forward Zone, which had been improved and maintained by the troops in the line, was good.' There were generally three lines, the third often consisting of small redoubts, the first not held continuously. The condition of 'the Battle Zone was fair, though still incomplete', in particular lacking 'dug-outs for machine gun posts' in Third Army's area. Having been in the area for nearly 12 months, Third Army 'had naturally developed its defences more thoroughly than the Fifth Army', who had taken over an extended line only in January. The Battle Zone similarly contained three lines with switch trenches, but again was not continuous, with centres of resistance. The Rear Zone in Third Army was 'wired throughout with two belts in front of the first line of trenches, and one belt of the second.'[24] 6th Division's own defence scheme has not survived. Marden observed that the hard frost of January had severely hampered digging, but that whilst a complete front and reserve trench existed in the Forward Zone, the support trenches 'hardly existed and dug-outs were notable by their absence' (this

21 M. Kitchen, *The German Offensives of 1918*, p.58.
22 Edmonds, op. cit. p.124.
23 War Diary, HQ IV Corps, Order dated 14 February 1918, TNA WO95/717. (Underlining in original).
24 Edmonds, op. cit. pp.123-4.

last remark not being entirely accurate given the activities of the engineers in the first three weeks in March). He added that 'a good corps line called the Vaulx-Morchies Line had been dug, the nearest portion a mile behind the reserve line', and 'this was held by the Pioneers and RE, owing to scarcity of numbers.' To the rear of this, 25th Division was held across IV Corps to inject into the Battle Zone where needed. Third Army had 27.5 of 80 battalions in the three corps engaged on 21 March in the Forward Zone. 6th Division had all three brigades in line, and each had the equivalent of a battalion in the Forward Zone, and two in the Battle Zone. 'With battalions at just over half-strength, and with the undulating nature of the ground', however, 'the defence resolved itself everywhere into a succession of posts with very limited field of fire.'[25]

6th Division's front of 4,500 yards was on a forward slope opposite the villages of Quéant and Pronville, and No Man's Land averaged three-quarters of a mile in width (see Map 12, colour section). 51st Division was to the south and 59th Division to the north. The countryside was downland 'of well-defined broad spurs and narrow valleys (like the fingers of a partially opened hand).' The Hirondelle (Noreuil) valley lay on the division's left (north), the Lagnicourt valley in the centre, and the Morchies valley in the south. These merged 'into the broad transverse valley' on the enemy's side of No Man's Land, and there was good observation of Quéant and Bourlon Wood to the right. 'All the advantages of ground lay with the defence', Marden concluded,[26] adding wistfully that the position would 'have been almost impregnable had there been sufficient time to complete it, and had there been separate troops for counter-attack.'[27] Despite its broader positive observations on the defences in the Third Army area, the *Official History* was particularly scathing concerning the defences in 6th Division's area. James Edmonds noted that 'its Forward Zone was difficult to hold, being exposed to enemy view and direct fire', and had 'less depth than was the case on most other parts of the line, especially in front of Lagnicourt and northwards, where it was only 500 yards.' Edmonds also claimed that there had been a dispute between the commanders of the two divisions that had previously held the area as to the best method of defence, 'with the unfortunate result that the necessary work had never been completed.' He lamented the absence of shelters and dugouts (which in the final analysis would have been of limited assistance), poor protection for machine guns, and that 'in places there was no reserve line, or only such as had been constructed in a hurry.' Indeed, Edmonds claimed that one battalion commander of 6th Division described the sector 'as "the most disgusting" he had ever met, with little cover to fall back on.'[28]

25 Marden, op. cit. p.45.
26 Marden, op. cit. p.44-5.
27 Marden, op. cit. p.45.
28 Edmonds, op. cit. p.224.

The enemy would attack using an intense bombardment that had, like that of the British at Cambrai, not required registration. They would then employ the so-called 'storm troop' tactics that they had utilised initially effectively on 30 November 1917 (yet which had proved to run out of steam as resistance was increasingly met). The first objective was for *Army Group Crown Prince Rupprecht* to trap British forces in the Cambrai salient and then, secondly, to push on towards Péronne and Arras. If the tactics employed were highly effective for break-in, the 'Michael' offensive, and its planned successors, were operationally bankrupt. Even with its reinforcements from the East, a breakthrough was unlikely, especially as the lack of real attention to logistics meant that crossing the old Somme battlefields would become a practical nightmare. If it was hoped that a series of tactical victories in successive offensives would bring the Allies to the negotiating table, then such hopes were to be misplaced. On the ground on 21 March however, facing the two divisions of IV Corps were three divisions of *XI Corps,* three divisions of *XIV Reserve Corps* and five divisions of *VI Reserve Corps, Seventeenth Army*, commanded by General Otto von Below.[29] With *Seventeenth Army's* 'success or failure stood or fell the whole "Michael" plan.'[30] They would attack with six divisions in the first line, two in the second and three in the third. The *Official History* notes 'the odds in the first instance were 3 to 1 and finally 11 to 3.'[31]

'Michael' 21-22 March 1918

Lieutenant-Colonel Bernard Prior of 9th Norfolk ventured out into No Man's Land on the night of the 20th and 'obtained the impression that this was no longer a false alarm.' In the enemy lines 'there was a stillness which at the same time was not a complete silence, just as if a large number of men were in position waiting in intense excitement and speaking to each other in whispers.'[32] Colonel Georg Bruchmüller's bombardment opened at 05.00.[33] The *Official History* describes that for 6th Division, this, 'especially on the centre and left, was particularly severe.'[34] 18 Brigade were on the right of the divisional front, 71 Brigade in the centre, and 16 Brigade on the left. 18 Brigade noted how the bombardment 'continued with uninterrupted fury for five

29 The victor of Caporetto, Otto von Below (1857-1944) was a capable general who had previously fought on the Eastern Front and in Macedonia. He had become the youngest German general to command an army in November 1914.
30 Edmonds, op. cit. p.151.
31 Edmonds, op. cit. p.221.
32 War Diary, 9th Battalion Norfolk Regiment, 'Diary of Lieutenant-Colonel B.H.L. Prior', TNA WO95/1623.
33 Georg Bruchmüller (1863-1948) was the German Army's artillery specialist. He had made his mark on the Eastern Front. On 21 March 6,608 guns fired 3.2 million rounds. Guns were silently registered, and a creeping barrage was fired with phosgene mixed with a lachrymatory gas, and smoke.
34 Edmonds, op. cit. p.225.

hours.'[35] 71 Brigade believed that 'there seemed to be such a large concentration of guns against us that there was no necessity for the enemy to lift his barrage from one line to another.'[36] The attack, when it came through the dense fog between 08.00 and 08.30 on 18 Brigade (times seem to have varied at different points on the line), 'was in long lines extended to two paces and at some 50 yards interval. Covered by from 10 to twelve such waves, the remainder of the troops advanced in artillery formation.'[37] 1st West Yorkshire were on the right of the 18 Brigade front, 2nd Durham Light Infantry on the right. 'Each battalion held the line with two companies in the front line and support, and two companies in the reserve line. The VM Line in front of Morchies was held by the 12th Field Company RE and one company 11th Leicestershire Pioneer Regiment.'[38] 11th Essex were in reserve.

The attack against 18 Brigade along the Morchies valley, 21 March 1918.

35 War Diary, HQ 18 Infantry Brigade, 'Narrative of the fighting on the 21st and 22nd March in front of Morchies', TNA WO95/1615.
36 War Diary, HQ 71 Infantry Brigade, 'Narrative of operations on 21st and 22nd March 1918', TNA WO95/1620.
37 War Diary, HQ 18 Infantry Brigade, 'Narrative of the fighting on the 21st and 22nd March in front of Morchies', TNA WO95/1615.
38 War Diary, HQ 18 Infantry Brigade, 'Narrative of the fighting on the 21st and 22nd March in front of Morchies', TNA WO95/1615.

The front companies of both 1st West Yorkshire and 2nd DLI had suffered very heavy casualties in the bombardment and were immediately overrun (although the *Official History* states that 'a platoon of the 1st West Yorkshire' in the Forward Zone, held out 'until about 5 P.M., it is believed.')[39] The enemy had relatively quickly overrun the Louverval Salient, which was defended by 51st Division, penetrated the support line of 153 Brigade to 18 Brigade's right by 10.00, and was thus able to turn on the West Yorkshire's flank. At 10.10 Colonel Boyall reported that the enemy threatened his support line.[40] The brigade had lost telephonic communication with its units at 07.00, the last runners had arrived a half hour later, and messages were now sent by pigeon. At 10.30 the battalion HQ of 2nd DLI was under attack but Second-Lieutenant Hubert McBain organised a counterattack, which drove the enemy back.[41] German machine-guns and ammunition were captured and turned on the enemy. Thus the DLI held on, but the enemy were bringing up artillery and they were under heavy machine gun fire. 11th Essex were ordered forward at 10.30, two companies to reinforce the West Yorkshires' threatened right flank, and at 11.45 one company was sent to reinforce the DLI. It was clear that the enemy had taken Lagnicourt to the left, and the brigade recorded that 'by 2.30 p.m. the situation was most critical, the 1st West Yorkshire Regt., 2nd Durham Light Infantry, 3 companies 11th Essex and one company 9th Norfolk, 71st Brigade, being practically surrounded.'[42] The brigade was in danger of ceasing to exist. At this point 6th Division issued orders for 71 and 18 Brigades to hold out in the Reserve Line. At 15.00, Colonel Boyall, now commanding all the surviving troops in contact with the enemy reported that if no reinforcements were received, 'the situation was hopeless and retirement impossible', ammunition was running low, but they indeed would 'fight it out to the last' in the Reserve Line.[43] The last message that brigade received was at 16.00, Boyall reporting the enemy within 40 yards of his HQ. It was relatively easy to staunch a frontal attack, but penetration to the flank was impossible to deal with. At 19.15, Boyall and Lieutenant-Colonel Brereton of 2nd DLI,[44] who were still holding out, retired to the VM Line, the rear

39 Edmonds, op. cit. p.225.
40 Alfred Morey Boyall had been a Regular captain of the West Yorkshire Regiment in August 1914, had served as Staff Captain and DAAG 1915-16, and had taken command of 1st West Yorkshire in November 1916.
41 Hubert McBain was awarded the Military Cross. 'He led a counter-attack and established a block in a trench at a very critical time. He held this position for four hours and greatly assisted his battalion to maintain its position. He showed great fearlessness and devotion to duty. In the afternoon he was wounded.' *Edinburgh Gazette*, 18 September 1918, p.3421.
42 War Diary, HQ 18 Infantry Brigade, 'Narrative of the fighting on the 21st and 22nd March in front of Morchies', TNA WO95/1615.
43 War Diary, HQ 18 Infantry Brigade, 'Narrative of the fighting on the 21st and 22nd March in front of Morchies', TNA WO95/1615.
44 Davis Lloyd Brereton was a Regular captain of the DLI in August 1914, had served as a Brigade Major in 1916, and had only taken command of the battalion in February 1918.

of the Battle Zone, the enemy following 300 yards to their rear. The remnants of the brigade were pitiful. Of 1st West Yorkshire, two officers and 98 ORs remained; from 2nd DLI there were three officers and 128 ORs, whilst 11th Essex could boast five officers and 140 ORs. Colonel Boyall appears to have been wounded and captured in this retreat, and Colonel Dumbell of 11th Essex took command of the VM Line.[45]

The attack against 71 Brigade at Lagnicourt, 21 March 1918. The picture is taken from the site of Bradford Reserve trench.

In 71 Brigade the 9th Norfolk were situated to the right and 2nd Sherwood Foresters on the left of the brigade front, whilst 1st Leicestershire were in reserve. 459 Field Company RE and one company of 11th Leicestershire were in the VM Line. The Sherwood Foresters were attacked at 09.12 and a general attack along the whole front began at 09.50. The Sherwoods actually held the enemy in the Forward Zone until 10.00, and then withdrew to the Support Line, which was soon overwhelmed. Marden credits the brigade with 'the only authenticated accounts of a successful resistance in the front system.'[46] Second-Lieutenant Herbert Taylor[47] described how

45 Charles Harold Dumbell had been a Regular captain of the Sherwood Foresters in August 1914, and had taken command of the unit in September 1917, holding it until the Armistice.
46 Marden, op. cit. p.46.
47 Herbert Gordon Taylor had been on the Western Front since November 1915 and had been commissioned from rank of sergeant in May 1917. He would be taken prisoner on 21 March.

SOS rockets in the fog brought no supporting fire, and Colonel Prior of 9th Norfolks was deeply frustrated that the trench mortars were only responding to SOS calls and that these, of course, were invisible. Taylor described how the advancing enemy 'made great use of machine guns and for his flanking fire had three men to a gun – one having the gun strapped on his back and dropping into a shell-hole or the like with it, while the second man fired from his back.'[48] The Sherwoods withdrew to the Reserve Line, but even here there had been severe casualties, and between 10.15 and 11.15 heavy fighting took place in Skipton Reserve (to the south-east of Lagnicourt), and Bradford Reserve (in front of Lagnicourt) where the 9th Norfolks would retire to. Whilst this was happening, the enemy, who had attacked in great strength up the Lagnicourt valley between 9th Norfolk and 16 Brigade, were advancing swiftly. The Skipton strong-point was penetrated on two occasions, but the enemy were driven out again by bombing attacks. In Bradford Reserve, Lieutenant-Colonel Prior noted that Captain Gerald Failes[49] 'rang up on the phone and reported that the enemy had attacked his position in great force and had been completely routed and that he could hold his trenches easily against any frontal attack.' Feeling 'considerably elated', Prior was returning to battalion HQ only to see 'a party of the enemy coming over the brow of the hill not 50 yards away.'[50] At 11.00 1st Leicestershire were ordered to send two companies forward to 9th Norfolk in Bradford Reserve, as what Prior had witnessed, of course, was the enemy's penetration between them and 16 Brigade. Bradford Reserve had to be given up, but the Sherwood Foresters in Skipton Reserve hung on. At 13.00 the enemy threated Skipton from Lagnicourt, and the trench was evacuated, and a defensive flank was formed to the west and south to the village by the Norfolks and Sherwoods in a wired communication trench, the Lagnicourt Switch. During this withdrawal, Major Hubert Tylden-Wright,[51] commanding the Sherwood Foresters, was wounded. Earlier, at 15.00, 16 Brigade reported that their Reserve Line was broken, and the enemy were pouring through to the north of Lagnicourt towards the VM Line. Worryingly, at 16.00 the enemy had secured a footing in the VM Line

48 H.C. Wylly, *1st and 2nd Battalions Sherwood Foresters (Nottinghamshire and Derbyshire Regiment) in the Great War*, Kindle Edition location 6453.

49 Gerald Watson Failes DSO MC had been a private in the Reserve Regiment of Cavalry, commissioned in February 1915. His DSO was awarded for this action. 'He showed good initiative in promptly moving all his Lewis guns to meet the direction of an enemy attack, breaking their attack up. He also led a bombing squad, successfully, rallied and reorganised stragglers, and by his fine example greatly conduced to the splendid resistance made by his men.' *London Gazette*, 13 September 1918, p.10865. Failes was killed in action on 15 April 1918.

50 War Diary, 9th Battalion Norfolk Regiment, 'Diary of Lieutenant-Colonel B.H.L. Prior', TNA WO95/1623. Prior met Failes later in the day and he claimed that his company had 'accounted for upwards of 2,000 of the enemy.'

51 Hubert Tylden-Wright was a captain of Nottinghamshire & Derbyshire Territorial ASC in August 1914. He had commanded the battalion as a lieutenant-colonel for four weeks in October-December 1917.

near Vaulx Wood, some 1,000 yards in the rear of the 18 Brigade units' positions. Although the enemy were ejected by 2nd South Lancashire of 75 Brigade in reserve, by 18.45 the Lagnicourt Switch was untenable, and the remnants of 9th Norfolk and 2nd Sherwood Foresters withdrew to the VM Line. That night, there were collected there 120 all ranks of 9th Norfolk, a similar number from the Sherwood Foresters, with 9 officers and 329 ORs of 1st Leicestershire. Colonel Prior sorted out each of the units and organised their companies for defence for the night.

The attack against 16 Brigade at Noreuil, 21 March 1918.

16 Brigade was on the division's left and had 2nd York & Lancaster in line on the brigade right, 1st King's Shropshire Light Infantry to the left, and 1st Buffs in reserve. The attack developed just after 08.00, the enemy proceeding up the L'Hirondelle valley to the left and the Lagnicourt valley to the right. The company of 2nd York & Lancasters in the Forward Zone were nearly all killed or wounded by the barrage, and only 15 ORs made their way back as the attack on the left of 71 Brigade advanced. No infantry attack developed, however, from the front. Lieutenant-Colonel Blunt alleged that his C and D Companies watched as the garrison of neighbouring battalion, 9th Norfolk, in the Reserve Line (Bradford Reserve) 'surrendered without fighting, being plainly visible leaving the trench with their hands up as the enemy approached.'[52]

52 War Diary, 2nd Battalion York & Lancaster Regiment, 'Report of operations in Vaux

This failure allowed the enemy to reach Lagnicourt, the surrender presumably taking place to the left of where Captain Failes was making his stand. The enemy was thus able to attack the right flank of Blunt's battalion, and the company there were beaten back. The enemy was sequentially penetrating his front to the right as they advanced, and all Blunt could do was form a defensive flank there as the enemy poured towards Lagnicourt. Blunt eventually was forced to withdraw holding defensive flanks both right and left.

On the left, B Company of 1st King's Shropshire Light Infantry in the Forward Zone had been smashed by the barrage and the remnants, officerless, fell back. Meanwhile the enemy had swiftly reached Noreuil, 500 yards behind the Reserve Line, 59th Division to the left having been pushed back, and the battalion, like the York and Lancasters, was being attacked in its flank, this time to the left. Colonel Horace Smith set off with three platoons in what must have been a hopeless venture in counterattack towards Noreuil, only to end up a prisoner of war.[53] The War Diary describes how after inflicting 'enormous losses on the enemy', the remainder of the battalion that did not retire, 'seeing themselves surrounded, determined to fight to the last.' This appears to have occurred in Lagnicourt Trench, 'little more than a ditch',[54] stretched between Noreuil and Lagnicourt. Fifty-five survivors of the battalion finally gathered in the VM Line under a lieutenant, their retreat having been covered by four machine-guns 'which continued firing until the enemy was within forty yards of them.'[55] (In contrast, Lance-Corporal Thomas Brookbank's two guns were taken in the fog without firing a single shot).[56] 1st Buffs, who had not been thrust forward to support the other two battalions, were intact, observed at 15.20 'a race for the occupation of the VAULX MORCHIES LINE' between a counterattacking battalion, 8th Border Regiment, 75 Brigade, who were attached as 6th Division's reserve, (aided by parties from the Divisional Bombing School) 'and the advanced troops of the enemy', approaching behind a creeping barrage and supported by aircraft. The Borders reached their goal first, the enemy being held up by wire. The Germans reached the VM Line in 16 Brigade's area near Vaulx Wood, but were ejected by the 11th Leicesters, the divisional pioneers, swapping spades for rifles. Lance-Corporal Brookbank described the VM line as only waist deep with little frontal protection. Setting up his gun on the parapet, one of the day's many acts of heroism unfolded in front of him, the enemy advancing a thousand yards away:

Area', March 1918, TNA WO95/1610.

53 Horace Mackenzie Smith was a Regular major of 1st KSLI in August 1914 and had been depot major. He commanded 5th KSLI until July 1915, 15th Royal Fusiliers for three months in mid-1916, and 1st KSLI from February 1918.

54 Edmonds, op. cit. p.227.

55 Edmonds, op. cit. p.227.

56 T. & M. Brookbank, *A Soldier of the 6th Division*, p.24.

> My attention was drawn to a team of six horses with a gun limber and spare outrider galloping towards the on-coming enemy, they became temporarily out of sight in a fold in the ground with only the heads of the riders to be seen. Suddenly, they were on their way back at full gallop drawing an 18 pounder gun behind the limber which they had limbered up right under the nose and in full sight of the still advancing enemy troops. I felt so proud of the operation I felt like throwing my steel helmet in the air.[57]

Two battalions of 40th Division arrived on the left to shore up the damaged right wing of 59th Division, and the situation thus stabilised on 6th Division's left. The problems presented to 16 Brigade has caused them to retire to the VM Line some five hours before 18 Brigade, whose stiff resistance had left them in a perilous position, the most exposed brigade of 59th, 6th, or 51st Divisions.

General Marden, who throughout the day could do very little other than to shuffle his very limited reserves, gave the enemy much credit. 'Fog favoured the Germans in that it prevented us seeing when the attack was launched', but praise was due for 'the skill they evinced and the dash with which they pushed forward and brought up successive waves of attackers.' By concentrating on the L'Hirondelle Valley to the left, the Lagnicourt Valley in the centre, and the Morchies Valley on the right 'they avoided much of the fire which they would have encountered on the broad spurs, and thus worked round and isolated the garrisons on the latter.'[58] The *Official History* speaks of 'a firm stand' being made by 6th Division 'against heavy odds', but at cost. In addition to infantry losses, 'fifty percent of the divisional artillery were put out of action early in the day.'[59] The division's fatalities totalled 714 (606 infantry, 49 RFA, 21 MGC, 29 RE and 9 RAMC). 51st Division to the right had suffered 394, and 59th Division to the left suffered 906, the highest total of the whole day. 6th Division's total fatalities were the fourth highest of the 18 attacked.[60] The fact was, however, that these losses had not been in vain – the enemy had failed to break through. *Seventeenth Army* 'seem to have exhausted their initial momentum early in the afternoon', and the enemy had been taken aback, in that the British 'had offered unexpectedly strong resistance.'[61] Tactically the enemy's methods had been successful. The bombardment had caused massive casualties in the Forward Zone. Then, 'the men of the advanced groups had slung rifles and made no attempt to use them, trusting to ... bombs.' Reaching a British defensive position, 'they hurled their bombs and at once jumped in to settle the defenders with club or bayonet.' The complete lack of a frontal attack on 16 Brigade, and the virtual surrounding of 18 Brigade, demonstrates the success

57 Brookbank,op. cit. p.25.
58 Marden, op. cit. p.46.
59 Edmonds, op. cit. p.225.
60 D. Tattersfield, 'The Kaiser's Battle – A Statistical Re-Analysis.'
61 Edmonds, op. cit. p.262, German source not given.

of infiltration made doubly successful by the cloaking fog. 'The next parties pushed on through gaps and then came others to deal with the centres of resistance by means of machine guns, flame projectors, trench mortars and field guns.'[62] Later attacks in the day and on the following day did not, however, match the sophistication of the morning, the enemy advancing en masse. In retrospect, the Germans themselves were critical of the operations against IV Corps. 'On the 21st, German O.H.L. let its basic strategic idea drop into the background, not being able to believe with full confidence in the possible success of this idea … it sent no fresh forces to the heavily engaged *Seventeenth Army*.'[63]

Marden wrote that 'the night was quiet, both sides preparing for the next day's struggle.'[64] It may have been quiet in terms of absence of fighting, but it is unlikely that any staff officer at his HQ slept. On the division's left, where 'practically the whole of the 178th Brigade had disappeared from the battle',[65] it was understood that the enemy occupied the VM line northwards for some 500 yards, and reassurance must have been felt at 01.00 on the 22nd when it was learnt that 40th Division would be relieving the right of the 59th. 75 Brigade (25th Division) was at Marden's disposal, 8th Border already having been used to support 16 Brigade. 2nd South Lancashire were sent to 71 Brigade, with 11th Cheshire moving in the morning to support 18 Brigade. At 05.00 Marden learnt that the 'Composite Battalion of Corps Reinforcement Camp' had moved into his reserve, and even more cheering news at 06.50 that 41st Division was concentrating to take over from the 6th.[66] Another long day of heavy fighting remained, however.

On the 22nd, 18 Brigade now had 74 Brigade (25th Division) supporting 153 Brigade of 51st Division on its right, and the three formations merged their HQs. At 15.00 a heavy bombardment opened on the VM Line, and half an hour later the left flank of 11th Leicestershire was penetrated and by 16.00 the enemy had machine-guns firing into 71 Brigade's flank from the rear. At 16.30 2nd Durham Light Infantry were attacked, and a counter-attack led by Second-Lieutenant James Eccles drove the enemy back,[67] but although a renewed attack was held by men lying in shell-holes, bombs were nearly exhausted, and a third attack drove the Durhams and the remnants of 1st West Yorkshire, now totalling only some 50 men in all, back through Morchies, onto 74 Brigade holding a line to the rear of the village. As the enemy began pouring through to the right, the brigades began to withdraw. Only 11th Essex could summon enough men to join 74, 75 and 153 Brigades in checking the enemy advance. The

62 Edmonds, op. cit. p.262-3.
63 Edmonds, op. cit. p.262, quoting *Militär Wochenblatt*, March 1928.
64 Marden, op. cit. p.48.
65 Edmonds, op. cit. p231.
66 War Diary, HQ 6th Division, 'Narrative of Operations on 21st and 22nd March', TNA WO95/1584.
67 James Edward Eccles had arrived on the Western Front in April 1915 and had been commissioned in May 1917.

fact that the line held was due not least to a counter-attack by the 25 tanks of 2nd Tank Battalion, one of three such battalions in Third Army reserve. Covered by 256th Brigade RFA, who fired 20,600 rounds in four hours over open sights, firing smoke shells at this point, they advanced towards Morchies, and the enemy retired. Only nine of the 25 tanks, with 30 percent of the crews, came out of action.[68] 18 Brigade had totalled 1,787 other ranks and 79 officers in the trenches on the morning of the 21st – on the morning of the 23rd, 110 other ranks and eight officers remained.[69]

In the centre, 71 Brigade had spent its night reorganising its line, and became aware at 08.30 that 16 Brigade to their left were under attack. This assault reached their front at 09.00 but was repulsed. Further attacks continued between 10.00 and 13.00, and the line was only broken at Vaulx Wood and 2nd South Lancashire were forced back to form a defensive to the south of the wood. Steadily as the afternoon progressed, however, attacks drove the brigade out of the VM Line towards the companies of the Corps Reinforcement Battalion to the rear of the wood, who had been both waiting to prevent any enemy breakthrough and digging trenches. Marden had sent the CRE, Lieutenant-Colonel Goldney, out at 08.30 that morning to site and arrange for the digging of these positions in anticipation of a breakthrough. As the shelling began that morning, Colonel Prior of 9th Norfolk recorded that his men, without rations were 'so worn out that they were indifferent to shellfire.' Liaising with Captain Kenneth Bion of the 2nd Sherwood Foresters,[70] Prior totted up that he had perhaps 80 men and the Sherwoods some 100. Colonel Francis Latham of 1st Leicesters asked Prior to bring the two units into line to his left.[71] Confusion reigned as to what was happening, but Prior became painfully aware that 'the sky line on the whole of our front became a mass of moving field grey figures.' He was able to describe the nature of the enemy attack in detail. Ahead of the main bulk he could see small groups pushing forward. These were not scouts, as Prior first thought, but 'machine gunners armed with light machine guns.' He observed 'one group of 3 men advance to within 3 or 400 yards of our men and they must have been at least a mile if not more in front of their main infantry advance.' The attack was proceeding diagonally to Prior's front, and he could see that 'the formation adopted was very similar to our "artillery formation", and the men were well extended.[72] Prior was wounded at this

68 Edmonds, op. cit. p.310.

69 War Diary, HQ 18 Infantry Brigade, 'Narrative of the fighting on the 21st and 22nd March in front of Morchies', TNA WO95/1615.

70 Kenneth Norman Bion had been commissioned in March 1915. All sources record him as being killed on 21 March, but Prior was liaising with him on the morning of the 22nd, and the war diary of 2nd Sherwood Foresters has him killed that day. He was shot in the head as the unit withdrew.

71 Francis Latham was a captain of 1st Leicestershire in August 1914. He would briefly command 9th Norfolk in September 1916, then 9th Suffolk from that point until February 1918, moving immediately to command 1st Leicestershire until the Armistice.

72 War Diary, 9th Battalion Norfolk Regiment, 'Diary of Lieutenant-Colonel B.H.L. Prior', TNA WO95/1623.

point, and was not in command when, under Captains Failes and Bion, the Norfolks and Sherwoods were forced to pull back. 1st Leicestershire were the last to leave the VM Line. They were subjected to heavy machine-gun fire from the front; the right (where 18 Brigade had been forced back); the left (where the Norfolks and Sherwoods had given way); and from the left rear. They had formed blocks at either end of their section of the VM Line, but no bombs were left. 'As soon as the men lined the parapet they were shot down by machine-gun bullets from the rear.'[73] At 16.10 they filed down a trench towards Morchies. This was covered by several enemy machine-gun, causing multiple casualties, but there was no other route. To complete their misery, as they withdrew over the ridge to the west of Morchies, they were caught by a 4.2-inch barrage. The units of the brigade fell back on 74 Brigade, and this line held, given the tank attack in support. On the morning of the 23rd, in terms of its infantry, 71 Brigade comprised eleven officers and 252 ORs.

The enemy attack fell on 16 Brigade at 10.00, breaking through at Vaulx Wood. The bombardment prior to this was ineffective as the brigade had withdrawn its troops from the VM Line to small rifle-pits to the rear. 25th Division's counterattack pushed the Germans back, but was delivered to the right of the wood, which did not relieve the pressure on 16 Brigade to the left of the wood. A defensive flank to the wood was formed, pushed back on the eastern edge of Vaux-Vralcourt village. The enemy was sandwiched between two defensive flanks (2nd South Lancashire holding that to the right) and could not progress. The *Official History* quotes a German account:

> The losses mount up. The German appetite for attack dwindles. Thoughts of Verdun came back to recollection; can it be that the attack has run itself to a standstill on the second day? Watches show that it is past 2 P.M. Not a move relieves the horrible stagnation.[74]

At 14.00 the attack witnessed by Prior fell on the brigade at the corner of the VM Line and the defensive flank. A wedge was driven between 8th Border Regiment and 1st Buffs, whose flank was up in the air, and they, too, had to pivot to the rear on Vaulx village. 40th Division now fell back to the brigade's left, and they were ordered to conform, but could not as 40th Division had retired so swiftly. The brigade now had both flanks exposed. Under the weight of continued attacks they withdrew by 18.00 to the Beugny–Ytres, or Army Line, which had been dug that day. 2nd York & Lancaster, 150 strong at the start of the day, covered the withdrawal with close fighting in Vaulx village – they were almost surrounded by the time they followed the rest of the brigade to safety. The day's fighting on this part of front had been vicious. Marden noted that the 'sunken road which contained the Headquarters of the 16th

73 H. C. Wylly, *History of the 1st & 2nd Battalions the Leicestershire Regiment in the Great War*, pp.69-70.
74 Edmonds, op. cit. citing Goes.

and 71st Infantry Brigades changed hand three times.'[75] 16 Brigade's casualties for March were 52 officers and 1,131 ORs.

	Killed		Wounded		Missing	
	Officers	ORs	Officers	ORs	Officers	ORs
1st Buffs	1	27	3	103	2	66
1st KSLI		8	4	22	17	469
2nd York & Lancaster	4	36	10	45	6	310
16th TM Battery				1	1	31
1st West Yorkshire	1	9	3	21	19	540
11th Essex	5	32	6	104	6	281
2nd DLI	1	16	7	60	20	509
18th TM Battery				2	1	22
9th Norfolk	4	31	7	158	8	173
1st Leicestershire	6	32	4	84	11	335
2nd Sherwood Foresters	3	5	7	9	10	476
71st TM Battery		5		7	1	16
6th Btn MGC	3	10	4	65	7	206
12th Field Coy RE	1	11	1	29		7
459th Field Coy RE	1	1		11		
509th Field Coy RE		5		12		4
6th Signal Coy RE		1		6		5
209th Divnl Employment Coy						3

Table 11.1: IV Corps estimate of 6th Division casualties 21-22 March 1918.

That night, 6th Division were relieved by the 41st. Marden reports the casualties as 3,900 out of a trench strength of 5,000 infantry – 78 percent. The extent of the casualties as they were understood by IV Corps at the end of March 1918 are detailed in Table 11.1 – the number of troops listed as missing is remarkable. The losses of 6th Machine Gun Battalion, whose guns had been pushed forward onto parapets to hold up the advancing enemy are also notable.

However desperate matters had been, IV Corps had held the enemy, and Ludendorff and Crown Prince Rupprecht called off *Seventeenth Army*'s push towards Arras on the

75 Marden, op. cit. p.48.

23rd. Pursuing success where it was to be had, they were ordered to join in the attack on Fifth Army, which had been successful, with an aim now to drive a wedge between the French and British. The enemy attack would now head into the broken wastes of the old Somme battlefield. 6th Division would not be part of this. Having carried out a defence which can justly be called heroic and having mounted a more effective defence than the divisions on either of their flanks, on 25 March they entrained for the Ypres salient once more, where decimated divisions were collected to recover. They would not enjoy rest.

'Georgette' 9-29 April 1917

Although 'Michael' was the first and main effort of the German assaults, it was not the only one planned. 'Georgette' would take place next, a thrust against the British positions before the River Lys, hopefully weakened by the need to send forces south. It opened on 9 April. Thirdly there would be a push north and south of Arras, 'Mars.' The latter was abandoned in favour of two alternative offensives, 'Blücher–Yorck', targeted at the Chemin des Dames, which would open on 27 May. This attack would fall mainly on the French and, again, would hopefully draw forces away from the Channel. 'Gneisenau' (Battle of the Matz), commenced on 9 June, and was merely an exploitation of the tactical success of the previous offensive. Lastly, there was 'Marneschütz–Reims', an attack east and west of Reims, on 15 July. Each attack, although initially successful, ground to a halt more quickly. 'Michael' would last 14 days; 'Georgette' would endure longest, at 20 days; 'Blücher–Yorck' was shorter, at seven days; 'Gneisenau' even briefer, lasting five days; whilst the Reims offensive would only be sustainable for two days.

The division now formed part of XXII Corps, and at the start of April 16 and 18 Brigades took over the front from Broodseinde south to Polygon Wood, 71 Brigade southwards from Reutel. Prior to this, the King had inspected representatives of each unit in Steenvorde on the 28th, 'asking them questions on what had happened and what they had done' in the 'Michael' operation.[76] The Ypres Salient was (in their view unfortunately) well known to the division from 1915-16. The general situation was grim. 1st Buffs observed that in the wake of the Third Battle of Ypres, the 'battle line is a desolate waste of mire and shell holds. The only communication being possible by trench boards and wooden roads, even the landscape seems changed from when the B(attalio)n was last here nearly 2 years ago.'[77] Thomas Brookbank described how movement was only possible at night, 'when we all had to walk these bridges in the dark' and 'they were constantly swept by machine gun fire.' The conditions for the troops were dismal: 'Always cold and damp with wet feet, we tie old rubber sheets

76 War Diary, HQ 71 Infantry Brigade, 28 March 1918, TNA WO95/1620.
77 War Diary, 1st Battalion Buffs, 30 March 1918, WO95/1608.

about our feet to help keep them as dry as possible.'[78] Marden was equally bleak about the state of the divisions in the Salient. These had 'been brought up to a respectable strength by drafts from all sources – wounded men belonging to other formations, RASC, Labour Battalions etc.', claiming that many 'had received no training in infantry weapons or methods of fighting.'[79] Within the records of 6th Division, however, there are no complaints noted concerning their quality. Thus in 18 Brigade, infantry trench strength in 18 Brigade was 80 officers and 1867 ORs immediately prior to 21 March, and 34 officers and 577 ORs on the 26th, whist at the end of the month the trench strength stood at 40 officers and 1333 ORs. Other brigades were not as well off. The ration strength of 71 Brigade had been 110 officers and 2,465 ORs on 1st March, and 53 officers and 759 ORs on the 31st.

The 'Georgette' offensive would fall on the line south of the division on 9 April, its northern end being the Messines Ridge. In the early hours of the 10th a German deserter reported that there would be an attack at 05.00. The information was very specific. *7th Division* would attack with its right on the Becelaere-Menin road. A high state of readiness was affected, and the enemy positions were bombarded, but no attack materialised. Later that day, as Messines fell, 6th Division made preparations for a further attack on 11th, and although fighting continued that day around Wytschaete, and the enemy advanced to within six miles of Hazebrouck, again no attack developed. On the 13th, 71 Brigade were ordered to move south to support 25th Division, IX Corps (see Map 13, colour section). Heavy fighting was going on around Neuve Eglise, south of Mount Kemmel, when they arrived. They took up positions between Neuve Eglise and Dranoutre the following day. Towards the end of the 14th preparations were being made to counter-attack the enemy who had now taken Neuve Eglise, but instead a withdrawal was ordered, 71 Brigade covering the whole of what was now 49th Division's front, some 3,200 yards, whilst the retirement was achieved. At 13.45 on the 15th, an intense barrage came down upon the British front line. 71 Brigade had all its units up, 9th Norfolk on the right, 1st Leicestershire in the centre, and 2nd Sherwood Foresters to the right. The infantry attack fell at 14.30 upon 9th Norfolk at Crucifix Hill (or Corner), some 2,500 yards west of Neuve Eglise. After half an hour's fighting, the enemy had established a footing in the front line but was pushed out by the reserve company in a successful counter-attack, who then had to hold a defensive flank to their right where 59th Division had been pushed back. The enemy pressed hard with heavy machine guns and the Norfolks, much depleted, were forced to fall back on 1st Leicesteshire, 1,500 yards south of Dranoutre. Lieutenant Albert Muggeridge, a platoon commander in B Company of the Leicesters, had his platoon in a series of shell-holes, and described the 'terrific bombardment' developing in intensity as the day went on, with 'our position … further harassed by enemy aircraft which flew low.' The German infantry advanced downhill 'in small masses' which

78 Brookbank, op. cit. pp.27-8.
79 Marden, op. cit. p.53.

'made an easy target for our fire.' They had, however, a 'small field gun in an advanced position and it was doing much damage.' Muggeridge's company was twice forced to reorganise its line, and confusion abounded, with 'verbal messages of a contradictory nature ... continually being passed along.'[80] That night the brigade retired to the western slopes of Mount Kemmel, in support to 49th Division.[81]

Mount Kemmel, it was so ordered, had to be held at all cost. Heavy fighting ensued on the 16th, but the brigade, although it moved companies up, did not come into action, and this situation persisted for the next three days, until 49th Division were relieved by the French. General Brown recorded 'a trying week' during which 'very little sleep was got' as the battalions were 'lying out in the open prepared to counter-attack at very short notice, and at no time were they under cover, either from shell-fire or weather.' Shell-fire accounted for most of the casualties, the two front companies of 9th Norfolk having been virtually wiped out, the rest suffering heavily in the counter-attack which had restored the line.[82] The brigade suffered six officers and 55 ORs killed, with 19 officers and 404 ORs wounded, whilst two officers and 293 ORs were missing. The total casualties came to 779, whereas three weeks earlier the brigade had only totalled 812 officers and other ranks.

Meanwhile, on 16 April, the British line in the Salient had been withdrawn, in response to the progress made by the enemy to the south of Ypres. This was a moment of high tension for machine-gunner Thomas Brookbank, withdrawing at 16.00 in daylight. 'At four p.m. figures could be seen running as fast as their legs could carry them. Our loads were quite heavy, and it was exhausting running along the duckboard bridges.' Reaching the appointed rendezvous, the guns were loaded on limbers: 'At full gallop, riders lashing their horses for more speed, we have five miles to go down the Menin road.' After a mile, the enemy began to shell them. 'Through the Menin Gate ... we went still at full stretch gallop for at that time and moment with shells bursting all around.' Brookbank and his fellows had been astride the boxes of ammunition: 'For days after we could not walk properly ... we were ... most severely shaken; so much that all of us suffered from tummy trouble, diarroea and looseness making life even more unpleasant for several days afterwards.'[83] When Mount Kemmel was lost by the French 28th Division on 25 April (no mean achievement on the part of the enemy), the outpost line was drawn in. 6th Division now held a line from the west end of Zillebeke Lake north to White Chateau near Hellfire Corner. They were roughly 2,000 yards west of Hooge, taken at such cost in August 1915, and now surrendered to the enemy. A further German attack to cut off the Ypres Salient, which did not involve the division, was halted on the 29th. 'Georgette', like 'Michael', had failed.

80 A.H. Muggeridge, Private Papers, IWM Docs 8493.
81 Comprising 100 and 148 Infantry Brigades and 'Wyatt's Force.'
82 War Diary, HQ 71 Infantry Brigade, 'Narrative of operations 14th to 20th April, 1918', TNE WO95/1620.
83 Brookbank, op. cit. pp.31-2.

Between 11 and 14 May the division relieved the 19th Division to the south, now holding the line from Zillebeke Lake to Elzenwalle. The French *14th Division* was to their right.[84] The division began raiding again, 11th Essex targeting Manor Farm on the 19th, and 2nd Durham Light Infantry carrying out a two-company raid east of Bedford House on the 22nd. On the 27th, however, a German attack drove the French back out of their positions in Ridge Wood almost to Dickebush Lake. This exposed the division's right flank, and Marden ordered elements of 2nd DLI up to be ready to hold a defensive flank, and the divisional artillery to put down a barrage. At mid-day, despite continual confusion as to what the position of the French actually was, II Corps ordered the division to assist the French in counter-attacking. General Craufurd, commanding 18 Brigade, Lieutenant-Colonel Dumbell, commanding 11th Essex, and Major Hill-Dillon, the GSO2 (Lieutenant-Colonel Grove, the GSO1, already having visited the French two hours earlier), went to the HQ of *14th Division*, and a joint plan was worked out. This was modified in the early evening, as the position became clearer, and the two GOCs conferred to achieve this.[85] During the attack on the following morning, Second-Lieutenant James Willett and a French interpreter were constantly moving between the battalion the French HQ,[86] and the *13th Battalion, Chasseurs Alpins*, arriving overnight (with the *47th Battalion*) to relieve the exhausted French division, attached one officer and ten ORs to 11th Essex for liaison purposes.[87] It was a model of inter-allied communication.

11th Essex attacked at 04.00 under a barrage of French and British guns, and were on their objective within two hours, although there were no French troops to their right. It appears that the *13th Chasseurs* had issued their orders hurriedly, only 75 minutes before jump-off, and their forming up line ran diagonally across the line of advance of the Essex unit. To add to the French woes, *47th Chasseurs*, attacking on the right of the *13th*, simply did not put in an appearance. This meant that Colonel Dumbell had to utilise the platoons of 2nd DLI that had been ordered up the previous day to fill in gaps between his unit and the overstretched *13th Chasseurs*. At the end of the day the line stabilised, but 11th Essex had lost nine ORs killed, with five officers and 124 ORs wounded. It had been a hard day's fighting. Following two more raids by 1st Leicestershire (night of 4/5 June) and 2nd York & Lancaster (unsuccessfully on 5 June), the division was relieved on 7 June, although the 71st Trench Mortar Battery

84 Commanded by General Philipot, who as a major commanding a battalion of Algerian Skirmishers had contained the Moroccan mutiny in Fez in 1912.

85 War Diary, HQ 6th Infantry Division, 27 May 1918, TNA WO95/1584.

86 James Cecil Hubert 'Jock' Willett MC was commissioned from 10th Essex in May 1917 and had been on the Western Front since May 1915. He was a keen athlete, and would live until 1985, when he was 88. His MC would be awarded for his work on 17 October 1918, the opening day of the Battle of the Selle.

87 War Diary, 11th Battalion Essex Regiment, 'Diary of Operations for 26th, 27th, 28th and 29th May 1918', TNA WO95/1616.

remained behind an extra night to assist the French forward on the 8th to further the recovery of the lost ground.

The division then enjoyed three weeks out of the line. During this period, one brigade was always at Dirty Bucket Camp, north of Brandhoek, working on rear lines of defence; one brigade was training in the St. Jan-ter-Biezen area, to the west of Poperinghe; and the remaining brigade was at musketry practice at Cormette, near Tilques. During this period the 18th Trench Mortar Battery were lent to the French *7th Division* to assist a raid on 19 June. On 27 June the Division came under the control of XIX Corps and relived the French *Chasseurs* (*46th Division*) in the Dickebush area. Marden notes that this area was 'a very unpleasant front', the enemy's position on Mount Kemmel, to the south-west, making 'movement, even in the rear lines, impossible by day, and practically all work of which there was plenty, had to be done by night.'

The French *46th Division* had never completely restored the line at Dickebush, if not for want of trying, and this task would now fall to 6th Division. They did not have to mount raids to identify the opposition, as they now had the benefit of a rash of deserters from the enemy lines. On 1 July a sergeant of *174 Infantry Regiment, 31st Division*, arrived in the division's lines at Ridge Wood. An Alsatian, he was 'communicative, but lacking in knowledge', and had deserted because of 'the harsh treatment meted out to his countrymen at Beverloo training camp.' A private of the same unit, also from Alsace, deserted the following night and was 'able to give a considerable amount of information regarding the enemy dispositions opposite our front.' Yet another Alsatian from this unit deserted on the 5th,[88] confirming 'dispositions, order of battle etc.' Three more arrived in the division's lines on the 10th, one of whom was 'unusually intelligent and gave much useful information.' A further two arrived the following day and 'confirmed the order of battle previously given and the relief of the 8th Division by the 11th Bavarian Division.' The *174 Regiment* had lost eight deserters in 11 days. The fact that the initial sergeant had been 'combed out', and the sheer numbers of deserters, must have been a heartening indication of both the state of morale and the scraping of the bottom of barrels.[89]

It was deemed important to recover the position at Ridge Wood and north to Elzenwalle, a front of approximately 2,000 yards, not only from the point of view of the observation it afforded the enemy, but also as 'the ground formed a sort of funnel up which the enemy could dribble and assemble unseen for an attack N. in the direction of Ypres and S. towards Kemmel', posing the danger of rolling up the British flank. The French attacks had been heralded by preceding bombardment and had ground to halt in the face of machine-gun fire from a multiplicity of advantageous locations. The use of tanks being ruled out, Marden was of the opinion a surprise attack might well succeed as there was only 500 yards to cover and the wire was not dense. The attack

88 *31st Division* was raised in the Lower Alsace and was regarded as mediocre.
89 War Diary, HQ 6th Infantry Division, 1, 2, 5 10 & 11 July 1918, TNA WO95/1584.

would be made by 1st West Yorkshire on the right, 2nd DLI in the centre and two companies of 1st Middlesex, 33rd Division, on the left. A complex creeping barrage at 100 yards every three minutes was fired by 80 18-pounders, curved to allow converging flank attacks, overlaid by Stokes mortars. The RAF were successful with photography, and the heavy artillery successfully neutralised the machine-gun positions, whilst howitzers of 41st Division blinded the observatories on Mount Kemmel. Counter-attacks from three directions were expected, and artillery and machine-gun fire was arranged to neutralise these. Trenches were camouflaged to conceal the concentration of infantry. After over 14 weeks of being on the defensive back foot, the division was once more involved in a minutely prepared (if minor) offensive operation. Marden observed that 'the energy and keenness displayed by the two attacking battalions and by the 11th Essex, who assisted very materially in the preliminary arrangements, were beyond praise.'[90]

The attack was supposed to begin at 06.00, but there was an 'unfortunate mistake' in respect of the creeping barrage. 'Two batteries opened at Zero minus 4, others followed at intervals up to Zero, with the result that the whole barrage was ragged.'[91] The assault waves left their trenches as soon as the barrage opened. The enemy were completely surprised, and only a few of the outposts, mainly in Ridge Wood, where the going was very difficult, offered any resistance. Despite the preparations, the enemy made no counter-attack, and concentrations of German troops were broken up by artillery fire. Seven enemy officers, 341 ORs, 25 machine guns and three trench mortars were captured. There were large concentrations of trench mortar ammunition found, which suggested that the Germans had been intending to renew their attack. Within 6th Division, two officers and 28 ORs lost their lives, four officers and 209 other ranks were wounded, with 19 ORs missing.[92] The casualties would have been less if the barrage had gone as planned.

The 6th Division would remain in this part of the Ypres sector until 24 August. On 17 July the enemy were seen putting out white posts parallel to their front line and prisoners' statements stated that Second Army would be attacked on the 18th. No attack developed. Two more deserters of *166 Infantry Regiment* who arrived in the division's lines on the 20th insisted that the preparations for this attack were now to be complete by the 21st. Marden called his brigade commanders in for a conference on the 21st, and artillery counter-preparation took place and the division took its battle positions on the 22nd. Again no attack materialised. On 2 August 1st Buffs carried out a four platoon raid under a barrage (including smoke) on Brasserie Farm, opposite

90 War Diary, HQ 6th Infantry Division, 'Report on the Operations of 14th July 1918, near Elzenwalle and Ridge Wood', TNA WO95/1584.

91 War Diary, HQ 6th Infantry Division, 'Report on the Operations of 14th July 1918, near Elzenwalle and Ridge Wood', TNA WO95/1584. Even a Court of Enquiry could not unearth the reason for the mishap.

92 War Diary, HQ 18 Infantry Brigade, 'Report on the attack carried out 14th July 1918 on Ridge Wood and Elzenwalle', TNA WO95/1615.

Ridge Wood, brigades to each side carrying out a demonstration, and took nine prisoners of *153 Infantry Regiment*, *8th Division*, although only three made it back to the British lines, the remainder killed by their own side's fire. Indeed, the raiders suffered 49 casualties, including the battalion Medical Officer, Captain Kingsmill Jones.[93] The *8th Division*, regarded as first-class, had replaced the *31st Division* who had provided the previous Alsatian deserters. The enemy remained very active throughout August on the division's front, and on the night of 8/9 August 18 Brigade assisted 41st Division, to the right of the 6th, in two minor enterprises. One was successful, the other not. One company of 1st West Yorkshire, led by Captain Walter Marshall,[94] participated in an operation to gain a higher footing on the north-western slope of the Vierstraat Ridge, to reduce enemy observation and take positions used for harassing machine gun fire. Attacking from muddy and water-logged trenches under a well-coordinated barrage, the company found that the enemy had pushed at least five machine-guns out in front of their line and, the creeping barrage having missed them, they fought well. Two officers with a few men each reached the enemy front line, both the officers being wounded, and one crawled back, the other having to be carried. The company suffered 52 casualties. In the more successful operation, two platoons of 2nd Durham Light Infantry, commanded by Lieutenant John Forsyth,[95] attacked to keep the line joined up with the new 41st Division front under a Stokes mortar barrage and reached their objective with only 13 casualties. Five casualties were incurred by 2/106th American Infantry Regiment, who were in the front-line trenches and who did not advance.[96]

Since 24 July 1918, the 27th American Division had been attached to the 6th and 41st Division for training, and relations between the two divisions were happy and close. The Americans relieved 6th Division from 21 August and the division proceeded for rest and training to the Wizernes area. On the 30th the enemy began to withdraw from the Lys salient, and the Americans advanced over the ground over which 6th Division had struggled in the preceding months. The division's last attacks had taken place on 8 August, the day of the opening of the Battle of Amiens, the start of what

93 War Dairy, HQ 16 Infantry Brigade, 2 August 1918, TNA WO95/1607. Kingsmill Williams Jones, having trained as a doctor in Dublin, joined 3rd East Lancashire Field Ambulance in February 1912, and had arrived in France in September 1914. He had been awarded the DSO for his work at Hooge in August 1915 (see Chapter 3), where he was wounded, and he was wounded again in September 1916 and later gassed. Jones was hit in the arm but continued to move about, bandaging the wounded, until hit in the head by machine gun fire.

94 Walter Kinsman Marshall MC was an officer of the 4th Battalion, attached to the 1st, and had been on the Western Front since May 1916.

95 John Dalton Forsyth MC had been commissioned into 25th Northumberland Fusiliers in June 1916.

96 War Diary, HQ 18th Infantry Brigade, 'Provisional narrative of attacks carried out by 18th Infantry Brigade 8th August 1918', TNA WO95/1615.

would become known as the Hundred Days. After their time in rest, 6th Division would move south to join Fourth Army, the spearhead of that victorious campaign.

Influenza Pandemic 1918

The British Army was never free of influenza during the First World War. In 1917 there were 28,980 admissions, and between January and May 1918 cases averaged at around 3,000 per month, although in April and May there were localized outbreaks of the coming pandemic in First and Second Armies, particularly in the latter towards the end of May. 6th Division were in Second Army to during this period, until early September. In June, however, there were 31,138 and in July 25,480 cases. Second Army admitted 1,921 cases to Casualty Clearing Stations during the week ending 12 June, and 3,851 the following week. Figures returned to normal in August and September, but in October there were 30,097 and in November 23,021 cases, the week ending 2 November being the peak of incidence, the peak of deaths occurring the following week.[97]

On 6 May, the Assistant Director of Medical Services of 6th Division noted 'some cases of high temp(erature), headaches, abd(ominal) pains and vomiting … high temps 101° to 103°.' On 12 May it was noted that of the 265 sick admissions the previous week, 140 were of the new illness – 'a specific disease now occurring … most cases come from YPRES … dugouts in ramparts.' The ADMS pondered: 'Is this an abdominal type of influenza or is it due to after effects of gas shelling? Difficult to decide ….'[98] On 25 May it was clear that it was influenza: 'Over 400 admissions for this influenza admitted during month, nearly 50% of admissions.'[99] By 8 June 16th Field Ambulance were requesting more tents to accommodate sickness cases. Two days later, '2 extra-large Hospital NISSEN Wards' were made available.[100] On 12 June when the senior Medical Officers and AAQMQ of II Corps visited to discuss the epidemic, 300 cases had been reported in 24 hours. All battalions in the division the following day had sick parades of between 20 and 50 flu cases and all were admitted. This did not cause undue concern, however, as 'there is plenty of accommodation at present, & all patients are being bathed and changed clothes.'[101] Five lorries were

97 W.G. Macpherson, W.P. Herringham, T.R. Elliott & A. Balfour, *Medical Services – Diseases of the War, Vol 1*, pp.174-5.

98 One theory is that a similar outbreak of 'prurulent bronchitis' in the British base at Etaples in winter 1916 may have led to slow spread emerging in early 1918. (See J.S. Oxford, 'The so-called Great Spanish Influenza pandemic of 1918 may have originated in France in 1916' p.1857.) Other theories hold that the virus was a much more rapidly mutating type and originated in the USA in January/February, being spread from the point of arrival of American troops in France, Brest.

99 War Diary, ADMS 6th Infantry Division, May 1918, TNA WO95/1593.

100 War Diary, ADMS 6th Infantry Division, 10 June 1918, TNA WO95/1593.

101 War Diary, ADMS 6th Infantry Division, 14 June 1918, TNA WO95/1593.

sent on the 14th to collect cases from 71 Brigade, on a day when there were 280 flu admissions. By that week's end there had been 901 flu cases out of 1,002 sickness admissions. Crowding in tents and huts was considered the reason for the rapid spread. Reassuringly, however, it was observed that 'cases recover in 3 to 5 days', and on 23 June it was happily recorded 'the epidemic of influenza is now on the wane and large numbers are being returned to duty daily.'[102] 6th Division therefore appears to have been one of the earliest and more badly affected formations in June, but one of the least badly affected in July. There is no mention of fatalities, which matches the general picture of few fatalities in this round of the disease.

The influenza virus mutated during the summer months, leading to a much more serious outbreak with considerable mortality from pulmonary complications, peaking in the BEF in October/November. Sickness rates in 6th Division were not unusual during October, and on 26 October the ADMS made his first reference to the new illness: 'Paper on Influenza is coming out & precautions taken … it is said to be very virulent & causes many deaths.'[103] On 2 November, in the BEF's week of highest incidence, it was noted: 'Sickness confined to diarrhoea (from cold and exposure) & some P(yrexia) U(known) O(rigin)s, but not many.' On 24 November this theme continued: 'Sicknesss is not high just now, influenza slight.'[104] Sanitary precautions were marked, and cases in Field Ambulances were inspected for distinguishing signs. On 12 December on the March to the Rhine, the village of Harze was found to be beset by 'haemorrhagic pneumonia" and avoided. On 28 February it was (no doubt thankfully) recorded that 'a severe epidemic of influenza is occurring throughout the Army but so far this Div(ision) has only had a few cases.'[105]

6th Division therefore suffered badly from the first wave and hardly at all during the second wave. During the first wave the division was not engaged in major operations, and the medical services were not overwhelmed. During its operations at the River Selle (see Chapter 13) its combat effectiveness remained absolutely unimpaired by sickness levels that were not out of the ordinary.

Conclusion

It is, once more, difficult to assess the division's morale at the opening of the *Kaiserschlacht*. Importantly, it had not been involved in the Salient in 1917, and hence had escaped what Alexander Watson describes as 'the weariness and distrust of the staff catalysed by the Third Ypres Offensive.'[106] In addition to not having suffered this demoralisation, the division's experience of the Battle of Cambrai had been

102 War Diary, ADMS 6th Infantry Division, 23 June 1918, TNA WO95/1593.
103 War Diary, ADMS 6th Infantry Division, 26 October 1918, TNA WO95/1593.
104 War Diary, ADMS 6th Infantry Division, 24 November 1918, TNA WO95/1593.
105 War Diary, ADMS 6th Infantry Division, 28 February 1919, TNA WO95/1593.
106 A. Watson, *Enduring the Great War*, p.154.

largely positive, particularly in terms of 20th November. In respect of the German counterattack, the division being in the centre of the British position, escaped the fury of 30 November. Only one brigade was heavily engaged in the last stages of the counterattack and fought with determination. Although understrength on 21 March 1918, the division's robust and heroic performance (more effective than the divisions on either side) reflects good morale and troops with reasonable experience. Those efforts were not the high water mark of the division's tactical development, but they certainly realised the extent of its mettle.

The overwhelming of 55th Division on 30 November 1917, likely caused by poorly trained replacements for 7,000 losses at Ypres, certainly showed the danger posed by divisions thus reinforced. This was indeed the situation that 6th Division was in at the opening of 'Georgette', and it was probably lucky that the weight of that attack did not fall on it as a whole. They were, in the Ypres sector, thrust again and again into hasty defensive efforts, and equally hasty minor offensive actions. These actions, fortunately, did not see the terrible intensity of 21 March. The ability to carry out the thoroughly planned Ridge Wood operation must have been balm to the souls of Marden and Grove, for whom control and organisation were central principles. It reflects the division's recovery. Despite its mood no doubt being lowered by a return to the miserable conditions of the Salient, it had the summer to recoup and train before being thrust into the Hundred Days campaign. This period of training before the division moved south would be essential in terms of bringing reinforcements up to scratch. Its progress through the Hundred Days would involve three major set piece attacks, the first two sandwiching several days of semi-mobile warfare. The division's experience, as ever, would be mixed, reflecting the truth of Peter Simkins' statement: 'It would be highly misleading to claim that the "Hundred Days' was a period of undiluted success for the BEF.'[107]

107 P. Simkins, '"Building Blocks": Aspects of Command and Control at Brigade level in the BEF's Offensive Operations, 1916-1918', in G. Sheffield & D. Todman (eds.), *Command and Control on the Western Front*, p. 165.

12

The Hundred Days – At the *Siegfriedstellung*

By 5 September 1918 the division was concentrated in the Heilly–Ribemont–Franvillers area on the River Ancre, south-west of Albert.[1] Over the next few days it continued training in open warfare. It became part of IX Corps, Fourth Army. Fourth Army would be the spearhead of the British advance during the 96 days of advance known as the Hundred Days campaign that followed the success of the all-arms triumph that was the Battle of Amiens on 8 August. IX Corps had been reconstituted under Sir Walter Braithwaite at the end of July,[2] and arrived in Fourth Army on 4 September. From Amiens, Fourth Army had progressed across the old Somme battlefield and on 29 August held a line on the Somme river/canal. It captured Péronne on 1 September, and progressed to hold a twelve mile front, which, as 6th Division moved into line, stretched from the west of Épehy in the north to Holnon Wood in the south, the latter some three and a half miles west of St Quentin. The army faced the outer defences of the Hindenburg Line.

Advanced Hindenburg System – Holnon

The Advanced Hindenburg System had originally been an outpost line, and not intended for defence against a set-piece attack. Essential to the advancing British in terms of observation over the Main Hindenburg System it had been significantly strengthened since the spring of 1917. In front of this, however, lay the old British Main Line, with strongly fortified locations, and which it was thought 'would probably be difficult to capture unless his (the enemy's) morale was very low'.[3] 32nd Division

1 The Divisional HQ war diaries have not survived for the months of September and October.
2 Sir Walter Pipon Braithwaite had commanded 62nd Division from December 1915 to August 1918 and, despite a mixed performance on the staff on Gallipoli, would prove a competent divisional then corps commander. The other divisions were the 1st, 32nd and 46th.
3 J.E. Edmonds, *Military Operations France and Belgium 1918, Volume IV*, p.458.

had followed the enemy to Holnon and St Quentin Wood (the latter the northern part of the former) to the east of which was the old British Main Line, and 6th Division relieved them on the night of 13/14 September. 1st Division were to their north and the French *34th Division* to the south.

A major assault on these outer defences was planned for 18 September, but prior to this 1st and 6th Divisions were tasked with advancing the line to the east of the woods, taking Holnon village itself. This was to be achieved by 18 Brigade. 11th Essex held a line through the eastern part of the woods, covering the divisional front. The enemy were holding, lightly it was believed, a line of trenches to the east of the woods, but a more significant and more strongly held system lay between the woods and Holnon village. 11th Essex were to take these positions and secure the high ground 1,000 yards north east of the village. 'A guarantee was understood to have been received from the 34th French Division that during this operation the 59th French Regiment would secure at the same time the commanding position South of HOLNON, known as ROUND HILL, and also the BOIS DE SAVY'.[4] On the 14th, three companies of the 11th Essex pushed through the woods and established an outpost line beyond its edge. Here they were shelled and bombarded with Yellow Cross (mustard) gas, although no casualties were sustained.[5] The following day they patrolled actively and established strongpoints, albeit now suffering over 50 casualties. The French, however, failed to capture Round Hill, and 18 Brigade stated: 'It is doubtful whether they ever started. It transpired that this Regiment was very tired and had been in the line too long and suffered too many casualties to be of any use as a fighting unit'.[6] With the hill still in enemy hands, 6th Division's positions were dominated by machine-guns and excellent artillery observation. Indeed, the front trenches were almost unapproachable during daylight. Despite this, the divisional front was now reorganised on a two battalion basis, 1st West Yorkshire taking up position on the right of 11th Essex. As soon as they established themselves in the trenches on the north-east edge of the woods, the Essex unit was subject to 'promiscuous shelling' with both Yellow and Blue Cross gas.[7] Battalion HQ was bombarded with 4.2-inch shells within an hour

4 War Diary, HQ 18 Infantry Brigade, 'Narrative of Operations 14th September to 28th September 1918', TNA WO95/1615.

5 Yellow Cross gas, in fact not strictly speaking a gas, was so named after the warning marking on the shell and nicknamed owing to its odour of mustard or horseradish in its impure form. Its constituent was dichlorodiethyl sulphide, an oily liquid. First used by the Germans at Ypres on 12 July 1917, on detonation the shells, bursting with a dull plop, sprayed the liquid in a seven to ten metre radius, and induced skin blistering and severe conjunctivitis and would render ground uninhabitable owing to the time which it took to evaporate. Morale, discipline and training were major factors in combating mustard gas rather than special protection.

6 War Diary, HQ 18 Infantry Brigade, 'Narrative of Operations 14th September to 28th September 1918', TNA WO95/1615.

7 Blue Cross gas, diphenylchloroarsine, was not in itself designed to cause death or injury, but to penetrate respirator filters using a fine particulate dust, causing uncontrollable

of being established. This was a testament to the well-sited observation positions of the Hindenburg outpost system. There were 57 casualties, nearly all gas, the following day. 'Gas poisoning mainly arose from (the) drenched condition of (the) woods, made worse by sunlight'.[8] A further attack was ordered for the 17th to secure the start line for the assault of the whole of Fourth Army, now scheduled for the 18th (see Map 14, colour section).

The 11th Essex and 1st West Yorkshire attacked at 05.30 on the 17th,[9] again in conjunction with 1st Division to the north and the French *2/59th Regiment* to the south. Both battalions assaulted with two companies in front and two in support. The units had assembled during a violent thunderstorm. 1st West Yorkshire advanced successfully behind the creeping barrage (there was no preliminary bombardment), not so 11th Essex. The enemy put down an accurate and heavy counter-barrage exactly on the battalion's forming up trenches, and B and D Companies suffered very heavy casualties before they could even set off. They regrouped and set off under Second-Lieutenant Alexander Akerman,[10] and he and a mere eight men arrived at a point 100 yards short of Badger Copse, 1,500 yards north-east of St Quentin Wood. Here the tiny party was heavily shelled and machine-gunned, and only three men returned, leaving Akerman amongst the dead. The other attacking company reached a sunken road 1,000 yards north of Holnon, and held this position. 1st West Yorkshire's objectives included Holnon itself. The two attacking companies, B and D, suffered heavy casualties from machine-guns on both flanks, and little news filtered back, although by 10.00 aircraft reported that the attackers held outposts east of the village. One company of the 2nd Durham Light Infantry was sent to mop-up Holnon, but this effort ended in failure with heavy casualties. The outposts remained uncontactable, and, as the regimental history states, 'of what happened to the gallant West Yorkshires it is impossible to say'.[11] 11th Essex did not record their casualties for the day. 1st West Yorkshire lost 14 officers (one killed) and 221 ORs (16 known to be dead and 86 missing). Beginning these operations, the three battalions of 18 Brigade had a combined fighting strength of 122 officers and 2,835 men, and a combined trench strength of 58 officers and 1,857 ORs. 1st West Yorkshire's losses were from a trench strength of 20 officers and 590 ORs. The casualties were mainly caused by machine-guns on Round Hill, which the French had again failed to clear, and at a barricade across the road beyond the village. The *Official History* notes that Brigadier-General

sneezing and coughing which would force the wearer to remove their respirator and hence succumb to lethal diphosgene shells. The British had, however, developed a good particulate filter.

8 War Diary, 11th Battalion Essex Regiment, 15/16 September 1918, TNA WO95/1616.

9 Marden's history incorrectly states this attack occurred on the 16th.

10 Born in 1895, Alexander Grant Akerman was commissioned on 30 October 1917. He had arrived on the Western Front in August 1915, serving with the Royal Engineers, where he achieved the rank of corporal.

11 E. Wyrall, *The West Yorkshire Regiment in the War 1914-1918, Volume Two*, p.332.

Craufurd had sent a copy of his orders to the French infantry commander but had been told by a staff officer 'that the weather was too bad and the French were not going to attack. In this decision they persisted and made no movement of any sort', despite the general commanding the division giving assurances of their attack.[12] The start line for the 18th was not secured, therefore, and as Marden remarks: 'The situation at the end of the 17th was therefore unsatisfactory on the right, but it was impossible to put off the general attack, and arrangements had to be improvised.' Adding to 6th Division's problems was the fact that the woods, which covered most of the division's 2,500 yard front were 'so drenched with gas shells and the tracks so bad' that the attacking 16 and 71 Brigades had to make a detour north and south of the woods to reach their start positions 'and this naturally fatigued the troops and hindered communication and supply'.[13]

The attack of the 18th, the Battle of Epéhy, was to be undertaken by the whole of Fourth Army in conjunction with the *XXXVI Corps* of the First French Army. The weather had been poor for aerial observation, but by the 17th aeroplane photographs of the enemy defences to a depth of 4,000 yards had been taken and swiftly distributed down to NCO level. The three phases of the operation involved the capture of the enemy's first line of defence (the old British Main Line), followed by the second line of defence (old British Outpost Line), and an exploitation phase to establish Fourth Army in the Advanced Hindenburg System where possible. (There was to be no line of exploitation for 6th Division, however). III Corps would attack in the north, at Épehy itself, the Australian Corps in the centre, and IX Corps in the south. Fourteen German divisions opposed Fourth Army, two in reserve. IX Corps General Staff records indicate no intelligence concerning the opposition. The *Official History* and Montgomery's history of Fourth Army indicate that the opposition offered to IX Corps at different points over these days was given by *25th* and *79th Reserve Divisions* and in particular between Gricourt and Selency by the *197th* and *11th Divisions,* the latter being 6th Division's principal opponents.[14] At this point in the war, the *25th Reserve Division* was rated at somewhere between second and third class, the *79th Reserve* as third class, the *197th* as third class and the *11th* a good second-class division.[15] Given these ratings, they defended well, but 6th Division was facing the best formation.

There was to be no preliminary bombardment, reliance being placed on "the effect of surprise, a powerful artillery concentration including intense counter-battery work, and the assistance of tanks at points where the resistance was expected to be most pronounced'.[16] Zero was at 05.20, and the infantry followed a creeping barrage

12 Edmonds, op. cit. *Vol IV*, p.475.
13 T.O. Marden, *A Short History of the Sixth Division*, p.60.
14 Edmonds, op. cit, sketch 26.
15 Anon. *Histories of the Two Hundred and Fifty-One Divisions of the German Army which Participated in the War (1914-1918).*
16 A. Montgomery, *The Story of the Fourth Army in the Battles of the Hundred Days*, p.124.

moving at 100 yards every three minutes. The start time and rate of creep was standard for Fourth Army. Marden described the ground over which his division would attack:

> Standing on the east edge of the wood, a bare glacis-like slope devoid of cover, except for two or three shell-trap copses, stretched away for 3,000 yards to the high ground overlooking St. Quentin. There was no sign of life and very few trenches could be seen, though it was known that they were there as the Fifth Army had held the position in March 1918. It was found afterwards that the Germans had camouflaged their trenches with thistles, which here covered the ground to a height in many places of eighteen inches. At the highest point about the centre of the Divisional area of attack was a network of trenches known later as the Quadrilateral – a name of bad omen to the 6th Division and which, like its namesake on the Somme, could be reinforced under cover from the back slopes of the hill. An examination of the battlefield after the 24th September also revealed several narrow sunken roads filled with wire. The position was one of great natural strength, and in addition the whole of the right was dominated by heights in the area to be attacked by the French.[17]

The Advanced Hindenburg System at Holnon. The picture is taken from the edge of St Quentin Wood, over 'the bare glacis-like slope'.

17 Marden, op. cit. p.60.

On the 18th, smoke and rain would obscure any landmarks indicated by the aerial photos. The early part of the night had been fine, but it was raining heavily when the attack was launched. 'The light was bad; the ground was soft and slippery, and consequently not suitable for the tanks, of which a certain number were "ditched" in the deep sunken roads and high embankments'.[18] Fourth Army would use only 23 tanks in the attack, six being allotted to IX Corps, two of which were designated for the attack on the Quadrilateral. This was a 'system of trenches enclosing a group of cottages which had themselves been turned into a keep. The eastern face was a high bank tunnelled for the passage of troops and guns'.[19] It was about 500 yards across, and there was also a quarry in its centre. Douai Trench, its western face and which extended both north and south from it, commanded Holnon village. The position lay on an east-west spur to the west of Fayet and to the south of the high ground it had been hoped 11th Essex would capture four days earlier. To the north of this nameless hill lay the fortified village of Fresnoy-le-Petit, also to be attacked by two tanks. The assault was thus being made on a horseshoe of high ground flanked by two strongpoints. As previously observed, 500 yards to the south of the division's advance lay Round Hill, still untaken by the French, and to its south-east lay Manchester Hill, where Lieutenant-Colonel Wilfrith Elstob and 16th Manchester had fought and died on 21 March 1918. Both provided observation over the right of the division's attack.

The 71 Brigade would attack on the flank of the whole of Fourth Army, their left directed at the Quadrilateral, their right at Holnon and the village of Selency, 700 yards to its east. 2nd DLI were attached to clear Holnon. Yet again, however, the French *88th Regiment* failed to take Round Hill. The DLI attacked in two waves (A and D Companies), successfully passing through the village, whereupon the enemy machine-guns and rifles began to exert their toll from their vantage point. By the time the two companies had debouched from the village, only one officer was left standing. The enemy then began to try to work round towards the rear of the battalion, and, threatened with being cut off, the survivors of the DLI withdrew to their starting point. At noon, B Company attempted to clear the village, but was driven back by machine-gun fire and gas shelling. In order to protect this exposed flank division, 2nd Life Guards Machine Gun Battalion was placed in depth on high ground near Holnon.

On the left of the 71 Brigade attack, against the Quadrilateral, 2nd Sherwood Foresters immediately took 40 prisoners, but found the enemy in great strength, with numerous well-positioned machine guns, and the wire 'unusually thick and but little damaged by our artillery'. After 08.00 the right company was reported in Douai Trench, which ran south-west from the Quadrilateral between Holnon and Selency. Of the two tanks operating in support, one ditched, whilst the other attacked the Quadrilateral directly. After inflicting casualties, it burst into flames and had to

18 Montgomery, op. cit. p.125.
19 Edmonds, op. cit. *Vol IV*, p.478.

be abandoned. 9th Norfolk, who were to advance to the second objective, had set off at 09.00, but were pushed away to the right by fire from the Quadrilateral, one company achieving Douai Trench. After repeated attempts by the Sherwoods on the Quadrilateral, the fighting ground to a halt.[20]

The 16 Brigade, attacking on the division's left, had struggled to get into position. The assembly area of 2nd York & Lancaster was inaccessible until after dark on the 17th, and 13 out of 16 guides were killed. The assembly places for the other two battalions could not be fixed till dusk – no landmarks could be seen and even if they had been noted, the smoke of the barrage concealed them during the attack. 'The brigade therefore attacked "into the blue", and the fact that there was not much loss of direction speaks well for the leading'. Indeed, in all the September attacks, 'success was due to Company and Platoon leaders and their men … it was a "soldiers' battle"'.[21] 2nd York & Lancaster were to take the first objective, a line of trenches running from Fresnoy south to the Quadrilateral, where 1st Buffs would pass through them to Gricourt, 1,000 yards beyond, 1st King's Shropshire Light Infantry to their left. Setting off at 05.20 'under a splendid creeping barrage', by 06.30 the leading companies of the York and Lancasters had taken their objectives. At 10.00, however, 'a determined enemy counter attack' drove them back out of Fresnoy itself.[22] Of the two tanks directed at Fresnoy, one failed to start, and the other was seen entering the village, whereafter the attacking troops saw it no more. Too weak to retaliate, the battalion held the trenches to the south, but had suffered 216 casualties. 1st Buffs lost direction in advancing but came up against the York and Lancasters stalled, and fire from Fresnoy and the Quadrilateral prevented further forward movement. 1st KSLI were prevented from advancing by the fire from Fresnoy, describing the fighting as 'very bitter' and confused, and all three battalions became intermingled. Casualties mounted and Brigadier-General Walker ordered the line consolidated and set about reorganising his front. He placed Lieutenant-Colonel James Robertson (2nd York & Lancaster) in command of the eight companies in the front line,[23] Major Lyndon Morris (1st KSLI) in command of the four companies in support,[24] and Lieutenant-Colonel Rowland Power, (1st Buffs) in command of brigade reserve.[25]

20 H.C. Wylly, *The 1st and 2nd Battalions the Sherwood Foresters in the Great War*, Kindle edition location 7295.

21 War Diary, HQ 16 Infantry Brigade, 16th I.B. No. G.O. 38/310, TNA WO95/1607.

22 War Diary, 2nd Battalion York & Lancaster, 18 September 1918, TNA WO95/1610.

23 James Robert Robertson had been a Regular captain of the Bedfordshire Regiment in August 1914. From July 1917 he had variously commanded 8th Bedfordshire, 1/4th Leicestershire, 3/1st Cambridgeshire, and 2nd York & Lancaster.

24 Lyndon Henry Morris, a Territorial captain on the 4th Shropshire Light Infantry in August 1914, would command until the Armistice.

25 Rowland Edward Power had commanded 2/4th Yorkshire Light Infantry from April 1917, and the battalion in which he had started the war as a captain from December 1917 until the Armistice.

To the north, much greater success had been achieved, but whilst 1st Division on the left of the 6th had taken its first objective comfortably, it could make little progress beyond Fresnoy, the creeping barrage moving faster than the troops could keep up. At the end of the day, all the troops were exhausted, but just before midnight, orders were received to renew the attack at 05.30 the following morning. Given the state of 6th Division's forces on the ground: 'It was apparent that the greatest difficulty would be experienced in co-ordinating the attack'.[26] At Zero a creeping barrage was put down, but the enemy resistance was even stronger than the previous day, commencing an artillery and machine-gun barrage before the attackers had even left their jumping-off trenches. The attack made no progress at all. 16 Brigade withdrew its troops from the front line for the barrage on the Quadrilateral, and in attacking, 9th Norfolk established themselves in Douai Trench (where 16 Brigade were in residence further north) but no further progress was made bar 2nd DLI finally clearing Holnon. To this point, the division had captured six officers and 264 ORs, as well as 65 machine guns. Marden notes that 'the enemy's artillery was very strong, and, with the thick Hindenburg wire in front of it, was placed close to their front line, and was enabled thus to do considerable execution on our back areas'.[27] If this was indeed the case, the question arises as to why Fourth Army's artillery had not achieved more effective counter-battery fire.

Marden held conferences with his brigadiers daily during these operations, and over the days that followed preparations were made for another assault, a heavy artillery shoot being conducted on the Quadrilateral for three hours on the 22nd, over 1,000 shells being delivered, but the enemy artillery responded strongly. Between the 20th and the 23rd, 11th Leicestershire, the divisional pioneers, laboured in the front line constructing jumping-off positions, with the Royal Engineers assisting and working on roads.[28] The renewed attack was made on September 24th, again the objective being to take the high ground containing the Advanced Hindenburg System prior to any attack on the Hindenburg Line itself, the assault on which had been set for 29 September, an order issued by GHQ on the 22nd. 6th Division were, once more, under the cosh of a timetable beyond their control. 18 Brigade had relieved the 16th, and were in place between the Quadrilateral and Holnon, with 1st Leicestershire attached, whilst 16 Brigade remained in line. The 1st Division would again attack on the left, now being responsible for taking Fresnoy and Gricourt, the French *XXXVI Corps* inserting a fresh division to the right, the *171st Regiment* abutting the British. A fresh battalion of Mark V tanks from 5th Brigade Tank Corps was allotted to IX Corps (specifically requested by Marden), and eight were attached to 6th Division, directed at Selency, the

26 War Diary, HQ 16 Infantry Brigade, 16th I.B. No. G.O. 38/310, TNA WO95/1607.
27 Marden, op. cit. pp. 61-2.
28 In the middle of this the CRE, Lieutenant-Colonel George Goldney, was sent home to the UK, 35 year-old Lieutenant-Colonel Harry Alexander Lewis Hall taking over on the 23rd. Hall had started the war a captain of Royal Engineers and had served as brigade-major from May 1917 to January 1918.

Quadrilateral, and the elusive high ground to its north. The RAF would cooperate by carrying out ground attack on the enemy trenches from Zero.

The attack of 11th Essex against the Quadrilateral, 23 September 1918.

In 18 Brigade, 11th Essex were to seize the Quadrilateral, supported by four tanks, and 1st West Yorkshire and 2nd DLI were to take Douai Trench, Selency Chateau and Selency itself, to the Quadrilateral's south. Attacking at 05.00, the wire proved problematic, but by 07.00 C Company of 11th Essex had attained the south-west corner of the Quadrilateral, whilst A had forced their way in at the northern corner. All four tanks supporting the Essex unit's assault, however, had been knocked out by direct hits from field guns. A bombing attack down Douai Trench, the western face, failed due to its narrowness and the fact it was full of wire, and all A Company's officers were by now wounded. Continual close quarter fighting secured part of Epicure Alley, the southern face. By night, when C Company were relieved, the enemy still held much of the position, especially the northern trench which dominated the southern face, being on higher ground. Fighting continued into the night and only by 08.30 on the 25th was Douai Trench, the western face, secured. Bit by bit the Essex battalion worked forward down Epicure Alley, taking it by 2.30, and Etretat Trench, the eastern face, was in British hands by 15.50. At 20.00 the whole of the Quadrilateral was secure. German officers captured there 'admitted they had fully expected to hold it indefinitely'.[29]

29 Marden, op. cit. p.63.

Despite the fact that the French had now successfully taken Round Hill, Manchester Hill still eluded them, and 1st West Yorkshire and 2nd DLI were both held up by their portion of Douai Trench. The West Yorkshires, in the centre of the brigade attack, lost direction in the smoke and mist, came under heavy fire, and fell back. The attacking companies of 2nd DLI met belts of thick and virtually uncut wire, and 'eventually the entire two companies became casualties or were captured. Nothing more was seen of any officers or men ... except a few dead who were eventually found in the vicinity of the trench'. At 10.30, however, two companies of 1st Leicestershire attacked through the DLI and 1st West Yorkshire simultaneously rushed Douai Trench, and the whole position was at last taken. The success of this final assault 'was largely due to the fact that the attackers followed the barrage so closely that they reached the parapet at the same moment that it lifted from the trench',[30] and hence the enemy had no time to recover and mount their machine guns. Douai Trench was found to be replete with many machine-guns 'with quantities of empty cartridge cases lying beside each one'.[31] The cost of success was high, however. 18 Brigade suffered 17 officer and 850 other rank casualties during the day.

To the north, 16 Brigade attacked with 2nd York & Lancaster, and 1st KSLI. Of the four tanks supporting them, only one reached the objective. The wire was again uncut, but the tired troops hacked their way through, and 2nd York & Lancaster captured two 77mm guns at the point of the bayonet, one light trench mortar and 22 machine-guns, as well as nine enemy officers and 300 ORs. The battalion itself suffered 145 casualties, but even had the energy to assist 3 Brigade capture Gricourt in the afternoon and repel an enemy counter-attack the following day. 1st KSLI achieved their objectives despite heavy opposition and the fact that the Quadrilateral to their right was not taken that day on the face that abutted them.

General Walker reflected upon the operations, stating firmly: 'By far the most important lesson emphasised by our experiences is the vital necessity of allowing time for orders, for concerted action, to reach Units'. He noted that 2nd York & Lancasters only had 10 minutes warning of assisting 3 Brigade in the capture of Gricourt. Of this operation, Archibald Montgomery, MGGS Fourth Army, wrote: 'Ably planned at short notice by the brigade commander' (i.e. 3 Brigade) the attack 'well exemplifies the value of initiative by subordinate commanders'.[32] What was one commander's 'short notice' was another's 'far too short notice'. In describing a 'soldier's battle', the progress of which was largely beyond the influence of brigade HQ, Walker wrote that his HQ's activities were concentrated on: (i) Reorganizing units that had got mixed up; (ii) Relieving the most tired troops; (iii) Collecting a reserve; (iv) Issuing

30 H.C. Wylly, *History of the 1st & 2nd Battalions the Leicestershire Regiment in the Great War*, p.84.
31 War Diary, HQ 18 Infantry Brigade, 'Narrative of Operations 14th September to 28th September 1918', TNA WO95/1615.
32 Montgomery, op. cit. p.143.

orders for consolidation; and (v) Collating information on the positions on flanks, and informing units thereof.

Clearly 6th Division had had a very tough time. As at the previous struggle for a Quadrilateral, the division's battle was only part of a multiple division operation across an entire army, and the timings were set for the whole force, impossible to adjust in respect of local issues. And 6th Division had very specific local issues. Walter Braithwaite acknowledged on 19 September that both 1st and 6th Divisions 'have had considerable difficulties to overcome', and that 'it may be difficult' for the 6th to take Selency and the Quadrilateral unless the French Army took Manchester Hill.[33] The emphasis on French failures was therefore no excuse on the part of 6th Division. Secondly, there was a partial failure on the part of the artillery. Round and Manchester Hills were not suppressed after the failure of the French attacks, although this would have been a task primarily for the French Army artillery, and as noted, support from the French having been promised was not always forthcoming. Three heavy batteries (6-inch howitzer or 60-pounder) had been attached to the division for the attack on the 18th, under Marden's direct authority. The destructive fire, however, was clearly inadequate. Given that the positions were very heavily wired, it would appear that insufficient artillery effort was devoted to either weight or accuracy in cutting this obstacle (the had been no preliminary bombardment preceding the 18th, in an attempt maintain secrecy concerning the movement of batteries). The 4.5-inch howitzers were relied upon to cut wire during the advance. The Quadrilateral was only subject to sustained bombardment on 22 September, after two failed assaults (a position horribly reminiscent of the same-named place on the Somme). It is significant that after proper artillery preparation, it was successfully taken. Also, the very active enemy artillery indicates that counter-battery fire was inadequate (this likely a weather-related issue). Lastly, in terms of suppression, the creeping barrage of 100 yards every three minutes completely lost its purpose if wire was uncut and held troops up, or stout resistance was met. (This problem would rear its head again at the Selle on 17 October, as would the matter of accuracy of destructive fire). Fourth Army amassed 750 18-pounders; 228 4.5-inch howitzers; 240 6-inch howitzers; 120 60-pounders; and 150 heavier guns/howitzers for the Battle of Epéhy. These resources being stretched across its entire front, despite the evident riches in heavy artillery, they were insufficient to crack a nut such as the Quadrilateral. In the final analysis, however, there was the independent will of the enemy, in this case bent on stern resistance and backed by powerful and accurate artillery, all situated in a perfectly-sited and very strong defensive system.

Having defended well, the enemy's defences were eventually fractured, and over the next three days the division's patrols gradually gained ground into the Advanced Hindenburg System, capturing 10 officers, 372 ORs, four guns, 15 trench mortars and 53 machine-guns. By the 30th, when the French relived the division, the village of Fayet, 500 yards from the Hindenburg Line, was surrounded on three sides. On

33 War Diary, HQ IX Corps, G.384/305/81, 19 September 1918, TNA WO95/837.

the 29th of September, of course, the 46th Division of IX Corps further north had successfully and famously broken the Hindenburg Line itself, 1st Division forming a defensive flank to their right, the cooperation of 6th Division not being required.

Beyond the Beaurevoir – Fonsomme line – Mannequin and Doon Hills

Having ruptured the main Hindenburg Position itself, Fourth Army's task was now to fight its way through the Hindenburg Support Positions, on the eastern edge of which was the final enemy prepared defensive position, the Masnières – Beaurevoir – Fonsomme line. This 'consisted of two trenches with concrete emplacements every two or three hundred yards and with machine-gun nests scattered behind it'.[34] The Germans had offered stiff resistance to Fourth Army, and to the north, had not fallen back in front of Third Army. The Army largely secured the Beaurevoir Line on 3 October (although Third Army to the north and the French Army to the south both failed). On the 4th, IX Corps was ordered to take Mannequin Hill and Doon Hill to the north-east of its front, these lying beyond the Beaurevoir Line between Montbrehain and Sequehart (see Map 15, colour section). No progress was made. Patrols made their way up the slopes of Mannequin on the 5th but were repelled. This eminence commanded Montbrehain to the north, although by the end of the 5th this village had been secured, the last Australian action of the war. GHQ then ordered a renewed offensive that after a day's postponement would take place on the 8th. To progress into open country, however, a major effort would have to be made as the enemy had still not withdrawn and was holding their positions to the east of the Beaurevoir line which they had just lost.

On IX Corps front, still abutting the French, the attack would be made by 6th Division, who had enjoyed four days of rest. On the right was 16 Brigade (with 139 Brigade of 46th Division attached), 71 Brigade attacking on the left. To the division's right was the French *42nd Division,* lying a little to the rear. On their left was the 30th American Division, 2,000 yards ahead, linked to 6th Division by a series of posts that lay on the railway line that ran south-west from Montbrehain. The division's left flank was protected, its right was open and potentially vulnerable. The *Official History* observes that 'Major-General Marden had a difficult task'.[35] Marden's own description of the geography facing the division notes how: 'The position to be attacked consisted of high rolling downs with deep traverse valleys, giving good cover for supports and forward guns, and on the right a broad longitudinal valley closed by a ridge on which stood the village of Méricourt'.[36] The *Official History* was sarcastic concerning Marden's 'other difficulty' (other than topography, that is), in that the

34 J.E. Edmonds & R. Maxwell-Hyslop, *Military Operations – France and Belgium 1918*, Vol V, p.158.
35 Edmonds & Maxwell-Hyslop, op. cit. *Vol V*, p.189.
36 Marden, op. cit. *Vol V*, p.65.

French *XV Corps* who would be on the southern side of this valley, 'did not intend to advance, if at all, until fifty minutes (6 a.m.) after the British; nor did it intend to advance as far, and thus the right of the 6th Division would be left exposed to grave danger of counter-attack'.[37] The French had not secured their jumping-off line, and attacked once more on the 6th, improving their position, but were still not in line. Marden decided to solve this problem, meeting with his brigade commanders on the morning of the 6th, by deciding 'to leave the valley severely alone to start with, merely smoking by guns and bombs from aeroplanes the Méricourt Ridge and attacking all along the high ground to the north',[38] i.e. the Mannequin Hill-Doon Hill ridge. As the two allies advanced (which the French did despite the Official Historian's comments), Whippet tanks and the 1st West Yorkshires would attack from the high ground against the Méricourt Ridge cutting off enemy positions in the valley. To support this difficult assault, Marden described the weight of artillery as 'immense'.[39] The 6th Divisional artillery and two further brigades[40] were to move forward behind the infantry to support exploitation and ward off counter-attack. This would be a typical tactical move from now on in the campaign. It was further hoped that cavalry would be pushed through to advance to Le Cateau.

The attack against the Mannequin Hill/Doon Hill ridge, 8 October 1918.

37 Edmonds & Maxwell-Hyslop, op. cit. *Vol V*, pp.189-190.
38 Marden, op. cit. p.65.
39 Marden, op. cit. p.66.
40 5th Brigade RHA and 232nd Brigade RFA.

In 16 Brigade, 1st King's Shropshire Light Infantry would lead the attack,[41] followed by 1st Buffs and 2nd York & Lancaster. The Buffs would pass through the KSLI to take the objective (the division as a whole having to advance 4,000 yards), the York and Lancasters carrying out the attack on Méricourt and forming a defensive flank to the valley whilst 1st West Yorkshire mopped up. During the night patrols were pushed out to ensure there were no enemy outposts between the front line and the point where the barrage would fall. First, however, two machine-gun posts beyond Sequehart on the road leading down the valley had to be secured to avoid their enfilading the right flank of the 16 Brigade advance. 1/1st Monmouthshire, the divisional pioneers of 46th Division were tasked with this. B Company made the attack, the two leading platoons being virtually wiped out. The CO, Lieutenant-Colonel John Jenkins, organized a second unsuccessful attack, dying of wounds sustained. 6th Division troops eventually worked round the position cutting it off and forced the enemy to surrender.

16 Brigade set off at 05.10. The objective for 1st KSLI was a sunken road to the east of Mannequin Hill. A and B Companies formed up on two platoon fronts on a taped line 30 yards west of the barrage line. 1st Buffs formed up to their rear, with 2nd York & Lancaster behind them. Little opposition was met, and large numbers of prisoners were soon being sent back. The objective for 1st Buffs was Beauregard Farm on the flanks of Doon Hill to an area to the north of Fresnoy. After initial good progress, the two officers commanding the leading companies were wounded,[42] and the front line was being shelled heavily. Reinforcements stabilised the situation, 105 casualties having been sustained. As expected, the right flank remained problematic. The French *47th Division* had been held up at Cerise Wood, 1,000 yards to the south-east of Sequehart, i.e. to the rear of 16 Brigade's start line. They succeeded in mastering this location by 08.45, and Lieutenant-Colonel Weber, 2 Brigade RFA, moved his guns up behind 1st KSLI to assist the advance in the valley. It was hoped that the attack of the 2nd York & Lancasters would turn the resisting enemy's flank, but 'the creeping barrage for this attack, however, was never put down, being apparently held up while the artillery concerned waited for news of the French or of our readiness to attack'.[43] The unit could not get forward because of enfilade fire, even though 16th Trench Mortar Battery were able to put one enemy machine-gun team out of action with a direct hit. General Walker ordered the barrage to take place, but his orders were not executed. The battle thus became stationary. Even after the French had pushed on, the York & Lancasters could not advance on Méricourt for fear of being caught in any barrage. Meanwhile, 1st West Yorkshire had become involved in a difficult struggle. Their leading A and C Companies came under enfilade machine-gun fire and could

41 6th Division's War Diary, orders etc. are missing for October, and no orders exist in 16 Brigade's War Diary.

42 Captains V.N. Moss and G.F.Hamilton.

43 War Diary, HQ 16 Infantry Brigade, 'Narrative of Active Operations Undertaken by 16th Infantry Brigade from 8th to 10th October Inclusive', TNA WO95/1607.

not take Mannequin Wood in the valley to the south of Mannequin Hill, two of the three Whippet tanks who were in support breaking down before they arrived at this location, the third being put out of action. A third attempt after the wood was shelled for half an hour from 12.50 by 2 Brigade RFA was successful, however, (reflecting the good practice of pushing field artillery forward), and the defending enemy were taken prisoner, as were troops preparing a counter-attack, seven officers and 249 ORs in all. These captures were allegedly made by a mere 15 men of the 1st West Yorkshires, who had advanced protected by smoke. In addition to the artillery, B Company 6th Battalion MGC had combined with the Lewis guns of 1st KSLI and put two enemy machine gun teams out of action. Other spoils included a field gun, four trench mortars, four anti-tank rifles, ten heavy and 11 light machine-guns. Seventy-eight casualties were sustained by the West Yorkshires. The battle then began to move again, the enemy falling back under the cover of machine-gun fire, and all units pushed patrols forward, 1st West Yorkshire now advancing in conjunction with the French. By nightfall, Méricourt, at the head of the problematic valley, was in British hands.

On the left, 71 Brigade formed up on lines taped by 489 Field Company RE two hours before jump-off, 9th Norfolk on the left, 2nd Sherwood Foresters on the right. The latter, advancing on the three company front, described the barrage as 'most effective and accurate'. Advancing in the shadow of Mannequin Hill, forward posts were quickly overcome, and the copses allowed the unit to keep direction. Resistance was encountered in the sunken roads and particularly at Doon Mill. Doon Copse, 500 yards to the east of the mill, had a machine-gun post in the right hand corner. Although technically in the area of 9th Norfolks, the Sherwood Foresters used perfect *SS143* tactics to outflank the position, where 80 prisoners and five machine guns were captured, most in a deep dug-out. In a similar strongpoint, 100 prisoners were taken. Doon Mill itself was captured without much difficulty, another 100 prisoners being bagged, the unit still keeping up with the barrage.

Lieutenant George Grossmith,[44] commanding D Company 1st Leicestershire, who were in support, reached the sunken road, the first objective. Here his men came under machine-gun fire from Mannequin Hill to the right rear and dropped into the sunken road on which the enemy had good range. Having sustained about 50 percent casualties (although a number were likely stragglers), Grossmith got his men moving again. Their advance was not easy. They pushed on, having to mop up machine gun posts missed by the first wave of troops, Grossmith himself navigating entirely by compass. Of the enemy, 'their morale seemed quite broken', he remarked. Five hundred yards from Doon Hill 'most of us were half choked with smoke, gas and powder fumes, and our breath came in short gasps'.[45] Reduced to 20 in number, he

44 George Wilfred Grossmith MC was commissioned in April 1915. Wounded at Loos in 1915, he would survive the war to reach the age of 99.

45 G.W. Grossmith, Private Papers, IWM Docs 11013.

halted his men, and located the CO of 2nd Sherwood Foresters, Lieutenant-Colonel Hudson, who gave him directions. He returned to his men and headed for the Doon Hill ridge. He now encountered cavalry, Scots Greys, and realised there was a lower ridge and a basin before the ridge which Hudson had directed him to occupy. The cavalry were reluctant to proceed without the infantry occupying this lower ridge, which Grossmith attempted to do, but the machine gun fire was too accurate. He remained where he was and consolidated his position.

Although units were being encouraged at this point in the war to press on regardless of unsupported flanks, the delay involved in the adjacent Buffs' leapfrog manoeuvre resulted in the Sherwoods' battalion HQ being exposed to flanking fire, and Lieutenant Erwin, the acting adjutant was (amongst others) hit. 24 Brigade RFA moved up to assist exploitation, and as noted cavalry were pushed up. The attack could not be progressed as 77mm guns some 600 to 1,000 yards ahead were shelling the unit over open sights. Marden later described how the attached squadron of Royal Scots Greys (5th Cavalry Brigade), 'worked round and made a gallant attempt to gallop the guns, but were stopped by close range gun-fire'.[46] These, of course, were the horse soldiers encountered by Grossmith, and Marden and Grossmith's descriptions do not quite marry up. A gap also existed between the right of 71 and the left of 16 Brigades, which had to be covered by the machine guns attached to 1st Leicestershire who were in support. The Sherwood Foresters had captured five officers and 450 ORs, as well as six field guns and 15 machine-guns. Their casualties totalled nine officers and 152 ORs, 28 of the casualties being fatal. The advance of the 9th Norfolks proved more straightforward, the American 118th Regiment of 30th Division keeping reasonable pace, and both units achieved exploitation.

The day had been one in which 6th Division made its first advances against an enemy who was not properly entrenched, and they proved well able to force the enemy back, capturing over 30 officers and 1,100 ORs. Yet the day had been hard fought, the enemy, as would be the case throughout the later stage of the Hundred Days, basing their defence on automated fire, firing over ground which they were very familiar with. In support of the progressing infantry, 6th Battalion Machine Gun Corps had pushed two companies forward, deploying its guns on the right flank with sections following the leading infantry. The war diary of the Trench Mortar Batteries is missing, but it is clear that they did the same. Further, for the first time the division (although none of the October war diaries survive) was able to push field artillery batteries up in the wake of the advance of some 4,000 yards. Whilst the tanks had failed, the division also operated with cavalry (if also unsuccessfully). Battle was becoming more mobile.

46 Marden, op. cit. p.67.

Conclusion

The experiences of 6th Division before and beyond the Hindenburg Line represent a game of two halves. With respect to the Advanced Hindenburg Positions, the enemy were occupying very well sited, entrenched and fortified positions. These were held with determined resistance. 6th Division were probably facing the most difficult defensive nut to crack and were opposed by the best division on the whole Army front. Their difficulties were compounded by the French failure to take the defensive positions which overlooked their right. Until firepower was concentrated, the 'weapons system' failed to do its job to get the infantry forward. This it largely succeeded in during the attacks on Mannequin and Doon Hills though, again, the failures of the French on the right created problems. As the division was now advancing much more into open country it was able to use its firepower more flexibly to mitigate this. Over the next nine days it would play another game of two halves – attacks over open country followed by another set piece battle against an enemy using topography to its advantage.

13

The Hundred Days – At the River Selle

The combined attack by Third and Fourth Armies on the 8th was so successful that by the evening Cambrai could no longer be held. The German *Second Army* recorded that: 'The penetration of the enemy had progressed so that it became impossible to hold the enemy in this line for any length of time … the right flank of the army seemed seriously threatened. It was necessary to withdraw into the HERMANN position.' This had been hastily prepared behind the River Selle, which lay to the east. At 23.00 'the main body of the divisions in line started to move; the rearguards followed at 2:30 A.M. Posts remained in contact with the enemy.'[1] Sir Henry Rawlinson wrote hopefully on 8 October: 'I have given objectives for another 10,000 yard advance and may quite likely pull it off.'[2] To hold the British on 9 October, 'strong rearguards, well provided with artillery and machine-guns',[3] were left on a line utilising railway embankments, woods etc. Beyond these temporary posts the River Selle (and the *Hermann Stellung* on its east banks) was not the only geographical barrier. Whilst it would not face the River Selle itself, IX Corps was opposed by significant topographical features that favoured the enemy. These included the large Andigny Forest at its junction with the French Army, and a dominating ridge of high ground, the Bellevue spur, which lay between the forest and the source of the Selle. The *Hermann Stellung* stretched across the front of both these obstacles.

Pursuit to the Selle 9-12 October

If they could have seen through the heavy mist at dawn on 9 October 1918 the units of IX Corps would have looked out on a landscape that for a distance of some three miles

1 War Diary, HQ German *Second Army*, 8 October 1918, *United States Army in the World War Vol. 7*, p.890.
2 Sir H. Rawlinson, War Journal, 8 October 1918, Churchill College RWLN 1/11.
3 Order, HQ German *Second Army*, 'Withdrawal of Front', 8 October 1918, *USAWW Vol. 7*, p.891.

of open country was almost completely devoid of the German Army. The landscape over which the Pursuit was to be conducted comprised rolling farmland of big fields, with gentle valleys and rises. It was, however, dotted with woods, some of them large; and was criss-crossed by the well-developed Le Cateau-St Quentin railway system, with its branch lines, cuttings and embankments. The villages of the area were long straggling affairs that offered limited defensive value, there being only one sizeable town, Bohain. Fourth Army were optimistic, Sir Henry Rawlinson hopeful that 'if our victory were followed up at once, the cavalry might be given the opportunity, denied to them on the 8th, of completing the rout of the enemy.'[4]

The attack resumed at 05.20 with two objectives, the first being about 4,500 yards ahead, with exploitation to a second objective, a further 2,500 yards on (see Map 15, colour section). This, as far as 6th Division were concerned, involved capturing Bohain. The division no longer abutted the French, as 46th Division had come into line on their right. 16 and 71 Brigades still held the division's front, right and left, both 'very tired' from the previous day's fighting. The two brigades had been ordered overnight to cede part of their front to the 46th Division and in turn take over part of the front of the 30th American Division. These 'almost impossible' orders were successfully carried out in the pitch dark.[5] A creeping barrage was fired which lasted 71 minutes, whereupon six brigades of field artillery followed the infantry.[6] Although the French to the right of IX Corps would only begin their attack at 10.00, and 46th Division had proceeded without much regard to them keeping up, 6th Division was instructed that it was 'particularly important that the left flank of the Corps keep level with the advance of the II American Corps' on the left.[7]

Within 16 Brigade, a depleted 1st King's Shropshire Light Infantry (only six officers remained at the end of the day) received their orders to lead the attack at midnight. They were in position only just in time but arrived at their objective, Jonnecourt Farm, some 4,000 yards away 40 minutes later, despite the fog, sending back only three prisoners. They then pushed on to the railway which lay just to the west of Bohain where at 10.00 they began to be subject to erratic shelling.[8] When it became evident that 71 Brigade on their left had pushed on into Bohain, 16 Brigade was ordered to exploit further, but darkness precluded this. 71 Brigade fielded 1st

4 A. Montgomery, *The Story of the Fourth Army in the Battles of the Hundred Days*, p.197.
5 T.O. Marden, *A Short History of the Sixth Division*, p.68.
6 War Diary, Commander Royal Artillery 6th Division, Operation Order, 8 October 1918, TNA WO95/1591. Edmonds and Maxwell-Hyslop, *Military Operations France and Belgium 1918, Vol. 5*, p.213. 6th Division were supported by two RFA brigades of 6th Division, and four Army brigades.
7 War Diary, HQ IX Corps, Order No.144, 8 October 1918, TNA WO95/837.
8 The unit would attack again on 17 October, but whilst the war diary does not report reinforcement in terms of other ranks, Captain A.B. Rogers returned from leave on the 12th, and the unit was loaned two second-lieutenants from 1st Buffs, and two from 2nd York & Lancaster. They received a glut of 14 officers on the 19th.

Leicestershire and 9th Norfolk, right and left. Orders were received only at 01.40 on 9 October and the brigade found the assembly 'exceedingly difficult', having to carry out a relief involving taking over part of the American front on a 'very black night' across a 'considerable tract of unknown country.'[9] Lieutenant George Grossmith, 1st Leicestershire, reported that his CO only returned with orders to battalion HQ (a hole in the side of a sunken road with tarpaulins across) at 03.30 – this left only one hour and 50 minutes to reposition the battalion.[10] Both battalions advanced in fog with one section of field artillery attached. The Leicesters, progressing behind the creeping barrage, reached Jonnecourt Farm without loss, capturing one anti-tank gun. After they had passed through, two explosions, likely booby traps, occurred. They pressed on to the railway, but like the other units, were met with heavy machine-gun fire. Demonstrating their mastery of *SS143* tactics, C Company, under the personal command of the CO Lieutenant-Colonel Francis Latham, attempted to outflank the enemy with a captured light machine-gun from the north, whilst the second-in-command, Major John Herring-Cooper, with a Lewis gun section, moved to outflank them from the south.[11] Having a covered line of retreat, approximately 100 of the enemy were able to flee. Although by 18.00 the operation had been successful, it had not been without cost. The adjutant, Second-Lieutenant Douglas Sims, was mortally wounded whilst drafting orders for A Company to join the manoeuvre.[12] The paucity of prisoners (about 10) reflected the successful enemy withdrawal, although two heavy and three light machine-guns, as well as a 'dart machine', were amongst the spoils.[13]

As per Rawlinson's wishes, 5th Cavalry Brigade had sought to make progress. 12th Lancers moved up to Jonnecourt Farm behind 1st Leicesters, and reconnaissances were made, with much loss of direction in the fog, to see if the railway line could be turned from the north in the American Corps area. Being met with strong machine-gun fire, the patrols turned back. Just after midday a wildly optimistic order was received from Fourth Army for IX Corps to seize the Bellevue spur, at least 7,500 yards ahead of the position reached, with the cavalry to exploit to Wassigny a further 5,500 yards beyond. This being impossible, some four hours later a further order was received to 'turn Bohain' from the north in the American area. This was known from the morning patrols to be impossible, and the cavalry hence made no further progress.[14]

9 War Diary, HQ 71 Infantry Brigade, 'Narrative of Operations – 8th to 11th October 1918,' TNA WO95/1620.

10 G.W. Grossmith, Private Papers, IWM Docs 11013.

11 Major John Gustavus Herring-Cooper, an Irish hockey international, served in 3rd Queen's Own Royal West Kent and had been commissioned in the Leicestershire Regiment in 1911.

12 Second-Lieutenant Douglas Henry Sims MC had commissioned from private in August 1917. The unit lost two officers killed, with 20 casualties in the ranks, of whom five were fatalities.

13 War Diary, 1st Battalion Leicestershire Regiment, 9 October 1918, TNA WO95/1622.

14 War Diary, HQ 5th Cavalry Brigade, 9 October 1918, TNA WO95/1138.

The logic of the first order was impeccable. In seizing the Bellevue spur, the Selle position would be turned. The fact was that at that moment Fourth Army HQ was out of touch with the effectiveness of the enemy rearguards.

It was 9th Norfolk who would take Bohain that day. The orders to take over part of the line from the Americans were some of the last to arrive, yet they somehow managed to start on time. The unit advanced uneventfully behind the barrage to high ground to the north of Jonnecourt Farm and, working round to the north, sent out a patrol which at 13.00 found Bohain to be seemingly empty. The Norfolks pushed on in the spirit of Rawlinson's midday orders, but matters were not straightforward. It was not until 18.00 that they had finally managed to drive the enemy rearguard from the town and secure the eastern edges. The unit had advanced nearly 6,000 yards and captured 15 prisoners, one light trench mortar and a 4.2 inch howitzer for the loss of five other ranks killed. The Norfolks had also liberated 4,500 French inhabitants, being 'mobbed by a hysterical crowd of men women and children, almost delirious in their joy',[15] some of whom had been without food for three days.[16] Lieutenant Grossmith entered Bohain and described how:

> Hundreds of civilians came running up the streets towards us and shook hands and kissed us and made a great fuss. It was all rather pathetic. They were chiefly old men, women and girls, and even young boys were very few. They had been sheltering in the cellars during our bombardment and the German evacuation and were hysterical with joy at their liberation.[17]

Although 'little wilful destruction' had been carried out, at every cross-roads in Bohain a mine had been blown, stretching across the street from side to side, 'while the houses on either side had collapsed.'[18]

In respect of Rawlinson's high hopes of midday, the Bellevue spur remained unreachable in the distance. Little progress had been made beyond the rearguard line the enemy had held during the morning, with one exception, the capture of Bohain. A discontinuity remained in the line that night. 2nd Sherwood Foresters of 16 Brigade, who had relieved 9th Norfolk, controlled Bohain, whilst on their right flank, units of 46th Division remained on the railway, some 1,500 yards to the rear. The Germans had put up stout resistance based, again, on a machine-gun defence, and it had taken much longer to master this than had been expected, even if the infantry tactics used were effective.

15 R.E. Priestley, *Breaking the Hindenburg Line – The Story of the 46th (North Midland) Division*, p.130.
16 Montgomery, op. cit. p.197.
17 Grossmith, op. cit.
18 Priestley, op. cit. p.130.

Fourth Army issued orders at 19.30 on the 9th for IX Corps to secure the high ground north and south of Andigny-les-Fermes on the Bellevue spur.[19] The Official Historian noted in relation to this optimism that the British were 'uncertain, of course, whether the enemy was holding' their new position on the eastern bank 'merely by rearguards or was meaning to stand.'[20] On the morning of the 10th mist and rain unhelpfully 'prevented any observation of the enemy's movements',[21] and in particular no aeroplane observation was possible before midday which might have shed light on the German intentions. With the 'probability of the enemy retiring for some distance', both the 46th and 6th Divisions 'were re-organised into an advanced guard formation with one Inf[antry] B[riga]de in the line and two in support', with one mixed brigade of artillery allotted to each division in the line.[22] 46th Division pushed on towards Riquerval Wood, the easternmost aspect of the Andigny Forest (where they met stiff resistance), whilst to the north of the wood 6th Division rested 16 Brigade and continued with 71 Brigade, which had D Company 6th Battalion MGC attached. 1st Leicestershire advanced on the right, with 2nd Sherwood Foresters on the left. There was no covering barrage, but 24 Brigade RFA bombarded houses, copses and sunken roads that might contain resistance. Little was met by either unit. Having taken eight prisoners, 1st Leicestershire, due to the lack of progress by 46th Division, formed a defensive flank to Riquerval Wood. 5th Cavalry Brigade again sent the 12th Lancers forward, and they pushed patrols forward beyond the infantry, whilst the Sherwood Foresters on the left covered some 5,000 yards arriving at Vaux-Andigny somewhat later than the Americans on their left. They noted that 'the country was practically untouched, and the farms were still occupied by civilians and the country in cultivation.'[23] For the Sherwoods, 'the long-hoped-for open warfare had begun.'[24]

The objectives set by Fourth Army for IX Corps on the 11th were Andigny-les-Fermes on the Bellevue spur and Riquerval Wood.[25] 46th Division would make no progress. In 6th Division, 71 Brigade advanced to the north of the wood without a barrage, fire again being directed only on centres of likely opposition. The Americans on the left being more advanced, the brigade front was extended, and all three units were employed. 1st Leicestershire were on the right, 9th Norfolk were in the centre, with 2nd Sherwood Foresters on the left. 'It was soon discovered however that the

19 XIII Corps were ordered to take Le Cateau and II American Corps to cross the Selle. This would not be achieved until 17 October.
20 Edmonds and Maxwell-Hyslop, op. cit. p.234.
21 Montgomery, op. cit. p.200.
22 War Diary, HQ IX Corps, 9 October 1918, TNA WO95/837.
23 War Diary, 2nd Battalion Sherwood Foresters, 10 October 1918, TNA WO95/1624.
24 H.C. Wylly, *The First and Second Battalions The Sherwood Foresters (Nottinghamshire and Derbyshire Regiment) in the Great War*, p.181.
25 War Diary, HQ Fourth Army, Message G.340 10 October 1918, TNA WO95/439.

enemy's resistance had very much stiffened',[26] the brigade encountering some trenches and wire on the northern aspect of Riquerval Wood and on the ridge that barred the approach to the Bellevue spur. As the Sherwoods noted, whilst the German line had been located by patrols the previously night, 'it was not known that the enemy had a continuous and very skilfully concealed entrenched and wired position on the ridge, or that he meant to hold it with all his energy.'[27]

The 1st Leicestershire had one section of field artillery, two sections of machine-guns, and one section of Stokes mortars attached. This support was insufficient in the absence of a barrage, and they were only able to advance some 400 yards before having to go to ground due to heavy machine-gun fire. From his position Lieutenant Grossmith could see how 'the leading wave of B Company lay 200 yards out on the hillside, which was swept by machine gun fire from the opposite ridge.'[28] The unit's trench strength at the end of the day was only 12 officers and 356 other ranks, which indicates the degree of depletion. 5th Tank Battalion had made nine tanks available to 6th Division and sent five. Two had mechanical trouble, one long before it reached the line, another breaking down coming back. Two came up behind 1st Leicesters but could not suppress the machine guns in the absence of a barrage. The tanks then operated towards Riquerval Wood, but were soon spotted by enemy observation balloons and heavily shelled, one tank receiving a direct hit.[29] In the centre, 9th Norfolk had received their orders to attack at 05.30 only at 03.15, and after a hastily called conference the battalion was guided over the unfamiliar ground at 04.15. Attacking at 05.30, they soon met machine-gun fire and became aware that the flanking battalions were held up. Their advance was halted whilst artillery fire was brought to bear on the offending machine-guns. At 12.50 orders were issued to continue towards the farm on the Bellevue spur in conjunction with the Sherwood Foresters, and two tanks having arrived ten minutes later, these were sent forward to deal with any machine-gun nests. Infantry followed the tanks, but the barrage called to support the advance fell short, and they were forced to retire to their original line, where they remained. On the left, 2nd Sherwood Foresters recorded that the enemy was 'evidently expecting' the advance,[30] and whilst forming up they were subjected to an artillery barrage. The delay caused by this enemy counter-barrage meant that the attacking troops had to cross the exposed shallow valley in front of the ridge in daylight. Battalion HQ, with two 18-pounder guns attached, had followed up the two attacking companies, B and D. The artillery observer, situated on higher ground, only now became aware of the strength of the enemy position, in front of which the Sherwoods were about to debouch, completely unaware of their danger. D Company

26 War Diary, HQ 71 Infantry Brigade, 'Narrative of Operations – 8th to 11th October 1918,' TNA WO95/1620.
27 Wylly, op. cit. p.181.
28 Grossmith, op. cit.
29 War Diary, HQ 5th Tank Battalion, 11 October 1918, TNA WO95/111.
30 War Diary, 2nd Battalion Sherwood Foresters, 11 October 1918, TNA WO95/1624.

was recalled, but B could not be reached. The unsuspecting troops, in two waves, walked into withering fire. To the observing battalion HQ, 'the Company seemed to melt away.' Many of the soldiers were hit and fell, 'the rest, unable to face the hail of bullets, lay down.' The enemy thereafter 'contented himself with only firing if any attempted to crawl forward of back.'[31] It was clearly impossible to cross the 500 yards of valley. The companies on the right attempted to assist the Norfolks but could make no progress. The support company was transferred to the left to assist the Americans, and it was planned to outflank the Bellevue spur in conjunction with them. This was impossible, and at the end of the day the Sherwoods remained in a sunken road on top of the small ridge, a position they viewed as a 'death trap' due to continuing German artillery and machine-gun fire. 'Darkness soon gave the longed for cover, and rations and water could be sent up to the troops at last.'[32] Between 6 and 11 October 2nd Sherwood Foresters had lost two officers and 47 other ranks killed, with seven officers and 145 other ranks wounded with nine other ranks missing. At nightfall on the 11th 'two companies were commanded by second-lieutenants who had never been in action before, and one by a lieutenant who had practically no experience.'[33] It had been a deeply frustrating day – at the furthest extent, 6th Division had advanced 1,500 yards. IX Corps acknowledged that progress had been 'very slow … as the enemy had reinforced his line with a fresh Division which had been resting for a month.'[34]

Despite having observed that the enemy was clearly making a stand, on 12 October IX Corps made two attempts to improve its position. It is interesting that Montgomery, in his history of Fourth Army, neglects to mention these attempts. Both are reminiscent of small unit actions on the Somme in late July 1916, where a position which not been taken by a stronger force on one day was attacked by a weaker force the next. Both were predictably abortive. Thus, 46th Division failed again to make any progress towards Riquerval Wood. In 6th Division, 18 Brigade, which had not taken part in the Pursuit, had brought into the line. Their task was to advance, particularly on the left, and pull level with the Americans in Vaux-Andigny. As the brigade war diary noted, their line was 'very much dominated by a minor spur running North for about 1,500 yards from REGINCOURT [*sic*].'[35] This spur, which had been impossible to attain the previous day, formed the western edge of the valley that lay between the attacking units and the dominating Bellevue spur. It was the objective of an attack carried out at 16.30 on the 12th by 2nd Durham Light Infantry on the left and 11th Essex on the right. The Essex unit had a trench strength of 16 officers and 401 other ranks, the DLI being better off having 28 officers and 631 other ranks. The danger posed by the ridge was clearly known – 2nd Sherwood Foresters had come to grief

31 Wylly, op. cit. p.182.
32 Wylly, op. cit. p.182.
33 Wylly, op. cit. p.182.
34 War Diary, HQ IX Corps, 9 October 1918, TNA WO95/837.
35 War Diary, HQ 18 Infantry Brigade, 12 October 1918, TNA WO95/1615.

there 24 hours previously. An artillery barrage therefore concentrated on the wire and trenches on this ridge for 15 minutes before moving 100 yards every four minutes in four lifts. By this time it would be dusk, and the ridge could be consolidated in darkness. Meanwhile, heavy artillery was to pound the Bellevue spur to the rear, with machine-guns firing in enfilade from Vaux-Andigny.

The DLI attacked with only one company.[36] They attained the ridge but ran into their own barrage, were pushed to the right by it and even so, could not locate 11th Essex who had failed to penetrate the wire. They were driven back by machine-gun fire and bombing.[37] As 18 Brigade reported, in front of the Essex battalion: 'The wire was hidden from view, and unfortunately it was found that the barrage had been placed too far back, and had thus missed the wire.' Despite the unusual jump-off time, the enemy counter-barrage came down as soon as the British barrage lifted, just in front of the start line. The units of 18 Brigade were leaping into the unknown: 'The maps of this area were most indifferent, and many copses existed which were not shown.'[38] In addition to being uncut, the wire itself was much stronger than expected, consisting of 'two formidable and strongly constructed belts.'[39] The enemy was also found to have dug a series of trenches in front.[40] In an event horribly reminiscent of much earlier operations, after they had overcome the enemy outposts in front of the wire, one platoon tried to force its way through the gap cut by the Germans for access, on which machine-guns were naturally trained.[41] 2nd DLI suffered one officer and 47 other rank casualties,[42] 11th Essex lost three officers and 65 other ranks. Major Alistair Saunders, commanding the Essex unit,[43] was the only CO who attacked that day who lodged anything approaching critical observations. He wrote, underlining his remarks three times: 'It is essential that the Division on our right progresses before we advance in this sector. Otherwise enemy can shoot right up valley. This will be readily realised by seeing the ground as the maps are very inaccurate.'[44]

36 2nd Durham Light Infantry were commanded by Lieutenant-Colonel Robert Villiers Turner DSO. A captain of the battalion in August 1914, he had commanded 13th DLI for two months in 1916, and the 2nd Battalion from 13 July 1918.
37 War Diary 2nd Battalion Durham Light Infantry, 12 October 1918, TNA WO95/1617.
38 Marden, op. cit. p.69.
39 War Diary, HQ 18 Infantry Brigade, 'Account of Minor Operation', 12 October 1918 TNA WO95/1615.
40 Marden, op. cit. p.69.
41 War Diary, 11th Battalion Essex Regiment, Preliminary Report on Operations, 12 October 1918 TNA WO95/1616.
42 One officer was wounded, with 42 ORs wounded, four killed and one missing.
43 Alistair Grant Saunders, commissioned in October 1914, was commanding in the absence of Lieutenant-Colonel C. Dumbell, the latter having gone to brigade HQ to assist General Craufurd who had been injured in a dump explosion.
44 War Diary, 11th Battalion Essex Regiment, 'Preliminary Report on Operations, 12 October 1918,' TNA WO95/1616.

6th Division in Semi-open Warfare

Historians have alternately used the words 'open', 'semi-open' and 'mobile' to describe the warfare of the Hundred Days. Mobile warfare for the BEF fell between two technological stools. The cavalry was an arm about to leave the 20th Century battlefield in the face of rapid development of firepower; armour and communications were not sufficiently developed to achieve what in another 22 years would be the shape of mobile warfare. At best, the BEF could only achieve semi-mobility in warfare that was semi-open. This does not mean, however, that they lacked an effective formula.

The so-called Pursuit to the Selle of 9 October 1918 was one of the most extensive displays of all-arms warfare on the move in the whole of the Great War. Infantry, mobile artillery, machine-guns and light trench mortars, cyclists, and tanks were used across the whole front to drive in the enemy's rearguards. In the XIII Corps attack towards Le Cateau, the main cavalry thrust with attached armoured cars attempted (but failed) to achieve Haig's longed-for breakthrough near Le Cateau. The cavalry attached to 6th Division were certainly easily constrained. The contribution of the RAF in ground attack during the Pursuit is difficult to assess, as it was restricted by weather, and offered no recorded assistance to the division. Tanks did not pursue, and in 6th Division's area even failed to drive the enemy back from relatively temporary positions through both vulnerability and mechanical issues. The infantry proved the true weapon of the Pursuit to the Selle, with their mobile supporting companions in arms. The reasons for the failure of the combination of arms to set in motion a true pursuit was largely down to the degree and nature of the enemy resistance. 6th Division's infantry could be halted in their tracks by a determined machine-gun defence judiciously using topography. The enemy's will to resist and key aspects of its defensive firepower was neither broken nor exhausted. They were determined to control their withdrawal, and successfully protected much of their matériel, notably their ordnance. The paucity of prisoners taken by 6th Division in comparison with 8 October and the degree of resistance offered is a good indication of this. Semi-mobile or semi-open warfare at the Selle was achieved only to the extent that the enemy allowed them to do so. In attempting to overcome the enemy's independent will, effective communication, essentially in quick decision making in this type of warfare, was increasingly reliant on primitive means. Command and control was inevitably hampered.

In recognising failure, IX Corps noted on the 12th that 'over the last few days three fresh Divisions had come into the line opposite the Corps front.' Whilst the enemy were indeed reinforced, Fourth Army had become a victim of hubris. In the (false) belief that the Germans were on the run, Army and corps pressured their divisions into hasty operations based on little intelligence, and 6th Division fell painfully foul of this in front of the Bellevue spur. They were thus drawn into the old problem of single battalion attacks or assaults by weak and tired units on narrow fronts, directed at formidable obstacles.

Logistics and Engineering during the Hundred Days

Reviewing land transportation in the war, Colonel M.G. Taylor, Assistant Director of Movements, concluded: 'Transportation was the cause of our greater difficulties – not fighting power, leadership, or the more active side of military training.'[45] Even before the Hundred Days campaign began, when GHQ became aware that the German offensives had petered out and an enemy withdrawal to the Hindenburg Line seemed possible, the Quartermaster General stated: 'The problem of effective pursuit will largely be one of supplies and transport.'[46] Railways would have to be pushed forward, and roads and bridges onwards from the railheads reconstructed as rapidly as possible. Rob Thompson states that: 'The most important part of the engineering and logistical learning curve, certainly in relation to victory in 1918, was the German withdrawal to the Hindenburg Line in spring 1917.'[47] Thompson points out that the BEF had begun the war as a mobile force with flexible transport and supply. The logistics system had then grown on an ad hoc basis. The collapse of that system on the Somme in 1916 had led to the appointment of Sir Eric Geddes, civilian railwayman turned Director-General of Transportation, who remodelled logistic procedures to make them effective for positional warfare. He concentrated on railways, both standard gauge and light, to reliably send 'divisional pack' to railheads. 6th Division's logistical responsibility in positional warfare was simply to shift divisional pack, ammunition etc. from railheads and distribute. Advancing over the devastated areas in 1917, however, it was understood that more decentralisation of transport to corps and division would be required, i.e. more reliance on motor transport and roads. Logistics would effectively dictate operations – tempo of attack in more mobile warfare would depend on the pushing forward of railways and roads. In terms of the latter, it was accepted that 30 miles was 'the maximum that could be reasonably be expected from motorized and horse-drawn supply columns.'[48] Lorries would become the increasingly crucial link between railhead and the fighting as the distance between the two expanded late in the Hundred Days. And as roads were pushed forward, the need for roadstone increased, which in turn placed its own demands on rail transport. In comparison to the BEF's developing understanding, the German advance in the spring offensives of 1918 were logistically naïve. In contrast with the enemy's poorly supported thrust, the BEF successfully supported the massive demands of all its five armies advancing at once, by settling 'on the less glamorous, but more logistically feasible, limited-objective set-piece attack – the correct choice at the time.'[49]

45 M.G. Taylor, 'Land Transportation in the Late War', p.700.
46 War Diary, QMG Branch, 'Explanatory Review July 1918', TNA WO95/39.
47 R. Thompson, 'The Empire Strikes Back', p.7.
48 I.M. Brown, *British Logistics on the Western Front 1914-1919*, p.143.
49 Brown, op. cit. p.198-202.

Sir Henry Rawlinson was anxious about rail supply for Fourth Army as the Hundred Days campaign progressed. It was not capacity that troubled him, rather reconstruction. On 5 September he first confided to his journal: 'My chief anxiety is to get the railways through in time' – in that case for the attack on the Hindenburg Line – describing them as the 'governing factor.'[50] As 6th Division began their attacks at Holnon, their railhead was at Brie (16 September), twelve miles behind their front line. They were able to use light railway relatively nearby. For the attack at the Selle on 17 October, the railhead was at Roisel, 23 miles behind the front line by road, and IX Corps was as dependent on horse transport as it was on MT. Indeed, the BEF became increasingly reliant on horse transport during the campaign and in hillier country there was animal exhaustion in the face of a cut in fodder. By the time of their final major attack on the 23rd, the railhead was at Essigny, south of Fresnoy, some 21 mile behind the front line by road. The diaries of neither the Divisional Train ASC or Divisional Ammunition Column survive for October 1918 to assess the degree of strain.

The administrative arrangements set out on 7 October, immediately prior to the push through the Beaurevoir Line, show ammunition and supplies being delivered to refilling points by MT and then on by horse. There was a divisional gun ammunition dump, and corps advanced, divisional, and left and right brigade small ammunition/grenade dumps. The AAQMG hoped to be provided with two supply tanks for the two front brigades. Only five lorries were available for the evacuation of wounded. In terms of the Royal Engineers, there were corps, main divisional and divisional forward dumps. MT went as far as the divisional dump and relied on horse transport from there. Water was an important concern. Eighteen wells were in working order, and there were two watering points for horses, one with a capacity of 1,200 horses per hour, the other with a capacity of 6,000. Four routes were deemed fit for MT and horse transport, but other routes were noted as mined.[51] Rob Thompson emphasises the transportation problems generated by 'munitions gourmets', i.e. artillery overdemand, and the delivery of unnecessary trench stores for the engineers.[52] Indeed, on 13 October the division's AAQMG ordered that: 'At the present time unless Ordnance Stores are actually required, and Units are in a position to accept same when received by DADOS, demands for them should not be submitted.'[53]

The distances from the railheads meant that supply was completely dependent on good roads. This made the work of the engineers and pioneers critical to the tempo of operations. On 8 October, during the push through the Beaurevoir line, whilst 11th

50 Rawlinson, op. cit. 5 & 6 September 1918.
51 War Diary, AAQMG 6th Infantry Division, Administrative Arrangements No. 16, 7 October 1918, TNA WO95/1587.
52 R. Thompson, 'The Empire Strikes Back', BCMH conference lecture 28 October 2018, London.
53 War Diary, AAQMG 6th Infantry Division, Administrative Instruction and Summary No. 21, 13 October 1918, TNA WO95/1587.

Leicestershire were working on roads, the main concern for the Royal Engineers was the establishment of water points – as noted above, those for horses being as crucial as those for the troops. This having been constructed, the division were informed that '5 Garford lorries would work all night carrying water forward to new water point, 11 water lorries were being sent up tonight & 12 at dawn tomorrow.'[54] As the Pursuit began, work continued on water points, and efforts commenced on the road that lay behind the division's advance (Bellenglise to Joncourt), the pioneers laying a dry weather track on either side. 459 Field Company moved forward with the infantry repairing wells and removing mines and booby traps, whilst 509 Company reconnoitered crossroads and assessed what repairs might be necessary to the Fresnoy – Bohain Road as it fell into the hands of the infantry. As the Pursuit ground to a halt, the engineers took stock of the craters the enemy had blown in the roads. The RE orders for the 12th list ten craters in order of importance, with 'all transport … to be made available for carting timber, stone etc. to the sites of craters', and by the following day Bohain was clear, even if the repair of craters was not permanently completed, this only being achieved on the 16th. Road construction/repair was staged: 'In the first instance repairs are to be made to take single way mechanical transport in wet weather. Subsequent improvements to be made to take double lorry transport',[55] (lorries causing more damage to roads than horse transport). The weather was a significant problem. By the 13th it was arranged that 'all lorries, tank carriers, tenders and cars will be provided with skid chains … as long as roads continue greasy.'[56] Tractors were stationed at three locations to assist ditched lorries. Stating the obvious, the AAQMG wrote to all that it was 'of paramount importance to keep M.T. traffic running on roads whatever their condition.'[57] The weather was not the only cause of hold-ups. On the 14th it was noted that 'several delay-action mines have been reported on our left. Search will therefore be made along roads for these and any suspicious work investigated.'[58] (Mines were regularly exploding to the rear under the newly repaired rail tracks, but these were not the division's responsibility, and could be repaired in 12 hours). In the attack of the 17th the field companies were tasked with advancing with the artillery brigades that followed the infantry, ensuring the roads were adequate for the guns to pass along. On the 21st, as the division prepared for what would be its last action, the engineers began work in yet another new area, companies were building bridges, clearing obstacles, erecting horse troughs, and preparing roads for motor transport.

54 War Diary, CRE 6th Division, 8 October 1918, TNA WO95/1594.
55 War Diary, CRE 6th Division, 'Works Instructions for 12-10-18', TNA WO95/1594.
56 War Diary, AAQMG 6th Infantry Division, Administrative Instruction and Summary No. 21, 13 October 1918, TNA WO95/1587.
57 War Diary, AAQMG 6th Infantry Division, Administrative Instruction and Summary No. 21, 13 October 1918, TNA WO95/1587.
58 War Diary, CRE 6th Division, 'Works Instructions for 14-10-18', TNA WO95/1594.

Winter was coming, and the heavy rain speeded the degradation of roads. Standard gauge railway would never get beyond the Selle, and beyond the Sambre-Oise Canal, the advance of Fourth Army was restricted to a brigade – Bethell's Force. The BEF was consuming supplies at an extraordinary rate, the railheads were falling behind, and the supply and engineering services were worn out. The imminence of winter meant that the need for winter accommodation would require 'a major and fundamental reorientation of supply.'[59] The BEF needed an Armistice as much as the enemy by 11 November.

Battle of the Selle, 17-24 October 1918

The defences at the Selle involved an outpost zone between 30 and 300 metres wide. There was then the main resistance line or *Hauptwiderstandlinie* (*HWL I*), sited along the railway embankments and cuttings east of the river and continuing across the Bellevue spur towards Riquerval Wood in wired trenches. Some 500 to 750 yards to the east was the *HWL II* or *Zwischenstellung* (Intermediate Position), which largely consisted of machine gun nests and rifle pits. Fourth Army found itself preparing for another major set-piece attack to overcome these defences. XIII and II American Corps would be crossing the river and assaulting the *HWL I* railway line position north of IX Corps. The attack of 6th Division would be part of a particularly complex assault, and to understand their role, the plan for the whole of IX Corps must be comprehended.

Walter Braithwaite's plans were inventive and ambitious. After the abortive frontal attacks on Riquerval Wood, this was to be subject to a 'Chinese attack', and the main 46th Division thrust would be made from a small area just beyond the southern outskirts of Vaux-Andigny down the valley beneath the Bellevue spur, to secure a defensive flank to the Andigny Forest. Rather than attack the Bellevue spur frontally, both 6th and 1st Divisions would debouch from a very small area of central Vaux-Andigny. The objective of 6th Division was the forcing of the *HWL I* and the taking of the Bellevue spur and part of the valley to the north, the Angin valley. The *HWL II* positions would be overcome by the rested 1st Division who would proceed to capture the villages beyond and exploit towards the Sambre-Oise Canal. The whole Andigny Forest would be pinched out by the end of the day, the French *XV Corps* attacking on its southern side. Although the plan avoided the mistakes of the latter part of the Pursuit, it was highly optimistic to believe these objectives could be achieved in one day.

Braithwaite met with Marden and his fellow divisional commanders on both 13 and 14 October agreeing the complex artillery plans outlined in Chapter Ten. After a two-day bombardment, the attack took place at 05.20 on 17 October in fog which lasted until late morning. 46th Division achieved their objectives despite fog and loss of

59 Thompson, op. cit. p.13.

the barrage. 6th Division's part in the assault was not easy. The front was narrow, only 1,500 yards, and five battalions were to debouche 'fan-wise from the village of Vaux-Andigny ... advancing 2,500-3,000 yards to a front of 5,000 yards.'[60] The right of the advance would be astride the Bellevue spur, the left in the Angin valley, to the line of the *HWL II* where 1st Division would pass then through. The barrage opened 200-300 yards in front of the infantry start line, lifting 100 yards every three minutes.[61] The main opposition was the *15th Reserve Division*, occupying the *HWL I* in front of Vaux-Andigny. This division was rated 'third class', and 'during 1918 the division was almost constantly in line holding defensive sectors, which it did with fair success.'[62] The right of the weak *24th Infantry Division* confronted the left of the division's advance to the *HWL II.* This division had been battered in Fourth Army's assault on the Beaurevoir-Fonsomme Line in the opening days of October. A Saxon division, it had been rated 'good' and a 'courageous adversary' in 1917, and although it was rated 'third class' in 1918 its performance in in the March offensive and on the defensive in August and October 'was above the average and would warrant a higher rating.'[63]

18 and 16 Brigades were in line, right and left. 16 Brigade, attacking along the Bellevue spur, suffered the misfortune of serious injury to their commander on the evening prior to the assault. Brigadier-General Harry Walker lost his left arm to a shell whilst standing behind brigade HQ. It was blown off 'so cleanly that his wrist watch was recovered by his orderly and was still going.'[64] The brigade laid out long direction tapes pointing in the initial direction, necessary as their starting line 'faced east-south-east, while its direction of advance was south-east.'[65] Both brigades had three tanks attached. On the right, in 18 Brigade, strongpoints had been allotted as targets for the tanks on the inter-brigade boundary. The forming up of all units was made difficult by the heavy enemy shelling with HE and phosgene gas which had begun two hours before zero. On the 600 yard frontage of 18 Brigade, expanding to 2,300 yards on the objective, two battalions advanced. 11th Essex were on the right, 2nd Durham Light Infantry on the left. The Essex unit advanced at Zero up the

60 Marden, op. cit. p.70.

61 In terms of the 18-pounder barrage, for the first three minutes, fire was 'intense'; from 3-9 'rapid'; from 9-112 'normal rate; from 112-129 half a round a minute. From 129-132 minutes the fire would be intense, this being a signal to the infantry that the barrage was about to move on; from 132-180 the rate of fire was 'normal'; and from 185-190 it was 'slow.' Shrapnel was fired first and after 4-5,000 yards HE was fired. One gun in each battery fired 50 percent smoke. Three hours after zero, two brigades of Field Artillery would move forward. (War Diary, 6th Infantry Division, 6th Division Artillery Instructions No. 5, 16 October 1918, TNA WO/95 1591).

62 *Histories of the Two Hundred and Fifty-One Divisions of the German Army which Participated in the War (1914-1918)*, p.257.

63 *Histories*, pp.345-6.

64 Marden, op. cit. p.70. Percy Brown, commanding the resting 71 Brigade took over until Brigadier-General William Braithwaite arrived on the 19th.

65 A. Montgomery, *The Story of the Fourth Army in the Battles of the Hundred Days*, p.212.

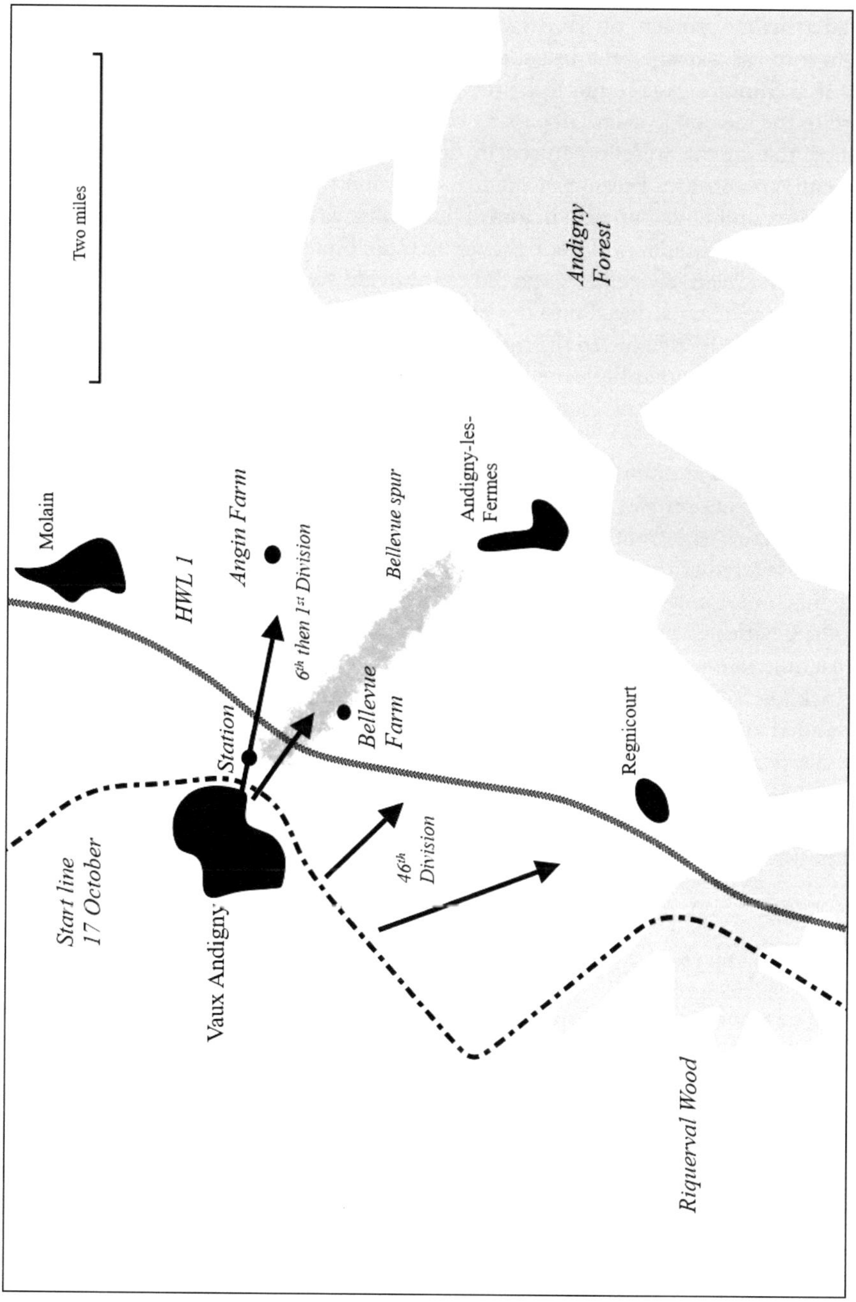

Map 13.1: Attack of IX Corps, the Battle of the Selle, 13 October 1918.

Bellevue spur on the right but soon met uncut wire and entrenchments. Uncut wire was a particular problem on 18 Brigade's front and dealing with it caused the Essex unit to lose the barrage. The brigade later concluded: 'The rate of the barrage (100 yards in 3 minutes) was found to be much too quick for Infantry to keep up having regard to the inevitable delays in passing obstacles even in slightly enclosed country.'[66] Further, the enemy were 'organised in depth and very cleverly arranged.' Despite advancing arm-in-arm because of the fog, direction was lost, and the right company of the Essex unit ended up well in 46th Division's area participating in the capture of Regnicourt. The shoulders of the Bellevue spur are broad – it was understandable that in the fog the relatively gentle slope did not provide sufficient warning to 11th Essex that they were being seduced into the valley below.

The attached tanks followed the right of the Essex assault off the spur, this depriving the infantry of support at Bellevue Farm. Here *III Battalion RIR 25* put up particularly stiff resistance, counterattacking and ejecting the elements of 11th Essex that had kept direction and secured a toehold. The company on the left shoulder of the spur also suffered misfortune when its company HQ was wiped out by a shell, and it was some time before cohesion was regained.[67] Before this was achieved, however, they had wandered across the front of the 2nd DLI advancing on their left. The enemy was then encountered at the *HWL II* in the Angin valley, 'organised in depth', and with many machine-guns. This position would hold up a number of units that morning. Captain Charles Clayton, a staff officer with 2 Brigade, described how 'dislodging' the machine gun nests created problems for command and control in the advance. 'In the thick fog … they were hard to locate and after each had been located it had to be surrounded and separately rushed.' This was time consuming and 'through a series of these disconnected operations the platoons got out of touch with each other.' Whilst they would ultimately arrive on the objective, it would be 'some time before their positions were known to their Battalion Commanders.'[68] The stalled Essex battalion was, however, carried forward by the leapfrogging units of 1st Division. The fog

66 War Diary, HQ 18 Infantry Brigade, 'Narrative of the Attack on the 17th October 1918,' TNA WO95/1615.

67 The company commander Captain Herbert Vincent Corbett was killed. A Cambridge student commissioned in October 1914, he had been severely wounded at Ypres in April 1915, and during his convalescence had finished his degree, returning to the Western Front only in June 1918. CSM Percy Alfred Strait MM was also killed. Platoon commander Second-Lieutenant James Cecil Hubert Willett MC and bar (commissioned from lance-corporal in May 1917) restored the situation. The bar to his MC was won during this action. The citation reads: 'For conspicuous gallantry and devotion to duty during an attack south-east of Vaux-Andigny on 17th October 1918. He was in command of the support company, and after his company had been used to reinforce the assaulting companies he spotted and charged an enemy post, capturing two machine-guns and twenty O.Rs. He did very excellent work during the whole operation.' (*London Gazette*, 4 October 1919, p.12257).

68 C.P. Clayton, *The Hungry One*, p.223.

lifting, both the lost tanks and infantry regained the ridge. Suffering 73 casualties, the unit had captured 115 prisoners, three trench mortars, two 77-mm guns, and 33 machine-guns.[69]

The stalled position of 11th Essex in the HWL1 in front of Bellevue Farm, 17 October 1918.

On the left of the attack on the shoulder of the ridge, 2nd DLI were immediately met by the enemy counter-barrage and ran into both opposition on the ground and a good deal of uncut wire. With loss of direction and contact, company commanders found command and control impossible. As Clayton noted, 'it became a case of separate platoons fighting on their own.'[70] Considerable time was lost cutting wire at the *HWL I* trenches on the Bellevue spur, where under heavy machine-gun fire a vicious bombing action took place. Consequently, as elsewhere, the barrage was lost. Sustaining heavy casualties as it drifted north, the attack completely lost steam in the Angin valley. The DLI were reinforced by two companies of 1st West Yorkshire, but the attack was only carried forward by the impetus of 1st Division.

69 War Diary, 11th Battalion Essex Regiment, 17 October 1918, TNA WO95/1616.
70 War Diary, 2nd Battalion Durham Light Infantry, 17 October 1918, TNA WO95/1617. Lieutenant T. Shepherd was killed, as was Second-Lieutenant Louis Pollock (commissioned in August 1918). Second-Lieutenants Ernest William Gillard (commissioned August 1918), J.G. Evans, and L.J. Harvey were wounded. 61 ORs were wounded, 15 killed and 8 missing.

Immediately to the north, 16 Brigade, facing *24th Infantry Division*, attacked with 1st King's Shropshire Light Infantry leading despite having been subject to particularly heavy gas shelling.[71] Protected by the barrage and covered by the fire of 60 machine-guns they debouched from Vaux-Andigny station. Both attacking battalions had one gun of 16th Trench Mortar Battery attached. A special map made from photos had been issued to each unit to show probable points of resistance. Unfortunately, a 'large number of M.G.s opened at zero minus 3 minutes, which caused a certain amount of anxiety among the attacking troops.'[72] They found the wire to be 'practically uncut', and the enemy 'holding his line almost entirely with machine-guns.' Despite this, they successfully took their sub-objective, the trench system of the *HWL I* running along the railway line which cut immediately across their advance. The initial task of the three attached tanks was to assist the Shropshires with this capture. They recorded that 'stubborn resistance was offered by the enemy at VAUX ANDIGNY Station' but that their tanks 'knocked out the machine-gunners here and … so allowed the Infantry to go forward.' By 06.30 the *HWL I* had been broken, and 1st Buffs passed through the Shropshires on the right,[73] their objective being the *HWL II*. The Buffs were aided in the poor visibility by having a railway running to their left. They observed that the fog had its benefits, 'parties of the enemy being come upon unaware' to be either killed or made prisoner, and in at least one case an enemy machine-gun was outflanked unobserved.[74] Not being held up by uncut wire, they regarded the barrage as 'excellent', and had avoided the enemy counter-barrage by starting forward a few minutes before zero and keeping close to their own barrage start line. Using flanking movements to overcome the resistance of *I Battalion RIR 25*, a counterattack by elements of four different German units was swept away.[75] Their advance cost 56 casualties in reaching the *HWL II*.[76] Following on the left were 2nd York & Lancaster. They were supported by the tanks who had been in action at Vaux-Andigny station, whose second task was

71 The battalion had been commanded since 10 October by Major Lyndon Henry Morris, a Territorial captain of the 4th Battalion in August 1914. The unit's casualties were 'about 25 percent, including 2nd Lieut. H.J. Taylor (The Buffs, attached) killed.' (W. de B. Wood, *The History of the King's Shropshire Light Infantry in the Great War*, p.62).

72 War Diary, HQ 16 Infantry Brigade, 17 October 1918, TNA WO95/1607.

73 The battalion was commanded that day by Major Lord Teynham, the CO Lieutenant-Colonel Roland Edward Power being on leave. Henry John Philip Sydney Roper-Curzon, 18th Baron Teynham, formally a yeomanry officer, was commissioned captain in December 1914.

74 War Diary, 1st Battalion East Kent Regiment, 17 October 1918, TNA WO95/1608. The battalion's strength at the start of the month was 33 officers and 817 ORs, and during the month suffered 16 officer and 244 OR casualties.

75 Including one reserve company from *I Battalion* and two from *II Battalion RIR 25* and *Battalion Dressler (IR 133)* from the *24th Division* (M. Whisler, 'Der Tommy Kommt', p.273).

76 Second-Lieutenants Edward Crewdson Pitt-Pitts (commissioned in May 1918), Charles Vincent, Edward Henry Ronca (commissioned in June 1918) and Harold James Taylor (commissioned in December 1917) were killed; and Second-Lieutenant Noel Adair

to assist in the capture of the high ground north of the railway, and to provide enfilade fire across the valley up which the 1st Buffs were advancing. The battalion arrived on their objective at approximately the same time as the Buffs, 09.15.[77] 16 Brigade had advanced 2,500 yards and captured five officers and 568 prisoners from 17 different units. The fighting had been 'in some places severe, as the enemy … resisted with considerable determination.'[78] The progress of 6th Division had been a story with two chapters, but it reached the *HWL II* as directed. And that was as much as virtually any formation did that day – no unit of XIII or II American Corps would get beyond the intermediate objective, and in XI Corps 1st Division only reached the first objective. It would not be until the morning of the 19th that Fourth Army would achieve the third objective set for the 17th, a line along the Sambre-Oise canal.

The Chief of Staff of the American 30th Division, Lieutenant-Colonel John Herr, made a serious allegation concerning 6th Division in an unpublished document.[79] He claimed to have contacted his 6th Division counterpart, presumably Thomas Grove the GSO 1, to coordinate the jump-off. In this conversation he was allegedly told that 'the 6th would not jump off despite orders to do so.'[80] Herr asserted that he was told: 'There is no use in concealing from you the truth, we just can't do it. We can make a bluff at starting off and open up with artillery fire, but we simply cannot make a real attack.'[81] Herr states that he passed this information to his divisional commander, Major-General Lewis, who in turn relayed it to the corps commander, Major-General Read. Read, Herr wrote, would not take the matter up with Rawlinson. What Herr alleges he was warned of, of course, did not happen. 6th Division, as has been seen, had a mixed experience that morning, but indeed jumped-off. 16 Brigade advanced in an exemplary fashion, but a difficult time was had on the front of 18 Brigade. Mark Whisler has commented that the published accounts, Montgomery's history of Fourth Army and Marden's history of 6th Division, as well as the IX Corps Narrative of Operations, 'seem to gloss over the 18th Brigade's problems.'[82] This is not entirely fair, as Marden specifically noted that it had to be 'carried forward by the oncoming waves of the 1st Division.'[83] All three of its leading battalions met with uncut wire

Harper (commissioned in June 1915) wounded. Five ORs were killed, 33 wounded and five gassed, with 13 missing.

77 The battalion war diary for the day of the attack is lost. The unit was commanded by Lieutenant-Colonel James Robert Robertson, who may well have been wounded that day as the unit was commanded two days later by the adjutant, Captain Ernest Edward Battle. Robertson had four battalion commands between July 1917 and 17 October 1918.

78 Montgomery, op. cit. p.213.

79 John K. Herr, 'My Personal Experiences and Observations in Connection with the Great War', John K. Herr Papers, United States Military Academy Archives, West Point, New York, cited in M. Yockelson, 'Brothers in Arms', p.312.

80 Yockelson, op. cit. p.302.

81 Herr, op. cit.

82 Whisler, op. cit. p.313.

83 Marden, op. cit. p.70.

and stiff opposition, lost the barrage, and had difficulty in keeping direction. This indeed caused a complete loss of impetus on the brigade front. The commentary in the brigade war diary located the problems some way down the chain of command. It was suggested that the 'regrettable delay' on the part of 2nd DLI was occasioned by 'lack of experience' of company commanders 'who did not realise that with a fresh Division about to leap-frog through it was essential to push on without delay were it at all possible to do so.'[84] (1st Cameron Highlanders noted the 'stickiness' of the 11th Essex companies who had not progressed beyond the *HWL I.* It is highly possible the same issues pertained). The position was much the same as that the division had found itself in at the Transloy Ridges in October 1916. After sustained heavy fighting and casualties, units had been reinforced without opportunity for further training of replacements and had been plunged into more heavy fighting. The difficulties of 18 Brigade no doubt have a number of different roots. The formation had indeed undergone an extremely hard time in the September fighting for the Quadrilateral. It had, however, been rested during the heavy fighting of 8 October, coming into line again for the doomed small operation of the 12th. Peter Simkins points to three issues, two of which are clearly training issues: 'The evidence … appears to suggest that the 18th Brigade may not have been as combat sharp as other formations in 6th Division and morale and leadership may have had something to do with this.'[85] Coupled with this was a marked artillery failure, and enemy resistance which was determined, backed with very accurate artillery support. It is clear, however, that if 18 Brigade had such problems, it did not extend across the whole division. It would be highly surprising if the division's GSO1 had said that the whole division would fail to go forward. This would not just represent an unthinkable lack of loyalty, there were also simply no general grounds in the division's previous performance for saying this. If anything, it was the 30th American Division who experienced difficulties on 17 October (as it had bordering 6th Division during the Pursuit and would again on the 18th and 19th), leaving the British flanks exposed rather than vice versa. The credibility of the remarks attributed to Colonel Grove seems highly questionable.

The Battle of the Selle was concluded on 19 October without the participation of 6th Division. The Selle operations as a whole were not over, however. Whilst the German *18th Army* had pulled back across the Sambre-Oise Canal on 18 September, to the north of Fourth Army the Third Army has at yet to cross the Selle. The German *2nd Army* was therefore still on the river north of Le Cateau with a flank that stretched back towards the Sambre-Oise Canal at Catillon. Third Army made its crossing on the 20th, and on the 23rd, Fourth and Third Armies would attack together, Rawlinson's formation driving in the enemy flank in a north-easterly direction towards Landrecies. The IX Corps would attack on the army's right, adjacent to the Sambre-Oise canal,

84 War Diary, HQ 18 Infantry Brigade, 'Narrative of the Attack on the 17 October 1918', TNA WO95/1615.
85 Peter Simkins, personal communication, email 10 March 2016.

XIII Corps on the left abutting Third Army. A Zero of 01.20 was agreed, suiting Third Army's practices.

The 1st Division assaulted on a 6,000 yard frontage to the right to take Catillon, and 6th Division on a frontage half that width to the left (see Map 16, colour section). 6th Division would progress along the south-eastern aspect of the Bois l'Evêque. Attached to IX Corps was the 301st American Tank Battalion organised in three sections of three Mark V tanks each, one further section being held in reserve. Specific tasks involving dealing with strongpoints were allotted. One section was attached to 1st Division which was then to drive due north to help 6th Division take Gimbremont Farm to the north-west of Catillon. Secondly, two sections would assist the 6th in the taking of an area of enclosures at le Planty, further to the north-west along the Bazeul-Catillon road from Gimbremont. These machines would then proceed north to the eastern edge of Bois l'Evêque. 2nd Tank Brigade, to which the Americans were attached, had had only two to three days for reconnaissance, and the information as to what lay behind the enemy's front line was limited. 'The BOIS L'EVEQUE was expected from civilian statements and photographs to be almost impassable for tanks, and this proved to be the case.' Wisely, none of the machines strayed therein. The front line being somewhat fluid, tank reconnaissance officers 'in more than one case walked through the line unawares and came under the fire of snipers or machine-guns.'[86]

6th Division faced a difficult prospect. The enemy had good artillery positions both in the substantial Bois l'Evêque and on the eastern bank of the Sambre and Oise Canal. The first opposed the left of the division's advance. Without suppression, the latter would enfilade their right. Indeed, 'the hostile artillery fire was more than had been encountered since the fighting about St. Quentin.' In the days prior to the attack 'the shelling of roads, farms and villages in our rear area and of artillery positions was continuous.'[87] The division's assembly, in particular, was subject to damaging HE and gas shelling. A model of thoroughness, General Marden held a conference with his brigade commanders and battalion COs three hours before zero to ensure that the plans for the attack, supported by seven brigades of field artillery and one heavy, were completely understood by all. 18 Brigade comprised the right of the divisional assault, which would take the rest of the high ground to the west of Catillon, cross the Catillon-Bazeul road, and press on up the west bank of the canal towards Ors, brushing the edge of the Bois l'Evêque. The 2nd Durham Light Infantry abutted the attack of 1st Division. The Durhams' assembly was subject to heavy enemy shelling between midnight and 01.00 which caused casualties and disorganisation in the two assaulting companies. Almost immediately on setting off in moonlight and thick mist, these two companies and their support were caught yet again by the counter-barrage, their commanders being wounded. The skill of the German artillery, hastily

86 War Diary, HQ 2nd Tank Brigade, 'Report on Operations 23rd and 24th October 1918,' TNA WO95/102.
87 Marden, op. cit. p.71.

sited on the east bank of the canal, was evident: 'The enemy barrage crept back with our advance and rested in three places.'[88] The bombardment left only small groups of infantry advancing up the eastern slope of the valley of the St Maurice stream to meet the enemy on the high ground that overlooked Catillon. Topping the crest they met machine-gun fire and wired hedges. Despite the degradation of command and control, the opposition was overcome and the Durhams reached the Catillon-Bazeul road. Here they were held up by fire from houses north-east of Catillon, and the disorganisation began to have a negative effect. Small parties of infantry from the three companies, some under officers, some under NCOs, fell back out of touch with each other. None, on their own, were strong enough to deal with the opposition. Four hours beyond jump-off the British troops were still being shelled with a mixture of high explosive and gas. Lieutenant-Colonel Reginald Turner, essentially in the dark as to what had transpired, ordered A Company forward from reserve.[89] The first three companies having drifted to the right, A Company passed to their left, and their impetus overcame the opposition on the road. Thus, without the planned help of the two sections of tanks in taking the stronghold at le Planty on their left, they had captured both the higher ground beyond the road and Gimbremont Farm itself by dawn. The day had ultimately been successful, and the battalion had performed much more effectively than on the 17th, but the Durhams had suffered 151 casualties. Over the next two days posts were pushed forward to Malmaison Farm and the Ors road, but Ors itself and a few remaining strongholds on the west bank of the canal would remain to be taken by 32nd Division on 4 November in the Battle of the Sambre.

The 1st West Yorkshire attacked on the brigade's left, also having to proceed down into the shallow valley of the St Maurice stream and uphill again. 'Tapes had been laid previously to direct the attack and compass bearings carefully worked out',[90] the morning fog and obscured moon making this an absolute necessity. The battalion was supported by tanks, a section of machine-guns and a trench mortar. The country was more difficult in front of the West Yorkshires than in front of the Durhams, and the unit progressed more slowly, albeit with less casualties. The tanks cleared passages through the thick hedges in some places and in others the infantry went at them with billhooks. Unfortunately, the inevitable delays caused by forcing passage led to the loss of the barrage and exposed the battalion to unsuppressed enemy machine-gun fire. Around 08.30, however, brigade received reports that the West Yorkshires were on the Catillon-Bazeul road and pushing forward with the co-operation of the tanks. One of the tanks had ditched within 200 yards of the road, but two progressed and 'an observer who saw these tanks in action reported that they practically cleared up the whole of the ground between R.10 and the BAZEUL-CATILLON road.' They thus

88 War Diary, 2nd Battalion Durham Light Infantry, 23 October 1918, TNA WO95/1617.
89 Reginald Turner DSO was retired territorial officer of the Sherwood Foresters in August 1914. He was promoted to command 6th Northamptonshire in March 1917.
90 E. Wyrall, *The West Yorkshire Regiment in the War 1914-1918*, p.377.

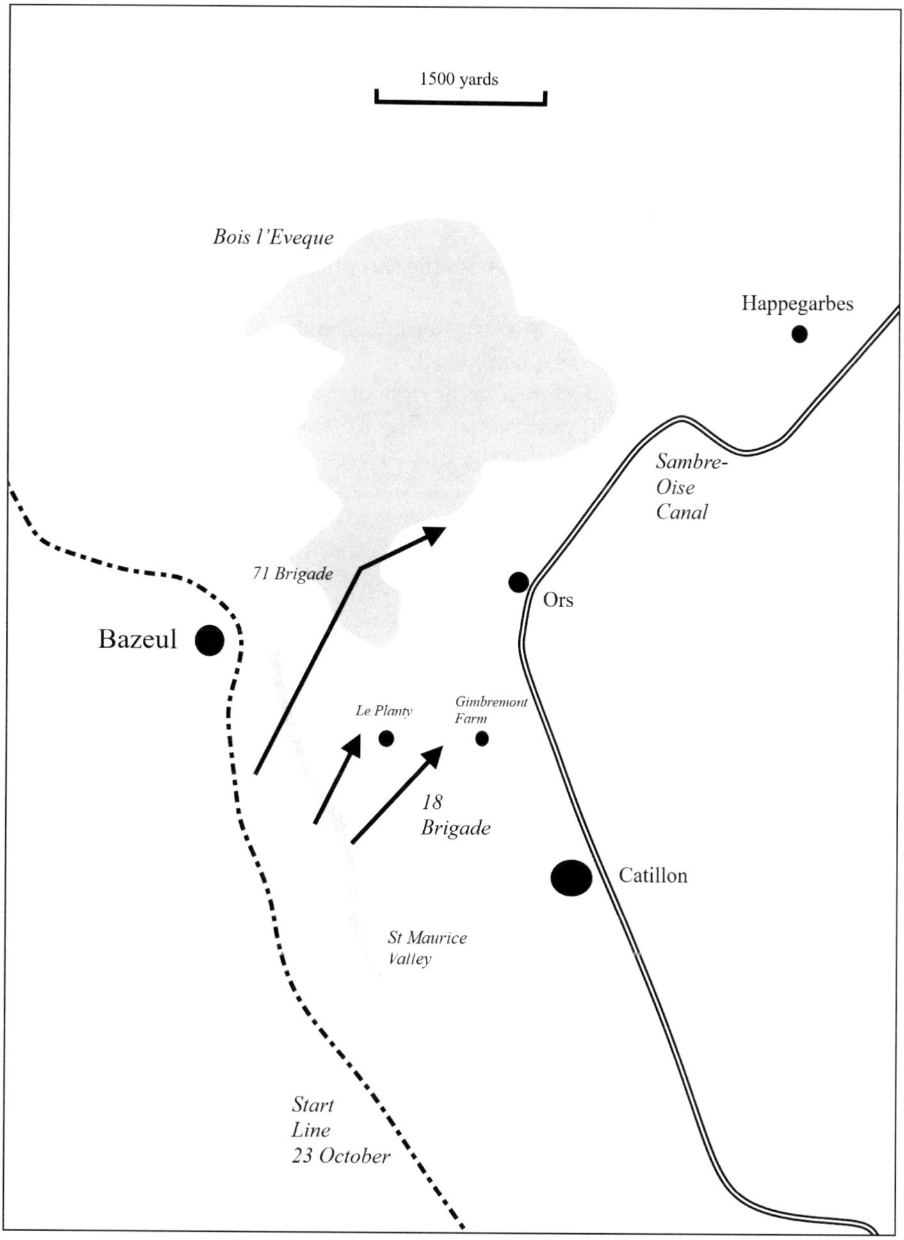

Map 13.2: The attack against the Bois l'Evêque, 23 October 1918.

cleared a distance nearly two-thirds of the way to Ors, abutting the southern tip of the Bois l'Evêque.[91] A defensive flank was put down to the left in the absence of contact with the adjacent battalion of 71 Brigade in the wood and by 15.00 the Yorkshire unit had advanced to the second objective, the Durhams on their right being ahead. The fighting that day had been expensive, costing 1st West Yorkshire 107 casualties. During the night they pushed their line out further and by 08.00 on the 24th were on the final objective positioned around the west of Ors. That night they sent out patrols onto the canal banks to find the enemy, with the exception of a few machine-guns and sniper posts, gone.

The left of the division's assault, facing the scrubland and remaining trees of the Bois l'Evêque, was made by 71 Brigade, temporarily commanded by the able Lieutenant-Colonel Latham of 1st Leicestershire. On the right of the brigade, 9th Norfolk fielded two companies, each on a 300 yard frontage. Their first objective lay some 300-400 yards beyond the south-east corner of the Bois l'Evêque. Despite the heavy shelling the battalion started well, but 'the first check occurred very soon, when many wired hedges and fences, in a close country of small fields, were met with and found to be almost unpassable.'[92] They had progressed no more than 400 yards. Opposition was strong. The advanced troops were 'at one time surrounded by the enemy and after fierce hand to hand fighting some were able to get back.'[93] A party of about 50, however, eventually arrived in the corner of the wood, and the barrage having been lost, dug in and awaited support on both flanks. By now, the Norfolks had fallen behind the progress of 1st Leicestershire, attacking on the brigade's left. The attached section of tanks had meanwhile reached the first objective but found themselves with no infantry to support. The 2nd Brigade Tank Corps later observed: 'The infantry was somewhat slow in following up the tanks, probably owing to the poor visibility and enclosed nature of the country.' Being under fire from machine-guns and a 77-mm gun, the tanks returned from whence they came. They had, however, 'reduced strong points and broke[n] paths through the hedges for the infantry.'[94] Two tanks were then ordered to report to Colonel Day of the Norfolks and deal with strong points in the orchards close to the wood that were holding progress up.

Bazeul being a centre for fruit-growing, immediately in front of 1st Leicestershire on the brigade's left 'were small orchards for a distance of 500 yards with thick hedges reinforced by wire, and although billhooks were used, the wire and the direction of the hedges soon caused the attacking lines to lose direction', and thus the barrage

91 War Diary, HQ 2nd Tank Brigade, 'Report on Operations 23rd and 24th October 1918', TNA WO95/102.
92 F.L. Petre, *The History of the Norfolk Regiment*, p.207.
93 War Diary, HQ IX Corps, 23 October 1918, TNA WO95/837.
94 War Diary, HQ 2nd Tank Brigade, 'Report on Operations 23rd and 24th October 1918,' TNA WO95/102. Across the whole of the 301st Tank Battalion there were only five casualties, all gassed.

was again lost.[95] By 05.00 the leading parties had only progressed 1,000 yards but had reached a ridge overlooking the wood. Communication proved a central problem across the division's front that morning. The Leicesters' CO Major Herring-Cooper had to go forward as the only information coming in about the progress of the attack was from the wounded proceeding to the rear. He was able to discern that his companies were on the first objective but was also clear that his right flank was in the air with no contact with the Norfolks. Referring matters to brigade, at 12.30 a company of 2nd Sherwood Foresters was ordered to push into the gap. Reports were received from division of the Germans moving east, with fires along the canal, and by 13.00 the enemy fire had slackened. During the afternoon the Leicesters were able to advance their line further into the wood which was 'very thick, a way having to be cut through it.'[96] The Sherwood Foresters pushed on to the second objective, their right resting on the railway line north-east of Ors.

The Leicesters and the company of Sherwood Foresters were now in front of the Norfolks, and the respite gave the latter battalion the chance to reform. General Marden and Colonel Latham, demonstrating both the inventiveness of front-line commanders displayed during the Hundred Days as well as devolved command, then decided to shift the Norfolks to the left round the rear of the Leicesters into 25th Division's area in order to attack the wood in a south-easterly direction. The line of this attack would follow paths and rides that ran across the previous line of advance rather than battling through the undergrowth. Darkness intervened before this inventive operation could be concluded, however. The 9th Norfolk were withdrawn that night, having suffered a hefty 136 casualties.

At 17.00 a contact patrol was able to report that the IX Corps line held the southern part of Bois l'Evêque with its farthest reach at a point on the railway line to the north of Ors. The corps had taken nearly all of its objectives in a day of heavy fighting. Fourth Army concluded that 6th Division's slow progress was 'due to the enemy's counter-preparation, which caused a certain amount of disorganisation resulting in the infantry being unable to keep up with the creeping barrage.'[97] The weight and skilled nature of the German counter-barrage had indeed caused significant casualties across the whole of the corps front. Although 6th Division experienced much more resistance than the 1st, the enemy's preparedness to withdraw was indicated by the fact that only 100 or so prisoners were taken. The Germans were bound to mount increased opposition facing 6th Division. Opposite 1st Division, they had largely withdrawn across the canal. Opposite the 6th, there was more of an imperative to

95 War Diary, 1st Battalion Leicestershire Regiment, 23 October 1918, TNA WO95/1622. During the period 20-24 October 1st Leicestershire suffered five officers wounded, eight other ranks killed, 90 wounded and 33 missing, a total of 131. Less the battle nucleus their strength had been 14 officers and 362 other ranks – they had therefore lost a third of their numbers.

96 War Diary, HQ IX Corps, 23 October 1918, TNA WO95/837.

97 War Diary, HQ Fourth Army, 23 October 1918, TNS WO95/439.

protect *2nd Army*'s flank. In addition to artillery fire there was yet another clear reason for the failure to achieve the furthest objectives that day. The nature of the countryside had changed once more. The enclosed fields which had been a feature of the fruit-growing east bank of the Selle in contrast to the west had become even more dense. The fact that the enemy had wired the hedges could not have been known (but might have been guessed). The nature of the countryside, however, was clear, and to a certain extent had been anticipated with the provision of billhooks. 6th Division also faced the Bois l'Evêque, and it was in the undergrowth where the trees had been felled that the enemy machine-gun nests were concealed. Whereas 1st Division attacking towards the canal could easily keep up with the barrage progression, 6th Division, given these obstacles, could not. The artillery of Fourth Army had learnt from the experiences of 17-19 October, and had allowed for a slower rate of progress, 100 yards in four rather than three minutes (the barrage had even progressed at 100 yards every six minutes in Bois l'Evêque), but it was still too fast for the terrain. The universal loss of the protective barrage exposed 6th Division to the enemy machine-guns and progress slowed.

On the 24th, Fourth Army tasked IX Corps with taking the objectives that had not been achieved the previous day. 71 Brigade of 6th Division had reached a line by night about half-way through the eastern corner of the Bois l'Evêque and was relieved by 16 Brigade which resumed the assault under a creeping barrage at 09.30. Generals Braithwaite and Marden, again models of thoroughness, visited the adjacent 25th Division the previous afternoon and returned to hold a conference with their own battalion commanders to ensure that the brigades of both divisions understood the attack.[98] A machine-gun barrage was put down on the south-east edge of the wood and the ground between the wood and the canal. The two attacking battalions formed up on the defensive flank maintained by XIII Corps through the centre of the wood during the night and attacked in a south-easterly direction. On the right, 2nd York & Lancaster met less opposition than had been offered the previous day and were on their objective by 11.30. 1st Shropshire Light Infantry attacked on the left. Barrage lifts that morning were 100 yards every six minutes due to the expected thickness of the scrub in the wood, but in fact progress proved relatively easy, and the advancing troops for once had to halt and wait for the barrage to move on. The unit's line was established on the objective on the right, but not on the left where 25th Division were struggling.[99] By the following day, the corps was on the canal south of Catillon and established in the western outskirts of the village itself, and was able to exploit Ors with patrols, but not occupy it. A small area of the eastern tip of Bois l'Evêque remained outside the British grasp, due to machine-gun fire from high ground to the east.

98 War Diary, HQ 16 Infantry Brigade, 23 October 1918, TNA WO95/1607.
99 War Diary 1st King's Shropshire Light Infantry, 24 October 1918, TNA WO95/1609.

The Battle of the Selle was over. On 31 October two Companies of 1st Buffs mounted an operation to seize a farm on the Happegarbes spur and the adjacent high ground, 3,000 yards west of Landrecies. Even this small objective was accompanied by a section of 6th Battalion MGC and two Stokes guns, and protected by a creeping barrage whilst heavy guns bombarded enemy positions on the railway line that ran along the canal. The attack was led by Lieutenant Louis Barber, and the tactics employed are hinted at in the statement: 'The attack was made on a two platoon frontage, 2 other platoons operating on either flank so as to protect the advance, and 3 platoons were retained in support.'[100] The barrage at first fell short, and all but six men in the leading platoon became casualties whilst forming up. The advance was then held up by enemy machine-gun fire, and it was not until four hours after jump-off that the right flanking platoon attacked with rifle grenades and the farm was captured (the high ground having been taken behind a correctly aligned barrage). A withdrawal had to be made from the farm when the enemy mounted a counter-attack following a bombardment by field guns, light and heavy trench mortars, but were resisted from further advance by Lewis guns and riflemen. Reserve platoons came up, the farm was bombarded by the Stokes guns, and then retaken at the point of the bayonet. Forty-one casualties had been sustained.

This action was to be the division's last in the First World War. It typified what might be called the 'true texture' of the fighting of the Hundred Days. The Buffs' strength on the day of the attack was 36 officers and 651 ORs. Thus despite depletion in September and October's heavy fighting they were being kept reasonably up to strength (six officers and 164 ORs would arrive the following month). Twenty-five year old Louis Walter Barber, who led the attack, had arrived on the Western Front on 1 May 1915 as a private with the Seaforth Highlanders, and had been commissioned on 14 February 1915. He had been promoted company commander (acting Captain) 15 days beforehand. Thus, despite the high casualty levels, the Buffs were able to field a very competent young officer with three years' experience of war. The assault was made using well practiced and competent infantry tactics, but all did not go well initially – the powerful artillery support was partly inaccurate. Such was the friction of war. Further, the enemy mounted a stiff resistance – they were evidently still far from a demoralised and beaten force. But it was the well-directed use of firepower that resisted the enemy, Lewis guns and rifles bringing them to a halt, whilst 'the light TM guns and Machine guns were invaluable in bringing the day's fighting to a successful conclusion.'[101] Barber had been awarded the MBE for 'an act of gallantry in the face of the enemy' in June 1918, but would be awarded the MC for his actions on 31 October:

100 War Diary, 1st Battalion Buffs, 'Report on Minor Operation near BOIS D'EVEQUE Oct 31st 1918', TNA WO95/1608.

101 War Diary, 1st Battalion Buffs, 'Report on Minor Operation near BOIS D'EVEQUE Oct 31st 1918', TNA WO95/1608.

> He was in command of two companies in an assault on a fortified farm and an adjoining wood east of the Bois L'Eveque, 30th October 1918. When the attack threatened to collapse he reorganised the line, and succeeded in capturing the objective. Later the enemy recaptured the farm, but he again reorganised his forces for a counter-attack, which drove the enemy out. Throughout the day he showed great gallantry and enterprise.

6th Division and the 'true texture' of the fighting of the Hundred Days

During the Hundred Days 6th Division participated in four set-piece attacks and had one period of semi-open warfare. The first period of set-piece operations, at Holnon, was as taxing apiece of trench warfare as they had experienced. The third, on 17 October at the Selle, showed them to be tired and depleted in an attack which took Fourth Army three days to achieve the objectives set for the first. Revisionist historians have tended to ascribe the overall success of the Hundred days to the 'weapons system.' This system's success at the Battle of Amiens on 8 August was a triumph the BEF was never to repeat, however – the shortcomings were evident at the Selle in particular. In the so-called Pursuit, the mobile elements, cavalry and armoured cars, would prove highly vulnerable to German firepower.[102] Airpower in reconnaissance and ground support was considerably frustrated. Between 9 and 16 October at the Selle there were only two days of significant flying because of rain and fog, rendering the BEF partially blind. The 'God of War', the artillery, also contributed less to the fighting than might be supposed. The two day preliminary bombardment before 17 October was based on assumed locations of potential lines of resistance and artillery rather than intelligence. It was seemingly ineffective as the wire was largely found to be intact across the whole front of Fourth Army. It was also tactically flawed – the barrage at 100 yards every three minutes moved too quickly when unreduced obstacles had to be overcome. Counter-battery fire was made largely impossible by the failure to fly and hence lack of intelligence, and the enemy's guns were very active and accurate. It was the mobile support of field guns pushed forward that was of most use to the infantry. In terms of armour, Fourth Army had about 60 tanks at the Selle, and these were able only to make occasional tactical differences, proving vulnerable to terrain and shellfire (as always), and suffering increasing breakdowns pushed forward in the advance. Communications became more and more difficult, and devolved command resulted pragmatically from this difficulty. Mobile firepower in the form of the Lewis gun, with Vickers and Stokes guns pushed forward on the flanks were the main adjuncts to the infantry advance (with the mobile field guns).

102 In attacking Gattigny Wood and Honnechy on 9 October in the XIII Corps area of IX Corps they sustained 57 dead and 338 wounded, as well as losing 401 horses. Armoured cars were insufficiently developed, their axles vulnerable to rough ground.

The 'Queen of the Battlefield', therefore, were often they key element of the 'weapons system.' As Peter Simkins has observed: 'For all the BEF's superior logistics, improved technology and highly effective combined armed tactics' during the final campaign, 'the doggedness and resilience of the British front line soldier remained as important – and perhaps even more important – than the methods he employed.'[103] This was partly possible because the army's infantry was not as youthful as some have supposed – only about 17 percent appear to have been aged 18-19 at the Selle, with a good leavening of seasoned junior leaders. The minor Happegarbes operation is therefore a good summary of much of the infantry experience of these later battles. Partially flawed artillery support coupled with persistent infantry using mobile firepower and effective tactics won the day, albeit at some cost.

The other part of the equation was of course, the independent will of the enemy. 6th Division's operations at Holnon and the Selle demonstrate conclusively that the German will to resist persisted much longer than might be supposed. The enemy's staff functions were intact during their retreat, continually reorganising units and formations, and both Holnon and the Selle demonstrate their inventive use of geography in defence. The Hindenburg Plan for *materialschlacht* of 1916 meant that automatic weapons existed in profusion, and they possessed ample ammunition for both machine-guns and artillery. Their infantry defence in the Hundred Days was predicated upon reduced numbers but an abundance of firepower. Further, the German machine-gunners were an elite group in their regiments. Sergeant Thomas Brookbank, giving a view from the ground, described the enemy as 'good fighting troops and put up a strong resistance, especially their machine-gunners.' The latter 'were excellent at selecting the best positions to get a good field of fire from which they played havoc with our advancing troops.'[104] Despite the haemorrhage of infantry in surrenders to the Allies and desertions on the lines of communication, a distilled group remained in the front-line who still possessed fighting spirit.

103 P. Simkins, *From the Somme to Victory*, p.206. For a wider discussion see P. Hodgkinson, *The Battle of the Selle*, pp.243-282.
104 T. & M. Brookbank, *A Soldier of 6th Division*, p.48.

Conclusion

On the day the Armistice was signed, Second-Lieutenant Clifford Carter of 2nd York & Lancaster described at Bohain how: 'The night was given over to revelry, in which the French joined. Bonfires were lit at every street corner and the whole countryside was ablaze with fires and star shells.'[1] IX Corps was then transferred to the Second Army for the March to the Rhine as part of the British Army of Occupation. It was organised into three infantry brigade groups, and a Divisional Troops group under the CRA. Marden described the advance, which began on 20 November, as 'the progression of a snake, the rear group moving forward at each advance to the area occupied the previous day by the leading group.'[2] The practicalities of logistics interfered with its progress, the enemy's destruction of roads, bridges and railways as encountered by the division at the Selle having been duplicated all along the route, and there were difficulties in feeding the leading divisions. Lieutenant Carter foraged for his officers' mess in any location he thought likely, including a convent. Staff officers proceeded by car in reconnaissance, and Engineers and Pioneers moved ahead mending roads and ensuring water supplies. Marden reported that 'once across the (Belgian) frontier the roads were splendid, the inhabitants most hospitable and enthusiastic.'[3] The 2nd York & Lancaster held a battalion concert on 27 November 'to which the civilians were invited. Two Belgians sang and one recited. It was the first really enjoyable time they had had for years.'[4] Tom Grove, the GSO1, described passing through Charleroi how 'we were cheered by all the small children along the road and many of the men took their hats off to us.'[5] The German frontier was crossed at Malmedy on 13 December 'with drums beating and colours flying', Clifford Carter noting that 'the 'crossing' was made with fixed bayonets 'marching to attention', the same procedure being adopted at each German town. 'We were "conquerors" and must

1 C. Carter, Private Papers, IWM Docs 7988.
2 T.O. Marden, *A Short History of the Sixth Division*, p.77.
3 Marden, op. cit. p.77.
4 War Diary, 2nd Battalion York & Lancaster Regiment, 27 November 1918, TNA WO95/1610.
5 T.T. Grove, 'It Happened by Chance', NAM 1963-08-14.

behave as such!', Carter added.[6] Marden described how 'the attitude of the population in Germany was servile and little hate could be felt.'[7] Carter noted how 'everything is very sombre … the civilians appear to be friendly, but I suppose they are making the best of a bad job. All the men and boys raise their hats to our Officers in the street.' Citizens were ordered to 'step off the footpath and walk in the road' when a soldier approached, also to remove their hats on the passing of British regimental colours, the playing of the British national anthem, or on encountering British officers.[8] Anxiety about reprisal eased and the division relaxed in their relations with the population.[9] The March to the Rhine was completed on 23 December when the head of the column reached Rondorf, south of Cologne, a distance of 220 miles having been covered. Headquarters were set up at Bruhl and the brigades distributed across the Divisional Occupation Zone which stretched back in a south-westerly direction. Here the activity was mainly educational and recreational, and demobilization began, the miners from 2nd York & Lancaster departing as early as 30 December. Thomas Brookbank, 6th Machine Gun Battalion, described how 'rules were laid down for both troops and civilians.' Troops were instructed not to fraternise, 'which did not always work when girls were around.' (Indeed by 18 January the division was experiencing an increase in cases of venereal disease and there was discussion of issuing prophylactics, a variety of which called 'Tripp' were purchased in Cologne, 1,000 on the first occasion).[10] The Rhineland Army shrank steadily, and on 15 March 6th Division ceased to exist, becoming the Midland Division under Major-General Sir C.P.A. Hull, who had served his war as a brigade and divisional commander, lastly with 56th Division.

Sir Henry Rawlinson wrote to General Marden on the division leaving Fourth Army in November 1918: 'The Division has passed through strenuous times and has seen some heavy fighting' (this at Holnon Wood and Vaux-Andigny), 'where the gallantry and determination of all ranks filled me with admiration.' He concluded: 'I congratulate most heartily you all on the victories you have won.'[11] Peter Simkins, in the context of the SHLM Battle Assessment Study, presents figures to demonstrate that 6th Division was the fifth most successful regular division out of nine in the Hundred Days campaign, with a success rate in attack of just under 63 percent, and the seventh most successful out of the nine who served in Fourth Army, where the average success rate in opposed attacks was nearly 71 percent. Of the 60 divisions active in the Hundred Days, it ranks 43rd in success in attack. Even if a perfect algorithm for analysing battlefield performance were achievable, this does not appear on the face of it to be an outstanding record, with an 'outright failure' rate of 25 percent. As Simkins notes, however: 'One might bear in mind that a failure rate of 25 percent in

6 Carter, op. cit.
7 Marden, op. cit. p.78.
8 T. & M. Brookbank, *A Soldier of 6th Division*, p.51.
9 Carter, op. cit.
10 War Diary, ADMS 6th Infantry Division, 18 January 1919, TNA WO95/1593.
11 Marden op. cit. pp. 76-7.

opposed attacks was by no means discreditable on the Western Front and, in any case, did not necessarily signify that a particular division was always ineffective.'[12] Indeed, the analysis cannot take into account the unique constellation of problems faced at Holnon, a significant element of Rawlinson's 'strenuous times.'

To attempt to categorise 6th Division as 'good, 'bad' or 'indifferent 'in terms of its performance is meaningless. Many formations could be described using these words at one time or other during the war. Like the whole BEF, the division's career was not even. Progress was dependent on things that were both within its control and things which were not. The Hooge operation in August 1915 was probably the best piece of operational planning for a set-piece attack carried out in the BEF in the war to that date, but this did not guarantee complete success. Its performance at the Quadrilateral on the Somme in September 1916 might be viewed as poor, yet the reasons for its two failed attacks were largely beyond its control and tell as much about the general inadequacies of the BEF's planning during this period as a whole. The formation's performance in the Battle of Morval two weeks later was faultless, yet the difference was due to no change within the division itself. 6th Division slogged away in places the spotlight of historiography has tended not to illuminate – the Battle of Armentières in 1914, when all eyes were on the First Battle of Ypres; 15 months in the Ypres salient during a period of no major offensive or defensive actions; and at Loos in April 1917, when the focus of historians has been on the Battle of Arras. The division's moment of purist heroism demonstrated in sheer tenacity and solid soldiering, was in its defence on 21-22 March 1918 against the 'Michael' offensive. In the Hundred Days, when Simkins' analysis suggests its performance was less than sparkling, it had the ill luck to be pitched against powerful defences held with obduracy. Its performance at the Selle, on 17 October 1918, shows a division tired by recent heavy fighting, and demonstrating some of the vagaries in performance induced by piecemeal reinforcement at a time when training was impossible by virtue of constant action.

Thomas Marden described a division 'which played no inconspicuous part in the Great War.'[13] 6th Division would not truly be described as 'conspicuous' in the Great War, either. Indeed, Marden's career prior to taking up the helm of the division is a model for the vagaries of both the division's performance and the conflict as a whole. A technocrat of war, with a mastery of detail, a concept of tight command, and a complete understanding of the new warfare, he never had success as a brigade commander, if exemplary victory constitutes such. Jonathan Krause's observation 'that a particular force can do everything "right" and still suffer defeat,'[14] rings so true concerning the

12 P. Simkins, 'Co-stars or Supporting Cast? British Divisions in the "Hundred Days", 1918', in P. Griffiths (ed.) *British Fighting Methods in the Great War*, p.58. Also personal communication.

13 Marden, op. cit. p.v.

14 Jonathan Krause, *Early Trench Tactics in the French Army: The Second Battle of Artois, May-June 1915*, p. 1.

division's progress. The soundest competence could not guarantee success in the face of both the friction of war and the independent will of a tenacious enemy. The division's losses of somewhere around 54,000 soldiers throughout the war testifies to this. As Stuart Mitchell observes: 'There can be no one set of prescribed bullet points for the BEF's learning process. It was a complex interplay between effective structure, battle-wise lower ranks, and good leadership that allowed the whole system to flourish.'[15] 6th Division is a mirror for the whole BEF – it had its defeats and victories. All of the components of the 'complete orchestra of war' learnt the trade of the new warfare, and in the end were victorious as part of a greater whole.

15 S.T.B. Mitchell, 'An Inter-Disciplinary Study of Learning in the 32nd Division on the Western Front, 1916-1918', p. 275.

Appendix I

Order of Battle
6th Division: 4 August 1914 -11 November 1918

Headquarters

General Officer Commanding

4 August 1914	Major-General J.L Keir (promoted)
27 May 1915	Major-General W.N. Congreve (promoted)
14 November 1915	Major-General C. Ross (replaced)
21 August 1917	Major-General T.O. Marden (to Armistice)

GSO1

4 August 1914	Colonel W.T. Furse (promoted)
29 December 1914	Lieutenant-Colonel J.S.M. Shea (promoted)
7 July 1915	Lieutenant-Colonel G.F. Boyd (promoted)
22 June 1916	Lieutenant-Colonel L.F. Renny (replaced)
24 March 1917	Lieutenant-Colonel T.T. Grove (to Armistice)

GSO2

4 August 1914	Lieutenant-Colonel J.T. Burnett-Stuart (promoted)
18 February 1915	Major W.E. Ironside (promoted)
29 February 1916	Major L.P. Evans (promoted)
6 March 1917	Major M. Beevor (promoted)
17 November 1917	Major W. Harris St John (replaced)
29 April 1918	Major S.S. Hill-Dillon (promoted)
16 June 1918	Major R.W. Barnett (killed in action)
24 August 1918	Major L.M. Taylor (to Armistice)

GSO3

4 August 1914	Captain A.T. Paley (promoted)
29 October 1914	Major W.E. Ironside (promoted)
18 February 1915	Captain T.T. Grove (promoted)
10 August 1915	Major A.B. Lawson (promoted)
6 December 1915	Captain H.D. Denison-Pender (promoted)
25 June 1916	Captain M.K. Wardle (promoted)

26 July 1917	Captain M. C. Bell (promoted)
2 November 1917	Major A.S. Wright (transferred)
22 May 1918	Captain J. Horlington (to Armistice)

Assistant Adjutant & Quartermaster General

4 August 1914	Colonel W. Campbell
6 October 1914	Major F.C. Dundas
14 October 1914	Colonel R. Wanless O'Gowan
15 February 1915	Lieutenant-Colonel R.S. May
6 February 1916	Lieutenant-Colonel M.R. Walsh
30 August 1917	Lieutenant-Colonel M.B. Savage
16 December 1917	Major C. Macfie
2 January 1918	Lieutenant-Colonel P. Hudson (to Armistice)

Deputy Assistant Adjutant General

4 August 1914	Major F.C. Dundas
1 November 1914	Captain G. Ogston
5 January 1916	Captain J.L. Watson
8 March 1916	Captain S.G.L. Bradley
23 March 1917	Major C. Macfie (to Armistice)

Deputy Assistant Quartermaster General

4 August 1914	Major A. Delavoye
15 January 1915	Major H.L. Nevill
27 February 1915	Major B. Atkinson
29 May 1915	Captain J.C. Dundas
14 October 1915	Major H. Street
17 January 1917	Captain R.B. Tower
22 May 1918	Colonel A.J. Hay (to Armistice)

Infantry

16 Infantry Brigade

General Officer Commanding

4 August 1914	Brigadier-General E.C. Ingouville-Williams (promoted)
17 June 1915	Brigadier-General C.L. Nicholson (promoted)
26 July 1916	Brigadier General W.L. Osborn (replaced)
26 October 1917	Brigadier-General H.A. Walker (wounded)
16 October 1918	Brigadier-General P.W. Brown (temporary)
19 October 1918	Brigadier-General W.G. Braithwaite (to Armistice)

Brigade Major

4 August 1914	Captain R.H. Mangles
12 February 1915	Captain H.R. Headlam
1 September 1915	Captain C.B. Costin
21 November 1915	Captain B.C.B. Tower
25 June 1916	Captain H.D. Denison-Pender
26 September 1916	Captain R.B. Leslie
14 October 1917	Captain N. F. Wellington
16 February 1918	Lieutenant S.H.D. Chamier
6 March 1918	Captain N. F. Wellington
19 April 1918	Captain J. Horlington
20 May 1918	Captain N.F. Wellington
5 June 1918	Captain E. Dryden (to Armistice)

1st Buffs

4 August 1914	Lieutenant-Colonel H.C. de la M. Hill (replaced)
15 November 1914	Lieutenant-Colonel R. McDouall (replaced)
21 December 1914	Lieutenant-Colonel J. Hasler (promoted)
26 February 1915	Lieutenant-Colonel R. McDouall (replaced)
31 July 1915	Lieutenant-Colonel E.H. Finch-Hatton (invalided)
5 October 1915	Captain E.G.F.L. Gould (replaced)
15 October 1915	Lieutenant-Colonel E.H. Finch-Hatton (invalided)
21 November 1915	Captain C. F. Cattley (replaced)
? December 1916	Lieutenant-Colonel E.G.F.L. Gould (replaced)
27 May 1916	Major H.W. Green (transferred to another active battalion)
2 June 1916	Lieutenant-Colonel E.H. Finch-Hatton (promoted)
13 July 1916	Lieutenant-Colonel H.W. Green (promoted)
26 November 1917	Major B. L. Strauss (killed in action)
1 December 1917	Major F.K. Hardy (replaced)
12 December 1917	Lieutenant-Colonel R.E. Power (to Armistice)

1st Leicestershire (to November 1915)

4 August 1914	Lieutenant-Colonel H.L. Croker (promoted)
21 March 1915	Major A.H. Buchanan-Dunlop (replaced)
1 June 1915	Lieutenant-Colonel H.S. Smith (killed in action/died of wounds)
25 October 1915	Lieutenant-Colonel A.H. Buchanan-Dunlop

(to 71 Brigade, 6th Division)

1st King's Shropshire Light Infantry

4 August 1914	Lieutenant-Colonel C.P. Higginson (wounded)
23 October 1914	Major E.B. Luard (replaced)

? November 1914	Major W.J. Rowan-Robinson (replaced)
1 December 1914	Lieutenant-Colonel J.A. Strick (transferred to staff)
5 August 1915	Lieutenant-Colonel E.B. Luard (invalided)
28 December 1915	Lieutenant-Colonel B.E. Murray (replaced)
20 March 1916	Lieutenant-Colonel E.B. Luard (died of wounds)
23 April 1916	Lieutenant-Colonel B.E. Murray (replaced)
17 October 1916	Lieutenant-Colonel C.F.B. Winterscale (replaced)
15 February 1918	Lieutenant-Colonel H.M. Smith (prisoner of war)
24 March 1918	Major H. de R. Morgan (replaced)
3 April 1918	Lieutenant-Colonel G. Meynell (invalided)
27 May 1918	Major E.A. Freeman (replaced)
9 June 1918	Lieutenant-Colonel D.H. Leslie (wounded)
17 July 1918	Major E.A. Freeman (invalided)
23 July 1918	Captain H.J. Colbourn (replaced)
8 August 1918	Lieutenant-Colonel C.H. Cautley (replaced)
29 August 1918	Lieutenant-Colonel G. Meynell (promoted)
9 October 1918	Lieutenant-Colonel L.H. Morris (to Armistice)

2nd York & Lancaster

4 August 1914	Lieutenant-Colonel E.C. Cobbold (invalided)
9 December 1914	Lieutenant-Colonel W.F. Clemson (promoted)
18 September 1915	Major G.McD. Pratt (replaced)
17 October 1915	Lieutenant-Colonel M.F. Halford (transferred to staff)
1 May 1916	Major H.P. Philby (killed in action)
18 May 1916	Captain R.P. Wood (replaced)
5 June 1916	Lieutenant-Colonel H.R. Headlam (promoted)
11 June 1916	Major E.L. Thomson (replaced)
30 June 1916	Lieutenant-Colonel A. St J. Blunt (wounded)
25 September 1916	Lieutenant-Colonel R.P. Wood (killed in action)
10 October 1916	Lieutenant-Colonel F. Lewis (replaced)
13 February 1917	Lieutenant-Colonel A. St J. Blunt (replaced)
22 April 1918	Lieutenant-Colonel J.R. Robertson (? wounded)
18 October 1918	Captain E.E. Battle (replaced)
25 October 1918	Major P.H.C. Collins (to Armistice)

5th Loyal North Lancashire (15 February 1915 to 11 June 1915)

15 February 1915	Lieutenant-Colonel G. Hesketh

8th Bedfordshire (17 November 1915 to February 1918)

27 September 1915	Lieutenant-Colonel J.S. Liddell (replaced)
14 January 1916	Lieutenant-Colonel H.C. Jackson (wounded)
18 April 1916	Lieutenant-Colonel W.R.H. Dann (wounded)
19 May 1916	Major D.McL. Hawkins (replaced)

2 June 1916	Lieutenant-Colonel Lord H.F. Montagu-Douglas-Scott (replaced)
4 April 1917	Lieutenant-Colonel A.O.V. Russell (Lord Ampthill) (replaced)
19 May 1917	Lieutenant-Colonel H.R. McCullagh (replaced)
15 June 1917	Lieutenant-Colonel R. le Huquet (replaced)
20 July 1917	Lieutenant-Colonel J.R. Robertson (transferred to another active battalion)
6 August 1917	Lieutenant-Colonel R. le Huquet (to disbandment)

16th Machine Gun Company (February 1916 to 1 March 1918)
16th Trench Mortar Battery (from 3 April 1916)

17 Infantry Brigade

(to 24th Division 14 October 1915)

General Officer Commanding

4 August 1914	Brigadier-General W.R.B. Doran (replaced)
11 February 1915	Brigadier-General G.M. Harper (promoted)
24 September 1915	Brigadier-General J.W.V. Carroll

Brigade Major

4 August 1914	Major A.D. Green
28 September 1914	Captain W.H.E. Segrave
1 June 1915	Captain H.V. Scott
4 September 1915	Captain A.N. Pope

1st Royal Fusiliers

4 August 1914	Lieutenant-Colonel R. Fowler-Butler (wounded)
31 July 1915	Lieutenant-Colonel B.G. Price

1st North Staffordshire

4 August 1914	Lieutenant-Colonel V.W. de Falbe

2nd Leinster

4 August 1914	Lieutenant-Colonel W.T.M. Reeve (wounded)
19 November 1914	Lieutenant-Colonel G.M. Bullen-Smith (replaced)
3 June 1915	Lieutenant-Colonel W.T.M. Reeve (invalided)
21 July 1915	Lieutenant-Colonel G.M. Bullen-Smith (invalided)
13 September 1915	Major R.A.H. Orpen-Palmer (replaced)
4 October 1915	Lieutenant-Colonel G.M. Bullen-Smith

3rd Rifle Brigade

4 August 1914	Lieutenant-Colonel R. Alexander (wounded)
13 October 1914	Lieutenant-Colonel C.H.C. Henniker
22 November 1914	Lieutenant-Colonel R. Alexander (died of wounds)
30 December 1914	Lieutenant-Colonel C.H.C. Henniker (invalided)
7 June 1915	Major R. Pigot

1/2nd London (from 21 February 1915)

30 September 1914	Lieutenant-Colonel J. Attenborough

18 Infantry Brigade

General Officer Commanding

4 August 1914	Brigadier-General W.N. Congreve (promoted)
30 May 1915	Brigadier-General H.S. Ainslie (replaced)
5 August 1915	Lieutenant-Colonel F.W. Towsey (acting)
15 August 1915	Brigadier-General R.J. Bridgford (incapacitated)
19 April 1916	Lieutenant-Colonel C.J. Hobkirk (acting)
29 April 1916	Brigadier-General W.K. McClintock (replaced)
13 June 1916	Brigadier-General H.S. Tew (replaced)
19 August 1916	Brigadier-General R.J. Bridgford (replaced)
15 September 1917	Brigadier-General G.S.G. Craufurd (to Armistice)

Brigade Major

4 August 1914	Captain R.F.H. Wallace
29 October 1914	Major A.T. Paley
17 July 1915	Major F.G. Maughan
26 October 1915	Captain T.G.B. Morgan-Grenville-Gavin
13 February 1917	Captain H.E. Pickering
1 April 1918	Captain H.C.E. Hull (to Armistice)

1st West Yorkshire

4 August 1914	Lieutenant-Colonel F.W. Towsey (wounded)
21 September 1914	Major G.G. Lang (wounded)
14 October 1914	Lieutenant-Colonel F.W. Towsey (invalided)
19 October 1914	Major G.G. Lang (replaced)
22 October 1914	Lieutenant-Colonel T.P. Barrington (replaced)
8 December 1914	Lieutenant-Colonel F.W. Towsey (promoted)
15 September 1915	Lieutenant-Colonel G.G. Lang (invalided)
11 November 1915	Lieutenant-Colonel G.H. Soames (replaced)
29 January 1916	Lieutenant-Colonel G.G. Lang (invalided)
18 September 1916	Lieutenant-Colonel H.M. Dillon (replaced)
31 October 1916	Lieutenant-Colonel A.M. Boyall (wounded & POW)

28 March 1918	Lieutenant-Colonel D.L. Weir (transferred to another active battalion)
21 May 1918	Lieutenant-Colonel G.B. Drew (invalided)
22 July 1918	Major E.W. Cannings (replaced)
29 July 1918	Lieutenant-Colonel D.L. Weir (to Armistice)

1st East Yorkshire (to November 1915)

4 August 1914	Lieutenant-Colonel R.E. Benson (killed in action/died of wounds)
20 September 1914	Lieutenant-Colonel W.H. Young (replaced)
11 November 1914	Lieutenant-Colonel W.H. Armstrong (wounded)
20 November 1914	Lieutenant-Colonel J.L.J. Clarke (promoted)

2nd Sherwood Foresters (to October 1915)

4 August 1914	Lieutenant-Colonel C.R. Crofton-Atkins (invalided)
7 October 1914	Lieutenant-Colonel P. Leveson-Gower (wounded)
5 August 1915	Lieutenant-Colonel C.J.W. Hobbs

(to 71 Brigade, 6th Division)

2nd Durham Light Infantry

4 August 1914	Lieutenant-Colonel B.W.L. McMahon (replaced)
4 January 1915	Lieutenant-Colonel J.A. Crosthwaite (replaced)
11 June 1915	Lieutenant-Colonel M.D. Goring-Jones (promoted)
16 January 1916	Lieutenant-Colonel A.E. Irvine (replaced)
28 August 1916	Lieutenant-Colonel H.R. Cumming (promoted)
14 September 1916	Lieutenant-Colonel A.E. Irvine (invalided)
25 December 1916	Major E.V. Manger (replaced)
10 February 1917	Lieutenant-Colonel A.E. Irvine (promoted)
15 August 1917	Lieutenant-Colonel H.R. McCullagh (replaced)
5 February 1918	Lieutenant-Colonel D.L. Brereton (replaced)
12 July 1918	Lieutenant-Colonel R.V. Turner (to Armistice)

1/16th London (12 November 1914 to 9 February 1916)

4 August 1914	Lieutenant-Colonel R. Shoolbred

11th Essex (from October 1915)

26 September 1915	Lieutenant-Colonel C.J. Hobkirk (promoted)
3 June 1916	Captain H.B. Harris (replaced)
8 June 1916	Lieutenant-Colonel H.W. Green (transferred to another active battalion)
29 June 1916	Lieutenant-Colonel F.G. Spring (temporary absence)
3 November 1916	Lieutenant-Colonel E.V. Manger (replaced)

10 December 1916	Lieutenant-Colonel F.G. Spring (promoted)
29 August 1917	Major J.P. Wylie (invalided)
31 August 1917	Major G.N. Stockdale (replaced)
16 September 1917	Lieutenant-Colonel C.H. Dumbell (temporary absence)
22 September 1918	Major A.G. Saunders (to Armistice)

14th Durham Light Infantry (from 28 November 1915 to February 1918)

14 October 1915	Lieutenant-Colonel G.F. Menzies (replaced)
10 October 1916	Lieutenant-Colonel J.B. Rosher (to disbandment)

18th Machine Gun Company (from January 1916)
18th Trench Mortar Battery (from 16 April 1916)

19 Infantry Brigade

(attached 12 October 1914 to 31 May 1915)

General Officer Commanding

5 September 1914	Brigadier-General Hon. F. Gordon

Brigade Major

5 September 1914	Captain C.P. Heywood
23 May 1915	Captain H.E.R.R. Braine

2nd Royal Welsh Fusiliers

4 August 1914	Lieutenant-Colonel H. Delme-Radcliffe (invalided)
27 October 1914	Lieutenant-Colonel O. de L. Williams

1st Scottish Rifles

4 August 1914	Lieutenant-Colonel P.R. Robertson

1st Middlesex

4 August 1914	Lieutenant-Colonel B.E. Ward (died of wounds)
21 October 1914	Lieutenant-Colonel F.G.M. Rowley (wounded)
30 October 1914	Captain H.P. Osborne (replaced)
29 November 1914	Lieutenant-Colonel W.C.C. Ash (replaced)
7 February 1915	Lieutenant-Colonel F.G.M. Rowley

2nd Argyll & Sutherland Highlanders

4 August 1914	Lieutenant-Colonel H.P. Moulton-Barrett (replaced)
3 November 1914	Captain H.G. Hyslop (replaced)
6 November 1914	Lieutenant-Colonel H.B. Kirk (replaced)
16 January 1915	Lieutenant-Colonel R.C. Gore

5th Scottish Rifles (from 19 November 1914)

4 August 1914	Lieutenant-Colonel R.J. Douglas

71 Infantry Brigade

(from 24th Division 11 October 1915)

General Officer Commanding

31 August 1915	Brigadier-General M.T. Shewen (replaced)
27 May 1916	Brigadier-General FitzJ. M. Edwards (invalided)
6 October 1916	Brigadier-General E. Feetham (promoted)
19 August 1917	Brigadier-General P.W. Brown (temporary absence)
16 October 1918	Lieutenant-Colonel F. Latham (acting)
19 October 1918	Brigadier-General P.W. Brown (to Armistice)

Brigade Major

22 May 1915	Major H.C.D. Jarrett
7 December 1915	Captain B. T. Burbury
20 June 1917	Captain A. Weyman
4 July 1918	Captain C. Allerton
12 July 1918	Captain J.F. Tamblyn
4 November 1918	Captain B.E. Davies (to Armistice)

1st Leicestershire

25 October 1915	Lieutenant-Colonel A.H. Buchanan-Dunlop (invalided)
2 February 1916	Lieutenant-Colonel R.H. Gillespie (invalided)
21 September 1916	Lieutenant-Colonel R.S. Dyer-Bennet (transferred to another active battalion)
13 December 1916	Lieutenant-Colonel R.H. Gillespie (invalided)
27 March 1917	Lieutenant-Colonel H.B. Brown (transferred to another active battalion)
3 May 1917	Lieutenant-Colonel R.H. Gillespie (replaced)
16 January 1918	Lieutenant-Colonel H.B. Brown (invalided)
17 January 1918	Lieutenant-Colonel D.L. Weir (replaced)
6 February 1918	Lieutenant-Colonel F. Latham (wounded)
29 April 1918	Major G.N. Wykes (invalided)
11 May 1918	Captain S.T. Hartshorne (replaced)
22 May 1918	Lieutenant-Colonel D.L. Weir (transferred to another active battalion)
26 July 1918	Lieutenant-Colonel F. Latham (transferred to another active battalion)
16 October 1918	Major J.G. Herring-Cooper (replaced)
26 October 1918	Lieutenant-Colonel J.H. Martin (to Armistice)

2nd Sherwood Foresters

5 August 1915	Lieutenant-Colonel C.J.W. Hobbs (wounded)
7 June 1916	Major E.R. Street (replaced)
3 August 1916	Lieutenant-Colonel C.J.W. Hobbs (died of wounds)
19 October 1916	Lieutenant-Colonel F.E. Bradshaw (wounded)
19 October 1917	Lieutenant-Colonel H. Tylden-Wright (replaced)
23 November 1917	Lieutenant-Colonel H.M. Milward (temporary absence)
23 January 1918	Major H. Tylden-Wright (replaced)
26 March 1918	Lieutenant-Colonel H.M. Milward (replaced)
20 September 1918	Lieutenant-Colonel C.E. Hudson (to Armistice)

9th Norfolk

21 September 1915	Lieutenant-Colonel E.H.D. Stracey (temporary absence)
13 August 1916	Lieutenant-Colonel F.E. Bradshaw (wounded)
16 September 1916	Major F. Lewis (replaced)
1 October 1916	Lieutenant-Colonel B.H.L. Prior (wounded)
10 December 1816	Major de la Poer (invalided)
15 December 1916	Lieutenant-Colonel R.S. Dyer-Bennet (invalided)
14 January 1917	Major T. Frederick
27 January 1917	Lieutenant-Colonel J.B.O. Trimble (transferred to another active battalion)
27 February 1917	Lieutenant-Colonel R.S. Dyer-Bennet (replaced)
10 March 1917	Lieutenant-Colonel E.H.D. Stracey (replaced)
24 March 1917	Lieutenant-Colonel B.H.L. Prior (gassed)
22 January 1917	Lieutenant-Colonel W.J. Spurrell (replaced)
10 March 1918	Lieutenant-Colonel B.H.L. Prior (wounded)
22 March 1918	Lieutenant-Colonel F.R. Day (replaced)
1 July 1918	Lieutenant-Colonel B.H.L. Prior (invalided)
23 August 1918	Lieutenant-Colonel F.R. Day (to Armistice)

9th Suffolk (to February 1918)

21 September 1915	Lieutenant-Colonel R.V.G. Brettell (wounded)
26 September 1915	Major F. G. Davies (replaced)
3 November 1915	Lieutenant-Colonel W.H.A. de la Pryme (wounded)
14 May 1916	Lieutenant-Colonel A.P. Mack (killed in action)
15 September 1916	Major M.F. Heigham (replaced)
28 September 1916	Lieutenant-Colonel F. Latham (temporary absence)
6 February 1917	Major M.F. Heigham (replaced)
24 February 1917	Major J.P. Wylie (replaced)
27 February 1917	Lieutenant-Colonel J.B.O. Trimble (replaced)
1 April 1917	Lieutenant-Colonel F. Latham (to disbandment)

8th Bedfordshire
27 September 1915 Lieutenant-Colonel J.S. Liddell

(to 16 Brigade, 6th Division 17 November 1915)
71st Machine Gun Company (from 14 March 1916)
71st Trench Mortar Battery (from April 1916)

Divisional Artillery

Brigadier-General Royal Artillery
4 August 1914 Brigadier-General W.L.H. Paget (promoted)
27 May 1915 Brigadier-General G. Humphreys (promoted)
21 June 1916 Brigadier-General E.S. Cleeve (sacked)
25 October 1916 Brigadier-General E.F. Delaforce (to Armistice)

2nd Brigade RFA
4 August 1914 Colonel W.A.M. Thompson
8 July 1915 Lieutenant-Colonel L.C.L. Oldfield
May 1916 Lieutenant-Colonel M.J. MacCarthy
21 June 1917 Lieutenant-Colonel W.H.F. Weber (to Armistice)

21, 42, & 53 batteries

24th Brigade RFA
4 August 1914 Lieutenant-Colonel C.E. Lawrie
27 May 1915 Lieutenant-Colonel W. Evans
1 March 1916 Lieutenant-Colonel J.A.C. Forsyth (to Armistice)

110, 111, & 112 batteries

38th Brigade RFA (to 14 January 1917)
4 August 1914 Lieutenant-Colonel R.F. Fox
30 January 1915 Lieutenant-Colonel L.M. Phillpotts
2 November 1915 Lieutenant-Colonel E.F. Calthrop
23 December 1915 Lieutenant-Colonel W.E. Clark
26 September 1916 Lieutenant-Colonel A. Mellor

24, 34 (to 15 February 1916), & 72 batteries

12th Howitzer Brigade (to 12 May 1916)
4 August 1914 Lieutenant-Colonel G. Humphreys
30 June 1915 Lieutenant-Colonel H.M. Davson

43, 86 & 87 batteries

24 Heavy Battery (to 17 April 1915)

4 August 1914	Major H.E.J. Brake
February 1915	Major E. Miles

Trench Mortar Batteries

Medium	X.6, Y.6, Z.6 (from 1 April 1916 to March 1918)
Heavy	W.6 (to 6 March 1918)

Anti-aircraft

No. 2 Pom-Pom Section (4 October to 16 December 1914)

6th Divisional Ammunition Column

4 August 1914	Lieutenant-Colonel G.A. Cardew
20 September 1914	Major G.A.S. Cape
September 1914	Lieutenant-Colonel E.R.H.J. Cloete
25 July 1915	Lieutenant-Colonel H.E.W. de Robeck
21 November 1916	Lieutenant-Colonel B. Allan (to Armistice)

Machine Gun Corps

6th Battalion MGC (from 1 March 1918)

1 March 1918	Lieutenant-Colonel J.B. Rosher (to Armistice)

192nd Machine Gun Company (from 15 December 1916)
16th Machine Gun Company
18th Machine Gun Company
71st Machine Gun Company

Army Ordnance Corps

Deputy Assistant Director Ordnance Services

October 1914	Major H.M. Howard
27 January 1915	Major F.H.P. O'Connor
19 November 1915	Major S.T. Hayley
27 December 1915	Major S.B. Winch
29 April 1917	Major R.G.P. Hare (to Armistice)

Royal Engineers

Commander Royal Engineers

4 August 1914	Lieutenant-Colonel G.C. Kemp (promoted)
15 August 1915	Lieutenant-Colonel A.G. Stevenson (promoted)
20 December 1915	Colonel T.A.H. Bigge (invalided)
6 January 1916	Captain R.H. Mackenzie (acting)
28 January 1916	Lieutenant-Colonel H.R.S. Christie
10 November 1916	Major A.C. Howard (acting)
29 November 1916	Major R.H. Mackenzie (acting)
2 January 1917	Lieutenant-Colonel G.F.B. Goldney
23 September 1918	Lieutenant-Colonel H.A.L. Hall (to Armistice)

Field Companies

12th

38th (to 7 April 1915)
1st London (509th) (from 23 December 1914)
2/2nd (459th) West Riding (from 13 October 1915)
6th Divisional Signal Company

Pioneers

11th Leicestershire (from 1 April 1916)

21 October 1915	Lieutenant-Colonel C. Turner (replaced)
26 October 1918	Lieutenant-Colonel R.H. Radford

Army Service Corps

6th Divisional Train

4 August 1914	Lieutenant-Colonel H. Davies
7 April 1918	Lieutenant-Colonel F.C.S. Norrington (to Armistice)

Royal Army Medical Corps

Assistant Director Medical Services

4 August 1914	Colonel H.O. Trevor
March 1915	Colonel B.H. Scott
March 1917	Colonel H.W. Grattan
October 1918	Colonel H.C.R. Hime (to Armistice)

16th Field Ambulance
Lieutenant-Colonel A.C. Fox

17th Field Ambulance
Lieutenant-Colonel J.P. Silver

18th Field Ambulance
Lieutenant-Colonel A.A. Watson

Army Veterinary Corps

Assistant Director of Veterinary Services

6 September 1914	Major H.M. Lenox-Conyngham
29 August 1915	Major R. Tindle
3 February 1918	Major R.F. Bett (to Armistice)

6th Mobile Veterinary Section

Labour Corps

No. 11 Divisional Employment Company (from 20 May 1917; into 209th Employment Company June 1917)

Mounted troops

C Squadron 19th Hussars (to 14 April 1915)
4 August 1914 Major H.O'S.F. Tanner

B Squadron 1st Northamptonshire Yeomanry (from 14 April 1915 to May 1916)
4 August 1914 Major C.B. Lowther

6th Cyclist Company (to 26 May 1916)
4 August 1914 Captain S.H. Dix

Assistant Provost Marshall

4 August 1914	Captain H.S. Rogers
3 March 1915	Major J.S.R. Tufton
5 August 1915	Captain O.H. North
10 October 1916	Captain S.H. Dix
16 October 1916	Captain A.J.D. Simey
7 September 1918	Captain W.A. Bignell

Senior Chaplains

Church of England	
July 1915	Rev. T.P. Moreton
October 1915	Rev. N. Talbot
May 1916	Rev. M. Ponsonby
November 1916	Rev. J.D. McCready
1 January 1917	Rev. L.G. Reed
8 July 1918	Rev. E.C. Hoskyns

Roman Catholic	
November 1916	Father J. FitzGibbon (killed)
September 1918	Father W. Keary

Appendix II

Infantry Casualties*

16 Brigade

		Officers			ORs		
		K	W	M	K	W	M
1914	Sept	2	5		12	66	5
	Oct	12	31		164	652	245
	Nov	2			25	135	1
	Dec		2		17	54	
1915	Jan				6	15	
	Feb		6		27	108	
	March	2	5		20	133	
	April		6		15	96	
	May	1	8		22	90	
	June	1	11		66	245	
	July	2	7		27	134	1
	Aug	12	25	2	142	669	83
	Sept	2	5		21	162	
	Oct	2	5		25	116	
	Nov		2		16	43	
	Dec	1	10		58	314	14
1916	Jan	1	1		12	55	
	Feb	1	3		14	74	1

	March		3		20	72	
	April	7	14	2	93	322	113
	May	3	10		47	189	1
	June				15	96	
	July	1	5		12	65	
	Aug	3	1		26	155	
	Sept	17	31		256	1038	152
	Oct	8	10		113	320	45
	Nov		1		2	5	2
	Dec		1		16	61	1
1917	Jan	2	1	1	8	17	1
	Feb		2		9	37	
	March	3	5	1	55	225	15
	April	9	27		160	747	24
	May	1	4		34	150	
	June	1	18	1	67	237	46
	July	4	7	1	43	140	5
	Aug				2	37	
	Sept	3	6		22	243	5
	Oct		3		28	109	2
	Nov	3	10		50	213	12
	Dec	5	17	1	66	242	46
1918	Jan		1			2	
	Feb				3	10	
	March	5	18	30	75	184	871
	April	3	6		20	112	2
	May	1	4		27	256	
	June		2		4	33	
	July	4	4		17	137	1
	Aug	2	2		25	125	11
	Sept	7	33	1	122	613	115
	Oct	11	25		96	669	
	Nov						
TOTAL		144	403	40	2222	10022	1820

17 Brigade

		Officers			ORs		
		K	W	M	K	W	M
1914	Sept	1	6	2	32	117	22
	Oct	10	21	3	174	683	301
	Nov		4		31	187	1
	Dec	2	4		31	158	6
1915	Jan	2	2		26	81	
	Feb		4		27	123	
	March	7	9		84	675	2
	April	1	8		45	156	
	May	1	5		28	152	
	June		9		51	303	
	July	2	8		39	244	
	Aug	6	14		73	414	1
	Sept		6		32	210	
	Oct	1			10	43	
TOTAL		33	100	5	683	3546	333

18 Brigade

		Officers			ORs		
		K	W	M	K	W	M
1914	Sept	19	21	10	155	447	436
	Oct	5	28	17	112	728	811
	Nov		4		33	122	
	Dec	2	3		21	86	4
1915	Jan	1	2		26	65	
	Feb	1			16	55	
	March	1	2		37	130	
	April	1	1	24	83		
	May	3			27	146	

	June	4	3	51	351		
	July	2	5	34	22		
	Aug	17	30		236	914	170
	Sept	1	8		50	197	
	Oct	2	7		54	239	1
	Nov	3	3		17	70	
	Dec	2	15		89	301	3
1916	Jan		6	1	31	126	
	Feb		6		39	265	1
	March		1		16	131	
	April	3	7	1	41	161	15
	May	1	5		36	185	
	June		6		27	91	
	July	2	2		2	16	
	Aug	1	4		36	154	1
	Sept	16	40	1	189	898	84
	Oct	5	26	6	110	469	172
	Nov					2	
	Dec			2	19	54	
1917	Jan	3	4		19	109	
	Feb		4		12	47	1
	March	1	8		33	181	12
	April	9	33	2	115	611	58
	May	1	11		22	201	8
	June	8	9		66	328	17
	July		5		24	142	2
	Aug	1	1		20	75	
	Sept	4	4		27	128	
	Oct		3		12	116	4
	Nov	2	4		12	123	21
	Dec	8	12	2	52	225	112
1918	Jan				2	6	
	Feb		1	1	6	28	

	March	7	16	46	57	187	1352
	April	3	16		40	340	
	May	1	19		31	283	14
	June		5		11	53	2
	July	3	10		42	293	25
	Aug	1	4		24	119	9
	Sept	9	47	2	144	858	159
	Oct	8	22	2	109	409	66
	Nov						
TOTAL		161	473	202	2755	10914	3560

19 Brigade

		Officers			ORs		
		K	W	M	K	W	M
1914	Sept						
	Oct	7	11	4	113	355	269
	Nov	2	12		44	308	
	Dec	1	3		15	56	
1915	Jan	1	1		14	60	1
	Feb	1	2		16	72	1
	March	2	3		23	85	
	April		3		15	67	
	May				17	35	
TOTAL		14	35	4	257	1038	271

71 Brigade

		Officers			ORs		
		K	W	M	K	W	M
1915	Oct	1	1		32	92	3
	Nov	3	3		11	33	
	Dec	2	9		28	218	5

1916	Jan	1			7	47	
	Feb	1	2		9	45	
	March				15	119	
	April	1	2		3	27	
	May	2	8		20	130	1
	June	1	4		3	39	2
	July		1		8	16	
	Aug	1	3	1	14	61	
	Sept	23	50	3	418	1328	163
	Oct	6	8	2	187	441	13
	Nov				3	6	
	Dec		2		6	26	1
1917	Jan		2		10	39	
	Feb	2	5		34	94	
	March	1	3		33	95	
	April		8	1	71	306	4
	May	1	9		52	159	
	June		3		22	129	
	July	1	7		17	85	
	Aug						
	Sept		3		29	198	
	Oct		6		26	109	
	Nov	5	13		55	270	5
	Dec		11		10	103	2
1918	Jan		2		7	11	1
	Feb				6	53	3
	March	13	15	26	79	273	1003
	April	6	19	2	66	485	293
	May		11		37	198	1
	June	1	3		4	62	
	July	1	7		33	129	1
	Aug		3		7	71	
	Sept	9	31	2	121	765	70

	Oct Nov	8	36 1		45	794 5	94
TOTAL		90	291	37	1528	7061	1665

Total divisional infantry casualties

Officers			ORs			TOTAL
K	W	M	K	W	M	
442	1302	288	7445	32581	7649	49707

* Compiled from brigade war diaries. Wounded totals include gas casualties.

Appendix III

Divisional Victoria Cross Awards

No. 7504 Private Henry May 1st Battalion The Cameronians (Scottish Rifles), 19 Infantry Brigade, at that time attached to 6th Division.

> For most conspicuous bravery near La Boutillerie, on 22nd October 1914, in voluntarily endeavouring to rescue, under very heavy fire, a wounded man, who was killed before he could save him, and subsequently, on the same day, in carrying a wounded officer a distance of 300 yards into safety whilst exposed to very severe fire.

London Gazette, 21 April 1915
Henry May was born 29 July 1885 in Bridgeton, Glasgow, to William and Maggie May. He attended Dalmarnock Public School in Bridgeton and after working as an apprentice mechanic, enlisted on 29 August 1902, serving in South Africa. Returning to work as a power loom mechanic, he was recalled from the Reserve on 5 August 1914. He had been wounded in the face by shrapnel at Ypres in November 1914. May was initially discharged from the Army on 28 August 1915, purportedly working as ammunitions factory inspector, but rejoined in 1918 and was commissioned lieutenant in the Army Service Corps, serving in North Russia in 1919. Following the war, May returned to work in the textiles industry. He died on 26 July 1941.

No. 9730 Private John Joseph Caffey, 2nd Battalion York & Lancaster Regiment.

> For most conspicuous bravery on 16th November 1915, near La Brique. A man of the West Yorkshire Regiment had been badly wounded, and was lying in the open unable to move, in full view of, and about 300 to 400 yards from, the enemy's trenches. Corporal Stirk, Royal Army Medical Corps, and Private Caffrey, at once started out to rescue him, but at the first attempt they were driven back by shrapnel fire. Soon afterwards they started again, under close sniping and machine-gun fire, and succeeded in reaching and bandaging the wounded man, but just as Corporal Stirk had lifted him on Private Caffrey's back he himself was shot in the head. Private Caffrey put down the wounded man, bandaged Corporal Stirk, and helped him back into safety. He then returned and brought in the man of the West Yorkshire Regiment. He had made three

> journeys across the open under close and accurate fire and had risked his own life to save others with the utmost coolness and bravery.

London Gazette, 22 January 1915
John Joseph Caffrey was born on 23 October 1891, leaving Ireland at an early age and settling in Nottingham where his father John, a bricklayer, originated from. He enlisted in 1910, having already served in the 7th Sherwood Foresters. He later was promoted sergeant and served in the VC Guard at the interment of the Unknown Warrior. After various jobs he was a member of the Home Guard during World War II, after which he worked as a commissionaire at Butlin's Holiday camp. He died in Derby on 22 February 1953.

No. 3/10133 Sergeant Arthur Frederic Saunders, 9th Battalion Suffolk Regiment.

> For most conspicuous bravery. When his officer had been wounded in the attack, he took charge of two machine-guns and a few men, and, although severely wounded in the thigh, closely followed the last four charges of another battalion, and rendered every possible support. Later, when the remains of the battalion which he had been supporting had been forced to retire, he stuck to his guns, continued to give clear orders, and by continuous firing did his best to cover the retirement.

London Gazette, 30 March 1916.
Born on 22 April 1878, Arthur Frederic Saunders joined the Royal Navy as a Boy, 2nd Class, at just under age 16. On 22 April 1896 he signed-up for continuous service with the Royal Navy for 12 years, which he completed in 1908, achieving the rank of Petty Officer (2nd Class). After leaving the Royal Navy he worked for the agricultural equipment company Ransomes, Sims & Jeffries. His award was not won serving with 6th Division, rather during the Battle of Loos. After medical attention and a period of convalescence, his leg had become 3 inches shorter therefore he wore a medical boot to aid his walking. He was discharged and returned to his pre-war employ, serving with the Home Guard during World War II. He died on 30 July 1947.

Second-Lieutenant Frank Bernard Wearne, llth Battalion Essex Regiment.

> For superb courage, leadership and self-sacrifice. On 28th June 1917, 2/Lieut. Wearne was in command of two sections on the left of a raiding party, whose objective was the German front line, east of Loos. He led his men into the objective against opposition, and by his magnificent example and daring, they held on to the German trench for one hour according to orders. Throughout the hour they were repeatedly counter-attacked, from their left down the trench and from their front over the open. Grasping the fact that if the left flank went, our men would have to give way, 2/Lieut. Wearne at a moment when the attack

> was being heavily pressed, and when matters were most critical, leapt on to the parapet and, followed by his left section, ran along the top of the trench, firing and throwing bombs at the enemy. This unexpected and daring manoeuvre threw the enemy back in disorder. Whilst on the top 2/Lieut. Wearne was severely wounded but refused to leave his men. He remained in the trench directing operations, organizing the defence and encouraging all. Just before the order to withdraw was given 2/Lieut. Wearne was severely hit for the second time, and when being brought away was hit for the third time and killed. His tenacity in remaining at his post, though severely wounded, and his magnificent fighting spirit enabled his men to hold on to the left flank; had this gone, the whole operation would have failed.

London Gazette, 5 August 1917
Born on 1 March 1894 in Fulham, Bernard Wearne attended Bromsgrove School and Corpus Christi College, Oxford. His father Frank was a wine merchant and lost two sons during the war. Bernard enlisted on 3 September 1914 in 18th Royal Fusiliers and was commissioned on 16 May 1915 in the Essex Regiment. He had been wounded in the right arm in July 1916 and spent six months convalescing.

Second-Lieutenant (Acting Captain) Arthur Lascelles, 3rd Battalion attached 14th Battalion Durham Light Infantry.

> At Masnieres on 3rd December 1917, showed the greatest courage, initiative, and devotion to duty when in command of his company. His company was in a very exposed position, and after a very heavy bombardment, during which Captain Lascelles was wounded, the enemy attacked in strong force, but was driven off, largely owing to the fine example set by this officer, who refused to allow himself to be dressed, but continued to encourage his men and organize the defence. Shortly afterwards the enemy again attacked and captured the trench, taking several of his men prisoners. Captain Lascelles at once jumped on to the parapet and, followed by the remainder of his company, twelve men, rushed across under very heavy machine-gun fire and drove over sixty of the enemy back, being wounded again, thereby saving a most critical situation. He then was untiring in re-organizing the position, but shortly afterwards the enemy again attacked and captured the trench and Captain Lascelles. Later he escaped, being wounded again in doing so. The remarkable determination and gallantry of this officer inspired everyone.

London Gazette, 11 January 1919.
Arthur Lascelles was born in Streatham on 12 October 1880, the family moving to Wales, both his parents John and Mary being Welsh. He was educated at Malvern and Uppingham Schools, went to study medicine at Edinburgh but emigrated to South Africa, fighting as a trooper in the Second Boer War., and against the Germans in

South-West Africa in 1914-15. He returned to Great Britain and was commissioned in the 3rd DLI in December 1915. After his wounding at Cambrai his right arm was badly damaged, but he retuned to service with the 15th DLI and was killed on 7 November 1918 at Limont-Fontaine.

Appendix IV

'Shot at Dawn'

Lance-Corporal	Alfred Atkinson	1st West Yorkshire	Desertion	02/03/1915
Private	Thomas Hope	2nd Leinster	Desertion	02/03/1915
Private	Ernest Kirk	1st West Yorkshire	Desertion	06/03/1915
Private	Alfred Eveleigh	1st Buffs	Desertion	24/02/1915
Private	Robert Gawler	1st Buffs	Desertion	24/02/1916
Private	George Hunter	2nd Durham Light Infantry	Desertion	02/07/1916
Private	William Nelson	14th Durham Light Infantry	Desertion	11/08/1916
Private	Harry Farr	1st West Yorkshire	Cowardice	18/10/1916
Private	Arthur Hamilton	14th Durham Light Infantry	Desertion	27/03/1917
Private	George Everill	1st North Staffordshire	Desertion	14/09/1917
Private	Wilfred Clarke	2nd Durham Light Infantry	Desertion	09/02/1918
Private	Joseph Nisbet	1st Leicestershire	Desertion	23/08/1918

Private (8014) Alfred Atkinson, 1st West Yorkshire
Alfred Atkinson had enlisted in 1905 (stating at his trial that 'this is the second time that I have answered the call of our country') and was promoted (acting) lance-corporal on active service. On 1 January 1915 the roll of Atkinson's platoon of D Company was called to march to trench duty, as previously warned, and he was found to be absent. On 15 February the Military Police apprehended him in a private house in Armentières, having dinner. Atkinson stated that on 31 December he went into town 'to see some friends', remained absent, came 'to think about the seriousness of my crime', but was 'ashamed' to return. He had apparently just won a sum of money gambling and had been drinking.[1] Atkinson made a statement in his own defence in the trial: 'Gentlemen, I cannot give an explanation (or) any reason for committing this offence, only that I must have taken leave of my natural senses', asking the court to 'treat me as lenient as law and nature will allow, as I leave two innocent lifes (sic) behind, a wife and child who will also share and suffer my punishment, which is the

1 J. Putkowski & J. Sykes, *Shot at Dawn*, p.35.

most striking feeling in nature.' He stated that he felt 'the shame of it to the bottom of my heart' and would 'willingly sacrifice my life to rub out the dark cloud that hangs over my head at the present moment.' He concluded: 'After all, gentlemen, the law says a life for a life.' Atkinson's eloquence paid off in court as whilst he was sentenced to death, the court recommended 'mercy' – evidence presented at the trial stated that 'during his service he has been a good character.' His CO described him as a 'good soldier' but gave the opinion that 'he stayed away to avoid the irksome duty of serving in the trenches.' Walter Congreve stated that 'the discipline of the battalion is now good, except that there is too much drunkenness', and confirmed the sentence 'because I consider it a bad case.' Sir John Keir agreed, as did Sir William Pulteney, General Smith-Dorrien stating that: 'The discipline of this Brigade is the worst in the Army and the discipline of the 1st West Yorkshires is the worst in that Brigade.' He opined that the 'offence of desertion to avoid duty in the trenches is not appreciated, for no capital punishment has been carried out in the 6th Division', and 'an example in the Division is very necessary.'[2] Atkinson was executed on 2 March 1915 at the Armentières Asylum. It was said of two members of the firing squad:

> When they came back, tough characters though they were supposed to be, they were sick, they screamed in their sleep, they vomited immediately after eating. All they could say was: 'The sight was horrible, made more so by the fact that we had shot one of our own men.'[3]

Atkinson is buried in Chapelle-d'Armentières Old Military Cemetery.

Private (9689) Thomas Hope – 2nd Leinster

Thomas Hope had enlisted in 1912 and was a 'fine athlete.' According to his CO he 'gave a good deal of trouble in his company through small absences', was 'very unreliable', and had absented himself whilst the battalion was mobilising at Cambridge, again on the Aisne (being awarded 56 days Field Punishment No. 1) and yet again, (being awarded a further three months F. P. No. 1). On 23 December 1914 he was detailed on a ration party leaving the trenches at l'Epinette for an 800 yard journey (it was snowing), and was not seen again until 9 February 1915, when he was found in the billets of the 1st Rifle Brigade in Armentières in a greatcoat with a lance-corporal's stripe and a police badge, being drunk and giving a false name. He was in the company of another private of 2nd Leinster, also drunk. In his defence, Hope stated: 'I was very much upset owing to the death of two of my brothers of which I had just heard. I had no intention of going absent when I left the trenches. It was a sudden impulse.' He claimed to have wandered into the enemy positions, being held for three days then taken to Lille, where he escaped during an attack into French trenches,

2 Atkinson, A. TNA WO71/402.
3 Putkowski & Sykes, op. cit. p.35.

where he stayed for two days. From there on he had supposedly been trying to locate his own regiment. His CO regarded him a 'bad example to other soldiers.' General Smith-Dorrien wrote that 'the brigade discipline is 2nd worse and the batt(alion) discipline also the 2nd worse in the army. The case is a very bad one.'[4] Hope was executed on 2 March 1915. His grave was subsequently lost, and he is commemorated on the Ploegsteert Memorial.

Putkowski and Sykes observe that he was 'the first of a number of offenders who claimed that the death of a relative had contributed to the commission of their offence.' They continue that: 'Research has shown that many deserters, executed in similar circumstances, did not make this fact known to the court.'[5] They did not seek to verify Hope's claims. If his brothers shared the same surname (an established Mullingar name) then there are only two candidates in the CWGC records, neither of whom, like Thomas, are Irish born. It is of course the case that the trench conditions were terrible in December 1914 in the area manned by 2nd Leinster. Hope's case was raised in the House of Commons in January 1916, when the Irish MP J.P Farrell asked whether:

> In the case of Private L. Hope (sic), sentenced to death for alleged desertion of the post of duty and executed in August last in France, the sentence was sanctioned in the manner provided by the Regulations; whether this man was not told at the time of his trial or until within 1½ hours of his execution of the sentence which was carried out on him; whether his company records show that, so far from being a coward or deserter, he had on several occasions needlessly exposed himself on the trench parapets defying the German snipers; whether he had the benefit of any advocate in his trial; and whether, in such cases, a prisoner condemned has any right of appeal or is given any chance to defend himself?[6]

Mr Harold Tennant (Undersecretary of State for War) replied that it was 'impractical to employ legal counsel in the field, and that Hope's sentence had been reviewed in the normal way, the soldier being told of his execution at least twelve hours before it was carried out.'[7]

Private (7981) Ernest Kirk – 1st West Yorkshire

Born in India, 25 year-old Ernest Kirk had enlisted in Lahore in 1905. He had earned the North West Frontier Medal for service in the 1908 Mohmand Campaign. His CO wrote that 'his conduct under fire was (no) different to the average private', although at his trial whilst his conduct was described as 'fair' he was also described as

4 Hope, T. WO71/401.
5 Putkowski & Sykes, op. cit. p.36.
6 *Hansard*, 12 January 1916.
7 Putkowski & Sykes, op. cit. pp.403-4.

'insubordinate.' He had been sentenced to two months Field Punishment No.1 on 21 November 1914 for 'drunkenness.' Very soon after he 'left the trenches to report sick at the Reg(imental) Dressing Station.' He was found in the attic of a house in Houplines on 21 February (in uniform and with his rifle) having been thought by civilians to be a spy. He told those who apprehended him that 'I have been absent about 2 weeks.' Kirk claimed that 'I heard my father was ill and that upset me. I did not mean to desert. I have been ill for about 5 weeks of my absence.' The court sentenced him to death without any recommendation for clemency. Brigadier-General Congreve described Kirk's actions as a 'bad case', and added that 'there is a great deal of drunkenness and absence resulting from it in this battalion, more than 2/3rds of it being composed of special reservists.' General Keir agreed that 'the amount of crime in this battalion is excessive.'[8]

Kirk was executed on 6 March 1915 at the Armentières Asylum and is buried in Chapelle-d'Armentières Old Military Cemetery. Of his 12 executioners it was stated: 'Men I had known for years as clean, decent, self-respecting soldiers, whose only offence was an occasional military "drunk", screamed out, begging not to be made into murderers.'[9]

Both Ernest Kirk and Alfred Atkinson were members of a battalion that had suffered severely from the enemy attack on the Aisne on 20 September, when 15 officers were killed, wounded or missing, with 71 other ranks known to have been killed, 110 wounded, and 436 missing. Both were serving Regulars, and Congreve's remarks about special reservists, who discipline was likely poorer, refers to the battalion overall. At the point of their desertion, the weather had rendered the conditions in the trenches appalling.

Private (8107) Alfred Edward Eveleigh – 1st Buffs

Alfred Eveleigh was born in 1888, the son of a blacksmith, and had enlisted in 1905 having previously been a grocer's assistant. He arrived in France on 20 September 1914. At the time of his offences he was in 14 Platoon D Company 1st Buffs on the Canal Bank, Ypres. On 18 January 1916 he deserted and was sentenced to death, commuted to '10 years penal servitude.' Some days later, when in a 'sulky temper', he absented himself from a digging party. His CO reported having 'let him down very lightly – with 14 days F.P. No. 2' (General Ross annotated Nicholson's report of the CO's remarks with 'this' (i.e. the second offence) 'is the result'). The CO advised that he warned him of the danger of reinstatement of the capital sentence, but within three hours, on 30 January, Eveleigh committed a fresh offence. He was warned at midday for a six day trench duty at 18.00, but when the platoon paraded, Eveleigh was absent. A search party was mounted, but he could not be found. He reported himself the following morning to the guard room at the Town Hall, Ypres and was arrested. In

8 Kirk, E. TNA WO71/403.
9 Putkowski & Sykes, op. cit. p.35.

his defence he claimed, 'no recollection' of having been warned for duty, and that he 'did not know that absence for one night would make me a deserter.' In being found guilty he called no witnesses as to his character. The previous sentence of death was reinstated. General Nicholson observed that 'this man had always been a good well-conducted soldier.' Eveleigh had in fact been crimed in August 1915 for 'making an improper reply to an NCO', and on 8 December 1915 had been found 'in Houtkerque without a pass ... improperly dressed.' Nicholson viewed the offence as 'deliberate', and that in addition to avoidance of duty, he intended 'to shew wilful defiance of authority and subordination in refusing to do anything which he might be ordered to.' The Earl of Cavan, in agreement, added: 'There have been a good many cases of desertion in the 1/Buffs.' Nicholson had stated 'the discipline of the battalion is excellent', with the caveat 'except as regards "Desertion" and "Absence without leave".'[10]

Eveleigh was executed on 24 February 1916, and is buried in White House Cemetery, Ypres.

Private (10095) Robert William Gawler – 1st Buffs

Born in 1895, Robert Gawler had enlisted in December 1913. In January 1915 he had been apprehended after breaking out of his billet, and in June had been late on parade He had previously, on 26 October 1915, been absent without leave and sentenced to three months Field Punishment No. 1. On 20 December 1915 he was found absent from a roll-call of D Company on parade for trench duty. The following day he presented himself to the Town Major in Ypres, 'sober and properly dressed', stating that he was absent from his unit but 'had been to the hospital to see some of his relatives who were wounded or sick.' At his trial he stated that he been buying cards in Poperinghe, returning to find his unit departed for the trenches, and as to where they were, no one could inform him. Further, on 1 January 1916 Gawler was in a party detailed to proceed from the trenches to a dump, carrying rations and RE materials. He was missing on return. On 23 January he was apprehended in Osterhove Camp, Boulogne, where he had been noticed over several days, claiming to be returning to his regiment having been on leave. He was found guilty of two charges of desertion and sentenced to death. General Nicholson noted that the Medical Officer had supported his claim of 'temporary lapse of memory' in respect of the first offence 'when taken in conjunction with his family antecedents into which he (the Medical Officer) had enquired.' Gawler had previously been in the Canterbury Union Workhouse with his father, a hawker. Two soldiers who knew him from Kent also reported that he had an epileptic sister and a grandfather 'in a home' with the same condition. His comrades reported that recently he had 'become morose and depressed.' His CO regarded him as having 'usually been an average well-conducted soldier', and that there was 'reasonable ground for doubt as to whether he is entirely responsible for his actions.' Brigadier General Nicholson was of the opinion that 'in view of the man's medical

10 Eveleigh, A.E. TNA WO71/449.

and family history' the death penalty should not be carried out. General Ross saw his actions as 'deliberate', overriding Nicholson's recommendation, and the Earl of Cavan concurred adding again that 'there have been several cases of desertion lately in this regiment.'[11] Mark Connelly has suggested that 'Nicholson had not underplayed the situation for five other men of the battalion were facing court martial on desertion charges, and this background situation probably represents the key to the case.'[12] The 'spate of ill-discipline', in Connelly's view, was due to the 'trying conditions of the winter of 1915-16', the location of the Buffs' trenches being particularly poor and D Company, to which both Gawler and Eveleigh belonged, D Company at one point having been detached from the rest of the battalion due to flooding.[13]

Gawler was executed with Alfred Eveleigh on 24 February 1916 at Burgomaster Farm, Ypres. The officer in charge of the firing squad 'was also upset as he knew Eveleigh from many years ago, and Gawler was only a boy.'[14] They are buried side by side in White House Cemetery.

Private (9170) George Hunter, 2nd Durham Light Infantry

Born in 1891, and a foundry worker, George Hunter enlisted on 31 August 1914, and went to the Western Front on 24 August 1915. He served first with 8th Entrenching Battalion from 11 September 1915 and the 2nd DLI from 28 October 1915. In Great Britain he had been convicted for drunkenness and disorderly behaviour (in a civil court) on 6 December 1914. On 4 March 1915 he was convicted for absence (sentenced to 35 days detention) and again on 13 August 1915 (seven days Field Punishment No. 2). There were ten other recorded cases of shorter periods of absence. Once on the Western Front he was sentenced to three months Field Punishment No. 1 for wounding himself in the left hand (24 December 1915) and one year's imprisonment (suspended) on 24 March 1916 for absence. His CO, Lieutenant-Colonel Irvine, stated that: 'As a fighting man this man is perfectly useless – he is very nervous and has no control over himself … not of normal mental development.' He was in hospital from September to November 1915 and again from 24 December 1915 to February 1916 (the latter related to shooting off his little finger). He went absent again on 23 April 1916 (when his unit was on the Canal Bank, Ypres), and was apprehended on 20 May 1916 at Easingwold with a pass made out by himself in another name. At his trial he described himself as having a 'wandering mind', but he had, of course, succeeded in crossing the Channel and returning to Great Britain. Irvine stated (in a somewhat contradictory way to his other remarks) that 'he knows perfectly what he is doing',

11 Gawler, R.W. TNA WO71/448.
12 M. Connelly, *Steady the Buffs!*, Kindle edition location 598.
13 Connelly, op. cit. location 637.
14 *Sussex History Forum* <http://sussexhistoryforum.co.uk/index.php?topic=14924.0> (Accessed 20 January 2019).

and that 'I cannot recommend him to mercy', but added that 'if he is sentenced to the extreme penalty he should be carefully examined by a specialist in mental diseases.'[15]

Hunter was executed on 2 July 1916 and is buried in Esquelbecq Military Cemetery. His widow and child were awarded pensions.

Private (14387) William Nelson, 14th Durham Light Infantry

Born in 1894 and a pre-war miner, William Barry Nelson went to the Western Front on 11 September 1915 and was wounded on the 26th at Loos in the hand, returning to his unit on 1 December. He deserted on the 24th, re-joining on 15 January 1916; again on 15 February 1916, re-joining on the 21st (sentenced to 10 years penal servitude); and again on 15 July 1916, have been found guilty on the 8th of stealing an officer's puttees. On that day he had been undergoing Field Punishment No. 1 and was warned to parade for the trenches at 20.00 but escaped when he asked to go to the canteen. He reappeared at the 6th Divisional Stores in Poperinghe on the 18th 'and asked for a night's sleep.' In his defence Nelson observed, 'I have had a lot of trouble at home, and my nerves are badly upset. My father is a prisoner in Germany and is losing his eyesight there through bad treatment. My mother died while I was in England leaving my sister aged 13 and my brother aged 10. I was the only one left. I had to leave them in (the) charge of a neighbour.[16] I had no intention of deserting. I did not realise what I was doing when I left the camp.' General Ross noted that: 'The discipline in the 14th D.L.I. is good. There have been few cases of desertion in this battalion. On the other hand, this is a bad case. Pte. Nelson is not a good fighting soldier. If the sentence is commuted in so grave a case as this it will encourage others to chance it.' His CO, Lieutenant-Colonel Menzies regarded his character as 'bad from a fighting point of view.'[17]

Nelson was executed on 11 August 1916 and is buried in Acheux British Cemetery.

Private (8871) Harry Farr, 1st West Yorkshire

Harry Farr had enlisted in May 1908, but was a reservist in August 1914, arriving on the Western Front with 2nd West Yorkshire on 5 November 1914. Four days earlier he had been crimed for overstaying his pass. After a failed attack under heavy shell fire on 9 May, Farr was invalided two days later with shellshock, and after recovery joined 1st West Yorkshire on 20 October 1915. At his trial, Sergeant Andrews added: 'The accused reported sick with nerves about April 1916. The Medical Officer retained him for a fortnight in the dressing station.' (During April the battalion was only in the trenches for a few days towards the end of the month, the whole division having been at rest). 'He reported again for the same cause on 22.7.16 and was retained for

15 Hunter, G. TNA WO71/480.
16 The truth concerning his father is impossible to establish. He had younger siblings aged as described, but there is no clearly identifiable death of his mother.
17 Nelson, W. TNA WO71/488.

the day, being discharged to duty the following day.' (On the 22nd the battalion had been in the trenches for two days, artillery being active on the first, the second being described as 'very quiet').[18]

On 16 September 1916 1st West Yorkshire entered the trenches opposite the Quadrilateral (see Chapter Four), following the first two failed attacks, scheduled to attack on the 18th. On the 17th, Farr presented himself at the divisional transport lines to RSM H. Laking,[19] who reported that Farr had appeared at 09.00 (the bombardment opened at 11.00) stating:

> He was sick and had fallen out from his Company the night previous on the march up to the trenches. He stated he could not find his Company Commander for permission to fall out. I ordered him to report sick at the Dressing Station. When he returned, he states they would not see him as he was not wounded. I then ordered him to proceed up to the battalion with the ration party which was going in the evening. The ration party paraded about 8pm. The accused was found and marched off with it. On arrival at the ration trench Q.M.S. Booth reported to me that the accused was missing. On returning to the Transport Line at about 11pm I saw the accused standing near a brazier. I asked him why he was there. He replied, 'I cannot stand it.' I asked him what he meant, and he again replied, 'I cannot stand it.' I told him he would have to go to the trenches that night. He replied, 'I cannot.' I ordered Company Q.M.S. Booth to take him up to the trenches under escort. After going 500 yards the accused commenced to scream and struggle with his escort. I again warned him that he would have to go to the trenches or be tried for cowardice. He replied, 'I am not fit to be in the trenches.' I then said I would take him to see a Medical Officer. He refused to go saying 'I will not go any further that way.' I ordered the escort to take him on. The accused again started struggling and screaming. I ordered the escort to leave him alone when he jumped up and ran back to the Transport Line. I placed him in the charge of a guard at the Transport.

Charged with cowardice, when questioned at his trial, Farr stated that he did not go and see the medical officer: 'Because being away from shell fire I felt better' (the Medical Officer being nearer to the front line). The MO who knew him was wounded and replaced on the 17th. That officer, Captain Williams, examined Farr for his trial and concluded 'that in my opinion both his general physical & mental conditions were ~~good~~ satisfactory.'[20] His company commander, Captain Wilson, however, wrote: 'I cannot say what has destroyed this man's nerves, but he has proved himself on many

18 War Diary, 1st Battalion West Yorkshire Regiment, April & July 1916, TNA WO95/1618.
19 C. Corns & J. Hughes-Wilson (*Blindfold and Alone*), mistakenly have this NCO as 'Haking', p.202.
20 Crossing out in original.

occasions incapable of keeping his head in action & likely to cause a panic. Apart from his behaviour under fire, his conduct & character are very good.'[21] Second-Lieutenant Marshall added: 'I have known the accused for the last six weeks. On working parties he has three times asked for leave to fall out and return to camp as he could not stand the noise of the artillery. He was trembling and did not appear in a fit state.' In reviewing the death sentence, Brigadier-General Bridgford noted that his CO was new and did not know Farr and offered no opinion. The Earl of Cavan concluded: 'The GOC 6th Div(ision) informs me that the men know the man is no good.' All the generals ignored the evidence of the officer who knew Farr best.[22] Whilst eleven percent of capital sentences were carried out during the war, only 3.3 percent of the 551 guilty verdicts for cowardice resulted in the sentence of death being carried out. Psychiatrist Simon Wessely offers the opinion that: 'It seems very probable that Farr was suffering from a psychiatric disorder, even if we do not know which one.'[23].

Farr was executed at Carnoy on 18 October 1916 and is commemorated on the Thiepval Memorial.

Private (39213) Arthur Hamilton, 14th Durham Light Infantry

Born between 1880-86 in Belfast,[24] Arthur Hamilton, a painter and decorator, was conscripted in October 1916, stating that that he had previously served in 5th KRRC in 1908. In December 1916 he was absent from Monkswearmouth Hospital for six days, and later crimed for being drunk and 'imperfectly dressed' in Hartlepool. He arrived on the Western Front on 10 January 1917 and joined the Training Company of 14th DLI on 15 January. Four days previously he had been charged with 'irregularity when on guard' and five days later with 'wilfully destroying gov(ernmen)t property.'

On 8 February, Hamilton's platoon was in Etna Crater, Cambrin Sector, and he absented himself from a group due to relieve comrades at the end of a sap. It was his first tour in the trenches. He was apprehended by the Military Police seven days later in Calais. At his trial for desertion he claimed that he had been intending to go to the dressing station having been suffering from 'trench feet & bronchitis for about 6 days previously … and was attending for medicine daily', also claiming to have been diagnosed with valvular disease of the heart. These latter two conditions, he stated, were diagnosed in Great Britain, although his physical condition on examination in October was assessed as good. He further claimed to have been discharged from the Royal Irish Fusiliers in 1912 after four months with VDH and 'enlarged toe joints.' He did not mention having previous service on attestation, or the diagnosis of heart disease, but the examining MO in October 1916 did indeed record his foot problems. He also claimed not to have been paid since November 'which made me feel very

21 Underlinings in original.
22 Farr, H. TNA WO71/509.
23 S. Wessely, 'The Life and Death of Private Harry Farr', p.443.
24 Three different ages are given in his service file, Hamilton, A. TNA WO363.

fed up', and to have been 'upset' by a 'bullying' challenge on his way out of the line. Lieutenant-Colonel Rosher described the discipline of the battalion as 'good' and Hamilton's behaviour as 'bad.' General Ross could 'see no extenuating circumstances', and General Horne, taking the view that 'Hamilton is an old soldier', presumed that he had acted deliberately.[25]

Hamilton was executed on 27 March 1917 and is buried in Noeux-les-Mines Communal Cemetery.

Private (8833) George Everill – 1st North Staffordshire

Born in 1889, and an ironworker, George Everill, attested in August 1914, having previously been discharged from the North Staffordshire Regiment in 1905, having lied about his age.[26] He was quickly promoted acting-sergeant, but subsequently posted as a private to 1st North Staffordshire on the Western Front on 2 May 1915. He had been required to forfeit six day's pay for overstaying his furlough in December 1914 and was convicted of 'breaking out of barracks' in February 1915. He is recorded as wounded on an unknown date. In November 1915 he was changed with insolence to an NCO. He was court-martialled for being absent without leave in February 1916 (his sentence commuted to three months Field Punishment No. 1). Eight days later he was convicted for insubordination; and again in April for disobeying an order (sentenced to two year's hard labour). He was court-martialled again twice in July 1917 for 'using threatening language to his superior officer' (sentenced to three year's penal servitude, commuted), and later in the month for disobeying an order; and yet again in August for the same offence. He was finally charged with desertion when on 24 August 1917, in the guard tent, he was warned to move with his unit from divisional support, but was missing on departure, leaving his rifle and equipment. The following day he was apprehended. At his trial he made no defence and called no character evidence.[27]

Everill was executed at Poperinghe on 14 September 1917 and is buried in Poperinghe New Military Cemetery.

Private (11606) Wilfred Clarke, 2nd Durham Light Infantry

Born in 1895, Wilfred Clarke, previously a railway labourer, had served in the 2nd then 3rd Battalion Durham Light Infantry since July 1913.[28] He went overseas in January 1916, by which time he had been convicted of 15 offences, mostly absence. He was convicted of six further offences in the field. In May 1916 he was charged with desertion (sentenced to 10 year's penal servitude, suspended); and again on 17 October 1917 when he was found absent from a parade for the trenches. He was arrested at

25 Hamilton, A. TNA WO71/550.
26 Everill, G. Service file, TNA WO363.
27 Everill, G. TNA WO71/593.
28 Clarke, W. Service file, TNA WO363.

Boulogne on 12 December. It was stated: 'Accused's Platoon sergeant has known him for 10 months. Says he is No. 1 of Lewis Gun Team, good in line and clean out of line. Accused once volunteered to go out and find lost patrol. C.O. reports accused good in line, unreliable out of line.' The acting CO continued: 'Has often volunteered and been on patrol.' Brigadier-General Craufurd, noting that 'the discipline of the regiment is good', and that Clarke had been 'twice absent from working parties in 1917', supported the death sentence, as did General Marden. General Byng added the comment: 'Suspended sentence seems to have had no beneficial effect.'[29]

Clarke was executed on 9 February 1918 and is buried in Bancourt British Cemetery.

Private (11682) Joseph Nisbet, 1st Leicestershire

Born in 1890, Joseph Nisbet was a Durham miner, who volunteered in September 1914. He went to the Western Front at the end of July 1915, and eight days later was convicted of 'quitting the ranks without permission.' In March 1916 he was crimed for disobeying an order; again in the same month for 'quitting the ranks'; and in May for disobeying an order once more (awarded the death sentence, commuted to two years' penal servitude in Rouen Prison). In December 1916 he was convicted for violence to the captain who had just sentenced him for a minor offence. He was subsequently incarcerated in Maidstone Prison and released on 12 April 1918. In June 1918 he was convicted once more of disobeying a command (being awarded 90 days Field Punishment No. 1). On 15 July he was absent from parade for the front line. He reported sick to the MO, complaining of 'pain', who pronounced him fit. Three days later he was found in a dug-out near Calais. At his trial, Nisbet claimed to have been 'ailing' since his return to the battalion, and in 'a dazed condition' on the day in question. His friend at the trial stated that he was 'certainly ill that particular night.' The CO, Lieutenant-Colonel Latham, wrote that:

> I am of opinion that it is distinctly bad for discipline to have a man of such little value as a soldier and with such a disgraceful record moving about with men who are doing their duty. A man of this sort must have a bad effect on the morale of any men who may come into contact with him.[30]

Nisbet was executed on 23 August 1918 and is buried in Nine Elms British Cemetery.

Overview

Perhaps unsurprisingly, given the nature of 6th Division, ten of those executed were from Regular battalions, with two from the same Service Battalion, 14th Durham Light Infantry. Eight had served in the pre-war years. Only one was a conscript and

29 Clarke, W. TNA WO71/678.
30 TNA WO71/663.

two of the three volunteers had done so on the outbreak of war. One soldier, Harry Farr, was clearly suffering from combat stress; and the mental health of another, George Hunter, was suspect. Whilst most had poor disciplinary records (Wilfred Clarke and Joseph Nisbet particularly so), in the late 1914/early 1915 cases it is likely that the very poor conditions at the time played a part. Inescapably, it must be concluded that the comments of General Officers indicate that example to others was the reason for carrying out the sentence.

Bibliography

I. ARCHIVE SOURCES

1. *The National Archives of the United Kingdom (TNA)*

1.1 War Diaries

War Diary, QMG Branch, TNA WO95/39.
War Diary, HQ 2nd Tank Brigade, TNA WO95/102.
War Diary, HQ 5th Tank Battalion, TNA WO95/111.
War Diary, HQ Second Army, TNA WO95/271.
War Diary, 174th Tunnelling Company, Royal Engineers, TNA WO95/404.
War Diary, HQ Fourth Army, TNA WO95/439.
War Diary, HQ I Corps, WO95/594.
War Diary, HQ III Corps, TNA WO95/668.
War Diary, DAQMG III Corps, TNA WO95/683.
War Diary, HQ IV Corps, TNA WO95/717.
War Diary, HQ IX Corps, TNA WO95/837.
War Diary, HQ XIV Corps, TNA WO95/911.
War Diary, AQMG XIV Corps, TNA WO95/914.
War Diary, HQ 5th Cavalry Brigade, TNA WO95/1138.
War Diary, HQ 1st Infantry Division, TNA WO95/1227.
War Diary, 1st Battalion Middlesex Regiment, TNA WO95/1365.
War Diary, HQ 6th Infantry Division, TNA WO95/1581, 1582, 1583 & 1584.
War Diary, AAQMG 6th Infantry Division, TNA WO95/1585, 1586 & 1587.
War Diary, CRA 6th Infantry Division, TNA WO95/1588, 1589, 1590 & 1591.
War Diary, ADMS 6th Infantry Division, TNA WO95/1592 & 1593.
War Diary, Commander Royal Engineers 6th Division, TNA WO95/1594.
War Diary, 2 Brigade Royal Field Artillery, WO95/1596.
War Diary, 12 Brigade Royal Field Artillery, WO95/1597.
War Diary, 38 Brigade Royal Field Artillery, WO95/1598.
War Diary, 6th Division Trench Mortar batteries, WO95/1598.

War Diary, 12 Field Company Royal Engineers, TNA WO95/1599.
War Diary, 38 Field Company Royal Engineers, TNA WO95/1599.
War Diary 459 Field Company Royal Engineers, TNA WO95/1599.
War Diary 509 Field Company Royal Engineers, TNA WO95/1600.
War Diary, 16 Field Ambulance, TNA WO95/1602.
War Diary, 17 Field Ambulance, TNA WO95/1602.
War Diary, 18 Field Ambulance, TNA WO95/1603.
War Diary, 16 Infantry Brigade, TNA WO95/1605, 1606 & 1607.
War Diary, 1st Battalion Buffs, TNA WO95/1608.
War Diary, 1st Battalion King's Shropshire Light Infantry, TNA WO95/1609.
War Diary, 2nd Battalion York & Lancaster Regiment, TNA WO95/1610.
War Diary, 8th Battalion Bedfordshire Regiment, TNA WO95/1611.
War Diary, 1st Battalion Leicestershire Regiment, TNA WO95/1611.
War Diary, HQ 17 Infantry Brigade, TNA WO95/1612.
War Diary, 2nd Battalion Leinster Regiment, TNA WO95/1612.
War Diary, 1st Battalion North Staffordshire Regiment, TNA WO95/1613.
War Diary, 3rd Battalion Rifle Brigade, TNA WO95/1613.
War Diary, 1st Battalion Royal Fusiliers, WO95/1613.
War Diary, 1st North Staffordshire Regiment, TNA WO95/1613.
War Diary, HQ 18 Infantry Brigade, TNA WO95/1614, 1615 & 1616.
War Diary, 11th Battalion Essex Regiment, TNA WO95/1616.
War Diary, 2nd Battalion Sherwood Foresters, TNA WO95/1616 & 1624.
War Diary, 2nd Battalion Durham Light Infantry, TNA WO95/1617.
War Diary, 14th Battalion Durham Light Infantry, TNA WO95/1617.
War Diary, 1st Battalion West Yorkshire Regiment, TNA WO95/1618.
War Diary, 1st Battalion East Yorkshire Regiment, TNA WO95/1618.
War Diary, HQ 71 Infantry Brigade, TNA WO95/1619 & 1620.
War Diary, 1st Battalion Leicestershire Regiment, TNA WO95/1621 & 1622.
War Diary, 9th Battalion Norfolk Regiment, TNA WO95/1623.
War Diary, 9th Battalion Suffolk Regiment, TNA WO95/1625.
War Diary, 10 Brigade Royal Field Artillery, TNA WO95/5117.

1.2 Service files

Private W. Clarke, TNA WO363.
Private G. Everill, TNA WO363.
Private A. Hamilton, TNA WO363.
Lieutenant-Colonel J.B. Rosher, TNA WO339/18477.
Lieutenant C.A. Smith, TNA WO 9339/78698.

1.3 Judge Advocate General's Office: Courts Martial Proceedings

Hope, T. WO71/401.
Atkinson, A. TNA WO71/402.
Kirk, E. TNA WO71/403.

Gawler, R.W. TNA WO71/448.
Eveleigh, A.E. TNA WO71/449.
Hunter, G. TNA WO71/480.
Nelson, W. TNA WO71/488.
Farr, H. TNA WO71/509.
Hamilton, A. TNA WO71/550.
Everill, G. TNA WO71/593.
Clarke, W. TNA WO71/678.

1.4 Other
W.L. Osborn to Official Historian, 28 January 1936, TNA CAB45/136.

Imperial War Museum
A. St. J. Blunt, Private Papers, IWM Docs 16149.
H. C. Boxer, Private Papers, IWM Docs 4891.
B.J. Brookes, Private Papers, IWM Docs 10825.
E. Buffey, Private Papers, IWM Docs 7104.
F.G. Chandler, Private Papers, IWM Docs 15460.
G. Clifthill, Private Papers, IWM Docs 2611.
J.W. Gamble, Private Papers, IWM Docs 12003.
K.M. Gaunt, Private Papers, IWM Docs 7490.
G.W. Grossmith, Private Papers, IWM Docs 11013.
M.V.B. Hill, Private Papers, IWM Docs 6370.
P.H. Jones, Private Papers, IWM Docs 12253.
J. du P. Langrishe, Private Papers, IWM Docs 15014.
J.A. Liddell, Private papers, IWM Docs 11126.
E.A. Luther, Private Papers, IWM Docs 12283.
F. Minter, Private Papers, IWM Docs 14360.
E.G. Morley, Private Papers, IWM Docs 2450.
A.H. Muggeridge, Private Papers, IWM Docs 8493.
C.L. Nicholson, Private Papers, IWM Docs 9975.
C.P. Quayle, Private Papers, IWM Docs 1955.
T.C. Rainbird, Private Papers, IWM Docs 11755.
E.E. Simeons, Private Papers, IWM Docs 2808.
E.K. Smith, Private Papers, IWM Docs 2535.
R.B. Wilkinson, Private Papers, IWM Docs 5761.
Fourth Army Papers, Vol. 5, IWM Docs 29537.

National Army Museum
T.T. Grove, 'It Happened by Chance', NAM 1963-08-14.

National Library of Scotland
Field-Marshal Sir Douglas Haig, Manuscript Diary, Acc. 3155.

Churchill College, Cambridge
Sir Henry Rawlinson, War Journal, RWLN 1/11 & 1/12.

II. OFFICIAL PUBLICATIONS

II.I British Official Histories

Anon. *Military Operations France and Belgium, 1916 – Appendices* (London: Macmillan, 1932).
C.F. Aspinall-Oglander, *Military Operations Gallipoli, Vol. 2* (London: Imperial War Museum, originally published 1932).
J.E. Edmonds, *Military Operations: France & Belgium 1914, Vol. 1* (London: Imperial War Museum, originally published 1933).
J.E. Edmonds, *Military Operations France and Belgium 1914, Vol. 2* (London: Imperial War Museum, originally published 1925).
J.E. Edmonds, *Military Operations France and Belgium 1915, Vol. 2* (London: Imperial War Museum, originally published 1928).
J.E. Edmonds, *Military Operations France and Belgium 1916, Vol. 1* (London: Imperial War Museum, originally published 1932).
J.E. Edmonds, *Military Operations France and Belgium 1917, Vol 2* (London: Imperial War Museum, originally published 1948).
J.E. Edmonds, *Military Operations France and Belgium 1918, Vol 1* (London: Imperial War Museum, originally published 1935).
J.E. Edmonds, *Military Operations France and Belgium, 1918, Vol. 4* (London: Imperial War Museum, originally published 1947).
J.E. Edmonds & R. Maxwell-Hyslop, *Military Operations – France and Belgium 1918, Vol V* (London: Imperial War Museum originally published 1947).
J.E Edmonds & G.C. Wynne, *Military Operations France and Belgium 1915 Vol. 1* (London: Imperial War Museum, originally published 1927).
C. Falls, *Military Operations France and Belgium 1917, Vol. 1* (London: Imperial War Museum, originally published 1940).
A.M. Henniker, *Transportation on the Western Front* (London: HMSO, 1937).
W.G. Macpherson, W.P. Herringham, T.R. Elliott & A. Balfour, *Medical Services – Diseases of the War, Vol 1* (London: HMSO, n.d.).
W. Miles, *Military Operations France and Belgium 1916, Vol. 2* (London: Imperial War Museum, originally published 1938).
W. Miles, *Military Operations France and Belgium 1917 – The Battle of Cambrai* (London: Imperial War Museum, originally published 1948).

II.II General Staff publications etc.

A.F. Becke, *Order of Battle of Divisions, Part 1.* (Great Britain: Committee of Imperial Defence. Historical Section, 1935).

General Staff, *Notes for Infantry Officers on Trench Warfare* (London: War Office, March 1916).

General Staff, *SS107 Notes on Minor Enterprises* (March 1916).

General Staff, *SS109 Training of Divisions for Offensive Action* (May 1916).

General Staff, *SS135 Instructions for the Training of Divisions for Offensive Action* (1918).

General Staff, *SS 135 The Training and Employment of Divisions* (January 1918).

General Staff, *SS135 The Division in Attack* (November 1918).

General Staff, *SS 143 The Training and Employment of Platoons* (1917 & 1918).

General Staff, *SS145 Notes on R.E. Preparations for, and the Employment of the R.E. in Offensive Operations* (February 1917).

General Staff, *SS152 Instructions for the Training of the British Armies in France* (June 1917).

General Staff, *SS159 Notes on Tactical Schemes Compiled by Fourth Army* (May 1917).

General Staff, *SS 169 Employment of 3-in Stokes Mortars in Recent Fighting* (1917).

General Staff, *SS 197 Tactical Employment of Lewis Guns*, (1918).

General Staff, *SS 204 Infantry and Tank Co-Operation and Training* (1918).

General Staff, *SS 214 Tanks and their Employment in Co-Operation with Other Arms* (1918).

General Staff, *SS 169 Employment of 3-in Stokes Mortars in Recent Fighting* (1917).

General Staff, *Artillery Notes No.9 No.3 Counter Battery Work* (1918).

War Office, *Field Service Regulations, Part I, Operations 1909* (Amendments 1912) (London, HMSO).

War Office, *Statistics of the Military Effort of the British Empire During the Great War 1914-1920* (London HMSO, 1922).

II.III United States of America

General Staff American Expeditionary Forces, *Histories of Two Hundred and Fifty-One Divisions of the German Army which Participated in the War (1914-1918)* (Washington, Government Printing Office, 1920).

III. PRINTED SOURCES

Anon. *The VC & DSO Book, Vol. 3 1916-1923*, (Uckfield: Naval & Military Press, n.d.).

R.V.K Applin, *Machine-Gun Tactics* (London: Hugh Rees, 1910).

C.W. Arnold (A. Wilson ed.), *The War Diary of an English Soldier* (Brighton: Reveille, 2014).

G. Ashurst, *My Bit* (Ramsbury: Crowood Press, 1987).

T. Ashworth, *Trench Warfare 1914-1918* (London: Pan, 2000).
E. Astill (ed.), *The Great War Diaries of Brigadier General Alexander Johnston 1914-1917* (Barnsley: Pen & Sword, 2007).
A. H. Atteridge, *History of the 17th (Northern) Division* (Glasgow: R. Maclehose, 1926).

P. Barton, P. Doyle and J. Vandewalle, *Beneath Flanders Fields* (Staplehurst: Spellmount, 2004).
R. Berkeley, *The History of the Rifle Brigade in the War of 1914-1918, Vol. I* (London: Rifle Brigade Club, 1927).
S. Bidwell & D. Graham, *Fire-Power – The British Army Weapons & Theories of War 1904-1945* (Barnsley: Pen & Sword, 2004).
E. Blunden, *Undertones of War* (London: Penguin, originally published 1928).
B. Bond & N. Cave, *Haig: A Re-appraisal 80 Years On* (Barnsley: Pen & Sword, 2009).
B. Bond & S. Robbins (eds), *Staff Officer: The Diaries of Walter Guinness (First Lord Moyne) 1914-1918* (London: Leo Cooper, 1987).
J. Bourne, *Who's Who in World War 1* (London: Routledge, 2001).
T. Bowman, *Irish Regiments in the Great War: Discipline and Morale* (Manchester: Manchester University Press, 2003).
T. & M. Brookbank, *A Soldier of the 6th Division* (Kibworth Beauchamp: Matador, 2016).
I. M. Brown, *British Logistics on the Western Front 1914-1919* (London: Praeger, 1998).
G. A Burgoyne (C. Davidson ed.), *The Burgoyne Diaries* (London: Harmsworth, 1985).

N. Cave, *Sanctuary Wood & Hooge* (London: Leo Cooper, 1993).
C. von Clausewitz (translated by J.J. Graham), *On War - Volume One* (1908 version, originally published 1832).
C. P. Clayton, *The Hungry One* (Gomer Press: Llandysul, 1978).
B. Congreve (T. Norman ed.), Armageddon Road (London: William Kimber, 1982).
M. Connelly, *Forward the Buffs!* (Oxford: Oxford University Press, 2006).
C. Corns and J. Hughes-Wilson, *Blindfold and Alone* (London: Cassell, 2001).
G. Corrigan, *Mud, Blood and Poppycock* (London: Cassell, 2004).
J. Costin, *Cambridgeshire Kitcheners* (Barnsley: Pen & Sword, 2016).
Crown Prince Rupprecht of Bavaria, *Mein Kriegstagebuch II* (Munich: Deutsche National Verlag, 1929).
Crown Prince Rupprecht of Bavaria, *Mein Kriegstagbuch, Vol. III* (Berlin: 1929).
F.P. Crozier, *A Brass Hat in No Man's Land* (London: Cape, 1930).

P. Dennis & J. Grey, *1918: Defining Victory* (Canberra: Department of Defence, 1999).
C. Duffy, *Through German Eyes: The British and the Somme 1916* (London: Weidenfeld & Nicolson, 2006).

J.D.P. French, *1914* (New York: Houghton Miflin, 1919),

P. Griffith, *Battle Tactics of the Western Front: The British Army's Art of Attack 1916-18* (London: Yale University Press, 1994).
A.D. Gristwood, *The Somme* (Columbia: University of South Carolina Press, 2006; originally published 1927).

B. Hammond, *Cambrai 1917* (London: Weidenfeld & Nicolson, 2008).
P. Hart, *The Somme* (London: Weidenfeld & Nicolson, 2005).
F.C. Hitchcock, "*Stand To*" (Uckfield: Naval & Military Press; originally published 1937)
P.E. Hodgkinson, *British Infantry Battalion Commanders in the First World War* (Farnham: Ashgate, 2015).
P. Hodgkinson, *The Battle of the Selle* (Solihull: Helion, 2017).
P. Hodgkinson, *The Resourceful Gunner* (Amazon Createspace: 2019).
R. Holmes, *Tommy* (London: Harper Collins, 2004).
M.M.L. Hudson, *Two Lives* (York: Wilton, 1992).
A.H. Hussey & D.S. Inman, *The Fifth Division in the Great War*, (London: Nisbet, 1921).
G. S. Hutchinson, *The Thirty-Third Division in France and Flanders 1915-1919* (London: Waterlow & Sons, 1921).

E. Ironside, *The Authorised Biography* (Stroud: The History Press, 2018).

S. Jones (ed.), *Stemming the Tide* (Solihull: Helion, 2013).
S. Jones (ed.), *Courage without Glory* (Solihull: Helion, 2015).
S. Jones (ed.), *At All Costs* (Solihull: Helion, 2018).

J. Keegan (ed.), *Churchill's Generals* (London: Warner Books, 1991).
P. Kendall, *Aisne 1914* (Stroud: History Press, 2012).
M. Kitchen, *The German Offensives of 1918* (Stroud: Tempus, 2001).
Jonathan Krause, *Early Trench Tactics in the French Army: The Second Battle of Artois, May-June 1915* (Farnham: Ashgate, 2013).

A. Leask, *Putty* (Solihull: Helion, 2015).
D. Lindsay, *Forgotten General: A Life of Andrew Thorne* (Salisbury: Michael Russell, 1987).
M. LoCicero, R. Mahoney & S. Mitchell, *A Military Transformed?* (Helion: Solihull, 2014).
L.L. Loewe, *Basil Henriques* (London: Routledge & Kegan Paul, 1976).
D. Lomas, *First Ypres 1914* (Oxford: Osprey, 1999).
F. von Lossberg (D.T. Zabecki & D.J. Biedekarkne (eds.), *Lossberg's War*, (Kentucky: University Press, 2017; originally published 1939).
T.O. Marden, *A Short History of the Sixth Division* (London: Hugh Rees, 1920).

T.O. Marden, *The History of the Welch Regiment, Vol. 2, 1914-1918* (Uckfield: Naval and Military; originally published 1932).
C. Messenger, *Call to Arms* (London: Weidenfeld & Nicholson, 2005).
W. Miles, *The Durham Forces in the Field 1914-18*, (Uckfield, Naval & Military; originally published 1920).
A. Montgomery, *The Story of the Fourth Army in the Battles of the Hundred Days* (London: Hodder & Stoughton, 1919).
F.A. Mumby (ed.), *The Great World War, Vol. IV* (London: Gresham, n.d.).
C.C.R. Murphy, *The History of the Suffolk Regiment 1914-1927* (London: Hutchinson, n.d.).

G.W.L. Nicholson, *Canadian Expeditionary Force 1914-1919* (Ottawa: Queens' Printer, 1962).
W. N. Nicholson, *Behind the Lines* (Stevenage: Strong Oak, originally published 1939).
T. Norman, *The Hell They Called High Wood* (London: William Kimber, 1984).

A. Palazzo, *Seeking Victory on the Western Front – The British Army & Chemical Warfare in World War I* (Lincoln: University of Nebraska Press, 2000).
F.L. Petre, *The History of the Norfolk Regiment* (Norwich: Jarrold & Sons, 1924).
W. Philpott, *Bloody Victory* (London: Little Brown, 2009).
G. Pratten, *Australian Battalion Commanders in the Second World War* (Melbourne: Cambridge University Press, 2009).
R.E. Priestley, *Breaking the Hindenburg Line – The Story of the 46th (North Midland) Division* (London: Fisher Unwin, 1919).
R. Prior and T. Wilson, *Command on the Western Front – The Military Career of Sir Henry Rawlinson 1914-1918* (Barnsley: Pen & Sword, 2004).
P. Prior & T. Wilson, *The Somme* (London: Yale University Press, 2005).
J. Putkowski & J. Sykes, *Shot at Dawn* (London: Leo Cooper, 1989).

B. Rawling, *Surviving Trench Warfare* (London: University of Toronto Press, 1992).
F. Richards, *Old Soldiers Never Die* (London: Faber, 1965).
S. Robbins, *British Generalship on the Western Front 1914-18* (Abingdon: Frank Cass, 2005).

M. Samuels, *Doctrine and Dogma* (Westport: Greenwood, 1992).
H.R. Sandilands, *The Fifth in the Great War* (Dover: G.W. Grigg, 1938).
G.D. Sheffield (ed.), *Leadership & Command: The Anglo-American Military Experience since 1861* (London: Brassey's, 1997).
G.D. Sheffield, *Forgotten Victory* (London: Headline, 2002).
G. Sheffield & J. Bourne (eds.), *Douglas Haig: War Diaries and Letters 1914-1918* (London: Weidenfeld & Nicolson, 2005).
G. Sheffield & P. Gray, *Changing War: The British Army, The Hundred Days Campaign and The Birth of the Royal Air Force, 1918* (London: Bloomsbury, 2013).

G. Sheffield and D. Todman (eds.), *Command and Control on the Western Front – The British Army's Experience 1914-18* (Staplehurst: Spellmount, 2004).
J. Sheldon, *The German Army at Cambrai* (Barnsley: Pen & Sword, 2009).
J. Sheldon, *The German Army at Ypres 1914 and the Battle for Flanders* (Barnsley: Pen & Sword, 2010).
P. Simkins, *From the Somme to Victory – The British Army's Experience on the Western Front 1916-1918* (Barnsley: Pen & Sword, 2014).
W.J. Slim, *Defeat into Victory* (London: Corgi, 1971).
J. Smyth, *Leadership in Battle* (Newton Abbot: David & Charles, 1975).
F.C. Stanley, *The History of the 89th Brigade 1914-1918* (Liverpool: Liverpool Daily Post, 1919).
H. Strachan, *The First World War – Volume 1: To Arms* (Oxford: Oxford University Press, 2001).
P. Strong & S. Marble, *Artillery in the Great War,* (Barnsley: Pen & Sword, 2011).

J. Terraine (ed.), *General Jack's Diary* (London: Cassell, 2000).

H. M. Urquhart, *Arthur Currie: The Biography of a Great Canadian* (Toronto: J.M. Dent, 1950).

A. Watson, *Enduring the Great War: Combat, Morale and Collapse in the German and British Armies 1914-1918* (Cambridge: Cambridge University Press, 2008).
W.C.C. Weetman, *The Sherwood Foresters in the Great War 1914-1919 – 1/8th Battalion* (Nottingham: Thomas Forman, 1920).
W. de B. Wood, *The History of the King's Shropshire Light Infantry in the Great War* (London: Medici Society, 1925).
H.C. Wylly, *The First and Second Battalions the Sherwood Foresters (Nottinghamshire and Derbyshire Regiment) in the Great War* (Aldershot: Gale & Polden, 1936).
H. C. Wylly, *History of the 1st & 2nd Battalions the Leicestershire Regiment in the Great War* (Aldershot: Gale & Polden, 1928).
E. Wyrall, *The West Yorkshire Regiment in the War 1914-1918* (London: Bodley Head, 1923).

IV. JOURNAL ARTICLES

V.W. Andrews, 'The Legend of the Admiral', *The Ypres Times*, (3) 1926, pp.70-1.
A.F. Becke, 'The Coming of the Creeping Barrage', *Journal of the Royal Artillery*, (58) 1931, pp.19-42.
J. Bourne, 'British Divisional Commanders during the Great War: First Thoughts', *Gun Fire: A Journal of First World War History*, (29) n.d.
D. Fletcher, 'The First Tank Action in History', *Stand To!*, (107) 2016, pp.4-7.
C. Hardy, 'Rewriting History – An Alternative Account of the Death of Lieutenant George Macpherson', *Stand To!* (89) 2010, pp.30-2.

T. Harvey, 'Turnover Amongst Brigade Commanders, 1917 – The Real Reasons?', *Stand To!*, (109) 2017, pp.97-105.
J.S. Oxford, 'The so-called Great Spanish Influenza pandemic of 1918 may have originated in France in 1916', *Phil. Trans. R. Soc. Lond.* (356) 2001, 1857-1859
D. Tattersfield, 'The Kaiser's Battle – A Statistical Re-Analysis', *Stand To!*, (111) 2018, pp.43-48.
C. Taylor, 'One Man and his Car (and Dog), *Stand To!*, (112) 2018, pp.22-6.
M.G Taylor, 'Land Transportation in the Late War', *Journal of the Royal United Services Institution*, (66) 1921, pp.699-722.
R. Thompson, '"The Empire Strikes Back" – BEF Logistic and Engineering Preparation and Development for the Advance to Victory, 1918', *Stand To!*, (113) 2018, pp.7-15.
M. Vego, 'Science vs the Art of War', *JFQ* (2012).
S. Wessely, 'The Life and Death of Private Harry Farr', *Journal of the Royal Society of Medicine*, (99) 2006, pp.440-443.

VI. THESES/UNPUBLISHED PAPERS

J. Bourne, 'British Generals on the Cusp of Victory, September 1918', paper presented at University of Wolverhampton, 3 March 2018.
A Geddes, 'Solly-Flood, GHQ, and Tactical Training in the BEF, 1916-1918', MA thesis University of Birmingham, (2007).
P.M. Harris, 'The Men who Planned the War', PhD thesis, King's College London (2013).
T. G. Harvey, 'The Battle of Hill 70 – 15-25 August 1917', MA dissertation University of Birmingham, (2006).
T. G. Harvey, '"An Army of Brigadiers" British Brigade Commanders at the Battle of Arras 1917', PhD thesis University of Birmingham (2015).
S.B.T. Mitchell, 'An Inter-Disciplinary Study of Learning in the 32nd Division on the Western Front, 1916-1918', PhD thesis, University of Birmingham, (2013).
A.J. Saunders, 'A Muse of Fire – British Trench Warfare Munitions, their Invention, Manufacture and Tactical Employment on the Western Front, 1914–18', PhD thesis Exeter University (2008).
A. Simpson, 'The Operational Role of British Corps Command on the Western Front', PhD thesis, University College, London (2001).
M. Whisler, 'Der Tommy Kommt' – British Expeditionary Force Campaign Orchestration and Fourth Army Operational Execution at the Battle of the Selle River, October 1918', Master of Military Studies thesis, United States Marine Corps Command and Staff College (2001).
M. Yockelson, 'Brothers in Arms?' The American and British Coalition on the Western Front 1918', PhD thesis Cranfield University (2006).

Index

Index of People

Index of Places

Index of Allied Military Units & Formations